BEAU FIELDING AND THE SHAM WIDOW.

THE

WITS AND BEAUX OF SOCIETY.

BY

GRACE AND PHILIP WHARTON,

AUTHORS OF "THE QUEENS OF SOCIETY."

With Illustrations from Drawings by

H. K. BROWNE AND JAMES GODWIN.

ENGRAVED BY THE BROTHERS DALZIEL.

NEW YORK:

HARPER & BROTHERS, PUBLISHERS,

FRANKLIN SQUARE.

1861.

PREFACE.

THE success of the "Queens of Society" will have pioneered the way for the "Wits and Beaux," with whom, during the holiday time of their lives, these fair ladies were so greatly associated. The "Queens," whether all wits or not, must have been the cause of wit in others; their influence over dandyism is notorious: their power to make or mar a man of fashion, almost historical. So far, a chronicle of the sayings and doings of the "Wits" is worthy to serve as a *pendent* to that of the "Queens:" happy would it be for society if the annals of the former could more closely resemble the biography of the latter. But it may not be so: men are subject to temptations, to failures, to delinquencies, to calamities, of which women can scarcely dream, and which they can only lament and pity.

Our "Wits," too—to separate them from the "Beaux"—were men who often took an active part in the stirring events of their day; they assumed to be statesmen, though, too frequently, they were only politicians. They were brave and loyal: indeed, in the time of the Stuarts, all the Wits were Cavaliers, as well as the Beaux. One hears of no repartee among Cromwell's followers; no dash, no merriment in Fairfax's staff; eloquence, indeed, but no wit in the Parliamentarians; and, in truth, in the second Charles's time, the king might have headed the list of the Wits himself—such a capital man as his Majesty is known to have been for a wet evening or a dull Sunday; such a famous teller of a story—such a perfect diner-out: no wonder that in his reign we had George Villiers, second Duke of Buckingham of that family, "mankind's epitome," who had every pretension to every accomplishment combined in himself. No wonder that we could attract De Grammont and Saint Evremond to our court; and own, somewhat to our discredit be it allowed, Rochester and Beau Fielding. Every reign has had its wits, but those in Charles's time were so numerous as to distinguish the era by an especial brilliancy. Nor let it be supposed that these annals do not contain a moral application. They show how little the sparkling attributes herein portrayed conferred happiness; how far more the rare, though certainly real touches of genuine feeling and strong affection, which appear here and there eveu in the lives of the most thoughtless "Wits and Beaux," elevate the character in youth, or console the spirit in age. They prove how wise has been that change in society which now repudiates the "Wit" as a distinct class, and requires general intelligence as a compensation for lost repartees, or long obsolete practical jokes.

"Men are not all evil:" so in the life of George Villiers, we find him kind-hearted and free from hypocrisy. His old servants—and the fact speaks in extenuation of one of our wildest Wits and Beaux—loved him faithfully. De Grammont, we all own, has little to redeem him except his good-nature: Rochester's latest days were almost hallowed by his penitence. Chesterfield is saved by his kindness to the Irish and his affection for his son. Horace Walpole had human affections, though a most inhuman pen: and Wharton was famous for his good-humor.

The periods most abounding in the Wit and the Beau have, of course, been those most exempt from wars and rumors of wars. The Restoration; the early period of the Augustan age; the commencement of the Hanoverian dynasty,—have all been enlivened by Wits and Beaux, who came to light like mushrooms after a storm of rain, as soon as the political horizon was clear. We have Congreve, who affected to be the Beau as well as the Wit; Lord Hervey, more of the courtier than the Beau—a Wit by inheritance—a peer, assisted into a pre-eminent position by royal preference, and consequent *prestige;* and all these men were the offspring of the particular state of the times in which they figured: at earlier periods, they would have been deemed effeminate; in later ones, absurd.

Then the scene shifts: intellect had marched forward gigantically: the world is grown exacting, disputatious, critical, and such men as Horace Walpole and Brinsley Sheridan appear; the characteristics of wit which adorned that age being well diluted by the feebler talents of Selwyn and Hook.

Of these, and others, "*table traits,*" and other traits, are here given: brief chronicles of *their* life's stage, over which a curtain has so long been dropped, are supplied carefully from well-established sources: it is with characters, not with literary history, that we deal; and do our best to make the portraitures life-like, and to bring forward old memories, which, without the stamp of antiquity, might be suffered to pass into obscurity.

Your Wit and your Beau, be he French or English, is no medieval personage: the aristocracy of the present day rank among his immediate descendants: he is a creature of a modern and an artificial age; and with his career are mingled many features of civilized life, manners, habits, and traces of family history which are still, it is believed, interesting to the majority of English readers, as they have long been to

GRACE and PHILIP WHARTON.

CONTENTS.

GEORGE VILLIERS, SECOND DUKE OF BUCKINGHAM.

Signs of the Restoration. — Samuel Pepys in his Glory. — A royal Company. — Pepys "ready to weep."—The Playmate of Charles II.—George Villiers' Inheritance.—Two gallant young Noblemen.—The brave Francis Villiers.—After the Battle of Worcester. —Disguising the King.—Villiers in Hiding.—He appears as a Mountebank.—Buckingham's Habits.—A daring Adventure.—Cromwell's saintly Daughter.—Villiers and the Rabbi.—The Buckingham Pictures and Estates.—York House.—Villiers returns to England.—Poor Mary Fairfax.—Villiers in the Tower.—Abraham Cowley, the Poet.—The greatest Ornament of Whitehall.—Buckingham's Wit and Beauty.—Flecknoe's Opinion of him.—His Duel with the Earl of Shrewsbury.—Villiers as a Poet.—As a Dramatist. —A fearful Censure!—Villiers' Influence in Parliament.—A Scene in the Lords.—The Duke of Ormond in Danger.—Colonel Blood's Outrages.—Wallingford House, and Ham House.—"Madame Ellen."—The Cabal.—Villiers again in the Tower.—A Change.—The Duke of York's Theatre.—Buckingham and the Princess of Orange.—His last Hours. —His Religion.—Death of Villiers.—The Duchess of Buckingham..............Page 13

COUNT DE GRAMMONT, ST. EVREMOND, AND LORD ROCHESTER.

De Grammont's Choice.—His Influence with Turenne.—The Church or the Army?—An Adventure at Lyons.—A brilliant Idea.—De Grammont's Generosity.—A Horse "for the Cards."—Knight-Cicisbeism.—De Grammont's first Love.—His witty Attacks on Mazarin.—Anne Lucie de la Mothe Houdancourt.—Beset with Snares.—De Grammont's Visits to England.—Charles II.—The Court of Charles II.—Introduction of Country-dances.—Norman Peculiarities.—St. Evremond, the handsome Norman.—The most beautiful Woman in Europe.—Hortense Mancini's Adventures.—Madame Mazarin's House at Chelsea.—Anecdote of Lord Dorset.—Lord Rochester in his Zenith.—His Courage and Wit.—Rochester's Pranks in the City.—Credulity, past and present.—"Dr. Bendo," and La Belle Jennings.—La Triste Heritiere.—Elizabeth, Countess of Rochester.—Retribution and Reformation.—Rochester's Exhortation to Mr. Fanshawe.—Little Jermyn.—An incomparable Beauty.—Anthony Hamilton, De Grammont's Biographer.—The Three Courts.—La Belle Hamilton.—De Grammont's Description of her.—Her practical Jokes. —The household Deity of Whitehall.—A Chaplain in Livery.—Le Mariage forcé.—De Grammont's last Hours.—What might he not have been?.......................... 49

BEAU FIELDING.

On Wits and Beaux.—Scotland Yard in Charles II.'s Day.—Orlando of "The Tatler."—Beau Fielding, Justice of the Peace.—Adonis in Search of a Wife.—The sham Widow.—Ways and Means.—Barbara Villiers, Lady Castlemaine.—Quarrels with the King.—The Beau's second Marriage.—The last Days of Fops and Beaux........................ 85

OF CERTAIN CLUBS AND CLUB-WITS UNDER ANNE.

The Origin of Clubs.—The Establishment of Coffee-houses.—The October Club.—The Beef-steak Club.—Of certain other Clubs.—The Kit-kat Club.—The Romance of the Bowl.—The Toasts of the Kit-kat.—The Members of the Kit-kat.—A good Wit, and a bad Architect.—"Well-natured Garth."—The Poets of the Kit-kat.—Charles Montagu, Earl of Halifax. — Chancellor Somers. — Charles Sackville, Lord Dorset. — Less celebrated Wits.. 95

WILLIAM CONGREVE.

When and where was he born?—The Middle Temple.—Congreve finds his Vocation.—Verses to Queen Mary.—The Tennis-court Theatre.—Congreve abandons the Drama.—Jeremy Collier.—The Immorality of the Stage.—Very improper Things.—Congreve's Writings.—Jeremy's Short Views.—Rival Theatres.—Dryden's Funeral.—A Tub-Preacher.—Horoscopic Predictions.—Dryden's Solicitude for his Son.—Congreve's Ambition.—Anecdote of Voltaire and Congreve.—The Profession of Mæcenas.—Congreve's private Life.—"Malbrook's" Daughter.—Congreve's Death and Burial.................. 109

BEAU NASH.

The King of Bath.—Nash at Oxford.—"My Boy Dick."—Offers of Knighthood.—Doing Penance at York.—Days of Folly.—A very romantic Story.—Sickness and Civilization. —Nash descends upon Bath.—Nash's Chef-d'œuvre.—The Ball.—Improvements in the Pump-room, etc.—A public Benefactor.—Life at Bath in Nash's Time.—A Compact with the Duke of Beaufort.—Gaming at Bath.—Anecdotes of Nash.—"Miss Sylvia."—A generous Act. — Nash's Sun setting. — A Panegyric. — Nash's Funeral. — His Characteristics .... Page 127

PHILIP, DUKE OF WHARTON.

Wharton's Ancestors—His early Years.—Marriage at sixteen.—Wharton takes leave of his Tutor.—The young Marquis and the old Pretender.—Frolics at Paris.—Zeal for the Orange Cause.—A Jacobite Hero.—The Trial of Atterbury.—Wharton's Defense of the Bishop.—Hypocritical Signs of Penitence.—Sir Robert Walpole duped.—Very trying. —The Duke of Wharton's "Whens."—Military Glory at Gibraltar.—"Uncle Horace." —Wharton to Uncle Horace. — The Duke's Impudence. — High Treason. — Wharton's ready Wit.—Last Extremities.—Sad Days in Paris.—His last Journey to Spain.—His Death in a Bernardine Convent........ 145

LORD HERVEY.

George II. arriving from Hanover.—His Meeting with the Queen.—Lady Suffolk.—Queen Caroline.—Sir Robert Walpole.—Lord Hervey.—A Set of fine Gentlemen.—An eccentric Race.—Carr, Lord Hervey.—A fragile Boy.—Description of George II.'s Family.—Anne Brett.—A bitter Cup.—The Darling of the Family.—Evenings at St. James's.—Frederick, Prince of Wales.—Amelia Sophia Walmoden.—Poor Queen Caroline!—Nocturnal Diversions of Maids of Honor.—Neighbor George's Orange-chest.—Mary Lepel, Lady Hervey.—Rivalry.—Hervey's Intimacy with Lady Mary.—Relaxations of the royal Household.—Bacon's Opinion of Twickenham.—A Visit to Pope's Villa.—The little Nightingale.—The Essence of small Talk.—Hervey's Affectation and Effeminacy.—Pope's Quarrel with Hervey and Lady Mary.—Hervey's Duel with Pulteney.—"The Death of Lord Hervey: a Drama."—Queen Caroline's last Drawing-room.—Her Illness and Agony. — A painful Scene. — The Truth discovered. — The Queen's dying Bequests. — The King's Temper. — Archbishop Potter is sent for. — The Duty of Reconciliation. — The Death of Queen Caroline.—A Change in Hervey's Life.—Lord Hervey's Death.—Want of Christianity.—Memoirs of his own Time........ 165

PHILIP DORMER STANHOPE, FOURTH EARL OF CHESTERFIELD.

The King of Table Wits.—Early Years.—Hervey's Description of his Person.—Resolutions and Pursuits.—Study of Oratory.—The Duties of an Embassador.—King George II.'s Opinion of his Chroniclers.—Life in the Country.—Melusina, Countess of Walsingham. —George II. and his Father's Will.—Dissolving Views.—Madame du Bouchet.—The Broad-bottomed Administration.—Lord Lieutenant of Ireland in time of Peril.—Reformation of the Calendar.—Chesterfield House.—Exclusiveness.—Recommending "Johnson's Dictionary."—"Old Samuel" to Chesterfield.—Defensive Pride of the "respectable Hottentot."—The Glass of Fashion.—Lord Scarborough's Friendship for Chesterfield. — The Death of Chesterfield's Son. — His Interest in his Grandsons. — "I must go and rehearse my Funeral."—Chesterfield's Will.—What is a Friend?—Les Manières nobles. —Letters to his Son........ 203

THE ABBÉ SCARRON.

An Eastern Allegory.—Who comes here?—A mad Freak and its Consequences.—Making an Abbé of him.—The May-fair of Paris.—Scarron's Lament to Pellisson.—The Office of the Queen's Patient.—"Give me a simple Benefice."—Scarron's Description of himself.—Improvidence and Servility.—The Society at Scarron's.—The witty Conversation. — Françoise D'Aubigné's Début. — The sad Story of La Belle Indienne. — Matrimonial Considerations.—"Scarron's Wife will live forever."—Petits Soupers.—Scarron's last Moments.—A Lesson for gay and grave 227

FRANCOIS, DUC DE LA ROCHEFOUCAULT AND THE DUC DE SAINT-SIMON.

Rank and Good-breeding. — The Hotel de Rochefoucault. — Racine and his Plays. — La Rochefoucault's Wit and Sensibility.—Saint-Simon's Youth.—Looking out for a Wife.— Saint-Simon's Court Life.—The History of Louise de la Vallière.—A mean Act of Louis Quatorze.—All has passed away!—Saint-Simon's Memoirs of his own Time........ 245

HORACE WALPOLE.

The Commoners of England.—Horace's Regret for the Death of his Mother.—"Little Horace" in Arlington Street.—Introduced to George I.—Characteristic Anecdote of George I. —Walpole's Education.—Schoolboy Days.—Boyish Friendships.—Companionship of Gray. — A dreary Doom. — Walpole's Description of youthful Delights. — Anecdote of

Pope and Frederick of Wales.—The Pomfrets.—Sir Thomas Robinson's Ball.—Political Squibs.—That "Rogue Walpole."—Sir Robert's Retirement from Office.—The splendid Mansion of Houghton.—Sir Robert's Love of Gardening.—What we owe to the "Grandes Tours."—George Vertue.—Men of one Idea.—The noble Picture-gallery at Houghton. —Sir Robert's Death.—The Granville Faction.—A very good Quarrel.—Twickenham.—Strawberry Hill.—The Recluse of Strawberry.—Portraits of the Digby Family.—Sacrilege. — Mrs. Damer's Models. — The Long Gallery at Strawberry.—The Chapel. — "A dirty little Thing."—The Society around Strawberry Hill.—Anne Seymour Conway.—A Man who never doubted.—Lady Sophia Fermor's Marriage.—Horace in Favor.—Anecdote of Sir William Stanhope. — A paper House. — Walpole's Habits. — Why did he not Marry?—"Dowagers as plenty as Flounders."—Catherine Hyde, Duchess of Queensberry.—Anecdote of Lady Granville.—Kitty Clive.—Death of Horatio Walpole.—George, third Earl of Orford.—A Visit to Houghton.—Family Misfortunes.—Poor Chatterton.—Walpole's Concern with Chatterton.—Walpole in Paris.—Anecdote of Madame Geoffrin. —"Who's that Mr. Walpole?"—The Miss Berrys.—Horace's two "Straw Berries."—Tapping a new Reign.—The Sign of the Gothic Castle.—Growing old with Dignity.—Succession to an Earldom.—Walpole's last Hours.—Let us not be ungrateful. . Page 255

GEORGE SELWYN.

A Love of Horrors.—Anecdotes of Selwyn's Mother.—Selwyn's College Days.—Orator Henley.—Selwyn's blasphemous Freak.—The Profession of a Wit.—The Thirst for Hazard. —Reynolds's Conversation-piece.—Selwyn's Eccentricities and Witticisms.—A most important Communication. — An amateur Headsman. — The Eloquence of Indifference. — Catching a Housebreaker.—The Family of the Selwyns.—The Man of the People.—Selwyn's parliamentary Career.—True Wit.—Some of Selwyn's witty Sayings.—The Sovereignty of the People.—On two Kinds of Wit.—Selwyn's Home for Children.—Mie-Mie, the little Italian. — Selwyn's little Companion taken from him. — His later Days and Death 307

RICHARD BRINSLEY SHERIDAN.

Sheridan a Dunce.—Boyish Dreams of literary Fame.—Sheridan in Love.—A Nest of Nightingales.—The Maid of Bath.—Captivated by Genius.—Sheridan's Elopement with "Cecilia."—His Duel with Captain Matthews.—Standards of Ridicule.—Painful family Estrangements.—Enters Drury Lane.—Success of the Famous "School for Scandal."—Opinions of Sheridan and his Influence.—The Literary Club.—Anecdote of Garrick's Admittance.—Origin of "the Rejected Addresses."—New Flights.—Political Ambition. —The gaming Mania.—Almack's.—Brookes'.—Black-balled.—Two Versions of the Election Trick.—St. Stephen's won.—Vocal Difficulties.—Leads a double Life.—Pitt's vulgar Attack.—Sheridan's happy Retort.—Grattan's Quip.—Sheridan's Sallies.—The Trial of Warren Hastings.—Wonderful Effect of Sheridan's Eloquence.—The supreme Effort. —The Star culminates.—Native Taste for Swindling.—A shrewd but graceless Oxonian.—Duns outwitted.—The Lawyer jockeyed.—Adventures with Bailiffs.—Sheridan's Powers of Persuasion.—House of Commons Greek.—Curious Mimicry.—The royal boon Companion.—Lights and Shadows of Depravity.—Street Frolics at Night.—An old Tale. —The Fray in St. Giles'.—Sheridan's gradual Downfall.—Unopened Letters.—An odd Incident.—Reckless Extravagance.—Sporting Ambition.—Like Father like Son.—A severe and witty Rebuke.—Convivial Excesses of a past Day.—Worth wins at last.—Bitter Pangs.—The Scythe of Death.—The fair, loving, neglected Wife.—Debts of Honor.—Drury Lane burned.—The Owner's Serenity.—Misfortunes never come singly.—The Whitbread Quarrel.—Ruined, undone, and almost forsaken.—The dead Man arrested.—The Stories fixed on Sheridan.—Extempore Wit and inveterate Talkers 329

BEAU BRUMMELL.

Two popular Sciences.—"Buck Brummell" at Eton.—Investing his Capital.—Young Cornet Brummell. — The Beau's Studio. — The Toilet. — "Creasing down." — Sneers and Snuff-boxes. — A great Gentleman. — Anecdotes of Brummell. — "Don't forget Brum: Goose at Four!"—Offers of Intimacy resented.—Never in Love.—Brummell out Hunting.—Anecdote of Sheridan and Brummell.—The Beau's poetical Efforts.—The Value of a crooked Sixpence. — The Breach with the Prince of Wales. — "Who's your fat Friend?"—The Climax is reached.—The Black-mail of Calais.—George the Greater and George the Less. — An extraordinary Step. — Down the Hill of Life. — A miserable Old Age.—In the Hospice du bon Sauveur.—O young Men of this Age, be warned! 381

THEODORE EDWARD HOOK.

The greatest of modern Wits.—What Coleridge said of Hook.—Hook's Family.—Redeeming Points.—Versatility.—Varieties of Hoaxing.—The Black-wafered Horse.—The Berners Street Hoax.—Success of the Scheme.—The Strop of Hunger.—Kitchen Examinations.—The wrong House.—Angling for an Invitation.—The Hackney-coach Device.—The Plots of Hook and Mathews.—Hook's Talents as an Improvisatore.—The Gift becomes his Bane. — Hook's Novels. — College Fun. — Baiting a Proctor. — The punning Faculty.—Official Life opens.—Troublesome Pleasantry.—Charge of Embezzlement.—

Misfortune.—Doubly disgraced.—No Effort to remove the Stain.—Attacks on the Queen. —An incongruous Mixture.—Specimen of the Ramsbottom Letters.—Hook's Scurrility. —Fortune and Popularity.—The End....................................Page 405

SYDNEY SMITH.

The "wise Wit."—Oddities of the Father.—Verse-making at Winchester.—Curate Life on Salisbury Plain.—Old Edinburgh.—Its social and architectural Features.—Making Love metaphysically.—The old Scottish Supper.—The Men of Mark passing away.—The Band of young Spirits.—Brougham's early Tenacity.—Fitting up Conversations.—"Old School" Ceremonies.—The Speculative Society.—A brilliant Set.—Sydney's Opinion of his Friends.—Holland House.—Preacher at the "Foundling."—Sydney's "Grammar of Life."—The Picture Mania.—A Living comes at last.—The Wit's Ministry.—The first Visit to Foston le Clay.—Country Quiet.—The universal Scratcher.—Country Life and Country Prejudice.—The genial Magistrate.—Glimpse of Edinburgh Society.—Mrs. Grant of Laggan.—A Pension Difficulty.—Jeffrey and Cockburn.—Craigcrook.—Sydney Smith's Cheerfulness.—His rheumatic Armor.—No Bishopric.—Becomes Canon of St. Paul's.—Anecdotes of Lord Dudley.—A sharp Reproof.—Sydney's Classification of Society.—Last Stroke of Humor.. 433

GEORGE BUBB DODINGTON, LORD MELCOMBE.

A dinner-giving lordly Poet.—A Misfortune for a Man of Society.—Brandenburgh House. —"The Diversions of the Morning."—Johnson's Opinion of Foote.—Churchill and the "Rosciad."—Personal Ridicule in its proper Light.—Wild Specimen of the Poet.—Walpole on Dodington's "Diary."—The best Commentary on a Man's Life.—Leicester House.—Grace Boyle.—Elegant Modes of passing Time.—A sad Day.—What does Dodington come here for?—The Veteran Wit, Beau, and Politician.—Defend us from our Executors and Editors.. 469

LIST OF ILLUSTRATIONS.

PAGE
BEAU FIELDING AND THE SHAM WIDOW .... (*Frontispiece.*)
VILLIERS IN DISGUISE—THE MEETING WITH HIS SISTER 24
DE GRAMMONT'S MEETING WITH LA BELLE HAMILTON 77
WHARTON'S ROGUISH PRESENT 149
A SCENE BEFORE KENSINGTON PALACE—GEORGE II. AND QUEEN CAROLINE 167
POPE AT HIS VILLA—DISTINGUISHED VISITORS 186
A ROYAL ROBBER 210
SCARRON AND THE WITS—FIRST APPEARANCE OF LA BELLE INDIENNE 237
STRAWBERRY HILL FROM THE THAMES 276
SELWYN ACKNOWLEDGES "THE SOVEREIGNTY OF THE PEOPLE" 322
THE FAMOUS "LITERARY CLUB" 340
A TREASURE FOR A LADY—SHERIDAN AND THE LAWYER 357
THE BEST THING BEAU BRUMMELL EVER SAID 396
THEODORE HOOK'S ENGINEERING FROLIC 417
A DROLL SCENE AT SYDNEY SMITH'S 448
SYDNEY SMITH'S WITTY ANSWER TO THE OLD PARISH CLERK 453

THE

WITS AND BEAUX OF SOCIETY.

GEORGE VILLIERS, SECOND DUKE OF BUCKINGHAM.

Samuel Pepys, the weather-glass of his time, hails the first glimpse of the Restoration of Charles II. in his usual quaint terms and vulgar sycophancy.

"To Westminster Hall," says he; "where I heard how the Parliament had this day dissolved themselves, and did pass very cheerfully through the Hall, and the Speaker without his mace. The whole Hall was joyful thereat, as well as themselves; and now they begin to talk loud of the king." And the evening was closed, he further tells us, with a large bonfire in the Exchange, and people called out, "God bless King Charles!"

This was in March, 1660; and during that spring, Pepys was noting down how he did not think it possible that "my Lord Protector," Richard Cromwell, should come into power again; how there were great hopes of the king's arrival; how Monk, the Restorer, was feasted at Mercers' Hall; (Pepys's own especial); how it was resolved that a treaty be offered to the king, privately; how he resolved to go to sea with "my lord;" and how, while they lay at Gravesend, the great affair which brought back Charles Stuart was virtually accomplished. Then, with various parentheses, inimitable in their way, Pepys carries on his narrative. He has left his father's "cutting-room" to take care of itself; and finds his cabin little, though his bed is convenient, but is certain, as he rides at anchor with "my lord" in the ship, that the king "must of necessity come in," and the vessel sails round and anchors in Lee Roads. "To the castles about Deal, where *our* fleet" (*our fleet*, the saucy son of a tailor!) "lay and anchored; great was the shoot of guns from the castles and ships, and our answers." Glorious Samuel! in his element, to be sure.

Then the wind grew high: he began to be "dizzy and squeamish;" nevertheless employed "Lord's Day" in looking through the lieutenant's glass at two good merchantmen, and the women in them, "being pretty handsome;" then in the afternoon he first saw Calais, and was pleased, though it was at a great distance. All eyes were looking across the Channel just then—for the king was at Flushing; and, though the "Fanatiques" still held their heads up high, and the Cavaliers also talked high on the other side, the cause that Pepys was bound to still gained ground.

Then "they begin to speak freely of King Charles;" churches in the city, Samuel declares, were setting up his arms; merchant-ships—more important in those days—were hanging out his colors. He hears, too, how the Mercers' Company were making a statue of his gracious Majesty, to set up in the Exchange. Ah! Pepys's heart is merry; he has forty shillings (some shabby perquisite) given him by Captain Cowes of the "Paragon;" and "my lord" in the evening "falls to singing" a song upon the Rump to the tune of the "Blacksmith."

The hopes of the Cavalier party are hourly increasing, and those of Pepys we may be sure also; for Pim, the tailor, spends a morning in his cabin "putting a great many ribbons to a sail." And the king is to be brought over suddenly, "my lord" tells him: and indeed it looks like it, for the sailors are drinking Charles's health in the streets of Deal, on their knees; "which, methinks," says Pepys, "is a little too much;" and "methinks" so, worthy Master Pepys, also.

Then, how the news of the Parliamentary vote of the king's declaration was received! Pepys becomes eloquent.

"He that can fancy a fleet (like ours) in her pride, with pendants loose, guns roaring, caps flying, and the loud '*Vive le Roi!*' echoed from one ship's company to another; he, and he only, can apprehend the joy this inclosed vote was received with, or the blessing he thought himself possessed of that bore it."

Next, orders come for "my lord" to sail forthwith to the king; and the painters and tailors set to work, Pepys superintending, "cutting out some pieces of yellow cloth in the fashion of a crown and C. R.; and putting it upon a fine sheet"—and that is to supersede the States' arms, and is finished and set up. And the next day, on May 14, the Hague is seen plainly by *us*, "my lord going up in his night-gown into the cuddy."

And then they land at the Hague; some "nasty Dutchmen" come on board to offer their boats, and get money, which Pepys does not like; and in time they find themselves in the Hague, "a most neat place in all respects;" salute the Queen of Bohemia and the Prince of Orange—afterward William III.—and find at their place of supper nothing but a "sallet" and two or three bones of mutton provided for ten of us, "which was very strange." Nevertheless, on they sail, having returned to the fleet, to Schevelling; and, on the 23d of the month, go to meet the king; who, "on getting into the boat, did kiss my lord with much affection." And "extraordinary press of good company," and great mirth all day, announced the Restoration. Nevertheless Charles's clothes had not been, till this time, Master Pepys is assured, worth forty shillings—and he, as a connoisseur, was scandalized at the fact.

And now, before we proceed, let us ask who worthy Samuel Pepys was, that he should pass such stringent comments on men and manners? His origin was lowly; his family ancient; his father having followed, until the Restoration, the calling of a tailor. Pepys, vulgar as he was, had nevertheless received a university education; first entering Trinity College, Cambridge, as a sizar. To our wonder we find him marrying furtively and independently; and his wife, of fifteen, was glad with her husband to take up an abode in the house of a relative, Sir Edward Montagu, afterward Earl of Sandwich, the "my lord" under whose shadow Samuel Pepys dwelt in reverence. By this nobleman's influence, Pepys forever left the "cutting-room;" he acted first as Secretary (always as toad-eater, one would fancy), then became a clerk in the Admiralty; and as such went, after the Restoration, to live in Seething Lane, in the parish of St. Olave, Hart Street—and in St. Olave his mortal part was ultimately deposited.

So much for Pepys. See him now, in his full-bottomed wig, and best cambric neckerchief, looking out for the king and his suit, who are coming on board the "Nazeby."

"Up, and made myself as fine as I could, with the linning stockings on, and wide canons that I bought the other day at the Hague." So began he the day. "All day nothing but lords and persons of honor on board, that we were exceeding full. Dined in great deal of state, the royalle company by themselves in the coache, which was a blessed sight to see." This royal company consisted of Charles, the Dukes of York and Gloucester, his brothers, the Queen of Bohemia, the Princess Royal, the Prince of Orange, afterward William III.—all of whose hands Pepys kissed, after dinner. The King and Duke of York changed the names of the ships. The "Rumpers," as Pepys called the Parliamentarians, had given one the name of the "Nazeby;" that was now christened the "Charles;" "Richard" was changed into "James." The "Speaker" into "Mary," the "Lambert" was "Henrietta," and so on. How merry the king must have been while he thus turned the

Roundheads, as it were, off the ocean; and how he walked here and there, up and down (quite contrary to what Samuel Pepys "expected"), and fell into discourse of his escape from Worcester, and made Samuel "ready to weep" to hear of his traveling four days and three nights on foot, up to his knees in dirt, with "nothing but a green coat and pair of breeches on" (worse and worse, thought Pepys), and a pair of country shoes that made his feet sore; and how, at one place, he was made to drink by the servants, to show he was not a Roundhead; and how, at another place—and Charles, the best teller of a story in his own dominions, may here have softened his tone—the master of the house, an inn-keeper, as the king was standing by the fire, with his hands on the back of a chair, kneeled down and kissed his hand "privately," saying he could not ask him who he was, but bid "God bless him, where he was going!"

Then, rallying after this touch of pathos, Charles took his hearers over to Fecamp, in France—thence to Rouen, where, he said, in his easy, irresistible way, "I looked so poor that the people went into the rooms before I went away, to see if I had not stolen something or other."

With what reverence and sympathy did our Pepys listen! but he was forced to hurry off to get Lord Berkeley a bed; and with "much ado" (as one may believe) he did get "him to bed with my Lord Middlesex;" so, after seeing these two peers of the realm in that undignified predicament—two in a bed—"to my cabin again," where the company were still talking of the king's difficulties, and how his Majesty was fain to eat a piece of bread and cheese out of a poor body's pocket; and, at a Catholic house, how he lay a good while "in the Priest's Hole, for privacy."

In all these hairbreadth escapes—of which the king spoke with infinite humor and good feeling—one name was perpetually introduced: George—George Villiers, *Villers*, as the royal narrator called him; for the name was so pronounced formerly. And well he might; for George Villiers had been his playmate, classfellow, nay, bedfellow sometimes, in priests' holes; their names, their haunts, their hearts, were all assimilated; and misfortune had bound them closely to each other. To George Villiers let us now turn; he is waiting for his royal master on the other side of the Channel—in England. And a strange character have we to deal with:

"A man so various, that he seemed to be
Not one, but all mankind's epitome:
Stiff in opinions, always in the wrong,
Was every thing by starts, and nothing long;

But, in the course of one revolving moon,
Was chemist, fiddler, statesman, and buffoon."*

Such was George Villiers: the Alcibiades of that age. Let us trace one of the most romantic, and brilliant, and unsatisfactory lives that has ever been written.

George Villiers was born at Wallingford House, in the parish of St. Martin's-in-the-Fields, on the 30th January, 1627. The Admiralty now stands on the site of the mansion in which he first saw the light. His father was George Villiers, the favorite of James I. and Charles I.; his mother, the Lady Katherine Manners, daughter and heiress of Francis, Earl of Rutland. Scarcely was he a year old, when the assassination of his father, by Felton, threw the affairs of his family into confusion. His mother, after the Duke of Buckingham's death, gave birth to a son, Francis; who was, subsequently, savagely killed by the Roundheads, near Kingston. Then the Duchess of Buckingham very shortly married again, and uniting herself to Randolph Macdonald, Earl of Antrim, became a rigid Catholic. She was therefore lost to her children, or rather, they were lost to her; for King Charles I., who had promised to be a "husband to her, and a father to her children," removed them from her charge, and educated them with the royal princes.

The youthful peer soon gave indications of genius; and all that a careful education could do, was directed to improve his natural capacity under private tutors. He went to Cambridge; and thence, under the care of a preceptor named Aylesbury, traveled into France. He was accompanied by his young, handsome, fine-spirited brother, Francis; and this was the sunshine of his life. His father had indeed left him, as his biographer Brian Fairfax expresses it, "the greatest name in England; his mother, the greatest estate of any subject." With this inheritance there had also descended to him the wonderful beauty, the matchless grace, of his ill-fated father. Great abilities, courage, fascination of manners, were also his; but he had not been endowed with firmness of character, but was at once energetic and versatile. Even at this age, the qualities which became his ruin were clearly discoverable.

George Villiers was recalled to England by the troubles which drove the King to Oxford, and which converted that academical city into a garrison, its under-graduates into soldiers, its ancient halls into barrack-rooms. Villiers was on this occasion entered at Christ Church: the youth's best feelings were aroused, and his loyalty was engaged to one to whom his father owed so much. He was now a young man

* Dryden.

of twenty-one years of age—able to act for himself; and he went heart and soul into the cause of his sovereign. Never was there a gayer, a more prepossessing Cavalier. He could charm even a Roundhead. The harsh and Presbyterian-minded Bishop Burnet, has told us that "he was a man of a noble presence; had a great liveliness of wit, and a peculiar faculty of turning every thing into ridicule, with bold figures and natural descriptions." How invaluable he must have been in the Common-rooms at Oxford, then turned into guard-rooms, his eye upon some unlucky volunteer Don, who had put off his clerkly costume for a buff jacket, and could not manage his drill. Irresistible as his exterior is declared to have been, the original mind of Villiers was even far more influential. De Grammont tells us, "he was extremely handsome, but still thought himself much more so than he really was; although he had a great deal of discernment, yet his vanities made him mistake some civilities as intended for his person which were only bestowed on his wit and drollery."

But this very vanity, so unpleasant in an old man, is only amusing in a younger wit. While thus a gallant of the court and camp, the young nobleman proved himself to be no less brave than witty. Juvenile as he was, with a brother still younger, they fought on the royalist side at Lichfield, in the storming of the Cathedral Close. For thus allowing their lives to be endangered, their mother blamed Lord Gerard, one of the Duke's guardians; while the Parliament seized the pretext of confiscating their estates, which were afterward returned to them, on account of their being under age at the time of confiscation. The youths were then placed under the care of the Earl of Northumberland, by whose permission they traveled in France and Italy, where they appeared—their estates having been restored—with princely magnificence. Nevertheless, on hearing of the imprisonment of Charles I. in the Isle of Wight, the gallant youths returned to England, and joined the army under the Earl of Holland, who was defeated near Nonsuch, in Surrey.

A sad episode in the annals of these eventful times is presented in the fate of the handsome, brave Francis Villiers. His murder, for one can call it by no other name, shows how keenly the personal feelings of the Roundheads were engaged in this national quarrel. Under most circumstances, Englishmen would have spared the youth, and respected the gallantry of the free young soldier, who, planting himself against an oak-tree which grew in the road, refused to ask for quarter, but defended himself against several assailants. But the name of Villiers was hateful in Puritan ears. "Hew them down, root and branch!" was the sentiment that actuated the soldiery. His very loveliness exasperated their vengeance. At last, "with nine wounds on his beautiful face and body," says Fairfax, "he was slain." "The oak-tree," writes the devoted servant, "is his monument," and the letters of F. V. were cut in it in his day. His body was conveyed by water to York House, and was entombed with that of his father, in the Chapel of Henry VII.

His brother fled toward St. Neot's, where he encountered a strange kind of peril. Tobias Rustat attended him; and "was with him in the rising in Kent for King Charles I., wherein the Duke was engaged; and they, being put to the flight, the Duke's helmet, by a brush under a tree, was turned upon his back, and tied so fast with a string under his throat, that without the present help of T. R.," writes Fairfax, "it had undoubtedly choked him, as I have credibly heard."*

While at St. Neot's, the house in which Villiers had taken refuge was surrounded with soldiers. He had a stout heart, and a dextrous hand; he took his resolution; rushed out upon his foes, killed the officer in command, galloped off and joined the Prince in the Downs.

The sad story of Charles I. was played out; but Villiers remained stanch, and was permitted to return and to accompany Prince Charles into Scotland. Then came the battle of Worcester in 1651: there Charles II. showed himself a worthy descendant of James IV. of Scotland. He resolved to conquer or die: with desperate gallantry the English Cavaliers and the Scotch Highlanders seconded the monarch's valiant onslaught on Cromwell's horse, whose invincible Life Guards were almost driven back by the shock. But they were not seconded; Charles II. had his horse twice shot under him, but, nothing daunted, he was the last to tear himself away from the field, and then only upon the solicitations of his friends.

Charles retired to Kidderminster that evening. The Duke of Buckingham, the gallant Lord Derby, Wilmot, afterward Earl of Rochester, and some others, rode near him. They were followed by a small body of horse. Disconsolately they rode on northward, a faithful band of sixty being resolved to escort his Majesty to Scotland. At length they halted on Kinver Heath, near Kidderminster, their guide having lost the

* The day after the battle at Kingston the Duke's estates were confiscated (8th July, 1648).—Nichols' History of Leicestershire, iii. 213; who also says that the Duke offered marriage to one of the daughters of Cromwell, but was refused. He went abroad in 1648, but returned with Charles II. to Scotland in 1650, and again escaped to France after the battle of Worcester, 1651. The sale of the pictures would seem to have commenced during his first exile.

way. In this extremity Lord Derby said that he had been received kindly at an old house in a secluded woody country, between Tong Castle and Brewood, on the borders of Staffordshire. It was named "Boscobel," he said; and that word has henceforth conjured up to the mind's eye the remembrance of a band of tired heroes riding through woody glades to an ancient house, where shelter was given to the worn-out horses and scarcely less harassed riders.

But not so rapidly did they in reality proceed. A Catholic family, named Giffard, were living at White-Ladies, about twenty-six miles from Worcester. This was only about half a mile from Boscobel: it had been a convent of Cistercian nuns, whose long white cloaks of old had once been seen, ghost-like, amid forest glades or on hillock green. The White-Ladies had other memories to grace it besides those of holy vestals or of unholy Cavaliers. From the time of the Tudors, a respectable family named Somers had owned the White-Ladies, and inhabited it since its white-garbed tenants had been turned out and the place secularized. "Somers's House," as it was called (though, more happily, the old name has been restored), had received Queen Elizabeth on her progress. The richly cultivated old conventual gardens had supplied the Queen with some famous pears, and, in the fullness of her approval of the fruit, she had added them to the City arms. At that time one of these vaunted pear-trees stood securely in the market-place of Worcester.

At the White-Ladies Charles rested for half an hour; and here he left his garters, waistcoat, and other garments, to avoid discovery, ere he proceeded. They were long kept as relics.

The mother of Lord Somers had been placed in this old house for security, for she was on the eve of giving birth to the future statesman, who was born in that sanctuary just at this time. His father at that very moment commanded a troop of horse in Cromwell's army, so that the risk the Cavaliers ran was imminent. The King's horse was led into the hall. Day was dawning; and the Cavaliers, as they entered the old conventual tenement, and saw the sunbeams on its walls, perceived their peril. A family of servants named Penderell held various offices there and at Boscobel. William took care of Boscobel; George was a servant at White-Ladies; Humphrey was the miller to that house; Richard lived close by, at Hebbal Grange. He and William were called into the royal presence. Lord Derby then said to them, "This is the King; have a care of him, and preserve him as thou didst me."

Then the attendant courtiers began undressing the King. They took off his buff-coat, and put on him a "noggon coarse shirt," and a green suit and another doublet—Richard Penderell's woodman's dress. Lord Wilmot cut his sovereign's hair with a knife, but Richard Penderell took up his shears and finished the work. "Burn it," said the king; but Richard kept the sacred locks. Then Charles covered his dark face with soot. Could any thing have taken away the expression of his half-sleepy, half-merry eyes?

They departed, and half an hour afterward Colonel Ashenhurst, with a troop of Roundhead horse, rode up to the White-Ladies. The King, meantime, had been conducted by Richard Penderell into a coppice-wood, with a bill-hook in his hands for defense and disguise. But his followers were overtaken near Newport; and here Buckingham, with Lords Talbot and Leviston, escaped, and henceforth, until Charles's wanderings were transferred from England to France, George Villiers was separated from the Prince. Accompanied by the Earls of Derby and Lauderdale, and by Lord Talbot, he proceeded northward, in hopes of joining General Leslie and the Scotch horse. But their hopes were soon dashed: attacked by a body of Roundheads, Buckingham and Lord Leviston were compelled to leave the high road, to alight from their horses, and to make their way to Bloore Park, near Newport, where Villiers found a shelter. He was soon, however, necessitated to depart: he put on a laborer's dress; he deposited his George, a gift from Henrietta Maria, with a companion, and set off for Billstrop, in Nottinghamshire, one Matthews, a carpenter, acting as his guide; at Billstrop he was welcomed by Mr. Hawley, a Cavalier; and from that place he went to Brookesby, in Leicestershire, the original seat of the Villiers family, and the birth-place of his father. Here he was received by Lady Villiers—the widow, probably, of his father's brother, Sir William Villiers—one of those contented country squires who not only sought no distinction, but scarcely thanked James I. when he made him a baronet. Here might the hunted refugee see, on the open battlements of the church, the shields on which were exhibited united quarterings of his father's family with those of his mother; here, listen to old tales about his grandfather, good Sir George, who married a serving-woman in his deceased wife's kitchen;* and that serving-woman became the leader of fash-

* Sir George Villiers's second wife was Mary, daughter of Antony Beaumont, Esq., of Glenfield (Nichols' Leicestershire, iii. 193), who was son of Wm. Beaumont, Esq., of Cole Orton. She afterward was married successively to Sir Wm. Rayner and Sir Thomas Compton, and was created Countess of Buckingham in 1618.

ions in the court of James. Here he might ponder on the vicissitudes which marked the destiny of the house of Villiers, and wonder what should come next.

That the spirit of adventure was strong within him, is shown by his daring to go up to London, and disguising himself as a mountebank. He had a coat made, called a "Jack Pudding Coat:" a little hat was stuck on his head, with a fox's tail in it, and cocks' feathers here and there. A wizard's mask one day, a daubing of flour another, completed the disguise it was then so usual to assume: witness the long traffic held at Exeter Change by the Duchess of Tyrconnel, Frances Jennings, in a white mask, selling laces and French gew-gaws, a trader to all appearance, but really carrying on political intrigues; every one went to chat with the "White Milliner," as she was called, during the reign of William and Mary. The Duke next erected a stage at Charing Cross—in the very face of the stern Rumpers, who, with long faces, rode past the sinful man each day as they came ambling up from the Parliament House. A band of puppet-players and violins set up their shows; and music covers a multitude of incongruities. The ballad was then the great vehicle of personal attack, and Villiers's dawning taste for poetry was shown in the ditties which he now composed, and in which he sometimes assisted vocally. While all the other Cavaliers were forced to fly, he thus bearded his enemies in their very homes: sometimes he talked to them face to face, and kept the sanctimonious citizens in talk till they found themselves sinfully disposed to laugh. But this vagrant life had serious evils: it broke down all the restraints which civilized society naturally and beneficially imposes. The Duke of Buckingham, Butler, the author of Hudibras, writes, "rises, eats, goes to bed by the Julian account, long after all others that go by the new style, and keeps the same hours with owls and the Antipodes. He is a great observer of the Tartar customs, and never eats till the great cham, having dined, makes proclamation that all the world may go to dinner. He does not dwell in his house, but haunts it like an evil spirit, that walks all night, to disturb the family, and never appears by day. He lives perpetually benighted, runs out of his life, and loses his time as men do their ways in the dark: and as blind men are led by their dogs, so he is governed by some mean servant or other that relates to his pleasures. He is as inconstant as the moon which he lives under; and although he does nothing but advise with his pillow all day, he is as great a stranger to himself as he is to the rest of the world. His mind entertains all things that come and go; but like guests and strangers, they are not welcome if they stay long. This lays

VILLIERS IN DISGUISE—THE MEETING WITH HIS SISTER.

him open to all cheats, quacks, and impostors, who apply to every particular humor while it lasts, and afterward vanish. He deforms nature while he intends to adorn her, like Indians that hang jewels in their lips and noses. His ears are perpetually drilling with a fiddlestick, and endures pleasures with less patience than other men do their pains."

The more effectually to support his character as a mountebank, Villiers sold mithridate and galbanum plasters: thousands of spectators and customers thronged every day to see and hear him. Possibly many guessed that beneath all this fantastic exterior some ulterior project was concealed; yet he remained untouched by the City Guards. Well did Dryden describe him:

> "Then all for women, painting, rhyming, drinking,
> Besides ten thousand freaks that died in thinking.
> Blest madman, who could every hour employ
> With something new to wish or to enjoy!"

His elder sister, Lady Mary Villiers, had married the Duke of Richmond, one of the loyal adherents of Charles I. The duke was, therefore, in durance at Windsor, while the duchess was to be placed under strict surveillance at Whitehall.

Villiers resolved to see her. Hearing that she was to pass into Whitehall on a certain day, he set up his stage where she could not fail to perceive him. He had something important to say to her. As she drew near, he cried out to the mob that he would give them a song on the Duchess of Richmond and the Duke of Buckingham: nothing could be more acceptable. "The mob," it is related, "stopped the coach and the duchess. . . . Nay, so outrageous were the mob, that they forced the duchess, who was then the handsomest woman in England, to sit in the boot of the coach, and to hear him sing all his impertinent songs. Having left off singing, he told them it was no more than reason that he should present the duchess with some of the songs. So he alighted from his stage, covered all over with papers and ridiculous little pictures. Having come to the coach, he took off a black piece of taffeta, which he always wore over one of his eyes, when his sister discovered immediately who he was, yet had so much presence of mind as not to give the least sign of mistrust; nay she gave him some very opprobrious language, but was very eager at snatching the papers he threw into her coach. Among them was a packet of letters, which she had no sooner got but she went forward, the duke, at the head of the mob, attending and hallooing her a good way out of the town."

A still more daring adventure was contemplated also by

this young, irresistible duke. Bridget Cromwell, the eldest daughter of Oliver, was, at that time, a bride of twenty-six years of age; having married, in 1647, the saintly Henry Ireton, Lord Deputy of Ireland. Bridget was the pattern heroine of the "*unco guid*," the quintessence of all propriety; the impersonation of sanctity; an ultra republican, who scarcely accorded to her father the modest title of Protector. She was esteemed by her party a "personage of sublime growth:" "humbled, not exalted," according to Mrs. Hutchinson, by her elevation: "nevertheless," says that excellent lady, "as my Lady Ireton was walking in the St. James's Park, the Lady Lambert, as proud as her husband, came by where she was, and as the present princess always hath precedency of the relict of the dead, so she put by my Lady Ireton, who, notwithstanding her piety and humility, was a little grieved at the affront."

After this anecdote one can not give much credence to this lady's humility: Bridget was, however, a woman of powerful intellect, weakened by her extreme, and to use a now common term, *crotchety* opinions. Like most *esprits forts*, she was easily imposed upon. One day this paragon saw a mountebank dancing on a stage in the most exquisite style. His fine shape, too, caught the attention of one who assumed to be above all folly. It is sometimes fatal to one's peace to look out of a window; no one knows what sights may rivet or displease. Mistress Ireton was sitting at her window unconscious that any one with the hated and malignant name of "Villiers" was before her. After some unholy admiration, she sent to speak to the mummer. The duke scarcely knew whether to trust himself in the power of the bloodthirsty Ireton's bride or not—yet his courage—his love of sport—prevailed. He visited her that evening: no longer, however, in his jack-pudding coat, but in a rich suit, disguised with a cloak over it. He wore still a plaster over one eye, and was much disposed to take it off, but prudence forbade; and thus he stood in the presence of the prim and saintly Bridget Ireton. The particulars of the interview rest on his statement, and they must not, therefore, be accepted implicitly. Mistress Ireton is said to have made advances to the handsome incognito. What a triumph to a man like Villiers, to have intrigued with my Lord Protector's sanctified daughter! But she inspired him with disgust. He saw in her the presumption and hypocrisy of her father; he hated her as Cromwell's daughter and Ireton's wife. He told her, therefore, that he was a Jew, and could not by his laws become the paramour of a Christian woman. The saintly Bridget stood amazed; she had imprudently let him into some of the most important secrets of her party. A Jew! It was dreadful! But how could a person of that persuasion be so strict, so strait-laced? She probably entertained all the horror of Jews which the Puritanical party cherished as a virtue; forgetting the lessons of toleration and liberality inculcated by Holy Writ. She sent, however, for a certain Jewish Rabbi to converse with the stranger. What was the Duke of Buckingham's surprise, on visiting her one evening, to see the learned doctor armed at all points with the Talmud, and thirsting for dispute, by the side of the saintly Bridget. He could noways meet such a body of controversy; but thought it best forthwith to set off for the Downs. Before he departed he wrote, however, to Mistress Ireton, on the plea that she might wish to know to what tribe of Jews he belonged. So he sent her a note written with all his native wit and point.*

Buckingham now experienced all the miseries that a man of expensive pleasures with a sequestrated estate is likely to endure. One friend remained to watch over his interests in England. This was John Traylman, a servant of his late father's; who was left to guard the collection of pictures made by the late duke, and deposited in York House. That collection was, in the opinion of competent judges, the third in point of value in England, being only inferior to those of Charles I. and the Earl of Arundel.

It had been bought, with immense expense, partly by the duke's agents in Italy, the Mantua Gallery supplying a great portion—partly in France—partly in Flanders; and to Flanders a great portion was destined now to return. Secretly and laboriously did old Traylman pack up and send off these treasures to Antwerp, where now the gay youth whom the aged domestic had known from a child was in want and exile. The pictures were eagerly bought by a foreign collector named Duart. The proceeds gave poor Villiers bread; but the noble works of Titian and Leonardo da Vinci, and others, were lost forever to England.

It must have been very irritating to Villiers to know that while he just existed abroad, the great estates enjoyed by his father were being subjected to pillage by Cromwell's soldiers, or sold for pitiful sums by the Commissioners appointed by Parliament to break up and annihilate many of the old properties in England. Burleigh-on-the-Hill, the stately seat on which the first duke had lavished thousands, had been taken by the Roundheads. It was so large, and presented so long a line of buildings that the Parliamentarians could not hold it

* This incident is taken from Madame Dunois' Memoirs, part i. p. 86.

without leaving in it a great garrison and stores of ammunition. It was therefore burnt, and the stables alone occupied; and those even were formed into a house of unusual size. York House was doubtless marked out for the next destructive decree. There was something in the very history of this house which might be supposed to excite the wrath of the Roundheads. Queen Mary (whom we must not, after Miss Strickland's admirable life of her, call Bloody Queen Mary, but who will always be best known by that unpleasant title) had bestowed York House on the See of York, as a compensation for York House, at Whitehall, which Henry VIII. had taken from Wolsey. It had afterward come into possession of the Keepers of the Great Seal. Lord Bacon was born in York House, his father having lived there; and the

"Greatest, wisest, meanest of mankind,"

built here an aviary which cost £300. When the Duke of Lennox wished to buy York House, Bacon thus wrote to him: "For this you will pardon me: York House is the house where my father died, and where I first breathed; and there will I yield my last breath, if it so please God and the King." It did not, however, please the King that he should; the house was borrowed only by the first Duke of Buckingham from the Archbishop of York, and then exchanged for another seat on the plea that the duke would want it for the reception of foreign potentates, and for entertainments given to royalty.

The duke pulled it down: and the house, which was erected as a temporary structure, was so superb that even Pepys, twenty years after it had been left to bats and cobwebs, speaks of it in raptures, as of a place in which the great duke's soul was seen in every chamber. On the walls were shields on which the arms of Manners and of Villiers—peacocks and lions—were quartered. York House was never, however, finished; but, as the lover of old haunts enters Buckingham Street in the Strand, he will perceive an ancient water-gate, beautifully proportioned, built by Inigo Jones—smoky, isolated, impaired—but still speaking volumes of remembrance of the glories of the assassinated duke, who had purposed to build the whole house in that style.

"*Yorschaux*," as he called it—York House—the French embassador had written word to his friends at home, "is the most richly fitted up of any that I saw." The galleries and state rooms were graced by the display of the Roman marbles, both busts and statues, which the first duke had bought from Rubens; while in the gardens the Cain and Abel of John of Bologna, given by Philip IV. of Spain to King Charles, and by him bestowed on the elder George Villiers, made that fair *pleasaunce* famous. It was doomed—as were what were called the "superstitious" pictures in the house—to destruction: henceforth all was in decay and neglect. "I went to see York House and gardens," Evelyn writes in 1655, "belonging to the former greate Buckingham, but now much ruined through neglect."

Traylman, doubtless, kept George Villiers the younger in full possession of all that was to happen to that deserted tenement in which the old man mourned for the departed, and thought of the absent.

The intelligence which he had soon to communicate was all-important. York House was to be occupied again; and Cromwell and his coadjutors had bestowed it on Fairfax. The blow was perhaps softened by the reflection that Fairfax was a man of generous temper; and that he had an only daughter, Mary Fairfax, young, and an heiress. Though the daughter of a Puritan, a sort of interest was attached, even by Cavaliers, to Mary Fairfax, from her having, at five years of age, followed her father through the civil wars on horseback, seated before a maid-servant; and having, on her journey, frequently fainted, and was so ill as to have been left in a house by the roadside, her father never expecting to see her again.

In reference to this young girl, then about eighteen years of age, Buckingham now formed a plan. He resolved to return to England disguised, and to offer his hand to Mary Fairfax, and so recover his property through the influence of Fairfax, He was confident of his own attractions; and, indeed, from every account, he appears to have been one of those reckless, handsome, speculative characters that often take the fancy of better men than themselves. "He had," says Burnet, "no sort of literature, only he was drawn into chemistry; and for some years he thought he was very near the finding of the philosopher's stone, which had the effect that attends on all such men as he was, when they are drawn in, to lay out for it. He had no principles of religion, virtue, or friendship; pleasure, frolic, or extravagant diversion was all he laid to heart. He was true to nothing; for he was not true to himself. He had no steadiness nor conduct; he could keep no secret, nor execute any design without spoiling it; he could never fix his thoughts, nor govern his estate, though then the greatest in England. He was bred about the king, and for many years he had a great ascendant over him; but he spoke of him to all persons with that contempt, that at last he drew a lasting disgrace upon himself. And he at length ruined both body and mind, fortune and reputation equally."

This was a sad prospect for poor Mary Fairfax, but certainly if in their choice

——— "Weak women go astray,
Their stars are more in fault than they,"

and she was less to blame in her choice than her father, who ought to have advised her against the marriage. Where and how they met is not known. Mary was not attractive in person: she was in her youth little, brown, and thin, but became a "short fat body," as De Grammont tells us, in her early married life; in the later period of her existence, she was described by the Vicomtesse de Longueville as a "little round crumpled woman, very fond of finery;" and she adds that, on visiting the duchess one day, she found her, though in mourning, in a kind of loose robe over her, all edged and laced with gold. So much for a Puritan's daughter.

To this insipid personage the duke presented himself. She soon liked him, and in spite of his outrageous infidelities, continued to like him after their marriage.

He carried his point: Mary Fairfax became his wife on the 6th of September, 1657, and, by the influence of Fairfax, his estate, or, at all events, a portion of the revenues, about £4000 a year, it is said, were restored to him. Nevertheless, it is mortifying to find that in 1672, he sold York House, in which his father had taken such pride, for £30,000. The house was pulled down; streets were erected on the gardens: George Street, Villiers Street, Duke Street, Buckingham Street, Off Alley, recall the name of the ill-starred George, first duke, and of his needy, profligate son; but the only trace of the real greatness of the family importance thus swept away is in the motto inscribed on the point of old Inigo's water-gate, toward the street: "*Fidei coticula crux.*" It is sad for all good royalists to reflect that it was not the rabid Roundhead, but a degenerate Cavalier, who sold and thus destroyed York House.

The marriage with Mary Fairfax, though one of interest solely, was not a *mésalliance:* her father was connected by the female side with the Earls of Rutland; he was also a man of a generous spirit, as he had shown, in handing over to the Countess of Derby the rents of the Isle of Man, which had been granted to him by the Parliament. In a similar spirit he was not sorry to restore York House to the Duke of Buckingham.

Cromwell, however, was highly exasperated by the nuptials between Mary Fairfax and Villiers, which took place at Nun-Appleton, near York, one of Fairfax's estates. The Protector had, it is said, intended Villiers for one of his own daughters.

Upon what plea he acted it is not stated; he committed Villiers to the Tower, where he remained until the death of Oliver, and the accession of Richard Cromwell.

In vain did Fairfax solicit his release: Cromwell refused it, and Villiers remained in durance until the abdication of Richard Cromwell, when he was set at liberty, but not without the following conditions, dated February 21st, 1658–9:—

"The humble petition of George Duke of Buckingham was this day read. Resolved that George Duke of Buckingham, now prisoner at Windsor Castle, upon his engagement upon his honor at the bar of this House, and upon the engagement of Lord Fairfax in £20,000, that the said duke shall peaceably demean himself for the future, and shall not join with, or abet, or have any correspondence with, any of the enemies of the Lord Protector, and of his Commonwealth, in any of the parts beyond the sea, or within this commonwealth, shall be discharged of his imprisonment and restraint; and that the Governor of Windsor Castle be required to bring the Duke of Buckingham to the bar of this House on Wednesday next, to engage his honor accordingly. Ordered, that the security of £20,000, to be given by the Lord Fairfax, on the behalf of the Duke of Buckingham, be taken in the name of His Highness the Lord Protector."

During his incarceration at Windsor, Buckingham had a companion, of whom many a better man might have been envious: this was Abraham Cowley, an old college friend of the duke's. Cowley was the son of a grocer, and owed his entrance into academic life to having been a King's Scholar at Westminster. One day he happened to take up from his mother's parlor window a copy of Spenser's "Faerie Queene." He eagerly perused the delightful volume, though he was then only twelve years old: and this impulse being given to his mind, became at fifteen a reciter of verses. His "Poetical Blossoms," published while he was still at school, gave, however, no foretaste of his future eminence. He proceeded to Trinity College, Cambridge, where his friendship with Villiers was formed; and where, perhaps, from that circumstance, Cowley's predilections for the cause of the Stuarts was ripened into loyalty.

No two characters could be more dissimilar than those of Abraham Cowley and George Villiers. Cowley was quiet, modest, sober, of a thoughtful, philosophical turn, and of an affectionate nature; neither boasting of his own merits nor depreciating others. He was the friend of Lucius Cary, Lord Falkland; and yet he loved, though he must have condemned, George Villiers. It is not unlikely that, while Cowley imparted his love of poetry to Villiers, Villiers may have inspired the pensive and blameless poet with a love of that display of wit then in vogue, and heightened that sense of humor which speaks forth in some of Cowley's productions. Few authors suggest so many new thoughts, really his own, as Cowley. "His works," it has been said, "are a flower-garden run to weeds, but the flowers are numerous and brilliant, and a search after them will well repay the pains of a collector who is not too indolent or fastidious."

As Cowley and his friend passed the weary hours in durance, many an old tale could the poet tell the peer of stirring times; for Cowley had accompanied Charles I. in many a perilous journey, and had protected Queen Henrietta Maria in her escape to France: through Cowley had the correspondence of the royal pair, when separated, been carried on. The poet had before suffered imprisonment for his loyalty; and, to disguise his actual occupation, had obtained the degree of Doctor of Medicine, and assumed the character of a physician, on the strength of knowing the virtues of a few plants.

Many a laugh, doubtless, had Buckingham at the expense of *Dr.* Cowley : however, in later days, the duke proved a true friend to the poet, in helping to procure for him the lease of a farm at Chertsey, from the queen, and here Cowley, rich upon £300 a year, ended his days.

For some time after Buckingham's release, he lived quietly and respectably at Nun-Appleton, with General Fairfax and the vapid Mary. But the Restoration—the first dawnings of which have been referred to in the commencement of this biography —ruined him, body and mind.

He was made a Lord of the Bedchamber, a Member of the Privy Council, and afterward Master of the Horse,* and Lord Lieutenant of Yorkshire. He lived in great magnificence at Wallingford House, a tenement next to York House, intended to be the habitable and useful appendage to that palace.

He was henceforth, until he proved treacherous to his sovereign, the brightest ornament of Whitehall. Beauty of person was hereditary: his father was styled the "handsomest-bodied man in England," and George Villiers the younger equaled George Villiers the elder in all personal accomplishments. When he entered the Presence-Chamber all eyes followed him; every movement was graceful and stately. Sir John Reresby pronounced him "to be the finest gentleman he ever saw." "He was born," Madame Dunois declared, "for gallantry and magnificence." His wit was faultless, but his manners engag-

* The duke became Master of the Horse in 1668: he paid £20,000 to the Duke of Albemarle for the post.

ing; yet his sallies often descended into buffoonery, and he spared no one in his merry moods. One evening a play of Dryden's was represented. An actress had to spout forth this line—

"My wound is great because it is so small!"

She gave it out with pathos, paused, and was theatrically distressed. Buckingham was seated in one of the boxes. He rose; all eyes were fixed upon a face well known in all gay assemblies; in a tone of burlesque he answered,

"Then 'twould be greater were it none at all."

Instantly the audience laughed at the duke's tone of ridicule, and the poor woman was hissed off the stage.

The king himself did not escape Buckingham's shafts; while Lord Chancellor Clarendon fell a victim to his ridicule; nothing could withstand it. There, not in that iniquitous gallery at Whitehall, but in the king's privy chambers, Villiers might be seen in all the radiance of his matured beauty. His face was long and oval, with sleepy, yet glistening eyes, over which large arched eyebrows seemed to contract a brow on which the curls of a massive wig (which fell almost to his shoulders) hung low. His nose was long, well formed, and flexible; his lips thin and compressed, and defined, as the custom was, by two very short, fine, black patches of hair, looking more like strips of sticking-plaster than a mustache. As he made his reverence his rich robes fell over a faultless form. He was a beau to the very fold of the cambric band round his throat; with long ends of the richest, closest point that was ever rummaged out from a foreign nunnery to be placed on the person of this sacrilegious sinner.

Behold, now, how he changes. Villiers is Villiers no longer. He is Clarendon, walking solemnly to the Court of the Star Chamber: a pair of bellows is hanging before him for the purse; Colonel Titus is walking with a fire-shovel on his shoulder, to represent a mace; the king, himself a capital mimic, is splitting his sides with laughter; the courtiers are fairly in a roar. Then how he was wont to divert the king with his descriptions! "Ipswich, for instance," he said, "was a town without inhabitants—a river it had without waters—streets without names; and it was a place where asses wore boots:" alluding to the asses, when employed in rolling Lord Hereford's bowling-green, having boots on their feet to prevent their injuring the turf.

Flecknoe, the poet, describes the duke at this period, in "Euterpe Revived"—

"The gallant'st person, and the noblest minde,
In all the world his prince could ever finde,
Or to participate his private cares,
Or bear the public weight of his affairs,
Like well-built arches, stronger with their weight,
And well-built minds, the steadier with their height;
Such was the composition and frame
O' the noble and the gallant Buckingham."

The praise, however, even in the duke's best days, was overcharged. Villiers was no "well-built arch," nor could Charles trust to the fidelity of one so versatile for an hour. Besides, the moral character of Villiers must have prevented him, even in those days, from bearing "the public weight of affairs."

A scandalous intrigue soon proved the unsoundness of Flecknoe's tribute. Among the most licentious beauties of the court was Anna Maria, Countess of Shrewsbury, the daughter of Robert Brudenel, Earl of Cardigan, and the wife of Francis, Earl of Shrewsbury: among many shameless women she was the most shameless, and her face seems to have well expressed her mind. In the round, fair visage, with its languishing eyes, and full, pouting mouth, there is something voluptuous and bold. The forehead is broad, but low; and the wavy hair, with its tendril curls, comes down almost to the fine arched eyebrows, and then, falling into masses, sets off white shoulders which seem to designate an inelegant amount of *embonpoint*. There is nothing elevated in the whole countenance, as Lely has painted her, and her history is a disgrace to her age and time.

She had numerous lovers (not in the refined sense of the word), and, at last, took up with Thomas Killigrew. He had been, like Villiers, a royalist: first a page to Charles I., next a companion of Charles II., in exile. He married the fair Cecilia Croft; yet his morals were so vicious that even in the Court of Venice to which he was accredited, in order to borrow money from the merchants of that city, he was too profligate to remain. He came back with Charles II., and was Master of the Revels, or King's Jester, as the court considered him, though without any regular appointment, during his life: the butt, at once, and the satirist of Whitehall.

It was Killigrew's wit and descriptive powers which, when heightened by wine, were inconceivably great, that induced Villiers to select Lady Shrewsbury for the object of his admiration. When Killigrew perceived that he was supplanted by Villiers, he became frantic with rage, and poured out the bitterest invectives against the countess. The result was that, one night, returning from the Duke of York's apartments at St. James's, three passes with a sword were made at him through his chair, and one of them pierced his arm. This, and other occurrences, at last aroused the attention of Lord Shrewsbury, who had hitherto never doubted his wife: he challenged the Duke of Buckingham; and his infamous wife, it is said, held her paramour's horse, disguised as a page. Lord Shrewsbury was killed,* and the scandalous intimacy went on as before. No one but the queen, no one but the Duchess of Buckingham, appeared shocked at this tragedy, and no one minded their remarks, or joined in their indignation: all moral sense was suspended, or wholly stifled; and Villiers gloried in his depravity, more witty, more amusing, more fashionable than ever; and yet he seems, by the best known and most extolled of his poems, to have had some conception of what a real and worthy attachment might be.

The following verses are to his "Mistress."

"What a dull fool was I
To think so gross a lie,
As that I ever was in love before!
I have, perhaps, known one or two,
With whom I was content to be
At that which they call keeping company.
But after all that they could do,
I still could be with more.
Their absence never made me shed a tear;
And I can truly swear,
That, till my eyes first gazed on you,
I ne'er beheld the thing I could adore.

"A world of things must curiously be sought:
A world of things must be together brought
To make up charms which have the power to move,
Through a discerning eye, true love;
That is a master-piece above
What only looks and shape can do;
There must be wit and judgment too,
Greatness of thought, and worth, which draw,
From the whole world, respect and awe.

"She that would raise a noble love must find
Ways to beget a passion for her mind;
She must be that which she to be would seem,
For all true love is grounded on esteem:
Plainness and truth gain more a generous heart
Than all the crooked subtleties of art.
She must be—what said I?—she must be *you*:
None but yourself that miracle can do.
At least, I'm sure, thus much I plainly see,
None but yourself e'er did it upon me.
'Tis you alone that can my heart subdue,
To you alone it always shall be true."

* The duel with the Earl of Shrewsbury took place on the 17th of January, 1667-8.

The next lines are also remarkable for the delicacy and happy turn of the expressions—

"Though Phillis, from prevailing charms,
Have forc'd my Delia from my arms,
Think not your conquest to maintain
By rigor or unjust disdain.
In vain, fair nymph, in vain you strive,
For Love doth seldom Hope survive.
My heart may languish for a time,
As all beauties in their prime
Have justified such cruelty,
By the same fate that conquered me.
When age shall come, at whose command
Those troops of beauty must disband—
A rival's strength once took away,
What slave's so dull as to obey?
But if you'll learn a noble way
To keep his empire from decay,
And there forever fix your throne,
Be kind, but kind to me alone."

Like his father, who ruined himself by building, Villiers had a monomania for bricks and mortar, yet he found time to write "The Rehearsal," a play on which Mr. Reed in his "Dramatic Biography" makes the following observation: "It is so perfect a masterpiece in its way, and so truly original, that, notwithstanding its prodigious success, even the task of imitation, which most kinds of excellence have invited inferior geniuses to undertake, has appeared as too arduous to be attempted with regard to this, which through a whole century stands alone, notwithstanding that the very plays it was written expressly to ridicule are forgotten, and the taste it was meant to expose totally exploded."

The reverses of fortune which brought George Villiers to abject misery were therefore, in a very great measure, due to his own misconduct, his depravity, his waste of life, his perversion of noble mental powers: yet in many respects he was in advance of his age. He advocated, in the House of Lords, toleration to Dissenters. He wrote a "Short Discourse on the Reasonableness of Men's having a Religion, or Worship of God;" yet, such was his inconsistency, that, in spite of these works, and of one styled a "Demonstration of the Deity," written a short time before his death, he assisted Lord Rochester in his atheistic poem upon "Nothing."

Butler, the author of Hudibras, too truly said of Villiers "that he had studied *the whole body of vice*;" a most fearful censure—a most significant description of a bad man. "His parts," he adds, "are disproportionate to the whole, and like a monster, he has more of some, and less of others, than he should have. He has pulled down all that nature raised in him, and built himself up again after a model of his own. He has dammed up all those lights that nature made into the noblest prospects of the world, and opened other little blind loopholes backward, by turning day into night, and night into day."

The satiety and consequent misery produced by this terrible life are ably described by Butler. And it was perhaps partly this wearied, worn-out spirit that caused Villiers to rush madly into politics for excitement. In 1666 he asked for the office of Lord President of the North; it was refused: he became disaffected, raised mutinies, and, at last, excited the indignation of his too-indulgent sovereign. Charles dismissed him from his office, after keeping him for some time in confinement. After this epoch little is heard of Buckingham but what is disgraceful. He was again restored to Whitehall, and, according to Pepys, even closeted with Charles, while the Duke of York was excluded. A certain acquaintance of the duke's remonstrated with him upon the course which Charles now took in Parliament. "How often have you said to me," this person remarked, "that the king was a weak man, unable to govern, but to be governed, and that you could command him as you liked? Why do you suffer him to do these things?"

"Why," answered the duke, "I do suffer him to do these things, that I may hereafter the better command him." A reply which betrays the most depraved principle of action, whether toward a sovereign or a friend, that can be expressed. His influence was for some time supreme, yet he became the leader of the opposition, and invited to his table the discontented peers, to whom he satirized the court, and condemned the king's want of attention to business. While the theatre was ringing with laughter at the inimitable character of Bayes in the "Rehearsal," the House of Lords was listening with profound attention to the eloquence that entranced their faculties, making wrong seem right, for Buckingham was ever heard with attention.

Taking into account his mode of existence, "which," says Clarendon, "was a life by night more than by day, in all the liberties that nature could desire and wit invent," it was astonishing how extensive an influence he had in both Houses of Parliament. His rank and condescension, the pleasantness of his humors and conversation, and the extravagance and keenness of his wit, unrestrained by modesty or religion, caused persons of all opinions and dispositions to be fond of his company, and to imagine that these levities and vanities would wear off with age, and that there would be enough of good left to make him useful to his country, for which he pretended a wonderful affection.

But this brilliant career was soon checked. The varnish over the hollow character of this extraordinary man was eventually rubbed off. We find the first hint of that famous coalition styled the *Cabal*, in Pepys's Diary, and henceforth the duke must be regarded as a ruined man.

"He" (Sir H. Cholmly) "tells me that the Duke of Buckingham his crimes, as far as he knows, are his being of a cabal with some discontented persons of the late House of Commons, and opposing the desires of the king in all his matters in that House; and endeavoring to become popular, and advising how the Commons' House should proceed, and how he would order the House of Lords. And he hath been endeavoring to have the king's nativity calculated; which was done, and the fellow now in the Tower about it. . . . This silly lord hath provoked, by his ill carriage, the Duke of York, my Lord Chancellor, and all the great persons, and therefore most likely will die."

One day, in the House of Lords, during a conference between the two Houses, Buckingham leaned rudely over the shoulder of Henry Pierrepont, Marquis of Dorchester. Lord Dorchester merely removed his elbow. Then the duke asked him if he was uneasy. "Yes," the marquis replied, adding, "the duke dared not do this if he were any where else." Buckingham retorted, "Yes, he would; and he was a better man than my lord marquis;" on which Dorchester told him that he lied. On this Buckingham struck off Dorchester's hat, seized him by the periwig, pulled it aside, and held him. The Lord Chamberlain and others interposed, and sent them both to the Tower. Nevertheless, not a month afterward, Pepys speaks of seeing the duke's play of "The Chances" acted at Whitehall. "A good play," he condescends to say, "I find it, and the actors most good in it; and pretty to hear Knipp sing in the play very properly 'All night I weepe,' and sung it admirably. The whole play pleases me well: and most of all, the sight of many fine ladies, among others, my Lady Castlemaine and Mrs. Middleton."

The whole management of public affairs was, at this period, intrusted to five persons, and hence the famous combination, the united letters of which formed the word "Cabal:"—Clifford, Arlington, Buckingham, Ashley, and Lauderdale. Their reprehensible schemes, their desperate characters, rendered them the opprobrium of their age, and the objects of censure to all posterity. While matters were in this state a daring outrage, which spoke fearfully of the lawless state of the times, was ascribed, though wrongly, to Buckingham. The Duke of Ormond, the object of his inveterate hatred, was at that time Lord Lieutenant of Ireland. Colonel Blood—a disaffected disbanded officer of the Commonwealth, who had been attainted for a conspiracy in Ireland, but had escaped punishment—came to England, and acted as a spy for the Cabal, who did not hesitate to countenance this daring scoundrel.

His first exploit was to attack the Duke of Ormond's coach one night in St. James's Street: to secure his person, bind him, put him on horseback after one of his accomplices, and carry him to Tyburn, where he meant to hang his grace. On their way, however, Ormond, by a violent effort, threw himself on the ground; a scuffle ensued: the duke's servants came up, and after receiving the fire of Blood's pistols, the duke escaped. Lord Ossory, the Duke of Ormond's son, on going afterward to court, met Buckingham, and addressed him in these words:

"My lord, I know well that you are at the bottom of this late attempt on my father; but I give you warning, if he by any means comes to a violent end, I shall not be at a loss to know the author. I shall consider you as an assassin, and shall treat you as such; and wherever I meet you I shall pistol you, though you stood behind the king's chair; and I tell it you in his majesty's presence, that you may be sure I shall not fail of performance."

Blood's next feat was to carry off from the Tower the crown jewels. He was overtaken and arrested; and was then asked to name his accomplices. "No," he replied, "the fear of danger shall never tempt me to deny guilt or to betray a friend." Charles II., with undignified curiosity, wished to see the culprit. On inquiring of Blood how he dared to make so bold an attempt on the crown, the bravo answered, "My father lost a good estate fighting for the crown, and I considered it no harm to recover it by the crown." He then told his majesty how he had resolved to assassinate him; how he had stood among the reeds in Battersea-fields with this design; how then a sudden awe had come over him: and Charles was weak enough to admire Blood's fearless bearing, and to pardon his attempt. Well might the Earl of Rochester write of Charles—

"Here lies my sovereign lord the king,
Whose word no man relies on;
Who never said a foolish thing,
And never did a wise one."

Notwithstanding Blood's outrages—the slightest penalty for which in our days would have been penal servitude for life—Evelyn met him, not long afterward, at Lord Clifford's, at dinner, when De Grammont and other French noblemen were entertained. "The man," says Evelyn, "had not only a daring, but a villainous unmerciful look, a false countenance; but very well-spoken, and dangerously insinuating."

Early in 1662, the Duke of Buckingham had been engaged in practices against the court: he had disguised deep designs by affecting the mere man of pleasure. Never was there such splendor as at Wallingford House—such wit and gallantry; such perfect good-breeding; such apparently open-handed hospitality. At those splendid banquets, John Wilmot, Earl of Rochester, "a man whom the muses were fond to inspire, but ashamed to avow," showed his "beautiful face," as it was called; and chimed in with that wit for which the age was famous. The frequenters at Wallingford House gloried in their indelicacy. "One is amazed," Horace Walpole observes, "at hearing the age of Charles II. called polite." The Puritans have affected to call every thing by a Scripture name; the new-comers affected to call every thing by its right name;

> "As if preposterously they would confess
> A forced hypocrisy in wickedness."

Walpole compares the age of Charles II. to that of Aristophanes—"which called its own grossness polite." How bitterly he decries the stale poems of the time as "a heap of senseless ribaldry;" how truly he shows that licentiousness weakens as well as depraves the judgment. "When Satyrs are brought to court," he observes, "no wonder the Graces would not trust themselves there."

The Cabal is said, however, to have been concocted, not at Wallingford House, but at Ham House, near Kingston-on-Thames.

In this stately old manor-house, the abode of the Tollemache family, the memory of Charles II. and of his court seems to linger still. Ham House was intended for the residence of Henry, Prince of Wales, and was built in 1610. It stands near the river Thames; and is flanked by noble avenues of elm and of chestnut trees, down which one may almost, as it were, hear the king's talk with his courtiers; see Arlington approach with the well-known patch across his nose; or spy out the lovely, childish Miss Stuart and her future husband, the Duke of Richmond, slipping behind into the garden, lest the jealous, mortified king should catch a sight of the "conscious lovers."

This stately structure was given by Charles II., in 1672, to the Duke and Duchess of Lauderdale: she, the supposed mistress of Cromwell; he, the cruel, hateful Lauderdale of the Cabal. This detestable couple, however, furnished with massive grandeur the apartments of Ham House. They had the ceilings painted by Verrio; the furniture was rich, and even the bellows and brushes in some of the rooms are of silver filigree. One room is furnished with yellow damask, still rich, though faded; the very seats on which Charles, looking around him, saw Clifford, Arlington, Buckingham, Ashley (the infamous Shaftesbury), and Lauderdale—and knew not, good easy man, that he was looking on a band of traitors—are still there. Nay, he even sat to Sir Peter Lely for a portrait for this very place—in which schemes for the ruin of the kingdom were concocted. All, probably, was smooth and pleasing to the monarch as he ranged down the fine gallery, ninety-two feet long; or sat at dinner amid his foes in that hall, surrounded with an open gallery; or disported himself on the river's green brink. Nay, one may even fancy Nell Gwynn taking a day's pleasure in this then lone and ever sweet locality. We hear her swearing, as she was wont to do, perchance at the dim looking-glasses, her own house in Pall Mall, given her by the king, having been filled up for the comedian, entirely, ceiling and all, with looking-glass. How bold and pretty she looked in her undress, even Pepys—no very sound moralist, though a vast hypocrite—tells us: Nelly, "all unready" was "very pretty, prettier far than he thought." But to see how she was "painted," would, he thought, "make a man mad."

"Madame Ellen," as after her *elevation*, as it was termed, she was called, might, since she held long a great sway over Charles's fancy, be suffered to scamper about Ham House—where her merry laugh perhaps scandalized the now saintly Duchess of Lauderdale, just to impose on the world; for Nell was regarded as the Protestant champion of the court, in opposition to her French rival, the Duchess of Portsmouth.

Let us suppose that she has been at Ham House, and is gone off to Pall Mall again, where she can see her painted face in every turn. The king has departed, and Killigrew, who, at all events, is loyal, and the true-hearted Duke of Richmond, all are away to London. In yon sanctimonious-looking closet, next to the duchess's bedchamber, with her psalter and her prayer-book on her desk, which is fixed to her great chair, and that very cane which still hangs there serving as her support from that closet, murmur and wrangle the component parts of that which was never mentioned without fear—the Cabal. They dare not trust themselves in the gallery; there is tapestry there, and we all know what coverts there are for eaves-droppers and spiders in tapestried walls; then the great cardinal spiders do so click there, are so like the death-watch, that Villiers, who is inveterately superstitious, will not abide there. The hall, with its inclosing galleries, and the buttery near, are manifestly unsafe. So they herd, nay, crouch, mutter, and concoct that fearful treachery which, as far as their country is concerned, has been a thing apart in our annals. Englishmen are turbulent, ambitious, unscrupulous; but the craft of Maitland, Duke of Lauderdale—the subtlety of Ashley, seem hardly conceivable either in a Scot or a Southern.

These meetings had their natural consequence. One leaves Lauderdale, Arlington, Ashley, and Clifford, to their fate. But the career of Villiers inspires more interest. He seemed born for better things. Like many men of genius, he was so credulous that the faith he pinned on one Heydon, an astrologer, at this time, perhaps buoyed him up with false hopes. Be it as it may, his plots now tended to open insurrection. In 1666 a proclamation had been issued for his apprehension—he having then absconded. On this occasion he was saved by the act of one whom he had injured grossly—his wife. She managed to outride the sergeant-at-arms, and to warn him of his danger. She had borne his infidelities, after the fashion of the day, as a matter of course: jealousy was then an impertinence—constancy, a chimera; and her husband, whatever his conduct, had ever treated her with kindness of manner: he had that charm, that attribute of his family, in perfection, and it had fascinated Mary Fairfax.

He fled, and played for a year successfully the pranks of his youth. At last, worn out, he talked of giving himself up to justice. "Mr. Fenn, at the table, says that he hath been taken by the watch two or three times of late, at unseasonable hours, but so disguised they did not know him; and when I come home, by and by, Mr. Lowther tells me that the Duke of Buckingham do dine publickly this day at Wadlow's, at the Sun Tavern; and is mighty merry, and sent word to the Lieutenant of the Tower, that he would come to him as soon as he had dined."

While in the Tower—to which he was again committed—Buckingham's pardon was solicited by Lady Castlemaine; on which account the king was very angry with her; called her a meddling "jade;" she calling him "fool," and saying if he was not a fool he never would suffer his best subjects to be imprisoned—referring to Buckingham. And not only did she ask his liberty, but the restitution of his places. No wonder there was discontent when such things were done, and public affairs were in such a state. We must again quote the graphic, terse language of Pepys:—"It was computed that the Parliament had given the king for this war only, besides all prizes, and besides the £200,000 which he was to spend of his own revenue, to guard the sea, above £5,000,000, and odd £100,000; which is a most prodigious sum. Sir H. Cholmly, as a true

English gentleman, do decry the king's expenses of his privy purse, which in King James's time did not rise to above £5000 a year, and in King Charles's to £10,000, do now cost us above £100,000, besides the great charge of the monarchy, as the Duke of York has £100,000 of it, and other limbs of the royal family."

In consequence of Lady Castlemaine's intervention, Villiers was restored to liberty—a strange instance, as Pepys remarks, of the "fool's play" of the age. Buckingham was now as presuming as ever: he had a theatre of his own, and he soon showed his usual arrogance by beating Henry Killigrew on the stage, and taking away his coat and sword; all very "innocently" done, according to Pepys. In July he appeared in his place in the House of Lords, as "brisk as ever," and sat in his robes, "which," says Pepys, "is a monstrous thing that a man should be proclaimed against, and put in the Tower, and released without any trial, and yet not restored to his places."

We next find the duke intrusted with a mission to France, in concert with Lords Halifax and Arlington. In the year 1680, he was threatened with an impeachment, in which, with his usual skill, he managed to exculpate himself by blaming Lord Arlington. The House of Commons passed a vote for his removal; and he entered the ranks of the opposition.

But this career of public meanness and private profligacy was drawing to a close. Alcibiades no longer—his frame wasted by vice—his spirits broken by pecuniary difficulties—Buckingham's importance visibly sank away. "He remained, at last," to borrow the words of Hume, "as incapable of doing hurt as he had ever been little desirous of doing good to mankind." His fortune had now dwindled down to £300 a year in land; he sold Wallingford House, and removed into the City.

And now the fruits of his adversity, not, we hope too late, began to appear. Like Lord Rochester, who had ordered all his immoral works to be burnt, Buckingham now wished to retrieve the past. In 1685 he wrote the religious works which form so striking a contrast with his other productions.

That he had been up to the very time of his ruin perfectly impervious to remorse, dead also to shame, is amply manifested by his conduct soon after his duel with the Earl of Shrewsbury.

Sir George Etherege had brought out a new play at the Duke of York's Theatre. It was called, "She Would if she Could." Plays in those days began at what we now consider our luncheon hour. Though Pepys arrived at the theatre at two o'clock—his wife having gone before—about a thousand people had been put back from the pit. At last, seeing his wife in the eighteen-penny-box, he "made shift" to get there, and there saw, "but lord!" (his own words are inimitable) "how dull, and how silly the play, there being nothing in the world good in it, and few people pleased in it. The king was there; but I sat mightily behind and could see but little, and hear not at all. The play being done, I into the pit to look for my wife, it being dark and raining, but could not find her; and so staid going between the two doors and through the pit an hour and half, I think, after the play was done; the people staying there till the rain was over, and to talk to one another. And among the rest, here was the Duke of Buckingham to-day openly in the pit; and there I found him with my Lord Buckhurst, and Sedley, and Etheridge the poet, the last of whom I did hear mightily find fault with the actors, that they were out of humor, and had not their parts perfect, and that Harris did do nothing, nor could so much as sing a ketch in it; and so was mightily concerned, while all the rest did, through the whole pit, blame the play as a silly, dull thing, though there was something very roguish and witty; but the design of the play, and end, mighty insipid."

Buckingham had held out to his Puritan friends the hope of his conversion for some years; and when they attempted to convert him, he had appointed a time for them to finish their work. They kept their promise, and found him in the most profligate society. It was indeed impossible to know in what directions his fancies might take him, when we find him believing in the predictions of a poor fellow, in a wretched lodging, near Tower Hill, who, having cast his nativity, assured the duke he would be king.

He had continued for years to live with the Countess of Shrewsbury, and two months after her husband's death, had taken her to his home. Then, at last, the Duchess of Buckingham indignantly observed, that she and the countess could not possibly live together. "So I thought, madam," was the reply. "I have therefore ordered your coach to take you to your father's." It has been asserted that Dr. Sprat, the duke's chaplain, actually married him to Lady Shrewsbury, and that his legal wife thenceforth was styled "The Duchess-dowager."

He retreated with his mistress to Claverdon, near Windsor, situated on the summit of a hill which is washed by the Thames. It is a noble building, with a great terrace in front, under which are twenty-six niches, in which Buckingham had intended to place twenty-six statues as large as life; and in the middle is an alcove, with stairs. Here he lived with the infamous countess, by whom he had a son, whom he styled Earl of Coventry (his second title), and who died an infant.

One lingers still over the social career of one whom Louis XIV. called "the only English gentleman he had ever seen." A capital retort was made to Buckingham by the Princess of Orange, during an interview, when he stopped at the Hague, between her and the Duke. He was trying diplomatically to convince her of the affection of England for the States. "We do not," he said, "use Holland like a mistress, we love her as a wife." "*Vraiment je crois que vous nous aimez comme vous aimez la vôtre*," was the sharp and clever answer.

On the death of Charles II., in 1685, Buckingham retired to the small remnant of his Yorkshire estates. His debts were now set down at the sum of £140,000. They were liquidated by the sale of his estates. He took kindly to a country life, to the surprise of his old comrade in pleasure, Etherege. "I have heard the news," that wit cried, alluding to this change, "with no less astonishment than if I had been told that the Pope had begun to wear a periwig and had turned beau in the seventy-fourth year of his age!"

Father Petre and Father Fitzgerald were sent by James II. to convert the duke to Popery. The following anecdote is told of their conference with the dying sinner: "We deny," said the Jesuit Petre, "that any one can be saved out of our Church. Your grace allows that our people may be saved." "No, curse ye," said the duke, "I make no doubt you will all be damned to a man!" "Sir," said the father, "I can not argue with a person so void of all charity." "I did not expect, my reverend father," said the duke, "such a reproach from you, whose whole reasoning was founded on the very same instance of want of charity to yourself."

Buckingham's death took place at Helmsby, in Yorkshire, and the immediate cause was an ague and fever, owing to having sat down on the wet grass after fox-hunting. Pope has given the following forcible, but inaccurate, account of his last hours, and the place in which they were passed:

"In the worst inn's worst room, with mat half hung,
The floors of plaster and the walls of dung,
On once a flock-bed, but repaired with straw,
With tape-tied curtains never meant to draw;
The George and Garter dangling from that bed,
Where tawdry yellow strove with dirty red,
Great Villiers lies: alas! how changed from him,
That life of pleasure and that soul of whim!
Gallant and gay, in Claverdon's proud alcove,
The bower of wanton Shrewsbury and love;
Or, just as gay, at council in a ring
Of mimic'd statesmen and their merry King.

No wit to flatter left of all his store,
No fool to laugh at, which he valued more
Then victor of his health, of fortune, friends,
And fame, this lord of useless thousands ends."

Far from expiring in the "worst inn's worst room," the duke breathed his last in Kirby Moorside, in a house which had once been the best in the place. Brian Fairfax, who loved this brilliant reprobate, has left the only authentic account on record of his last hours.

The night previous to the duke's death, Fairfax had received a message from him desiring him to prepare a bed for him in his house, Bishop Hill, in York. The next day, however, Fairfax was sent for to his master, whom he found dying. He was speechless, but gave the afflicted servant an earnest look of recognition.

The Earl of Arran, son of the Duke of Hamilton, and a gentleman of the neighborhood, stood by his bedside. He had then received the Holy Communion from a neighboring clergyman of the Established Church. When the minister came, it is said that he inquired of the duke what religion he professed. "It is," replied the dying man, "an insignificant question, for I have been a shame and a disgrace to all religions: if you can do me any good, pray do." When a Popish priest had been mentioned to him, he answered vehemently, "No, no!"

He was in a very low state when Lord Arran had found him. But though that nobleman saw death in his looks, the duke said he "felt so well at heart that he knew he could be in no danger."

He appeared to have had inflammation in the bowels, which ended in mortification. He begged of Lord Arran to stay with him. The house seems to have been in a most miserable condition, for in a letter from Lord Arran to Dr. Sprat, he says: "I confess it made my heart bleed to see the Duke of Buckingham in so pitiful a place, and so bad a condition, and what made it worse, he was not at all sensible of it, for he thought in a day or two he should be well; and when we reminded him of his condition, he said it was not as we apprehended. So I sent for a worthy gentleman, Mr. Gibson, to be assistant to me in this work; so we jointly represented his condition to him, who I saw was at first very uneasy; but I think we should not have discharged the duties of honest men if we had suffered him to go out of this world without desiring him to prepare for death." The duke joined heartily in the beautiful prayers for the dying, of our church, and yet there was a sort of selfishness and indifference to others manifest even at the last.

"Mr. Gibson," writes Lord Arran, "asked him if he had made a will, or if he would declare who was to be his heir? but to the first, he answered he had made none; and to the last, whoever was named he answered, 'No.' First, my lady duchess was named, and then I think almost every body that had any relation to him, but his answer always was, 'No.' I did fully represent my lady duchess' condition to him, but nothing that was said to him could make him come to any point."

In this "retired corner," as Lord Arran terms it, did the former wit and beau, the once brave and fine cavalier, the reckless plotter in after-life, end his existence. His body was removed to Helmsby Castle, there to wait the duchess' pleasure, being meantime embalmed. Not one farthing could his steward produce to defray his burial. His George and blue ribbon were sent to King James, with an account of his death.

In Kirby Moorside, the following entry in the register of burials records the event, which is so replete with a singular retributive justice—so constituted to impress and sadden the mind:—

"George Villus, Lord dooke of bookingham."

He left scarcely a friend to mourn his life; for to no man had he been true. He died on the 16th of April according to some accounts; according to others, on the third of that month, 1687, in the sixty-first year of his age. His body, after embalming, was deposited in the family vault in Henry VII.'s chapel.* He left no children, and his title was therefore extinct. The Duchess of Buckingham, of whom Brian Fairfax remarks, "that if she had none of the vanities, she had none of the vices of the court," survived him several years. She died in 1705, at the age of sixty-six, and was buried in the vault of the Villiers family, in the chapel of Henry VII.

Such was the extinction of all the magnificence and intellectual ascendency that at one time centred in this great and gifted family.

* Brian Fairfax states, that at his death (the Duke of Buckingham's) he charged his debts on his estate, leaving much more than enough to cover them. By the register of Westminster Abbey, it appears that he was buried in Henry VII.'s Chapel, 7th June, 1687.

COUNT DE GRAMMONT, ST. EVREMOND, AND LORD ROCHESTER.

It has been observed by a French critic, that the Mémoires de Grammont afford the truest specimens of French character in our language. To this it may be added, that the subject of that animated narrative was most completely French in principle, in intelligence, in wit that hesitated at nothing, in spirits that were never daunted, and in that incessant activity which is characteristic of his countrymen. Grammont, it was said, "slept neither night nor day;" his life was one scene of incessant excitement.

His father, supposed to have been the natural son of Henry the Great, of France, did not suppress that fact, but desired to publish it; for the morals of his time were so depraved, that it was thought to be more honorable to be the illegitimate son of a king that the lawful child of lowlier parents. Born in the Castle of Semeae, on the banks of the Garonne, the fame of two fair ancestresses, Corisande and Menadame, had entitled the family of De Grammont to expect in each successive member an inheritance of beauty. Wit, courage, good-nature, a charming address, and boundless assurance, were the heritage of Philibert de Grammont. Beauty was not his possession: good-nature, a more popular quality, he had in abundance:

> "His wit to scandal never stooping,
> His mirth ne'er to buffoonery drooping."

As Philibert grew up, the two aristocratic professions of France were presented for his choice: the army or the church. Neither of these vocations constitutes now the ambition of the high-born in France: the church, to a certain extent, retains its prestige, but the army, ever since officers have risen from the ranks, does not comprise the same class of men as in England. In the reign of Louis XIII., when De Grammont lived, it was otherwise. All political power was vested in the church. Richelieu was, to all purposes, the ruler of France, the dictator of Europe; and, with regard to the church, great men, at the head of military affairs, were daily proving to the world how much intelligence could effect with a small numerical power. Young men took one course or another; the sway of the cabinet, on the one hand, tempted them to the church; the brilliant exploits of Turenne, and of Condé, on the other, led them to the camp. It was merely the difference of dress between the two that constituted the distinction: the soldier might be as pious as the priest, the priest was sure to be as worldly as the soldier; the soldier might have ecclesiastical preferment; the priest sometimes turned out to fight.

Philibert de Grammont chose to be a soldier. He was styled the Chevalier de Grammont, according to custom, his father being still living. He fought under Turenne, at the siege of Trino. The army in which he served was beleaguering that city when the gay youth from the banks of the Garonne joined it, to aid it not so much by his valor as by the fun, the raillery, the off-hand anecdote, the ready, hearty companionship which lightened the soldier's life in the trenches: adieu to impatience, to despair, even to gravity. The very generals could not maintain their seriousness when the light-hearted De Grammont uttered a repartee—

"Sworn enemy to all long speeches,
Lively and brilliant, frank and free,
Author of many a repartee:
Remember, over all, that he
Was not renowned for storming breaches."

Where he came, all was sunshine, yet there breathed not a colder, graver man than the Calvinist Turenne: modest, serious, somewhat hard, he gave the young nobility who served under him no quarter in their shortcomings; but a word, a look, from De Grammont could make him, *malgré lui*, unbend. The gay chevalier's white charger's prancing, its gallant rider foremost in every peril, were not forgotten in after times, when De Grammont, in extreme old age, chatted over the achievements and pleasures of his youth.

Among those who courted his society in Turenne's army was Matta, a soldier of simple manners, hardy habits, and handsome person, joined to a candid, honest nature. He soon persuaded De Grammont to share his quarters, and there they gave splendid entertainments, which, Frenchman-like, De Grammont paid for out of the successes of the gaming-tables. But chances were against them; the two officers were at the mercy of their *maître d'hôtel*, who asked for money. One day, when De Grammont came home sooner than usual, he found Matta fast asleep. While De Grammont stood looking at him, he awoke, and burst into a violent fit of laughter.

"What is the matter?" cried the chevalier.

"Faith, chevalier," answered Matta, "I was dreaming that we had sent away our *maître d'hôtel*, and were resolved to live like our neighbors for the rest of the campaign."

"Poor fellow!" cried De Grammont. "So you are knocked down at once: what would have become of you if you had been reduced to the situation I was in at Lyons, four days before I came here? Come, I will tell you all about it."

"Begin a little farther back," cried Matta, "and tell me about the manner in which you first paid your respects to Cardinal Richelieu. Lay aside your pranks as a child, your genealogy, and all your ancestors together; you can not know any thing about them."

"Well," replied De Grammont, "it was my father's own fault that he was not Henry IV.'s son: see what the Grammonts have lost by this cross-grained fellow! Faith, we might have walked before the Counts de Vendôme at this very moment."

Then he went on to relate how he had been sent to Pau, to the college, to be brought up to the church, with an old servant to act both as his valet and his guardian. How his head was too full of gaming to learn Latin. How they gave him his rank at college, as the youth of quality, when he did not deserve it; how he traveled up to Paris to his brother to be polished, and went to court in the character of an abbé. "Ah, Matta, you know the kind of dress then in vogue. No, I would not change my dress, but I consented to draw over it a cassock. I had the finest head of hair in the world, well curled and powdered above my cassock, and below were my white buskins and spurs."

Even Richelieu, that hypocrite, he went on to relate, could not help laughing at the parti-colored costume, sacerdotal above, soldier-like below; but the cardinal was greatly offended—not with the absence of decorum, but with the dangerous wit, that could laugh in public at the cowl and shaven crown, points which constituted the greatest portion of Richelieu's sanctity.

De Grammont's brother, however, thus addressed the chevalier:—"Well, my little parson," said he, as they went home, "you have acted your part to perfection; but now you must choose your career. If you like to stick to the church, you will possess great revenues, and nothing to do; if you choose to go into the army, you will risk your arm or your leg, but in time you may be a major general with a wooden leg and a glass eye, the spectacle of an indifferent, ungrateful court. Make your choice."

The choice, Philibert went on to relate, was made. For the good of his soul, he renounced the church, but for his own advantage, he kept his abbacy. This was not difficult in days when secular abbés were common; nothing would induce him to change his resolution of being a soldier. Meantime he was perfecting his accomplishments as a fine gentleman, one of the requisites for which was a knowledge of all sorts of games. No matter that his mother was miserable at his decision. Had her son been an abbé, she thought he would have become a saint: nevertheless, when he returned home, with the air of a courtier and a man of the world, boy as he was, and the very impersonation of what might then be termed *la jeune France*, she was so enchanted with him that she consented to his going to the wars, attended again by Brinon, his valet, equerry, and mentor in one. Next in De Grammont's narrative came his adventure at Lyons, where he spent the 200 louis his mother had given Brinon for him, in play, and very nearly broke the poor old servant's heart; where he had duped a horse-dealer; and he ended by proposing plans, similarly *honorable*, to be adopted for their present emergencies.

The first step was to go to head-quarters, to dine with a certain Count de Cameran, a Savoyard, and invite him to supper. Here Matta interposed, "Are you mad?" he exclaimed. "Invite him to supper! we have neither money nor credit; we are ruined; and to save us you intend to give a supper!"

"Stupid fellow!" cried De Grammont. "Cameran plays at quinze: so do I: we want money. He has more than he knows what to do with: we give a supper, he pays for it. However," he added, "it is necessary to take certain precautions. You command the guards: when night comes on, order your *Sergent-de-place* to have fifteen or twenty men under arms, and let them lay themselves flat on the ground between this and head-quarters. Most likely we shall win this stupid fellow's money. Now the Piedmontese are suspicious, and he commands the horse. Now you know, Matta, you can not hold your tongue, and are very likely to let out some joke that will vex him. Supposing he takes it into his head that he is being cheated? He has always eight or ten horsemen: we must be prepared."

"Embrace me!" cried Matta, "embrace me! for thou art unparalleled. I thought you only meant to prepare a pack of cards and some false dice. But the idea of protecting a man who plays at quinze by a detachment of foot is excellent; thine own, dear chevalier!"

Thus, like some of Dumas' heroes, hating villainy as a matter of course, but being by no means ashamed to acknowledge it, the Piedmontese was asked to supper. He came. Nevertheless, in the midst of the affair, when De Cameran was losing as fast as he could, Matta's conscience touched him: he awoke from a deep sleep, heard the dice shaking, saw the poor Savoyard losing, and advised him to play no more.

"Don't you know, count, you *can not* win?"

"Why?" asked the count.

"Why, faith, because we are cheating you," was the reply.

The chevalier turned round impatiently, "Sieur Matta," he cried, "do you suppose it can be any amusement to Monsieur le Comte to be plagued with your ill-timed jests? For my part, I am so weary of the game that I swear by Jupiter I can scarcely play any more." Nothing is more distasteful to a losing gamester than a hint of leaving off; so the count entreated the chevalier to continue, and assured him that "Monsieur Matta might say what he pleased, for it did not give him the least uneasiness to continue."

The chevalier allowed the count to play upon credit, and that act of courtesy was taken very kindly: the dupe lost 1500 pistoles, which he paid the next morning, when Matta was sharply reprimanded for his interference.

"Faith," he answered, "it was a point of conscience with me; besides it would have given me pleasure to have seen his horse engaged with my infantry, if he had taken any thing amiss."

The sum thus gained set the spendthrifts up; and De Grammont satisfied his conscience by giving it away, to a certain extent, in charity. It is singular to perceive in the history of this celebrated man that moral taint of character which the French have never lost: this total absence of right reasoning on all points of conduct, is coupled in our Gallic neighbors with the greatest natural benevolence, with a generosity only kept back by poverty, with impulsive, impressionable dispositions, that require the guidance of a sound Protestant faith to elevate and correct them.

The chevalier hastened, it is related, to find out distressed comrades, officers who had lost their baggage, or who had been ruined by gaming; or soldiers who had been disabled in the trenches; and his manner of relieving them was as graceful and as delicate as the bounty he distributed was welcome. He was the darling of the army. The poor soldier knew him personally, and adored him; the general was sure to meet him in the scenes of action, and to seek his company in those of security.

And, having thus retrieved his finances, the gay-hearted chevalier used, henceforth, to make De Cameran go halves with him in all games in which the odds were in his own favor. Even the staid Calvinist, Turenne, who had not then renounced, as he did in after life, the Protestant faith, delighted in the off-hand merriment of the chevalier. It was toward the end of the siege of Trino, that De Grammont went to visit that general in some new quarters, where Turenne received him, surrounded by fifteen or twenty officers. According to the custom of the day, cards were introduced, and the general asked the chevalier to play.

"Sir," returned the young soldier, "my tutor taught me that when a man goes to see his friends it is neither prudent to leave his own money behind him nor civil to take theirs."

"Well," answered Turenne, "I can tell you you will find neither much money nor deep play among us; but that it can not be said that we allowed you to go off without playing, suppose we each of us stake a horse."

De Grammont agreed, and, lucky as ever, won from the officers some fifteen or sixteen horses, by way of a joke; but seeing several faces pale, he said, "Gentlemen, I should be sorry to see you go away from your general's quarters on foot; it will do very well if you all send me to-morrow your horses, except one, which I give for the cards."

The *valet-de-chambre* thought he was jesting. "I am serious," cried the chevalier. "*Parole d'honneur* I give a horse for the cards; and what's more, take which you please, only don't take mine."

"Faith," said Turenne, pleased with the novelty of the affair, "I don't believe a horse was ever before given for the cards."

Young people, and indeed old people, can perhaps hardly remember the time when, even in England, money used to be put under the candlesticks "for the cards," as it was said, but in fact for the servants, who waited. Winner or loser, the tax was to be paid, and this custom of vails was also prevalent in France.

Trino at last surrendered, and the two friends rushed from their campaigning life to enjoy the gayeties of Turin, at that time the centre of pleasure; and resolved to perfect their characters as military heroes—by falling in love, if respectably, well; if disreputably, well too, perhaps all the more agreeable, and venturesome, as they thought.

The court of Turin was then presided over by the Duchess of Savoy, *Madame Royale*, as she was called in France, the daughter of Henry IV. of France, the sister of Henrietta Maria of England. She was a woman of talent and spirit, worthy of her descent, and had certain other qualities which constituted a point of resemblance between her and her father; she was, like him, more fascinating than respectable.

The customs of Turin were rather Italian than French. At

that time every lady had her professed lover, who wore the liveries of his mistress, bore her arms, and sometimes assumed her very name. The office of the lover was, never to quit his lady in public, and never to approach her in private: to be on all occasions her esquire. In the tournament her chosen knight-cicisbeo came forth with his coat, his housings, his very lance distinguished with the ciphers and colors of her who had condescended to invest him with her preference. It was the remnant of chivalry that authorized this custom; but of chivalry demoralized—chivalry denuded of her purity, her respect, the chivalry of corrupted Italy, not of that which, perhaps fallaciously, we assign to the earlier ages.

Grammont and Matta enlisted themselves at once in the service of two beauties. Grammont chose for the queen of beauty, who was to "rain influence" upon him, Mademoiselle de St. Germain, who was in the very bloom of youth. She was French, and, probably, an ancestress of that all-accomplished Comte de St. Germain, whose exploits so dazzled successive European courts, and the fullest account of whom, in all its brilliant colors, yet tinged with mystery, is given in the Memoirs of Maria Antoinette, by the Marquise d'Adhémar, her lady of the bedchamber.

The lovely object of De Grammont's "first love" was a radiant brunette belle, who took no pains to set off by art the charms of nature. She had some defects: her black and sparkling eyes were small; her forehead, by no means "as pure as moonlight sleeping upon snow," was not fair, neither were her hands; neither had she small feet—but her form generally was perfect; her elbows had a peculiar elegance in them; and in old times to hold the elbow out well, and yet not to stick it out, was a point of early discipline. Then her glossy black hair set off a superb neck and shoulders; and, moreover, she was gay, full of mirth, life, complaisance, perfect in all the acts of politeness, and invariable in her gracious and graceful bearing.

Matta admired her; but De Grammont ordered him to attach himself to the Marquise de Senantes, a married beauty of the court; and Matta, in full faith that all Grammont said and did was sure to succeed, obeyed his friend. The chevalier had fallen in love with Mademoiselle de St. Germain at first sight, and instantly arrayed himself in her color, which was green, while Matta wore blue, in compliment to the marquise; and they entered the next day upon duty, at La Venerie, where the Duchess of Savoy gave a grand entertainment. De Grammont, with his native tact and unscrupulous mendacity, played his part to perfection; but his comrade, Matta, committed a hundred solecisms. The very second time he honored the marquise with his attentions, he treated her as if she were his humble servant: when he pressed her hand, it was a pressure that almost made her scream. When he ought to have ridden by the side of her coach, he set off, on seeing a hare start from her form; then he talked to her of partridges when he should have been laying himself at her feet. Both these affairs ended as might have been expected. Mademoiselle de St. Germain was diverted by Grammont, yet he could not touch her heart. Her aim was to marry; his was merely to attach himself to a reigning beauty. They parted without regret; and he left the then remote court of Turin for the gayer scenes of Paris and Versailles. Here he became as celebrated for his alertness in play as for his readiness in repartee; as noted for his intrigues as he afterward was for his bravery.

Those were stirring days in France. Anne of Austria, then in her maturity, was governed by Mazarin, the most artful of ministers, an Italian to the very heart's core, with a love of amassing wealth ingrafted in his supple nature that amounted to a monomania. The whole aim of his life was gain. Though gaming was at its height, Mazarin never played for amusement; he played to enrich himself; and when he played, he cheated.

The Chevalier de Grammont was rich, and Mazarin worshiped the rich. He was witty; and his wit soon procured him admission into the clique whom the wily Mazarin collected around him in Paris. Whatever were De Grammont's faults, he soon perceived those of Mazarin; he detected, and he detested the wily, grasping, serpent-like attributes of the Italian; he attacked him on every occasion on which a "wit combat" was possible; he gracefully showed Mazarin off in his true colors. With ease he annihilated him, metaphorically, at his own table. Yet De Grammont had something to atone for: he had been the adherent and companion in arms of Condé; he had followed that hero to Sens, to Nordlingen, to Fribourg, and had returned to his allegiance to the young king, Louis XIV., only because he wished to visit the court at Paris. Mazarin's policy, however, was that of pardon and peace—of duplicity and treachery—and the chevalier seemed to be forgiven on his return to Paris, even by Anne of Austria. Nevertheless, De Grammont never lost his independence; and he could boast in after life that he owed the two great cardinals who had governed France nothing that they could have refused. It was true that Richelieu had left him his abbacy; but he could not refuse it to one of De Grammont's rank. From Mazarin he had gained nothing except what he had won at play.

After Mazarin's death the chevalier intended to secure the favor of the king, Louis XIV., to whom, as he rejoiced to find, court alone was now to be paid. He had now somewhat rectified his distinctions between right and wrong, and was resolved to have no regard for favor unless supported by merit; he determined to make himself beloved by the courtiers of Louis, and feared by the ministers; to dare to undertake any thing to do good, and to engage in nothing at the expense of innocence. He still continued to be eminently successful in play, of which he did not perceive the evil, nor allow the wickedness; but he was unfortunate in love, in which he was equally unscrupulous and more rash than at the gaming-table.

Among the maids of honor of Anne of Austria was a young lady named Anne Lucie de la Mothe Houdancourt. Louis, though not long married, showed some symptoms of admiration for this *débutante* in the wicked ways of the court.

Gay, radiant in the bloom of youth and innocence, the story of this young girl presents an instance of the unhappiness which, without guilt, the sins of others bring upon even the virtuous. The queen-dowager, Anne of Austria, was living at St. Germains when Mademoiselle de la Mothe Houdancourt was received into her household. The Duchess de Noailles, at that time *Grande Maîtresse*, exercised a vigilant and kindly rule over the maids of honor; nevertheless, she could not prevent their being liable to the attentions of Louis: she forbade him however to loiter, or indeed even to be seen in the room appropriated to the young damsels under her charge; and when attracted by the beauty of Anne Lucie de la Mothe, Louis was obliged to speak to her through a hole behind a clock which stood in a corridor.

Anne Lucie, notwithstanding this apparent encouragement of the king's addresses, was perfectly indifferent to his admiration. She was secretly attached to the Marquis de Richelieu, who had, or pretended to have, honorable intentions toward her. Every thing was tried, but tried in vain, to induce the poor girl to give up all her predilections for the sake of a guilty distinction—that of being the king's mistress: even her *mother* reproached her with her coldness. A family council was held, in hopes of convincing her of her willfulness, and Anne Lucie was bitterly reproached by her female relatives; but her heart still clung to the faithless Marquis de Richelieu, who, however, when he saw that a royal lover was his rival, meanly withdrew.

Her fall seemed inevitable; but the firmness of Anne of Austria saved her from her ruin. That queen insisted on her being sent away; and she resisted even the entreaties of the queen, her daughter-in-law, and the wife of Louis XIV.; who, for some reason not explained, entreated that the young lady might remain at the court. Anne was sent away in a sort of disgrace to the convent of Chaïllot, which was then considered to be quite out of Paris, and sufficiently secluded to protect her from visitors. According to another account, a letter full of reproaches, which she wrote to the Marquis de Richelieu, upbraiding him for his desertion, had been intercepted.

It was to this young lady that De Grammont, who was then, in the very centre of the court, "the type of fashion and the mould of form," attached himself as an admirer who could condescend to honor with his attentions those whom the king pursued. The once gay girl was thus beset with snares: on one side was the king, whose disgusting preference was shown when in her presence by sighs and sentiment; on the other, De Grammont, whose attentions to her were importunate, but failed to convince her that he was in love; on the other was the time-serving, heartless De Richelieu, whom her reason condemned but her heart cherished. She soon showed her distrust and dislike of De Grammont: she treated him with contempt; she threatened him with exposure, yet he would not desist: then she complained of him to the king. It was then that he perceived that though love could equalize conditions, it could not act in the same way between rivals. He was commanded to leave the court. Paris, therefore, Versailles, Fontainebleau, and St. Germains were closed against this gay chevalier; and how could he live elsewhere? Whither could he go? Strange to say, he had a vast fancy to behold the man who, stained with the crime of regicide, and sprung from the people, was receiving magnificent embassies from continental nations, while Charles II. was seeking security in his exile from the power of Spain in the Low Countries. He was eager to see the Protector, Cromwell. But Cromwell, though in the height of his fame when beheld by De Grammont—though feared at home and abroad—was little calculated to win suffrages from a mere man of pleasure like De Grammont. The court, the city, the country, were in his days gloomy, discontented, joyless: a proscribed nobility was the sure cause of the thin though few festivities of the now lugubrious gallery of Whitehall. Puritanism drove the old jovial churchmen into retreat, and dispelled every lingering vestige of the old hospitality: long graces and long sermons, sanctimonious manners, and grim, sad faces, and sad-colored dresses, were not much to De Grammont's taste: he returned to France, and declared that he had gained no advantage from his travels. Nevertheless, either from choice or necessity, he made another trial of the damps and fogs of England.*

When he again visited our country, Charles II. had been two years seated on the throne of his father. Every thing was changed, and the British court was in its fullest splendor; while the rejoicings of the people of England at the Restoration were still resounding through the land.

If one could include royal personages in the rather gay than worthy category of the "wits and beaux of society," Charles II. should figure at their head. He was the most agreeable companion, and the worst king imaginable. In the first place he was, as it were, a citizen of the world; tossed about by fortune from his early boyhood; a witness at the tender age of twelve of the battle of Edge Hill, where the celebrated Harvey had charge of him and of his brother. That inauspicious commencement of a wandering life had perhaps been among the least of his early trials. The fiercest was his long residence as a sort of royal prisoner in Scotland. A traveled, humbled man, he came back to England with a full knowledge of men and manners, in the prime of his life, with spirits unbroken by adversity, with a heart unsoured by that "stern nurse," with a gayety that was always kindly, never uncourteous, ever more French than English; far more natural did he appear as the son of Henrietta Maria than as the offspring of the thoughtful Charles.

In person, too, the king was then agreeable; though rather what the French would call *distingué* than dignified; he was, however, tall, and somewhat elegant, with a long French face, which in his boyhood was plump and full about the lower part of the cheeks, but now began to sink into that well-known, lean, dark, flexible countenance, in which we do not, however, recognize the gayety of the man whose very name brings with it associations of wit, politeness, good company, and all the attributes of a first-rate wit, except the almost inevitable ill-nature. There is in the physiognomy of Charles II. that melancholy which is often observable in the faces of those who are mere men of pleasure.

De Grammont found himself completely in his own sphere at Whitehall, where the habits were far more French than English. Along that stately Mall, overshadowed with umbrageous trees, which retains—and it is to be hoped ever will retain—the old name of the "Birdcage Walk," one can picture to one's self the king walking so fast that no one can

* M. de Grammont visited England during the Protectorate. His second visit, after being forbidden the court by Louis XIV., was in 1662.

keep up with him; yet stopping from time to time to chat with some acquaintances. He is walking to Duck Island, which is full of his favorite water-fowl, and of which he has given St. Evremond the government. How pleasant is his talk to those who attend him as he walks along; how well the quality of good-nature is shown in his love of dumb animals; how completely he is a boy still, even in that brown wig of many curls, and with the George and Garter on his breast! Boy, indeed, for he is followed by a litter of young spaniels: a little brindled greyhound frisks beside him; it is for that he is ridiculed by the "*psalm*" sung at the Calves' Head Club: these favorites were cherished to his death.

> "His dogs would sit in council boards
> Like judges in their seats:
> We question much which had most sense,
> The master or the curs."

Then what capital stories Charles would tell, as he unbent at night amid the faithful, though profligate companions of his exile! He told his anecdotes, it is true, over and over again, yet they were always embellished with some fresh touch—like the repetition of a song which has been encored on the stage. Whether from his inimitable art, or from his royalty, we leave others to guess, but his stories bore repetition again and again: they were amusing, and even novel, to the very last.

To this seducing court did De Grammont now come. It was a delightful exchange from the endless ceremonies and punctilios of the region over which Louis XIV. presided. Wherever Charles was, his palace appeared to resemble a large hospitable house—sometimes town, sometimes country—in which every one did as he liked; and where distinctions of rank were kept up as a matter of convenience, but were only valued on that score.

Charles had modeled his court very much on the plan of that of Louis XIV., which he had admired for its gayety and spirit. Corneille, Racine, Molière, Boileau, were encouraged by *le Grand Monarque*. Wycherley and Dryden were attracted by Charles to celebrate the festivities, and to amuse the great and the gay. In other points De Grammont found a resemblance. The queen-consort, Catherine of Braganza, was as complacent to her husband's vices as the queen of Louis. These royal ladies were merely first sultanas, and had no right, it was thought, to feel jealousy or to resent neglect. Each returning Sabbath saw Whitehall lighted up, and heard the tabors sound for a *branle* (Anglicized "brawl"). This was a dance which mixed up every body, and called a brawl, from the foot being shaken to a quick time. Gayly did his Majesty perform it, leading to the hot exercise Anne Hyde, Duchess of York, stout and homely, and leaving Lady Castlemaine to his son the Duke of Monmouth. Then Charles, with ready grace, would begin the coranto, taking a single lady in this dance along the gallery. Lords and ladies one after another followed, and "very noble," writes Pepys, "and great pleasure it was to see." Next came the country dances, introduced by Mary, Countess of Buckingham, the grandmother of the graceful duke who is moving along the gallery; and she invented those once popular dances in order to introduce, with less chance of failure, her rustic country cousins, who could not easily be taught to carry themselves well in the brawl, or to step out gracefully in the coranto, both of which dances required practice and time. In all these dances the king shines the most, and dances much better than his brother the Duke of York.

In these gay scenes De Grammont met with the most fashionable belles of the court: fortunately for him they all spoke French tolerably; and he quickly made himself welcome among even the few—and few indeed there were—who plumed themselves upon untainted reputations. Hitherto those French noblemen who had presented themselves in England had been poor and absurd. The court had been thronged with a troop of impertinent Parisian coxcombs, who had pretended to despise every thing English, and who treated the natives as if they were foreigners in their own country. De Grammont, on the contrary, was familiar with every one: he ate, he drank, he lived, in short, according to the custom of the country that hospitably received him, and accorded him the more respect, because they had been insulted by others.

He now introduced the *petits soupers*, which have never been understood any where so well as in France, and which are even there dying out to make way for the less social and more expensive dinner; but, perhaps, he would even here have been unsuccessful, had it not been for the society and advice of the famous St. Evremond, who at this time was exiled in France and took refuge in England.

This celebrated and accomplished man had some points of resemblance with De Grammont. Like him, he had been originally intended for the church; like him he had turned to the military profession; he was an ensign before he was full sixteen; and had a company of foot given him after serving two or three campaigns. Like De Grammont, he owed the facilities of his early career to his being the descendant of an ancient and honorable family. St. Evremond was the Seigneur of St. Denis le Guast, in Normandy, where he was born.

Both these sparkling wits of society had at one time, and, in fact, at the same period, served under the great Condé; both were pre-eminent, not only in literature, but in games of chance. St. Evremond was famous at the University of Caen, in which he studied, for his fencing; and "St. Evremond's pass" was well known to swordsmen of his time; both were gay and satirical; neither of them pretended to rigid morals; but both were accounted men of honor among their fellow-men of pleasure. They were graceful, kind, generous.

In person St. Evremond had the advantage, being a Norman—a race which combines the handsomest traits of an English countenance with its blond hair, blue eyes, and fair skin. Neither does the slight tinge of the Gallic race detract from the attractions of a true, well-born Norman, bred up in that province which is called the Court-end of France, and polished in the capital. Your Norman is hardy, and fond of field-sports: like the Englishman, he is usually fearless; generous, but somewhat crafty. You may know him by the fresh color, the peculiar blue eye, long and large; by his joyousness and look of health, gathered up even in his own marshy country, for the Norman is well fed, and lives on rich pasture-land, with cheapness and plenty around him. And St. Evremond was one of the handsomest specimens of this fine locality (so mixed up as it is with *us*); and his blue eyes sparkled with humor; his beautifully-turned mouth was all sweetness; and his noble forehead, the whiteness of which was set off by thick dark eyebrows, was expressive of his great intelligence, until a wen grew between his eyebrows, and so changed all the expression of his face that the Duchess of Mazarin used to call him the "Old Satyr." St. Evremond was also Norman in other respects: he called himself a thorough Roman Catholic, yet he despised the superstitions of his church, and prepared himself for death without them. When asked by an ecclesiastic sent expressly from the court of Florence to attend his death-bed, if he "would be reconciled," he answered, "With all my heart; I would fain be reconciled to my stomach, which no longer performs its usual functions." And his talk, we are told, during the fortnight that preceded his death, was not regret for a life we should, in seriousness, call misspent, but because partridges and pheasants no longer suited his condition, and he was obliged to be reduced to boiled meats. No one, however, could tell what might also be passing in his heart. We can not always judge of a life, any more than of a drama, by its last scene; but this is certain, that in an age of blasphemy St. Evremond could not endure to hear religion insulted by ridicule. "Common decency," said this man of the world, "and a due regard to our fellow-creatures, would not permit it." He did not, it seems, refer his displeasure to a higher source —to the presence of the Omniscient—who claims from us all not alone the tribute of our poor frail hearts in serious moments, but the deep reverence of every thought in the hours of careless pleasure.

It was now St. Evremond who taught De Grammont to collect around him the wits of that court, so rich in attractions, so poor in honor and morality. The object of St. Evremond's devotion, though he had at the era of the Restoration passed his fiftieth year, was Hortense Mancini, once the richest heiress, and still the most beautiful woman in Europe, and a niece, on her mother's side, of Cardinal Mazarin's. Hortense had been educated, after the age of six, in France. She was Italian in her accomplishments, in her reckless, wild disposition, opposed to that of the French, who are generally calculating and wary even in their vices: she was Italian in the style of her surpassing beauty, and French to the core in her principles. Hortense, at the age of thirteen, had been married to Armand Duc de Meilleraye and Mayenne, who had fallen so desperately in love with this beautiful child, that he declared "if he did not marry her he should die in three months." Cardinal Mazarin, although he had destined his niece Mary to this alliance, gave his consent on condition that the duke should take the name of Mazarin. The cardinal died a year after this marriage, leaving his niece Hortense the enormous fortune of £1,625,000; yet she died in the greatest difficulties, and her corpse was seized by her creditors.

The Duc de Mayenne proved to be a fanatic, who used to waken his wife in the dead of the night to hear his visions; who forbade his child to be nursed on fast-days; and who believed himself to be inspired. After six years of wretchedness, poor Hortense petitioned for a separation and a division of property. She quitted her husband's home, and took refuge first in a nunnery, where she showed her unbelief or her irreverence, by mixing ink with holy water, that the poor nuns might black their faces when they crossed themselves; or, in concert with Madame de Courcelles, another handsome married woman, she used to walk through the dormitories in the dead of night, with a number of little dogs barking at their heels; then she filled two great chests that were over the dormitories with water, which ran over, and, penetrating through the chinks of the floor, wet the holy sisters in their beds. At length all this sorry gayety was stopped by a decree that Hortense was to return to the Palais Mazarin; and to remain there until the suit for a separation should be decided. That the result should be favorable was doubtful: therefore, one fine night in June, 1667, Hortense escaped. She dressed herself in male attire, and, attended by a female servant, managed to get through the gate of Paris, and to enter a carriage. Then she fled to Switzerland; and, had not her flight been shared by the Chevalier de Rohan, one of the handsomest men in France, one could hardly have blamed an escape from a half-lunatic husband. She was only twenty-eight when, after various adventures, she came in all her unimpaired beauty to England. Charles was captivated by her charms, and, touched by her misfortunes, he settled on her a pension of £4000 a year, and gave her rooms in St. James's. Waller sang her praise:

"When through the world fair Mazarine had run,
Bright as her fellow-traveler, the sun:
Hither at length the Roman eagle flies,
As the last triumph of her conquering eyes."

If Hortense failed to carry off from the Duchess of Portsmouth—then the star of Whitehall—the heart of Charles, she found, at all events, in St. Evremond one of those French, platonic, life-long friends, who, as Chateaubriand worshiped Madame Récamier, adored to the last the exiled niece of Mazarin. Every day, when in her old age and his, the warmth of love had subsided into the serener affection of pitying, and yet admiring friendship, St. Evremond was seen, a little old man in a black coif, carried along Pall Mall in a sedan chair, to the apartment of Madame Mazarin, in St. James's. He always took with him a pound of butter, made in his own little dairy, for her breakfast. When De Grammont was installed at the court of Charles, Hortense was, however, in her prime. Her house at Chelsea, then a country village, was famed for its society and its varied pleasures. St. Evremond has so well described its attractions that his words should be literally given. "Freedom and discretion are equally to be found there. Every one is made more at home than in his own house, and treated with more respect than at court. It is true that there are frequent disputes there, but they are those of knowledge and not of anger. There is play there, but it is inconsiderable, and only practiced for its amusement. You discover in no countenance the fear of losing, nor concern for what is lost. Some are so disinterested that they are reproached for expressing joy when they lose, and regret when they win. Play is followed by the most excellent repasts in the world. There you will find whatever delicacy is brought from France, and whatever is curious from the Indies. Even the commonest meats have the rarest relish imparted to them. There is neither a plenty which gives a notion of extravagance, nor a frugality that discovers penury or meanness."

What an assemblage it must have been! Here lolls Charles, Lord Buckhurst, afterward Lord Dorset, the laziest, in matters of business or court advancement—the boldest, in point of frolic and pleasure, of all the wits and beaux of his time. His youth had been full of adventure and of dissipation. "I know not how it is," said Wilmot, Lord Rochester, "but my Lord Dorset can do any thing, and is never to blame." He had, in truth, a heart; he could bear to hear others praised; he despised the arts of courtiers; he befriended the unhappy; he was the most engaging of men in manners, the most lovable and accomplished of human beings; at once poet, philanthropist, and wit; he was also possessed of chivalric notions, and of daring courage.

Like his royal master, Lord Dorset had traveled; and when made a gentleman of the bedchamber to Charles II., he was not unlike his sovereign in other traits; so full of gayety, so high-bred, so lax, so courteous, so convivial, that no supper was complete without him; no circle "the right thing," unless Buckhurst, as he was long called, was there to pass the bottle round, and to keep every one in good humor. Yet, he had misspent a youth in reckless immorality, and had even been in Newgate on a charge, a doubtful charge, it is true, of highway robbery and murder, but had been found guilty of manslaughter only. He was again mixed up in a disgraceful affair with Sir Charles Sedley. When brought before Sir Robert Hyde, then Chief Justice of the Common Pleas, his name having been mentioned, the judge inquired whether that was the Buckhurst lately tried for robbery? and when told it was, he asked him whether he had so soon forgotten his deliverance at that time: and whether it would not better become him to have been at his prayers begging God's forgiveness, than to come into such courses again?

The reproof took effect, and Buckhurst became what was then esteemed a steady man; he volunteered and fought gallantly in the fleet, under James Duke of York; and he completed his reform, to all outward show, by marrying Lady Falmouth.* Buckhurst, in society, the most good-tempered of men, was thus referred to by Prior, in his poetical epistle to Fleetwood Sheppard:

"When crowding folks, with strange ill faces,
Were making legs and begging places;

---

* The Earl of Dorset married Elizabeth, widow of Charles Berkeley, Earl of Falmouth, and daughter of Hervey Bagot, Esq., of Pipe Hall, Warwickshire, who died without issue. He married, 7th March, 1684-5, Lady Mary Compton, daughter of James Earl of Northampton.

And some with patents, some with merit,
Tired out my good Lord Dorset's spirit."

Yet his pen was full of malice, while his heart was tender to all. Wilmot, Lord Rochester, cleverly said of him:—

"For pointed satire I would Buckhurst chuse,
The best good man with the worst-natured muse."

Still more celebrated as a beau and wit of his time, was John Wilmot, Lord Rochester. He was the son of Lord Wilmot, the cavalier who so loyally attended Charles II. after the battle of Worcester; and, as the offspring of that loyalist, was greeted by Lord Clarendon, then Chancellor of the University of Oxford, when he took his degree as Master of Arts, with a kiss.* The young nobleman then traveled, according to custom; and then most unhappily for himself and for others, whom he corrupted by his example, he presented himself at the court of Charles II. He was at this time a youth of eighteen, and one of the handsomest persons of his age. The face of Buckhurst was hard and plain; that of De Grammont had little to redeem it but its varying intelligence; but the countenance of the young Earl of Rochester was perfectly symmetrical: it was of a long oval, with large, thoughtful, sleepy eyes; the eyebrows arched and high above them; the brow, though concealed by the curls of the now modest wig, was high and smooth; the nose, delicately shaped, somewhat aquiline; the mouth full, but perfectly beautiful, was set off by a round and well-formed chin. Such was Lord Rochester in his zenith; and as he came forward on state occasions, his false light curls hanging down on his shoulders—a cambric kerchief loosely tied, so as to let the ends, worked in point, fall gracefully down; his scarlet gown in folds over a suit of light steel armor—for men had become carpet knights then, and the coat of mail worn by the brave cavaliers was now less warlike, and was mixed up with robes, ruffles, and rich hose—and when in this guise he appeared at Whitehall, all admired; and Charles was enchanted with the simplicity, the intelligence, and modesty of one who was then an ingenuous youth, with good aspirations and a staid and decorous demeanor.

Woe to Lady Rochester—woe to the mother who trusted her son's innocence in that vitiated court! Lord Rochester forms one of the many instances we daily behold, that it is the inexperienced, the ignorant, who fall most deeply, as well as most early, into temptation. He soon lost every trace of virtue—of principle, even of deference to received notions of pro-

* Lord Rochester succeeded to the Earldom in 1659. It was created by Charles II. in 1652, at Paris.

priety. For a while there seemed hopes that he would not wholly fall: courage was his inheritance, and he distinguished himself in 1665, when, as a volunteer, he went in quest of the Dutch East India Fleet, and served with heroic gallantry under Lord Sandwich. And when he returned to court, there was a partial improvement in his conduct. He even looked back upon his former indiscretions with horror: he had now shared in the realities of life: he had grasped a high and honorable ambition; but he soon fell away—soon became almost a castaway. "For five years," he told Bishop Burnet, when on his death-bed, "I was never sober." His reputation as a wit must rest, in the present day, chiefly upon productions which have long since been condemned as unreadable. Strange to say, when not under the influence of wine, he was a constant student of classical authors, perhaps the worst reading for a man of his tendencies: all that was satirical and impure attracting him most. Boileau, among French writers, and Cowley among the English, were his favorite authors. He also read many books of physic; for long before thirty his constitution was so broken by his life, that he turned his attention to remedies, and to medical treatment; and it is remarkable how many men of dissolute lives take up the same sort of reading, in the vain hope of repairing a course of dissolute living. As a writer, his style was at once forcible and lively; as a companion, he was wildly vivacious: madly, perilously, did he outrage decency, insult virtue, profane religion. Charles II. liked him on first acquaintance, for Rochester was a man of the most finished and fascinating manners; but at length there came a coolness, and the witty courtier was banished from Whitehall. Unhappily for himself he was recalled, and commanded to wait in London until his majesty should choose to readmit him into his presence.

Disguises and practical jokes were the fashion of the day. The use of the mask, which was put down by proclamation soon after the accession of Queen Anne, favored a series of pranks with which Lord Rochester, during the period of his living concealed in London, diverted himself. The success of his scheme was perfect. He established himself, since he could not go to Whitehall, in the city. "His first design," De Grammont relates, "was only to be initiated into the mysteries of those fortunate and happy inhabitants; that is to say, by changing his name and dress, to gain admittance to their feasts and entertainments. . . . As he was able to adapt himself to all capacities and humors, he soon deeply insinuated himself into the esteem of the substantial wealthy aldermen, and into the affections of their more delicate, magnificent, and tender ladies; he made one in all their feasts, and at all their assemblies; and while in the company of the husbands, he declaimed against the faults and mistakes of government; he joined their wives in railing against the profligacy of the court ladies, and in inveighing against the king's mistresses: he agreed with them, that the industrious poor were to pay for these cursed extravagances; that the City beauties were not inferior to those at the other end of the town, . . . after which, to outdo their murmurings, he said, that he wondered Whitehall was not yet consumed by fire from heaven, since such rakes as Rochester, Killigrew, and Sidney were suffered there."

This conduct endeared him so much to the City, and made him so welcome at their clubs, that at last he grew sick of their cramming, and endless invitations.

He now tried a new sphere of action; and instead of returning, as he might have done, to the court, retreated into the most obscure corners of the metropolis; and again changing his name and dress, gave himself out as a German doctor, named Bendo, who professed to find out inscrutable secrets, and to apply infallible remedies; to know, by astrology, all the past, and to foretell the future.

If the reign of Charles was justly deemed an age of high civilization, it was also one of extreme credulity. Unbelief in religion went hand in hand with blind faith in astrology and witchcraft; in omens, divinations, and prophecies: neither let us too strongly despise, in these their foibles, our ancestors. They had many excuses for their superstitions; and for their fears, false as their hopes, and equally groundless. The circulation of knowledge was limited: the public journals, that part of the press to which we now owe inexpressible gratitude for its general accuracy, its enlarged views, its purity, its information, was then a meagre statement of dry facts; an announcement, not a commentary. "The Flying Post," the "Daily Courant," the names of which may be supposed to imply speed, never reached lone country places till weeks after they had been printed on their one duodecimo sheet of thin coarse paper. Religion, too, just emerging into glorious light from the darkness of popery, had still her superstitions; and the mantle that priestcraft had contrived to throw over her exquisite, radiant, and simple form, was not then wholly and finally withdrawn. Romanism still hovered in the form of credulity.

But now, with shame be it spoken, in the full noonday genial splendor of our Reformed Church, with newspapers, the leading articles of which rise to a level with our greatest didactic writers, and are competent even to form the mind as well as to amuse the leisure hours of the young readers: with every species of direct communication, we yet hold to fallacies from which the credulous in Charles's time would have shrunk in dismay and disgust. Table-turning, spirit-rapping, *clairvoyance*, Swedenborgianism, and all that family of follies, would have been far too strong for the faith of those who counted upon dreams as their guide, or looked up to the heavenly planets with a belief, partly superstitious, partly reverential, for their guidance; and in a dim and flickering faith trusted to their *stars*.

"Dr. Bendo," therefore, as Rochester was called—handsome, witty, unscrupulous, and perfectly acquainted with the then small circle of the court—was soon noted for his wonderful revelations. Chamber-women, waiting-maids, and shop-girls were his first customers; but, very soon, gay spinsters from the court came in their hoods and masks to ascertain, with anxious faces, their fortunes; while the cunning, sarcastic "Dr. Bendo," noted in his diary all the intrigues which were confided to him by these lovely clients. La Belle Jennings, the sister of Sarah, Duchess of Marlborough, was among his disciples; she took with her the beautiful Miss Price, and, disguising themselves as orange-girls, these young ladies set off in a hackney-coach to visit Dr. Bendo; but, when within half a street of the supposed fortune-teller's, were prevented by the interruption of a dissolute courtier named Brounker.

"Every thing by turns and nothing long." When Lord Rochester was tired of being an astrologer, he used to roam about the streets as a beggar: then he kept a footman who knew the Court well, and he used to dress him up in a red coat, supply him with a musket, like a sentinel, and send him to watch at the doors of all the fine ladies, to find out their goings on: afterward, Lord Rochester would retire to the country, and write libels on these fair victims, and, one day, offered to present the king with one of his lampoons; but, being tipsy, gave Charles, instead, one written upon himself.

At this juncture we read with sorrow Bishop Burnet's forcible description of his career:

"He seems to have freed himself from all impressions of virtue or religion, of honor or good-nature.... He had but one maxim, to which he adhered firmly, that he has to do every thing, and deny himself in nothing that might maintain his greatness. He was unhappily made for drunkenness, for he had drunk all his friends dead, and was able to subdue two or three sets of drunkards one after another; so it scarce ever appeared that he was disordered after the greatest drinking: an hour or two of sleep carried all off so entirely, that no sign of them remained. . . . This had a terrible conclusion."

Like many other men, Rochester might have been saved by being kept far from the scene of temptation. While he remained in the country he was tolerably sober, perhaps steady. When he approached Brentford on his route to London, his old propensities came upon him.

When scarcely out of his boyhood he carried off a young heiress, Elizabeth Mallet, whom De Grammont calls *La triste heritiere:* and triste, indeed, she naturally was. Possessed of a fortune of £2500 a year, this young lady was marked out by Charles II. as a victim for the profligate Rochester. But the reckless young wit chose to take his own way of managing the matter. One night, after supping at Whitehall, with Miss Stuart, the young Elizabeth was returning home with her grandfather, Lord Haly, when their coach was suddenly stopped near Charing Cross by a number of bravos, both on horseback and on foot—the "Roaring Boys and Mohawks," who were not extinct even in Addison's time. They lifted the affrighted girl out of the carriage, and placed her in one which had six horses; they then set off for Uxbridge, and were overtaken; but the outrage ended in marriage, and Elizabeth became the unhappy, neglected Countess of Rochester. Yet she loved him—perhaps in ignorance of all that was going on while *she* staid with her four children at home.

"If," she writes to him, "I could have been troubled at any thing, when I had the happiness of receiving a letter from you, I should be so, because you did not name a time when I might hope to see you, the uncertainty of which very much afflicts me. . . . Lay your commands upon me what I am to do, and though it be to forget my children, and the long hope I have lived in of seeing you, yet will I endeavor to obey you; or in the memory only torment myself, without giving you the trouble of putting you in mind that there lives a creature as

"Your faithful, humble servant."

And he, in reply: "I went away (to Rochester) like a rascal, without taking leave, dear wife. It is an unpolished way of proceeding, which a modest man ought to be ashamed of. I have left you a prey to your own imaginations among my relations, the worst of damnations. But there will come an hour of deliverance, till when, may my mother be merciful unto you! So I commit you to what I shall ensue, woman to woman, wife to mother, in hopes of a future appearance in glory. . . .

"Pray write as often as you have leisure, to your

"ROCHESTER."

To his son, he writes: "You are now grown big enough to be a man, if you can be wise enough; and the way to be truly wise is to serve God, learn your book, and observe the instructions of your parents first, and next your tutor, to whom I have entirely resigned you for this seven years; and according as you employ that time, you are to be happy or unhappy forever. I have so good an opinion of you, that I am glad to think you will never deceive me. Dear child, learn your book and be obedient, and you will see what a father I shall be to you. You shall want no pleasure while you are good, and that you may be good are my constant prayers."

Lord Rochester had not attained the age of thirty, when he was mercifully awakened to a sense of his guilt here, his peril hereafter. It seemed to many that his very nature was so warped that penitence in its true sense could never come to him; but the mercy of God is unfathomable; He judges not as man judges; He forgives, as man knows not how to forgive.

> "God, or kind Master, merciful as just,
> Knowing our frame, remembers man is dust:
> He marks the dawn of every virtuous aim,
> And fans the smoking flax into a flame;
> He hears the language of a silent tear,
> And sighs are incense from a heart sincere."

And the reformation of Rochester is a confirmation of the doctrine of a special Providence, as well as of that of a retribution even in this life.

The retribution came in the form of an early but certain decay; of a suffering so stern, so composed of mental and bodily anguish, that never was man called to repentance by a voice so distinct as Rochester. The reformation was sent through the instrumentality of one who had been a sinner like himself, who had sinned *with* him; an unfortunate lady, who, in her last hours, had been visited, reclaimed, consoled, by Bishop Burnet. Of this, Lord Rochester had heard. He was then, to all appearance, recovering from his last sickness. He sent for Burnet, who devoted to him one evening every week of that solemn winter when the soul of the penitent sought reconciliation and peace.

The conversion was not instantaneous; it was gradual, penetrating, effective, sincere. Those who wish to gratify curiosity concerning the death-bed of one who had so notoriously sinned, will read Burnet's account of Rochester's illness and death with deep interest; and nothing is so interesting as a death-bed. Those who delight in works of nervous thought and elevated sentiments will read it too, and arise from the perusal gratified. Those, however, who are true, contrite Christians will go still farther; they will own that few works so intensely touch the holiest and highest feelings; few so absorb the heart; few so greatly show the vanity of life; the unspeakable value of a purifying faith. "It is a book which the critic," says Dr. Johnson, "may read for its elegance, the philosopher for its arguments, the saint for its piety."

While deeply lamenting his own sins, Lord Rochester became anxious to redeem his former associates from theirs.

"When Wilmot, Earl of Rochester,"* writes William Thomas, in a manuscript preserved in the British Museum, "lay on his death-bed, Mr. Fanshawe came to visit him, with an intention to stay about a week with him. Mr. Fanshawe, sitting by the bedside, perceived his lordship praying to God, through Jesus Christ, and acquainted Dr. Radcliffe, who attended my Lord Rochester in this illness and was then in the house, with what he had heard, and told him that my lord was certainly delirious, for to his knowledge, he said, he believed neither in God nor in Jesus Christ. The doctor, who had often heard him pray in the same manner, proposed to Mr. Fanshawe to go up to his lordship to be further satisfied touching this affair. When they came to his room, the doctor told my lord what Mr. Fanshawe said, upon which his lordship addressed himself to Mr. Fanshawe to this effect: 'Sir, it is true, you and I have been very bad and profane together, and then I was of the opinion you mention. But now I am quite of another mind, and happy am I that I am so. I am very sensible how miserable I was while of another opinion. Sir, you may assure yourself that there is a Judge and a future state;' and so entered into a very handsome discourse concerning the last judgment, future state, etc., and concluded with a serious and pathetic exhortation to Mr. Fanshawe to enter into another course of life; adding that he (Mr. F.) knew him to be his friend; that he never was more so than at this time; and 'sir,' said he, 'to use a Scripture expression, I am not mad, but speak the words of truth and soberness.' Upon this Mr. Fanshawe trembled, and went immediately afoot to Woodstock, and there hired a horse to Oxford, and thence took coach to London."

There were other butterflies in that gay court; beaux without wit; remorseless rakes, incapable of one noble thought or high pursuit; and among the most foolish and fashionable of these was Henry Jermyn, Lord Dover. As the nephew of Henry Jermyn, Lord St. Albans, this young simpleton was

* Mr. William Thomas, the writer of this statement, heard it from Dr. Radcliffe, at the table of Speaker Harley (afterward Earl of Oxford), 16th June, 1702.

ushered into a court life with the most favorable auspices. Jermyn Street (built in 1667) recalls to us the residence of Lord St. Albans, the supposed husband of Henrietta Maria. It was also the centre of fashion when Henry Jermyn the younger was launched into its unholy sphere. Near Eagle Passage lived at that time La Belle Stuart, Duchess of Richmond; next door to her Henry Savile, Rochester's friend. The locality has since been purified by worthier associations: Sir Isaac Newton lived for a time in Jermyn Street, and Gray lodged there.

It was, however, in De Grammont's time, the scene of all the various gallantries which were going on. Henry Jermyn was supported by the wealth of his uncle, that uncle who, while Charles II. was starving at Brussels, had kept a lavish table in Paris: little Jermyn, as the younger Jermyn was called, owed much indeed to his fortune, which had procured him great *éclat* at the Dutch court. His head was large; his features small; his legs short; his physiognomy was not positively disagreeable, but he was affected and trifling, and his wit consisted in expressions learned by rote, which supplied him either with raillery or with compliments.

This petty, inferior being had attracted the regard of the Princess Royal—afterward Princess of Orange—the daughter of Charles I. Then the Countess of Castlemaine—afterward Duchess of Cleveland—became infatuated with him; he captivated also the lovely Mrs. Hyde, a languishing beauty, whom Sir Peter Lely has depicted in all her sleepy attractions, with her ringlets falling lightly over her snowy forehead and down to her shoulders. This lady was, at the time when Jermyn came to England, recently married to the son of the great Clarendon. She fell desperately in love with this unworthy being; but, happily for her peace, he preferred the honor (or dishonor) of being the favorite of Lady Castlemaine, and Mrs. Hyde escaped the disgrace she perhaps merited.

De Grammont appears absolutely to have hated Jermyn; not because he was immoral, impertinent, and contemptible, but because it was Jermyn's boast that no woman, good or bad, could resist him. Yet, in respect to their unprincipled life, Jermyn and De Grammont had much in common. The count was at this time an admirer of the foolish beauty, Jane Middleton; one of the loveliest women of a court where it was impossible to turn without seeing loveliness.

Mrs. Middleton was the daughter of Sir Roger Needham; and she has been described, even by the grave Evelyn, as a "famous, and, indeed, incomparable beauty." A coquette, she was, however, the friend of intellectual men; and it was probably at the house of St. Evremond that the count first saw her. Her figure was good; she was fair and delicate; and she had so great a desire, Count Hamilton relates, to "appear magnificently, that she was ambitious to vie with those of the greatest fortunes, though unable to support the expense."

Letters and presents now flew about. Perfumed gloves, pocket looking-glasses, elegant boxes, apricot paste, essences, and other small wares arrived weekly from Paris: English jewelry still had the preference, and was liberally bestowed; yet Mrs. Middleton, affected and somewhat precise, accepted the gifts but did not seem to encourage the giver.

The Count de Grammont, piqued, was beginning to turn his attention to Miss Warmestre, one of the queen's maids of honor, a lively brunette, and a contrast to the languid Mrs. Middleton, when, happily for him, a beauty appeared on the scene, and attracted him, by higher qualities than mere looks, to a real, fervent, and honorable attachment.

Among the few respected families of that period was that of Sir George Hamilton, the fourth son of James, Earl of Abercorn, and of Mary, granddaughter of Walter, eleventh Earl of Ormond. Sir George had distinguished himself during the civil wars: on the death of Charles I. he had retired to France, but returned, after the Restoration, to London, with a large family, all intelligent and beautiful.

From their relationship to the Ormond family, the Hamiltons were soon installed in the first circles of fashion. The Duke of Ormond's sons had been in exile with the king; they now added to the lustre of the court after his return. The Earl of Arran, the second, was a beau of the true Cavalier order; clever at games, more especially at tennis, the king's favorite diversion; he touched the guitar well; and made love *ad libitum*. Lord Ossory, his elder brother, had less vivacity but more intellect, and possessed a liberal, honest nature, and an heroic character.

All the good qualities of these two young noblemen seem to have been united in Anthony Hamilton, of whom De Grammont gives the following character:—"The elder of the Hamiltons, their cousin, was the man who, of all the court, dressed best; he was well made in his person, and possessed those happy talents which lead to fortune, and procure success in love: he was a most assiduous courtier, had the most lively wit, the most polished manners, and the most punctual attention to his master imaginable; no person danced better, nor was any one a more general lover—a merit of some account in a court entirely devoted to love and gallantry. It is not at all surprising that, with these qualities, he succeeded my Lord Falmouth in the king's favor."

The fascinating person thus described was born in Ireland: he had already experienced some vicissitudes, which were renewed at the Revolution of 1688, when he fled to France—the country in which he had spent his youth—and died at St. Germains in 1720, aged seventy-four. His poetry and his fairy tales are forgotten; but his "Memoirs of the Count de Grammont" is a work which combines the vivacity of a French writer with the truth of an English historian.

Ormond Yard, St. James's Square, was the London residence of the Duke of Ormond: the garden-wall of Ormond House took up the greater part of York Street: the Hamilton family had a commodious house in the same courtly neighborhood; and the cousins mingled continually. Here persons of the greatest distinction constantly met; and here the "Chevalier de Grammont," as he was still called, was received in a manner suitable to his rank and style; and soon regretted that he had passed so much time in other places; for, after he once knew the charming Hamiltons, he wished for no other friends.

There were three courts at that time in the capital; that at Whitehall, in the king's apartments; that in the queen's, in the same palace; and that of Henrietta Maria, the Queen Mother, as she was styled, at Somerset House. Charles's was pre-eminent in immorality, and in the daily outrage of all decency; that of the unworthy widow of Charles I. was just bordering on impropriety; that of Katherine of Braganza was still decorous, though not irreproachable. Pepys, in his Diary, has this passage:—"Visited Mrs. Ferrers, and stayed talking with her a good while, there being a little, proud, ugly, talking lady there, that was much crying up the queene-mother's court at Somerset House, above our queen's; there being before her no allowance of laughing and mirth that is at the other's; and, indeed, it is observed that the greatest court nowadays is there. Thence to Whitehall, where I carried my wife to see the queene in her presence-chamber; and the maydes of honour and the young Duke of Monmouth, playing at cards."

Queen Katherine, notwithstanding that the first words she was ever known to say in English were "*You lie!*" was one of the gentlest of beings. Pepys describes her as having a modest, innocent look, among all the demireps with whom she was forced to associate. Again we turn to Pepys, an anecdote of whose is characteristic of poor Katherine's submissive, uncomplaining nature:

"With Creed, to the King's Head ordinary; . . . . and a pretty gentleman in our company, who confirms my Lady Castlemaine's being gone from court, but knows not the reason; he told us of one wipe the queene, a little while ago, did give her, when she come in and found the queene under the dresser's hands, and had been so long. 'I wonder your majesty,' says she, 'can have the patience to sit so long a-dressing?' 'I have so much reason to use patience,' says the queene, 'that I can very well bear with it.'"

It was in the court of this injured queen that De Grammont went one evening to Mrs. Middleton's house: there was a ball that night, and among the dancers was the loveliest creature that De Grammont had ever seen. His eyes were riveted on this fair form; he had heard of, but never till then seen her whom all the world consented to call "La Belle Hamilton," and his heart instantly echoed the expression. From this time he forgot Mrs. Middleton, and despised Miss Warmestre: "he found," he said, that he "had seen nothing at court till this instant."

"Miss Hamilton," he himself tells us, "was at the happy age when the charms of the fair sex begin to bloom; she had the finest shape, the loveliest neck, and most beautiful arms in the world; she was majestic and graceful in all her movements; and she was the original after which all the ladies copied in their taste and air of dress. Her forehead was open, white, and smooth; her hair was well set, and fell with ease into that natural order which it is so difficult to imitate. Her complexion was possessed of a certain freshness, not to be equaled by borrowed colors; her eyes were not large, but they were lively, and capable of expressing whatever she pleased."* So far for her person; but De Grammont was, it seems, weary of mere external charms: it was the intellectual superiority that riveted his feelings, while his connoisseurship in beauty was satisfied that he had never yet seen any one so perfect.

"Her mind," he says, "was a proper companion for such a form: she did not endeavor to shine in conversation by those sprightly sallies which only puzzle, and with still greater care she avoided that affected solemnity in her discourses which produces stupidity; but, without any eagerness to talk, she just said what she ought, and no more. She had an admirable discernment in distinguishing between solid and false wit; and far from making an ostentatious display of her abilities, she was reserved, though very just in her decisions. Her sentiments were always noble, and even lofty to the highest extent, when there was occasion; nevertheless, she was less prepossessed with her own merit than is usually the case with those who have so much. Formed as we have described, she could not fail of commanding love; but so far was she from

* See De Grammont's Memoirs.

DE GRAMMONT'S MEETING WITH LA BELLE HAMILTON.

courting it, that she was scrupulously nice with respect to those whose merit might entitle them to form any pretensions to her."

Born in 1641, Elizabeth—for such was the Christian name of this lovely and admirable woman — was scarcely in her twentieth year when she first appeared at Whitehall. Sir Peter Lely was at that time painting the Beauties of the Court, and had done full justice to the intellectual and yet innocent face that riveted De Grammont. He had depicted her with her rich dark hair, of which a tendril or two fell on her ivory forehead, adorned at the back with large pearls, under which a gauze-like texture was gathered up, falling over the fair shoulders like a veil: a full corsage, bound by a light band either of ribbon or of gold lace, confining, with a large jewel or button, the sleeve on the shoulder, disguised somewhat the exquisite shape. A frill of fine cambric set off, while in whiteness it scarce rivaled, the shoulder and neck.

The features of this exquisite face are accurately described by De Grammont, as Sir Peter has painted them. "The mouth does not smile, but seems ready to break out into a smile. Nothing is sleepy, but every thing is soft, sweet, and innocent in that face so beautiful and so beloved."

While the colors were fresh on Lely's palettes, James Duke of York, that profligate who aped the saint, saw it, and henceforth paid his court to the original, but was repelled with fearless *hauteur*. The dissolute nobles of the court followed his example, even to the "lady-killer" Jermyn, but in vain. Unhappily for La Belle Hamilton, she became sensible to the attractions of De Grammont, whom she eventually married.

Miss Hamilton, intelligent as she was, lent herself to the fashion of the day, and delighted in practical jokes and tricks. At the splendid masquerade given by the queen she continued to plague her cousin, Lady Muskerry; to confuse and expose a stupid court beauty, a Miss Blaque; and at the same time to produce on the Count de Grammont a still more powerful effect than even her charms had done. Her success in hoaxing —which we should now think both perilous and indelicate— seems to have only riveted the chain, which was drawn around him more strongly.

His friend, or rather his foe, St. Evremond, tried in vain to discourage the chevalier from his new passion. The former tutor was, it appeared, jealous of its influence, and hurt that De Grammont was now seldom at his house.

De Grammont's answer to his remonstrances was very characteristic. "My poor philosopher," he cried, "you understand Latin well—you can make good verses—you are acquainted with the nature of the stars in the firmament—but you are wholly ignorant of the luminaries in the terrestrial globe."

He then announced his intention to persevere, notwithstanding all the obstacles which attached to the suit of a man without either fortune or character, who had been exiled from his own country, and whose chief mode of livelihood was dependent on the gaming-table.

One can scarcely read of the infatuation of La Belle Hamilton without a sigh. During a period of six years their marriage was in contemplation only; and De Grammont seems to have trifled inexcusably with the feelings of this once gay and ever lovely girl. It was not for want of means that De Grammont thus delayed the fulfillment of his engagement. Charles II., inexcusably lavish, gave him a pension of 1500 Jacobuses: it was to be paid to him until he should be restored to the favor of his own king. The fact was that De Grammont contributed to the pleasures of the court, and pleasure was the household deity of Whitehall. Sometimes, in those days of careless gayety, there were promenades in Spring Gardens, or the Mall; sometimes the court beauties sallied forth on horseback; at other times there were shows on the river, which then washed the very foundations of Whitehall. There in the summer evenings, when it was too hot and dusty to walk, Old Thames might be seen covered with little boats, filled with court and city beauties, attending the royal barges; collations, music, and fireworks completed the scene, and De Grammont always contrived some surprise—some gallant show: once a concert of vocal and instrumental music, which he had privately brought from Paris, struck up unexpectedly: another time, a collation brought from the same gay capital surpassed that supplied by the king. Then the count, finding that coaches with glass windows, lately introduced, displeased the ladies, because their charms were only partially seen in them, sent for the most elegant and superb *calèche* ever seen: it came after a month's journey, and was presented by De Grammont to the king. It was a royal present in price, for it had cost two thousand livres. The famous dispute between Lady Castlemaine and Miss Stuart, afterward Duchess of Richmond, arose about this *calèche*. The Queen and the Duchess of York appeared first in it in Hyde Park, which had then recently been fenced in with brick. Lady Castlemaine thought that the *calèche* showed off a fine figure better than the coach; Miss Stuart was of the same opinion. Both these grown-up babies wished to have the coach on the same day, but Miss Stuart prevailed.

The queen condescended to laugh at the quarrels of these

two foolish women, and complimented the Chevalier de Grammont on his present. "But how is it," she asked, "that you do not even keep a footman, and that one of the common runners in the street lights you home with a link?"

"Madam," he answered, "the Chevalier de Grammont hates pomp: my link-boy is faithful and brave." Then he told the queen that he saw she was unacquainted with the nation of link-boys, and related how that he had, at one time, had one hundred and sixty around his chair at night, and people had asked "whose funeral it was?" "As for the parade of coaches and footmen," he added, "I despise it. I have sometimes had five or six *valets-de-chambre*, without a single footman in livery except my chaplain."

"How!" cried the queen, laughing, "a chaplain in livery? surely he was not a priest."

"*Pardon*, Madame, a priest, and the best dancer in the world of the Biscayan jig."

"Chevalier," said the king, "tell us the history of your chaplain Poussatin."

Then De Grammont related how, when he was with the great Condé, after the campaign of Catalonia, he had seen among a company of Catalans, a priest in a little black jacket, skipping and frisking: how Condé was charmed, and how they recognized in him a Frenchman, and how he offered himself to De Grammont for his chaplain. De Grammont had not much need, he said, for a chaplain in his house, but he took the priest, who had afterward the honor of dancing before Anne of Austria, in Paris.

Suitor after suitor interfered with De Grammont's at last honorable address to La Belle Hamilton. At length an incident occurred which had very nearly separated them forever. Philibert de Grammont was recalled to Paris by Louis XIII. He forgot, Frenchman-like, all his engagements to Miss Hamilton, and hurried off. He had reached Dover, when her two brothers rode up after him. "Chevalier de Grammont," they said, "have you forgotten nothing in London?"

"I beg your pardon," he answered, "I forgot to marry your sister." It is said that this story suggested to Molière the idea of *Le Mariage forcé.* They were, however, married.

In 1669 La Belle Hamilton, after giving birth to a child, went to reside in France. Charles II., who thought she would pass for a handsome woman in France, recommended her to his sister Henrietta, Duchess of Orleans, and begged her to be kind to her.

Henceforth the Chevalier de Grammont and his wife figured at Versailles, where the Countess de Grammont was appointed *Dame de Palais.* Her career was less brilliant than in England. The French ladies deemed her haughty and old, and even termed her *une Anglaise insupportable.*

She had certainly too much virtue, and perhaps too much beauty still, for the Parisian ladies of fashion at that period to admire her.

She endeavored, in vain, to reclaim her libertine husband, and to call him to a sense of his situation when he was on his death-bed. Louis XIV. sent the Marquis de Dangeau to convert him, and to talk to him on a subject little thought of by De Grammont—the world to come. After the marquis had been talking for some time, De Grammont turned to his wife and said, "Countess, if you don't look to it, Dangeau will juggle you out of my conversion." St. Evremond said he would gladly die to go off with so successful a bon-mot.

He became, however, in time, serious, if not devout or penitent. Ninon de l'Enclos having written to St. Evremond that the Count de Grammont had not only recovered but had become devout, St. Evremond answered her in these words:

"I have learned with a great deal of pleasure that the Count de Grammont has recovered his former health and acquired a new devotion."*

A report having been circulated that De Grammont was dead, St. Evremond expressed deep regret. The report was contradicted by Ninon de l'Enclos. The count was then eighty-six years of age; "nevertheless he was," Ninon says, "so young that I think him as lively as when he hated sick people, and loved them after they had recovered their health;" a trait very descriptive of a man whose good-nature was always on the surface, but whose selfishness was deep as that of most wits and beaux, who are spoiled by the world, and

* "The Count de Grammont fell dangerously ill in the year 1696, of which the King (Louis XIV.) being informed, and knowing, besides, that he was inclined to libertinism, he was pleased to send the Marquis of Dangeau to see how he did, and to advise him to think of God. Hereupon Count de Grammont, turning toward his wife, who had ever been a very devout lady, told her, 'Countess, if you don't look to it, Dangeau will juggle you out of my conversion.' Madame de l'Enclos having afterward written to M. de St. Evremond that Count de Grammont was recovered, and turned devout, 'I have learned,' answered he to her, 'with a great deal of pleasure that Count de Grammont has recovered his former health, and acquired a new devotion. Hitherto I have been contented with being a plain, honest man; but I must do something more; and I only wait for your example to become a devotee. You live in a country where people have wonderful advantages of saving their souls: there, vice is almost as opposite to the mode as virtue; sinning passes for ill-breeding, and shocks decency and good manners as much as religion. Formerly it was enough to be wicked, now one must be a scoundrel withal, to be damned in France.'"

who, in return, distrust and deceive the spoilers. This long life of eighty-six years, endowed as De Grammont was with elasticity of spirits, good fortune, considerable talent, an excellent position, a wit that never ceased to flow in a clear current; with all these advantages, what might he not have been to society had his energy been well applied, his wit innocent, his talents employed worthily, and his heart as sure to stand muster as his manners?

BEAU FIELDING.

"Let us be wise, boys, here's a fool coming," said a sensible man, when he saw Beau Nash's splendid carriage draw up to the door. Is a beau a fool? Is a sharper a fool? Was Bonaparte a fool? If you reply "no" to the last two questions, you must give the same answer to the first. A beau is a fox, but not a fool—a very clever fellow, who, knowing the weakness of his brothers and sisters in the world, takes advantage of it to make himself a fame and a fortune. Nash, the son of a glass-merchant—Brummell, the hopeful of a small shopkeeper—became the intimates of princes, dukes, and fashionables; were petty kings of Vanity Fair, and were honored by their subjects. In the kingdom of the blind, the one-eyed man is king; in the realm of folly, the sharper is a monarch. The only proviso is, that the cheat come not within the jurisdiction of the law. Such a cheat is the beau or dandy, or fine gentleman, who imposes on his public by his clothes and appearance. *Bonâ-fide* monarchs have done as much; Louis XIV. won himself the title of Le Grand Monarque by his manners, his dress, and his vanity. Fielding, Nash, and Brummell did nothing more. It is not a question whether such roads to eminence be contemptible or not, but whether their adoption in one station of life be more so than in another. Was Brummell a whit more contemptible than "Wales?" Or is John Thomas, the pride and glory of the "Domestics' Free-and-Easy," whose whiskers, figure, face, and manner are all superb, one atom more ridiculous than your recognized beau? I trow not. What right, then, has your beau to a place among wits? I fancy Chesterfield would be much disgusted at seeing his name side by side with that of Nash in this volume; yet Chesterfield had no objection, when at Bath, to do homage to the king of that city, and may have prided himself on exchanging pinches from diamond-set snuff-boxes with that superb gold-laced dignitary in the Pump-room. Certainly, people who thought little of Philip Dormer Stanhope thought a great deal of the glass-merchant's reprobate son when he was in power, and submitted without a murmur to his impertinences. The fact is, that the beaux and the wits are more intimately connected than the latter would care to own: the wits have all been, or aspired to be, beaux, and beaux have had their fair share of wit; both lived for the same purpose—to shine in society; both used the same means, coats, and bon-mots. The only distinction is, that the garments of the beaux were better, and their sayings not so good as those of the wits; while the conversation of the wits was better, and their apparel not so striking as those of the beaux. So, my Lord Chesterfield, who prided yourself quite as much on being a fine gentleman as on being a fine wit, you can not complain at your proximity to Mr. Nash and others who *were* fine gentlemen, and would have been fine wits if they could.

Robert Fielding was, perhaps, the least of the beaux; but then, to make up for this, he belonged to a noble family; he married a duchess, and, what is more, he beat her. Surely in the kingdom of fools such a man is not to be despised. You may be sure he did not think he was, for was he not made the subject of two papers in "The Tatler," and what more could a man desire?

His father was a Suffolk squire, claiming relationship with the Earls of Denbigh, and, therefore, with the Hapsburgs, from whom the Beau and the Emperors of Austria had the common honor of being descended. Perhaps neither of them had sufficient sense to be proud of the greatest intellectual ornament of their race, the author of "Tom Jones;" but as our hero was dead before the humorist was born, it is not fair to conjecture what he might have thought on the subject.

It does not appear that very much is known of this great gem of the race of Hapsburg. He had the misfortune to be very handsome, and the folly to think that his face would be his fortune: it certainly stood him in good stead at times, but it also brought him into a lamentable dilemma.

His father was not rich, and sent his son to the Temple to study laws which he was only fitted to break. The young Adonis had sense enough to see that destiny did not beckon him to fame in the gloom of a musty law court, and removed a little farther up to the Thames, and the more fashionable region of Scotland Yard. Here, where now Z. 300 repairs to report his investigations to a Commissioner, the young dandies of Charles II.'s day strutted in gay doublets, swore hasty oaths of choice invention, smoked the true Tobago from huge pipe-bowls, and ogled the fair but not too bashful dames who passed to and fro in their chariots. The court took its name from the royalties of Scotland, who, when they visited the South, were there lodged as being conveniently near to Whitehall Palace. It is odd enough that the three architects, Inigo Jones, Vanbrugh, and Wren, all lived in this yard.

It was not to be supposed that a man who could so well

appreciate a handsome face and well-cut doublet as Charles II. should long overlook his neighbor, Mr. Robert Fielding, and in due course the Beau, who had no other diploma, found himself in the honorable position of a justice of the peace.

The emoluments of this office enabled Orlando, as "The Tatler" calls him, to shine forth in all his glory. With an enviable indifference to the future, he launched out into an expenditure which alone would have made him popular in a country where the heaviest purse makes the greatest gentleman. His lackeys were arrayed in the brightest yellow coats with black sashes—the Hapsburg colors. He had a carriage, of course, but like Sheridan, whom his gave so much trouble to pay for, it was hired, though drawn by his own horses. This carriage was described as being shaped like a sea-shell; and "The Tatler" calls it "an open tumbril of less size than ordinary, to show the largeness of his limbs and the grandeur of his personage to the best advantage." The said limbs were his especial pride: he gloried in the strength of his leg and arm; and when he walked down the street, he was followed by an admiring crowd, whom he treated with as much haughtiness as if he had been the emperor himself, instead of his cousin five hundred times removed. He used his strength to good or bad purpose, and was a redoubted fighter and bully, though good-natured withal. In the Mall, as he strutted, he was the cynosure of all female eyes. His dress had all the elegance of which the graceful costume of that period was capable, though Fielding did not, like Brummell, understand the delicacy of a quiet, but studied style. Those were simpler, somewhat more honest days. It was not necessary for a man to cloak his vices, nor be ashamed of his cloak. The beau then-a-day openly and arrogantly gloried in the grandeur of his attire; and bragging was a part of his character. Fielding was made by his tailor; Brummell made his tailor: the only point in common to both, was that neither of them paid the tailor's bill. The fine gentleman, under the Stuarts, was fine only in his lace and his velvet doublet; his language was coarse, his manners coarser, his vices the coarsest of all. No wonder when the king himself could get so drunk with Sedley and Buckhurst, as to be unable to give an audience appointed for; and when the chief fun of his two companions was to divest themselves of all the habiliments which civilization has had the ill taste to make necessary, and in that state run about the streets.

Orlando wore the finest ruffles and the heaviest sword; his wig was combed to perfection; and in his pocket he carried a little comb with which to arrange it from time to time, even as the dandy of to-day pulls out his whiskers or curls his mustache. Such a man could not be passed over; and accordingly he numbered half the officers and gallants of the town among his intimates. He drank, swore, and swaggered, and the snobs of the day proclaimed him "a complete gentleman."

His impudence, however, was not always tolerated. In the playhouses of the day, it was the fashion for some of the spectators to stand upon the stage, and the places in that position were chiefly occupied by young gallants. The ladies came most in masks; but this did not prevent Master Fielding from making his remarks very freely, and in no very refined strain to them. The modest damsels, whom Pope has described,

"The fair sat pouting at the courtier's play,
And not a mask went unimproved away:
The modest fan was lifted up no more,
And virgins smiled at what they blushed before,"

were not too coy to be pleased with the fop's attentions, and replied in like strain. The players were unheeded; the audience laughed at the improvised and natural wit, when carefully prepared dialogues failed to fix their attention. The actors were disgusted, and, in spite of Master Fielding's herculean strength, kicked him off the stage, with a warning not to come again.

The *rôle* of a beau is expensive to keep up; and our justice of the peace could not, like Nash, double his income by gaming. He soon got deep in debt, as every celebrated dresser has done. The old story, not new even in those days, was enacted, and the brilliant Adonis had to keep watch and ward against tailors and bailiffs. On one occasion they had nearly caught him; but, his legs being lengthy, he gave them fair sport as far as St. James's Palace, where the officers on guard rushed out to save their pet, and drove off the myrmidons of the law at the point of the sword.

But debts do not pay themselves, nor die, and Orlando with all his strength and prowess could not long keep off the constable. Evil days gloomed at no very great distance before him, and the fear of a sponging-house and debtors' prison compelled him to turn his handsome person to account. Had he not broken a hundred hearts already? had he not charmed a thousand pairs of beaming eyes? was there not one owner of one pair who was also possessed of a pretty fortune? Who should have the honor of being the wife of such an Adonis? who, indeed, but she who could pay highest for it; and who could pay with a handsome income but a well-dowered widow? A widow it must be—a widow it should be. Noble indeed was the sentiment which inspired this great man to sacrifice himself on the altar of Hymen for the good of his creditors. Ye young men in the Guards, who do this kind of thing every day—that is, every day that you can meet with a widow with the proper qualifications—take warning by the lamentable history of Mr. Robert Fielding, and never trust to "third parties."

A widow was found, fat, fair, and forty—and oh!—charm greater far than all the rest—with a fortune of sixty thousand pounds; this was a Mrs. Deleau, who lived at Whaddon in Surrey, and at Copthall Court in London. Nothing could be more charming; and the only obstacle was the absence of all acquaintance between the parties—for, of course, it was impossible for any widow, whatever her attractions, to be insensible to those of Robert Fielding. Under these circumstances, the Beau looked about for an agent, and found one in the person of a Mrs. Villars, hairdresser to the widow. He offered this person a handsome douceur in case of success, and she was to undertake that the lady should meet the gentleman in the most unpremeditated manner. Various schemes were resorted to: with the *alias*, for he was not above an *alias*, of Major General Villars, the Beau called at the widow's country house, and was permitted to see the gardens. At a window he espied a lady, whom he took to be the object of his pursuit—bowed to her majestically, and went away, persuaded he must have made an impression. But, whether the widow was wiser than wearers of weeds have the reputation of being, or whether the agent had really no power in the matter, the meeting never came off.

The hairdresser naturally grew anxious, the douceur was too good to be lost, and as the widow could not be had, some one must be supplied in her place.

One day while the Beau was sitting in his splendid "night-gown," as the morning-dress of gentlemen was then called, two ladies were ushered into his august presence. He had been warned of this visit, and was prepared to receive the yielding widow. The one, of course, was the hairdresser, the other a young, pretty, and *apparently* modest creature, who blushed much—though with some difficulty—at the trying position in which she found herself. The Beau, delighted, did his best to reassure her. He flung himself at her feet, swore, with oaths more fashionable than delicate, that she was the only woman he ever loved, and prevailed on the widow so far as to induce her to "call again to-morrow."

Of course she came, and Adonis was in heaven. He wrote little poems to her—for, as a gallant, he could of course make verses—serenaded her through an Italian donna, invited her to suppers, at which the delicacies of the season were served without regard to the purveyor's account, and to which, coy as she was, she consented to come, and clenched the engagement with a ring, on which was the motto, "Tibi Soli." Nay, the Beau had been educated, and had some knowledge of "the tongues," so that he added to these attentions the farther one of a song or two translated from the Greek. The widow ought to have been pleased, and was. One thing only she stipulated, namely, that the marriage should be private, lest her relations should forbid the banns.

Having brought her so far, it was not likely that the fortune-hunter would stick at such a mere trifle, and accordingly an entertainment was got up at the Beau's own rooms, a supper, suitable to the rank and wealth of the widow, provided by some obligingly credulous tradesman; a priest found —for, be it premised, our hero had changed so much of his religion as he had to change in the reign of James II., when Romanism was not only fashionable, but a sure road to fortune —and the mutually satisfied couple swore to love, honor, and obey one another till death them should part.

The next morning, however, the widow left the gentleman's lodgings, on the pretext that it was injudicious for her friends to know of their union at present, and continued to visit her sposo and sup somewhat amply at his chambers from time to time. We can imagine the anxiety Orlando now felt for a check-book at the heiress's bankers, and the many insinuations he may have delicately made, touching ways and means. We can fancy the artful excuses with which these hints were put aside by his attached wife. But the dupe was still in happy ignorance of the trick played on him, and for a time such ignorance was bliss. It must have been trying to him to be called on by Mrs. Villars for the promised douceur, but he consoled himself with the pleasures of hope.

Unfortunately, however, he had formed the acquaintance of a woman of a very different reputation to the real Mrs. Deleau, and the intimacy which ensued was fatal to him.

When Charles II. was wandering abroad, he was joined, among others, by a Mr. and Mrs. Palmer. The husband was a stanch old Romanist, with the qualities which usually accompanied that faith in those days—little respect for morality, and a good deal of bigotry. In later days he was one of the victims of Titus Oates, but escaped, and eventually died in Wales in 1705, after having been James II.'s embassador to Rome. This, in a few words, is the history of that Roger Palmer, afterward Lord Castlemaine, who sold his wife—not at Smithfield, but at Whitehall—to His Majesty King Charles II., for the sum of one peerage—an Irish one, taken on consideration.

Mrs. Palmer belonged to one of the oldest families in England, and could trace her descent to Pagan de Villiers, in the days of William Rufus, and a good deal farther among the nobles of Normandy. She was the daughter of William, second Viscount Grandison, and rejoiced in the appropriate name of Barbara, for she *could* be savage occasionally. She was very beautiful, and very wicked, and soon became Charles's mistress. On the Restoration she joined the king in England, and when the poor neglected queen came over, was foisted upon her as bedchamber-woman, in spite of all the objections of that ill-used wife. It was necessary to this end that she should be the wife of a peer; and her low-minded husband actually accepted the title of Earl of Castlemaine, well knowing to what he owed it. Pepys, who admired Lady Castlemaine more than any woman in England, describes the husband and wife meeting at Whitehall with a cold ceremonial bow; yet the husband *was* there, using the court power which his own shame procured for him. A quarrel between the two, strangely enough on the score of religion, her ladyship insisting that her child should be christened by a Protestant clergyman, while his lordship insisted on the ceremony being performed by a Romish priest, brought about a separation, and from that time Lady Castlemaine, lodged in Whitehall, began her empire over the king of England. That man, "who never said a foolish thing, and never did a wise one," was the slave of this imperious and most impudent of women. She forced him to settle on her an immense fortune, much of which she squandered at the basset-table, often staking a thousand pounds at a time, and sometimes losing fifteen thousand pounds a night.

Nor did her wickedness end here. We have some pity for one, who, like La Vallière, could be attracted by the attentions of a handsome fascinating prince: we pity, though we blame. But Lady Castlemaine was vicious to the very marrow: not content with a king's favor, she courted herself the young gallant of the town. Quarrels ensued between Charles and his mistress, in which the latter invariably came off victorious, owing to her indomitable temper; and the scenes recorded by De Grammont—when she threatened to burn down Whitehall, and tear her children in pieces—are too disgraceful for insertion. She forced the reprobate monarch to consent to all her extortionate demands; rifled the nation's pockets as well as his own; and at every fresh difference, forced Charles to give her some new pension. An intrigue with Jermyn, discovered and objected to by the king, brought on a fresh and more serious difference, which was only patched up by a patent of the Duchy of Cleveland. The Duchess of Cleveland was even worse than the Countess of Castlemaine. Abandoned in time by Charles, and detested by all people of any decent feeling, she consoled herself for the loss of a real king by taking up with a stage one. Hart and Goodman, the actors, were successively her cavalieri: the former had been a captain in the army; the latter a student at Cambridge. Both were men of the coarsest minds and most depraved lives. Goodman, in after years, was so reduced that, finding, as Sheridan advised his son to do, a pair of pistols handy, a horse saddled, and Hounslow Heath not a hundred miles distant, he took to the pleasant and profitable pastime of which Dick Turpin is the patron saint. He was all but hanged by his daring robberies, but unfortunately not quite so. He lived to suffer such indigence, that he and another rascal had but one under-garment between them, and entered into a compact that one should lie in bed while the other wore the article in question. Naturally enough the two fell out in time, and the end of Goodman—sad misnomer—was worse than his beginning: such was the gallant whom the imperious Duchess of Cleveland vouchsafed to honor.

The life of the once beautiful Barbara Villiers grew daily more and more depraved: at the age of thirty she retired to Paris, shunned and disgraced. After numerous intrigues, abroad and at home, she put the crowning point to her follies by falling in love with the handsome Fielding when she herself numbered sixty-five summers.

Whether the Beau still thought of fortune, or whether having once tried matrimony, he was so enchanted with it as to make it his cacoethes, does not appear: the legend explains not for what reason he married the antiquated beauty only three weeks after he had been united to the supposed widow. For a time he wavered between the two, but that time was short: the widow discovered his second marriage, claimed him, and in so doing revealed the well-kept secret that she was not a widow; indeed, not even the relict of John Deleau, Esq., of Whaddon, but a wretched adventurer of the name of Mary Wadsworth, who had shared with Mrs. Villars the plunder of the trick. The Beau tried to preserve his dignity, and throw over his duper, but in vain. The first wife reported the state of affairs to the second; and the duchess, who had been shamefully treated by Master Fielding, was only too glad of an opportunity to get rid of him. She offered Mary Wadsworth a pension of £100 a year, and the sum of £200 in ready money, to prove the previous marriage. The case came on, and Beau

Fielding had the honor of playing a part in a famous state trial.

With his usual impudence he undertook to defend himself at the Old Bailey, and hatched up some old story to prove that the first wife was married at the time of their union to one Brady; but the plea fell to the ground, and the fine gentleman was sentenced to be burnt in the hand. His interest in certain quarters saved him this ignominious punishment, which would, doubtless, have spoiled a limb of which he was particularly proud. He was pardoned: the real widow married a far more honorable gentleman, in spite of the unenviable notoriety she had acquired; the sham one was somehow quieted, and the duchess died some four years later, the more peacefully for being rid of her tyrannical mate.

Thus ended a pretty scandal of the day, in which all the parties were so disreputable that no one could feel any sympathy for a single one of them. How the dupe himself ended is not known. The last days of fops and beaux are never glorious. Brummell died in slovenly penury; Nash in contempt. Fielding lapsed into the dimmest obscurity; and as far as evidence goes, there is as little certainty about his death as of that of the Wandering Jew. Let us hope that he is not still alive: though his friends seem to have cared little whether he were so or not, to judge from a couple of verses written by one of them:

"If Fielding is dead,
And rests under this stone,
Then he is not alive
You may bet two to one.

"But if he's alive,
And does not lie there—
Let him live till he's hanged,
For which no man will care."

OF CERTAIN CLUBS AND CLUB-WITS UNDER ANNE.

I SUPPOSE that, long before the building of Babel, man discovered that he was an associative animal, with the universal motto, "*L'union c'est la force;*" and that association, to be of any use, requires talk. A history of celebrated associations, from the building society just mentioned down to the thousands which are represented by an office, a secretary, and a brass plate, in the present day, would give a curious scheme of the natural tendencies of man; while the story of their failures—and how many have not failed, sooner or later!—would be a pretty moral lesson to your anthropolaters who Babelize nowadays, and believe there is nothing which a company with capital can not achieve. I wonder what object there is, that two men can possibly agree in desiring, and which it takes more than one to attain, for which an association of some kind has not been formed at some time or other, since first the swarthy savage learned that it was necessary to unite to kill the lion which infested the neighborhood! Alack for human nature! I fear by far the larger proportion of the objects of associations would be found rather evil than good, and, certes, nearly all of them might be ranged under two heads, according as the passions of hate or desire found a common object in several hearts. Gain on the one hand—destruction on the other—have been the chief motives of clubbing in all time.

A delightful exception is to be found, though—to wit, in associations for the purpose of talking. I do not refer to parliaments and philosophical academies, but to those companies which have been formed for the sole purpose of mutual entertainment by interchange of thought.

Now, will any kind reader oblige me with a derivation of the word "Club?" I doubt if it is easy to discover. But one thing is certain, whatever its origin, it is, in its present sense, purely English in idea and in existence. Dean Trench points this out, and, noting the fact that no other nation (he might have excepted the Chinese) has any word to express this kind of association, he has, with very pardonable national pride, but unpardonably bad logic, inferred that the English are the most sociable people in the world. The contrary is true; nay, *was* true, even in the days of Addison, Swift, Steele—even in the days of Johnson, Walpole, Selwyn; ay, at all time since we have been a nation. The fact is, we are not the most sociable, but the most associative race; and the establishment of clubs is a proof of it. We can not, and never could, talk freely, comfortably, and generally, without a company for talking. Conversation has always been with us as much a business as railroad-making, or what not. It has always demanded certain accessories, certain condiments, certain stimulants to work it up to the proper pitch. "We all know" we are the cleverest and wittiest people under the sun; but then our wit has been stereotyped. France has no "Joe Miller;" for a bon-mot there, however good, is only appreciated historically. Our wit is printed, not spoken: our best wits behind an ink-horn have sometimes been the veriest logs in society. On the Continent clubs were not called for, because society itself was the arena of conversation. In this country, on the other hand, a man could only chat when at his ease; could only be at his ease among those who agreed with him on the main points of religion and politics, and even then wanted the aid of a bottle to make him comfortable. Our want of sociability was the cause of our clubbing, and therefore the word "club" is purely English.

This was never so much the case as after the Restoration. Religion and politics never ran higher than when a monarch, who is said to have died a papist because he had no religion at all during his life, was brought back to supplant a furious puritanical Protectorate. Then, indeed, it was difficult for men of opposite parties to meet without bickering; and society demanded separate meeting-places for those who differed. The origin of clubs in this country is to be traced to two causes—the vehemence of religion and political partisanship, and the establishment of coffee-houses. These certainly gave the first idea of clubbery. The taverns which preceded them had given the English a zest for public life in a small way. "The Mermaid" was, virtually, a club of wits long before the first real club was opened, and, like the clubs of the eighteenth century, it had its presiding geniuses in Shakspeare and Rare Ben.

The coffee-houses introduced somewhat more refinement and less exclusiveness. The oldest of these was the "Grecian." "One Constantine, a Grecian," advertised in "The Intelligencer" of January 23d, 1664–5, "that the right coffee bery or chocolate" might be had of him "as cheap and as good as is any where to be had for money," and soon after began to sell the said "coffee bery" in small cups at his own establishment in Devereux Court, Strand. Some two years later we have news of "Will's," the most famous, perhaps, of the coffee-houses. Here Dryden held forth with pedantic vanity; and here was laid the first germ of that critical acumen which has since become a distinguishing feature in English literature. Then, in the City, one Garraway, of Exchange Alley, first sold "tea in leaf and drink, made according to the directions of the most knowing, and travelers into those eastern countries;" and thus established the well-known Garraway's, whither, in Defoe's day, "foreign banquiers" and even ministers resorted, to drink the said beverage. "Robin's," "Jonathan's," and many another, were all opened about this time, and the rage for coffee-house life became general throughout the country.

In these places the company was of course of all classes and colors; but, as the conversation was general, there was naturally at first a good deal of squabbling, till, for the sake of peace and comfort, a man chose his place of resort according to his political principles; and a little later there were regular Whig and Tory coffee-houses. Thus, in Anne's day, "The Cocoanut," in St. James's Street, was reserved for Jacobites, while none but Whigs frequented "The St. James's." Still there was not sufficient exclusiveness; and as early as in Charles II.'s reign, men of peculiar opinions began to appropriate certain coffee-houses at certain hours, and to exclude from them all but approved members. Hence the origin of clubs.

The October Club was one of the earliest, being composed of some hundred and fifty rank Tories, chiefly country members of Parliament. They met at the "Bell," in King Street, Westminster, that street in which Spenser starved, and Dryden's brother kept a grocer's shop. A portrait of Queen Anne, by Dahl, hung in the club-room. This and the Kit-kat, the great Whig club, were chiefly reserved for politics; but the fashion of clubbing having once come in, it was soon followed by people of all fancies. No reader of the "Spectator" can fail to remember the ridicule to which this was turned by descriptions of imaginary clubs for which the qualifications were absurd, and of which the business, on meeting, was preposterous nonsense of some kind. The idea of such fraternities, as the Club of Fat Men, the Ugly Club, the Sheromp Club, the Everlasting Club, the Sighing Club, the Amorous Club, and others, could only have been suggested by real clubs almost as ridiculous. The names, too, were almost as fantastical as those of the taverns in the previous century, which counted "The Devil," and "The Heaven and Hell," among their numbers. Many derived their titles from the standing dishes preferred at supper, the Beefsteak and the Kit-kat (a sort of mutton-pie) for instance.

The Beefsteak Club, still in existence, was one of the most famous established in Anne's reign. It had at that time less of a political than a jovial character. Nothing but that excellent British fare, from which it took its name, was, at first, served at the supper-table. It was an assemblage of wits of every station, and very jovial were they supposed to be when the juicy dish had been discussed. Early in the century, Estcourt, the actor, was made providore to this club, and wore a golden gridiron as a badge of office, and is thus alluded to in Dr. King's "Art of Cookery" (1709):—

"He that of honor, wit, and mirth partakes,
May be a fit companion o'er beefsteaks;
His name may be to future times enrolled
In Estcourt's book, whose gridiron's framed of gold."

Estcourt was one of the best mimics of the day, and a keen satirist to boot: in fact he seems to have owed much of his success on the stage to his power of imitation, for while his own manner was inferior, he could at pleasure copy exactly that of any celebrated actor. He *would* be a player. At fifteen he ran away from home, and joining a strolling company, acted Roxana in woman's clothes; his friends pursued him, and, changing his dress for that of a girl of the time, he tried to escape them, but in vain. The histrionic youth was captured, and bound apprentice in London town; the "seven long years" of which did not cure him of the itch for acting. But he was too good a wit for the stage, and amused himself, though not always his audience, by interspersing his part with his own remarks. The great took him by the hand, and old Marlborough especially patronized him: he wrote a burlesque of the Italian operas then beginning to be in vogue; and died in 1712–13. Estcourt was not the only actor belonging to the Beefsteak, nor even the only one who had concealed his sex under emergency; Peg Woffington, who had made as good a boy as he had done a girl, was afterward a member of this club.

In later years the beefsteak was cooked in a room at the top of Covent Garden Theatre, and counted many a celebrated wit among those who sat around its cheery dish. Wilkes the blasphemer, Churchill, and Lord Sandwich, were all members of it at the same time. Of the last, Walpole gives us information in 1763 at the time of Wilkes' duel with Martin in Hyde Park. He tells us that at the Beefsteak Club Lord Sandwich talked so profusely, "that he drove harlequins out of the company." To the honor of the club be it added, that his lordship was driven out after the harlequins, and finally expelled: it is sincerely to be hoped that Wilkes was sent after his lordship. This club is now represented by one held behind the

Lyceum, with the thoroughly British motto, "Beef and Liberty:" the name was happily chosen, and therefore imitated. In the reign of George II. we meet with a "Rump-steak, or Liberty Club;" and somehow steaks and liberty seem to be the two ideas most intimately associated in the Britannic mind. Can any one explain it?

Other clubs there were under Anne—political, critical, and hilarious—but the palm is undoubtedly carried off by the glorious Kit-kat.

It is not every eating-house that is immortalized by a Pope, though Tennyson has sung "The Cock" with its "plump headwaiter," who, by the way, was mightily offended by the Laureate's verses—or pretended to be so—and thought it "a great liberty of Mr. ——, Mr. ——, what is his name? to put respectable private characters into his books." Pope, or some say Arbuthnot, explained the etymology of this club's extraordinary title:—

"Whence deathless Kit-kat took its name,
Few critics can unriddle;
Some say from pastry-cook it came,
And some from Cat and Fiddle.

"From no trim beaux its name it boasts,
Gray statesmen or green wits;
But from the pell-mell pack of toasts
Of old cats and young kits."

Probably enough the title was hit on at hap-hazard, and retained because it was singular, but as it has given a poet a theme, and a painter a name for pictures of a peculiar size, its etymology has become important. Some say that the pastry-cook in Shire Lane, at whose house it was held, was named Christopher Katt. Some one or other was certainly celebrated for the manufacture of that forgotten delicacy, a mutton-pie, which acquired the name of a Kit-kat.

"A Kit-kat is a supper for a lord,"

says a comedy of 1700, and certes it afforded at this club evening nourishment for many a celebrated noble profligate of the day. The supposed sign of the Cat and Fiddle (Kitt), gave another solution, but after all, Pope's may be satisfactorily received.

The Kit-kat was, *par excellence*, the Whig Club of Queen Anne's time: it was established at the beginning of the eighteenth century, and was then composed of thirty-nine members, among whom were the Dukes of Marlborough, Devonshire, Grafton, Richmond, and Somerset. In later days, it numbered the greatest wits of the age, of whom anon.

This club was celebrated more than any for its *toasts*.

Now, if men must drink—and sure the vine was given us for use, I do not say for abuse—they had better make it an occasion of friendly intercourse; nothing can be more degraded than the solitary sanctimonious toping in which certain of our Northern brethren are known to indulge. They had better give to the quaffing of that rich gift, sent to be a medicine for the mind, to raise us above the perpetual contemplation of worldly ills, as much of romance and elegance as possible. It is the opener of the heart, the awakener of nobler feelings of generosity and love, the banisher of all that is narrow, and sordid, and selfish; the herald of all that is exalted in man. No wonder that the Greeks made a god of Bacchus, that the Hindoo worshiped the mellow Soma, and that there has been scarce a poet who has not sung its praise. There was some beauty in the feasts of the Greeks, when the goblet was really wreathed with flowers; and even the German student, dirty and drunken as he may be, removes half the stain from his orgies with the rich harmony of his songs, and the hearty good-fellowship of his toasts. We drink still, perhaps we shall always drink till the end of time, but all the romance of the bowl is gone; the last trace of its beauty went with the frigid abandonment of the toast.

There was some excuse for wine when it brought out that now forgotten expression of good-will. Many a feud was reconciled in the clinking of glasses; just as many another was begun when the cup was drained too deeply. The first quarter of the last century saw the end of all the social glories of the wassail in this country, and though men drank as much fifty years later, all its poetry and romance had then disappeared.

It was still, however, the custom at that period to call on the name of some fair maiden, and sing her praises over the cup as it passed. It was a point of honor for all the company to join the health. Some beauties became celebrated for the number of their toasts; some even standing toasts among certain sets. In the Kit-kat Club the custom was carried out by rule, and every member was compelled to name a beauty, whose claims to the honor were then discussed, and if her name was approved, a separate bowl was consecrated to her, and verses to her honor engraved on it. Some of the most celebrated toasts had even their portraits hung in the club-room, and it was no slight distinction to be the favorite of the Kit-kat. When only eight years old, Lady Mary Wortley Montagu enjoyed this privilege. Her father, the Lord Dorchester, afterward Evelyn, Duke of Kingston, in a fit of caprice, proposed "the pretty little child" as his toast. The other members, who had never seen her, objected; the Peer sent for her, and there could no longer be any question. The forward little girl was handed from knee to knee, petted, probably, by Addison, Congreve, Vanbrugh, Garth, and many another famous wit. Another celebrated toast of the Kit-kat, mentioned by Walpole, was Lady Molyneux, who, he says, died smoking a pipe.

This club was no less celebrated for its portraits than for the ladies it honored. They, the portraits, were all painted by Kneller, and all of one size, which thence got the name of Kit-kat; they were hung round the club-room. Jacob Tonson, the publisher, was secretary to the club.

Defoe tells us the Kit-kat held the first rank among the clubs of the early part of the last century, and certainly the names of its members comprise as many wits as we could expect to find collected in one society.

Addison must have been past fifty when he became a member of the Kit-kat. His "Cato" had won him the general applause of the Whig party, who could not allow so fine a writer to slip from among them. He had long, too, played the courtier, and was "quite a gentleman." A place among the exclusives of the Kit-kat was only the just reward of such attainments, and he had it. I shall not be asked to give a notice of a man so universally known, and one who ranks rather with the humorists than the wits. It will suffice to say, that it was not till *after* the publication of the "Spectator," and some time after, that he joined our society.

Congreve I have chosen out of this set for a separate life, for this man happens to present a very average sample of all their peculiarities. Congreve was a literary man, a poet, a wit, a beau, and—what unhappily is quite as much to the purpose—a profligate. The only point he, therefore, wanted in common with most of the members, was a title; but few of the titled members combined as many good and bad qualities of the Kit-kat kind as did William Congreve.

Another dramatist, whose name seems to be inseparable from Congreve's, was that mixture of bad and good taste—Vanbrugh. This author of "The Relapse," the most licentious play ever acted, and builder of Blenheim, the ugliest house ever erected, was a man of good family, and Walpole counts him among those who "wrote genteel comedy, because they lived in the best company." We doubt the logic of this; but if it hold, how is it that Van wrote plays which the best company, even of that age, condemned, and neither good nor bad company can read in the present day without being shocked? If the conversation of the Kit-kat was any thing like that in this member's comedies, it must have been highly edifying.

However, I have no doubt Mr. Van passed for a gentleman, whatever his conversation, and he was certainly a wit, and apparently somewhat less licentious in his morals than the rest. Yet what Pope said of his literature may be said, too, of some acts of his life:

"How Van wants grace, who never wanted wit."

And his quarrel with "Queen Sarah" of Marlborough, though the duchess was by no means the most agreeable woman in the world to deal with, is not much to Van's honor. When the nation voted half a million to build that hideous mass of stone, the irregular and unsightly piling of which caused Walpole to say that the architect "had emptied quarries, rather than built houses," and Dr. Evans to write this epitaph for the builder—

"Lie heavy on him, Earth, for he
Laid many a heavy load on thee,"

Sarah haggled over "seven-pence halfpenny a bushel:" Van retorted by calling her "stupid and troublesome," and "that wicked woman of Marlborough," and after the duke's death, wrote that the duke had left her "twelve thousand pounds a year to keep herself clean and go to law." Whether she employed any portion of it on the former object we do not pretend to say, but she certainly spent as much as a miser could on litigation, Van himself being one of the unfortunates she attacked in this way.

The events of Vanbrugh's life were varied. He began life in the army, but in 1697 gave the stage "The Relapse." It was sufficiently successful to induce him to follow it up with the "Provoked Wife," one of the wittiest pieces produced in those days. Charles, Earl of Carlisle, Deputy Earl Marshal, for whom he built Castle Howard, made him Clarencieux King-at-arms in 1704, and he was knighted by George I., 9th September, 1714. In 1705 he joined Congreve in the management of the Haymarket, which he himself built. George I. made him Comptroller-general of the royal works. He had even an experience of the Bastile, where he was confined for sketching fortifications in France. He died in 1726, with the reputation of a good wit, and a bad architect. His conversation was, certainly, as light as his buildings were heavy.

Another member, almost as well known in his day, was Sir Samuel Garth, the physician, "well-natured Garth," as Pope called him. He won his fame by a satire on the apothecaries in the shape of a poem called "The Dispensary." When delivering the funeral oration over Dryden's body, which had been so long unburied that its odor began to be disagreeable, he mounted a tub, the top of which fell through and left the doctor in rather an awkward position. He gained admission to the Kit-kat in consequence of a vehement eulogy on King William, which he had introduced into his Harveian oration, in 1697.* It was Garth, too, who extemporized most of the verses which were inscribed on the toasting-glasses of their club, so that he may, *par excellence*, be considered the Kit-kat poet. He was the physician and friend of Marlborough, with whose sword he was knighted by George I., who made him his physician in ordinary. Garth was a very jovial man, and, some say, not a very religious one. Pope said he was as good a Christian as ever lived, "without knowing it." He certainly had no affectation of piety, and if charitable and good-natured acts could take a man to heaven, he deserved to go there. He had his doubts about faith, and is said to have died a Romanist. This he did in 1719, and the poor and the Kit-kat must both have felt his loss. He was perhaps more of a wit than a poet, although he has been classed at times with Gray and Prior; he can scarcely take the same rank as other verse-making doctors, such as Akenside, Darwin, and Armstrong. He seems to have been an active, healthy man—perhaps too much so for a poet—for it is on record that he ran a match in the Mall with the Duke of Grafton, and beat him. He was fond too, of a hard frost, and had a regular speech to introduce on that subject: "Yes, sir, 'fore Gad, very fine weather, sir—very wholesome weather, sir—kills trees, sir—very good for man, sir."

Old Marlborough had another intimate friend at the club, who was probably one of its earliest members. This was Arthur Maynwaring, a poet, too, in a way, but more celebrated at this time for his *liaison* with Mrs. Oldfield, the famous but disreputable actress, with whom he fell in love when he was forty years old, and whom he instructed in the niceties of elocution, making her rehearse her parts to him in private. Maynwaring was born in 1668, educated at Oxford, and destined to the bar, for which he studied. He began life as a vehement Jacobite, and even supported that party in sundry pieces; but like some others, he was easily converted, when, on coming to town, he found it more fashionable to be a Whig. He held two or three posts under the Government, whose cause he now espoused: had the honor of the dedication of "The Tatler" to him by Steele, and died suddenly in 1712. He divided his fortune between his sister and his mistress, Mrs. Oldfield, and his son by the latter. Mrs. Oldfield must have grown rich in her sinful career, for she could afford, when ill, to refuse to take

* The Kit-kat club was not founded till 1703.

her salary from the theatre, though entitled to it. She acted best in Vanbrugh's "Provoked Husband," so well, in fact, that the manager gave her an extra fifty pounds by way of acknowledgment.

Poetizing seems to have been as much a polite accomplishment of that age as letter-writing was of a later, and a smattering of science is of the present day. Gentlemen tried to be poets, and poets gentlemen. The consequence was, that both made fools of themselves. Among the poetasters who belonged to the Kit-kat, we must mention Walsh, a country gentleman, member of Parliament, and very tolerable scholar. He dabbled in odes, elegies, epitaphs, and all that small fry of the muse which was then so plentiful. He wrote critical essays on Virgil, in which he tried to make out that the shepherds in the days of the Roman poet were very well-bred gentlemen of good education! He was a devoted admirer and friend of Dryden, and he encouraged Pope in his earlier career so kindly that the little viper actually praised him! Walsh died somewhere about 1709 in middle life.

We have not nearly done with the poets of the Kit-kat. A still smaller one than Walsh was Stepney, who, like Garth, had begun life as a violent Tory and turned coat when he found his interest lay the other way. He was well repaid, for from 1692 to 1706 he was sent on no less than eight diplomatic missions, chiefly to German courts. He owed this preferment to the good luck of having been a school-fellow of Charles Montagu, afterward Earl of Halifax. He died about 1707, and had as grand a monument and epitaph in Westminster Abbey as if he had been a Milton or Dryden.

When you meet a dog trotting along the road, you naturally expect that his master is not far off. In the same way, where you find a poet, still more a poetaster, there you may feel certain you will light upon a patron. The Kit-kat was made up of Mæcenas's and their humble servants; and in the same club with Addison, Congreve, Vanbrugh, and the minor poets, we are not at all surprised to find Sir Robert Walpole, the Duke of Somerset, Halifax, and Somers.

Halifax was, *par excellence*, the Mæcenas of his day, and Pope described him admirably in the character of Bufo:

> "Proud as Apollo, on his forked hill,
> Sat full-blown Bufo, puff'd by every quill;
> *Fed with soft dedication* all day long,
> Horace and he went hand in hand in song."

The dedications poured in thickly. Steele, Tickell, Philips, Smith, and a crowd of lesser lights, raised my lord each one on a higher pinnacle; and in return the powerful minister was not forgetful of the douceur which well-tuned verses were accustomed to receive. He himself had tried to be a poet, and in 1703 wrote verses for the toasting-cups of the Kit-kat. His lines to a Dowager Countess of ****, are good enough to make us surprised that he never wrote any better. Take a specimen:

"Fair Queen of Fop-land in her royal style;
Fop-land the greatest part of this great isle!
Nature did ne'er so equally divide
A female heart 'twixt piety and pride:
Her waiting-maids prevent the peep of day,
And all in order at her toilet lay
Prayer-books, patch-boxes, sermon-notes, and paint,
At once t' improve the sinner and the saint."

A Mæcenas who paid for his dedications was sure to be well spoken of, and Halifax has been made out a wit and a poet, as well as a clever statesman. He reminds me of a young Oxford man whom I knew in my college-days, and who never walked down the street without half a dozen loafers touching their hats to him. It was affirmed that he distributed sundry crowns among them in consideration of this honor; and certainly, when he left the university, I never spoke of him to any of that order of nondescripts who infest a university town without being assured that Mr. A—— was "one of the right sort —a rale gen'l'man he was, and no mistake." Halifax got his earldom and the garter from George I., and died, after enjoying them less than a year, in 1715.

Chancellor Somers, with whom Halifax was associated in the impeachment case in 1701, was a far better man in every respect. His was probably the purest character among those of all the members of the Kit-kat. He was the son of a Worcester attorney, and born in 1652. He was educated at Trinity, Oxford, and rose purely by merit, distinguishing himself at the bar and on the bench, unwearied in his application to business, and an exact and upright judge. At school he was a terrible good boy, keeping to his book in play-hours. Throughout life his habits were simple and regular, and his character unblemished. He slept but little, and in later years had a reader to attend him at waking. With such habits he can scarcely have been a constant attender at the club; and as he died a bachelor, it would be curious to learn what ladies he selected for his toasts. In his later years his mind weakened, and he died in 1716 of apoplexy. Walpole calls him "one of those divine men who, like a chapel in a palace, remain unprofaned, while all the rest is tyranny, corruption, and folly."

A huge stout figure rolls in now to join the toasters in

Shire Lane. In the puffy, once handsome face, there are signs of age, for its owner is past sixty; yet he is dressed in superb fashion; and in an hour or so, when the bottle has been diligently circulated, his wit will be brighter and keener than that of any young man present. I do not say it will be repeatable, for the talker belongs to a past age, even coarser than that of the Kit-kat. He is Charles Sackville,* famous as a companion of the merriest and most disreputable of the Stuarts, famous—or, rather, infamous—for his mistress, Nell Gwynn, famous for his verses, for his patronage of poets, and for his wild frolics in early life, when Lord Buckhurst. Rochester called him

"The best good man with the worst-natured muse;"

and Pope says he was

"The scourge of pride, though sanctified or great,
Of fops in learning and of knaves in state;"

Our sailors still sing the ballad which he is said to have written on the eve of the naval engagement between the Duke of York and Admiral Opdam, which begins—

"To all you ladies now on land
We men at sea indite."

With a fine classical taste and a courageous spirit, he had in early days been guilty of as much iniquity as any of Charles's profligate court. He was one of a band of young libertines who robbed and murdered a poor tanner on the high-road, and were acquitted, less on account of the poor excuse they dished up for this act than of their rank and fashion. Such fine gentlemen could not be hanged for the sake of a mere workman in those days—no! no! Yet he does not seem to have repented of this transaction, for soon after he was engaged with Sedley and Ogle in a series of most indecent acts at the Cock Tavern in Bow Street, where Sedley, in "birthday attire," made a blasphemous oration from the balcony of the house. In later years he was the pride of the poets: Dryden and Prior, Wycherley, Hudibras, and Rymer, were all encouraged by him, and repaid him with praises. Pope and Dr. King were no less bountiful in their eulogies of the Mæcenas. His conversation was so much appreciated that gloomy William III. chose him as his companion, as merry Charles had done before. The famous Irish ballad, which my Uncle Toby was always humming, "Lillibullero bullen-a-lah," but which Percy attributes to the Marquis of Wharton, another member of the Kit-kat, was said to have been written by Buckhurst. He retained his wit to the last; and Congreve, who visited him when he was dying, said, "Faith, he stutters more

* For some notice of Lord Dorset, see p. 72.

wit than other people have in their best health." He died at Bath in 1706.

Buckhurst does not complete the list of conspicuous members of this club, but the remainder were less celebrated for their wit. There was the Duke of Kingston, the father of Lady Mary Wortley Montagu; Granville, who imitated Waller, and attempted to make his "Myra" as celebrated as the court-poet's Saccharissa, who, by the way, was the mother of the Earl of Sunderland; the Duke of Devonshire, whom Walpole calls "a patriot among the men, a gallant among the ladies," and who founded Chatsworth; and other noblemen, chiefly belonging to the latter part of the seventeenth century, and all devoted to William III., though they had been bred at the courts of Charles and James.

With such an array of wits, poets, statesmen, and gallants, it can easily be believed that to be the toast of the Kit-kat was no slight honor; to be a member of it à still greater one; and to be one of its most distinguished, as Congreve was, the greatest. Let us now see what title this conceited beau and poet had to that position.

WILLIAM CONGREVE.

When "Queen Sarah" of Marlborough read the silly epitaph which Henrietta, Duchess of Marlborough, had written and had engraved on the monument she set up to Congreve, she said, with one of the true Blenheim sneers, "I know not what *happiness* she might have in his company, but I am sure it was no *honor*," alluding to her daughter's eulogistic phrases.

Queen Sarah was right, as she often was when condemnation was called for; and however amusing a companion the dramatist may have been, he was not a man to respect, for he had not only the common vices of his age, but added to them a foppish vanity, toadyism, and fine-gentlemanism (to coin a most necessary word), which we scarcely expect to meet with in a man who sets up for a satirist.

It is the fate of greatness to have falsehoods told of it, and of nothing in connection with it more so than of its origin. If the converse be true, Congreve ought to have been a great man, for the place and time of his birth are both subjects of dispute. Oh, happy Gifford! or happy Croker! why did you not—perhaps you did—go to work to set the world right on this matter—you, to whom a date discovered is the highest palm (no pun intended, I assure you) of glory, and who would rather Shakspeare had never written "Hamlet," or Homer the "Iliad," than that some miserable little forgotten scrap which decided a year or a place should have been consigned to flames before it fell into your hands? Why did you not bring the thunder of your abuse and the pop-gunnery of your satire to bear upon the question, "How, when, and where was William Congreve born?"

It was Lady Morgan, I think, who first "saw the light" (that is, if she was born in the daytime) in the Irish Channel. If it had been only some one more celebrated, we should have had by this time a series of philosophical, geographical, and ethnological pamphlets to prove that she was English or Irish, according to the fancies or prejudices of the writers. It was certainly a very Irish thing to do, which is one argument for the Milesians, and again it was done in the Irish Channel, which is another and a stronger one; and altogether we are not inclined to go into forty-five pages of recondite facts and fine-drawn arguments, mingled with the most vehement abuse of any body who ever before wrote on the subject, to prove that this country had the honor of producing her ladyship—the Wild Irish Girl. We freely give her up to the sister island. But not so William Congreve, though we are equally indifferent to the honor in his case.

The one party, then, assert that he was born in this country, the other that he breathed his first air in the Emerald Isle. Whichever be the true state of the case, we, as Englishmen, prefer to agree in the commonly received opinion that he came into this wicked world at the village of Bardsea or Bardsey, not far from Leeds in the county of York. Let the Bardseyans immediately erect a statue to his honor, if they have been remiss enough to neglect him heretofore.

But our difficulties are not ended, for there is a similar doubt about the year of his birth. His earliest biographer assures us he was born in 1672, and others that he was baptized three years before, in 1669. Such a proceeding might well be taken as proof of his Hibernian extraction, and accordingly we find Malone supporting the earlier date, producing, of course, a certificate of baptism to support himself; and as we have a very great respect for his authority, we beg also to support Mr. Malone.

This being settled, we have to examine who were his parents; and this is satisfactorily answered by his earliest biographer, who informs us that he was of a very ancient family, being "the only surviving son of William Congreve, Esq. (who was second son to Richard Congreve, Esq., of Congreve and Stretton in that county)," to wit, Yorkshire. Congreve *père* held a military command, which took him to Ireland soon after the dramatist's birth, and thus young William had the incomparable advantage of being educated at Kilkenny, and afterward at Trinity, Dublin, the "silent sister," as it is commonly called at our universities.

At the age of nineteen, this youth sought the classic shades of the Middle Temple, of which he was entered a student, but by the honorable society of which he was never called to the bar; but whether this was from a disinclination to study "Coke upon Lyttelton," or from an incapacity to digest the requisite number of dinners, the devouring of which qualify a young gentleman to address an enlightened British jury, we have no authority for deciding. He was certainly not the first, nor the last, young Templar who has quitted special pleading on a crusade to the heights of Parnassus, and he began early to try the nib of his pen and the color of his ink in a novel. Eheu! how many a novel has issued from the dull, dirty chambers of that same Temple! The waters of the

Thames just there seem to have been augmented by a mingled flow of sewage and Helicon, though the former is undoubtedly in the greater proportion. This novel, called "Incognita; or Love and Duty Reconciled," seems to have been—for I confess that I have not read more than a chapter of it, and hope I never may be forced to do so—great rubbish, with good store of villains and ruffians, love-sick maidens who tune their lutes—always conveniently at hand—and love-sick gallants who run their foes through the body with the greatest imaginable ease. It was, in fact, such a novel as James might have written, had he lived a century and a half ago. It brought its author but little fame, and accordingly he turned his attention to another branch of literature, and in 1693 produced "The Old Bachelor," a play of which Dryden, his friend, had so high an opinion that he called it the "best first-play he had ever read." However, before being put on the stage it was submitted to Dryden, and by him and others prepared for representation, so that it was well fathered. It was successful enough, and Congreve thus found his vocation. In his dedication—a regular piece of flummery of those days, for which authors were often well paid, either in cash or interest—he acknowledges a debt of gratitude to Lord Halifax, who appears to have taken the young man by the hand.

The young Templar could do nothing better now than write another play. Play-making was as fashionnble an amusement in those days of Old Drury, the only patented theatre then, as novel-writing is in 1860; and when the young ensign, Vanbrugh, could write comedies and take the direction of a theatre, it was no derogation to the dignity of the Staffordshire squire's grandson to do as much. Accordingly, in the following year he brought out a better comedy, "The Double Dealer," with a prologue which was spoken by the famous Anne Bracegirdle. She must have been eighty years old when Horace Walpole wrote of her to that other Horace—Mann: "Tell Mr. Chute that his friend Bracegirdle breakfasted with me this morning. As she went out and wanted her clogs, she turned to me and said: 'I remember at the playhouse they used to call, Mrs. Oldfield's chair! Mrs. Barry's clogs! and Mrs. Bracegirdle's pattens!'" These three ladies were all buried in Westminster Abbey, and, except Mrs. Cibber, the most beautiful and most sinful of them all—though they were none of them spotless—are the only actresses whose ashes and memories are hallowed by the place, for we can scarcely say that they do *it* much honor.

The success of "The Double Dealer" was at first moderate, although that highly respectable woman, Queen Mary, honored it with her august presence, which forthwith called up verses of the old adulatory style, though with less point and neatness than those addressed to the Virgin Queen:

"Wit is again the care of majesty,"

said the poet, and

"Thus flourished wit in our forefathers' age,
And thus the Roman and Athenian stage.
Whose wit is best, we'll not presume to tell,
But this we know, our audience will excell;
For never was in Rome, nor Athens seen
So fair a circle, and so bright a queen."

But this was not enough, for when Her Majesty departed for another realm in the same year, Congreve put her into a highly eulogistic pastoral, under the name of Pastora, and made some compliments on her, which were considered the finest strokes of poetry and flattery combined, that an age of addresses and eulogies could produce.

"As lofty pines o'ertop the lowly steed,
So did her graceful height all nymphs exceed.
To which excelling height she bore a mind
Humble as osiers, bending to the wind.
* * * * *
I mourn Pastora dead; let Albion mourn,
And sable clouds her chalkie cliffs adorn."

This play was dedicated to Lord Halifax, of whom we have spoken, and who continued to be Congreve's patron.

The fame of the young man was now made; but in the following year it was destined to shine out more brilliantly still. Old Betterton—one of the best Hamlets that ever trod the stage, and of whom Booth declared that when he was playing the Ghost to his Hamlet, his look of surprise and horror was so natural, that Booth could not for some minutes recover himself—was now a veteran in his sixtieth year. For forty years he had walked the boards and made a fortune for the patentees of Drury. It was very shabby of them, therefore, to give some of his best parts to younger actors. Betterton was disgusted, and determined to set up for himself, to which end he managed to procure another patent, turned the Queen's Court in Portugal Row, Lincoln's Inn, into a theatre, and opened it on the 30th of April, 1695. The building had been before used as a theatre in the days of the Merry Monarch, and Tom Killegrew had acted here some twenty years before; but it had again become a "tennis-quatre of the lesser sort," says Cibber, and the new theatre was not very grand in fabric. But Betterton drew to it all the best actors and actresses of his former company; and Mrs. Barry and Mrs. Bracegirdle remained true to the old man. Congreve, to his honor, espoused the same cause, and the theatre opened with his play of "Love for Love," which was more successful than either of the former. The veteran himself spoke the prologue, and fair Bracegirdle the epilogue, in which the poet thus alluded to their change of stage:

> "And thus our audience, which did once resort
> To shining theatres to see our sport,
> Now find us tost into a tennis-court.
> Thus from the past, we hope for future grace:
> I beg it—
> And some here know I have *a begging face.*"

The king himself completed the success of the opening by attending it, and the theatre in Lincoln's Inn Fields might have ruined the older house, if it had not been for the rapidity with which Vanbrugh and Cibber, who wrote for Old Drury, managed to concoct their pieces; while Congreve was a slower, though perhaps better, writer. "Love for Love" was hereafter a favorite of Betterton's, and when in 1709, a year before his death, the company gave the old man—then in ill health, poor circumstances, and bad spirits—a benefit, he chose this play, and himself, though more than seventy, acted the part of Valentine, supported by Mrs. Bracegirdle as Angelina, and Mrs. Barry as Frail.

The young dramatist, with all his success, was not satisfied with his fame, and resolved to show the world that he had as much poetry as wit in him. This he failed to do; and, like better writers, injured his own fame, by not being contented with what he had. Congreve—the wit, the dandy, the man about town—took it into his head to write a tragedy. In 1697 "The Mourning Bride" was acted at the Tennis Court Theatre. The author was wise enough to return to his former muse, and some time after produced his best piece, so some think, "The Way of the World," which was also performed by Betterton's company; but, alas! for overwriting—that cacoethes of imprudent men—it was almost hissed off the stage. Whether this was owing to a weariness of Congreve's style, or whether at the time of its first appearance Collier's attacks, of which anon, had already disgusted the public with the obscenity and immorality of this writer, I do not know; but, whatever the cause, the consequence was that Mr. William Congreve, in a fit of pique, made up his mind never to write another piece for the stage—a wise resolution, perhaps—and to turn fine gentleman instead. With the exception of composing a masque called the "Judgment of Paris," and an opera, "Gemele," which was never performed, he kept this resolution very honestly; and so Mr. William Congreve's career as a playwright ends at the early age of thirty.

But though he abandoned the drama, he was not allowed to retire in peace. There was a certain worthy, but peppery little man, who, though a Jacobite and a clergyman, was stanch and true, and as superior in character—even, indeed, in vigor of writing—to Congreve, as Somers was to every man of his age. This was Jeremy Collier, to whom we owe it that there is any English drama fit to be acted before our sisters and wives in the present day. Jeremy, the peppery, purged the stage in a succession of Jeremiads.

Born in 1650, educated at Cambridge as a poor scholar, ordained at the age of twenty-six, presented three years later with the living of Ampton, near Bury St. Edmunds, Jeremy had two qualities to recommend him to Englishmen—respectability and pluck. In an age when the clergy were as bad as the blackest sheep in their flocks, Jeremy was distinguished by purity of life; in an age when the only safety lay in adopting the principles of the Vicar of Bray, Jeremy was a Nonjuror, and of this nothing could cure him. The Revolution of 1688 was scarcely effected, when the fiery little partisan published a pamphlet, which was rewarded by a residence of some months in Newgate, *not* in the capacity of chaplain. But he was scarcely let out, when again went his furious pen, and for four years he continued to assail the new government, till his hands were shackled and his mouth closed in the prison of "The Gate-house." Now, see the character of the man. He was liberated upon giving bail, but had no sooner reflected on this liberation than he came to the conclusion that it was wrong, by offering security, to recognize the authority of magistrates appointed by a usurper, as he held William to be, and voluntarily surrendered himself to his judges. Of course he was again committed, but this time to the King's Bench, and would doubtless in a few years have made the tour of the London prisons, if his enemies had not got tired of trying him. Once more at liberty, he passed the next three years in retirement.

After 1693, Jeremy Collier's name was not brought before the public till 1696, when he publicly absolved Sir John Friend and Sir William Perkins, at their execution, for being concerned in a plot to assassinate King William. His "Essays on Moral Subjects" were published in 1697; 2d vol., 1705; 3d vol., 1709. But the only way to put out a firebrand like this is to let it alone, and Jeremy, being no longer persecuted, began, at last, to think the game was grown stupid, and gave it up. He was a well-meaning man, however, and as long as he had the luxury of a grievance, would injure no one.

He found one now in the immorality of his age, and if he had left politics to themselves from the first, he might have done much more good than he did. Against the vices of a court and courtly circles it was useless to start a crusade single-handed; but his quaint clever pen might yet dress out a powerful Jeremiad against those who encouraged the licentiousness of the people. Jeremy was no Puritan, for he was a Nonjuror and a Jacobite, and we may, therefore, believe that the cause was a good one, when we find him adopting precisely the same line as the Puritans had done before him. In 1698 he published, to the disgust of all Drury and Lincoln's Inn, his "Short View of the Immorality and Profaneness of the English Stage, together with the Sense of Antiquity upon this Argument."

While the King of Naples is supplying his ancient Venuses with gowns, and putting his Marses and Herculeses into pantaloons, there are—such are the varieties of opinion—respectable men in this country who call Paul de Kock the greatest moral writer of his age, and who would yet like to see "The Relapse," "Love for Love," and the choice specimens of Wycherley, Farquhar, and even of Beaumont and Fletcher, acted at the Princess's and the Haymarket in the year of grace 1860. I am not writing "A Short View" of this or any other moral subject; but this I must say—the effect of a sight or sound on a human being's silly little passions must of necessity be relative. You and I can read "Don Juan," Lewis's "Monk," the plays of Congreve, and any or all of the publications of Holywell Street, without more than disgust at their obscenity and admiration for their beauties. But could we be pardoned for putting these works into the hands of "sweet seventeen," or making Christmas presents of them to our boys? Ignorance of evil is, to a certain extent, virtue: let boys be boys in purity of mind as long as they can: let the unrefined "great unwashed" be treated also much in the same way as young people. I maintain that to a coarse mind all improper ideas, however beautifully clothed, suggest only sensual thoughts—nay, the very modesty of the garments makes them the more insidious—the more dangerous. I would rather give my boy John, Massinger, or Beaumont and Fletcher, whose very improper things "are called by their proper names," than let him dive in the prurient innuendo of these later writers.

But there is no need to argue the question—the public has decided it long since, and except in indelicate ballets and occasional rather *French* passages in farce, our modern stage is free from immorality. Even in Garrick's days, when men were not much more refined than in those of Queen Anne, it was found impossible to put the old drama on the stage without considerable weeding. Indeed I doubt if even the liberal upholder of Paul de Kock would call Congreve a moral writer; but I confess I am not a competent judge, for, *risum teneatis*, my critics, I have not read his works since I was a boy, and what is more, I have no intention of reading them. I well remember getting into my hands a large thick volume, adorned with miserable woodcuts, and bearing on its back the title "Wycherley, Congreve, Vanbrugh, and Farquhar." I devoured it at first with the same avidity with which one might welcome a bottle-imp, who at the hour of one's dullness turned up out of the carpet and offered you delights new and old for nothing but a tether on your soul; and with a like horror, boy though I was, I recoiled from it when any better moment came. It seemed to me, when I read this book, as if life were too rotten for any belief, a nest of sharpers, adulterers, cut-throats, and prostitutes. There was none—as far as I remember—of that amiable weakness, of that better sentiment, which in Ben Jonson or Massinger reconcile us to human nature. If truth be a test of genius, it must be a proof of true poetry, that man is not made uglier than he is. Nay, his very ugliness loses its intensity and falls upon our diseased tastes, for want of some goodness, some purity and honesty to relieve it. I will not say that there is none of this in Congreve. I only know that my recollection of his plays is like that of a vile nightmare, which I would not for any thing have return to me. I have read, since, books as bad, perhaps worse in some respects, but I have found the redemption here and there. I would no more place Shandy in any boy's hands than Congreve and Farquhar; and yet I can read Tristram again and again with delight; for amid all that is bad there stand out Trim and Toby, pure specimens of the best side of human nature, coming home to us and telling us that the world is not all bad. There may be such touches in "Love for Love," or "The Way of the World"—I know not and care not. To my remembrance Congreve is but a horrible nightmare, and may the fates forbid I should be forced to go through his plays again.

Perhaps, then, Jeremy was not far wrong when he attacked these specimens of the drama with an unrelenting Nemesis; but he was not before his age. It was less the obvious coarseness of these productions with which he found fault than their demoralizing tendency in a direction which we should now, perhaps, consider innocuous. Certainly the Jeremiad overdid it, and like a swift but not straight bowler at cricket, he sent balls which no wicket-keeper could stop, and which, therefore, were harmless to the batter. He did not want boldness. He attacked Dryden, now close upon his grave; Congreve, a young man, Vanbrugh, Cibber, Farquhar, and the rest, all alive, all in the zenith of their fame, and all as popular as writers could be. It was as much as if a man should stand up to-day and denounce Dickens and Thackeray, with the exception that well-meaning people went along with Jeremy, whereas very few would do more than smile at the zeal of any one who tilted against our modern pets. Jeremy, no doubt, was bold, but he wanted tact, and so gave his enemy occasion to blaspheme. He made out cases where there were none, and let alone what we moderns should denounce. So Congreve took up the cudgels against him with much wit and much coarseness, and the two fought out the battle in many a pamphlet and many a letter. But Jeremy was not to be beat. His "Short View" was followed by "A Defense of the Short View," a "Second Defense of the Short View," "A Farther Short View," and, in short, a number of "Short Views," which had been better merged into one "Long Sight." Jeremy grew coarse and bitter; Congreve coarser and bitterer; and the whole controversy made a pretty chapter for the "Quarrels of Authors." But the Jeremiad triumphed in the long run, because, if its method was bad, its cause was good, and a succeeding generation voted Congreve immoral. Enough of Jeremy. We owe him a tribute for his pluck, and though no one reads him in the present day, we may be thankful to him for having led the way to a better state of things.*

Congreve defended himself in eight letters addressed to Mr. Moyle, and we can only say of them, that, if any thing, they are yet coarser than the plays he would excuse.

The works of the young Templar, and his connection with Betterton, introduced him to all the writers and wits of his day. He and Vanbrugh, though rivals, were fellow-workers, and our glorious Haymarket Theatre, which has gone on at times when Drury and Covent Garden have been in despair, owes its origin to their confederacy. But Vanbrugh's theatre was on the site of the present Opera House, and *the* Haymarket was set up as a rival concern. Vanbrugh's was built in 1705, and met the usual fate of theatres, being burnt down some eighty-four years after. It is curious enough that this house, destined for the "legitimate drama"—often a very illegitimate performance—was opened by an opera set to *Italian* music, so that "Her Majesty's" has not much departed from the original cast of the place.

* Dryden, in the Preface to his Fables, acknowledged that Collier "had, in many points, taxed him justly."

Perhaps Congreve's best friend was Dryden. This man's life and death are pretty well known, and even his funeral has been described time and again. But Corinna—as she was styled—gave of the latter an account which has been called romantic, and much discredited. There is a deal of characteristic humor in her story of the funeral, and as it has long been lost sight of, it may not be unpalatable here: Dryden died on May-day, 1701, and Lord Halifax* undertook to give his body a *private* funeral in Westminster Abbey.

"On the Saturday following," writes Corinna, "the Company came. The Corps was put into a Velvet Hearse, and eighteen Mourning Coaches filled with Company attending. When, just before they began to move, Lord Jeffreys,† with some of his rakish Companions, coming by, in Wine, ask'd whose Funeral? And being told: 'What!' cries he, 'shall Dryden, the greatest Honour and Ornament of the Nation, be buried after this private Manner? No, Gentlemen! let all that lov'd Mr. Dryden, and honour his Memory, alight, and join with me in gaining my Lady's Consent, to let me have the Honour of his Interment, which shall be after another manner than this, and I will bestow £1000 on a Monument in the Abbey for him.' The Gentlemen in the Coaches, not knowing of the Bishop of Rochester's Favour, nor of Lord Halifax's generous Design (these two noble Spirits having, out of Respect to the Family, enjoin'd Lady Elsabeth and her Son to keep their Favour concealed to the World, and let it pass for her own Expense), readily came out of the Coaches, and attended Lord Jeffreys up to the Lady's Bed-side, who was then sick. He repeated the Purport of what he had before said, but she absolutely refusing, he fell on his knees, vowing never to rise till his Request was granted. The rest of the Company, by his Desire, kneeled also; she being naturally of a timorous Disposition, and then under a sudden surprise, fainted away. As soon as she recover'd her speech, she cry'd, 'No, no!' 'Enough, gentlemen,' replied he (rising briskly), 'My Lady is very good, she says, Go, go!' She repeated her former Words with all her Strength, but alas in vain! her feeble Voice was lost in their Acclamations of Joy! and Lord Jeffreys order'd the Hearsemen to carry the Corps to Russell's, an undertaker in Cheapside, and leave it there, till he sent orders for the Embalment, which, he added, should be after the Royal Manner. His directions were obey'd, the Company dispersed, and Lady Elsabeth and Mr. Charles remained Inconsolable. Next Morn-

* Charles Montagu, Earl of Halifax. Lord Halifax was born in 1661, and died in 1715. He was called "Mouse Montagu."

† Son of Judge Jeffries: satirized by Pope under the name of "Bufo."

ing Mr. Charles waited on Lord Halifax, etc., to excuse his Mother and self, by relating the real Truth. But neither his Lordship nor the Bishop would admit of any Plea; especially the latter, who had the Abbey lighted, the ground open'd, the Choir attending, an Anthem ready set, and himself waiting for some Hours without any Corps to bury. Russell, after three Days' Expectance of Orders for Embalment, without receiving any, waits on Lord Jeffreys, who, pretending Ignorance of the Matter, turn'd it off with an ill-natured Jest, saying, 'Those who observed the orders of a drunken Frolick, deserved no better; that he remembered nothing at all of it, and he might do what he pleased with the Corps.' On this Mr. Russell waits on Lady Elsabeth and Mr. Dryden; but alas! it was not in their power to answer. The season was very hot, the Deceas'd had liv'd high and fast; and being corpulent, and abounding with gross Humours, grew very offensive. The Undertaker, in short, threaten'd to bring home the Corps, and set it before the Door. It can not be easily imagin'd what grief, shame, and confusion seized this unhappy Family. They begged a Day's Respite, which was granted. Mr. Charles wrote a very handsome Letter to Lord Jeffreys, who returned it with this cool Answer, 'He knew nothing of the Matter, and would be troubled no more about it.' He then addressed the Lord Halifax and Bishop of Rochester, who were both too justly tho' unhappily incensed, to do anything in it. In this extreme distress, Dr. Garth, a man who entirely lov'd Mr. Dryden, and was withal a Man of Generosity and great Humanity, sends for the Corps to the College of Physicians in Warwick Lane, and proposed a Funeral by subscription, to which himself set a most noble example. Mr. Wycherley, and several others, among whom must not be forgotten Henry Cromwell, Esq., Captain Gibbons, and Mr. Christopher Metcalfe, Mr. Dryden's Apothecary and intimate Friend (since a Collegiate Physician), who with many others contributed most largely to the Subscription; and at last a Day, about three Weeks after his Decease, was appointed for the Interment at the Abbey. Dr. Garth pronounced a fine Latin Oration over the Corps at the College; but the audience being numerous, and the Room large, it was requisite the Orator should be elevated, that he might be heard. But as it unluckily happen'd there was nothing at hand but an old Beer-Barrel, which the Doctor with much good-nature mounted; and in the midst of his Oration, beating Time to the Accent with his Foot, the Head broke in, and his Feet sunk to the Bottom, which occasioned the malicious Report of his Enemies, 'That he was turned a Tub-Preacher.' However, he finished the Oration with a superior grace and genius, to the loud Acclamations of Mirth, which inspir'd the mix'd or rather Mob-Auditors. The Procession began to move, a numerous Train of Coaches attended the Hearse: But, good God! in what Disorder can only be express'd by a Sixpenny Pamphlet, soon after publish'd, entitled 'Dryden's Funeral.' At last the Corps arrived at the Abbey, which was all unlighted. No Organ played, no Anthem sung; only two of the Singing boys preceded the Corps, who sung an Ode of Horace, with each a small candle in their Hand. The Butchers and other Mob broke in like a Deluge, so that only about eight or ten Gentlemen could gain Admission, and those forced to cut the Way with their drawn Swords. The Coffin in this Disorder was let down into Chaucer's Grave, with as much Confusion, and as little Ceremony, as was possible; every one glad to save themselves from the Gentlemen's Swords, or the Clubs of the Mob. When the Funeral was over, Mr. Charles sent a Challenge to Lord Jeffreys, who refusing to answer it, he sent several others, and went often himself, but could neither get a letter deliver'd, nor Admittance to speak to him, that he resolved, since his Lordship refused to answer him like a gentleman, he would watch an Opportunity to meet him, and fight off hand, tho' with all the Rules of Honor; which his Lordship hearing, left the Town, and Mr. Charles could never have the satisfaction to meet him, tho' he sought it till his Death with the utmost Application."

Dryden was, perhaps, the last man of learning that believed in astrology; though an eminent English author, now living, and celebrated for the variety of his acquirements, has been known to procure the casting of horoscopes, and to consult a noted "astrologer," who gives opinions for a small sum. The coincidences of prophecy are not more remarkable than those of star-telling; and Dryden and the author I have referred to were probably both captivated into belief by some fortuitous realization of their horoscopic predictions. Nor can we altogether blame their credulity, when we see biology, table-turning, rapping, and all the family of impostures, taken up seriously in our own time.

On the birth of his son Charles, Dryden immediately cast his horoscope. The following account of Dryden's paternal solicitude for his son, and its result, may be taken as embellished, if not apocryphal. Evil hour, indeed—Jupiter, Venus, and the Sun were "all under the earth;" Mars and Saturn were in square: eight, or a multiple of it, would be fatal to the child—the square foretold it. In his eighth, his twenty-third, or his thirty-second year, he was certain to die, though he might possibly linger on to the age of thirty-four. The stars did all they could to keep up their reputation. When the boy was eight years old he nearly lost his life by being buried under a heap of stones out of an old wall, knocked down by a stag and hounds in a hunt. But the stars were not to be beaten; and though the child recovered, went in for the game a second time in his twenty-third year, when he fell, in a fit of giddiness, from a tower, and, to use Lady Elsabeth's words, was "mash'd to a mummy." Still the battle was not over, and the mummy returned in due course to its human form, though considerably disfigured. Mars and Saturn were naturally disgusted at his recovery, and resolved to finish the disobedient youth. As we have seen, he in vain sought his fate at the hand of Jeffreys; but we must conclude that the offended constellations took Neptune in partnership, for in due course the youth met with a watery grave.

After abandoning the drama, Congreve appears to have come out in the light of an independent gentleman. He was already sufficiently introduced into literary society; Pope, Steele, Swift, and Addison were not only his friends but his admirers, and we can well believe that their admiration was considerable, when we find the one dedicating his "Miscellany," the other his translation of the "Iliad," to a man who was qualified neither by rank nor fortune to play Mæcenas.

At what time he was admitted to the Kit-kat I am not in a position to state, but it must have been after 1715, and by that time he was a middle-aged man, his fame was long since achieved; and whatever might be thought of his works and his controversy with Collier, he was recognized as one of the literary stars at a period when the great courted the clever, and wit was a passport to any society. Congreve had plenty of that, and probably at the Kit-kat was the life of the party when Vanbrugh was away or Addison in a graver mood. Untroubled by conscience, he could launch out on any subject whatever; and his early life, spent in that species of so-called gayety which was then the routine of every young man of the world, gave him ample experience to draw upon. But Congreve's ambition was greater than his talents. No man so little knew his real value, or so grossly asserted one which he had not. Gay, handsome, and in good circumstances, he aspired to be, not Congreve the poet, not Congreve the wit, not Congreve the man of mind, but simply Congreve the fine gentleman. Such humility would be charming if it were not absurd. It is a vice of scribes to seek a character for which they have little claim. Johnson was as proud or prouder of his hunting than he was of his dictionary; Moore loved to be thought a diner-out rather than a poet; even Byron affected the fast man when he might have been content with the name of "genius;" but Congreve went farther, and was ashamed of being poet, dramatist, genius, or what you will. An anecdote of him, told by Voltaire, who may have been an "awfu' liar," but had no temptation to invent in such a case as this, is so consistent with what we gather of the man's character, that one can not but think it is true.

The philosopher of Ferney was anxious to see and converse with a brother dramatist of such celebrity as the author of "The Way of the World." He expected to find a man of a keen satirical mind, who would join him in a laugh against humanity. He visited Congreve, and naturally began to talk of his works. The fine gentleman spoke of them as trifles utterly beneath his notice, and told him, with an affectation which perhaps was sincere, that he wished to be visited as a gentleman, not as an author. One can imagine the disgust of his brother dramatist. Voltaire replied, that had Mr. Congreve been nothing more than a gentleman, he should not have taken the trouble to call on him, and therewith retired with an expression of merited contempt.

It is only in the present day that authorship is looked upon as a profession, though it has long been one. It is amusing to listen to the sneers of men who never wrote a book, or who, having written, have gained thereby some more valuable advantage than the publisher's check. The men who talk with horror of writing for money, are glad enough if their works introduce them to the notice of the influential, and aid them in procuring a place. In the same way, Congreve was not at all ashamed of fulsome dedications, which brought him the favor of the great. Yet we may ask, if, the laborer being worthy of his hire, and the labor of the brain being the highest, finest, and most exhausting that can be, the man who straightforwardly and without affectation takes guineas from his publisher, is not honester than he who counts upon an indirect reward for his toil? Fortunately, the question is almost settled by the example of the first writers of the present day; but there are still people who think that one should sit down to a year's—ay ten years'—hard mental work, and expect no return but fame. Whether such objectors have always private means to return to, or whether they have never known what it is to write a book, we do not care to examine, but they are to be found in large numbers among the educated; and indeed, to this present day, it is held by the upper classes to be utterly derogatory to write for money.

Whether this was the feeling in Congreve's day or not is

not now the question. Those were glorious days for an author, who did not mind playing the sycophant a little. Instead of having to trudge from door to door in Paternoster Row, humbly requesting an interview, which is not always granted—instead of sending that heavy parcel of MS., which costs you a fortune for postage, to publisher after publisher, till it is so often "returned with thanks" that you hate the very sight of it, the young author of those days had a much easier and more comfortable part to play. An introduction to an influential man in town, who again would introduce you to a patron, was all that was necessary. The profession of Mæcenas was then as recognized and established as that of doctor or lawyer. A man of money could always buy brains; and most noblemen considered an author to be as necessary a part of his establishment as the footmen who ushered them into my lord's presence. A fulsome dedication in the largest type was all that he asked; and if a writer were sufficiently profuse in his adulation, he might dine at Mæcenas's table, drink his sack and canary without stint, and apply to him for cash whenever he found his pockets empty. Nor was this all: if a writer were sufficiently successful in his works to reflect honor on his patron, he was eagerly courted by others of the noble profession. He was offered, if not hard cash, as good an equivalent, in the shape of a comfortable government sinecure; and if this was not to be had, he was sometimes even lodged and boarded by his obliged dedicatee. In this way he was introduced into the highest society; and if he had wit enough to support the character, he soon found himself *facile princeps* in a circle of the highest nobility in the land. Thus it is that in the clubs of the day we find title and wealth mingling with wit and genius; and the writer who had begun life by a cringing dedication, was now rewarded by the devotion and assiduity of the men he had once flattered. When Steele, Swift, Addison, Pope, and Congreve were the kings of their sets, it was time for authors to look and talk big. Eheu! those happy days are gone!

Our dramatist, therefore, soon discovered that a good play was the key to a good place, and the Whigs took care that he should have it. Oddly enough, when the Tories came in they did not turn him out. Perhaps they wanted to gain him over to themselves; perhaps, like the Vicar of Bray, he did not mind turning his coat once or twice in a lifetime. However this may be, he managed to keep his appointment without offending his own party; and when the latter returned to power, he even induced them to give him a comfortable little sinecure, which went by the name of Secretary to the Island of Jamaica, and raised the income from his appointments to £1200 a year.

From this period he was little before the public. He could afford now to indulge his natural indolence and selfishness. His private life was perhaps not worse than that of the majority of his contemporaries. He had his intrigues, his mistresses, the same love of wine, and the same addiction to gluttony. He had the reputation of a wit, and with wits he passed his time, sufficiently easy in his circumstances to feel no damping to his spirits in the cares of this life. The Island of Jamaica probably gave him no further trouble than that of signing a few papers from time to time, and giving a receipt for his salary. His life, therefore, presents no very remarkable feature, and he is henceforth known more on account of his friends than for aught he may himself have done. The best of these friends was Walter Moyle, the scholar, who translated parts of Lucian and Xenophon, and was pretty well known as a classic. He was a Cornish man of independent means, and it was to him that Congreve addressed the letters in which he attempted to defend himself from the attacks of Collier.

It was not to be expected that a wit and a poet should go through life without a platonic, and accordingly we find our man not only attached, but devoted to a lady of great distinction. This was no other than Henrietta, Duchess of Marlborough, the daughter of "Malbrook" himself, and of the famous "Queen Sarah." Henrietta was the eldest daughter, and there was no son to inherit the prowess of Churchill and the parsimony of his wife. The nation—to which, by the way, the Marlboroughs were never grateful—would not allow the title of their pet warrior to become extinct, and a special Act of Parliament gave to the eldest daughter the honors of the duchy.* The two Duchesses of Marlborough hated each other cordially. Sarah's temper was probably the main cause of their bickering; but there is never a feud between parent and child in which both are not more or less blamable.

The Duchess Henrietta conceived a violent fancy for the wit and poet, and whatever her husband, Lord Godolphin, may have thought of it, the connection ripened into a most intimate friendship, so much so that Congreve made the duchess not only his executrix, but the sole residuary legatee of all his property.† His will gives us some insight into the toadying character of the man. Only four near relations are mentioned as legatees, and only £540 is divided among them; whereas, after leaving £200 to Mrs. Bracegirdle, the actress; £100, "and all my apparel and linnen of all sorts" to a Mrs. Rooke, he divides the rest between his friends of the nobil-

* See Burke's "Peerage."

† The Duchess of Marlborough received £10,000 by Mr. Congreve's will.

ity, Lords Cobham and Shannon, the Duchess of Newcastle, Lady Mary Godolphin, Colonel Churchill (who receives "twenty pounds, together with my gold-headed cane"), and, lastly, "to the poor of the parish," the magnificent sum of *ten pounds*. "Blessed are those who give to the rich;" these words must surely have expressed the sentiment of the worldly Congreve.

However, Congreve got something in return from the Duchess Henrietta, which he might not have received from "the poor of the parish," to wit, a monument, and an inscription on it written by her own hand. I have already said what "Queen Sarah" thought of the latter, and, for the rest, those who care to read the nonsense on the walls of Westminster Abbey can decide for themselves as to the honor the poet received from his titled friend.

The latter days of William Congreve were passed in wit and gout: the wine, which warmed the one probably brought on the latter. After a course of ass's milk, which does not seem to have done him much good, the ex-dramatist retired to Bath, a very fashionable place for departing life in, under easy and elegant circumstances. But he not only drank of the springs beloved of King Bladud, of apocryphal memory, but even went so far as to imbibe the snail-water, which was then the last species of quack cure in vogue. This, probably, dispatched him. But it is only just to that disagreeable little reptile that infests our gardens, and whose slime was supposed to possess peculiarly strengthening properties, to state that his death was materially hastened by being overturned when driving in his chariot. He was close upon sixty, had long been blind from cataracts in his eyes, and as he was no longer either useful or ornamental to the world in general, he could perhaps be spared. He died soon after this accident in January, 1729. He had the sense to die at a time when Westminster Abbey, being regarded as a mausoleum, was open to receive the corpse of any one who had a little distinguished himself, and even of some who had no distinction whatever. He was buried there with great pomp, and his dear duchess set up his monument. So much for his body. What became of the soul of a dissolute, vain, witty, and unprincipled man, is no concern of ours. *Requiescat in pace*, if there is any peace for those who are buried in Westminster Abbey.

BEAU NASH.

"There is nothing new under the sun," said Walpole, by way of a very original remark. "No," whispered George Selwyn, "nor under the grandson either."

Mankind, as a body, has proved its silliness in a thousand ways, but in none, perhaps, so ludicrously as in its respect for a man's coat. He is not always a fool that knows the value of dress; and some of the wisest and greatest of men have been dandies of the first water. King Solomon was one and Alexander the Great was another; but there never was a more despotic monarch, nor one more humbly obeyed by his subjects, than the King of Bath, and he won his dominions by the cut of his coat. But as Hercules was killed by a dress-shirt, so the beaux of the modern world have generally ruined themselves by their wardrobes, and brought remorse to their hearts, or contempt from the very people who once worshiped them. The husband of Mrs. Damer, who appeared in a new suit twice a day, and whose wardrobe sold for £15,000, blew his brains out at a coffee-house. Beau Fielding, Beau Nash, and Beau Brummell all expiated their contemptible vanity in obscure old age of want and misery. As the world is full of folly, the history of a fool is as good a mirror to hold up to it as another; but in the case of Beau Nash the only question is, whether he or his subjects were the greater fools. So now for a picture of as much folly as could well be crammed into that hot basin in the Somersetshire hills, of which more anon.

It is a hard thing for a man not to have had a father—harder still, like poor Savage, to have one whom he can not get hold of; but perhaps it is hardest of all, when you have a father, and that parent a very respectable man, to be told that you never had one. This was Nash's case, and his father was so little known, and so seldom mentioned, that the splendid Beau was thought almost to have dropped from the clouds, ready dressed and powdered. He dropped in reality from any thing but a heavenly place—the shipping-town of Swansea: so that Wales can claim the honor of having produced the finest beau of his age.

Old Nash was, perhaps, a better gentleman than his son; but with far less pretensions. He was a partner in a glass-manufactory. The Beau, in after years, often got rallied on the inferiority of his origin, and the least obnoxious answer he ever made was to Sarah of Marlborough, as rude a creature as himself, who told him he was ashamed of his parentage. "No, madam," replied the King of Bath, "I seldom mention my father, in company, not because I have any reason to be ashamed of him, but because he has some reason to be ashamed of me." Nash, though a fop and a fool, was not a bad-hearted man, as we shall see. And if there were no other redeeming point in his character, it is a great deal to say for him, that in an age of toadyism, he treated rank in the same manner as he did the want of it, and did his best to remove the odious distinctions which pride would have kept up in his dominions. In fact, King Nash may be thanked for having, by his energy in this respect, introduced into society the first elements of that middle class which is found alone in England.

Old Nash—whose wife, by the way, was niece to that Colonel Poyer who defended Pembroke Castle in the days of the first Revolution—was one of those silly men who want to make gentlemen of their sons, rather than good men. He had his wish. His son Richard was a very fine gentleman, no doubt; but, unfortunately, the same circumstances that raised him to that much-coveted position, also made him a gambler and a profligate. Oh! foolish papas, when will you learn that a Christian snob is worth ten thousand irreligious gentlemen? When will you be content to bring up your boys for heaven rather than for the brilliant world? Nash, senior, sent his son first to school and then to Oxford, to be made a gentleman of. Richard was entered at Jesus College, the haunt of the Welsh. In my day, this quiet little place was celebrated for little more than the humble poverty of its members, one third of whom rejoiced in the cognomen of Jones. They were not renowned for cleanliness, and it was a standing joke with us silly boys, to ask at the door for "that Mr. Jones who had a tooth-brush." If the college had the same character then, Nash must have astonished its dons, and we are not surprised that in his first year they thought it better to get rid of him.

His father could ill afford to keep him at Oxford, and fondly hoped he would distinguish himself. "My boy Dick" did so at the very outset, by an offer of marriage to one of those charming sylphs of that academical city, who are always on the look-out for credulous undergraduates. The affair was discovered, and Master Richard, who was not seventeen, was removed from the University.* Whether he ever, in after

* Warner ("History of Bath," p. 366) says, "Nash was removed from Oxford by his friends."

life, made another offer, I know not, but there is no doubt that he *ought* to have been married, and that the connections he formed in later years were far more disreputable than his first love affairs.

The worthy glass-manufacturer having failed to make his son a gentleman in one way, took the best step to make him a blackguard, and, in spite of the wild inclinations he had already evinced, bought him a commission in the army. In this new position the incipient Beau did every thing but his duty; dressed superbly, but would not be in time for parade; spent more money than he had, but did not obey orders; and finally, though not expelled from the army, he found it convenient to sell his commission, and return home, after spending the proceeds.

Papa was now disgusted, and sent the young Hopeless to shift for himself. What could a well-disposed, handsome youth do to keep body and, not soul, but clothes together? He had but one talent, and that was for dress. Alas, for our degenerate days! When we are pitched upon our own bottoms, we must work; and that is a highly ungentlemanly thing to do. But in the beginning of the last century, such a degrading resource was quite unnecessary. There were always at hand plenty of establishments where a youth could obtain the necessary funds to pay his tailor, if fortune favored him; and if not, he could follow the fashion of the day, and take to what the Japanese call "the happy Dispatch." Nash probably suspected that he had no brains to blow out, and he determined the more resolutely to make fortune his mistress. He went to the gaming-table, and turned his one guinea into ten, and his ten into a hundred, and was soon blazing about in gold lace, and a new sword, the very delight of dandies.

He had entered his name, by way of excuse, at the Temple, and we can quite believe that he ate all the requisite dinners, though it is not so certain that he paid for them. He soon found that a fine coat is not so very far beneath a good brain in worldly estimation, and when, on the accession of William the Third, the Templars, according to the old custom, gave his Majesty a banquet, Nash, as a promising Beau, was selected to manage the establishment. It was his first experience of the duties of an M. C., and he conducted himself so ably on this occasion that the king even offered to make a knight of him. Probably Master Richard thought of his empty purse, for he replied with some of that assurance which afterward stood him in such good stead, "Please your majesty, if you intend to make me a knight, I wish I may be one of your poor knights of Windsor, and then I shall have a fortune, at least able to support my title." William did not see the force of this argument, and Mr. Nash remained Mr. Nash till the day of his death. He had another chance of the title, however, in days when he could have better maintained it, but again he refused. Queen Anne once asked him why he declined knighthood. He replied: "There is Sir William Read, the mountebank, who has just been knighted, and I should have to call him 'brother.'" The honor was, in fact, rather a cheap one in those days, and who knows whether a man who had done such signal service to his country did not look forward to a peerage? Worse men than even Beau Nash have had it.

Well, Nash could afford to defy royalty, for he was to be himself a monarch of all he surveyed, and a good deal more; but before we follow him to Bath, let us give the devil his due—which, by the way, he generally gets—and tell a pair of tales in the Beau's favor.

Imprimis, his accounts at the Temple were £10 deficient. Now I don't mean that Nash was not as great a liar as most of his craft, but the truth of this tale rests on the authority of the "Spectator," though Nash took delight in repeating it.

"Come hither, young man," said the Benchers, coolly: "whereunto this deficit?"

"Pri'thee, good masters," quoth Nash, "that £10 was spent on making a man happy."

"A man happy, young sir, pri'thee explain."

"Odds donners," quoth Nash, "the fellow said in my hearing that his wife and bairns were starving, and £10 would make him the happiest man *sub sole*, and on such an occasion as His Majesty's accession could I refuse it him?"

Nash was, proverbially, more generous than just. He would not pay a debt if he could help it, but would give the very amount to the first friend that begged it. There was much ostentation in this, but then my friend Nash *was* ostentatious. One friend bothered him day and night for £20 that was owing to him, and he could not get it. Knowing his debtor's character, he hit, at last, on a happy expedient, and sent a friend to *borrow* the money "to relieve his urgent necessities." Out came the bank-note, before the story of distress was finished. The friend carried it to the creditor, and when the latter again met Nash, he ought to have made him a pretty compliment on his honesty.

Perhaps the King of Bath would not have tolerated in any one else the juvenile frolics he delighted in after years to relate of his own early days. When at a loss for cash he would do any thing, but work, for a fifty pound note, and having, in one of his trips, lost all his money at York, the Beau undertook to "do penance" at the minster door for that sum. He accordingly arrayed himself—not in sackcloth and ashes, but —in an able-bodied blanket, and nothing else, and took his stand at the porch just at the hour when the dean would be going in to read service. "He, ho," cried that dignitary, who knew him, "Mr. Nash in masquerade?" "Only a Yorkshire penance, Mr. Dean," quoth the reprobate; "for keeping bad company, too," pointing therewith to the friends who had come to see the sport.

This might be tolerated, but when, in the eighteenth century, a young man emulates the hardiness of Godiva, without her merciful heart, we may not think quite so well of him. Mr. Richard Nash, Beau Extraordinary to the Kingdom of Bath, once rode through a village in that costume of which even our first parent was rather ashamed, and that, too, on the back of a cow! The wager was, I believe, considerable. A young Englishman did something more respectable, yet quite as extraordinary, at Paris, not a hundred years ago, for a small bet. He was one of the stoutest, thickest-built men possible, yet being but eighteen, had neither whisker nor mustache to masculate his clear English complexion. At the Maison Dorée one night he offered to ride in the Champs Elysées in a lady's habit, and not be mistaken for a man. A friend undertook to dress him, and went all over Paris to hire a habit that would fit his round figure. It was hopeless for a time, but at last a good-sized body was found, and added thereto, an ample skirt. Félix dressed his hair with *mainte* plats and a *net*. He looked perfect, but in coming out of the hairdresser's to get into his fly, unconsciously pulled up his skirt and displayed a sturdy pair of well-trowsered legs. A crowd—there is always a ready crowd in Paris—was waiting, and the laugh was general. This hero reached the horse-dealer's—"mounted," and rode down the Champs. "A very fine woman that," said a Frenchman in the promenade, "but what a back she has!" It was in the return bet to this that a now well-known diplomat drove a goat-chaise and six down the same fashionable resort, with a monkey, dressed as a footman, in the back seat. The days of folly did not, apparently, end with Beau Nash.

There is a long lacune in the history of this worthy's life, which may have been filled up by a residence in a sponging-house, or by a temporary appointment as billiard-marker; but the heroic Beau accounted for his disappearance at this time in a much more romantic manner. He used to relate that he was once asked to dinner on board a man-of-war under orders for the Mediterranean, and that such was the affection the officers entertained for him, that, having made him drunk—no difficult matter—they weighed anchor, set sail, and carried the successor of King Bladud away to the wars. Having gone so far, Nash was not the man to neglect an opportunity for imaginary valor. He therefore continued to relate that, in the apocryphal vessel, he was once engaged in a yet more apocryphal encounter, and wounded in the leg. This was a little too much for the good Bathonians to believe, but Nash silenced their doubts. On one occasion, a lady who was present when he was telling this story, expressed her incredulity.

"I protest, madam," cried the Beau, lifting his leg up, "it is true, and if I can not be believed, your ladyship may, if you please, receive further information, and feel the ball in my leg."

Wherever Nash may have passed the intervening years, may be an interesting speculation for a German professor, but is of little moment to us. We find him again, at the age of thirty, taking first steps toward the complete subjugation of the kingdom he afterward ruled.

There is, among the hills of Somersetshire, a huge basin formed by the river Avon, and conveniently supplied with a natural gush of hot water, which can be turned on at any time for the cleansing of diseased bodies. This hollow presents many curious anomalies: though sought for centuries for the sake of health, it is one of the most unhealthily-situated places in the kingdom; here the body and the pocket are alike cleaned out, but the spot itself has been noted for its dirtiness since the days of King Bladud's wise pigs; here, again, the diseased flesh used to be healed, but the healthy soul within it speedily besickened; you came to cure gout and rheumatism, and caught in exchange dice-fever.

The mention of those pigs reminds me that it would be a shameful omission to speak of this city without giving the story of that apocryphal British monarch, King Bladud. But let me be the one exception; let me respect the good sense of the reader, and not insult him by supposing him capable of believing a mythic jumble of kings, and pigs, and dirty marshes, which he will, if he cares to, find at full length in any "Bath Guide"—price sixpence.

But whatever be the case with respect to the Celtic sovereign, there is, I presume, no doubt, that the Romans were here, and probably the centurions and tribunes cast the *alea* in some pristine assembly-room, or wagged their plumes in some well-built Pump-room, with as much spirit of fashion as the full-bottomed-wigged exquisites in the reign of King Nash. At any rate Bath has been in almost every age a common centre for health-seekers and gamesters—two antipodal races who always flock together—and if it has from time to time declined, it has only been for a period. Saxon churls and Norman lords were too sturdy to catch much rheumatic gout: crusaders had better things to think of than their imaginary ailments; good health was in fashion under Plantagenets and Tudors; doctors were not believed in; even empirics had to praise their wares with much wit, and Morrison himself must have mounted a bank and dressed in Astleyian costume in order to find a customer; sack and small-beer were harmless, when homes were not comfortable enough to keep earl or churl by the fireside, and "out-of-doors" was the proper drawing-room for a man: in short, sickness came in with civilization, indisposition with immoral habits, fevers with fine-gentlemanliness, gout with greediness, and valetudinarianism—there *is* no Anglo-Saxon word for that—with what we falsely call refinement. So, whatever Bath may have been to pampered Romans, who over-ate themselves, it had little importance to the stout, healthy Middle Ages, and it was not till the reign of Charles II. that it began to look up. Doctors and touters—the two were often one in those days—thronged there, and fools were found in plenty to follow them. At last the blessed countenance of portly Anne smiled on the pig-styes of King Bladud. In 1703 she went to Bath, and from that time "people of distinction" flocked there. The assemblage was not perhaps very brilliant or very refined. The visitors danced on the green, and played privately at hazard. A few sharpers found their way down from London; and at last the Duke of Beaufort instituted an M. C. in the person of Captain Webster—Nash's predecessor—whose main act of glory was in setting up gambling as a public amusement. It remained for Nash to make the place what it afterward was, when Chesterfield could lounge in the Pump-room and take snuff with the Beau; when Sarah of Marlborough, Lord and Lady Hervey, the Duke of Wharton, Congreve, and all the little-great of the day thronged thither rather to kill time with less ceremony than in London, than to cure complaints more or less imaginary.

The doctors were only less numerous than the sharpers; the place was still uncivilized; the company smoked and lounged without etiquette, and played without honor; the place itself lacked all comfort, all elegance, and all cleanliness.

Upon this delightful place, the avatâr of the God of Etiquette, personified in Mr. Richard Nash, descended somewhere about the year 1705, for the purpose of regenerating the barbarians. He alighted just at the moment that one of the doctors we have alluded to, in a fit of disgust at some slight on the part of the town, was threatening to destroy its reputation, or, as he politely expressed it, "to throw a toad into the spring." The Bathonians were alarmed and in consternation, when young Nash, who must have already distinguished himself as a macaroni, stepped forward and offered to render the angry physician impotent. "We'll charm his toad out again with music," quoth he. He evidently thought very little of the watering-place, after his town experiences, and prepared to treat it accordingly. He got up a band in the Pump-room, brought thither in this manner the healthy as well as the sick, and soon raised the renown of Bath as a resort for gayety as well as for mineral waters. In a word, he displayed a surprising talent for setting every thing and every body to rights, and was, therefore, soon elected, by tacit voting, the King of Bath.

He rapidly proved his qualifications for the position. First he secured his Orphean harmony by collecting a band subscription, which gave two guineas a piece to six performers; then he engaged an official pumper for the Pump-room; and lastly, finding that the bathers still gathered under a booth to drink their tea and talk their scandal, he induced one Harrison to build assembly-rooms, guaranteeing him three guineas a week to be raised by subscription.

All this demanded a vast amount of impudence on Mr. Nash's part, and this he possessed to a liberal extent. The subscriptions flowed in regularly, and Nash felt his power increase with his responsibility. So, then, our minor monarch resolved to be despotic, and in a short time laid down laws for the guests, which they obeyed most obsequiously. Nash had not much wit, though a great deal of assurance, but these laws were his *chef-d'œuvre.* Witness some of them:

1. "That a visit of ceremony at first coming and another at going away, are all that are expected or desired by ladies of quality and fashion—except impertinents.

4. "That no person takes it ill that any one goes to another's play or breakfast, and not theirs—except captious nature.

5. "That no gentleman give his ticket for the balls to any but gentlewomen. N.B.—Unless he has none of his acquaintance.

6. "That gentlemen crowding before the ladies at the ball, show ill manners; and that none do so for the future except such as respect nobody but themselves.

9. "That the younger ladies take notice how many eyes observe them. N.B.—This does not extend to the *Have-at-alls.*

10. "That all whisperers of lies and scandal be taken for their authors."

Really this law of Nash's must have been repealed some time or other at Bath. Still more that which follows:

11. "That repeaters of such lies and scandal be shunned by all company, except such as have been guilty of the same crime."

There is a certain amount of satire in these Lycurgus statutes that shows Nash in the light of an observer of society; but, query, whether any frequenter of Bath would not have devised as good?

The dances of those days must have been somewhat tedious. They began with a series of minuets, in which, of course, only one couple danced at a time, the most distinguished opening the ball. These solemn performances lasted about two hours, and we can easily imagine that the rest of the company were delighted when the country dances, which included every body, began. The ball opened at six; the country dances began at eight: at nine there was a lull for the gentlemen to offer their partners tea; in due course the dances were resumed, and at eleven Nash held up his hand to the musicians, and under no circumstances was the ball allowed to continue after that hour. Nash well knew the value of early hours to invalids, and he would not destroy the healing reputation of Bath for the sake of a little more pleasure. On one occasion the Princess Amelia implored him to allow one dance more. The despot replied, that his laws were those of Lycurgus, and could not be abrogated for any one. By this we see that the M. C. was already an autocrat in his kingdom.

Nor is it to be supposed that his majesty's laws were confined to such merely professional arrangements. Not a bit of it; in a very short time his impudence gave him undenied right of interference with the coats and gowns, the habits and manners, even the daily actions of his subjects, for so the visitors at Bath were compelled to become. *Si parva licet componere magnis*, we may admit that the rise of Nash and that of Napoleon were owing to similar causes. The French emperor found France in a state of disorder, with which sensible people were growing more and more disgusted; he offered to restore order and propriety; the French hailed him, and gladly submitted to his early decrees; then, when he had got them into the habit of obedience, he could make what laws he liked, and use his power without fear of opposition. The Bath emperor followed the same course, and it may be asked whether it does not demand as great an amount of courage, assurance, perseverance, and administrative power to subdue several hundreds of English ladies and gentlemen as to rise supreme above some millions of French republicans. Yet Nash experienced less opposition than Napoleon; Nash reigned longer, and had no infernal machine prepared to blow him up.

Every body was delighted with the improvements in the Pump-room, the balls, the promenades, the chairmen—the *Rouge* ruffians of the mimic kingdom—whom he reduced to submission, and therefore nobody complained when Emperor Nash went farther, and made war upon the white aprons of the ladies and the boots of the gentlemen. The society was in fact in a very barbarous condition at the time, and people who came for pleasure liked to be at ease. Thus ladies lounged into the balls in their riding-hoods or morning dresses, gentlemen in boots with their pipes in their mouths. Such atrocities were intolerable to the late frequenter of London society, and in his imperious arrogance the new monarch used actually to pull off the white aprons of ladies who entered the assembly-rooms with that *dégagé* article, and throw them upon the back seats. Like the French emperor again, he treated high and low in the same manner, and when the Duchess of Queensberry appeared in an apron, coolly pulled it off, and told her it was only fit for a maid-servant. Her grace made no resistance.

The men were not so submissive; but the M. C. turned them into ridicule, and whenever a gentleman appeared at the assembly-rooms in boots, would walk up to him, and in a loud voice remark, "Sir, I think you have forgot your horse." To complete his triumph, he put the offenders into a song called "Trentinella's Invitation to the Assembly."

"Come one and all,
To Hoyden Hall,
For there's the assembly this night;
None but prude fools,
Mind manners and rules;
We Hoydens do decency slight.

"Come trollops and slatterns,
Cockt hats and white aprons;
This best our modesty suits:
For why should not we
In a dress be as free
As Hogs-Norton squires in boots?"

and as this was not enough, got up a puppet-show of a sufficient coarseness to suit the taste of the time, in which the practice of wearing boots was satirized.

His next onslaught was upon that of carrying swords; and in this respect Nash became a public benefactor, for in those days, though Chesterfield was the writer on etiquette, people were not well-bred enough to keep their tempers, and rivals for a lady's hand at a minuet, or gamblers who disputed over their cards, invariably settled the matter by an option between suicide or murder under the polite name of duel. The M. C. wisely saw that these affairs would bring Bath into bad repute, and determined to supplant the rapier by the less dangerous cane. In this he was for a long time opposed, until a notorious torch-light duel between two gamblers, of whom one was run through the body, and the other, to show his contrition, turned Quaker, brought his opponents to a sense of the danger of a weapon always at hand; and henceforth the sword was abolished.

These points gained, the autocrat laid down rules for the employment of the visitors' time, and these, from setting the fashion to some, soon became a law to all. The first thing to be done was, sensibly enough, the *ostensible* object of their residence in Bath, the use of the baths. At an early hour four lusty chairmen waited on every lady to carry her, wrapped in flannels, in

"A little black box, just the size of a coffin,"

to one of the five baths. Here, on entering, an attendant placed beside her a floating tray, on which were set her handkerchief, bouquet, and *snuff-box*, for our great-great-grandmothers *did* take snuff; and here she found her friends in the same bath of naturally hot water. It was, of course, a reunion for society on the plea of health; but the early hours and exercise secured the latter, whatever the baths may have done. A walk in the Pump-room, to the music of a tolerable band, was the next measure; and there, of course, the gentlemen mingled with the ladies. A coffee-house was ready to receive those of either sex; for that was a time when madame and miss lived a great deal in public, and English people were not ashamed of eating their breakfast in public company. These breakfasts were often enlivened by concerts paid for by the rich and enjoyed by all.

Supposing the peacocks now to be dressed out and to have their tails spread to the best advantage, we next find some in the public promenades, others in the reading-rooms, the ladies having their clubs as well as the men; others riding; others, perchance, already gambling. Mankind and womankind then dined at a reasonable hour, and the evening's amusements began early. Nash insisted on this, knowing the value of health to those, and they were many at that time, who sought Bath on its account. The balls began at six, and took place every Tuesday and Friday, private balls filling up the vacant nights. About the commencement of his reign, a theatre was built, and whatever it may have been, it afterward became celebrated as the nursery of the London stage, and now, *O tempo passato!* is almost abandoned. It is needless to add that the gaming-tables were thronged in the evenings.

It was at them that Nash made the money which sufficed to keep up his state, which was vulgarly regal. He drove about in a chariot, flaming with heraldry, and drawn by six grays, with outriders, running footmen, and all the appendages which made an impression on the vulgar minds of the visitors of his kingdom. His dress was magnificent; his gold lace unlimited, his coats ever new; his hat alone was always of the same color—*white;* and as the Emperor Alexander was distinguished by his purple tunic and Brummell by his bow, Emperor Nash was known all England over by his white hat.

It is due to the King of Bath to say that, however much he gained, he always played fair. He even patronized young players, and after fleecing them, kindly advised them to play no more. When he found a man fixed upon ruining himself, he did his best to keep him from that suicidal act. This was the case with a young Oxonian, to whom he had lost money, and whom he invited to supper, in order to give him his parental advice. The fool would not take the Beau's counsel, and "came to grief." Even noblemen sought his "protection." The Duke of Beaufort entered on a compact with him to save his purse, if not his soul. He agreed to pay Nash ten thousand guineas, whenever he lost the same amount at a sitting. It was a comfortable treaty for our Beau, who accordingly watched his grace. Yet it must be said, to Nash's honor, that he once saved him from losing eleven thousand, when he had already lost eight, by reminding him of his compact. Such was play in those days! It is said that the duke had afterward to pay the fine, from losing the stipulated sum at Newmarket.

He displayed as much honesty with the young Lord Townshend, who lost to him his whole fortune, his estate, and even his carriage and horses—what madmen are gamblers—and actually canceled the whole debt, on condition my lord should pay him £5000 whenever he chose to claim it. To Nash's honor it must be said that he never came down upon the nobleman during his life. He claimed the sum from his executors, who paid it. "Honorable to both parties."

But an end was put to the gaming at Bath and every where else—*except in a royal palace*, and Nash swore that, as he was a king, Bath came under the head of the exceptions—by an Act of Parliament. Of course Nash and the sharpers who frequented Bath—and their name was Legion—found means to evade this law for a time, by the invention of new games. But this could not last, and the Beau's fortune went with the death of the dice.

Still, however, the very prohibition increased the zest for play for a time, and Nash soon discovered that a private table was more profitable than a public one. He entered into an arrangement with an old woman at Bath, in virtue of which he was to receive a fourth share of the profits. This was probably not the only "hell"-keeping transaction of his life, and he had once before quashed an action against a cheat in consideration of a handsome bonus; and, in fact, there is no saying what amount of dirty work Nash would not have done for a hundred or so, especially when the game of the table was shut up to him. The man was immensely fond of money; he liked to show his gold-laced coat and superb new waistcoat in the Grove, the Abbey Ground, and Bond Street, and to be known as Le Grand Nash. But on the other hand, he did not love money for itself, and never hoarded it. It is, indeed, something to Nash's honor, that he died poor. He delighted, in the poverty of his mind, to display his great thick-set person to the most advantage; he was as vain as any fop, without the affectation of that character, for he was always blunt and free-spoken, but, as long as he had enough to satisfy his vanity, he cared nothing for mere wealth. He had generosity, though he neglected the precept about the right hand and the left, and showed some ostentation in his charities. When a poor ruined fellow at his elbow saw him win at a throw £200, and murmured "How happy that would make me!" Nash tossed the money to him, and said, "Go and be happy then." Probably the witless beau did not see the delicate satire implied in his speech. It was only the triumph of a gamester. On other occasions he collected subscriptions for poor curates and so forth, in the same spirit, and did his best toward founding a hospital, which has since proved of great value to those afflicted with rheumatic gout. In the same spirit, though himself a gamester, he often attempted to win young and inexperienced boys, who came to toss away their money at the rooms, from seeking their own ruin; and, on the whole, there was some goodness of heart in this gold-laced bear.

That he was a bear there are anecdotes enough to show, and whether true or not, they sufficiently prove what the reputation of the man must have been. Thus, when a lady, afflicted with a curvature of the spine, told him that "She had come *straight* from London that day," Nash replied with utter heartlessness, "Then, ma'am, you've been damnably warpt on the road." The lady had her revenge, however, for meeting the beau one day in the Grove, as she toddled along with her dog, and being impudently asked by him, if she knew the name of Tobit's dog, she answered quickly, "Yes, sir, his name was Nash, and a most impudent dog he was too."

It is due to Nash to state that he made many attempts to put an end to the perpetual system of scandal, which from some hidden cause seems always to be connected with mineral springs; but as he did not banish the old maids, of course he failed. Of the young ladies and their reputation he took a kind of paternal care, and in that day they seem to have needed it, for even at nineteen, those who had any money to lose, staked it at the tables with as much gusto as the wrinkled, puckered, greedy-eyed "single woman," of a certain or uncertain age. Nash protected and cautioned them, and even gave them the advantage of his own unlimited experience. Witness, for instance, the care he took of "Miss Sylvia," a lovely heiress who brought her face and her fortune to enslave some and enrich others of the loungers of Bath. She had a terrible love of hazard, and very little prudence, so that Nash's good offices were much needed in the case. The young lady soon became the standing toast at all the clubs and suppers, and lovers of her, or her ducats, crowded round her; but though at that time she might have made a brilliant match, she chose, as young women will do, to fix her affections upon one of the worst men in Bath, who, naturally enough, did not return them. When this individual, as a climax to his misadventures, was clapt into prison, the devoted young creature gave the greater part of her fortune in order to pay off his debts, and falling into disrepute from this act of generosity, which was, of course, interpreted after a worldly fashion, she seems to have lost her honor with her fame, and the fair Sylvia took a position which could not be creditable to her. At last the poor girl, weary of slights, and overcome with shame, took her silk sash and hanged herself. The terrible event made a nine hours'—*not* nine days'—sensation in Bath, which was too busy with mains and aces to care about the fate of one who had long sunk out of its circles.

When Nash reached the zenith of his power, the adulation he received was somewhat of a parody on the flattery of courtiers. True, he had his bards from Grub Street who sang his praises, and he had letters to show from Sarah of Marlborough and others of that calibre, but his chief worshipers were cooks, musicians, and even imprisoned highwaymen—one of whom disclosed the secrets of the craft to him—who wrote him dedications, letters, poems and what not. The good city of Bath set up his statue, and did Newton and Pope* the great honor

* A full-length statue of Nash was placed between busts of Newton and Pope.

of playing "supporters" to him, which elicited from Chesterfield some well-known lines:

"This statue placed the busts between
Adds to the satire strength;
Wisdom and Wit are little seen,
But Folly at full length."

Meanwhile his private character was none of the best. He had in early life had one attachment, besides that unfortunate affair for which his friends had removed him from Oxford, and in that had behaved with great magnanimity. The young lady had honestly told him that he had a rival; the Beau sent for him, settled on her a fortune equal to that her father intended for her, and himself presented her to the favored suitor. Now, however, he seems to have given up all thoughts of matrimony, and gave himself up to mistresses, who cared more for his gold than for himself. It was an awkward conclusion to Nash's generous act in that one case, that before a year had passed, the bride ran away with her husband's footman; yet, though it disgusted him with ladies, it does not seem to have cured him of his attachment to the sex in general.

In the height of his glory Nash was never ashamed of receiving adulation. He was as fond of flattery as Le Grand Monarque—and he paid for it too—whether it came from a prince or a chairman. Every day brought him some fresh meed of praise in prose or verse, and Nash was always delighted.

But his sun was to set in time. His fortune went when gaming was put down, for he had no other means of subsistence. Yet he lived on: he had not the good sense to die; and he reached the patriarchal of eighty-seven. In his old age he was not only garrulous, but bragging: he told stories of his exploits in which he, Mr. Richard Nash, came out as the first swordsman, swimmer, leaper, and what not. But by this time people began to doubt Mr. Richard Nash's long bow, and the yarns he spun were listened to with impatience. He grew rude and testy in his old age; suspected Quin, the actor, who was living at Bath, of an intention to supplant him; made coarse, impertinent repartees to the visitors at that city, and in general raised up a dislike to himself. Yet, as other monarchs have had their eulogists in sober mind, Nash had his in one of the most depraved; and Anstey, the low-minded author of "The New Bath Guide," panegyrized him a short time after his death in the following verses:

"Yet here no confusion—no tumult is known;
Fair order and beauty establish their throne;

For order, and beauty, and just regulation,
Support all the works of this ample creation.
For this, in compassion to mortals below,
The gods, their peculiar favor to show,
Sent Hermes to Bath in the shape of a beau:
That grandson of Atlas came down from above
To bless all the regions of pleasure and love;
To lead the fair nymph thro' the various maze,
Bright beauty to marshal, his glory and praise;
To govern, improve, and adorn the gay scene,
By the Graces instructed, and Cyprian queen:
As when in a garden delightful and gay,
Where Flora is wont all her charms to display,
The sweet hyacinthus with pleasure we view,
Contend with narcissus in delicate hue;
The gard'ner, industrious, trims out his border,
Puts each odoriferous plant in its order;
The myrtle he ranges, the rose and the lily,
With iris, and crocus, and daffa-down-dilly;
Sweet peas and sweet oranges all he disposes,
At once to regale both your eyes and your noses.
Long reign'd the great Nash, this omnipotent lord,
Respected by youth, and by parents ador'd;
For him not enough at a ball to preside,
The unwary and beautiful nymph would he guide;
Oft tell her a tale, how the credulous maid
By man, by perfidious man, is betrayed;
Taught Charity's hand to relieve the distress'd,
While tears have his tender compassion express'd,
But alas! he is gone, and the city can tell
How in years and in glory lamented he fell.
Him mourn'd all the Dryads on Claverton's mount;
Him Avon deplor'd, him the nymph of the fount,
The crystalline streams.
Then perish his picture—his statue decay—
A tribute more lasting the Muses shall pay.
If true, what philosophers all will assure us,
Who dissent from the doctrine of great Epicurus,
That the spirit's immortal (as poets allow):
In reward of his labors, his virtue and pains,
He is footing it now in the Elysian plains,
Indulg'd, as a token of Proserpine's favor,
To preside at her balls in a cream-color'd beaver.
Then peace to his ashes—our grief be suppress'd,
Since we find such a phœnix has sprung from his nest:
Kind Heaven has sent us another professor,
Who follows the steps of his great predecessor."

The end of the Bath Beau was somewhat less tragical than that of his London successor—Brummell. Nash, in his old age and poverty, hung about the clubs and supper-tables, button-holed youngsters, who thought him a bore, spun his long yarns, and tried to insist on obsolete fashions, when near the end of his life's century.

The clergy took more care of him than the youngsters.

They heard that Nash was an octogenarian, and likely to die in his sins, and resolved to do their best to shrive him. Worthy and well-meaning men accordingly wrote him long letters, which, if he read, the Beau must have had more patience than we can lay claim to. There was, however, a great deal of hell-fire in these effusions, and there was nothing which Nash dreaded so much. As long as there was immediate fear of death, he was pious and humble; the moment the fear had passed, he was jovial and indifferent again. His especial delight, to the last, seems to have been swearing against the doctors, whom he treated like the individual in Anstey's "Bath Guide," shying their medicines out of window upon their own heads. But the wary old Beckoner called him in, in due time, with his broken, empty-chested voice; and Nash was forced to obey. Death claimed him—and much good it got of him—in 1761, at the age of eighty-seven: there are few beaux who lived so long.

Thus ended a life, of which the moral lay, so to speak, out of it. The worthies of Bath were true to the worship of Folly, whom Anstey so well, though indelicately, describes as there conceiving Fashion; and though Nash, old, slovenly, disrespected, had long ceased to be either beau or monarch, treated his huge, unlovely corpse with the honor due to the great—or little. His funeral was as glorious as that of any hero, and far more showy, though much less solemn, than the burial of Sir John Moore. Perhaps for a bit of prose flummery, by way of contrast to Wolfe's lines on the latter event, there is little to equal the account in a contemporary paper: "Sorrow sate upon every face, and even children lisped that their sovereign was no more. The awfulness of the solemnity made the deepest impression on the minds of the distressed inhabitants. The peasant discontinued his toil, the ox rested from the plow, all nature seemed to sympathize with their loss, and the muffled bells rung a peal of bob-major."

The Beau left little behind him, and that little not worth much, even including his renown. Most of the presents which fools or flatterers had made him, had long since been sent *chèz ma tante;* a few trinkets and pictures, and a few books, which probably he had never read, constituted his little store.*

Bath and Tunbridge—for he had annexed that lesser kingdom to his own—had reason to mourn him, for he had almost made them what they were; but the country has not much cause to thank the upholder of gaming, the institutor of silly

* In the "Annual Register" (vol. v. p. 37), it is stated that a pension of ten guineas a month was paid to Nash during the latter years of his life by the Corporation of Bath.

fashion, and the high-priest of folly. Yet Nash was free from many vices we should expect to find in such a man. He did not drink, for instance; one glass of wine, and a moderate quantity of small beer, being his allowance for dinner. He was early in his hours, and made others sensible in theirs. He was generous and charitable when he had the money; and when he had not he took care to make his subjects subscribe it. In a word, there have been worse men and greater fools; and we may again ask whether those who obeyed and flattered him were not more contemptible than Beau Nash himself.

So much for the powers of impudence and a fine coat!

PHILIP, DUKE OF WHARTON.

If an illustration were wanted of that character unstable as water which shall not excel, this duke would at once supply it: if we had to warn genius against self-indulgence—some clever boy against extravagance—some poet against the bottle—this is the "shocking example" we should select: if we wished to show how the most splendid talents, the greatest wealth, the most careful education, the most unusual advantages, may all prove useless to a man who is too vain or too frivolous to use them properly, it is enough to cite that nobleman, whose acts gained for him the name of the *infamous* Duke of Wharton. Never was character more mercurial, or life more unsettled than his; never, perhaps, were more changes crowded into a fewer number of years, more fame and infamy gathered into so short a space. Suffice it to say, that when Pope wanted a man to hold up to the scorn of the world, as a sample of wasted abilities, it was Wharton that he chose, and his lines rise in grandeur in proportion to the vileness of the theme:

"Wharton, the scorn and wonder of our days,
Whose ruling passion was a love of praise.
Born with whate'er could win it from the wise,
Women and fools must like him or he dies;
Though raptured senates hung on all he spoke,
The club must hail him master of the joke.
Shall parts so various aim at nothing new?
He'll shine a Tully and a Wilmot too.
* * * *
Thus with each gift of nature and of art,
And wanting nothing but an honest heart;
Grown all to all, from no one vice exempt,
And most contemptible, to shun contempt;
His passion still, to covet general praise,
His life to forfeit it a thousand ways;
A constant bounty which no friend has made;
An angel tongue which no man can persuade;
A fool with more of wit than all mankind;
Too rash for thought, for action too refined."

And then those memorable lines—

"A tyrant to the wife his heart approved,
A rebel to the very king he loved;
He dies, sad outcast of each church and state;
And, harder still! flagitious, yet not great."

Though it may be doubted if the "lust of praise" was the

cause of his eccentricities, so much as an utter restlessness and instability of character, Pope's description is sufficiently correct, and will prepare us for one of the most disappointing lives we could well have to read.

Philip, Duke of Wharton, was one of those men of whom an Irishman would say, that they were fortunate before they were born. His ancestors bequeathed him a name that stood high in England for bravery and excellence. The first of the house, Sir Thomas Wharton, had won his peerage from Henry VIII. for routing some 15,000 Scots with 500 men, and other gallant deeds. From his father the marquis he inherited much of his talents; but for the heroism of the former, he seems to have received it only in the extravagant form of foolhardiness. Walpole remembered, but could not tell where, a ballad he wrote on being arrested by the guard in St. James's Park, for singing the Jacobite song, "The King shall have his own again," and quotes two lines to show that he was not ashamed of his own cowardice on the occasion:

"The duke he drew out half his sword—
The guard drew out the rest."

At the siege of Gibraltar, where he took up arms against his own king and country, he is said to have gone alone one night to the very walls of the town, and challenged the outpost. They asked him who he was, and when he replied, openly enough, "The Duke of Wharton," they actually allowed him to return without either firing on or capturing him. The story seems somewhat apocryphal, but it is quite possible that the English soldiers may have refrained from violence to a well-known madcap nobleman of their own nation.

Philip, son of the Marquis of Wharton, at that time only a baron, was born in the last year but one of the seventeenth century, and came into the world endowed with every quality which might have made a great man, if he had only added wisdom to them. His father wished to make him a brilliant statesman, and, to have a better chance of doing so, kept him at home, and had him educated under his own eye. He seems to have easily and rapidly acquired a knowledge of classical languages; and his memory was so keen that when a boy of thirteen he could repeat the greater part of the "Æneid" and of Horace by heart. His father's keen perception did not allow him to stop at classics; and he wisely prepared him for the career to which he was destined by the study of history, ancient and modern, and of English literature, and by teaching him, even at that early age, the art of thinking and writing on any given subject, by proposing themes for essays. There is certainly no surer mode of developing the reflective and reasoning powers of the mind; and the boy progressed with a rapidity which was almost alarming. Oratory, too, was of course cultivated, and to this end the young nobleman was made to recite before a small audience passages from Shakspeare, and even speeches which had been delivered in the House of Lords, and we may be certain he showed no bashfulness in this display.

He was precocious beyond measure, and at sixteen was a man. His first act of folly—or, perhaps, *he* thought of manhood—came off at this early age. He fell in love with the daughter of a Major General Holmes; and though there is nothing extraordinary in that, for nine tenths of us have been love-mad at as early an age, he did what fortunately very few do in a first love affair, he married the adored one. Early marriages are often extolled, and justly enough, as safeguards against profligate habits, but this one seems to have had the contrary effect on young Philip. His wife was in every sense too good for him: he was madly in love with her at first, but soon shamefully and openly faithless. Pope's line,

"A tyrant to the wife his heart approved,"

requires explanation here. It is said that she did not present her boy-husband with a son for three years after their marriage, and on this child he set great value and great hopes. About that time he left his wife in the country, intending to amuse himself in town, and ordered her to remain behind with the child. The poor deserted woman well knew what was the real object of this journey, and could not endure the separation. In the hope of keeping her young husband out of harm, and none the less because she loved him very tenderly, she followed him soon after, taking the little Marquis of Malmsbury, as the young live branch was called, with her. The duke was, of course, disgusted, but his anger was turned into hatred, when the child, which he had hoped to make his heir and successor, caught in town the small-pox, and died in infancy. He was furious with his wife, refused to see her for a long time, and treated her with unrelenting coldness.

The early marriage was much to the distaste of Philip's father, who had been lately made a marquis, and who hoped to arrange a very grand "alliance" for his petted son. He was, in fact, so much grieved by it, that he was fool enough to die of it in 1715, and the marchioness survived him only about a year, being no less disgusted with the licentiousness which she already discovered in her Young Hopeful.

She did what she could to set him right, and the young married man was shipped off with a tutor, a French Huguenot, who was to take him to Geneva to be educated as a Protestant and a Whig. The young scamp declined to be either. He was taken, by way of seeing the world, to the petty courts of Germany, and of course to that of Hanover, which had kindly sent us the worst family that ever disgraced the English throne, and by the various princes and grand dukes received with all the honors due to a young British nobleman.

The tutor and his charge settled at last at Geneva, and my young Lord amused himself with tormenting his strict guardian. Walpole tells us that he once roused him out of bed only to borrow a pin. There is no doubt that he led the worthy man a sad life of it; and to put a climax to his conduct, ran away from him at last, leaving with him, by way of hostage, a young bear-cub—probably quite as tame as himself—which he had picked up somewhere, and grown very fond of—birds of a feather, seemingly—with a message, which showed more wit than good-nature, to this effect: "Being no longer able to bear with your ill usage, I think proper to be gone from you; however, that you may not want company, I have left you the bear, as the most suitable companion in the world that could be picked out for you."

The tutor had to console himself with a *tu quoque*, for the young scapegrace had found his way to Lyons in October, 1716, and then did the very thing his father's son should not have done. The Chevalier de St. George, the Old Pretender, James III., or by whatever other *alias* you prefer to call him, having failed in the attempt "to have his own again" in the preceding year, was then holding high court in high dudgeon at Avignon. Any adherent would, of course, be welcomed with open arms; and when the young marquis wrote to him to offer his allegiance, sending with his letter a fine entire horse as a peace offering, he was warmly responded to. A person of rank was at once dispatched to bring the youth to the ex-regal court; he was welcomed with much enthusiasm, and the empty title of Duke of Northumberland at once, most kindly, conferred on him. However, the young marquis does not seem to have *goûté* the exile's court, for he staid there one day only, and returning to Lyons, set off to enjoy himself at Paris. With much wit, no prudence, and a plentiful supply of money, which he threw about with the recklessness of a boy just escaped from his tutor, he could not fail to succeed in that capital; and, accordingly, the English received him with open arms. Even the embassador, Lord Stair, though he had heard rumors of his wild doings, invited him repeatedly to dinner, and did his best, by advice and warning, to keep him out of harm's way. Young Philip had a horror of

WHARTON'S ROGUISH PRESENT.

preceptors, paid or gratuitous, and treated the plenipotentiary with the same coolness as he had served the Huguenot tutor. When the former, praising the late marquis, expressed—by way of a slight hint—a hope "that he would follow so illustrious an example of fidelity to his prince, and affection to his country, by treading in the same steps," the young scamp replied, cleverly enough, "That he thanked his excellency for his good advice, and as his excellency had also a worthy and deserving father, he hoped he would likewise copy so bright an example, and tread in all his steps;" the pertness of which was pertinent enough, for old Lord Stair had taken a disgraceful part against his sovereign in the massacre of Glencoe.

His frolics at Paris were of the most reckless character for a young nobleman. At the embassador's own table he would occasionally send a servant to some one of the guests, to ask him to join in the Old Chevalier's health, though it was almost treason at that time to mention his name even. And again, when the windows at the embassy had been broken by a young English Jacobite, who was forthwith committed to Fort l'Evêque, the harebrained marquis proposed, out of revenge, to break them a second time, and only abandoned the project because he could get no one to join him in it. Lord Stair, however, had too much sense to be offended at the follies of a boy of seventeen, even though that boy was the representative of a great English family; he, probably, thought it would be better to recall him to his allegiance by kindness and advice, than, by resenting his behavior, to drive him irrevocably to the opposite party; but he was doubtless considerably relieved when, after leading a wild life in the capital of France, spending his money lavishly, and doing precisely every thing which a young English nobleman ought not to do, my lord marquis took his departure in December, 1716.

The political education he had received now made the unstable youth ready and anxious to shine in the State; but being yet under age, he could not, of course, take his seat in the House of Lords. Perhaps he was conscious of his own wonderful abilities; perhaps, as Pope declares, he was thirsting for praise, and wished to display them; certainly he was itching to become an orator, and as he could not sit in an English Parliament, he remembered that he had a peerage in Ireland, as Earl of Rathfernhame and Marquis of Catherlogh, and off he set to see if the Milesians would stand upon somewhat less ceremony. He was not disappointed there. "His brilliant parts," we are told by contemporary writers, but rather, we should think, his reputation for wit and eccentricity, "found favor in the eyes of Hibernian quicksilvers, and in spite of his years, he was admitted to the Irish House of Lords."

When a friend had reproached him, before he left France, with infidelity to the principles so long espoused by his family, he is reported to have replied, characteristically enough, that "he had pawned his principles to Gordon, the Chevalier's banker, for a considerable sum, and, till he could repay him, he must be a Jacobite; but when that was done, he would again return to the Whigs." It is as likely as not that he borrowed from Gordon on the strength of the Chevalier's favor, for though a marquis in his own right, he was even at this period always in want of cash; and on the other hand, the speech, exhibiting the grossest want of any sense of honor, is in thorough keeping with his after-life. But whether he paid Gordon on his return to England—which is highly improbable—or whether he had not honor enough to keep his compact—which is extremely likely—there is no doubt that my lord marquis began, at this period, to qualify himself for the post of parish weathercock to St. Stephens.

His early defection to a man who, whether rightful heir or not, had that of romance in his history which is even now sufficient to make our young ladies "thorough Jacobites" at heart, was easily to be excused, on the plea of youth and high spirit. The same excuse does not explain his rapid return to Whiggery—in which there is no romance at all—the moment he took his seat in the Irish House of Lords. There is only one way to explain the zeal with which he now advocated the Orange cause: he must have been either a very designing knave, or a very unprincipled fool. As he gained nothing by the change but a dukedom for which he did not care, and as he cared for little else that the government could give him, we may acquit him of any very deep motives. On the other hand, his life and some of his letters show that, with a vast amount of bravado, he was sufficiently a coward. When supplicated, he was always obstinate; when neglected, always supplicant. Now it required some courage in those days to be a Jacobite. Perhaps he cared for nothing but to astonish and disgust every body with the facility with which he could turn his coat, as a hippodromist does with the ease with which he changes his costume. He was a boy and a peer, and he would make pretty play of his position. He had considerable talents, and now, as he sat in the Irish House, devoted them entirely to the support of the government.

For the next four years he was employed, on the one hand in political, on the other in profligate, life. He shone in both; and was no less admired, by the wits of those days, for his speeches, his arguments, and his zeal, than for the utter disregard of public decency he displayed in his vices. Such a promising youth, adhering to the government, merited some mark of its esteem, and accordingly, before attaining the age of twenty-one, he was raised to a dukedom. Being of age, he took his seat in the English House of Lords, and had not been long there before he again turned coat, and came out in the light of a Jacobite hero. It was now that he gathered most of his laurels.

The Hanoverian monarch had been on the English throne some six years. Had the Chevalier's attempt occurred at this period, it may be doubted if it would not have been successful. The "Old Pretender" came too soon, the "Young Pretender" too late. At the period of the first attempt, the public had had no time to contrast Stuarts and Guelphs: at that of the second, they had forgotten the one and grown accustomed to the other; but at the moment when our young duke appeared on the boards of the senate, the vices of the Hanoverians were beginning to draw down on them the contempt of the educated and the ridicule of the vulgar; and perhaps no moment could have been more favorable for advocating a restoration of the Stuarts. If Wharton had had as much energy and consistency as he had talent and impudence, he might have done much toward that desirable, or undesirable, end.

The grand question at this time before the House was the trial of Atterbury, Bishop of Rochester, demanded by Sir Robert Walpole. The man had a spirit almost as restless as his defender. The son of a man who might have been the original of the Vicar of Bray, he was very little of a poet, less of a priest, but a great deal of a politician. He was born in 1662, so that at this time he must have been nearly sixty years old. He had had by no means a hard life of it, for family interest, together with eminent talents, procured him one appointment after another, till he reached the bench, at the age of fifty-one, in the reign of Anne. He had already distinguished himself in several ways, most, perhaps, by controversies with Hoadly, and by sundry high-church motions. But after his elevation, he displayed his principles more boldly, refused to sign the Declaration of the Bishops, which was somewhat servilely made to assure George the First of the fidelity of the Established Church, suspended the curate of Gravesend for three years because he allowed the Dutch to have a service performed in his church, and even, it is said, on the death of Anne, offered to proclaim King James III., and head a procession himself in his lawn sleeves. The end of this and other vagaries was, that in 1722, the Government sent him to the Tower, on suspicion of being connected with a plot in favor of the Old Chevalier. The case excited no little attention, for it was long since a bishop had been charged with high treason; it was added that his jailers used him rudely; and, in short, public sympathy rather went along with him for a time. In March, 1723, a bill was presented to the Commons, for "inflicting certain pains and penalties on Francis, Lord Bishop of Rochester," and it passed that House in April; but when carried up to the Lords, a defense was resolved on. The bill was read a third time on May 15th, and on that occasion the Duke of Wharton, then only twenty-four years old, rose and delivered a speech in favor of the bishop. This oration far more resembled that of a lawyer summing up the evidence than of a parliamentary orator enlarging on the general issue. It was remarkable for the clearness of its argument, the wonderful memory of facts it displayed, and the ease and rapidity with which it annihilated the testimony of various witnesses examined before the House. It was mild and moderate, able and sufficient, but seems to have lacked all the enthusiasm we might expect from one who was afterward so active a partisan of the Chevalier's cause. In short, striking as it was, it can not be said to give the duke any claim to the title of a great orator; it would rather prove that he might have made a first-rate lawyer. It shows, however, that had he chosen to apply himself diligently to politics, he might have turned out a great leader of the Opposition.

Neither this speech nor the bishop's able defense saved him; and in the following month he was banished the kingdom, and passed the rest of his days in Paris.

Wharton, however, was not content with the House as an arena of political agitation. He was now old enough to have matured his principles thoroughly, and he completely espoused the cause of the exiled family. He amused himself with agitating throughout the country, influencing elections, and seeking popularity by becoming a member of the Wax-chandlers' Company. It is a proof of his great abilities, so shamefully thrown away, that he now, during the course of eight months, issued a paper, called "The True Briton," every Monday and Friday, written by himself, and containing varied and sensible arguments in support of his opinions, if not displaying any vast amount of original genius. This paper, on the model of "The Tatler," "The Spectator," etc., had a considerable sale, and attained no little celebrity, so that the Duke of Wharton acquired the reputation of a literary man as well as of a political leader.

But, whatever he might have been in either capacity, his disgraceful life soon destroyed all hope of success in them. He was now an acknowledged wit about town, and, what was then almost a recognized concomitant of that character, an acknowledged profligate. He scattered his large fortune in the most reckless and foolish manner: though married, his moral conduct was as bad as that of any bachelor of the day; and such was his extravagance and open licentiousness, that, having wasted a princely revenue, he was soon caught in the meshes of Chancery, which very sensibly vested his fortune in the hands of trustees, and compelled him to be satisfied with an income of twelve hundred pounds a year.

The young rascal now showed hypocritical signs of penitence—he was always an adept in that line—and protested he would go abroad and live quietly, till his losses should be retrieved. There is little doubt that, under this laudable design, he conceived one of attaching himself closer to the Chevalier party, and even espousing the faith of that unfortunate prince, or pretender, whichever he may have been. He set off for Vienna, leaving his wife behind to die, in April, 1726. He had long since quarreled with her, and treated her with cruel neglect, and at her death he was not likely to be much afflicted. It is said, that, after that event, a ducal family offered him a daughter and large fortune in marriage, and that the Duke of Wharton declined the offer, because the latter was to be tied up, and he could not conveniently tie up the former. However this may be, he remained a widower for a short time: we may be sure, not long.

The hypocrisy of going abroad to retrench was not long undiscovered. The fascinating scapegrace seems to have delighted in playing on the credulity of others; and Walpole relates that, on the eve of the day on which he delivered his famous speech for Atterbury, he sought an interview with the minister, Sir Robert Walpole, expressed great contrition at having espoused the bishop's cause hitherto, and a determination to speak against him the following day. The minister was taken in, and at the duke's request, supplied him with all the main arguments, pro and con. The duper, having got these well into his brain—one of the most retentive—repaired to his London haunts, passed the night in drinking, and the next day produced all the arguments he had digested, *in the bishop's favor.*

At Vienna he was well received, and carried out his private mission successfully, but was too restless to stay in one place, and soon set off for Madrid. Tired now of politics, he took a turn at love. He was a poet after a fashion, for the pieces he has left are not very good: he was a fine gentleman, always spending more money than he had, and is said to have been handsome. His portraits do not give us this impression: the features are not very regular; and though not coarse are certainly *not* refined. The mouth, somewhat sensual, is still much firmer than his character would lead us to expect; the nose sharp at the point, but cogitative at the nostrils; the eyes long but not large; while the raised brow has all that openness which he displayed in the indecency of his vices, but not in any honesty in his political career. In a word, the face is not attractive. Yet he is described as having had a brilliant complexion, a lively, varying expression, and a charm of person and manner that was quite irresistible. Whether on this account, or for his talents and wit, which were really shining, his new Juliet fell as deeply in love with him as he with her.

She was maid of honor—and a highly honorable maid—to the Queen of Spain. The Irish regiments long employed in the Spanish service had become more or less naturalized in that country, which accounts for the great number of thoroughly Milesian names still to be found there, some of them, as O'Donnell, owned by men of high distinction. Among other officers who had settled with their families in the Peninsula was a Colonel O'Byrne, who, like most of his countrymen there, died penniless, leaving his widow with a pension and his daughter without a sixpence. It can well be imagined that an offer from an English duke was not to be sneezed at by either Mrs. or Miss O'Byrne; but there were some grave obstacles to the match. The duke was a Protestant. But what of that? he had never been encumbered with religion, nor even with a decent observance of its institutions, for it is said that, when in England, at his country seat, he had, to show how little he cared for respectability, made a point of having the hounds out on a Sunday morning. He was not going to lose a pretty girl for the sake of a faith with which he had got disgusted ever since his Huguenot tutor tried to make him a sober Christian. He had turned coat in politics, and would now try his weathercock capabilities at religion. Nothing like variety, so Romanist he became.

But this was not all: his friends on the one hand objected to his marrying a penniless girl, and hers, on the other, warned her of his disreputable character. But when two people have made up their minds to be one, such trifles as these are of no consequence. A far more trying obstacle was the absolute refusal of her Most Catholic Majesty to allow her maid of honor to marry the duke.

It is a marvel that after the life of dissipation he had led, this man should have retained the power of loving at all. But every thing about him was extravagant, and now that he entertained a virtuous attachment, he was as wild in it as he had been reckless in less respectable connections. He must have been sincere at the time, for the queen's refusal was followed by a fit of depression that brought on a low fever. The queen heard of it, and, touched by the force of his devotion, sent him a cheering message. The moment was not to be lost, and, in spite of his weak state, he hurried to court, threw himself at her Majesty's feet, and swore he must have his lady-love or die. Thus pressed, the queen was forced to consent, but warned him that he would repent of it. The marriage took place, and the couple set off to Rome.

Here the Chevalier again received him with open arms, and took the opportunity of displaying his imaginary sovereignty by bestowing on him the Order of the Garter—a politeness the duke returned by wearing while there the no less unrecognized title of Duke of Northumberland, which "His Majesty" had formerly conferred on him. But James III., though no saint, had more respect for decent conduct than his father and uncle; the duke ran off into every species of excess, got into debt as usual—

"When Wharton's just, and learns to pay his debts,
And reputation dwells at Mother Brett's,
* * * *
Then, Celia, shall my constant passion cease,
And my poor suff'ring heart shall be at peace,"

says a satirical poem of the day, called "The Duke of Wharton's *Whens*"—was faithless to the wife he had lately been dying for; and, in short, such a thorough blackguard, that not even the Jacobites could tolerate him, and they turned him out of the Holy City till he should learn not to bring dishonor on the court of their fictitious sovereign.

The duke was not the man to be much ashamed of himself, though his poor wife may now have begun to think her late mistress in the right, and he was probably glad of an excuse for another change. At this time, 1727, the Spaniards were determined to wrest Gibraltar from its English defenders, and were sending thither a powerful army under the command of Los Torres. The duke had tried many trades with more or less success, and now thought that a little military glory would tack on well to his highly honorable biography. At any rate there was novelty in the din of war, and for novelty he would go any where. It mattered little that he should fight against his own king and own countrymen: he was not half blackguard enough yet, he may have thought; he had played traitor for some time, he would now play rebel outright—the game *was* worth the candle.

So what does my lord duke do but write a letter (like the Chinese behind their mud walls, he was always bold enough when well secured under the protection of the post, and was more absurd in ink even than in action) to the King of Spain, offering him his services as a volunteer against "Gib." Whether his Most Catholic Majesty thought him a traitor, a madman, or a devoted partisan of his own, does not appear, for without waiting for an answer—waiting was always too dull work for Wharton—he and his wife set off for the camp before Gibraltar, introduced themselves to the Conde in command, were received with all the honor—let us say honors—due to a duke, and established themselves comfortably in the ranks of the enemy of England. But all the duke's hopes of prowess were blighted. He had good opportunities. The Conde de los Torres made him his aid-de-camp, and sent him daily into the trenches to see how matters went on. When a defense of a certain Spanish out-work was resolved upon, the duke, from his rank, was chosen for the command. Yet in the trenches he got no worse wound than a slight one on the foot from a splinter of a shell, and this he afterward made an excuse for not fighting a duel with swords; and as to the out-work, the English abandoned the attack, so that there was no glory to be found in the defense. He soon grew weary of such inglorious and rather dirty work as visiting trenches before a stronghold; and well he might; for if there be one thing duller than another and less satisfactory, it must be digging a hole out of which to kill your brother mortals; and thinking he should amuse himself better at the court, he set off for Madrid. Here the king, by way of reward for his brilliant services in doing nothing, made him *colonel aggregate*—whatever that may be—of an Irish regiment; a very poor aggregate, we should think. But my lord duke wanted something livelier than the command of a lot of Hispaniolized Milesians; and having found the military career somewhat uninteresting, wished to return to that of politics. He remembered with gusto the frolic life of the Holy City, and the political excitement in the Chevalier's court, and sent off a letter to "His Majesty James III.," expressing, like a rusticated Oxonian, his penitence for having been so naughty the last time, and offering to come and be very good again. It is to the praise of the Chevalier de St. George that he had worldly wisdom enough not to trust the gay penitent. He was tired, as every body else was, of a man who could stick to nothing, and did not seem to care about seeing him again. Accordingly he replied in true kingly style, blaming him for having taken up arms against their common country, and telling him in polite language—as a policeman does a riotous drunkard—that he had better go home. The duke thought so too, was not at all offended at the letter, and set off, by way of returning toward his Penates, for Paris, where he arrived in May, 1728.

Horace Walpole—not *the* Horace—but "Uncle Horace," or "old Horace," as he was called, was then embassador to the court of the Tuileries. Mr. Walpole was one of the Houghton "lot," a brother of the famous minister Sir Robert, and though less celebrated, almost as able in his time. He had distinguished himself in various diplomatic appointments, in Spain, at Hanover and the Hague, and having successfully tackled Cardinal Fleury, the successor of the Richelieus and Mazarins at Paris, he was now in high favor at home. In after years he was celebrated for his duel with Chetwynd, who, when "Uncle Horace" had in the House expressed a hope that the question might be carried, had exclaimed, "I hope to see you hanged first!" "You hope to see me hanged first, do you?" cried Horace, with all the ferocity of the Walpoles; and thereupon, seizing him by the most prominent feature of his face, shook him violently. This was matter enough for a brace of swords and coffee for four, and Mr. Chetwynd had to repent of his remark after being severely wounded. In those days our honorable House of Commons was as much an arena of wild beasts as the American Senate of to-day.

To this minister our noble duke wrote a hypocritical letter, which, as it shows how the man *could* write penitently, is worth transcribing.

"Lions, June 28, 1728.

"Sir,—Your excellency will be surpris'd to receive a letter from me; but the clemency with which the government of England has treated me, which is in a great measure owing to your brother's regard to my father's memory, makes me hope that you will give me leave to express my gratitude for it.

"Since his present majesty's accession to the throne I have absolutely refused to be concerned with the Pretender or any of his affairs; and during my stay in Italy have behav'd myself in a manner that Dr. Peters, Mr. Godolphin, and Mr. Mills can declare to be consistent with my duty to the present king. I was forc'd to go to Italy to get out of Spain, where, if my true design had been known, I should have been treated a little severely.

"I am coming to Paris to put myself entirely under your excellency's protection; and hope that Sir Robert Walpole's good-nature will prompt him to save a family which his generosity induced him to spare. If your excellency would permit me to wait upon you for an hour, I am certain you would be convinc'd of the sincerity of my repentance for my former madness, would become an advocate with his majesty to grant me his most gracious pardon, which it is my comfort I shall never be required to purchase by any step unworthy of a man of honor. I do not intend, in case of the king's allowing me to pass the evening of my days under the shadow of his royal protection, to see England for some years, but shall remain in France or Germany, as my friends shall advise, and enjoy country sports till all former stories are buried in oblivion. I beg of your excellency to let me receive your orders at Paris, which I will send to your hostel to receive. The Dutchess of Wharton, who is with me, desires leave to wait on Mrs. Walpole, if you think proper. I am, etc."

After this, the embassador could do no less than receive him; but he was somewhat disgusted when on leaving him the duke frankly told him—forgetting all about his penitent letter, probably, or too reckless to care for it—that he was going to dine with the Bishop of Rochester—Atterbury himself then living in Paris—whose society was interdicted to any subject of King George. The duke, with his usual folly, touched on other subjects equally dangerous, his visit to Rome, and his conversion to Romanism; and, in short, disgusted the cautious Mr. Walpole. There is something delightfully impudent about all these acts of Wharton's; and had he only been a clown at Drury Lane instead of an English nobleman, he must have been successful. As it is, when one reads the petty hatred and humbug of those days, when liberty of speech was as unknown as any other liberty, one can not but admire the impudence of his Grace of Wharton, and wish that most dukes, without being as profligate, would be as free-spoken.

With six hundred pounds in his pocket, our young Lothario now set up house at Rouen, with an establishment "equal," say the old-school writers, "to his position, but not to his means." In other words, he undertook to live in a style for which he could not pay. Twelve hundred a year may be enough for a duke, as for any other man, but not for one who considers a legion of servants a necessary appendage to his position. My lord duke, who was a good French scholar, soon found an ample number of friends and acquaintances, and not being particular about either, managed to get through his half-year's income in a few weeks. Evil consequence: he was assailed by duns. French duns have never read their Bible, and know nothing about forgiving debtors; "your money first, and then my pardon," is their motto. My lord duke soon found this out. Still he had an income, and could pay them all off in time. So he drank and was merry, till one fine day came a disagreeable piece of news, which startled him considerably. The government at home had heard of his doings, and determined to arraign him for high treason.

He could expect little else, for had he not actually taken up arms against his sovereign?

Now Sir Robert Walpole was, no doubt, a bear. He was not a man to love or sympathize with; but he *was* good-natured at bottom. Our "frolic grace" had reason to acknowledge this. He could not complain of harshness in any measures taken against him, and he had certainly no claim to consideration from the government he had treated so ill. Yet Sir Robert was willing to give him every chance; and so far did he go, that he sent over a couple of friends to him to induce him only to ask pardon of the king, with a promise that it would be granted. For sure the Duke of Wharton's character was anomalous. The same man who had more than once humiliated himself when unasked, who had written to Walpole's brother the letter we have read, would not now, when entreated to do so, write a few lines to that minister to ask mercy. Nay, when the gentlemen in question offered to be content even with a letter from the duke's valet, he refused to allow the man to write. Some people may admire what they will believe to be firmness, but when we review the duke's character and subsequent acts, we can not attribute this refusal to any thing but obstinate pride. The consequence of this folly was a stoppage of supplies, for as he was accused of high treason, his estate was of course sequestrated. He revenged himself by writing a paper, which was published in "Mist's Journal," and which, under the cover of a Persian tale, contained a species of libel on the government.

His position was now far from enviable; and, assailed by duns, he had no resource but to humble himself, not before those he had offended, but before the Chevalier, to whom he wrote in his distress, and who sent him £2000, which he soon frittered away in follies. This gone, the duke begged and borrowed, for there are some people such fools that they would rather lose a thousand pounds to a peer than give sixpence to a pauper, and many a tale was told of the artful manner in which his grace managed to cozen his friends out of a louis or two. His ready wit generally saved him.

Thus on one occasion an Irish toady invited him to dinner; the duke talked of his wardrobe, then sadly defective; what suit should he wear? The Hibernian suggested black velvet. "Could you recommend a tailor?" "Certainly." Snip came, an expensive suit was ordered, put on, and the dinner taken.

In due course the tailor called for his money. The duke was not a bit at a loss, though he had but a few francs to his name. "Honest man," quoth he, "you mistake the matter entirely. Carry the bill to Sir Peter; for know that whenever I consent to wear another man's livery, my master pays for the clothes," and inasmuch as the dinner-giver was an Irishman, he did actually discharge the account.

At other times he would give a sumptuous entertainment, and in one way or another induce his guests to pay for it. He was only less adroit in coining excuses than Theodore Hook, and had he lived a century later, we might have a volume full of anecdotes to give of his ways and no means. Meanwhile his unfortunate duchess was living on the charity of friends, while her lord and master, when he could get any one to pay for a band, was serenading young ladies. Yet he was jealous enough of his wife at times, and once sent a challenge to a Scotch nobleman, simply because some silly friend asked him if he had forbidden his wife to dance with the lord. He went all the way to Flanders to meet his opponent; but, perhaps fortunately for the duke, Marshal Berwick arrested the Scotchman, and the duel never came off.

Whether he felt his end approaching, or whether he was sick of vile pleasures which he had recklessly pursued from the age of fifteen, he now, though only thirty years of age, retired for a time to a convent, and was looked on as a penitent and devotee. Penury, doubtless, cured him in a measure, and poverty, the porter of the gates of heaven, warned him to look forward beyond a life he had so shamefully misused. But it was only a temporary repentance; and when he left the religious house, he again rushed furiously into every kind of dissipation.

At length, utterly reduced to the last extremities, he bethought himself of his colonelcy in Spain, and determined to set out to join his regiment. The following letter from a friend who accompanied him will best show what circumstances he was in:

"Paris, June 1st, 1729.

"Dear Sir,—I am just returned from the Gates of Death, to return you Thanks for your last kind Letter of Accusations, which I am persuaded was intended as a seasonable Help to my Recollection, at a Time that it was necessary for me to send an Inquisitor General into my Conscience, to examine and settle all the Abuses that ever were committed in that little Court of Equity; but I assure you, your long Letter did not lay so much my Faults as my Misfortunes before me, which believe me, dear ———, have fallen as heavy and as thick upon me as the Shower of Hail upon us two in E—— Forest, and has left me much at a Loss which way to turn myself. The Pilot of the Ship I embarked in, who industriously ran upon every Rock, has at last split the Vessel, and so much of a sudden, that the whole Crew, I mean his Domesticks, are all left to swim for their Lives, without one friendly Plank to assist them to Shore. In short, he left me sick, in Debt, and without a Penny; but as I begin to recover, and have a little Time to think, I can't help considering myself, as one whisk'd up behind a Witch upon a Broomstick, and hurried over Mountains and Dales through confus'd Woods and thorny Thickets, and when the Charm is ended, and the poor Wretch dropp'd in a Desart, he can give no other Account of his enchanted Travels, but that he is much fatigued in Body and Mind, his Cloaths torn, and worse in all other Circumstances, without being of the least Service to himself or any body else. But I will follow your Advice with an active Resolution, to retrieve my bad Fortune, and almost a Year miserably misspent.

"But notwithstanding what I have suffered, and what my Brother Mad-man has done to undo himself, and every body who was so unlucky to have the least Concern with him, I could not but be movingly touch'd at so extraordinary a Vicissitude of Fortune, to see a great Man fallen from that shining Light, in which I beheld him in the House of Lords, to such a Degree of Obscurity, that I have observ'd the meanest Commoner here decline, and the Few he would sometimes fasten on, to be tired of his Company; for you know he is but a bad Orator in his Cups, and of late he has been but seldom sober.

"A week before he left Paris, he was so reduced, that he had not one single Crown at Command, and was forc'd to thrust in with any Acquaintance for a Lodging: Walsh and I have had him by Turns, all to avoid a Crowd of Duns, which he had of all Sizes, from Fourteen hundred Livres to Four, who hunted him so close, that he was forced to retire to some of the neighboring Villages for Safety. I, sick as I was, hurried about Paris to raise Money, and to St. Germain's to get him Linen; I bought him one Shirt and a Cravat, which with 500 Livres, his whole Stock, he and his Duchess, attended by one Servant, set out for Spain. All the News I have heard of them since is that a Day or two after, he sent for Captain Brierly, and two or three of his Domesticks, to follow him; but none but the Captain obey'd the Summons. Where they are now, I can't tell; but fear they must be in great Distress by this time, if he has no other Supplies; and so ends my Melancholy Story. I am, etc."

Still his good-humor did not desert him; he joked about their poverty on the road, and wrote an amusing account of their journey to a friend, winding up with the well-known lines:

> "Be kind to my remains, and oh! defend,
> Against your judgment, your departed friend."

His mind was as vigorous as ever, in spite of the waste of many debauches; and when recommended to make a new translation of "Telemachus," he actually devoted one whole day to the work; the next he forgot all about it. In the same manner he began a play on the story of Mary Queen of Scots, and Lady M. W. Montagu wrote an epilogue for it, but the piece never got beyond a few scenes. His genius, perhaps, was not for either poetry or the drama. His mind was a keen, clear one, better suited to argument and to grapple tough polemic subjects. Had he but been a sober man, he might have been a fair, if not a great writer. The "True Briton," with many faults of license, shows what his capabilities were. His absence of moral sense may be guessed from the fact that in a poem on the preaching of Atterbury, he actually compares the bishop to our Savior himself!

At length he reached Bilboa and his regiment, and had to live on the meagre pay of eighteen pistoles a month. The Duke of Ormond, then an exile, took pity on his wife, and supported her for a time: she afterward rejoined her mother at Madrid.

Meanwhile, the year 1730 brought about a salutary change in the duke's morals. His health was fast giving way from the effects of divers excesses; and there is nothing like bad health for purging a bad soul. The end of a misspent life was fast drawing near, and he could only keep it up by broth with eggs beaten up in it. He lost the use of his limbs, but not of his gayety. In the mountains of Catalonia he met with a mineral spring which did him some good; so much, in fact, that he was able to rejoin his regiment for a time. A fresh attack sent him back to the waters; but on his way he was so violently attacked that he was forced to stop at a little village. Here he found himself without the means of going farther, and in the worst state of health. The monks of a Bernardine convent took pity on him and received him into their house. He grew worse and worse; and in a week died on the 31st of May, without a friend to pity or attend him, among strangers, and at the early age of thirty-two.

Thus ended the life of one of the cleverest fools that have ever disgraced our peerage.

LORD HERVEY.

THE village of Kensington was disturbed in its sweet repose one day, more than a century ago, by the rumbling of a ponderous coach and six, with four outriders and two equerries kicking up the dust; while a small body of heavy dragoons rode solemnly after the huge vehicle. It waded, with inglorious struggles, through a deep mire of mud, between the Palace and Hyde Park, until the cortége entered Kensington Park, as the gardens were then called, and began to track the old road that led to the red-brick structure to which William III. had added a higher story, built by Wren. There are two roads by which coaches could approach the house: "one," as the famous John, Lord Hervey, wrote to his mother, "so convex, the other so concave, that, by this extreme of faults, they agree in the common one of being, like the high-road, impassable." The rumbling coach, with its plethoric steeds, toils slowly on, and reaches the dismal pile, of which no association is so precious as that of its having been the birth-place of our loved Victoria Regina. All around, as the emblazoned carriage impressively veers round into the grand entrance, savors of William and Mary, of Anne, of Bishop Burnet and Harley, Atterbury and Bolingbroke. But those were pleasant days compared to those of the second George, whose return from Hanover in this mountain of a coach is now described.

The panting steeds are gracefully curbed by the state coachman in his scarlet livery, with his cocked hat and gray wig underneath it: now the horses are foaming and reeking as if they had come from the world's end to Kensington, and yet they have only been to meet King George on his entrance into London, which he has reached from Helvoetsluys, on his way from Hanover, in time, as he expects, to spend his birthday among his English subjects.

It is Sunday, and repose renders the retirement of Kensington and its avenues and shades more sombre than ever. Suburban retirement is usually so. It is noon; and the inmates of Kensington Palace are just coming forth from the chapel in the palace. The coach is now stopping, and the equerries are at hand to offer their respectful assistance to the diminutive figure that, in full Field-marshal regimentals, a cocked hat stuck crosswise on his head, a sword dangling even down to his heels, ungraciously heeds them not, but stepping down, as the great iron gates are thrown open to receive him, looks neither like a king nor a gentleman. A thin, worn face, in which weakness and passion are at once pictured; a form buttoned and padded up to the chin; high Hessian boots without a wrinkle; a sword and a swagger, no more constituting him the military character than the "your majesty" from every lip can make a poor thing of clay a king. Such was George II.: brutal even to his submissive wife. Stunted by nature, he was insignificant in form, as he was petty in character; not a trace of royalty could be found in that silly, tempestuous physiognomy, with its hereditary small head: not an atom of it in his made-up, paltry little presence; still less in his bearing, language, or qualities.

The queen and her court have come from chapel, to meet the royal absentee at the great gate: the consort, who was to his gracious majesty like an elder sister rather than a wife, bends down, not to his knees, but yet she bends, to kiss the hand of her royal husband. She is a fair, fat woman, no longer young, scarcely comely; but with a charm of manners, a composure, and a *savoir faire* that causes one to regard her as mated, not matched to the little creature in that cocked hat, which he does not take off even when she stands before him. The pair, nevertheless, embrace; it is a triennial ceremony performed when the king goes or returns from Hanover, but suffered to lapse at other times; but the condescension is too great; and Caroline ends, where she began, "gluing her lips" to the ungracious hand held out to her in evident ill-humor.

They turn, and walk through the court, then up the grand staircase, into the queen's apartment. The king has been swearing all the way at England and the English, because he has been obliged to return from Hanover, where the German mode of life and new mistresses were more agreeable to him than the English customs and an old wife. He displays, therefore, even on this supposed happy occasion, one of the worst outbreaks of his insufferable temper, of which the queen is the first victim. All the company in the palace, both ladies and gentlemen, are ordered to enter: he talks to them all, but to the queen he says not a word.

She is attended by Mrs. Clayton, afterward Lady Sundon, whose lively manners and great good-temper and good-will—lent out like leasehold to all, till she saw what their friendship might bring—are always useful at these *tristes rencontres.* Mrs. Clayton is the amalgamating substance between chemical agents which have, of themselves, no cohesion; she covers

A SCENE BEFORE KENSINGTON PALACE—GEORGE II. AND QUEEN CAROLINE.

with address what is awkward; she smooths down with something pleasant what is rude; she turns off—and her office in that respect is no sinecure at that court—what is indecent, so as to keep the small majority of the company who have respectable notions in good humor. To the right of Queen Caroline stands another of her majesty's household, to whom the most deferential attention is paid by all present: nevertheless, she is the queen of the court, but not the queen of the royal master of that court. It is Lady Suffolk, the mistress of King George II., and long mistress of the robes to Queen Caroline. She is now past the bloom of youth, but her attractions are not in their wane; but endured until she had attained her seventy-ninth year. Of a middle height, well made, extremely fair, with very fine light hair, she attracts regard from her sweet fresh face, which had in it a comeliness independent of regularity of feature. According to her invariable custom, she is dressed with simplicity; her silky tresses are drawn somewhat back from her snowy forehead, and fall in long tresses on her shoulders, not less transparently white. She wears a gown of rich silk, opening in front to display a chemisette of the most delicate cambric, which is scarcely less delicate than her skin. Her slender arms are without bracelets, and her taper fingers without rings. As she stands behind the queen, holding her majesty's fan and gloves, she is obliged, from her deafness, to lean her fair face with its sunny hair first to the right side, then to the left, with the helpless air of one exceedingly deaf—for she had been afflicted with that infirmity for some years; yet one can not say whether her appealing looks, which seem to say, "Enlighten me, if you please"—and the sort of softened manner in which she accepts civilities which she scarcely comprehends, do not enhance the wonderful charm which drew every one who knew her toward this frail, but passionless woman.

The queen forms the centre of the group. Caroline, daughter of the Marquis of Brandenburgh-Anspach, notwithstanding her residence in England of many years, notwithstanding her having been, at the era at which this biography begins, ten years its queen—is still German in every attribute. She retains, in her fair and comely face, traces of having been handsome; but her skin is deeply scarred by the cruel small-pox. She is now at that time of life when Sir Robert Walpole even thought it expedient to reconcile her to no longer being an object of attraction to her royal consort. As a woman, she has ceased to be attractive to a man of the character of George II.; but, as a queen, she is still, as far as manners are concerned, incomparable. As she turns to address various members of the assembly, her style is full of sweetness as well as of courtesy; yet on other occasions she is majesty itself. The tones of her voice, with its still foreign accent, are most captivating; her eyes penetrate into every countenance on which they rest. Her figure, plump and matronly, has lost much of its contour; but is well suited for her part. Majesty in woman should be *embonpoint.* Her hands are beautifully white, and faultless in shape. The king always admired her bust; and it is, therefore, by royal command, tolerably exposed. Her fair hair is upraised in full short curls over her brow; her dress is rich, and distinguished in that respect from that of the Countess of Suffolk. "Her good Howard"—as she was wont to call her when, before her elevation to the peerage, she was lady of the bedchamber to Caroline, had, when in that capacity, been often subjected to servile offices, which the queen, though apologizing in the sweetest manner, delighted to make her perform. "My good Howard" having one day placed a handkerchief on the back of her royal mistress, the king, who half worshiped his intellectual wife, pulled it off in a passion, saying, "Because you have an ugly neck yourself, you hide the queen's!" All, however, that evening was smooth as ice, and perhaps as cold also. The company are quickly dismissed, and the king, who has scarcely spoken to the queen, retires to his closet, where he is attended by the subservient Caroline, and by two other persons.

Sir Robert Walpole, prime minister, has accompanied the king, in his carriage, from the very entrance of London, where the famous statesman met him. He is now the privileged companion of their majesties, in their seclusion for the rest of the evening. His cheerful face, in its full evening disguise of wig and tie, his invariable good-humor, his frank manners, his wonderful sense, his views, more practical than elevated, sufficiently account for the influence which this celebrated minister obtained over Queen Caroline, and the readiness of King George to submit to the tie. But Sir Robert's great source of ascendency was his temper. Never was there in the annals of our country a minister so free of access: so obliging in giving, so unoffending when he refused; so indulgent and kind to those dependent on him; so generous, so faithful to his friends, so forgiving to his foes. This was his character under one phase: even his adherents sometimes blamed his easiness of temper; the impossibility in his nature to cherish the remembrance of a wrong, or even to be roused by an insult. But, while such were the amiable traits of his character, history has its lists of accusations against him for corruption of the most shameless description. The end of this veteran statesman's career is well known. The fraudulent contracts which he gave, the peculation and profusion of the secret service money, his undue influence at elections, brought around his later life a storm, from which he retreated into the Upper House, when created Earl of Orford. It was before this timely retirement from office that he burst forth in these words: "I oppose nothing; give in to every thing; am said to do every thing, and to answer for every thing; and yet, God knows, I dare not do what I think is right."

With his public capacity, however, we have not here to do: it is in his character of a courtier that we view him following the queen and king. His round, complacent face, with his small glistening eyes, arched eyebrows, and with a mouth ready to break out aloud into a laugh, are all subdued into a respectful gravity as he listens to King George grumbling at the necessity for his return home. No English cook could dress a dinner; no English cook could select a dessert; no English coachman could drive, nor English jockey ride; no Englishman—such were his habitual taunts—knew how to come into a room; no Englishwoman understood how to dress herself. The men, he said, talked of nothing but their dull politics, and the women of nothing but their ugly clothes. Whereas, in Hanover, all these things were at perfection: men were patterns of politeness and gallantry; women, of beauty, wit, and entertainment. His troops there were the bravest in the world; his manufacturers the most ingenious; his people, the happiest: in Hanover, in short, plenty reigned, riches flowed, arts flourished, magnificence abounded, every thing was in abundance that could make a prince great, or a people blessed.

There was one standing behind the queen who listened to these outbreaks of the king's bilious temper, as he called it, with an apparently respectful solicitude, but with the deepest disgust in his heart. A slender, elegant figure, in a court suit, faultlessly and carefully perfect in that costume, stands behind the queen's chair. It is Lord Hervey. His lofty forehead, his features, which have a refinement of character, his well-turned mouth, and full and dimpled chin, form his claims to that beauty which won the heart of the lovely Mary Lepel; while the somewhat thoughtful and pensive expression of his physiognomy, when in repose, indicated the sympathizing, yet, at the same time, satirical character of one who won the affections, perhaps unconsciously, of the amiable Princess Caroline, the favorite daughter of George II.

A general air of languor, ill concealed by the most studied artifice of countenance, and even of posture, characterizes Lord Hervey. He would have abhorred robustness; for he belonged to the clique then called Maccaronis; a set of fine gentlemen, of whom the present world would not be worthy, tricked out for show, fitted only to drive out fading majesty in a state coach; exquisite in every personal appendage, too fine for the common usages of society; *point-device*, not only in every curl and ruffle, but in every attitude and step; men with full satin roses on their shining shoes; diamond tablet rings on their forefingers; with snuff-boxes, the worth of which might almost purchase a farm; lace worked by the delicate fingers of some religious recluse of an ancestress, and taken from an altar-cloth; old point-lace, dark as coffee-water could make it; with embroidered waistcoats, wreathed in exquisite tambour-work round each capacious lappet and pocket; with cut steel buttons that glistened beneath the courtly wax-lights: with these and fifty other small but costly characteristics that established the reputation of an aspirant Maccaroni. Lord Hervey was, in truth, an effeminate creature: too dainty to walk; too precious to commit his frame to horseback; and prone to imitate the somewhat recluse habits which German rulers introduced within the court: he was disposed to candle-light pleasures and cockney diversions; to Marybone and the Mall, and shrinking from the athletic and social recreations which, like so much that was manly and English, were confined almost to the English squire *pur et simple* after the Hanoverian accession; when so much degeneracy for a while obscured the English character, debased its tone, enervated its best races, vilified its literature, corrupted its morals, changed its costume, and degraded its architecture.

Beneath the effeminacy of the Maccaroni, Lord Hervey was one of the few who united to intense *finery* in every minute detail, an acute and cultivated intellect. To perfect a Maccaroni it was in truth advisable, if not essential, to unite some smattering of learning, a pretension to wit, to his super-dandyism; to be the author of some personal squib, or the translator of some classic. Queen Caroline was too cultivated herself to suffer fools about her, and Lord Hervey was a man after her own taste: as a courtier he was essentially a fine gentleman; and, more than that, he could be the most delightful companion, the most sensible adviser, and the most winning friend in the court. His ill health, which he carefully concealed, his fastidiousness, his ultra delicacy of habits, formed an agreeable contrast to the coarse robustness of "Sir Robert," and constituted a relief after the society of the vulgar, strong-minded minister, who was born for the hustings and the House of Commons rather than for the courtly drawing-room.

John Lord Hervey, long vice-chamberlain to Queen Caroline, was, like Sir Robert Walpole, descended from a commoner's family, one of those good old squires who lived, as Sir Henry Wotton says, "without lustre and without obscurity." The Duchess of Marlborough had procured the elevation of the Herveys of Ickworth to the peerage. She happened to be intimate with Sir Thomas Felton, the father of Mrs. Hervey, afterward Lady Bristol, whose husband, at first created Lord Hervey, and afterward Earl of Bristol, expressed his obligations by retaining as his motto, when raised to the peerage, the words "Je n'oublieray jamais," in allusion to the service done him by the Duke and Duchess of Marlborough.

The Herveys had always been an eccentric race; and the classification of "men, women, and Herveys," by Lady Mary Wortley Montagu, was not more witty than true. There was in the whole race an eccentricity which bordered on the ridiculous, but did not imply want of sense or of talent. Indeed this third species, "the Herveys," were more gifted than the generality of "men and women." The father of Lord Hervey had been a country gentleman of good fortune, living at Ickworth, near Bury in Suffolk, and representing the town in Parliament, as his father had before him, until raised to the peerage. Before that elevation he had lived on in his own county, uniting the character of the English squire, in that fox-hunting county, with that of a perfect gentleman, a scholar, and a most admirable member of society. He was a poet also, affecting the style of Cowley, who wrote an elegy upon his uncle, William Hervey, an elegy compared to Milton's "Lycidas" in imagery, music, and tenderness of thought. The shade of Cowley, whom Charles II. pronounced, at his death, to be "the best man in England," haunted this peer, the first Earl of Bristol. He aspired especially to the poet's *wit;* and the ambition to be a wit flew like wildfire among his family, especially infecting his two sons, Carr, the elder brother of the subject of this memoir, and Lord Hervey.

It would have been well could the Earl of Bristol have transmitted to his sons his other qualities. He was pious, moral, affectionate, sincere; a consistent Whig of the old school, and, as such, disapproving of Sir Robert Walpole, of the standing army, the corruptions, and that doctrine of expediency so unblushingly avowed by the ministers.

Created Earl of Bristol in 1714, the heir-apparent to his titles and estates was the elder brother, by a former marriage, of John, Lord Hervey; the dissolute, clever, whimsical Carr, Lord Hervey. Pope, in one of his satirical appeals to the *second* Lord Hervey, speaks of his friendship with Carr, "whose early death deprived the family" (of Hervey) "of as much wit and honor as he left behind him in any part of it." The *wit* was a family attribute, but the *honor* was dubious: Carr was as deistical as any Maccaroni of the day, and, perhaps, more dissolute than most: in one respect he has left behind him a celebrity which may be as questionable as his wit, or his honor; he is reputed to be the father of Horace Walpole, and if we accept presumptive evidence of the fact, the statement is clearly borne out, for in his wit, his indifference to religion, to say the least, his satirical turn, his love of the world, and his contempt of all that was great and good, he strongly resembles his reputed son; while the levity of Lady Walpole's character, and Sir Robert's laxity and dissoluteness, do not furnish any reasonable doubt to the statement made by Lady Louisa Stuart, in the introduction to Lord Wharncliffe's "Life of Lady Mary Wortley Montagu." Carr, Lord Hervey, died early, and his half-brother succeeded him in his title and expectations.

John, Lord Hervey, was educated first at Westminster School, under Dr. Freind, the friend of Mrs. Montagu; thence he was removed to Clare Hall, Cambridge: he graduated as a nobleman, and became M. A. in 1715.

At Cambridge Lord Hervey might have acquired some manly prowess; but he had a mother who was as strange as the family into which she had married, and who was passionately devoted to her son: she evinced her affection by never letting him have a chance of being like other English boys. When his father was at Newmarket, Jack Hervey, as he was called, was to ride a race, to please his father; but his mother could not risk her dear boy's safety, and the race was won by a jockey. He was as precious and as fragile as porcelain: the elder brother's death made the heir of the Herveys more valuable, more effeminate, and more controlled than ever by his eccentric mother. A court was to be his hemisphere, and to that all his views, early in life, tended. He went to Hanover to pay his court to George I.: Carr had done the same, and had come back enchanted with George, the heir-presumptive, who made him one of the lords of the bedchamber. Jack Hervey also returned full of enthusiasm for the Prince of Wales, afterward George II., and the princess; and that visit influenced his destiny.

He now proposed making the grand tour, which comprised Paris, Germany, and Italy. But his mother again interfered: she wept, she exhorted, she prevailed. Means were refused, and the stripling was recalled to hang about the court, or to loiter at Ickworth, scribbling verses, and causing his father uneasiness lest he should be too much of a poet, and too little of a public man.

Such was his youth: disappointed by not obtaining a commission in the Guards, he led a desultory, butterfly-like life; one day at Richmond with Queen Caroline, then Princess of Wales; another, at Pope's villa, at Twickenham; sometimes in the House of Commons, in which he succeeded his elder brother as member for Bury; and, at the period when he has been described as forming one of the quartette in Queen Caroline's closet at St. James's, as vice-chamberlain to his partial and royal patroness.

His early marriage with Mary Lepel, the beautiful maid of honor to Queen Caroline, insured his felicity, though it did not curb his predilections for other ladies.

Henceforth Lord Hervey lived all the year round in what were then called lodgings, that is, apartments appropriated to the royal household, or even to others, in St. James's, or at Richmond, or at Windsor. In order fully to comprehend all the intimate relations which he had with the court, it is necessary to present the reader with some account of the family of George II. Five daughters had been the female issue of his majesty's marriage with Queen Caroline. Three of these princesses, the three elder ones, had lived, during the life of George I., at St. James's with their grandfather; who, irritated by the differences between him and his son, then Prince of Wales, adopted that measure rather as showing his authority than from any affection to the young princesses. It was, in truth, difficult to say which of these royal ladies was the most unfortunate.

Anne, the eldest, had shown her spirit early in life while residing with George I.; she had a proud, imperious nature, and her temper was, it must be owned, put to a severe test. The only time that George I. did the English the *honor* of choosing one of the beauties of the nation for his mistress, was during the last year of his reign. The object of his choice was Anne Brett, the eldest daughter of the infamous Countess of Macclesfield by her second husband. The neglect of Savage, the poet, her son, was merely one passage in the iniquitous life of Lady Macclesfield. Endowed with singular taste and judgment, consulted by Colley Cibber on every new play he produced, the mother of Savage was not only wholly destitute of all virtue, but of all shame. One day, looking out of the window, she perceived a very handsome man assaulted by some bailiffs who were going to arrest him: she paid his debt, released, and married him. The hero of this story was Colonel Brett, the father of Anne Brett.

The child of such a mother was not likely to be even decently respectable; and Anne was proud of her disgraceful pre-eminence and of her disgusting and royal lover. She was dark, and her flashing black eyes resembled those of a Spanish beauty. Ten years after the death of George I., she found a husband in Sir William Leman, of Northall, and was announced, on that occasion, as the half-sister of Richard Savage.

To the society of this woman, when at St. James's, as "Mistress Brett," the three princesses were subjected: at the same time the Duchess of Kendal, the king's German mistress, occupied other lodgings at St. James's.

Miss Brett was to be rewarded with the coronet of a countess for her degradation, the king being absent on the occasion at Hanover; elated by her expectations, she took the liberty, during his majesty's absence, of ordering a door to be broken out of her apartment into the royal garden, where the princesses walked. The Princess Anne, not deigning to associate with her, commanded that it should be forthwith closed. Miss Brett imperiously reversed that order. In the midst of the affair, the king died suddenly, and Anne Brett's reign was over, and her influence soon as much forgotten as if she had never existed. The Princess Anne was pining in the dullness of her royal home, when a marriage with the Prince of Orange, was proposed for the consideration of his parents. It was a miserable match as well as a miserable prospect, for the prince's revenue amounted to no more than £12,000 a year; and the state and pomp to which the Princess Royal had been accustomed could not be contemplated on so small a fortune. It was still worse in point of that poor consideration, happiness. The Prince of Orange was both deformed and disgusting in his person, though his face was sensible in expression; and if he inspired one idea more strongly than another when he appeared in his uniform and cocked hat, and spoke bad French, or worse English, it was that of seeing before one a dressed-up baboon.

It was a bitter cup for the princess to drink, but she drank it; she reflected that it might be the only way of quitting a court where, in case of her father's death, she would be dependent on her brother Frederick, or on that weak prince's strong-minded wife. So she consented, and took the dwarf; and that consent was regarded by a grateful people, and by all good courtiers, as a sacrifice for the sake of Protestant principles, the House of Orange being, *par excellence*, at the head of the orthodox dynasties of Europe. A dowry of £80,000 was forthwith granted by an admiring Commons—just double what had ever been given before. That sum was happily lying in the exchequer, being the purchase-money of some lands in St. Christopher's which had lately been sold; and

King George was thankful to get rid of a daughter whose haughtiness gave him trouble. In person, too, the princess royal was not very ornamental to the court. She was ill-made, with a propensity to grow fat: her complexion, otherwise very fine, was marked with the small-pox; she had, however, a lively, clean look—one of her chief beauties—and a certain royalty of manner.

The Princess Amelia died, as the world thought, single, but consoled herself with various love flirtations. The Duke of Newcastle made love to her, but her affections were centred on the Duke of Grafton, to whom she was privately married, as is confidently asserted.

The Princess Caroline was the darling of her family. Even the king relied on her truth. When there was any dispute, he used to say, "Send for Caroline; she will tell us the right story."

Her fate had its clouds. Amiable, gentle, of unbounded charity, with strong affections, which were not suffered to flow in a legitimate channel, she became devotedly attached to Lord Hervey: her heart was bound up in him; his death drove her into a permanent retreat from the world. No debasing connection existed between them; but it is misery, it is sin enough to love another woman's husband—and that sin, that misery, was the lot of the royal and otherwise virtuous Caroline.

The Princess Mary, another victim to conventionalities, was united to Frederick, Landgrave of Hesse Cassel; a barbarian, from whom she escaped, whenever she could, to come, with a bleeding heart, to her English home. She was, even Horace Walpole allows, "of the softest, mildest temper in the world," and fondly beloved by her sister Caroline, and by the "Butcher of Culloden," William, Duke of Cumberland.

Louisa became Queen of Denmark in 1746, after some years' marriage to the Crown Prince. "We are lucky," Horace Walpole writes on that occasion, "in the death of kings."

The two princesses who were still under the paternal roof were contrasts. Caroline was a constant invalid, gentle, sincere, unambitious, devoted to her mother, whose death nearly killed her. Amelia affected popularity, and assumed the *esprit fort*—was fond of meddling in politics, and after the death of her mother, joined the Bedford faction, in opposition to her father. But both these princesses were outwardly submissive when Lord Hervey became the Queen's chamberlain.

The evenings at St. James's were spent in the same way as those at Kensington.

Quadrille formed her majesty's pastime, and, while Lord

Hervey played pools of cribbage with the Princess Caroline and the maids of honor, the Duke of Cumberland amused himself and the Princess Amelia at "buffet." On Mondays and Fridays there were drawing-rooms held; and these receptions took place, very wisely, in the evening.

Beneath all the show of gayety and the freezing ceremony of those stately occasions, there was in that court as much misery as family dissensions, or, to speak accurately, family hatreds can engender. Endless jealousies, which seem to us as frivolous as they were rabid; and contentions, of which even the origin is still unexplained, had long severed the queen from her eldest son. George II. had always loved his mother: his affection for the unhappy Sophia Dorothea was one of the very few traits of goodness in a character utterly vulgar, sensual, and entirely selfish. His son, Frederick, Prince of Wales, on the other hand, hated his mother. He loved neither of his parents; but the queen had the pre-eminence in his aversion.

The king, during the year 1736, was at Hanover. His return was announced, but under circumstances of danger. A tremendous storm arose just as he was prepared to embark at Helvoetsluys. All London was on the look-out, weather-cocks were watched; tides, winds, and moons formed the only subjects of conversation; but no one of his majesty's subjects were so demonstrative as the Prince of Wales, and his cheerfulness, and his triumph even, on the occasion, were of course resentfully heard of by the queen.

During the storm, when anxiety had almost amounted to fever, Lord Hervey dined with Sir Robert Walpole. Their conversation naturally turned on the state of affairs, prospectively. Sir Robert called the Prince a "poor, weak, irresolute, false, lying, contemptible wretch." Lord Hervey did not defend him, but suggested that Frederick, in case of his father's death, might be more influenced by the queen than he had hitherto been. "Zounds, my lord," interrupted Sir Robert, "he would tear the flesh off her bones with red-hot irons sooner! The distinctions she shows to you, too, I believe, would not be forgotten. Then the notion he has of his great riches, and the desire he has of fingering them, would make him pinch her, and pinch her again, in order to make her buy her ease, till she had not a groat left."

What a picture of a heartless and selfish character! The next day the queen sent for Lord Hervey, to ask him if he knew the particulars of a great dinner which the prince had given to the lord mayor the previous day, while the whole country, and the court in particular, was trembling for the safety of the king, his father. Lord Hervey told her that the prince's speech at the dinner was the most ingratiating piece of popularity ever heard; the healths, of course, as usual. "Heavens!" cried the queen: "popularity always makes me sick, but *Fritz's* popularity makes me vomit! I hear that yesterday, on the prince's side of the House, they talked of the king's being cast away with the same *sang froid* as you would talk of an overturn; and that my good son strutted about as if he had been already king. Did you mark the airs with which he came into my drawing-room in the morning? though he does not think fit to honor me with his presence, or *ennui* me with his wife's, of an evening. I felt something here in my throat that swelled and half choked me."

Poor Queen Caroline! with such a son, and such a husband, she must have been possessed of a more than usual share of German imperturbability to sustain her cheerfulness, writhing, as she often was, under the pangs of a long-concealed disorder, of which eventually she died. Even on the occasion of the king's return in time to spend his birthday in England, the queen's temper had been sorely tried. Nothing had ever vexed her more than the king's admiration for Amelia Sophia Walmoden, who, after the death of Caroline, was created Countess of Yarmouth. Madame Walmoden had been a reigning belle among the young married women at Hanover, when George II. visited that country in 1735. Not that her majesty's affections were wounded; it was her pride that was hurt by the idea that people would think that this Hanoverian lady had more influence than she had. In other respects the king's absence was a relief: she had the *éclat* of the regency; she had the comfort of having the hours which her royal torment decreed were to be passed in amusing his dullness, to herself; she was free from his "quotidian sallies of temper, which," as Lord Hervey relates, "let it be charged by what hand it would, used always to discharge its hottest fire, on some pretense or other, upon her."

It is quite true that from the first dawn of his preference for Madame Walmoden, the king wrote circumstantial letters of fifty or sixty pages to the queen, informing her of every stage of the affair; the queen, in reply, saying that she was only *one* woman, and an old woman, and adding, "that he might love *more and younger women.*" In return, the king wrote, "You must love the Walmoden, for she loves *you*;" a civil insult, which he accompanied with so minute a description of his new favorite, that the queen, had she been a painter, might have drawn her portrait at a hundred miles' distance.

The queen, subservient as she seemed, felt the humiliation.

Such was the debased nature of George II. that he not only wrote letters unworthy of a man to write, and unfit for a woman to read, to his wife, but he desired her to show them to Sir Robert Walpole. He used to "tag several paragraphs," as Lord Hervey expresses it, with these words, "*Montrez ceci, et consultez la-dessus de gros homme*," meaning Sir Robert. But this was only a portion of the disgusting disclosures made by the vulgar, licentious monarch to his too degraded consort.

In the bitterness of her mortification the queen consulted Lord Hervey and Sir Robert as to the possibility of her losing her influence, should she resent the king's delay in returning. They agreed, that her taking the "*fière* turn" would ruin her with her royal consort; Sir Robert adding, that if he had a mind to flatter her into her ruin, he might talk to her as if she were twenty-five, and try to make her imagine that she could bring the king back by the apprehension of losing her affection. He said it was now too late in her life to try new methods; she must persist in the soothing, coaxing, submissive arts which had been practiced with success, and even press his majesty to bring this woman to England! "He taught her," says Lord Hervey, "this hard lesson till she *wept*." Nevertheless, the queen expressed her gratitude to the minister for his advice. "My lord," said Walpole to Hervey, "she laid her thanks on me so thick that I found I had gone too far, for I am never so much afraid of her rebukes as of her commendations."

Such was the state of affairs between this singular couple. Nevertheless, the queen, not from attachment to the king, but from the horror she had of her son's reigning, felt such fears of the prince's succeeding to the throne as she could hardly express. He would, she was convinced, do all he could to ruin and injure her in case of his accession to the throne.

The consolation of such a friend as Lord Hervey can easily be conceived, when he told her majesty that he had resolved, in case the king had been lost at sea, to have retired from her service, in order to prevent any jealousy or irritation that might arise from his supposed influence with her majesty. The queen stopped him short, and said, "No, my lord, I should never have suffered that; you are one of the greatest pleasures of my life. But did I love you less than I do, or less like to have you about me, I should look upon the suffering you to be taken from me as such a meanness and baseness that you should not have stirred an inch from me. You," she added, "should have gone with me to Somerset House" (which was hers in case of the king's death). She then told him she should have begged Sir Robert Walpole on her knees not to have sent in his resignation.

The animosity of the Prince of Wales to Lord Hervey augmented, there can be no doubt, his unnatural aversion to the queen, an aversion which he evinced early in life. There was a beautiful, giddy maid of honor, who attracted not only the attention of Frederick, but the rival attentions of other suitors, and among them, the most favored was said to be Lord Hervey, notwithstanding that he had then been for some years the husband of one of the loveliest ornaments of the court, the sensible and virtuous Mary Lepel. Miss Vane became eventually the avowed favorite of the prince, and after giving birth to a son, who was christened FitzFrederick Vane, and who died in 1736, his unhappy mother died a few months afterward. It is melancholy to read a letter from Lady Hervey to Mrs. Howard, portraying the frolic and levity of this once joyous creature, among the other maids of honor; and her strictures show at once the unrefined nature of the pranks in which they indulged, and her once sobriety of demeanor.

She speaks, on one occasion, in which, however, Miss Vane did not share the nocturnal diversion, of some of the maids of honor being out in the winter all night in the gardens at Kensington—opening and rattling the windows, and trying to frighten people out of their wits; and she gives Mrs. Howard a hint that the queen ought to be informed of the way in which her young attendants amused themselves. After levities such as these, it is not surprising to find poor Miss Vane writing to Mrs. Howard, with complaints that she was unjustly aspersed, and referring to her relatives, Lady Betty Nightingale and Lady Hewet, in testimony of the falsehood of reports which, unhappily, the event verified.

The prince, however, never forgave Lord Hervey for being his rival with Miss Vane, nor his mother for her favors to Lord Hervey. In vain did the queen endeavor to reconcile Fritz, as she called him, to his father; nothing could be done in a case where the one was all dogged selfishness, and where the other, the idol of the opposition party, as the prince had ever been, so *legère de tête* as to swallow all the adulation offered to him, and to believe himself a demigod. "The queen's dread of a rival," Horace Walpole remarks, "was a feminine weakness: the behavior of her eldest son was a real thorn." Some time before his marriage to a princess who was supposed to augment his hatred of his mother, Frederick of Wales had contemplated an act of disobedience. Soon after his arrival in England, Sarah, Duchess of Marlborough, hearing that he was in want of money, had sent to offer him her granddaughter,

Lady Diana Spencer, with a fortune of £100,000. The prince accepted the young lady, and a day was fixed for his marriage in the duchess's lodge at the Great Park, Windsor. But Sir Robert Walpole getting intelligence of the plot, the nuptials were stopped. The duchess never forgave either Walpole or the royal family, and took an early opportunity of insulting the latter. When the Prince of Orange came over to marry the princess royal, a sort of boarded gallery was erected from the windows of the great drawing-room of that palace, and was constructed so as to cross the garden to the Lutheran chapel in the Friary, where the duchess lived. The Prince of Orange being ill, went to Bath, and the marriage was delayed for some weeks. Meantime the windows of Marlborough House were darkened by the gallery. "I wonder," cried the old duchess, "when my neighbor George will take away his orange-chest!" the structure, with its pent-house roof, really resembling an orange-chest.

Mary Lepel, Lady Hervey, whose attractions, great as they were, proved insufficient to rivet the exclusive admiration of the accomplished Hervey, had become his wife in 1720, some time before her husband had been completely enthralled with the gilded prison doors of a court. She was endowed with that intellectual beauty calculated to attract a man of talent: she was highly educated, of great talent; possessed of *savoir faire*, infinite good temper, and a strict sense of duty. She also derived from her father, Brigadier Lepel, who was of an ancient family in Sark, a considerable fortune. Good and correct as she was, Lady Hervey viewed with a fashionable composure the various intimacies formed during the course of their married life by his lordship.

The fact is, that the aim of both was not so much to insure their domestic felicity as to gratify their ambition. Probably they were disappointed in both these aims—certainly in one of them: talented, indefatigable, popular, lively, and courteous, Lord Hervey, in the House of Commons, advocated in vain, in brilliant orations, the measures of Walpole. Twelve years, fourteen years elapsed, and he was left in the somewhat subordinate position of vice-chamberlain, in spite of that high order of talents which he possessed, and which would have been displayed to advantage in a graver scene. The fact has been explained: the queen could not do without him; she confided in him; her daughter loved him; and his influence in that court was too powerful for Walpole to dispense with an aid so valuable to his own plans. Some episodes in a life thus frittered away, until, too late, promotion came, alleviated his existence, and gave his wife only a passing uneasiness, if even indeed they imparted a pang.

One of these was his dangerous passion for Miss Vane; another, his platonic attachment to Lady Mary Wortley Montagu.

While he lived on the terms with his wife which is described even by the French as being a "*Ménage de Paris*," Lord Hervey found in another quarter the sympathies which, as a husband, he was too well-bred to require. It is probable that he always admired his wife more than any other person, for she had qualities that were quite congenial to the tastes of a wit and a beau in those times. Lady Hervey was not only singularly captivating, young, gay, and handsome; but a complete model also of the polished, courteous, high-bred woman of fashion. Her manners are said by Lady Louisa Stuart to have "had a foreign tinge, which some called affected; but they were gentle, easy, and altogether exquisitely pleasing." She was in secret a Jacobite—and resembled in that respect most of the fine ladies in Great Britain. Whiggery and Walpolism were vulgar: it was *haut ton* to take offense when James II. was anathematized, and quite good taste to hint that some people wished well to the Chevalier's attempts: and this way of speaking owed its fashion probably to Frederick of Wales, whose interest in Flora Macdonald, and whose concern for the exiled family, were among the few amiable traits of his disposition. Perhaps they arose from a wish to plague his parents, rather than from a greatness of character foreign to this prince.

Lady Hervey was in the bloom of youth, Lady Mary in the zenith of her age, when they became rivals: Lady Mary had once excited the jealousy of Queen Caroline when Princess of Wales.

"How becomingly Lady Mary is dressed to-night," whispered George II. to his wife, whom he had called up from the card-table to impart to her that important conviction. "Lady Mary always dresses well," was the cold and curt reply.

Lord Hervey had been married about seven years when Lady Mary Wortley Montagu reappeared at the court of Queen Caroline, after her long residence in Turkey. Lord Hervey was thirty-three years of age; Lady Mary was verging on forty. She was still a pretty woman, with a piquant, neat-featured face; which does not seem to have done any justice to a mind at once masculine and sensitive, nor to a heart capable of benevolence—capable of strong attachments, and of bitter hatred.

Like Lady Hervey, she lived with her husband on well-bred terms: there existed no quarrel between them; no avowed ground of coldness; it was the icy boundary of frozen feeling that severed them; the sure and lasting though polite destroyer of all bonds, indifference. Lady Mary was full of repartee, of poetry, of anecdote, and was not averse to admiration; but she was essentially a woman of common sense, of views enlarged by travel, and of ostensibly good principles. A woman of delicacy was not to be found in those days, any more than other productions of the nineteenth century: a telegraphic message would have been almost as startling to a courtly ear as the refusal of a fine lady to suffer a *double entendre.* Lady Mary was above all scruples, and Lord Hervey, who had lived too long with George II. and his queen to have the moral sense in perfection, liked her all the better for her courage—her merry, licentious jokes, and her putting things down by their right names, on which Lady Mary plumed herself: she was what they term in the north of England "Emancipated." They formed an old acquaintance with a confidential, if not a tender friendship; and that their intimacy was unpleasant to Lady Hervey was proved by her refusal—when, after the grave had closed over Lord Hervey, late in life, Lady Mary ill, and broken down by age, returned to die in England—to resume an acquaintance which had been a painful one to her.

Lord Hervey was a martyr to illness of an epileptic character; and Lady Mary gave him her sympathy. She was somewhat of a doctor—and being older than her friend, may have had the art of soothing sufferings, which were the worse because they were concealed. While he writhed in pain, he was obliged to give vent to his agony by alleging that an attack of cramp bent him double: yet he lived by rule—a rule harder to adhere to than that of the most conscientious homeopath in the present day. In the midst of court gayeties and the duties of office, he thus wrote to Dr. Cheyne:

. . . "To let you know that I continue one of your most pious votaries, and to tell you the method I am in. In the first place, I never take wine nor malt drink, nor any liquid but water and milk-tea; in the next, I eat no meat but the whitest, youngest, and tenderest, nine times in ten nothing but chicken, and never more than the quantity of a small one at a meal. I seldom eat any supper, but if any, nothing absolutely but bread and water; two days in the week I eat no flesh; my breakfast is dry biscuit, not sweet, and green tea; I have left off butter as bilious; I eat no salt, nor any sauce but bread-sauce."

Among the most cherished relaxations of the royal household were visits to Twickenham, while the court was at Richmond. The River Thames, which has borne on its waves so much misery in olden times—which was the highway from the Star-chamber to the Tower—which has been belabored in our days with so much wealth, and sullied with so much impurity; that river, whose current is one hour rich as the stream of a

POPE AT HIS VILLA—DISTINGUISHED VISITORS.

gold river, the next hour foul as the pestilent church-yard—was then, especially between Richmond and Teddington, a glassy, placid stream, reflecting on its margin the chestnut-trees of stately Ham, and the reeds and wild flowers which grew undisturbed in the fertile meadows of Petersham.

Lord Hervey, with the ladies of the court, Mrs. Howard as their chaperon, delighted in being wafted to that village, so rich in names which give to Twickenham undying associations with the departed great. Sometimes the effeminate valetudinarian, Hervey, was content to attend the Princess Caroline to Marble Hill only, a villa residence built by George II. for Mrs. Howard, and often referred to in the correspondence of that period. Sometimes the royal barge, with its rowers in scarlet jackets, was seen conveying the gay party; ladies in slouched hats, pointed over fair brows in front, with a fold of sarcenet round them, terminated in a long bow and ends behind—with deep falling mantles over dresses never cognizant of crinoline: gentlemen, with cocked hats, their bag-wigs and ties appearing behind; and beneath their puce-colored coats, delicate silk tights and gossamer stockings were visible, as they trod the mossy lawn of the Palace Gardens at Richmond, or, followed by a tiny greyhound, prepared for the lazy pleasures of the day.

Sometimes the visit was private; the sickly Princess Caroline had a fancy to make one of the group who are bound to Pope's villa. Twickenham, where that great little man had, since 1715, established himself, was pronounced by Lord Bacon to be the finest place in the world for study. "Let Twitnam Park," he wrote to his steward, Thomas Bushell, "which I sold in my younger days, be purchased, if possible, for a residence for such deserving persons to study in (since I experimentally found the situation of that place much convenient for the trial of my philosophical conclusions)—expressed in a paper sealed, to the trust—which I myself had put in practice, and settled the same by act of parliament, if the vicissitudes of fortune had not intervened and prevented me."

Twickenham continued, long after Bacon had penned this injunction, to be the retreat of the poet, the statesman, the scholar; the haven where the retired actress and broken novelist found peace; the abode of Henry Fielding, who lived in one of the back streets; the temporary refuge, from the world of London, of Lady Mary Wortley Montagu, and the life-long home of Pope.

Let us picture to ourselves a visit from the princess to Pope's villa: As the barge, following the gentle bendings of the river, nears Twickenham, a richer green, a summer brightness, indicates it is approaching that spot of which even Bishop Warburton says that the "beauty of the owner's poetic genius appeared to as much advantage in the disposition of these romantic materials as in any of his best-contrived poems." And the loved toil which formed the quincunx, which perforated and extended the grotto until it extended across the road to a garden on the opposite side—the toil which showed the gentler parts of Pope's better nature—has been respected, and its effects preserved. The enameled lawn, green as no other grass save that by the Thames side is green, is swept still by the light boughs of the famed willow. Every memorial of the bard was treasured by the gracious hands into which, after 1744, the classic spot fell—those of Sir William Stanhope.

In the subterranean passage this verse appears; adulatory, it must be confessed:

"The humble roof, the garden's scanty line,
Ill suit the genius of the bard divine;
But fancy now assumes a fairer scope,
And Stanhope's plans unfold the soul of Pope."

It should have been Stanhope's "gold"—a metal which was not so abundant, nor indeed so much wanted in Pope's time as in our own.

As the barge is moored close to the low steps which lead up from the river to the villa, a diminutive figure, then in its prime (if prime it *ever* had), is seen moving impatiently forward. By that young-old face, with its large lucid speaking eyes that light it up, as does a rushlight in a cavern—by that twisted figure with its emaciated legs—by the large, sensible mouth, the pointed, marked, well-defined nose—by the wig, or hair pushed off in masses from the broad forehead and falling behind in tresses—by the dress, that loose, single-breasted black coat—by the cambric band and plaited shirt, without a frill, but fine and white, for the poor poet has taken infinite pains that day in self-adornment—by the delicate ruffle on that large thin hand, and still more by the clear, most musical voice which is heard welcoming his royal and noble guests, as he stands bowing low to the Princess Caroline, and bending to kiss hands—by that voice which gained him more especially the name of the little nightingale—is Pope at once recognized, and Pope in the perfection of his days, in the very zenith of his fame.

One would gladly have been a sprite to listen from some twig of that then stripling willow which the poet had planted with his own hand, to the talk of those who chatted for a while under its shade, before they went in-doors to an elegant dinner at the usual hour of twelve. How delightful to hear, unseen, the repartees of Lady Mary Wortley Montagu, who comes down, it is natural to conclude, from her villa near to that of Pope. How fine a study might one not draw of the fine gentleman and the wit in Lord Hervey, as he is commanded by the gentle Princess Caroline to sit on her right hand; but his heart is across the table with Lady Mary! How amusing to observe the dainty but not sumptuous repast contrived with Pope's exquisite taste, but regulated by his habitual economy—for his late father, a worthy Jacobite hatter, erst in the Strand, disdained to invest the fortune he had amassed, from the extensive sale of cocked hats, in the Funds, over which a Hanoverian stranger ruled; but had lived on his capital of £20,000, as spendthrifts do (without either moral, religious, or political reasons), as long as it lasted him; yet *he* was no spendthrift. Let us look, therefore, with a liberal eye, noting, as we stand, how that fortune, in league with nature, who made the poet crooked, had maimed two of his fingers, such time as, passing a bridge, the poor little poet was overturned into the river, and he would have been drowned, had not the postillion broken the coach window and dragged the tiny body through the aperture. We mark, however, that he generally contrives to hide this defect, as he would fain have hidden every other from the lynx eyes of Lady Mary, who knows him, however, thoroughly, and reads every line of that poor little heart of his, enamored of her as it was.

Then the conversation! How gladly would we catch here some drops of what must have been the very essence of small-talk, and small-talk is the only thing fit for early dinners! Our host is noted for his easy address, his engaging manners, his delicacy, politeness, and a certain tact he had of showing every guest that he was welcome in the choicest expressions and most elegant terms. Then Lady Mary! how brilliant is her slightest turn! how she banters Pope—how she gives *double entendre* for *double entendre* to Hervey! How sensible, yet how gay is all she says; how bright, how cutting, yet how polished is the *equivoque* of the witty, high-bred Hervey! He is happy that day—away from the coarse, passionate king, whom he hated with a hatred that burns itself out in his lordship's "Memoirs;" away from the somewhat exacting and pitiable queen; away from the hated Pelham, and the rival Grafton.

And conversation never flags when all, more or less, are congenial; when all are well-informed, well-bred, and resolved to please. Yet there is a canker in that whole assembly; that canker is a want of confidence: no one trusts the other; Lady Mary's encouragement of Hervey surprises and shocks the

Princess Caroline, who loves him secretly; Hervey's attentions to the queen of letters scandalize Pope, who soon afterward makes a declaration to Lady Mary. Pope writhes under a lash, just held over him by Lady Mary's hand. Hervey feels that the poet, though all suavity, is ready to demolish him at any moment, if he can; and the only really happy and complacent person of the whole party is, perhaps, Pope's old mother, who sits in the room next to that occupied for dinner, industriously spinning.

This happy state of things came, however, as is often the case, in close intimacies, to a painful conclusion. There was too little reality, too little earnestness of feeling, for the friendship between Pope and Lady Mary, including Lord Hervey, to last long. His lordship had his affectations, and his effeminate nicety was proverbial. One day being asked at dinner if he would take some beef, he is reported to have answered, "Beef? oh, no! faugh! don't you know I never eat beef, nor *horse*, nor curry, nor any of those things?" Poor man! it was probably a pleasant way of turning off what he may have deemed an assault on a digestion that could hardly conquer any solid food. This affectation offended Lady Mary, whose *mot*, that there were three species, "Men, women, and Herveys," implies a perfect perception of the eccentricities even of her gifted friend, Lord Hervey, whose mother's friend she had been, and the ob ject of whose admiration she undoubtedly was.

Pope, who was the most irritable of men, never forgot or forgave even the most trifling offense. Lady Bolingbroke truly said of him, that he played the politician about cabbages and salads, and every body agrees that he could hardly tolerate the wit that was more successful than his own. It was about the year 1725 that he began to hate Lord Hervey with such a hatred as only he could feel; it was unmitigated by a single touch of generosity or of compassion. Pope afterward owned that his acquaintance with Lady Mary and with Hervey was discontinued, merely because they had too much wit for him. Toward the latter end of 1732, "The Imitation of the Second Satire of the First Book of Horace," appeared, and in it Pope attacked Lady Mary with the grossest and most indecent couplet ever printed: she was called Sappho, and Hervey, Lord Fanny; and all the world knew the characters at once.

In retaliation for this satire, appeared "Verses to the Imitator of Horace;" said to have been the joint production of Lord Hervey and Lady Mary. This was followed by a piece entitled "Letter from a Nobleman at Hampton Court to a Doctor of Divinity." To this composition Lord Hervey, its sole author, added these lines, by way, as it seems, of extenuation.

Pope's first reply was in a prose letter, on which Dr. Johnson has passed a condemnation. "It exhibits," he says, "nothing but tedious malignity." But he was partial to the Herveys, Thomas and Henry Hervey, Lord Hervey's brothers, having been kind to him—"If you call a dog *Hervey*," he said to Boswell, "I shall love him."

Next came the epistle to Dr. Arbuthnot, in which every infirmity and peculiarity of Hervey are handed down in calm, cruel irony, and polished verses, to posterity. The verses are almost too disgusting to be revived in an age which disclaims scurrility. After the most personal rancorous invective, he thus writes of Lord Hervey's conversation:

"His wit all see-saw between this and *that*—
Now high, now low—now *master* up, now *miss*—
And he himself one vile antithesis.
* * * *
Fop at the toilet, flatterer at the board,
Now trips a lady, and now struts a lord.
Eve's tempter, thus the rabbins have expressed—
A cherub's face—a reptile all the rest.
Beauty that shocks you, facts that none can trust,
Wit that can creep, and pride that bites the dust."

"It is impossible," Mr. Croker thinks, "not to admire, however we may condemn, the art by which acknowledged wit, beauty, and gentle manners, the queen's favor, and even a valetudinary diet, are travestied into the most odious offenses."

Pope, in two lines, pointed to the intimacy between Lady Mary and Lord Hervey:

"Once, and but once, this heedless youth was hit,
And liked that dangerous thing, a female wit."

Nevertheless, he *afterward* pretended that the name *Sappho* was not applied to Lady Mary, but to women in general; and acted with a degree of mean prevarication which greatly added to the amount of his offense.

The quarrel with Pope was not the only attack which Lord Hervey had to encounter. Among the most zealous of his foes was Pulteney, afterward Lord Bath, the rival of Sir Robert Walpole, and the confederate with Bolingbroke in opposing that minister. The "Craftsman," a paper in the Whig interest, contained an attack on Pulteney, written with great ability, by Hervey. It provoked a *Reply* from Pulteney. In this composition he spoke of Hervey as "a thing below contempt," and ridiculed his personal appearance in the grossest terms. A duel was the result, the parties meeting behind Arlington House, in Piccadilly, where Mr. Pulteney had the satisfaction of almost running Lord Hervey through with his sword. Luckily the poor man slipped down, so the blow was evaded, and the seconds interfered: Mr. Pulteney then embraced Lord Hervey, and expressing his regret for their quarrel, declared that he would never again, either in speech or writing, attack his lordship. Lord Hervey only bowed, in silence; and thus they parted.

The queen having observed what an alteration in the palace Lord Hervey's death would cause, he said he could guess how it would be, and he produced "The Death of Lord Hervey; or, a Morning at Court; a Drama:" the idea being taken, it is thought, from Swift's verses on his own death, of which Hervey might have seen a surreptitious copy. The following scene will give some idea of the plot and structure of this amusing little piece. The part allotted to the Princess Caroline is in unison with the idea prevalent of her attachment to Lord Hervey:

ACT I.

SCENE: *The Queen's Gallery. The time, nine in the morning.*

Enter the QUEEN, PRINCESS EMILY, PRINCESS CAROLINE, *followed by* LORD LIFFORD, *and* MRS. PURCEL.

Queen. Mon Dieu, quelle chaleur! en vérité on étouffé. Pray open a little those windows.

Lord Lifford. Hasa your Majesty heara de news?

Queen. What news, my dear Lord?

Lord Lifford. Dat my Lord Hervey, as he was coming last night to *tone*, was rob and murdered by highwaymen and tron in a ditch.

Princess Caroline. Eh! grand Dieu!

Queen [*striking her hand upon her knee*]. Comment est-il véritablement mort? Purcel, my angel, shall I not have a little breakfast?

Mrs. Purcel. What would your Majesty please to have?

Queen. A little chocolate, my soul, if you give me leave, and a little sour cream, and some fruit. [*Exit* MRS. PURCEL.

Queen [*to Lord Lifford*]. Eh bien! my Lord Lifford, dites-nous un peu comment cela est arrivé. I can not imagine what he had to do to be putting his nose there. Seulement pour un sot voyage avec ce petit mousse, eh bien?

Lord Lifford. Madame, on sçait quelque chose de celai de Mon. Maran, qui d'abord qu'il a vu les voleurs s'est enfin et venu à grand galoppe à Londres, and after dat a wagoner take up the body and put it in his cart.

Queen [*to* PRINCESS EMILY]. Are you not ashamed, Amalie, to laugh?

Princess Emily. I only laughed at the cart, mamma.

Queen. Oh! that is a very fade plaisanterie.

Princess Emily. But if I may say it, mamma, I am not very sorry.

Queen. Oh! fie donc! Eh bien! my Lord Lifford! My God! where is this chocolate, Purcel?

As Mr. Croker remarks, Queen Caroline's breakfast-table, and her parentheses, reminds one of the card-table conversation of Swift:

"The Dean's dead: (pray what are trumps?)
Then Lord have mercy on his soul!
(Ladies, I'll venture for the vole.)

Six Deans, they say, must bear the pall;
(I wish I knew what king to call.)

Fragile as was Lord Hervey's constitution, it was his lot to witness the death-bed of the queen, for whose amusement he had penned the jeu d'esprit just quoted, in which there was, perhaps, as much truth as wit.

The wretched Queen Caroline had, during fourteen years, concealed from every one, except Lady Sundon, an incurable disorder, that of hernia. In November (1737) she was attacked with what we should now call English cholera. Dr. Tessier, her house-physician, was called in, and gave her Daffey's elixir, which was not likely to afford any relief to the deep-seated cause of her sufferings. She held a drawing-room that night for the last time, and played at cards, even cheerfully. At length she whispered to Lord Hervey, "I am not able to entertain people." "For heaven's sake, madam," was the reply, "go to your room: would to heaven the king would leave off talking of the Dragon of Wantley, and release you!" The Dragon of Wantley was a burlesque on the Italian opera, by Henry Carey, and was the theme of the fashionable world.

The next day the queen was in fearful agony, very hot, and willing to take any thing proposed. Still she did not, even to Lord Hervey, avow the real cause of her illness. None of the most learned court physicians, neither Mead nor Wilmot, were called in. Lord Hervey sat by the queen's bedside, and tried to soothe her, while the Princess Caroline joined in begging him to give her mother something to relieve her agony. At length, in utter ignorance of the case, it was proposed to give her some snakeroot, a stimulant, and, at the same time, Sir Walter Raleigh's cordial; so singular was it thus to find that great mind still influencing a court. It was that very medicine which was administered by Queen Anne of Denmark, however, to Prince Henry; that medicine which Raleigh said, "would cure him, or any other, of a disease, except in case of poison."

However, Ranby, house-surgeon to the king, and a favorite of Lord Hervey's, assuring him that a cordial with this name or that name was mere quackery, some usquebaugh was given instead, but was rejected by the queen soon afterward. At last Raleigh's cordial was administered, but also rejected about an hour afterward. Her fever, after taking Raleigh's cordial, was so much increased, that she was ordered instantly to be bled.

Then, even, the queen never disclosed the fact that could alone dictate the course to be pursued. George II., with more feeling than judgment, slept on the outside of the queen's bed all that night; so that the unhappy invalid could get no rest, nor change her position, not daring to irritate the king's temper.

The next day the queen said touchingly to her gentle, affectionate daughter, herself in declining health, "Poor Caroline! you are very ill, too; we shall soon meet again in another place."

Meantime, though the queen declared to every one that she was sure nothing could save her, it was resolved to hold a *levée*. The foreign ministers were to come to court, and the king, in the midst of his real grief, did not forget to send word to his pages to be sure to have his last new ruffles sewed on the shirt he was to put on that day; a trifle which often, as Lord Hervey remarks, shows more of the real character than events of importance, from which one frequently knows no more of a person's state of mind than one does of his natural gait from his dancing.

Lady Sundon was, meantime, ill at Bath, so that the queen's secret rested alone in her own heart. "I have an ill," she said, one evening, to her daughter Caroline, "that nobody knows of." Still, neither the princess nor Lord Hervey could guess at the full meaning of that sad assertion.

The famous Sir Hans Sloane was then called in; but no remedy except large and repeated bleedings was suggested, and blisters were put on her legs. There seems to have been no means left untried by the faculty to hasten the catastrophe—thus working in the dark.

The king now sat up with her whom he had so cruelly wounded in every nice feeling. On being asked, by Lord Hervey, what was to be done in case the Prince of Wales should come to inquire after the queen? he answered in the following terms, worthy of his ancestry—worthy of himself. It is difficult to say which was the most painful scene, that in the chamber where the queen lay in agony, or without, where the curse of family dissensions came like a ghoul to hover near the bed of death, and to gloat over the royal corpse. This was the royal dictum: "If the puppy should, in one of his impertinent airs of duty and affection, dare to come to St. James's, I order you to go to the scoundrel, and tell him I wonder at his impudence for daring to come here; that he has my orders already, and knows my pleasure, and bid him go about his business; for his poor mother is not in a condition to see him act his false, whining, cringing tricks now, nor am I in a humor to bear with his impertinence; and bid him trouble me with no more messages, but get out of my house."

In the evening, while Lord Hervey sat at tea in the queen's

outer apartment with the Duke of Cumberland, a page came to the duke to speak to the prince in the passage. It was to prefer a request to see his mother. This message was conveyed by Lord Hervey to the king, whose reply was uttered in the most vehement rage possible. "This," said he, "is like one of his scoundrel tricks; it is just of a piece with his kneeling down in the dirt before the mob to kiss her hand at the coach door when she came home from Hampton Court to see the princess, though he had not spoken one word to her during her whole visit. I always hated the rascal, but now I hate him worse than ever. He wants to come and insult his poor dying mother; but she shall not see him; you have heard her, and all my daughters have heard her, very often this year at Hampton Court desire me if she should be ill, and out of her senses, that I would never let him come near her; and while she had her senses she was sure she should never desire it. No, no! he shall not come and act any of his silly plays here."

In the afternoon the queen said to the king, she wondered the *Griff*, a nickname she gave to the prince, had not sent to inquire after her yet; it would be so like one of his *paroitres*. "Sooner or later," she added, "I am sure we shall be plagued with some message of that sort, because he will think it will have a good air in the world to ask to see me; and, perhaps, hopes I shall be fool enough to let him come, and give him the pleasure of seeing the last breath go out of my body, by which means he would have the joy of knowing I was dead five minutes sooner than he could know it in Pall Mall."

She afterward declared that nothing would induce her to see him except the king's absolute commands. "Therefore, if I grow worse," she said, "and should I be weak enough to talk of seeing him, I beg you, sir, to conclude that I doat—or rave."

The king, who had long since guessed at the queen's disease, urged her now to permit him to name it to her physicians. She begged him not to do so; and for the first time, and the last, the unhappy woman spoke peevishly and warmly. Then Ranby, the house-surgeon, who had by this time discovered the truth, said, "There is no more time to be lost; your majesty has concealed the truth too long; I beg another surgeon may be called in immediately."

The queen, who had, in her passion, started up in her bed, lay down again, turned her head on the other side, and, as the king told Lord Hervey, "shed the only tear he ever saw her shed while she was ill."

At length, too late, other and more sensible means were resorted to: but the queen's strength was failing fast. It must have been a strange scene in that chamber of death. Much as the king really grieved for the queen's state, he was still sufficiently collected to grieve also lest Richmond Lodge, which was settled on the queen, should go to the hated *Griff*;* and he actually sent Lord Hervey to the lord chancellor to inquire about that point. It was decided that the queen could make a will, so the king informed her of his inquiries, in order to set her mind at ease, and to assure her it was impossible that the prince could in any way benefit pecuniarily from her death. The Princess Emily now sat up with her mother. The king went to bed. The Princess Caroline slept on a couch in the antechamber, and Lord Hervey lay on a mattress on the floor at the foot of the Princess Caroline's couch.

On the following day (four after the first attack) mortification came on, and the weeping Princess Caroline and Lord Hervey were informed that the queen could not hold out many hours. Lord Hervey was ordered to withdraw. The king, the Duke of Cumberland, and the queen's four daughters alone remained, the queen begging them not to leave her until she expired; yet her life was prolonged many days.

When alone with her family, she took from her finger a ruby ring, which had been placed on it at the time of the coronation, and gave it to the king. "This is the last thing," she said, "I have to give you; naked I came to you, and naked I go from you; I had every thing I ever possessed from you, and to you whatever I have I return." She then asked for her keys, and gave them to the king. To the Princess Caroline she intrusted the care of her younger sisters; to the Duke of Cumberland, that of keeping up the credit of the family. "Attempt nothing against your brother, and endeavor to mortify him by showing superior merit," she said to him. She advised the king to marry again; he heard her in sobs, and with much difficulty got out this sentence: "*Non, j'aurai des maitresses.*" To which the queen made no other reply than "*Ah, mon Dieu! cela n'empêche pas.*" "I know," says Lord Hervey, in his Memoirs, "that this episode will hardly be credited, but it is literally true."

She then fancied she could sleep. The king kissed her, and wept over her; yet when she asked for her watch, which hung near the chimney, that she might give him the seal to take care of, his brutal temper broke forth. In the midst of his tears he called out, in a loud voice, "Let it alone! *mon Dieu!* the queen has such strange fancies; who should meddle with your seal? It is as safe there as in my pocket."

The queen then thought she could sleep, and, in fact, sank to rest. She felt refreshed on awakening and said, "I wish it

* Prince Frederick.

was over; it is only a reprieve to make me suffer a little longer; I can not recover, but my nasty heart will not break yet." She had an impression that she should die on a Wednesday: she had, she said, been born on a Wednesday, married on a Wednesday, crowned on a Wednesday, her first child was born on a Wednesday, and she had heard of the late king's death on a Wednesday.

On the ensuing day she saw Sir Robert Walpole. "My good Sir Robert," she thus addressed him, "you see me in a very indifferent situation. I have nothing to say to you but to recommend the king, my children, and the kingdom to your care."

Lord Hervey, when the minister retired, asked him what he thought of the queen's state.

"My lord," was the reply, "she is as much dead as if she was in her coffin; if ever I heard a corpse speak, it was just now in that room!"

It was a sad, an awful death-bed. The Prince of Wales having sent to inquire after the health of his dying mother, the queen became uneasy lest he should hear the true state of her case, asking "if no one would send those ravens," meaning the prince's attendants, "out of the house. They were only," she said, "watching her death, and would gladly tear her to pieces while she was alive." While thus she spoke of her son's courtiers, that son was sitting up all night in his house in Pall Mall, and saying, when any messenger came in from St. James's, "Well, sure, we shall soon have good news, she can not hold out much longer." And the princesses were writing letters to prevent the princess royal from coming to England, where she was certain to meet with brutal unkindness from her father, who could not endure to be put to any expense. Orders were, indeed, sent to stop her if she set out. She came, however, on pretense of taking the Bath waters; but George II., furious at her disobedience, obliged her to go direct to and from Bath without stopping, and never forgave her.

Notwithstanding her predictions, the queen survived the fatal Wednesday. Until this time no prelate had been called in to pray by her majesty, nor to administer the Holy Communion; and as people about the court began to be scandalized by this omission, Sir Robert Walpole advised that the Archbishop of Canterbury should be sent for: his opinion was couched in the following terms, characteristic at once of the man, the times, and the court:

"Pray, madam," he said to the Princess Emily, "let this farce be played; the archbishop will act it very well. You may bid him be as short as you will: it will do the queen no hurt, no more than any good; and it will satisfy all the wise and good fools who will call us atheists if we don't pretend to be as great fools as they are."

Unhappily, Lord Hervey, who relates this anecdote, was himself an unbeliever; yet the scoffing tone adopted by Sir Robert seems to have shocked even him.

In consequence of this advice, Archbishop Potter prayed by the queen morning and evening, the king always quitting the room when his grace entered it. Her children, however, knelt by her bedside. Still the whisperers who censured were unsatisfied—the concession was thrown away. Why did not the queen receive the communion? Was it, as the world believed, either "that she had reasoned herself into a very low and cold assent to Christianity?" or "that she was heterodox;" or "that the archbishop refused to administer the sacrament until she should be reconciled to her son?" Even Lord Hervey, who rarely left the antechamber, has only by his silence proved that she did *not* take the communion. That antechamber was crowded with persons who, as the prelate left the chamber of death, crowded around, eagerly asking, "Has the queen received?" "Her Majesty," was the evasive reply, "is in a heavenly disposition:" the public were thus deceived. Among those who were near the queen at this solemn hour was Dr. Butler, author of the "Analogy." He had been made clerk of the closet, and became, after the queen's death, Bishop of Bristol. He was in a remote living in Durham, when the queen, remembering that it was long since she had heard of him, asked the Archbishop of York "whether Dr. Butler was dead?" "No, madam," replied that prelate (Dr. Blackburn), "but he is buried;" upon which she had sent for him to court. Yet he was not courageous enough, it seems, to speak to her of her son and of the duty of reconciliation; whether she ever sent the prince any message or not is uncertain; Lord Hervey is silent on that point, so that it is to be feared that Lord Chesterfield's line,

> "And, unforgiving, unforgiven, dies!"

had but too sure a foundation in fact; so that Pope's sarcastic verses—

> "Hang the sad verse on Carolina's urn,
> And hail her passage to the realms of rest;
> All *parts performed*, and *all* her children blest,"

may have been but too just, though cruelly bitter. The queen lingered till the 20th of November. During that interval of agony her consort was perpetually boasting to every one of her virtues, her sense, her patience, her softness, her delicacy; and ending with the praise, "*Comme elle soutenoit sa dignité avec grace, avec politesse, avec douceur!*" Nevertheless he scarcely ever went into her room. Lord Hervey states "that he did, even in this moving situation, *snub* her for something or other she did or said." One morning, as she lay with her eyes fixed on a point in the air, as people sometimes do when they want to keep their thoughts from wandering, the king coarsely told her "she looked like a calf which had just had its throat cut." He expected her to die in state. Then, with all his bursts of tenderness he always mingled his own praises, hinting that though she was a good wife, he knew he had deserved a good one, and remarking, when he had extolled her understanding, that he did not "think it the worse for her having kept him company so many years." To all this Lord Hervey listened with, doubtless, well-concealed disgust; for cabals were even then forming for the future influence that might or might not be obtained.

The queen's life, meantime, was softly ebbing away in this atmosphere of selfishness, brutality, and unbelief. One evening she asked Dr. Tessier impatiently how long her state might continue?

"Your Majesty," was the reply, "will soon be released."

"So much the better," the queen calmly answered.

At ten o'clock that night, while the king lay at the foot of her bed, on the floor, and the Princess Emily on a couch-bed in the room, the fearful death-rattle in the throat was heard. Mrs. Purcel, her chief and old attendant, gave the alarm: the Princess Caroline and Lord Hervey were sent for; but the princess was too late, her mother had expired before she arrived. All the dying queen said was, "I have now got an asthma; open the window:" then she added, "*Pray!*" That was her last word. As the Princess Emily began to read some prayers, the sufferer breathed her last sigh. The Princess Caroline held a looking-glass to her lips, and finding there was no damp on it, said, "'Tis over!" Yet she shed not one tear upon the arrival of that event, the prospect of which had cost her so many heart-rending sobs.

The king kissed the lifeless face and hands of his often-injured wife, and then retired to his own apartment, ordering that a page should sit up with him for that and several other nights, for his majesty was afraid of apparitions, and feared to be left alone. He caused himself, however, to be buried by the side of his queen, in Henry VII.'s chapel, and ordered that one side of his coffin and of hers should be withdrawn; and in that state the two coffins were discovered not many years ago.

With the death of Queen Caroline, Lord Hervey's life, as to court, was changed. He was afterward made lord privy seal, and had consequently to enter the political world, with the disadvantage of knowing that much was expected from a man of so high a reputation for wit and learning. He was violently opposed by Pelham, Duke of Newcastle, who had been adverse to his entering the ministry; and since, with Walpole's favor, it was impossible to injure him by fair means, it was resolved to oppose Lord Hervey by foul ones. One evening, when he was to speak, a party of fashionable Amazons, with two duchesses—her grace of Queensberry and her grace of Ancaster—at their head, stormed the House of Lords and disturbed the debate with noisy laughter and sneers. Poor Lord Hervey was completely daunted, and spoke miserably. After Sir Robert Walpole's fall Lord Hervey retired. The following letter from him to Lady Mary Wortley Montagu fully describes his position and circumstances:

"I must now," he writes to her, "since you take so friendly a part in what concerns me, give you a short account of my natural and political health; and when I say I am still alive, and still privy seal, it is all I can say for the pleasure of one or the honor of the other; for since Lord Orford's retiring, as I am too proud to offer my service and friendship where I am not sure they will be accepted of, and too inconsiderable to have those advances made to me (though I never forgot or failed to return any obligation I ever received), so I remained as illustrious a nothing in this office as ever filled it since it was erected. There is one benefit, however, I enjoy from this loss of my court interest, which is, that all those flies which were buzzing about me in the summer sunshine and full ripeness of that interest, have all deserted its autumnal decay, and from thinking my natural death not far off, and my political demise already over, have all forgot the death-bed of the one and the coffin of the other."

Again he wrote to her a characteristic letter:

"I have been confined these three weeks by a fever, which is a sort of annual tax my detestable constitution pays to our detestable climate at the return of every spring; it is now much abated, though not quite gone off."

He was long a helpless invalid; and on the 8th of August, 1743, his short, unprofitable, brilliant, unhappy life was closed. He died at Ickworth, attended and deplored by his wife, who had ever held a secondary part in the heart of the great wit and beau of the court of George II. After his death his son George returned to Lady Mary all the letters she had written to his father: the packet was sealed; an assurance was at the same time given that they had not been read. In acknowledging this act of attention, Lady Mary wrote that "she could almost regret that he had not glanced his eye over a correspondence which might have shown him what so young a man might perhaps be inclined to doubt—the possibility of a long and steady friendship subsisting between two persons of different sexes without the least mixture of love."

Nevertheless, some expressions of Lord Hervey seem to have bordered on the tender style, when writing to Lady Mary in such terms as these. She had complained that she was too old to inspire a passion (a sort of challenge for a compliment), on which he wrote: "I should think any body a great fool that said he liked spring better than summer, merely because it is further from autumn, or that they loved green fruit better than ripe only because it was further from being rotten. I ever did, and believe ever shall, like woman best—

'Just in the noon of life—those golden days,
When the mind ripens ere the form decays.'"

Certainly this looks very unlike a pure Platonic, and it is not to be wondered at that Lady Hervey refused to call on Lady Mary, when, long after Lord Hervey's death, that fascinating woman returned to England. A wit, a courtier at the very fount of all politeness, Lord Hervey wanted the genuine source of all social qualities—Christianity. That moral refrigerator which checks the kindly current of neighborly kindness, and which prevents all genial feelings from expanding, produced its usual effect—misanthrophy. Lord Hervey's lines, in his "Satire after the manner of Persius," describes too well his own mental canker:

"Mankind I know, their motives and their art,
Their vice their own, their virtue best apart,
Till played so oft, that all the cheat can tell,
And dangerous only when 'tis acted well."

Lord Hervey left in the possession of his family a manuscript work, consisting of memoirs of his own time, written in his own autograph, which was clean and legible. This work, which has furnished many of the anecdotes connected with his court life in the foregoing pages, was long guarded from the eye of any but the Hervey family, owing to an injunction given in his will by Augustus, third Earl of Bristol, Lord Hervey's son, that it should not see the light until after the death of His Majesty George III. It was not therefore published until 1848, when they were edited by Mr. Croker. They are referred to both by Horace Walpole, who had heard of them, if he had not seen them, and by Lord Hailes, as affording the most intimate portraiture of a court that has ever been presented to the English people. Such a delineation as Lord Hervey has left ought to cause a sentiment of thankfulness in every British heart for not being exposed to such influences, to such examples as he gives, in the present day, when goodness, affection, purity, benevolence, are the household deities of the court of our beloved, inestimable Queen Victoria.

PHILIP DORMER STANHOPE, FOURTH EARL OF CHESTERFIELD.

The subject of this memoir may be thought by some rather the modeler of wits than the original of that class; the great critic and judge of manners rather than the delight of the dinner-table; but we are told to the contrary by one who loved him not. Lord Hervey says of Lord Chesterfield that he was "allowed by every body to have more conversable entertaining table-wit than any man of his time; his propensity to ridicule, in which he indulged himself with infinite humor and no distinction; and his inexhaustible spirits, and no discretion; made him sought and feared—liked and not loved—by most of his acquaintance."

This formidable personage was born in London on the 2d day of September, 1694. It was remarkable that the father of a man so vivacious, should have been of a morose temper; all the wit and spirit of intrigue displayed by him remind us of the frail Lady Chesterfield, in the time of Charles II.*—that lady who was looked on as a martyr because her husband was jealous of her; "a prodigy," says De Grammont, "in the city of London," where indulgent critics endeavor to excuse his lordship on account of his bad education, and mothers vowed that none of their sons should ever set foot in Italy, lest they should "bring back with them that infamous custom of laying restraint on their wives."

Even Horace Walpole cites Chesterfield as the "witty earl:" apropos to an anecdote which he relates of an Italian lady, who said that she was only four-and-twenty; "I suppose," said Lord Chesterfield, "she means four-and-twenty stone."

By his father the future wit, historian, and orator was utterly neglected; but his grandmother, the Marchioness of Halifax, supplied to him the place of both parents, his mother —her daughter, Lady Elizabeth Saville—having died in his childhood. At the age of eighteen, Chesterfield, then Lord Stanhope, was entered at Trinity Hall, Cambridge. It was one of the features of his character to fall at once into the tone of the society into which he happened to be thrown. One can hardly imagine his being "an absolute pedant," but such

* The Countess of Chesterfield here alluded to was the second wife of Philip, second Earl of Chesterfield. Philip Dormer, fourth Earl, was grandson of the second Earl, by his third wife.

was, actually, his own account of himself: "When I talked my best, I quoted Horace; when I aimed at being facetious, I quoted Martial; and when I had a mind to be a fine gentleman, I talked Ovid. I was convinced that none but the ancients had common sense; that the classics contained every thing that was either necessary, useful, or ornamental to men; and I was not even without thoughts of wearing the toga virilis of the Romans, instead of the vulgar and illiberal dress of the moderns."

Thus, again, when in Paris, he caught the manners, as he had acquired the language, of the Parisians. "I shall not give you my opinion of the French, because I am very often taken for one of them, and several have paid me the highest compliment they think it in their power to bestow—which is, 'Sir, you are just like ourselves.' I shall only tell you that I am insolent; I talk a great deal; I am very loud and peremptory; I sing and dance as I walk along; and, above all, I spend an immense sum in hair-powder, feathers, and white gloves."

Although he entered Parliament before he had attained the legal age, and was expected to make a great figure in that assembly, Lord Chesterfield preferred the reputation of a wit and a beau to any other distinction. "Call it vanity, if you will," he wrote in after life to his son, "and possibly it was so; but my great object was to make every man and every woman love me. I often succeeded; but why? by taking great pains."

According to Lord Hervey's account he often even sacrificed his interest to his vanity. The description given of Lord Chesterfield by one as bitter as himself implies, indeed, that great pains were requisite to counterbalance the defects of nature. Wilkes, one of the ugliest men of his time, used to say, that with an hour's start he would carry off the affections of any woman from the handsomest man breathing. Lord Chesterfield, according to Lord Hervey, required to be still longer in advance of a rival.

"With a person," Hervey writes, "as disagreeable as it was possible for a human figure to be without being deformed, he affected following many women of the first beauty and the most in fashion. He was very short, disproportioned, thick, and clumsily made; had a broad, rough-featured, ugly face, with black teeth, and a head big enough for a Polyphemus. One Ben Ashurst, who said a few good things, though admired for many, told Lord Chesterfield once, that he was like a stunted giant—which was a humorous idea and really apposite."

Notwithstanding that Chesterfield, when young, injured both soul and body by pleasure and dissipation, he always found time for serious study: when he could not have it otherwise, he took it out of his sleep. How late soever he went to bed, he resolved always to rise early; and this resolution he adhered to so faithfully, that at the age of fifty-eight he could declare that for more than forty years he had never been in bed at nine o'clock in the morning, but had generally been up before eight. He had the good sense, in this respect, not to exaggerate even this homely virtue. He did not rise with the dawn, as many early risers pride themselves in doing, putting all the engagements of ordinary life out of their usual beat, just as if the clocks had been set two hours forward. The man who rises at four in this country, and goes to bed at nine, is a social and family nuisance.

Strong good sense characterized Chesterfield's early pursuits. Desultory reading he abhorred. He looked on it as one of the resources of age, but as injurious to the young in the extreme. "Throw away," thus he writes to his son, "none of your time upon those trivial, futile books, published by idle necessitous authors for the amusement of idle and ignorant readers."

Even in those days such books "swarm and buzz about one:" "flap them away," says Chesterfield, "they have no sting." The earl directed the whole force of his mind to oratory, and became the finest speaker of his time. Writing to Sir Horace Mann, about the Hanoverian debate (in 1743, Dec. 15), Walpole praising the speeches of Lords Halifax and Sandwich, adds, "I was there, and heard Lord Chesterfield make the finest oration I ever heard there." This from a man who had listened to Pulteney, to Chatham, to Carteret, was a singularly valuable tribute.

While a student at Cambridge, Chesterfield was forming an acquaintance with the Hon. George Berkeley, the youngest son of the second Earl of Berkeley, and remarkable rather as being the second husband of Lady Suffolk, the favorite of George II., than from any merits or demerits of his own.

This early intimacy probably brought Lord Chesterfield into the close friendship which afterward subsisted between him and Lady Suffolk, to whom many of his letters are addressed.

His first public capacity was a diplomatic appointment: he afterward attained to the rank of an embassador, whose duty it is, according to a witticism of Sir Henry Wotton's, "*to lie* abroad for the good of his country;" and no man was in this respect more competent to fulfill these requirements than Chesterfield. Hating both wine and tobacco, he had smoked and drunk at Cambridge, "to be in the fashion;" he gamed at the Hague, on the same principle; and, unhappily, gaming became a habit and a passion. Yet never did he indulge it when acting, afterward, in a ministerial capacity. Neither when Lord Lieutenant of Ireland, or as Under-secretary of State, did he allow a gaming-table in his house. On the very night that he resigned office he went to *White's*.

The Hague was then a charming residence: among others who, from political motives, were living there, were John Duke of Marlborough and Queen Sarah, both of whom paid Chesterfield marked attention. Naturally industrious, with a ready insight into character—a perfect master in that art which bids us keep one's thoughts close, and our countenances open, Chesterfield was admirably fitted for diplomacy. A master of modern languages and of history, he soon began to like business. When in England, he had been accused of having "a need of a certain proportion of talk in a day:" "that," he wrote to Lady Suffolk, "is now changed into a need of such a proportion of writing in a day."

In 1728 he was promoted: being sent as embassador to the Hague, where he was popular, and where he believed his stay would be beneficial both to soul and body, there being "fewer temptations, and fewer opportunities to sin," as he wrote to Lady Suffolk, "than in England." Here his days passed, he asserted, in doing the king's business very ill—and his own still worse: sitting down daily to dinner with fourteen or fifteen people; while at five the pleasures of the evening began with a lounge on the Voorhoot, a public walk planted by Charles V.: then, either a very bad French play, or a "reprise quadrille," with three ladies, the youngest of them fifty, and the chance of losing, perhaps, three florins (besides one's time) —lasted till ten o'clock; at which time "His Excellency" went home, "reflecting with satisfaction on the innocent amusements of a well-spent day, that left nothing behind them," and retired to bed at eleven, "with the testimony of a good conscience."

All, however, of Chesterfield's time was not passed in this serene dissipation. He began to compose "The History of the Reign of George II." at this period. About only half a dozen characters were written. The intention was not confined to Chesterfield: Carteret and Bolingbroke entertained a similar design, which was completed by neither. When the subject was broached before George II., he thus expressed himself: and his remarks are the more amusing as they were addressed to Lord Hervey, who was, at that very moment, making his notes for that bitter chronicle of his majesty's reign, which has been ushered into the world by the late Wilson Croker—"They will all three," said King George II., "have about as much truth in them as the *Mille et Une Nuits.* Not but I shall like to read Bolingbroke's, who of all those rascals and knaves that have been lying against me these ten years has certainly the best parts, and the most knowledge. He is a scoundrel, but he is a scoundrel of a higher class than Chesterfield. Chesterfield is a little, tea-table scoundrel, that tells little womanish lies to make quarrels in families; and tries to make women lose their reputations, and make their husbands beat them, without any object but to give himself airs; as if any body could believe a woman could like a dwarf baboon."

Lord Hervey gave the preference to Bolingbroke: stating as his reason, that "though Lord Bolingbroke had no idea of wit, his satire was keener than any one's. Lord Chesterfield, on the other hand, would have a great deal of wit in them; but, in every page you would see he intended to be witty: every paragraph would be an epigram. *Polish*, he declared, would be his bane;" and Lord Hervey was perfectly right.

In 1732 Lord Chesterfield was obliged to retire from his embassy on the plea of ill-health, but, probably, from some political cause. He was in the opposition against Sir Robert Walpole on the Excise Bill; and felt the displeasure of that all-powerful minister by being dismissed from his office of High Steward.

Being badly received at court, he now lived in the country; sometimes at Buxton, where his father drank the waters, where he had his recreations, when not persecuted by two young brothers, Sir William Stanhope and John Stanhope, one of whom performed "tolerably ill upon a broken hautboy, and the other something worse upon a cracked flute." There he won three half-crowns from the curate of the place, and a shilling from "Gaffer Foxeley" at a cock-match. Sometimes he sought relaxation in Scarborough, where fashionable beaux "danced with the pretty ladies all night," and hundreds of Yorkshire country bumpkins "played the inferior parts; and, as it were, only tumble, while the others dance upon the high ropes of gallantry." Scarborough was full of Jacobites: the popular feeling was then all rife against Sir Robert Walpole's excise scheme. Lord Chesterfield thus wittily satirized that famous measure:

"The people of this town are, at present, in great consternation upon a report they have heard from London, which, if true, they think will ruin them. They are informed, that considering the vast consumption of these waters, there is a design laid of *excising* them next session; and, moreover, that as bathing in the sea is become the general practice of both sexes, and as the kings of England have always been allowed to be masters of the seas, every person so bathing shall be gauged, and pay so much per foot square as their cubical bulk amounts to."

In 1733, Lord Chesterfield married Melusina, the supposed niece, but, in fact, the daughter of the Duchess of Kendal, the mistress of George I. This lady was presumed to be a great heiress, from the dominion which her mother had over the king. Melusina had been created (for life) Baroness of Aldborough, county Suffolk, and Countess of Walsingham, county Norfolk, nine years previous to her marriage.

Her father being George I., as Horace Walpole terms him, "rather a good sort of man than a shining king," and her mother "being no genius," there was probably no great attraction about Lady Walsingham except her expected dowry.

During her girlhood Melusina resided in the apartments at St. James's—opening into the garden; and here Horace Walpole describes his seeing George I., in the rooms appropriated to the Duchess of Kendal, next to those of Melusina Schulemberg, or, as she was then called, the Countess of Walsingham. The Duchess of Kendal was then very "lean and ill-favored." "Just before her," says Horace, "stood a tall, elderly man, rather pale, of an aspect rather good-natured than august: in a dark tie-wig, a plain coat, waistcoat, and breeches of snuff colored cloth, with stockings of the same color, and a blue ribbon over all. That was George I."

The Duchess of Kendal had been maid of honor to the Electress Sophia, the mother of George I., and the daughter of Elizabeth of Bohemia. The duchess was always frightful; so much so that one night the electress, who had acquired a little English, said to Mrs. Howard, afterward Lady Suffolk, glancing at Mademoiselle Schulemberg, "Look at that *mawkin*, and think of her being my son's passion!"

The duchess, however, like all the Hanoverians, knew how to profit by royal preference. She took bribes; she had a settlement of £3000 a year. But her daughter was eventually disappointed of the expected bequest from her father, the king.*

In the apartments at St. James's Lord Chesterfield for some time lived, when he was not engaged in office abroad; and

* In the "Annual Register" for 1774, p. 20, it is stated that as George I. had left Lady Walsingham a legacy which his successor did not think proper to deliver, the Earl of Chesterfield was determined to recover it by a suit in Chancery, had not his majesty, on questioning the Lord Chancellor on the subject, and being answered that he could give no opinion extra-judicially, thought proper to fulfill the bequest.

A ROYAL ROBBER.

there he dissipated large sums in play. It was here, too, that Queen Caroline, the wife of George II., detected the intimacy that existed between Chesterfield and Lady Suffolk. There was an obscure window in Queen Caroline's apartments, which looked into a dark passage, lighted only by a single lamp at night. One Twelfth Night Lord Chesterfield, having won a large sum at cards, deposited it with Lady Suffolk, thinking it not safe to carry it home at night. He was watched, and his intimacy with the mistress of George II. thereupon inferred. Thenceforth he could obtain no court influence; and, in desperation, he went into the opposition.

On the death of George I., a singular scene, with which Lord Chesterfield's interests were connected, occurred in the Privy Council. Dr. Wake, Archbishop of Canterbury, produced the king's will, and delivered it to his successor, expecting that it would be opened and read in the council; what was his consternation when his majesty, without saying a word, put it into his pocket, and stalked out of the room with real German imperturbability! Neither the astounded prelate nor the subservient council ventured to utter a word. The will was never more heard of: rumor declared that it was burnt. The contents, of course, never transpired; and the legacy of £40,000, said to have been left to the Duchess of Kendal, was never more spoken of, until Lord Chesterfield, in 1733, married the Countess of Walsingham. In 1743, it is said, he claimed the legacy, in right of his wife, the Duchess of Kendal being then dead: and was "quieted" with £20,000, and got, as Horace Walpole observes, nothing from the duchess—"except his wife."

The only excuse that was urged to extenuate this act, on the part of George II., was that his royal father had burned two wills which had been made in his favor. These were supposed to be the wills of the Duke and Duchess of Zell and of the Electress Sophia. There was not even common honesty in the house of Hanover at that period.

Disappointed in his wife's fortune, Lord Chesterfield seems to have cared very little for the disappointed heiress. Their union was childless. His opinion of marriage appears very much to have coincided with that of the world of malcontents who rush, in the present day, to the court of Judge Cresswell, with "dissolving views." On one occasion, he writes thus: "I have at last done the best office that can be done to most married people; that is, I have fixed the separation between my brother and his wife, and the definitive treaty of peace will be proclaimed in about a fortnight."

Horace Walpole related the following anecdote of Sir William Stanhope (Chesterfield's brother) and his lady, whom he calls a "fond couple." After their return from Paris, when they arrived at Lord Chesterfield's house at Blackheath, Sir William, who had, like his brother, a cutting, polite wit, that was probably expressed with the "allowed simper" of Lord Chesterfield, got out of the chaise and said, with a low bow, "Madame, I hope I shall never see your face again." She replied, "Sir, I will take care that you never shall;" and so they parted.

There was little probability of Lord Chesterfield's participating in domestic felicity, when neither his heart nor his fancy were engaged in the union which he had formed. The lady to whom he was really attached, and by whom he had a son, resided in the Netherlands: she passed by the name of Madame du Bouchet, and survived both Lord Chesterfield and her son. A permanent provision was made for her, and a sum of five hundred pounds bequeathed to her, with these words: "as a small reparation for the injury I did her." "Certainly," adds Lord Mahon, in his Memoir of his illustrious ancestor, "a small one."

For some time Lord Chesterfield remained in England, and his letters are dated from Bath, from Tonbridge, from Blackheath. He had, in 1726, been elevated to the House of Lords upon the death of his father. In that assembly his great eloquence is thus well described by his biographer:*

"Lord Chesterfield's eloquence, the fruit of much study, was less characterized by force and compass than by elegance and perspicuity, and especially by good taste and urbanity, and a vein of delicate irony which, while it sometimes inflicted severe strokes, never passed the limits of decency and propriety. It was that of a man who, in the union of wit and good sense with politeness, had not a competitor. These qualities were matured by the advantage which he assiduously sought and obtained, of a familiar acquaintance with almost all the eminent wits and writers of his time, many of whom had been the ornaments of a preceding age of literature, while others were destined to become those of a later period."

The accession of George II., to whose court Lord Chesterfield had been attached for many years, brought him no political preferment. The court had, however, its attractions, even for one who owed his polish to the belles of Paris, and who was almost always, in taste and manners, more foreign than English. Henrietta, Lady Pomfret, the daughter and heiress of John, Lord Jeffreys, the son of Judge Jeffreys, was at that time the leader of fashion.

* Lord Mahon, now Earl of Stanhope, if not the most eloquent, one of the most honest historians of our time.

Six daughters, one of them Lady Sophia, surpassingly lovely, recalled the perfections of that ancestress, Arabella Fermor, whose charms Pope has so exquisitely touched in the "Rape of the Lock." Lady Sophia became eventually the wife of Lord Carteret, the minister, whose talents and the charms of whose eloquence constituted him a sort of rival to Chesterfield. With all his abilities, Lord Chesterfield may be said to have failed both as a courtier and as a political character, as far as permanent influence in any ministry was concerned, until in 1744, when what was called the "Broad-bottomed administration" was formed, when he was admitted into the cabinet. In the following year, however, he went, for the last time, to Holland, as embassador, and succeeded beyond the expectations of his party in the purposes of his embassy. He took leave of the States-General just before the battle of Fontenoy, and hastened to Ireland, where he had been nominated Lord Lieutenant previous to his journey to Holland. He remained in that country only a year; but long enough to prove how liberal were his views—how kindly the dispositions of his heart.

Only a few years before Lord Chesterfield's arrival in Dublin, the Duke of Shrewsbury had given as a reason for accepting the vice-regency of that country (of which King James I. had said, there was "more ado" than with any of his dominions), "that it was a place where a man had business enough to keep him from falling asleep, and not enough to keep him awake."

Chesterfield, however, was not of that opinion. He did more in one year than the duke would have accomplished in five. He began by instituting a principle of impartial justice. Formerly, Protestants had alone been employed as "managers;" the Lieutenant was to see with Protestant eyes, to hear with Protestant ears.

"I have determined to proscribe no set of persons whatever," says Chesterfield, "and determined to be governed by none. Had the Papists made any attempt to put themselves above the law, I should have taken good care to have quelled them again. It was said my lenity to the Papists had wrought no alteration either in their religious or their political sentiments. I did not expect that it would; but surely that was no reason for cruelty toward them."

Often by a timely jest Chesterfield conveyed a hint, or even shrouded a reproof. One of the ultra-zealous informed him that his coachman was a Papist, and went every Sunday to mass. "Does he indeed? I will take care he never drives me there," was Chesterfield's cool reply.

It was at this critical period, when the Hanoverian dynasty was shaken almost to its downfall by the insurrection in Scotland of 1745, that Ireland was imperiled: "With a weak or wavering, or a fierce and headlong Lord Lieutenant—with a Grafton or a Strafford," remarks Lord Mahon, "there would soon have been a simultaneous rising in the Emerald Isle." But Chesterfield's energy, his lenity, his wise and just administration saved the Irish from being excited into rebellion by the emissaries of Charles Edward, or slaughtered, when conquered, by the "Butcher," and his tiger-like dragoons. When all was over, and that sad page of history in which the deaths of so many faithful adherents of the exiled family are recorded, had been held up to the gaze of bleeding Caledonia, Chesterfield recommended mild measures, and advised the establishment of schools in the Highlands; but the age was too narrow-minded to adopt his views. In January, 1748, Chesterfield retired from public life. "Could I do any good," he wrote to a friend, "I would sacrifice some more quiet to it; but convinced as I am that I can do none, I will indulge my ease, and preserve my character. I have gone through pleasures while my constitution and my spirits would allow me. Business succeeded them; and I have now gone through every part of it without liking it at all the better for being acquainted with it. Like many other things, it is most admired by those who know it least. . . . I have been behind the scenes both of pleasure and business; I have seen all the coarse pulleys and dirty ropes which exhibit and move all the gaudy machines; and I have seen and smelt the tallow candles which illuminate the whole decoration, to the astonishment and admiration of the ignorant multitude. . . . My horse, my books, and my friends will divide my time pretty equally."

He still interested himself in what was useful; and carried a Bill in the House of Lords for the Reformation of the Calendar, in 1751. It seems a small matter for so great a mind as his to accomplish, but it was an achievement of infinite difficulty. Many statesmen had shrunk from the undertaking; and even Chesterfield found it essential to prepare the public, by writing in some periodical papers on the subject. Nevertheless the vulgar outcry was vehement: "Give us back the eleven days we have been robbed of!" cried the mob at a general election. When Bradley was dying, the common people ascribed his sufferings to a judgment for the part he had taken in that "impious transaction," the alteration of the calendar. But they were not less *bornès* in their notions than the Duke of Newcastle, then prime minister. Upon Lord Chesterfield giving him notice of his bill, that bustling premier, who had been in a hurry for forty years, who never "walked but always ran," greatly alarmed, begged Chesterfield not to stir matters that had been long quiet; adding, that he did not like "new-fangled things." He was, as we have seen, overruled, and henceforth the New Style was adopted; and no special calamity has fallen on the nation, as was expected, in consequence. Nevertheless, after Chesterfield had made his speech in the House of Lords, and when every one had complimented him on the clearness of his explanation—"God knows," he wrote to his son, "I had not even attempted to explain the bill to them; I might as soon have talked Celtic or Sclavonic to them, as astronomy. They would have understood it full as well." So much for the "Lords" in those days!

After his *furore* for politics had subsided, Chesterfield returned to his ancient passion for play. We must linger a little over the still brilliant period of his middle life, while his hearing was spared; while his wit remained, and the charming manners on which he had formed a science, continued; and before we see him in the mournful decline of a life wholly given to the world.

He had now established himself in Chesterfield House. Hitherto his progenitors had been satisfied with Bloomsbury Square, in which the Lord Chesterfield mentioned by De Grammont resided; but the accomplished Chesterfield chose a site near Audley Street, which had been built on what was called Mr. Audley's land, lying between Great Brook Field and the "Shoulder of Mutton Field." And near this locality with the elegant name, Chesterfield chose his spot, for which he had to wrangle and fight with the Dean and Chapter of Westminster, who asked an exorbitant sum for the ground. Isaac Ware, the editor of "Palladio," was the architect to whom the erection of this handsome residence was intrusted. Happily, it is still untouched by any *renovating* hand. Chesterfield's favorite apartments, looking on the most spacious private garden in London, are just as they were in his time; one especially, which he termed the "finest room in London," was furnished and decorated by him. "The walls," says a writer in the "Quarterly Review," "are covered half way up with rich and classical stores of literature; above the cases are in close series the portraits of eminent authors, French and English, with most of whom he had conversed; over these, and immediately under the massive cornice, extend all round in foot-long capitals the Horatian lines:

"Nunc . veterum . libris . Nunc . somno . et . inertibus . Horis.
Lucen . solicter . jucunda . oblivia . vitea.

"On the mantle-pieces and cabinets stand busts of old orators, interspersed with voluptuous vases and bronzes, antique or Italian, and airy statuettes in marble or alabaster of nude or semi-nude opera nymphs."

What Chesterfield called the "cannonical pillars" of the house were columns brought from Cannons, near Edgeware, the seat of the Duke of Chandos. The antechamber of Chesterfield House has been erroneously stated as the room in which Johnson waited the great lord's pleasure. That state of endurance was probably passed by "Old Samuel" in Bloomsbury.

In this stately abode—one of the few, the very few, that seem to hold *noblesse* apart in our leveling metropolis—Chesterfield held his assemblies of all that London, or indeed England, Paris, the Hague, or Vienna, could furnish of what was polite and charming. Those were days when the stream of society did not, as now, flow freely, mingling with the grace of aristocracy the acquirements of hard-working professors: there was then a strong line of demarkation; it had not been broken down in the same way as now, when people of rank and wealth live in rows, instead of inhabiting hotels set apart. Paris has sustained a similar revolution, since her gardens were built over, and their green shades, delicious, in the centre of that hot city, are seen no more. In the very Faubourg St. Germain, the grand old hotels are rapidly disappearing, and with them something of the exclusiveness of the higher orders. Lord Chesterfield, however, triumphantly pointing to the fruits of his taste, and distribution of his wealth, witnessed in his library at Chesterfield House, the events which time produced. He heard of the death of Sarah, Duchess of Marlborough, and of her bequest to him of twenty thousand pounds, and her best and largest brilliant diamond ring, "out of the great regard she had for his merit, and the infinite obligations she had received from him." He witnessed the change of society and of politics which occurred when George II. expired, and the Earl of Bute, calling himself a descendant of the house of Stuart, "and humble enough to be proud of it," having quitted the Isle of Bute, which Lord Chesterfield calls "but a little south of Nova Zembla," took possession, not only of the affections, but even of the senses of the young king, George III., who, assisted by the widowed Princess of Wales (supposed to be attached to Lord Bute), was "lugged out of the seraglio," and "placed upon the throne."

Chesterfield lived to have the honor of having the plan of "Johnson's Dictionary" inscribed to him, and the dishonor of neglecting the great author. Johnson, indeed, denied the truth of the story which gained general belief, in which it was asserted that he had taken a disgust at being kept waiting in the earl's antechamber, the reason being assigned that his lordship "had company with him;" when at last the door opened, and forth came Colley Cibber. Then Johnson—so report said—indignant, not only for having been kept waiting, but also for *whom*, went away, it was affirmed, in disgust; but this was solemnly denied by the doctor, who assured Boswell that his wrath proceeded from continual neglect on the part of Chesterfield.

While the Dictionary was in progress, Chesterfield seemed to forget the existence of him, whom, together with other literary men, he affected to patronize.

He once sent him ten pounds, after which he forgot Johnson's address, and said "the great author had changed his lodgings." People who really wish to benefit others can always discover where they lodge. The days of patronage were then expiring, but they had not quite ceased, and a dedication was always to be in some way paid for.

When the publication of the Dictionary drew near, Lord Chesterfield flattered himself that, in spite of all his neglect, the great compliment of having so vast an undertaking dedicated to him would still be paid, and wrote some papers in the "World," recommending the work, more especially referring to the "plan," and terming Johnson the "dictator," in respect to language: "I will not only obey him," he said, "as my dictator, like an old Roman, but like a modern Roman, will implicitly believe in him as my pope."

Johnson, however, was not to be propitiated by those "honeyed words." He wrote a letter couched in what he called "civil terms," to Chesterfield, from which we extract the following passages:

"When, upon some slight encouragement, I first visited your lordship, I was overpowered, like the rest of mankind, by the enchantment of your address; and could not forbear to wish that I might boast myself *vainqueur du vainqueur de la terre*—that I might obtain that regard for which I saw the world contending; but I found my attendance so little encouraged, that neither pride nor modesty would suffer me to continue it. When I had once addressed your lordship in publick, I had exhausted all the art of pleasing which a retired and uncourtly scholar can possess. I had done all that I could; and no man is well pleased to have his all neglected, be it ever so little.

"Seven years, my lord, have now passed, since I waited in your outward room, or was repulsed from your door, during which time I have been pushing on my work through difficulties, of which it is useless to complain, and have brought it, at last, to the verge of publication without one act of assistance, one word of encouragement, or one smile of favour: such treatment I did not expect, for I never had a patron before. . . . . Is not a patron, my lord, one who looks with unconcern on a man who is struggling for life in the water, and, when he has reached ground, encumbers him with help? The notice which you have been pleased to take of my labours, had it been early, had been kind; but it has been delayed till I am indifferent, and cannot enjoy it; till I am solitary, and cannot impart it; till I am known, and do not want it. I hope it is no very cynical asperity not to confess obligations where no benefit has been received, or to be unwilling that the publick should consider me as owing that to a patron which Providence has enabled me to do for myself."

The conduct of Johnson, on this occasion, was approved by most manly minds, except that of his publisher, Mr. Robert Dodsley; Dr. Adams, a friend of Dodsley, said he was sorry that Johnson had written that celebrated letter (a very model of polite contempt). Dodsley said he was sorry too, for he had a property in the Dictionary, to which his lordship's patronage might be useful. He then said that Lord Chesterfield had shown him the letter. "I should have thought," said Adams, "that Lord Chesterfield would have concealed it." "Pooh!" cried Dodsley, "do you think a letter from Johnson could hurt Lord Chesterfield? not at all, sir. It lay on his table where any one might see it. He read it to me; said, 'this man has great powers,' pointed out the severest passages, and said, 'how well they were expressed.'" The art of dissimulation, in which Chesterfield was perfect, imposed on Mr. Dodsley.

Dr. Adams expostulated with the doctor, and said Lord Chesterfield declared he would part with the best servant he had, if he had known that he had turned away a man who was "*always* welcome." Then Adams insisted on Lord Chesterfield's affability, and easiness of access to literary men. But the sturdy Johnson replied, "Sir, that is not Lord Chesterfield; he is the proudest man existing." "I think," Adams rejoined, "I know one that is prouder; you, by your own account, are the prouder of the two." "But mine," Johnson answered, with one of his happy turns, "was *defensive* pride." "This man," he afterward said, referring to Chesterfield, "I thought had been a lord among wits, but I find he is only a wit among lords."

In revenge, Chesterfield in his Letters depicted Johnson, it is said, in the character of the "respectable Hottentot." Among other things he observed of the Hottentot, "he throws his meat any where but down his throat." This being remarked to Johnson, who was by no means pleased at being immortalized as the Hottentot—"Sir," he answered, "Lord Chesterfield never saw me eat in his life."

Such are the leading points of this famous and lasting controversy. It is amusing to know that Lord Chesterfield was not always precise as to directions to his letters. He once directed to Lord Pembroke, who was always swimming, "To the Earl of Pembroke, in the Thames, over against Whitehall." This, as Horace Walpole remarks, "was sure of finding him within a certain fathom."

Lord Chesterfield was now admitted to be the very "glass of fashion," though age, and, according to Lord Hervey, a hideous person, impeded his being the "mould of form." "I don't know why," writes Horace Walpole, in the dog-days, from Strawberry Hill, "but people are always more anxious about their hay than their corn, or twenty other things that cost them more: I suppose my Lord Chesterfield, or some such dictator, made it fashionable to care about one's hay. Nobody betrays solicitude about getting in his rents." "The prince of wits," as the same authority calls him—"his entrance into the world was announced by his *bon-mots*, and his closing lips dropped repartees that sparkled with his juvenile fire."

No one, it was generally allowed, had such a force of table-wit as Lord Chesterfield; but while the "Graces" were ever his theme, he indulged himself without distinction or consideration in numerous sallies. He was, therefore, at once sought and feared; liked but not loved; neither sex, nor relationship, nor rank, nor friendship, nor obligation, nor profession, could shield his victim from what Lord Hervey calls "those pointed, glittering weapons, that seemed to shine only to a stander-by, but cut deep into those they touched."

He cherished "a voracious appetite for abuse;" fell upon every one that came in his way, and thus treated each one of his companions at the expense of the other. To him Hervey, who had probably often smarted, applied the lines of Boileau:

> "Mais c'est un petit fou qui se croit tout permis,
> Et qui pour un bon mot va perdre vingt amis."

Horace Walpole (a more lenient judge of Chesterfield's merits) observes that "Chesterfield took no less pains to be the phœnix of fine gentlemen, than Tully did to qualify himself as an orator. Both succeeded: Tully immortalized his name; Chesterfield's reign lasted a little longer than that of a fashionable beauty." It was, perhaps, because, as Dr. Johnson said, all Lord Chesterfield's witty sayings were puns, that even this brilliant wit failed to please, although it amused and surprised its hearers.

Notwithstanding the contemptuous description of Lord Chesterfield's personal appearance by Lord Hervey, his portraits represent a handsome, though hard countenance, well-marked features, and his figure and air appear to have been elegant. With his commanding talents, his wonderful brilliancy and fluency of conversation, he would perhaps sometimes have been even tedious, had it not been for his invariable cheerfulness. He was always, as Lord Hervey says, "present" in his company. Among the few friends who really loved this thorough man of the world, was Lord Scarborough, yet no two characters were more opposite. Lord Scarborough had judgment, without wit: Chesterfield wit, and no judgment; Lord Scarborough had honesty and principle; Lord Chesterfield had neither. Every body liked the one, but did not care for his company. Every one disliked the other, but wished for his company. The fact was, Scarborough was "splendid and absent;" Chesterfield, "cheerful and present:" wit, grace, attention to what is passing, the surface, as it were, of a highly-cultured mind, produced a fascination that all the honor and respectability in the court of George II. could not compete with.

In the earlier part of Chesterfield's career, Pope, Bolingbroke, Hervey, Lady Mary Wortley Montagu, and, in fact, all that could add to the pleasures of the then early dinner-table, illumined Chesterfield House by their wit and gayety. Yet in the midst of this exciting life, Lord Chesterfield found time to devote to the improvement of his natural son, Philip Stanhope, a great portion of his leisure. His celebrated Letters to that son did not, however, appear during the earl's life; nor were they in any way the source of his popularity as a wit, which was due to his merits in that line alone.

The youth to whom these letters, so useful, and yet so objectionable, were addressed, was intended for a diplomatist. He was the very reverse of his father: learned, sensible, and dry; but utterly wanting in the graces, and devoid of eloquence. As an orator, therefore, he failed; as a man of society, he must also have failed; and his death, in 1768, some years before that of his father, left that father desolate and disappointed. Philip Stanhope had attained the rank of envoy to Dresden, where he expired.

During the five years in which Chesterfield dragged out a mournful life after this event, he made the painful discovery that his son had married, without confiding that step to the father to whom he owed so much. This must have been almost as trying as the awkward, ungraceful deportment of him whom he mourned. The world now left Chesterfield ere he had left the world. He and his contemporary, Lord Tyrawley, were now old and infirm. "The fact is," Chesterfield wittily said, "Tyrawley and I have been dead these two years, but we don't choose to have it known."

"The Bath," he wrote to his friend Dayrolles, "did me more good than I thought any thing could do me; but all that good does not amount to what builders call half-repairs, and only keeps up the shattered fabric a little longer than it would have stood without them; but take my word for it, it will stand but a very little while longer. I am now in my grand climacteric, and shall not complete it. Fontenelle's last words at a hundred and three were, *Je souffre d'être:* deaf and infirm as I am, I can with truth say the same thing at sixty-three. In my mind it is only the strength of our passions, and the weakness of our reason, that makes us so fond of life; but when the former subside and give way to the latter, we grow weary of being, and willing to withdraw. I do not recommend this train of serious reflections to you, nor ought you to adopt them. . . . You have children to educate and provide for, you have all your senses, and can enjoy all the comforts both of domestic and social life. I am in every sense *isolé*, and have wound up all my bottoms; I may now walk off quietly, without missing nor being missed."

The kindness of his nature, corrupted as it was by a life wholly worldly, and but little illumined in its course by religion, shone now in his care of his two grandsons, the offspring of his lost son, and of their mother, Eugenia Stanhope. To her he thus wrote:

"The last time I had the pleasure of seeing you, I was so taken up in playing with the boys, that I forgot their more important affairs. How soon would you have them placed at school? When I know your pleasure as to that, I will send to Monsieur Perny, to prepare every thing for their reception. In the mean time, I beg that you will equip them thoroughly with clothes, linen, etc., all good, but plain; and give me the amount, which I will pay; for I do not intend, from this time forward, the two boys should cost you one shilling."

He lived, latterly, much at Blackheath, in the house which, being built on Crown land, has finally become the Ranger's lodge; but which still sometimes goes by the name of Chesterfield House. Here he spent large sums, especially on pictures, and cultivated Cantaloupe melons; and here, as he grew older, and became permanently afflicted with deafness, his chief companion was a useful friend, Solomon Dayrolles—one of those indebted hangers-on whom it was an almost invariable custom to find, at that period, in great houses—and perhaps too frequently in our own day.

Dayrolles, who was employed in the embassy under Lord Sandwich at the Hague, had always, to borrow Horace Walpole's ill-natured expression, "been a led-captain to the Dukes of Richmond and Grafton, used to be sent to auctions for them, and to walk in the parks with their daughters, and once went dry-nurse in Holland with them. He has belonged, too, a good deal to my Lord Chesterfield, to whom I believe he owes this new honor, 'that of being minister at the Hague,' as he had before made him black-rod in Ireland, and gave the ingenious reason, that he had a black face." But the great "dictator" in the empire of politeness was now in a slow but sure decline. Not long before his death he was visited by Monsieur Suard, a French gentleman, who was anxious to see "*l'homme le plus aimable, le plus poli et le plus spirituel des trois royaumes*," but who found him fearfully altered; morose, from his deafness, yet still anxious to please. "It is very sad," he said with his usual politeness, "to be deaf, when one would so much enjoy listening. I am not," he added, "so philosophic as my friend the Président de Montesquieu, who says, 'I know how to be blind, but I do not yet know how to be deaf.'" "We shortened our visit," says M. Suard, "lest we should fatigue the earl." "I do not detain you," said Chesterfield, "for I must go and rehearse my funeral." It was thus that he styled his daily drive through the streets of London.

Lord Chesterfield's wonderful memory continued till his latest hour. As he lay, gasping in the last agonies of extreme debility, his friend, Mr. Dayrolles, called in to see him half an hour before he expired. The politeness which had become part of his very nature did not desert the dying earl. He managed to say, in a low voice, to his valet, "Give Dayrolles a chair." This little trait greatly struck the famous Dr. Warren, who was at the bedside of this brilliant and wonderful man. He died on the 24th of March, 1773, in the 79th year of his age.

The preamble to a codicil (Feb. 11, 1773) contains the following striking sentences, written when the intellect was impressed with the solemnity of that solemn change which comes alike to the unreflecting and to the heart-stricken holy believer:

"I most humbly recommend my soul to the extensive mercy of that Eternal, Supreme, Intelligent Being who gave it me; most earnestly, at the same time, deprecating his justice. Satiated with the pompous follies of this life, of which I have had an uncommon share, I would have no posthumous ones displayed at my funeral, and therefore desire to be buried in the next burying-place to the place where I shall die, and limit the whole expense of my funeral to £100."

His body was interred, according to his wish, in the vault of the chapel in South Audley Street, but it was afterward removed to the family burial-place in Shelford Church, Nottinghamshire.

In his will he left legacies to his servants.* "I consider them," he said, "as unfortunate friends; my equals by nature, and my inferiors only in the difference of our fortunes." There was something lofty in the mind that prompted that sentence.

His estates reverted to a distant kinsman, descended from a younger son of the first earl; and it is remarkable, on looking through the Peerage of Great Britain, to perceive how often this has been the case in a race remarkable for the absence of virtue. Interested marriages, vicious habits, perhaps account for the fact; but retributive justice, though it be presumptuous to trace its course, is every where.

He had so great a horror in his last days of gambling, that in bequeathing his possessions to his heir, as he expected, and godson, Philip Stanhope, he inserts this clause:

"In case my said godson, Philip Stanhope, shall at any time hereinafter keep, or be concerned in keeping of, any race-horses, or pack of hounds, or reside one night at Newmarket, that infamous seminary of iniquity and ill-manners, during the course of the races there; or shall resort to the said races; or shall lose, in any one day, at any game or bet whatsoever, the sum of £500, then, in any the cases aforesaid, it is my express will that he, my said godson, shall forfeit and pay, out of my estate, the sum of £5000 to and for the use of the Dean and Chapter of Westminster."

When we say that Lord Chesterfield was a man who had *no friend*, we sum up his character in those few words. Just after his death, a small but distinguished party of men dined together at Topham Beauclerk's. There was Sir Joshua Reynolds; Sir William Jones, the orientalist; Bennet Langton; Steevens; Boswell; Johnson. The conversation turned on Garrick, who, Johnson said, had friends, but no friend. Then Boswell asked, what is a friend? One who comforts and supports you, while others do not. "Friendship, you know, sir, is the cordial drop to make the nauseous draught of life go down." Then one of the company mentioned Lord Chesterfield as one who had no friend; and Boswell said: "Garrick was pure gold, but beat out to thin leaf, Lord Chesterfield was

* Two years' wages were left to the servants.

tinsel." And, for once, Johnson did not contradict him. But not so do we judge Lord Chesterfield. He was a man who acted on false principles through life; and those principles gradually undermined every thing that was noble and generous in character; just as those deep underground currents, noiseless in their course, work through fine-grained rock, and produce a chasm. Every thing with Chesterfield was self: for self, and for self alone, were agreeable qualities to be assumed; for self, was the country to be served, because that country protects and serves us; for self, were friends to be sought and cherished, as useful auxiliaries, or pleasant accessories: in the very core of the cankered heart, that advocated this corrupting doctrine of expediency, lay unbelief; that worm which never died in the hearts of so many illustrious men of that period—the refrigerator of the feelings.

One only gentle and genuine sentiment possessed Lord Chesterfield, and that was his love for his son. Yet in this affection the worldly man might be seen in mournful colors. He did not seek to render his son good; his sole desire was to see him successful: every lesson that he taught him, in those matchless Letters which have carried down Chesterfield's fame to us when his other productions have virtually expired, exposes a code of dissimulation which Philip Stanhope, in his marriage, turned upon the father to whom he owed so much care and advancement. These Letters are, in fact, a complete exposition of Lord Chesterfield's character and views of life. No other man could have written them; no other man have conceived the notion of existence being one great effort to deceive, as well as to excel, and of society forming one gigantic lie. It is true they were addressed to one who was to enter the maze of a diplomatic career, and must be taken, on that account, with some reservation.

They have justly been condemned on the score of immorality; but we must remember that the age in which they were written was one of lax notions, especially among men of rank, who regarded all women accessible, either from indiscretion or inferiority of rank, as fair game, and acted accordingly. But while we agree with one of Johnson's bitterest sentences as to the immorality of Chesterfield's letters, we disagree with his styling his code of manners the manners of a dancing-master. Chesterfield was in himself a perfect instance of what he calls *les manières nobles;* and this even Johnson allowed.

"Talking of Chesterfield," Johnson said, "his manner was exquisitely elegant, and he had more knowledge than I expected." Boswell: "Did you find, sir, his conversation to be of a superior sort?" Johnson: "Sir, in the conversation which

I had with him, I had the best right to superiority, for it was upon philology and literature."

It was well remarked how extraordinary a thing it was that a man who loved his son so entirely should do all he could to make him a rascal. And Foote even contemplated bringing on the stage a father who had thus tutored his son; and intended to show the son an honest man in every thing else, but practicing his father's maxims upon him, and cheating him.

"It should be so contrived," Johnson remarked, referring to Foote's plan, "that the father should be the *only* sufferer by the son's villainy, and thus there would be poetical justice." "Take out the immorality," he added, on another occasion, "and the book (Chesterfield's Letters to his Son) should be put into the hands of every young gentleman."

We are inclined to differ, and to confess to a moral taint throughout the whole of the Letters; and even had the immorality been expunged, the false motives, the deep, invariable advocacy of principles of expediency would have poisoned what otherwise might be of effectual benefit to the minor virtues of polite society.

THE ABBÉ SCARRON.

THERE is an Indian or Chinese legend, I forget which, from which Mrs. Shelley may have taken her hideous idea of Frankenstein. We are told in this allegory that, after fashioning some thousands of men after the most approved model, endowing them with all that is noble, generous, admirable, and lovable in man or woman, the eastern Prometheus grew weary in his work, stretched his hand for the beer-can, and draining it too deeply, lapsed presently into a state of what Germans call "other-man-ness." There is a simpler Anglo-Saxon term for this condition, but I spare you. The eastern Prometheus went on seriously with his work, and still produced the same perfect models, faultless alike in brain and leg. But when it came to the delicate finish, when the last touches were to be made, his hand shook a little, and the more delicate members went awry. It was thus that instead of the power of seeing every color properly, one man came out with a pair of optics which turned every thing to green, and this verdancy probably transmitted itself to the intelligence. Another, to continue the allegory, whose tympanum had slipped a little under the unsteady fingers of the man-maker, heard every thing in a wrong sense, and his life was miserable, because, if you sang his praises, he believed you were ridiculing him, and if you heaped abuse upon him, he thought you were telling lies of him.

But as Prometheus Orientalis grew more jovial, it seems to have come into his head to make mistakes on purpose. "I'll have a friend to laugh with," quoth he; and when warned by an attendant Yaksha, or demon, that men who laughed one hour often wept the next, he swore a lusty oath, struck his thumb heavily on a certain bump in the skull he was completing, and holding up his little doll, cried, "Here is one who will laugh at every thing!"

I must now add what the legend neglects to tell. The model laugher succeeded well enough in his own reign, but he could not beget a large family. The laughers who never weep, the real clowns of life, who do not, when the curtain drops, retire, after an infinitesimal allowance of "cordial," to a half-starved, complaining family, with brats that cling round his parti-colored stockings, and cry to him—not for jokes—but for bread, these laughers, I say, are few and far between. You should, therefore, be doubly grateful to me for introducing to you now one of the most famous of them; one who, with all right and title to be lugubrious, was the merriest man of his age.

On Shrove Tuesday, in the year 1638, the good city of Mans was in a state of great excitement: the carnival was at its height, and every body was gone mad for one day before turning pious for the long, dull forty days of Lent. The market-place was filled with maskers in quaint costumes, each wilder and more extravagant than the last. Here were magicians with high peaked hats covered with cabalistic signs, here Eastern sultans of the medieval model, with very fierce looks and very large cimeters: here Amadis de Gaul with a wagging plume a yard high, here Pantagruel, here harlequins, here Huguenots ten times more lugubrious than the despised sectaries they mocked, here Cæsar and Pompey in trunk hose and Roman helmets, and a mass of other notabilities who were great favorites in that day, appeared.

But who comes here? What is the meaning of these roars of laughter that greet the last mask who runs into the market-place? Why do all the women and children hurry together, calling up one another, and shouting with delight? What is this thing? Is it some new species of bird thus covered with feathers and down? In a few minutes the little figure is surrounded by a crowd of boys and women, who begin to pluck him of his borrowed plumes, while he chatters to them like a magpie, whistles like a song-bird, croaks like a raven, or in his natural character showers a mass of funny nonsense on them, till their laughter makes their sides ache. The little wretch is literally covered with small feathers from head to foot, and even his face is not to be recognized. The women pluck him behind and before; he dances round and tries to evade their fingers. This is impossible; he breaks away, runs down the market pursued by a shouting crowd, is again surrounded, and again subjected to a plucking process. The bird must be stripped; he must be discovered. Little by little his back is bared, and little by little is seen a black jerkin, black stockings, and, wonder upon wonder! the bands of a canon. Now they have cleared his face of its plumage, and a cry of disgust and shame hails the disclosure. Yes, this curious masker is no other than a reverend abbé, a young canon of the cathedral of Mans! "This is too much—it is scandalous—it is disgraceful. The church must be respected, the sacred order must not descend to such frivolities." The people, lately laughing, are now furious at the shameless abbé, and not his liveliest wit can save him; they threaten and cry shame on him, and in terror of his life, he beats his way through the crowd, and takes to his heels. The mob follows hooting and savage. The little man is nimble; those well-shaped legs—*qui ont si bien dansé*—stand him in good stead. Down the streets, and out of the town go hare and hounds. The pursuers gain on him—a bridge, a stream filled with tall reeds, and delightfully miry, are all the hope of refuge he sees before him. He leaps gallantly from the bridge in among the osiers, and has the joy of listening to the disappointed curses of the mob, when reaching the stream their quarry is nowhere to be seen. The reeds conceal him, and there he lingers till nightfall, when he can issue from his lurking-place and escape from the town.

Such was the mad freak which deprived the Abbé Scarron of the use of his limbs for life. His health was already ruined when he indulged in this caprice; the damp of the river brought on a violent attack, which closed with palsy, and the gay young abbé had to pay dearly for the pleasure of astonishing the citizens of Mans. The disguise was easily accounted for—he had smeared himself with honey, ripped open a feather-bed, and rolled himself in it.

This little incident gives a good idea of what Scarron was in his younger days—ready at any time for any wild caprice.

Paul Scarron was the son of a Conseiller du Parlement of good family, resident in Paris. He was born in 1610, and his early days would have been wretched enough, if his elastic spirits had allowed him to give way to misery. His father was a good-natured, weak-minded man, who on the death of his first wife married a second, who, as one hen will peck at another's chicks, would not, as a stepmother, leave the little Paul in peace. She was continually putting her own children forward, and ill treating the late "anointed" son. The father gave in too readily, and young Paul was glad enough to be set free from his unhappy home. There may be some excuse in this for the licentious living to which he now gave himself up. He was heir to a decent fortune, and of course thought himself justified in spending it beforehand. Then, in spite of his quaint little figure, he had something attractive about him, for his merry face was good-looking, if not positively handsome. If we add to this, spirits as buoyant as an Irishman's —a mind that not only saw the ridiculous wherever it existed, but could turn the most solemn and awful themes to laughter, a vast deal of good-nature, and not a little assurance—we can understand that the young Scarron was a favorite with both men and women, and among the reckless pleasure-seekers of the day soon became one of the wildest. In short, he was a fast young

Parisian, with as little care for morality or religion as any youth who saunters on the Boulevards of the French capital to this day.

But his stepmother was not content with getting rid of young Paul, but had her eye also on his fortune, and therefore easily persuaded her husband that the service of the church was precisely the career for which the young reprobate was fitted. There was an uncle who was Bishop of Grenoble, and a canonry could easily be got for him. The fast youth was compelled to give into this arrangement, but declined to take full orders; so that while drawing the revenue of his stall, he had nothing to do with the duties of his calling. Then, too, it was rather a fashionable thing to be an abbé, especially a gay one. The position placed you on a level with people of all ranks. Half the court was composed of love-making ecclesiastics, and the *soutane* was a kind of diploma for wit and wickedness. Viewed in this light, the church was as jovial a profession as the army, and the young Scarron went to the full extent of the letter allowed to the black gown. It was only such stupid superstitious louts as those of Mans, who did not know any thing of the ways of Paris life, who could object to such little freaks as he loved to indulge in.

The merry little abbé was soon the delight of the Marais. This distinct and antiquated quarter of Paris was then the May-fair of that capital. Here lived in ease, and contempt of the bourgeoisie, the great, the gay, the courtier, and the wit. Here Marion de Lorme received old cardinals and young abbés; here were the salons of Madame de Martel, of the Comtesse de la Suze, who changed her creed in order to avoid seeing her husband in this world or the next, and the famous —or infamous—Ninon de l'Enclos; and at these houses young Scarron met the courtly Saint-Evremond, the witty Sarrazin, and the learned, but arrogant Voiture. Here he read his skits and parodies, here travestied Virgil, made epigrams on Richelieu, and poured out his indelicate but always laughable witticisms. But his indulgences were not confined to intrigues; he also drank deep, and there was not a pleasure within his reach, which he ever thought of denying himself. He laughed at religion, thought morality a nuisance, and resolved to be merry at all costs.

The little account was brought in at last. At the age of five-and-twenty his constitution was broken up. Gout and rheumatism assailed him alternately or in leash. He began to feel the annoyance of the constraint they occasioned; he regretted those legs which had figured so well in a ronde or a minuet, and those hands which had played the lute to dames more fair than modest; and, to add to this, the pain he suffered was not slight. He sought relief in gay society, and was cheerful in spite of his sufferings. At length came the Shrove Tuesday and the feathers; and the consequences were terrible. He was soon a prey to doctors, whom he believed in no more than in the church of which he was so great a light. His legs were no longer his own, so he was obliged to borrow those of a chair. He was soon tucked down into a species of dumb-waiter on castors, in which he could be rolled about in a party, just as the late Lady Charleville was. In front of this chair was fastened a desk, on which he wrote; for too wise to be overcome by his agony, he drove it away by cultivating his imagination, and in this way some of the most fantastic productions in French literature were composed by this quaint little abbé.

Nor was sickness his only trial now. Old Scarron was a citizen, and had, what was then criminal, sundry ideas of the liberty of the nation. He saw with disgust the tyranny of Richelieu, and joined a party in the Parliament to oppose the cardinal's measures. He even had the courage to speak openly against one of the court edicts; and the pitiless cardinal, who never overlooked any offense, banished him to Touraine, and naturally extended his animosity to the conseiller's son. This happened at a moment at which the cripple believed himself to be on the road to favor. He had already won that of Madame de Hautefort, on whom Louis XIII. had set his affections, and this lady had promised to present him to Anne of Austria. The father's honest boldness put a stop to the son's intended servility, and Scarron lamented his fate in a letter to Pellisson:

"O mille écus, par malheur retranchés,
Que vous pouviez m'épargner de péchés!
Quand un valet me dit, tremblant et hâve,
Nous n'avons plus de bûches dans la cave
Que pour aller jusqu'à demain matin,
Je peste alors sur mon chien de destin,
Sur le grand froid, sur le bois de la grève,
Qu'on vend si cher, et qui si-tôt s'achève.
Je jure alors, et méme je médis
De l'action de mon père étourdi,
Quand sans songer à ce qu'il allait faire
Il m'ébaucha sous un astre contraire,
Et m'acheva par un discours maudit
Qu'il fit depuis sur un certain édit."

The father died in exile: his second wife had spent the greater part of the son's fortune, and secured the rest for her own children. Scarron was left with a mere pittance, and, to complete his troubles, was involved in a lawsuit about the property. The cripple, with his usual impudence, resolved to plead his own cause, and did it only too well; he made the judges laugh so loud that they took the whole thing to be a farce on his part, and gave—most ungratefully—judgment against him.

Glorious days were those for the penniless, halcyon days for the toady and the sycophant. There was still much of the old oriental munificence about the court, and sovereigns like Mazarin and Louis XIV. granted pensions for a copy of flattering verses, or gave away places as the reward of a judicious speech. Sinecures were legion, yet to many a holder they were no sinecures at all, for they entailed constant servility and a complete abdication of all freedom of opinion.

Scarron was nothing more than a merry buffoon. Many another man has gained a name for his mirth, but most of them have been at least independent. Scarron seems to have cared for nothing that was honorable or dignified. He laughed at every thing but money, and at that he smiled, though it is only fair to say that he was never avaricious, but only cared for ease and a little luxury.

When Richelieu died, and the gentler, but more subtle Mazarin mounted his throne, Madame de Hautefort made another attempt to present her *protégé* to the queen, and this time succeeded. Anne of Austria had heard of the quaint little man who could laugh over a lawsuit in which his whole fortune was staked, and received him graciously. He begged for some place to support him. What could he do? What was he fit for? "Nothing, your majesty, but the important office of The Queen's Patient; for that I am fully qualified." Anne smiled, and Scarron from that time styled himself "par la grace de Dieu, le malade de la Reine." But there was no stipend attached to this novel office. Mazarin procured him a pension of 500 crowns. He was then publishing his "Typhon, or the Gigantomachy," and dedicated it to the cardinal, with an adulatory sonnet. He forwarded the great man a splendidly-bound copy, which was accepted with nothing more than thanks. In a rage the author suppressed the sonnet and substituted a satire. This piece was bitterly cutting, and terribly true. It galled Mazarin to the heart, and he was undignified enough to revenge himself by canceling the poor little pension of £60 per annum which had previously been granted to the writer. Scarron having lost his pension, soon afterward asked for an abbey, but was refused. "Then give me," said he, "a simple benefice, so simple, indeed, that all its duties will be comprised in believing in God." But Scarron had the satisfaction of gaining a great name among the cardinal's many enemies, and with none more so than De Retz, then *coadju-*

*teur** to the Archbishop of Paris, and already deeply implicated in the Fronde movement. To insure the favor of this rising man, Scarron determined to dedicate to him a work he was just about to publish, and on which he justly prided himself as by far his best. This was the "Roman Comique," the only one of his productions which is still read. That it should be read, I can quite understand, on account not only of the ease of its style, but of the ingenuity of its improbable plots, the truth of the characters, and the charming bits of satire which are found here and there, like gems, amid a mass of mere fun. The scene is laid at Mans, the town in which the author had himself perpetrated his chief follies; and many of the characters were probably drawn from life, while it is likely enough that some of the stories were taken from facts which had there come to his knowledge. As in many of the romances of that age, a number of episodes are introduced into the main story, which consists of the adventures of a strolling company. These are mainly amatory, and all indelicate, while some are positively dirty, and as coarse as any thing in French literature. Scarron had little of the clear wit of Rabelais to atone for this; but he makes up for it, in a measure, by the utter absurdity of some of his incidents. Not the least curious part of the book is the Preface, in which he gives a description of himself, in order to contradict, as he affirms, the extravagant reports circulated about him, to the effect that he was set upon a table in a cage, or that his hat was fastened to the ceiling by a pulley, that he might "pluck it up or let it down, to do compliment to a friend, who honored him with a visit." This description is a tolerable specimen of his style, and we give it in the quaint language of an old translation, published in 1741:

"I am past thirty, as thou may'st see by the back of my Chair. If I live to be forty, I shall add the Lord knows how many Misfortunes to those I have already suffered for these eight or nine Years last past. There was a Time when my Stature was not to be found Fault with, tho' now 'tis of the smallest. My Sickness has taken me shorter by a Foot. My Head is somewhat too big, considering my Height; and my Face is full enough, in all Conscience, for one that carries such a Skeleton of a Body about him. I have Hair enough on my Head not to stand in need of a Peruke; and 'tis gray, too, in spight of the Proverb. My Sight is good enough, tho' my Eyes are large; they are of a blue Color, and one of them is sunk deeper into my Head than the other, which was occasion'd by my leaning on that Side. My Nose is well enough mounted. My Teeth, which in the Days of Yore look'd like

* *Coadjuteur.*—A high office in the Church of Rome.

a Row of square Pearl, are now of an Ashen Color; and in a few Years more, will have the Complexion of a Small-coal Man's Saturday Shirt. I have lost one Tooth and a half on the left Side, and two and a half precisely on the right; and I have two more that stand somewhat out of their Ranks. My Legs and Thighs, in the first place, compose an obtuse Angle, then a right one, and lastly an acute. My Thighs and Body make another; and my Head, leaning perpetually over my Belly, I fancy makes me not very unlike the Letter Z. My Arms are shortened, as well as my Legs; and my Fingers as well as my Arms. In short, I am a living Epitome of human Misery. This, as near as I can give it, is my Shape. Since I am got so far, I will e'en tell thee something of my Humor. Under the Rose, be it spoken, Courteous Reader, I do this only to swell the Bulk of my Book, at the Request of the Bookseller—the poor Dog, it seems, being afraid he should be a Loser by this Impression, if he did not give Buyer enough for his Money."

This allusion to the publisher reminds us that, on the suppression of his pension—on hearing of which Scarron only said, "I should like, then, to suppress myself"—he had to live on the profits of his works. In later days it was Madame Scarron herself who often carried them to the bookseller's, when there was not a penny in the house. The publisher was Quinet, and the merry wit, when asked whence he drew his income, used to reply with mock haughtiness, "De mon Marquisat de Quinet." His comedies, which have been described as mere burlesques—I confess I have never read them, and hope to be absolved—were successful enough, and if Scarron had known how to keep what he made, he might sooner or later have been in easy circumstances. He knew neither that nor any other art of self-restraint, and, therefore, was in perpetual vicissitudes of riches and penury. At one time he could afford to dedicate a piece to his sister's greyhound, at another he was servile in his address to some prince or duke.

In the latter spirit, he humbled himself before Mazarin, in spite of the publication of his "Mazarinade," and was, as he might have expected, repulsed. He then turned to Fouquet, the new Surintendant de Finances, who was liberal enough with the public money, which he so freely embezzled, and extracted from him a pension of 1600 francs (about £64). In one way or another, he got back a part of the property his stepmother had alienated from him, and obtained a prebend in the diocese of Mans, which made up his income to something more respectable.

He was now able to indulge to the utmost his love of society. In his apartment, in the Rue St. Louis, he received all the leaders of the Fronde, headed by De Retz, and bringing with them their pasquinades on Mazarin, which the easy Italian read and laughed at and pretended to heed not at all. Politics, however, was not the staple of the conversation at Scarron's. He was visited as a curiosity, as a clever buffoon, and those who came to see, remained to laugh. He kept them all alive by his coarse, easy, impudent wit; in which there was more vulgarity and dirtiness than ill-nature. He had a fund of *bonhommie*, which set his visitors at their ease, for no one was afraid of being bitten by the chained dog they came to pat. His salon became famous; and the admission to it was a diploma of wit. He kept out all the dull, and ignored all the simply great. Any man who could say a good thing, tell a good story, write a good lampoon, or mimic a fool, was a welcome guest. Wits mingled with pedants, courtiers with poets. Abbés and gay women were at home in the easy society of the cripple, and circulated freely round his dumb-waiter.

The ladies of the party were not the most respectable in Paris, yet some who were models of virtue met there, without a shudder, many others who were patterns of vice. Ninon de l'Enclos—then young—though age made no alteration in *her*—and already slaying her scores, and ruining her hundreds of admirers, there met Madame de Sévigné, the most respectable, as well as the most agreeable, woman of that age. Mademoiselle de Scudéry, leaving, for the time, her twelve-volume romance, about Cyrus and Ibrahim, led on a troop of Molière's Précieuses Ridicules, and here recited her verses, and talked pedantically to Pellisson, the ugliest man in Paris, of whom Boileau wrote:

"L'or même à Pellisson donne un teint de beauté."

Then there was Madame de la Sablière, who was as masculine as her husband the marquis was effeminate; the Duchesse de Lesdiguières, who was so anxious to be thought a wit that she employed the Chevalier de Méré to make her one; and the Comtesse de la Suze, a clever but foolish woman.

The men were poets, courtiers, and pedants. Ménage with his tiresome memory, Montreuil and Marigni the song-writers, the elegant De Grammont, Turenne, Coligni, the gallant Abbé Têtu, and many another celebrity, thronged the rooms where Scarron sat in his curious wheelbarrow.

The conversation was decidedly light; often, indeed, obscene, in spite of the presence of ladies; but always witty. The hostility of Scarron to the reigning cardinal was a great recommendation, and when all else flagged, or the cripple had an unusually sharp attack, he had but to start with a line of his "Mazarinade," and out came a fresh lampoon, a new caricature, or fresh rounds of wit fired off at the Italian, from the well-filled cartridge-boxes of the guests, many of whom kept their *mots* ready made up for discharge.

But a change came over the spirit of the paralytic's dream. In the Rue St. Louis, close to Scarron's, lived a certain Madame Neuillant, who visited him as a neighbor, and one day excited his curiosity by the romantic history of a mother and daughter, who had long lived in Martinique, who had been ruined by the extravagance and follies of a reprobate husband and father; and were now living in great poverty—the daughter being supported by Madame de Neuillant herself. The good-natured cripple was touched by this story, and begged his neighbor to bring the unhappy ladies to one of his parties. The evening came; the abbé was, as usual, surrounded by a circle of lady-wits, dressed in the last fashions, flaunting their fans, and laughing merrily at his sallies. Madame de Neuillant was announced, and entered, followed by a simply-dressed lady, with the melancholy face of one broken down by misfortunes, and a pretty girl of fifteen. The contrast between the new-comers and the fashionable *habituées* around him at once struck the abbé. The girl was not only badly, but even shabbily dressed, and the shortness of her gown showed that she had grown out of it, and could not afford a new one. The *grandes dames* turned upon her their eye-glasses, and whispered comments behind their fans. She was very pretty, they said, very interesting, elegant, lady-like, and so on; but, *parbleu!* how shamefully *mal mise!* The new-comers were led up to the cripple's dumb-waiter, and the *grandes dames* drew back their ample petticoats as they passed. The young girl was overcome with shame; their whispers reached her; she cast down her pretty eyes, and growing more and more confused, she could bear it no longer, and burst into tears. The abbé and his guests were touched by her shyness, and endeavored to restore her confidence. Scarron himself leaned over, and whispered a few kind words in her ear; then breaking out into some happy pleasantry, he gave her time to recover her composure. Such was the first *début*, in Parisian society, of Françoise d'Aubigné, who was destined, as Madame Scarron, to be afterward one of its leaders, and, as Madame de Maintenon, to be its ruler.

Some people are cursed with bad sons—some with erring daughters. Françoise d'Aubigné was long the victim of a wicked father. Constans d'Aubigné belonged to an old and honorable family, and was the son of that famous old Hugue-

SCARRON AND THE WITS—FIRST APPEARANCE OF LA BELLE INDIENNE.

not general, Théodore-Agrippa d'Aubigné, who fought for a long time under Henry of Navarre, and in his old age wrote the history of his times. To counterbalance this distinction, the son Constans brought all the discredit he could on the family. After a reckless life, in which he squandered his patrimony, he married a rich widow, and then, it is said, contrived to put her out of the way. He was imprisoned as a murderer, but acquitted for want of evidence. The story goes, that he was liberated by the daughter of the governor of the jail, whom he had seduced in the prison, and whom he married when free. He sought to retrieve his fortune in the island of Martinique, ill-treated his wife, and eventually ran away and left her and her children to their fate. They followed him to France, and found him again incarcerated. Madame d'Aubigné was foolishly fond of her good-for-nothing spouse, and lived with him in his cell, where the little Françoise, who had been born in prison, was now educated.

Rescued from starvation by a worthy Huguenot aunt, Madame de Villette, the little girl was brought up as a Protestant, and a very stanch one she proved for a time. But Madame d'Aubigné, who was a Romanist, would not allow her to remain long under the Calvinistic lady's protection, and sent her to be converted by her godmother, the Madame de Neuillant above mentioned. This woman, who was as merciless as a woman can be, literally broke her into Romanism, treated her like a servant, made her groom the horses, and comb the maid's hair, and when all these efforts failed, sent her to a convent to be finished off. The nuns did by specious reasoning what had been begun by persecution, and young Françoise, at the time she was introduced to Scarron, was a highly respectable member of "the only true church."

Madame d'Aubigné was at this time supporting herself by needle-work. Her sad story won the sympathy of Scarron's guests, who united to relieve her wants. *La belle Indienne*, as the cripple styled her, soon became a favorite at his parties, and lost her shyness by degrees. Ninon de l'Enclos, who did not want heart, took her by the hand, and a friendship thus commenced between that inveterate Laïs and the future wife of Louis XIV. which lasted till death.

The beauty of Françoise soon brought her many admirers, among whom was even one of Ninon's slaves; but as marriage was not the object of these attentions, and the young girl would not relinquish her virtue, she remained for some time unmarried, but respectable. Scarron was particularly fond of her, and well knew that, portionless as she was, the poor girl would have but little chance of making a match.

His kindness touched her, his wit charmed her; she pitied his infirmities, and, as his neighbor, frequently saw and tried to console him. On the other hand the cripple, though forty years old, and in a state of health which it is impossible to describe, fell positively in love with the young girl, who alone of all the ladies who visited him combined wit with perfect modesty. He pitied her destitution. There was mutual pity, and we all know what passion that feeling is akin to.

Still, for a paralytic, utterly unfit for marriage in any point of view, to offer to a beautiful young girl, would have seemed ridiculous, if not unpardonable. But let us take into account the difference in ideas of matrimony between ourselves and the French. We must remember that marriage has always been regarded among our neighbors as a contract for mutual benefit, into which the consideration of money of necessity entered largely. It is true that some qualities are taken as equivalents for actual cash: thus, if a young man has a straight and well-cut nose, he may sell himself at a higher price than young Lefèvre there with the hideous pug; if a girl is beautiful, the marquis will be content with some thousands of francs less for her dower than if her hair were red or her complexion irreclaimably brown. If Julie has a pretty foot, a *svelte* waist, and can play the piano thunderingly, or sing in the charmingest soprano, her ten thousand francs are quite as acceptable as those of stout, awkward, glum-faced Jeannette. The faultless boots and yellow kids of young Adolphe counterbalance the somewhat apocryphal vicomté of ill-kempt and ill-attired Henri.

But then there must be *some* fortune. A Frenchman is so much in the habit of expecting it, that he thinks it almost a crime to fall in love where there is none. Françoise, pretty, clever, agreeable as she was, was penniless, and even worse, she was the daughter of a man who had been imprisoned on suspicion of murder, and a woman who had gained her livelihood by needle-work. All these considerations made the fancy of the merry abbé less ridiculous, and Françoise herself being sufficiently versed in the ways of the world to understand the disadvantage under which she labored, was less amazed and disgusted than another girl might have been, when, in due course, the cripple offered her himself and his dumb-waiter. He had little more to give—his pension, a tiny income from his prebend and his Marquisat de Quinet.

The offer of the little man was not so amusing as other episodes of his life. He went honestly to work; represented to her what a sad lot would hers be, if Madame de Neuillant died, and what were the temptations of beauty without a penny. His arguments were more to the point than delicate, and he talked to the young girl as if she was a woman of the world. Still, she accepted him, cripple as he was.

Madame de Neuillant made no objection, for she was only too glad to be rid of a beauty who ate and drank, but did not marry.

On the making of the contract, Scarron's fun revived. When asked by the notary what was the young lady's fortune, he replied: "Four louis, two large wicked eyes, one fine figure, one pair of good hands, and lots of mind." "And what do you give her?" asked the lawyer. "Immortality," replied he, with the air of a bombastic poet. "The names of the wives of kings die with them—that of Scarron's wife will live forever!"

His marriage obliged him to give up his canonry, which he sold to Ménage's man-servant, a little bit of simony which was not even noticed in those days. It is amusing to find a man who laughed at all religion, insisting that his wife should make a formal avowal of the Romish faith. Of the character of this marriage we need say no more than that Scarron had at that time the use of no more than his eyes, tongue, and hands. Yet such was then, as now, the idea of matrimony in France, that the young lady's friends considered her fortunate.

Scarron in love was a picture which amazed and amused the whole society of Paris, but Scarron married was still more curious. The queen, when she heard of it, said that Françoise would be nothing but a useless bit of furniture in his house. She proved not only the most useful appendage he could have, but the salvation alike of his soul and his reputation. The woman who charmed Louis XIV. by her good sense, had enough of it to see Scarron's faults, and prided herself on reforming him as far as it was possible. Her husband had hitherto been the great Nestor of indelicacy, and when he was induced to give it up, the rest followed his example. Madame Scarron checked the license of the abbé's conversation, and even worked a beneficial change in his mind.

The joviality of their parties still continued. Scarron had always been famous for his *petits soupers*, the fashion of which he introduced, but as his poverty would not allow him to give them in proper style, his friends made a picnic of it, and each one either brought or sent his own dish of ragout, or whatever it might be, and his own bottle of wine. This does not seem to have been the case after the marriage, however; for it is related as a proof of Madame Scarron's conversational powers, that, when one evening a poorer supper than usual was served, the waiter whispered in her ear, "Tell them another story, Madame, if you please, for we have no joint to-night." Still both guests and host could well afford to dispense with the coarseness of the cripple's talk, which might raise a laugh, but must sometimes have caused disgust, and the young wife of sixteen succeeded in making him purer both in his conversation and his writings.

The household she entered was indeed a villainous one. Scarron rather gloried in his early delinquencies, and, to add to this, his two sisters had characters far from estimable. One of them had been maid of honor to the Princesse de Conti, but had given up her appointment to become the mistress of the Duc de Trêmes. The laugher laughed even at his sister's dishonor, and allowed her to live in the same house on a higher *étage*. When, on one occasion, some one called on him to solicit the lady's interest with the duke, he coolly said, "You are mistaken; it is not I who know the duke; go up to the next story." The offspring of this connection he styled "his nephews after the fashion of the Marais." Françoise did her best to reclaim this sister and to conceal her shame, but the laughing abbé made no secret of it.

But the laugher was approaching his end. His attacks became more and more violent: still he laughed at them. Once he was seized with a terrible choking hiccough, which threatened to suffocate him. The first moment he could speak he cried, "If I get well, I'll write a satire on the hiccough." The priests came about him, and his wife did what she could to bring him to a sense of his future danger. He laughed at the priests and at his wife's fears. She spoke of hell. "If there is such a place," he answered, "it won't be for me, for without you I must have had my hell in this life." The priest told him, by way of consolation, that "God had visited him more than any man." "He does me too much honor," answered the mocker. "You should give him thanks," urged the ecclesiastic. "I can't see for what," was the shameless answer.

On his death-bed he parodied a will, leaving to Corneille "two hundred pounds of patience; to Boileau (with whom he had a long feud), the gangrene; and to the Academy, the power to alter the French language as they liked." His legacy in verse to his wife is grossly disgusting, and quite unfit for quotation. Yet he loved her well, avowed that his chief grief in dying was the necessity of leaving her, and begged her to remember him sometimes, and to lead a virtuous life.

His last moments were as jovial as any. When he saw his friends weeping around him he shook his head and cried,

"I shall never make you weep as much as I have made you laugh." A little later a softer thought of hope came across him. "No more sleeplessness, no more gout," he murmured; "the Queen's patient will be well at last." At length the laugher was sobered. In the presence of death, at the gates of a new world, he muttered, half afraid, "I never thought it was so easy to laugh at death," and so expired. This was in October, 1660, when the cripple had reached the age of fifty.

Thus died a laugher. It is unnecessary here to trace the story of his widow's strange rise to be the wife of a king. Scarron was no honor to her, and in later years she tried to forget his existence. Boileau fell into disgrace for merely mentioning his name before the king. Yet Scarron was in many respects a better man than Louis; and, laugher as he was, he had a good heart. There is a time for mirth and a time for mourning, the Preacher tells us. Scarron never learned this truth, and he laughed too much and too long. Yet let us not end the laugher's life in sorrow:

"It is well to be merry and wise," etc.

Let us be merry as the poor cripple, who bore his sufferings so well, and let us be wise too. There is a lesson for gay and grave in the life of Scarron, the laugher.

FRANCOIS, DUC DE LA ROCHEFOUCAULT, AND THE DUC DE SAINT-SIMON.

The precursor of Saint-Simon, the model of Lord Chesterfield, this ornament of his age belonged, as well as Saint-Simon, to that state of society in France which was characterized—as Lord John Russell, in his "Memoirs of the Duchess of Orleans," tells us—by an idolatry of power and station. "God would not condemn a person of that rank," was the exclamation of a lady of the old *régime*, on hearing that a notorious sinner, "Pair de France," and one knows not what else, had gone to his account impenitent and unabsolved; and though the sentiment may strike us as profane, it was, doubtless, genuine.

Rank, however, was often adorned by accomplishments which, like an exemption from rules of conduct, it almost claimed as a privilege. Good-breeding was a science in France; natural to a peasant, even, it was studied as an epitome of all the social virtues. "*N'être pas poli*" was the sum total of all dispraise: a man could only recover from it by splendid valor or rare gifts; a woman could not hope to rise out of that Slough of Despond to which good-breeding never came. We were behind all the arts of civilization in England, as François de Rochefoucault (we give the orthography of the present day) was in his cradle. This brilliant personage, who combined the wit and the moralist, the courtier and the soldier, the man of literary tastes and the sentimentalist *par excellence*, was born in 1613. In addition to his hereditary title of duc, he had the empty honor, as Saint-Simon calls it, of being Prince de Marsillac, a designation which was lost in that of *De la Rochefoucault*—so famous even to the present day. As he presented himself at the court of the regency, over which Anne of Austria nominally presided, no youth there was more distinguished for his elegance or for the fame of his exploits during the wars of the Fronde than this youthful scion of an illustrious house. Endowed by nature with a pleasing countenance, and, what was far more important in that fastidious region, an air of dignity, he displayed wonderful contradictions in his character and bearing. He had, says Madame de Maintenon, "*beaucoup d'esprit, et peu de savoir;*" an expressive phrase. "He was," she adds, "pliant in nature, intriguing, and cautious;" nevertheless she never, she declares, possessed a more steady friend, nor one more confiding and better adapted to advise. Brave as he was, he held personal valor, or affected to do so, in light estimation. His ambition was to rule others. Lively in conversation, though naturally pensive, he assembled around him all that Paris or Versailles could present of wit and intellect.

The old Hôtel de Rochefoucault, in the Rue de Seine, in the Faubourg St. Germain, in Paris, still grandly recalls the assemblies in which Racine, Boileau, Madame de Sévigné, the La Fayettes, and the famous Duchesse de Longueville, used to assemble. The time-honored family of De la Rochefoucault still preside there; though one of its fairest ornaments, the young, lovely, and pious Duchesse de la Rochefoucault of our time, died in 1852—one of the first known victims to diphtheria in France, in that unchanged old locality. There, where the De Longuevilles, the Mazarins, and those who had formed the famous council of state of Anne of Austria had disappeared, the poets and wits who gave to the age of Louis XIV. its true brilliancy, collected around the Duc de la Rochefoucault. What a scene it must have been, in those days when, as Buffon said of the earth in spring, "*tout fourmille de vie!*" Let us people the salon of the Hôtel de Rochefoucault with visions of the past; see the host there, in his chair, a martyr to the gout, which he bore with all the cheerfulness of a Frenchman, and picture to ourselves the great men who were handing him his cushion, or standing near his *fauteuil*.

Racine's joyous face may be imagined as he comes in fresh from the College of Harcourt. Since he was born in 1639, he had not arrived at his zenith till La Rochefoucault was almost past his prime. For a man at thirty-six in France can no longer talk prospectively of the departure of youth; it is gone. A single man of thirty, even in Paris, is "*un vieux garçon*:" life begins too soon and ends too soon with those pleasant sinners, the French. And Racine, when he was first routed out of Port Royal, where he was educated, and presented to the whole Faubourg St. Germain, beheld his patron, La Rochefoucault, in the position of a disappointed man. An early adventure of his youth had humbled, perhaps, the host of the Hôtel de Rochefoucault. At the battle of St. Antoine, where he had distinguished himself, a musket ball had nearly deprived him of sight. On this occasion he had quoted these lines, taken from the tragedy of "*Alcyonnée*." It must, however, be premised that the famous Duchesse de Longueville had urged him to engage in the wars of the Fronde. To her these lines were addressed:

"Pour mériter son cœur, pour plaire à ses beaux yeux,
J'ai fait la guerre aux Rois, je l'aurais faite aux dieux."

But now he had broken off his intimacy with the duchesse, and he therefore parodied these lines:

"Pour ce cœur inconstant, qu'enfin je connais mieux,
J'ai fait la guerre aux Rois, j'en ai perdue les yeux."

Nevertheless La Rochefoucault was still the gay, charming, witty host and courtier. Racine composed, in 1660, his "*Nymphe de Seine*," in honor of the marriage of Louis XIV., and was then brought into notice of those whose notice was no empty compliment, such as, in our day, illustrious dukes pay to more illustrious authors, by asking them to be jumbled in a crowd at a time when the rooks are beginning to caw. We catch, as they may, the shadow of a dissolving water-ice, or see the exit of an unattainable tray of negus. No; in the days of Racine, as in those of Halifax and Swift in England, solid fruits grew out of fulsome praise; and Colbert, then minister, settled a pension of six hundred livres, as francs were called in those days (twenty-four pounds), on the poet. And with this the former pupil of Port Royal was fain to be content. Still he was so poor that he *almost* went into the church, an uncle offering to resign him a priory of his order if he would become a regular. He was a candidate for orders, and wore a sacerdotal dress when he wrote the tragedy of "Theagenes," and that of the "Frères Ennemis," the subject of which was given him by Molière.

He continued, in spite of a quarrel with the saints of Port Royal, to produce noble dramas from time to time, but quitted theatrical pursuits after bringing out (in 1677) "Phèdre," that *chef-d'œuvre* not only of its author, but, as a performance, of the unhappy but gifted Rachel. Corneille was old, and Paris looked to Racine to supply his place, yet he left the theatrical world forever. Racine had been brought up with deep religious convictions; they could not, however, preserve him from a mad, unlawful attachment. He loved the actress Champmesle: but repentance came. He resolved not only to write no more plays, but to do penance for those already given to the world. He was on the eve of becoming, in his penitence, a Carthusian friar, when his religious director advised marriage instead. He humbly did as he was told, and united himself to the daughter of a treasurer for France, of Amiens, by whom he had seven children. It was only at the request of Madame de Maintenon that he wrote "Esther" for the convent of St. Cyr, where it was first acted.

His death was the result of his benevolent, sensitive nature.

Having drawn up an excellent paper on the miseries of the people, he gave it to Madame de Maintenon to read it to the king. Louis, in a transport of ill-humor, said, "What! does he suppose because he is a poet that he ought to be minister of state?" Racine is said to have been so wounded by this speech that he was attacked by a fever and died. His decease took place in 1699, nineteen years after that of La Rochefoucault, who died in 1680.

Among the circle whom La Rochefoucault loved to assemble was Boileau, Despréaux, and Madame de Sévigné—the one whose wit and the other whose grace completed the delights of that salon. A life so prosperous as La Rochefouçault's had but one cloud—the death of his son, who was killed during the passage of the French troops over the Rhine. We attach to the character of this accomplished man the charms of wit; we may also add the higher attractions of sensibility. Notwithstanding the worldly and selfish character which is breathed forth in his "Maxims and Reflections," there lay at the bottom of his heart true piety. Struck by the death of a neighbor, this sentiment seems even on the point of being expressed; but, adds Madame de Sévigné, and her phrase is untranslatable, "*il n'est pas effleuré.*"

All has passed away! the *Fronde* has become a memory, not a realized idea. Old people shake their heads, and talk of Richelieu; of his gorgeous palace at Rueil, with its lake and its prison thereon, and its mysterious dungeons, and its avenues of chestnuts, and its fine statues; and of its cardinal, smiling, while the worm that never dieth is eating into his very heart; a seared conscience, and playing the fine gentleman to fine ladies in a rich stole, and with much garniture of costly lace; while beneath all is the hair shirt, that type of penitence and sanctity which he ever wore as a salvo against all that passion and ambition that almost burst the beating heart beneath that hair shirt. Richelieu has gone to his fathers. Mazarin comes on the scene; the wily, grasping Italian. He too vanishes; and forth, radiant in youth, and strong in power, comes Louis, and the reign of politeness and periwigs begins.

The Duc de Saint-Simon, perhaps the greatest portrait-painter of any time, has familiarized us with the greatness, the littleness, the graces, the defects of that royal actor on the stage of Europe, whom his own age entitled Louis the Great. A wit, in his writings, of the first order—if we comprise under the head of wit the deepest discernment, the most penetrating satire—Saint-Simon was also a soldier, philosopher, a reformer, a Trappist, and, eventually, a devotee. Like all young men who wished for court favor, he began by fighting: Louis cared little for carpet knights. He entered, however, into a scene which he has chronicled with as much fidelity as our journalists do a police report, and sat quietly down to gather up observations—not for his own fame, not even for the amusement of his children or grandchildren—but for the edification of posterity yet a century afar off his own time. The treasures were buried until 1829.

A word or two about Saint-Simon and his youth. At nineteen he was destined by his mother to be married. Now every one knows how marriages are managed in France, not only in the time of Saint-Simon, but even to the present day. A mother, or an aunt, or a grandmother, or an experienced friend, looks out; be it for son, be it for daughter, it is the business of her life. She looks and she finds: family, suitable; fortune, convenient; person, *pas mal;* principles, Catholic, with a due abhorrence of heretics, especially English ones. After a time, the lady is to be looked at by the unhappy *prétendû;* a church, a mass, or vespers, being very often the opportunity agreed. The victim thinks she will do. The proposal is discussed by the two mammas; relatives are called in; all goes well; the contract is signed; then, a measured acquaintance is allowed: but no *tête-à-têtes;* no idea of love. "What! so indelicate a sentiment before marriage! Let me not hear of it," cries mamma, in a sanctimonious panic. "Love! *Quelle bêtise!*" adds *mon père.*

But Saint-Simon, it seems, had the folly to wish to make a marriage of inclination. Rich, *pair de France*, his father—an old *roué*, who had been page to Louis XIII.—dead, he felt extremely alone in the world. He cast about to see whom he could select. The Duc de Beauvilliers had eight daughters; a misfortune, it may be thought, in France or any where else. Not at all: three of the young ladies were kept at home, to be married; the other five were at once disposed of, as they passed the unconscious age of infancy, in convents. Saint-Simon was, however, disappointed. He offered, indeed; first for the eldest, who was not then fifteen years old; and finding that she had a vocation for a conventual life, went on to the third, and was going through the whole family, when he was convinced that his suit was impossible. The eldest daughter happened to be a disciple of Fénélon's, and was on the very eve of being vowed to Heaven.

Saint-Simon went off to La Trappe, to console himself for his disappointment. There had been an old intimacy between Monsieur La Trappe and the father of Saint-Simon; and this friendship had induced him to buy an estate close to the ancient abbey where La Trappe still existed. The friendship became hereditary; and Saint-Simon, though still a youth, revered and loved the penitent recluse of *Ferté au Vidame*, of which Lamartine has written so grand and so poetical a description.

Let us hasten over his marriage with Mademoiselle de Lorges, who proved a good wife. It was this time a grandmother, the Maréchale de Lorges, who managed the treaty; and Saint-Simon became the happy husband of an innocent blonde, with a majestic air, though only fifteen years of age. Let us hasten on, passing over his presents; his six hundred louis, given in a corbeille full of what he styles "galanteries;" his mother's donation of jewelry; the midnight mass, by which he was linked to the child who scarcely knew him; let us lay all that aside, and turn to his court life.

It was at this juncture that Louis XIV., who had hitherto dressed with great simplicity, indicated that he desired his court should appear in all possible magnificence. Instantly the shops were emptied. Even gold and silver appeared scarcely rich enough. Louis himself planned many of the dresses for any public occasion. Afterward he repented of the extent to which he had permitted magnificence to go, but it was then impossible to check the excess.

Versailles, henceforth in all its grandeur, contains an apartment which is called, from its situation, and the opportunities it presents of looking down upon the actors of the scene around, *L'Œil de Bœuf.* The revelations of the Œil de Bœuf, during the reign of Louis XV., form one of the most amazing pictures of wickedness, venality, power misapplied, genius polluted, that was ever drawn. No one that reads that infamous book can wonder at the revolution of 1789. Let us conceive Saint-Simon to have taken his stand here, in this region, pure in the time of Louis XIV., comparatively, and note we down his comments on men and women.

He has journeyed up to court from La Trappe, which has fallen into confusion and quarrels, to which the most saintly precincts are peculiarly liable.

The history of Mademoiselle de la Vallière was not, as he tells us, of his time. He hears of her death, and so indeed does the king, with emotion. She expired in 1710, in the Rue St. Jacques, at the Carmelite convent, where, though she was in the heart of Paris, her seclusion from the world had long been complete. Among the nuns of the convent none was so humble, so penitent, so chastened as this once lovely Louise de la Vallière, now, during a weary term of thirty-five years, "Marie de la Miséricorde." She had fled from the scene of her fall at one-and-thirty years of age. Twice had she taken refuge among the "blameless vestals," whom she envied as the broken-spirited envy the passive. First, she escaped from the torture of witnessing the king's passion for Madame de Montespan, by hiding herself among the Benedictine sisters at St. Cloud. Thence the king fetched her in person, threatening to order the cloister to be burnt. Next, Lauzun, by the command of Louis, sought her, and brought her *avec main forte.* The next time she fled no more; but took a public farewell of all she had too fondly loved, and throwing herself at the feet of the queen, humbly entreated her pardon. Never since that voluntary sepulture had she ceased, during those long and weary years, to lament—as the heart-stricken can alone lament—her sins. In deep contrition she learned the death of her son by the king, and bent her head meekly beneath the chastisement.

Three years before her death the triumphant Athénée de Montespan had breathed her last at Bourbon. If Louis XIV. had nothing else to repent of, the remorse of these two women ought to have wrung his heart. Athénée de Montespan was a youthful, innocent beauty, fresh from the seclusion of provincial life, when she attracted the blighting regards of royalty. A *fête* was to be given; she saw, she heard that she was its object. She entreated her husband to take her back to his estate in Guyenne, and to leave her there till the king had forgotten her. Her husband, in fatal confidence, trusted her resistance, and refused her petition. It was a life-long sorrow; and he soon found his mistake. He lived and died passionately attached to his wife, but never saw her after her fall.

When she retired from court, to make room for the empire of the subtle De Maintenon, it was her son, the Duc de Maine, who induced her, not from love, but from ambition, to withdraw. She preserved, even in her seclusion in the country, the style of a queen, which she had assumed. Even her natural children by the king were never allowed to sit in her presence, on a *fauteuil*, but were only permitted to have small chairs. Every one went to pay her court, and she spoke to them as if doing them an honor; neither did she ever return a visit, even from the royal family. Her fatal beauty endured to the last: nothing could exceed her grace, her tact, her good sense in conversation, her kindness to every one.

But it was long before her restless spirit could find real peace. She threw herself on the guidance of the Abbé de la Tour; for the dread of death was ever upon her. He suggested a terrible test of her penitence. It was, that she should entreat her husband's pardon, and return to him. It was a fearful struggle with herself, for she was naturally haughty and high spirited; but she consented. After long agonies of hesitation, she wrote to the injured man. Her letter was couched in the most humble language; but it received no reply. The Marquis de Montespan, through a third person, intimated to her that he would neither receive her, nor see her, nor hear her name pronounced. At his death she wore widow's weeds; but never assumed his arms, nor adopted his liveries.

Henceforth, all she had was given to the poor. When Louis meanly cut down her pension, she sent word that she was sorry for the poor, not for herself; they would be the losers. She then humbled herself to the very dust: wore the hardest cloth next her fair skin; had iron bracelets; and an iron girdle, which made wounds on her body. Moreover, she punished the most unruly members of her frame: she kept her tongue in bounds; she ceased to slander; she learned to bless. The fear of death still haunted her; she lay in bed with every curtain drawn, the room lighted up with wax candles; while she hired watchers to sit up all night, and insisted that they should never cease talking or laughing, lest, when she woke, the fear of *death* might come over her affrighted spirit.

She died at last after a few hours' illness, having just time to order all her household to be summoned, and before them to make a public confession of her sins. As she lay expiring, blessing God that she died far away from the children of her adulterous connection, the Comte d'Antin, her only child by the Marquis de Montespan, arrived. Peace and trust had then come at last to the agonized woman. She spoke to him about her state of mind, and expired.

To Madame de Maintenon the event would, it was thought, be a relief; yet she wept bitterly on hearing of it. The king showed, on the contrary, the utmost indifference, on learning that one whom he had once loved so much was gone forever.

All has passed away! The *Œil de Bœuf* is now important only as being pointed out to strangers; Versailles is a show-place, not a habitation. Saint-Simon, who lived until 1775, was truly said to have turned his back on the new age, and to live in the memories of a former world of wit and fashion. He survived until the era of the "Encyclopédia" of Voltaire and Jean-Jacques Rousseau. He lived, indeed, to hear that Montesquieu was no more. How the spirit of Louis XIV. spoke in his contemptuous remarks on Voltaire, whom he would only call Arouet: "The son of my father's and my own notary."

At length, after attaining his eightieth year, the chronicler, who knew the weaknesses, the vices, the peculiarities of mankind, even to a hair's breadth, expired; having long given up the court and occupied himself, while secluded in his country-seat, solely with the revising and amplification of his wonderful Memoirs.

No works, it has been remarked, since those of Sir Walter Scott, have excited so much sensation as the Memoirs of his own time, by the soldier, embassador, and *Trappist*, Duc de Saint-Simon.

HORACE WALPOLE.

"Had this elegant writer," remarks the compiler of "Walpoliana," "composed memoirs of his own life, an example authorized by eminent names, ancient and modern, every other pen must have been dropped in despair, so true was it that 'he united the good sense of Fontenelle with the Attic salt and graces of Count Anthony Hamilton.'"

But "Horace" was a man of great literary modesty, and always undervalued his own efforts. His life was one of little incident: it is his character, his mind, the society around him, the period in which he shone, that give the charm to his correspondence, and the interest to his biography.

Besides, he had the weakness common to several other fine gentlemen who have combined letters and *haut ton*, of being ashamed of the literary character. The vulgarity of the court, its indifference to all that was not party writing, whether polemical or political, cast a shade over authors in his time.

Never was there, beneath all his assumed Whig principles, a more profound aristocrat than Horace Walpole. He was, by birth, one of those well-descended English gentlemen who have often scorned the title of noble, and who have repudiated the notion of merging their own ancient names in modern titles. The commoners of England hold a proud pre-eminence. When some low-born man entreated James I. to make him a gentleman, the well-known answer was, "Na, na, I canna! I could mak thee a lord, but none but God Almighty can mak a gentleman."

Sir Robert Walpole, afterward minister to George II., and eventually Lord Orford, belonged to an ancient family in Norfolk; he was a third son, and was originally destined for the church, but the death of his elder brethren having left him heir to the family estate, in 1698, he succeeded to a property which ought to have yielded him £2000 a year, but which was crippled with various incumbrances. In order to relieve himself of these, Sir Robert married Catherine Shorter, the granddaughter of Sir John Shorter, who had been illegally and arbitrarily appointed Lord Mayor of London by James II.

Horace was her youngest child, and was born in Arlington Street, on the 24th of September, 1717, O. S. Six years afterward he was inoculated for the small-pox, a precaution which he records as worthy of remark, since the operation had then only recently been introduced by Lady Mary Wortley Montagu from Turkey.

He is silent, however, naturally enough, as to one important point—his real parentage. The character of his mother was by no means such as to disprove an assertion which gained general belief: this was, that Horace was the offspring, not of Sir Robert Walpole, but of Carr, Lord Hervey, the eldest son of the Earl of Bristol, and the elder brother of Lord Hervey whose "Memoirs of the Court of George II." are so generally known. Carr, Lord Hervey, was witty, eccentric, and sarcastic: and from him Horace Walpole is said to have inherited his wit, his eccentricity, his love of literature, and his profound contempt for all mankind, excepting only a few members of a cherished and exclusive *clique*.

In the Notes of his life which Horace Walpole left for the use of his executor, Robert Berry, Esq., and of his daughter, Miss Berry, he makes this brief mention of Lady Walpole: "My mother died in 1737." He was then twenty years of age.

But beneath this seemingly slight recurrence to his mother, a regret which never left him through life was buried. Like Cowper, he mourned, as the profoundest of all sorrows, the loss of that life-long friend.

"My mother, when I learn'd that thou wast dead,
Say, wast thou conscious of the tears I shed?
Hovered thy spirit o'er thy sorrowing son?
Wretch even then, life's journey just begun."

Although Horace in many points bore a strong resemblance to Sir Robert Walpole, he rarely if ever received from that jovial, heartless, able man, disgrace as he was to the English aristocracy, any proof of affection. An outcast from his father's heart, the whole force of the boy's love centred in his mother; yet in after life no one reverenced Sir Robert Walpole so much as his supposed son. To be adverse to the minister was to be adverse to the unloved son who cherished his memory. What "my father" thought, did, and said, was law; what his foes dared to express was heresy. Horace had the family mania strong upon him: the world was made for Walpoles, whose views were never to be controverted, nor whose faith impugned. Yet Horace must have witnessed, perhaps without comprehending it, much disunion at home. Lady Walpole, beautiful and accomplished, could not succeed in riveting her husband to his conjugal duties. Gross licentiousness was the order of the day, and Sir Robert was among the most licentious: he left his lovely wife to the perilous attentions of all the young courtiers who fancied that by courting the Premier's wife they could secure Walpole's good offices. Sir Robert, according to Pope, was one of those who—

> "Never made a friend in private life,
> And was, besides, a tyrant to his wife."

At all events, if not a tyrant, he was indifferent to those circumstances which reflected upon him, and were injurious to her. He was conscious that he had no right to complain of any infidelity on her part, and he left her to be surrounded by men whom he knew to be profligates of the most dangerous pretensions to wit and elegance.

It was possibly not unfrequently that Horace, his mother's pet, gleaned in the drawing-rooms of Arlington Street his first notions of that *persiflage* which was the fashion of the day. We can fancy him a precocious, old-fashioned little boy, at his mother's apron-string, while Carr, Lord Hervey, was paying his devoirs; we see him gazing with wondering eyes at Pulteney, Earl of Bath, with his blue ribbon across his laced coat; while compassionating friends, observing the pale-faced boy in that hot-house atmosphere, in which both mind and body were like forced plants, prophesied that "little Horace" could not possibly live to be a man.

He survived, however, two sisters, who died in childhood, and became dearer and dearer to his fond mother.

In his old age, Horace delighted in recalling anecdotes of his infancy: in these his mother's partiality largely figured. Brought up among courtiers and ministers, his childish talk was all of kings and princes; and he was a gossip both by inclination and habit. His greatest desire in life was to see the king—George I., and his nurses and attendants augmented his wish by their exalted descriptions of the grandeur which he affected, in after life, to despise. He entreated his mother to take him to St. James's. When relating the incidents of the scene in which he was first introduced to a court, Horace Walpole speaks of the "infinite good-nature of his father, who never thwarted any of his children," and "suffered him," he says, "to be too much indulged."

Some difficulties attended the fruition of the forward boy's wish. The Duchess of Kendal was jealous of Sir Robert Walpole's influence with the king; her aim was to bring Lord Bolingbroke into power. The childish fancy was, nevertheless, gratified: and under his mother's care he was conducted to the apartments of the Duchess of Kendal in St. James's.

"A favor so unusual to be asked by a boy of ten years old," he afterward wrote in his "Reminiscences," "was still too slight to be refused to the wife of the first minister and her darling child." However, as it was not to be a precedent, the interview was to be private, and at night.

It was ten o'clock in the evening when Lady Walpole, leading her son, was admitted into the apartments of Melusina de Schulenberg, Countess of Walsingham, who passed under the name of the Duchess of Kendal's niece, but who was, in fact, her daughter, by George I. The polluted rooms in which Lady Walsingham lived were afterward occupied by the two mistresses of George II.—the Countess of Suffolk, and Madame de Walmoden, Countess of Yarmouth.

With Lady Walsingham, Lady Walpole and her little son waited until, notice having been given that the king had come down to supper, he was led into the presence of "that good sort of man," as he calls George I. That monarch was pleased to permit the young courtier to kneel down and kiss his hand. A few words were spoken by the august personage, and Horace was led back into the adjoining room.

But the vision of that "good sort of man" was present to him when, in old age, he wrote down his recollections for his beloved Miss Berry. By the side of a tall, lean, ill-favored old German lady—the Duchess of Kendal—stood a pale, short, elderly man, with a dark tie-wig, in a plain coat and waistcoat; these and his breeches were all of snuff-colored cloth, and his stockings of the same color. By the blue ribbons alone could the young subject of this "good sort of man" discern that he was in the presence of majesty. Little interest could be elicited in this brief interview, yet Horace thought it his painful duty, being also the son of a prime minister, to shed tears when, with the other scholars of Eton College, he walked in the procession to the proclamation of George II. And no doubt he was one of *very* few personages in England whose eyes were moistened for that event. Nevertheless, there was something of *bonhommie* in the character of George I. that one misses in his successor. His love of punch, and his habit of becoming a little tipsy over his private dinners with Sir Robert Walpole, were English as well as German traits, and were regarded almost as condescensions; and then he had a kind of slow wit, that was turned upon the venial officials whose perquisites were at their disgraceful height in his time.

"A strange country this," said the monarch, in his most clamorous German: "one day, after I came to St. James's, I looked out of the window, and saw a park, with walks, laurels, etc.; these they told me were mine. The next day Lord Chetwynd, the ranger of *my* park, sends me a brace of carp out of my canal; I was told, thereupon, that I must give five guineas to Lord Chetwynd's porter for bringing me my *own* fish, out of my *own* canal, in my *own* park!" In spite of some agreeable qualities, George I. was, however, any thing but a "good sort of man." It is difficult how to rank the two first Georges; both were detestable as men, and scarcely tolerable as monarchs. The foreign deeds of George I. were stained with the supposed murder of Count Konigsmark: the English career of George II. was one of the coarsest profligacy. Their example was infamous.

His father's only sister having become the second wife of Charles Lord Townshend, Horace was educated with his cousins; and the tutor selected was Edward Weston, the son of Stephen, Bishop of Exeter: this preceptor was afterward engaged in a controversy with Dr. Warburton, concerning the "Naturalization of the Jews." By that learned, haughty disputant, he is termed "a gazetteer by profession—by inclination a Methodist." Such was the man who guided the dawning intellect of Horace Walpole. Under his care he remained until he went, in 1727, to Eton. But Walpole's was not merely a scholastic education: he was destined for the law—and, on going up to Cambridge, was obliged to attend lectures on civil law. He went from Eton to King's College—where he was, however, more disposed to what are termed accomplishments than to deep reading. At Cambridge he even studied Italian: at home he learned to dance and fence; and took lessons in drawing from Bernard Lens, drawing-master to the Duke of Cumberland and his sisters. It is not to be wondered at that he left Cambridge without taking a degree.

But fortune was lying, as it were, in wait for him; and various sinecures had been reserved for the Minister's youngest son: first, he became Inspector of the Imports and Exports in the Customs; but soon resigned that post to be Usher of the Exchequer. "And as soon," he writes, "as I became of age I took possession of two other little patent places in the Exchequer, called Comptroller of the Pipe, and Clerk of the Estreats. They had been held for me by Mr. Fane."

Such was the mode in which younger sons were then provided for by a minister; nor has the unworthy system died out in our time, although greatly modified.

Horace was growing up meantime, not an awkward, but a somewhat insignificant youth, with a short, slender figure: which always retained a boyish appearance when seen from behind. His face was commonplace, except when his really expressive eyes sparkled with intelligence, or melted into the sweetest expression of kindness. But his laugh was forced and uncouth: and even in his smile there was a hard, sarcastic expression that made one regret that he smiled.

He was now in possession of an income of £1700 annually, and he looked naturally to the Continent, to which all young members of the aristocracy repaired, after the completion of their collegiate life.

He had been popular at Eton: he was also, it is said, both beloved and valued at Cambridge. In reference to his Etonian days he says, in one of his letters: "I can't say I am sorry I was never quite a schoolboy: an expedition against bargemen, or a match at cricket, may be very pretty things to recollect; but, thank my stars, I can remember things that are very near as pretty. The beginning of my Roman history was spent in the asylum, or conversing in Egeria's hallowed grove; not in thumping and pummeling King Amulius's herdsmen."*

"I remember," he adds, "when I was at Eton, and Mr. Bland had set me on an extraordinary task, I used sometimes to pique myself upon not getting it, because it was not immediately my school business. What! learn more than I was absolutely forced to learn! I felt the weight of learning that; for I was a blockhead, *and pushed above my parts*."†

Popular among his schoolfellows, Horace formed friendships at Eton which mainly influenced his after life. Richard West, the son of West, Lord Chancellor of Ireland, and the grandson, on his mother's side, of Bishop Burnet: together with a youth named Assheton—formed, with the poet Gray, and Horace himself, what the young wit termed the "Quadruple Alliance." Then there was the "triumvirate," George Montagu, Charles Montagu, and Horace—next came George Selwyn and Hanbury Williams; lastly, a retired, studious youth, a sort of foil to all these gay, brilliant young wits—a certain William Cole, a lover of old books, and of quaint prints. And in all these boyish friendships, some of which were carried from Eton to Cambridge, may be traced the foundation of the Horace Walpole, of Strawberry Hill and of Berkeley Square. To Gray he owed his ambition to be learned, if possible—poetical, if nature had not forbidden; to the Montagus, his dash and spirit; to Sir Hanbury Williams, his turn for *jeux d'esprit*, as a part of the completion of a fine gentleman's education; to George Selwyn, his appreciation of what was then considered wit—but which we moderns are not worthy to appreciate. Lord Hertford and Henry Conway, Walpole's cousins, were also his schoolfellows; and for them he evinced throughout his long life a warm regard. William Pitt, Lord Chatham—chiefly remembered at Eton for having been flogged for being out of bounds—was a contemporary, though not an intimate of Horace Walpole's at Eton.

* Life by Warburton, p. 70. † Ibid. p. 63.

His regard for Gray did him infinite credit: yet never were two men more dissimilar as they advanced in life. Gray had no aristocratic birth to boast; and Horace dearly loved birth, refinement, position, all that comprises the cherished term "quality." Thomas Gray, more illustrious for the little his fastidious judgment permitted him to give to the then critical world, than many have been in their productions of volumes, was born in Cornhill—his father being a worthy citizen. He was just one year older than Walpole, but an age his senior in gravity, precision, and in a stiff resolution to maintain his independence. He made one fatal step, fatal to his friendship for Horace, when he forfeited—by allowing Horace to take him and pay his expenses during a long continental tour—his independence. Gray had many points which made him vulnerable to Walpole's shafts of ridicule; and Horace had a host of faults which excited the stern condemnation of Gray. The author of the "Elegy"—which Johnson has pronounced to be the noblest ode in our language—was one of the most learned men of his time, "and was equally acquainted with the elegant and profound paths of science, and that not superficially, but thoroughly; knowing in every branch of history, both natural and civil, as having read all the original historians of England, France, and Italy; a great antiquarian, who made criticism, metaphysics, morals, and politics a principal part of his plan of study—who was uncommonly fond of voyages and travels of all sorts—and who had a fine taste in painting, prints, architecture, and gardening."

What a companion for a young man of taste and sympathy! but the friends were far too clever long to agree. Gray was haughty, impatient, intolerant of the peculiarities of others, according to the author of "Walpoliana:" doubtless he detected the vanity, the actual selfishness, the want of earnest feeling in Horace, which had all been kept down at school, where boys are far more unsparing Mentors than their betters. In vain did they travel *en prince*, and all at Walpole's expense: in vain did they visit courts, and receive affability from princes: in vain did he of Cornhill participate for a brief period in the attentions lavished on the son of a British Prime Minister: they quarreled—and we almost reverence Gray for it, more especially when we find the author of "Walpoliana" expressing his conviction that "had it not been for this idle indulgence of his hasty temper, Mr. Gray would immediately on his return home have received, as usual, a pension or office from Sir Robert Walpole." We are inclined to feel contempt for the anonymous writer of that amusing little book.

After a companionship of four years, Gray, nevertheless, returned to London. He had been educated with the expectation of being a barrister; but finding that funds were wanting to pursue a legal education, he gave up a set of chambers in the Temple, which he had occupied previous to his travels, and retired to Cambridge.

Henceforth what a singular contrast did the lives of these once fond friends present. In the small, quaint rooms of Peter-House,* Gray consumed a dreary celibacy, consoled by the Muse alone, who—if other damsels found no charms in his somewhat priggish, wooden countenance, or in his manners, replete, it is said, with an unpleasant consciousness of superiority—never deserted him. His college existence, varied only by his being appointed Professor of Modern History, was, for a brief space, exchanged for an existence almost as studious in London. Between the years 1759 and 1762, he took lodgings, we find, in Southampton Row—a pleasant locality then, opening to the fields—in order to be near the British Museum, at that time just opened to the public. Here his intense studies were, it may be presumed, relieved by the lighter task of perusing the Harleian Manuscripts; and here he formed the acquaintance of Mason, a dull, affected poet, whose celebrity is greater as the friend and biographer of Gray, than even as the author of those verses on the death of Lady Coventry, in which there are, nevertheless, some beautiful lines. Gray died in college—a doom that, next to ending one's days in a jail or a convent, seems the dreariest. He died of the gout: a suitable, and, in that region and in those three-bottle days, almost an inevitable disease; but there is no record of his having been intemperate.

While Gray was poring over dusty manuscripts, Horace was beginning that career of prosperity which was commenced by the keenest enjoyment of existence. He has left us, in his Letters, some brilliant passages, indicative of the delights of his boyhood and youth. Like him, we linger over a period still fresh, still hopeful, still generous in impulse—still strong in faith in the world's worth—before we hasten on to portray the man of the world, heartless, not wholly, perhaps, but wont to check all feeling till it was well-nigh quenched; little-minded; bitter, if not spiteful; with many acquaintances and scarce one friend—the Horace Walpole of Berkeley Square and Strawberry Hill.

"Youthful passages of life are," he says, "the chippings of Pitt's diamond, set into little heart-rings with mottoes; the stone itself more worth, the filings more gentle and agreeable. Alexander, at the head of the world, never tasted the true

* Gray migrated to Pembroke in 1756.

pleasure that boys of his age have enjoyed at the head of a school. Little intrigues, little schemes and policies, engage their thoughts; and at the same time that they are laying the foundation for their middle age of life, the mimic republic they live in furnishes materials of conversation for their latter age; and old men can not be said to be children a second time with greater truth from any one cause, than their living over again their childhood in imagination."

Again: "Dear George, were not the playing-fields at Eton food for all manner of flights? No old maid's gown, though it had been tormented into all the fashions from King James to King George, ever underwent so many transformations as these poor plains have in my idea. At first I was contented with tending a visionary flock, and sighing some pastoral name to the echo of the cascade under the bridge. . . As I got further into Virgil and Clelia, I found myself transported from Arcadia to the garden of Italy; and saw Windsor Castle in no other view than the *Capitoli immobile saxum.*"

Horace Walpole's humble friend Assheton was another of those Etonians who were plodding on to independence, while he, set forward by fortune and interest, was accomplishing reputation. Assheton was the son of a worthy man, who presided over the Grammar School at Lancaster, upon a stipend of £32 a year. Assheton's mother had brought to her husband a small estate. This was sold to educate the "boys:" they were both clever and deserving. One became the fellow of Trinity College; the other, the friend of Horace, rose into notice as the tutor of the young Earl of Plymouth; then became a D.D., and a fashionable preacher in London; was elected preacher at Lincoln's Inn; attacked the Methodists; and died, at fifty-three, at variance with Horace—this Assheton, whom once he had loved so much.

Horace, on the other hand, after having seen all that was most exclusive, attractive, and lofty, both in art and nature, came home without bringing, he declares, "one word of French or Italian for common use." A country tour in England delighted him: the populousness, the ease in the people also, charmed him. "Canterbury was a paradise to Modena, Reggio, or Parma." He had, before he returned, perceived that nowhere except in England was there the distinction of "middling people;" he now found that nowhere but in England were middling houses. "How snug they are!" exclaims this scion of the exclusives. Then he runs on into an anecdote about Pope and Frederick, Prince of Wales. "Mr. Pope," said the prince, "you don't love princes." "Sir, I beg your pardon." "Well, you don't love kings, then." "Sir, I own

I like the lion better before his claws are grown." The "Horace Walpole" began now to creep out: never was he really at home except in a court atmosphere. Still he assumed, even at twenty-four, to be the boy.

"You won't find me," he writes to Harry Conway, "much altered, I believe; at least outwardly. I am not grown a bit shorter or fatter, but am just the same long, lean creature as usual. Then I talk no French but to my footman; nor Italian, but to myself. What inward alterations may have happened to me you will discover best; for you know 'tis said, one never knows that one's self. I will answer, that that part of it that belongs to you has not suffered the least change—I took care of that. For *virtù*, I have a little to entertain you—it is my sole pleasure. I am neither young enough nor old enough to be in love."

Nevertheless, it peeps out soon after that the "Pomfrets" are coming back. Horace had known them in Italy. The Earl and Countess and their daughters were just then the very pink of fashion; and even the leaders of all that was exclusive in the court. Half in ridicule, half in earnest, are the remarks which, throughout all the career of Horace, incessantly occur. "I am neither young enough nor old enough to be in love," he says; yet that he was in love with one of the lovely Fermors is traditionary still in the family—and that tradition pointed at Lady Juliana, the youngest, afterward married to Mr. Penn. The Earl of Pomfret had been master of the horse to Queen Caroline: Lady Pomfret, lady of the bedchamber. "My Earl," as the countess styled him, was apparently a supine subject to her ladyship's strong will and wrong-headed ability—which she, perhaps, inherited from her grandfather, Judge Jeffreys; she being the daughter and heiress of that rash young Lord Jeffreys who, in a spirit of braggadocia, stopped the funeral of Dryden on its way to Westminster, promising a more splendid procession than the poor, humble cortège—a boast which he never fulfilled. Lady Sophia Fermor, the eldest daughter, who afterward became the wife of Lord Carteret, resembled, in beauty, the famed Mistress Arabella Fermor, the heroine of the "Rape of the Lock." Horace Walpole admired Lady Sophia—whom he christened Juno—much. Scarcely a letter *drips* from his pen—as a modern novelist used to express it*—without some touch of the Pomfrets. Thus to Sir Horace Mann, then a diplomatist at Florence:

"Lady Pomfret I saw last night. Lady Sophia has been ill with a cold; her head is to be dressed French, and her body

* The accomplished novelist, Mrs. Gore, famous for her facility.

English, for which I am sorry, her figure is so fine in a robe. She is full as sorry as I am."

Again, at a ball at Sir Thomas Robinson's, where four-and-twenty couples danced country-dances, in two sets, twelve and twelve, "there was Lady Sophia, handsomer than ever, but a little out of humor at the scarcity of minuets;" however, as usual, dancing more than any body, and as usual too, she took out what men she liked, or thought the best dancers." . . . . "We danced; for I country-danced till four, then had tea and coffee, and came home." Poor Horace! Lady Sophia was not for a younger son, however gay, talented, or rich.

His pique and resentment toward her mother, who had higher views for her beautiful daughter, begins at this period to show itself, and never dies away.

Lady Townshend was the wit who used to gratify Horace with tales of her whom he hated—Henrietta Louisa, Countess of Pomfret.

"Lady Townshend told me an admirable history: it is of *our friend* Lady Pomfret. Somebody that belonged to the Prince of Wales said, they were going to *court;* it was objected that they ought to say to Carlton House; that the only *court* is where the king resides. Lady P., with her paltry air of significant learning and absurdity, said, 'Oh, Lord! is there no *court* in England but the king's? Sure, there are many more! There is the *Court* of Chancery, the *Court* of Exchequer, the *Court* of King's Bench, etc.' Don't you love her? Lord Lincoln does her daughter—Lady Sophia Fermor. He is come over, and met me and her the other night; he turned pale, spoke to her several times in the evening, but not long, and sighed to me at going away. He came over all alone; and not only his Uncle Duke (the Duke of Newcastle) but even Majesty is fallen in love with him. He talked to the king at his levee, without being spoken to. That was always thought high treason; but I don't know how the gruff gentleman liked it. And then he had been told that Lord Lincoln designed to have made the campaign, if we had gone to war; in short, he says Lord Lincoln is the handsomest man in England."

Horace was not, therefore, the only victim to a mother's ambition: there is something touching in the interest he from time to time evinces in poor Lord Lincoln's hopeless love. On another occasion, a second ball of Sir Thomas Robinson's, Lord Lincoln, out of prudence, dances with Lady Caroline Fitzroy, Mr. Conway taking Lady Sophia Fermor. "The two couple were just admirably mismatched, as every body soon perceived, by the attentions of each man to the woman he did not dance with, and the emulation of either lady: it was an admirable scene."

All, however, was not country dancing: the young man, "too old and too young to be in love," was to make his way as a wit. He did so, in the approved way in that day of irreligion, in a political squib. On July 14th, 1742, he writes in his Notes, "I wrote the '*Lessons for the Day;*' the 'Lessons for the Day' being the first and second chapters of the 'Book of Preferment.'" Horace was proud of this *brochure*, for he says it got about surreptitiously, and was "the original of many things of that sort." Various *jeux d'esprit* of a similar sort followed. A "Sermon on Painting," which was preached before Sir Robert Walpole, in the gallery at Houghton, by his chaplain; "Patapan, or the Little White Dog," imitated from La Fontaine. No. 38 of the "Old England Journal," intended to ridicule Lord Bath; and then, in a magazine, was printed his "Scheme for a Tax on Message Cards and Notes." Next, the "Beauties," which was also handed about, and got into print. So that without the vulgarity of publishing, the reputation of the dandy writer was soon noised about. His religious tenets may or may not have been sound; but at all events the tone of his mind assumed at this time a very different character to that reverent strain in which, when a youth at college, he had apostrophized those who bowed their heads beneath the vaulted roof of King's College, in his eulogium in the character of Henry VI.

"Ascend the temple, join the vocal choir,
Let harmony your raptured souls inspire.
Hark how the tuneful, solemn organs blow,
Awfully strong, elaborately slow;
Now to yon empyrean seats above
Raise meditation on the wings of love.
Now falling, sinking, dying to the moan
Once warbled sad by Jesse's contrite son;
Breathe in each note a conscience through the sense,
And call forth tears from soft-eyed Penitence."

In the midst of all his gayeties, his successes, and perhaps his hopes, a cloud hovered over the destinies of his father. The opposition, Horace saw, in 1741, wished to ruin his father "by ruining his constitution." They wished to continue their debates on Saturdays, Sir Robert's only day of rest, when he used to rush to Richmond New Park, there to amuse himself with a favorite pack of beagles. Notwithstanding the minister's indifference to this, his youngest son, Horace, felt bitterly what he considered a persecution against one of the most corrupt of modern statesmen.

"Trust me, if we fall, all the grandeur, all the envied grandeur of our house, will not cost me a sigh: it has given me no pleasure while we have it, and will give me no pain when I part with it. My liberty, my ease, and choice of my own friends and company, will sufficiently counterbalance the crowds of Downing Street. I am so sick of it all, that if we are victorious or not, I propose leaving England in the spring."

The struggle was not destined to last long. Sir Robert was forced to give up the contest and be shelved with a peerage. In 1742, he was created Earl of Orford, and resigned. The wonder is that, with a mortal internal disease to contend with, he should have faced his foes so long. Verses ascribed to Lord Hervey ended, as did all the squibs of the day, with a fling at that "rogue Walpole."

"For though you have made that rogue Walpole retire,
You are out of the frying-pan into the fire:
But since to the Protestant line I'm a friend,
I tremble to think how these changes may end."

Horace, in spite of affected indifference, felt his father's downfall poignantly. He went, indeed, to court, in spite of a cold, taken in an unaired house; for the prime minister now quitted Downing Street for Arlington Street. The court was crowded, he found, with old ladies, the wives of patriots who had not been there for "these twenty years," and who appeared in the accoutrements that were in vogue in Queen Anne's time. "Then," he writes, "the joy and awkward jollity of them is inexpressible! They titter, and, wherever you meet them, are always looking at their watches an hour before the time. I met several on the birthday (for I did not arrive time enough to make clothes), and they were dressed in all the colors of the rainbow. They seem to have said to themselves, twenty years ago, 'Well, if ever I do go to court again, I will have a pink and silver, or a blue and silver;' and they keep their resolutions."

Another characteristic anecdote betrays his ill-suppressed vexation:

"I laughed at myself prodigiously the other day for a piece of absence. I was writing, on the king's birthday, and being disturbed with the mob in the street, I rang for the porter, and with an air of grandeur, as if I was still at Downing Street, cried, 'Pray send away those marrow-bones and cleavers!' The poor fellow, with the most mortified air in the world, replied, 'Sir, they are not at *our* door, but over the way, at my Lord Carteret's.' 'Oh!' said I, 'then let them alone; may be, he does not dislike the noise!' I pity the poor porter, who sees all his old customers going over the way too."

The retirement of Sir Robert from office had an important

effect on the tastes and future life of his son Horace. The minister had been occupying his later years in pulling down his old ancestral house at Houghton, and in building an enormous mansion, which has since his time been, in its turn, partially demolished. When Harley, Earl of Oxford, was known to be erecting a great house for himself, Sir Robert had remarked that a minister who did so committed a great imprudence. When Houghton was begun, Sir Hynde Aston reminded Sir Robert of this speech. "You ought to have recalled it to me before," was the reply; "for before I began building, it might have been of use to me."

This famous memorial of Walpolean greatness, this splendid folly, constructed, it is generally supposed, on public money, was inhabited by Sir Robert only ten days in summer, and twenty days in winter; in the autumn, during the shooting season, two months. It became almost an eyesore to the quiet gentry, who viewed the palace with a feeling of their own inferiority. People as good as the Walpoles lived in their gable-ended, moderate-sized mansions; and who was Sir Robert, to set them at so immense a distance?

To the vulgar comprehension of the Premier, Houghton, gigantic in its proportions, had its purposes. He there assembled his supporters; there, for a short time, he entertained his constituents and coadjutors with a magnificent, jovial hospitality, of which he, with his gay spirits, his humorous, indelicate jokes, and his unbounded good-nature, was the very soul. Free conversation, hard drinking, were the features of every day's feast. Pope thus describes him:

"Seen him, I have, but in his happier hour,
Of social pleasure, ill exchanged for power;
Seen him uncumbered with the venal tribe,
Smile without art, and win without a bribe."

Amid the coarse taste one gentle refinement existed: this was the love of gardening, both in its smaller compass and in its nobler sense of landscape gardening. "This place," Sir Robert, in 1743, wrote to General Churchill, from Houghton, "affords no news, no subject of entertainment or amusement; for fine men of wit and pleasure about town understand neither the language and taste, nor the pleasure of the inanimate world. My flatterers here are all mutes: the oaks, the beeches, the chestnuts, seem to contend which best shall please the lord of the manor. They can not deceive; they will not lie. I in sincerity admire them, and have as many beauties about me as fill up all my hours of dangling, and no disgrace attending me, from sixty-seven years of age. Within doors we come a little nearer to real life, and admire, upon the almost speaking canvas, all the airs and graces the proudest ladies can boast."

In these pursuits Horace cordially shared. Through his agency, Horace Mann, still at Florence, selected and purchased works of art, which were sent either to Arlington Street, or to form the famous Houghton Collection, to which Horace so often refers in that delightful work, his "Anecdotes of Painting."

Among the embellishments of Houghton, the gardens were the most expensive.

"Sir Robert has pleased himself," Pulteney, Earl of Bath, wrote, "with erecting palaces and extending parks, planting gardens in places to which the very earth was to be transported in carriages, and embracing cascades and fountains whose water was only to be obtained by aqueducts and machines, and imitating the extravagance of Oriental monarchs, at the expense of a free people whom he has at once impoverished and betrayed."

The ex-minister went to a great expense in the cultivation of plants, bought Uvedale's "Hortus Siccus;" and received from Bradley, the Professor of Botany at Cambridge, the tribute of a dedication, in which it was said that "Sir Robert had purchased one of the finest collections of plants in the kingdom."

What was more to his honor still, was Sir Robert's preservation of St. James's Park for the people. Fond of out-door amusements himself, the Premier heard, with dismay, a proposal on the part of Queen Caroline, to convert that ancient park into a palace garden. "She asked my father," Horace Walpole relates, "what the alteration might possibly cost." "*Only three crowns*," was the civil, witty, candid answer. The queen was wise enough to take the hint. It is possible she meant to convert the park into gardens that should be open to the public as at Berlin, Manheim, and even the Tuileries. Still it would not have been ours.

Horace Walpole owed, perhaps, his love of architecture and his taste for gardening, partly to the early companionship of Gray, who delighted in those pursuits. Walpole's estimation of pictures, medals, and statues, was however the fruit of a long residence abroad. We are apt to rail at continental nations; yet had it not been for the occasional intercourse with foreign nations, art would have altogether died out among us. To the "Grandes Tours," performed as a matter of course by our young nobility in the most impressionable period of their lives, we owe most of our noble private collections. Charles I. and Buckingham, renewed, in their travels in Spain, the efforts previously made by Lord Arundel and Lord Pembroke, to embellish their country seats. Then came the rebellion; and like a mighty rushing river, made a chasm in which much perished. Art languished in the reign of the second Charles, excepting in what related to portrait-painting. Evelyn stood almost alone in his then secluded and lovely retirement at Wotton; apart in his undying exertions still to arrest the Muses ere they quitted forever English shores. Then came the deadly blank of William's icy influence. The reign of Anne was conspicuous more for letters than for art: architecture, more especially, was vulgarized under Vanbrugh. George I. had no conception of any thing abstract: taste, erudition, science, art, were like a dead language to his common sense, his vulgar profligacy, and his personal predilections. Neither George II. nor his queen had an iota of taste, either in language, conduct, literature, or art. To be vulgar was *haut ton;* to be refined, to have pursuits that took one from low party gossip, or heterodox disquisitions upon party, was esteemed odd: every thing original was cramped; every thing imaginative was sneered at; the enthusiasm that is elevated by religion was unphilosophic; the poetry that is breathed out from the works of genius was not comprehended.

It was at Houghton, under the roof of that monster palace, that Horace Walpole indulged that taste for pictures which he had acquired in Italy. His chief coadjutor, however, as far as the antiquities of painting are concerned, was George Vertue, the eminent engraver. Vertue was a man of modest merit, and was educated merely as an engraver; but, conscious of talent, studied drawing, which he afterward applied to engraving. He was patronized both by the vain Godfrey Kneller, and by the intellectual Lord Somers: his works have more fidelity than elegance, and betray in every line the antiquary rather than the genius. Vertue was known to be a first-rate authority as to the history of a painter; he was admitted and welcomed into every great country house in England; he lived in an atmosphere of vertù; every line a dilettante collector wrote, every word he uttered, was minuted down by him; he visited every collection of rarities; he copied every paper he could find relative to art; registers of wills and registers of parishes, for births and deaths were his delight; sales his recreation. He was the "Old Mortality" of pictures in this country. No wonder that his compilations were barely contained in forty volumes, which he left in manuscript. Human nature has singular varieties: here was a man who expended his very existence in gathering up the works of others, and died without giving to the world one of his own. But Horace

Walpole has done him justice. After Vertue's death he bought his manuscripts from his widow. In one of his pocket-books was contained the whole history of this man of one idea. Vertue began his collection in 1713, and worked at it until his death in 1757, forty-four years.

He died in the belief that he should one day publish an unique work on painting and painters: such was the aim of his existence, and his study must have been even more curious than the wonderfully crammed small house at Islington, where William Upcott, the "Old Mortality" in his line, who saved from the housemaid's fire-lighting designs the MSS. of Evelyn's Life and Letters, which he found tossing about in the old gallery at Wotton, near Dorking, passed his days. Like Upcott, like Palissy, Vertue lived and died under the influence of one isolated aim, effort, and hope.

In these men the cherished and amiable monomania of gifted minds was realized. Upcott had every possible autograph from every known hand in his collection; Palissy succeeded in making glazed china; but Vertue left his ore to the hands of others to work out into shape, and the man who moulded his crude materials was Horace Walpole. His forty volumes were shaped into a readable work, as curious and accurate in facts as it is flippant and prejudiced in style and opinions.

Walpole's "Anecdotes of Painting" are the foundation of all our small amount of knowledge as to what England has done formerly to encourage art.

One may fancy the modest, ingenious George Vertue arranging first, and then making a catalogue of the Houghton Gallery: Horace, a boy still, in looks, with a somewhat chubby face, admiring and following: Sir Robert, in a cocked hat, edged with silver lace, a curled short wig, a loose coat, also edged with silver lace, and with a half-humorous expression on his vulgar conntenance, watching them at intervals, as they paraded through the hall, a large square space, adorned with bas-reliefs and busts, and containing a bronze copy of the Laocoon, for which Sir Robert (or rather we English) paid a thousand pounds; or they might be seen hopping speedily through the ground-floor apartments where there could be little to arrest the footsteps of the medieval-minded Vertue. Who but a courtier could give one glance to a portrait of George I., though by Kneller? Who that *was* a courtier in that house would pause to look at the resemblance, also by Kneller, of the short-lived, ill-used Catherine Shorter, the Premier's first wife—even though he still endured it in his bedroom? a mute reproach for his neglect and misconduct. So let us hasten to the yellow dining-room where presently we may admire the works of Titian, Guido, Vanderwerf, and last, not least, eleven portraits by Vandyck, of the Wharton family, which Sir Robert bought at the sale of the spendthrift Duke of Wharton.

Then let us glance at the saloon, famed for the four large "Market Pieces," as they were called, by Rubens and Snyders: let us lounge into what were called the Carlo Maratti and the Vandyck rooms; step we also into the green velvet bed-chamber, the tapestry-room, the worked bed-chamber; then comes another dining-room: in short, we are lost in wonder at this noble collection, which cost £40,000.

Many of the pictures were selected and bargained for by Vertue, who, in Flanders, purchased the Market Pieces referred to, for £428; but did not secure the "Fish Market," and the "Meat Market," by the same painter. In addition to the pictures, the stateliness and beauty of the rooms were enhanced by rich furniture, carving, gilding, and all the subsidiary arts which our grandfathers loved to add to high merit in design or coloring. Besides his purchases, Sir Robert received presents of pictures from friends, and expectant courtiers; and the gallery at Houghton contained at last 222 pictures. To our sorrow now, to our disgrace then, this splendid collection was suffered to go out of the country: Catherine, Empress of Russia, bought it for £40,000, and it adorns the Hermitage Palace of St. Petersburg.

After Sir Robert's retirement from power, the good qualities which he undoubtedly possessed, seemed to reappear when the pressure of party feeling was withdrawn. He was fast declining in health when the insurrection of 1745 was impending. He had warned the country of its danger in his last speech, one of the finest ever made in the House of Lords: after that effort his voice was heard no more. The gallant, unfortunate Charles Edward was then at Paris, and that scope of old experience

> "Which doth attain
> To somewhat of prophetic strain,"

showed the ex-minister of Great Britain that an invasion was at hand. It was on this occasion that Frederick, Prince of Wales, took Sir Robert, then Lord Orford, by the hand, and thanked him for his zeal in the cause of the royal family. Walpole returned to Norfolk, but was summoned again to London to afford the ministry the benefit of his counsels. Death, however, closed his prosperous but laborious life. He suffered agonies from the stone; large doses of opium kept him in a state of stupor, and alone gave him ease; but his strength failed, and he was warned to prepare himself for his decease. He bore the announcement with great fortitude, and took leave of his children in perfect resignation to his doom. He died on the 28th of March, 1745.

Horace Walpole—whatsoever doubts may rest on the fact of his being Lord Orford's son or not—writes feelingly and naturally upon this event, and its forerunner, the agonies of disease. He seems, from the following passages in his letters to Sir Horace Mann, to have devoted himself incessantly to the patient invalid: on his father having rallied, he thus expresses himself:

"You have heard from your brother the reason of my not having written to you so long. I have been out but twice since my father fell into this illness, which is now near a month, and all that time either continually in his room, or obliged to see multitudes of people; for it is wonderful how every body of all kinds has affected to express their concern for him! He has been out of danger this week; but I can't say he mended at all perceptibly till these last three days. His spirits are amazing, and his constitution more; for Dr. Hulse said honestly from the first, that if he recovered it would be from his own strength, not from their art. How much more," he adds, mournfully, "he will ever recover, one scarce dare hope about; for us, he is greatly recovered; for himself—" He then breaks off.

A month after we find him thus referring to the parent still throbbing in mortal agony on the death-bed, with no chance of amendment:

"How dismal a prospect for him, with the possession of the greatest understanding in the world, not the least impaired, to lie without any use of it! for to keep him from pains and restlessness, he takes so much opiate that he is scarce awake four hours of the four-and-twenty; but I will say no more of this."

On the 29th of March he again wrote to his friend in the following terms:

"I begged your brothers to tell you what it is impossible for me to tell you. You share in our common loss! Don't expect me to enter at all upon the subject. After the melancholy two months that I have passed, and in my situation, you will not wonder I shun a conversation which could not be bounded by a letter, a letter that would grow into a panegyric or a piece of a moral; improper for me to write upon, and too distressful for us both! a death is only to be felt, never to be talked upon by those it touches."

Nevertheless, the world soon had Horace Walpole for her own again; during Lord Orford's last illness, George II.

thought of him, it seems, even though the "Granvilles" were the only people tolerated at court. That famous *clique* comprised the secretly adored of Horace (Lady Grenville once), Lady Sophia Fermor.

"The Granville faction," Horace wrote, before his father's death, "are still the constant and only countenanced people at court. Lord Winchelsea, one of the disgraced, played at court at Twelfth-night, and won; the king asked him next morning how much he had for his own share. He replied, 'Sir, about a quarter's salary.' I liked the spirit, and was talking to him of it the next night at Lord Granville's. 'Why yes,' said he, 'I think it showed familiarity at least: tell it your father, I don't think he will dislike it.'"

The most trifling incidents divided the world of fashion and produced the bitterest rancor. Indeed, nothing could exceed the frivolity of the great, except their impertinence. For want of better amusements, it had become the fashion to make conundrums, and to have printed books full of them, which were produced at parties. But these were peaceful diversions. The following anecdote is worthy of the times of George II. and of Frederick of Wales:

"There is a very good quarrel," Horace writes, "on foot, between two duchesses: she of Queensberry sent to invite Lady Emily Lenox to a ball: her grace of Richmond, who is wonderfully cautious since Lady Caroline's elopement (with Mr. Fox), sent word 'she could not determine.' The other sent again the same night: the same answer. The Queensberry then sent word that she had made up her company, and desired to be excused from having Lady Emily's; but at the bottom of the card wrote, 'Too great trust.' There is no declaration of war come out from the other duchess; but I believe it will be made a national quarrel of the whole illegitimate royal family."

Meantime, Houghton was shut up: for its owner died £50,000 in debt, and the elder brother of Horace, the second Lord Orford, proposed, on entering it again, after keeping it closed for some time, to enter upon "new, and then very unknown economy, for which there was great need:" thus Horace refers to the changes.

It was in the South Sea scheme that Sir Robert Walpole had realized a large sum of money, by selling out at the right moment. In doing so he had gained 1000 per cent. But he left little to his family, and at his death Horace received a legacy only of £5000, and a thousand pounds yearly, which he was to draw (for doing nothing), from the collector's place in the Custom House; the surplus to be divided between his brother

STRAWBERRY HILL FROM THE THAMES.

Edward and himself: this provision was afterward enhanced by some money which came to Horace and his brothers from his uncle Captain Shorter's property; but Horace was not at this period a rich man, and perhaps his not marrying was owing to his dislike of fortune-hunting, or to his dread of refusal.

Two years after his father's death he took a small house at Twickenham: the property cost him nearly £14,000; in the deeds he found that it was called Strawberry Hill. He soon commenced making considerable additions to the house—which became a sort of raree-show in the latter part of the last, and until a late period in this, century.

Twickenham—so called, according to the antiquary Norden, because the Thames, as it flows near it, seems from the islands to be divided into two rivers—had long been celebrated for its gardens, when Horace Walpole, the generalissimo of all bachelors, took Strawberry Hill. "Twicknam is as much as Twynam," declares Norden, "a place scytuate between two rivers." So fertile a locality could not be neglected by the monks of old, the great gardeners and tillers of land in ancient days; and the Manor of Twickenham was consequently given to the monks of Christ Church, Canterbury, by King Edred, in 491; who piously inserted his anathema against any person—whatever their rank, sex, or order—who should infringe the rights of these holy men. "May their memory," the king decreed, with a force worthy of the excommunicator-wholesale, Pius IX., "be blotted out of the Book of Life; may their strength continually waste away, and be there no restorative to repair it!" Nevertheless, there were in the time of Lysons, a hundred and fifty acres of fruit-gardens at Twickenham: the soil being a sandy loam, raspberries grew plentifully. Even so early as Queen Elizabeth's days, Bishop Corbet's father had a nursery-garden at Twickenham—so that King Edred's curse seems to have fallen as powerlessly as it may be hoped all subsequent maledictions may do.

In 1698, one of the Earl of Bradford's coachmen built a small house on a piece of ground, called in old works, Strawberry-Hill-Shot; lodgings were here let, and Colley Cibber became one of the occupants of the place, and here wrote his Comedy called "Refusal; or the Ladies' Philosophy." The spot was so greatly admired that Talbot, Bishop of Durham, lived eight years in it, and the Marquis of Carnarvon succeeded him as a tenant: next came Mrs. Chenevix, a famous toy-woman. She was probably a French woman, for Father Courayer—he who vainly endeavored to effect a union between the English and the Gallican churches—lodged here some time. Horace Walpole bought up Mrs. Chenevix's lease, and afterward the fee-simple; and henceforth became the busiest, if not the happiest, man in a small way in existence.

We now despise the poor, over-ornate miniature Gothic style of Strawberry Hill; we do not consider with what infinite pains the structure was enlarged into its final and well-known form. In the first place, Horace made a tour to collect models from the chief cathedral cities in England; but the building required twenty-three years to complete it. It was begun in 1753, and finished in 1776. Strawberry Hill had one merit, every thing was in keeping: the internal decorations, the screens, the niches, the chimney-pieces, the book-shelves, were all Gothic; and most of these were designed by Horace himself; and, indeed, the description of Strawberry Hill is too closely connected with the annals of his life to be dissevered from his biography. Here he gathered up his mental forces to support and amuse himself during a long life, sometimes darkened by spleen, but rarely by solitude; for Horace, with much isolation of the heart, was, to the world, a social being.

What scandal, what trifles, what important events, what littleness of mind, yet what stretch of intellect were henceforth issued by the recluse of Strawberry, as he plumed himself on being styled, from that library of "Strawberry!" Let us picture to ourselves the place, the persons—put on, if we can, the sentiments and habits of the retreat; look through its loop-holes, not only on the wide world beyond, but into the small world within; and face the fine gentleman author in every period of his varied life.

"The Strawberry Gazette," Horace once wrote to a fine and titled lady, "is very barren of weeds." Such, however, was rarely the case. Peers, and still better, peeresses—politicians, actors, actresses—the poor poet who knew not where to dine, the Mæcenas who was "fed with dedications"—the belle of the season, the demirep of many, the antiquary, and the dilettanti—painters, sculptors, engravers, all brought news to the "Strawberry Gazette;" and incense, sometimes wrung from aching hearts, to the fastidious wit who professed to be a judge of all material and immaterial things—from a burlesque to an Essay on History or Philosophy—from the construction of Mrs. Chenevix's last new toy to the mechanism of a clock made in the sixteenth century, was lavished there.

It is noonday: Horace is showing a party of guests from London over Strawberry: enter we with him, and let us stand in the great parlor before a portrait by Wright of the Minister to whom all courts bowed. "That is my father, Sir Robert, in profile," and a vulgar face in profile is always seen at its vulgarest; and the *nez-retroussé*, the coarse mouth, the double chin, are most forcibly exhibited in this limning by Wright; who did not, like Reynolds, or like Lawrence, cast a *nuance* of gentility over every subject of his pencil. Horace—can we not hear him in imagination?—is telling his friends how Sir Robert used to celebrate the day on which he sent in his resignation, as a fête; then he would point out to his visitors a Conversation-piece, one of Reynolds's earliest efforts in small life, representing the second Earl of Edgecumbe, Selwyn, and Williams—all wits and beaux, and *habitués* of Strawberry. Colley Cibber, however, was put in cold marble in the anteroom; respect very *Horatian*, for no man knew better how to rank his friends than the recluse of Strawberry. He hurries the lingering guests through the little parlor, the chimney-piece of which was copied from the tomb of Ruthall, Bishop of Durham, in Westminster Abbey. Yet how he pauses complacently to enumerate what has been done for him by titled belles: how these dogs, modeled in terra-cotta, are the production of Anne Damer; a water-color drawing by Agnes Berry; a landscape with gipsies by Lady Di Beauclerk; all platonically devoted to our Horace; but he dwells long, and his bright eyes are lighted up as he pauses before a case, looking as if it contained only a few apparently faded, of no-one-knows-who (or by whom) miniatures; this is a collection of Peter Oliver's best works—portraits of the Digby family.

How sadly, in referring to these invaluable pictures, does one's mind revert to the day when, before the hammer of Robins had resounded in these rooms—before his transcendent eloquence had been heard at Strawberry—Agnes Strickland, followed by all eyes, pondered over that group of portraits: how, as she slowly withdrew, we of the commonalty scarce worthy to look, gathered around the spot again, and wondered at the perfect life, the perfect coloring, proportion, and keeping of those tiny vestiges of a by-gone generation!

Then Horace—we fear it was not till his prime was past, and a touch of gout crippled his once active limbs—points to a picture of Rose, the gardener (well named), presenting Charles II. with a pine-apple. Some may murmur a doubt whether pine-apples were cultivated in cold Britain so long since. But Horace enforces the fact; "the likeness of the king," quoth he, "is too marked, and his features are too well known to doubt the fact;" and then he tells "how he had received a present the last Sunday of fruit—and from whom."

They pause next on Sir Peter Lely's portrait of Cowley—next on Hogarth's Sarah Malcolm, the murderess of her mistress; then—and doubtless, the spinster ladies are in fault here for the delay—on Mrs. Damer's model of two kittens, pets, though, of Horace Walpole's—for he who loved few human beings was, after the fashion of bachelors, fond of cats.

They ascend the staircase: the domestic adornments merge into the historic. We have Francis I.—not himself, but his armor; the chimney-piece, too, is a copy from the tomb-works of John, Earl of Cornwall, in Westminster Abbey; the stone-work from that of Thomas, Duke of Clarence, at Canterbury.

Stay a while: we have not done with sacrilege yet; worse things are to be told, and we walk with consciences not unscathed into the Library, disapproving in secret but flattering vocally. Here the very spirit of Horace seemed to those who visited Strawberry before its fall to breathe in every corner. Alas! when we beheld that library, it was half filled with chests containing the MSS. of his letters; which were bought by that enterprising publisher of learned name, Richard Bentley, and which have since had adequate justice done them by first-rate editors. There they were: the "Strawberry Gazette" in full; one glanced merely at the yellow paper, and clear, decisive hand, and then turned to see what objects he, who loved his books so well, collected for his especial gratification. Mrs. Damer again! how proud he was of her genius—her beauty, her cousinly love for himself; the wise way in which she bound up the wounds of her breaking heart when her profligate husband shot himself, by taking to occupation—perhaps, too, by liking cousin Horace indifferently well. He put her models forward in every place. Here was her Osprey Eagle in terra-cotta, a masterly production; there a *couvre-fire*, or *cur-few*, imitated and modeled by her. Then the marriage of Henry VI. figures on the wall: near the fire is a screen of the first tapestry ever made in England, representing a map of Surrey and Middlesex; a notion of utility combined with ornament, which we see still exhibited in the Sampler in old-fashioned, middle-class houses; that poor posthumous, base-born child of the tapestry, almost defunct itself; and a veritable piece of antiquity.

Still more remarkable in this room was a quaint-faced clock, silver gilt, given by Henry VIII. to Anne Boleyn; which perchance, after marking the moments of her festive life, struck unfeelingly the hour of her doom.

But the company are hurrying into a little ante-room, the ceiling of which is studded with stars in mosaic; it is therefore called jocularly, the "Star Chamber;" and here stands a cast of the famous bust of Henry VII., by Torregiano, intended for the tomb of that sad-faced, long-visaged monarch, who always looks as if royalty had disagreed with him.

Next we enter the Holbein Chamber. Horace hated bishops and archbishops, and all the hierarchy; yet here again we behold another prelatical chimney-piece—a frieze taken from the tomb of Archbishop Warham, at Canterbury. And here, in addition to Holbein's picture of Mary Tudor, Duchess of Suffolk, and of her third husband, Adrian Stokes, are Vertue's copies of Holbein, drawings of that great master's pictures in Buckingham House: enough—let us hasten into the Long Gallery. Those who remember Sir Samuel Merrick and his gallery at Goodrich Court will have traced in his curious, somewhat gewgaw collections of armor, antiquities, faded portraits, and mock horses, much of the taste and turn of mind that existed in Horace Walpole.

The gallery, which all who recollect the sale at Strawberry Hill must remember with peculiar interest, sounded well on paper. It was 56 feet long, 17 high, and 13 wide; yet was neither long enough, high enough, nor wide enough to inspire the indefinable sentiment by which we acknowledge vastness. We beheld it the scene of George Robins's triumphs—crowded to excess. Here strolled Lord John Russell; there, with heavy tread, walked Daniel O'Connell. Hallam, placid, kindly, gentle—the prince of book-worms—moved quickly through the rooms, pausing to raise a glance to the ceiling—copied from one of the side aisles of Henry VII.'s Chapel—but the fretwork is gilt, and there is a *petitesse* about the Gothic which disappoints all good judges.

But when Horace conducted his courtly guests into this his mind-vaunted vaulted gallery, he had sometimes George Selwyn at his side; or Gray—in his gracious moods; or, in his old age, "my niece, the Duchess of Gloucester," leaned on his arm. What strange associations, what brilliant company!—the associations can never be recalled there again; nor the company reassembled. The gallery, like every thing else, has perished under the pressure of debt. He who was so particular, too, as to the number of those who were admitted to see his house—he who stipulated that four persons only should compose a party, and one party alone be shown over each day—how would he have borne the crisis, could he have foreseen it, when Robins became, for the time, his successor, and was the temporary lord of Strawberry; the dusty, ruthless, wondering, depreciating mob of brokers—the respectable host of publishers—the starving army of martyrs, the authors—the fine ladies, who saw nothing there comparable to Howell and James's—the antiquaries, fishing out suspicious antiquities—the painters, clamorous over Kneller's profile of Mrs. Barry—the virtuous indignant mothers, as they passed by the portraits of the Duchess de la Vallière, and of Ninon de l'Enclos, and remarked, or at all events they *might* have remarked, that the company on the floor was scarcely much more respectable than the company on the walls—the fashionables, who herded together, impelled by caste, that free-masonry of social life, enter the Beauclerk closet to look over Lady Di's scenes from the "Mysterious Mother"—the players and dramatists, finally, who crowded round Hogarth's sketch of his "Beggars' Opera," with portraits, and gazed on Davison's likeness of Mrs. Clive: how could poor Horace have tolerated the sound of their irreverent remarks, the dust of their shoes, the degradation of their fancying that they might doubt his spurious-looking antiquities, or condemn his improper-looking ladies on their canvas? How, indeed, could he? For those parlors, that library, were peopled in his days with all those who could enhance his pleasures, or add to their own, by their presence. When Poverty stole in there, it was irradiated by Genius. When painters hovered beneath the fretted ceiling of that library, it was to thank the oracle of the day, not always for large orders, but for powerful recommendations. When actresses trod the Star Chamber, it was as modest friends, not as audacious critics on Horace, his house, and his pictures.

Before we call up the spirits that were familiar at Strawberry—ere we pass through the garden-gate, the piers of which were copied from the tomb of Bishop William de Luda, in Ely Cathedral—let us glance at the chapel, and then a word or two about Walpole's neighbors and anent Twickenham.

The front of the chapel was copied from Bishop Audley's tomb at Salisbury. Four panels of wood, taken from the Abbey of St. Edmund's Bury, displayed the portraits of Cardinal Beaufort, of Humphrey, Duke of Gloucester, and of Archbishop Kemp. So much for the English church.

Next was seen a magnificent shrine in mosaic, from the church of St. Mary Maggiore, in Rome. This was the work of the noted Peter Cavalini, who constructed the tomb of Edward the Confessor in Westminster Abbey. The shrine had figured over the sepulchre of four martyrs, who rested beneath it in 1257; then the principal window in the chapel was brought from Bexhill in Surrey; and displayed portraits of Henry III. and his queen.

It was not every day that gay visitors traveled down the dusty roads from London to visit the recluse at Strawberry; but Horace wanted them not, for he had neighbors. In his youth he had owned for his playfellow the ever witty, the precocious, the all-fascinating Lady Mary Wortley Montagu. "She was," he wrote, "a playfellow of mine when we were children. She was always a dirty little thing. This habit continued with her. When at Florence, the Grand Duke gave her apartments in his palace. One room sufficed for every thing; and when she went away, the stench was so strong that they were obliged to fumigate the chamber with vinegar for a week."

Let not the scandal be implicitly credited. Lady Mary, dirty or clean, resided occasionally, however, at Twickenham. When the admirable Lysons composed his "Environs of London," Horace Walpole was still living—it was in 1795—to point out to him the house in which his brilliant acquaintance lived. It was then inhabited by Dr. Morton. The profligate and clever Duke of Wharton lived also at Twickenham.

Marble Hill was built by George II., for the Countess of Suffolk, and Henry, Earl of Pembroke, was the architect. Of later years, the beautiful and injured Mrs. Fitzherbert might be seen traversing the greensward, which was laved by the then pellucid waters of the Thames. The parish of Twickenham, in fact, was noted for the numerous characters who have, at various times, lived in it; Robert Boyle, the great philosopher; James Craggs, Secretary of State; Lord George Germaine; Lord Bute—are strangely mixed up with the old memories which circle around Twickenham.

One dark figure in the background of society haunts us also: Lady Macclesfield, the cruel mother of Savage, polluted Twickenham by her evil presence.

Let us not dwell on her name, but recall, with somewhat of pride, that the names of that knot of accomplished, intellectual women, who composed the neighborhood of Strawberry, were all English; those who loved to revel in all its charms of society and intellect were our justly-prized countrywomen.

Foremost in the bright constellation was Anne Seymour Conway, too soon married to the Hon. John Damer. She was one of the loveliest, the most enterprising, and the most gifted women of her time—thirty-one years younger than Horace, having been born in 1748. He doubtless liked her the more that no ridicule could attach to his partiality, which was that of a father to a daughter, in so far as regarded his young cousin. She belonged to a family dear to him, being the daughter of Field Marshal Henry Seymour Conway: then she was beautiful, witty, a courageous politician, a heroine, fearless of losing caste by aspiring to be an artist. She was, in truth, of our own time rather than of that. The works which she left at Strawberry are scattered; and if still traceable, are probably in many instances scarcely valued. But in that lovely spot, hallowed by the remembrance of Mrs. Siddons, who lived there in some humble capacity—say maid, say companion—in Guy's Cliff House, near Warwick—noble traces of Anne Damer's genius are extant: busts of the majestic Sally Siddons; of Nature's aristocrat, John Kemble; of his brother Charles—arrest many a look, call up many a thought of Anne Damer and her gifts: her intelligence, her warmth of heart, her beauty, her associates. Of her powers Horace Walpole had the highest opinion. "If they come to Florence," he wrote, speaking of Mrs. Damer's going to Italy for the winter, "the great duke should beg Mrs. Damer to give him something of her statuary; and it would be a greater curiosity than any thing in his Chamber of Painters. She has executed several marvels since you saw her; and has lately carved two colossal heads for the bridge at Henley, which is the most beautiful in the world, next to the Ponte di Trinità, and was principally designed by her father, General Conway."

No wonder that he left to this accomplished relative the privilege of living, after his death, at Strawberry Hill, of which she took possession in 1797, and where she remained twenty years; giving it up, in 1828, to Lord Waldegrave.

She was, as we have said, before her time in her appreciation of what was noble and superior, in preference to that which gives to caste alone its supremacy. During her last years she bravely espoused an unfashionable cause; and disregarding the contempt of the lofty, became the champion of the injured and unhappy Caroline of Brunswick.

From his retreat at Strawberry, Horace Walpole heard all that befell the object of his flame, Lady Sophia Fermor. His letters present from time to time such passages as these; Lady Pomfret, whom he detested, being always the object of his satire:

"There is not the least news; but that my Lord Carteret's wedding has been deferred on Lady Sophia's (Fermor's) falling dangerously ill of a scarlet fever; but they say it is to be next Saturday. She is to have £1600 a year jointure, £400 pin-money, and £2000 of jewels. Carteret says he does not intend to marry the mother (Lady Pomfret) and the whole family. What do you think my Lady intends?"

Lord Carteret, who was the object of Lady Pomfret's successful generalship, was at this period, 1744, fifty-four years of age, having been born in 1690. He was the son of George, Lord Carteret, by Grace, daughter of the first Earl of Bath, of the line of Granville—a title which became eventually his. The fair Sophia, in marrying him, espoused a man of no ordinary attributes. In person, Horace Walpole, after the grave had closed over one whom he probably envied, thus describes him:

> "Commanding beauty, smoothed by cheerful grace,
> Sat on each open feature of his face.
> Bold was his language, rapid, glowing, strong,
> And science flowed spontaneous from his tongue:
> A genius seizing systems, slighting rules,
> And void of gall, with boundless scorn of fools."

After having been Lord Lieutenant of Ireland, Carteret attended his royal master in the campaign, during which the battle of Dettingen was fought. He now held the reins of government in his own hands as premier. Lord Chesterfield has described him as possessing quick precision, nice decision, and unbounded presumption. The Duke of Newcastle used to say of him that he was a "man who never doubted."

In a subsequent letter we find the sacrifice of the young and lovely Sophia completed. Ambition was the characteristic of her family: and she went, not unwillingly, to the altar. The whole affair is too amusingly told to be given in other language than that of Horace:

"I could tell you a great deal of news," he writes to Horace Mann, "but it would not be what you would expect. It is not of battles, sieges, and declarations of war; nor of invasions, insurrections, and addresses: it is the god of love, not he of war, who reigns in the newspapers. The town has made up a list of six-and-thirty weddings, which I shall not catalogue to you. But the chief entertainment has been the nuptials of our great Quixote (Carteret) and the fair Sophia. On the point of matrimony, she fell ill of a scarlet fever, and was given over, while he had the gout, but heroically sent her word, that if she was well, he *would* be well. They corresponded every day, and he used to plague the cabinet council with reading her letters to them. Last night they were married; and as all he does must have a particular air in it, they supped at Lord Pomfret's. At twelve, Lady Granville (his mother) and all his family went to bed, but the porter: then my lord went home, and waited for her in the lodge. She came alone, in a hackney-chair, met him in the hall, and was led up the back stairs to bed. What is ridiculously lucky is, that Lord Lincoln goes into waiting to-day, and will be to present her!"

The event was succeeded by a great ball at the Duchess of Richmond's, in honor of the bride, Lady Carteret paying her ladyship the "highest honors," which she received in the "highest state." "I have seen her," adds Horace, "but once, and found her just what I expected, *très grande dame*, full of herself, and yet not with an air of happiness. She looks ill, and is grown lean, but is still the finest figure in the world. The mother (Lady Pomfret) is not so exalted as I expected; I fancy Carteret has kept his resolution, and does not marry her too."

While this game was being played out, one of Walpole's most valued neighbors, Pope, was dying of dropsy, and every evening a gentle delirium possessed him. Again does Horace return to the theme, ever in his thoughts—the Carterets: again does he recount their triumphs and their follies.

"I will not fail"—still to Horace Mann—"to make your compliments to the Pomfrets and Carterets. I see them seldom, but I am in favor; so I conclude, for my Lady Pomfret told me the other night that I said better things than any body. I was with them all at a subscription-ball at Ranelagh last week, which my Lady Carteret thought proper to look upon as given to her, and thanked the gentlemen, who were not quite so well pleased at her condescending to take it to herself. I did the honors of all her dress. 'How charming your ladyship's cross is! I am sure the design was your own!' 'No, indeed; my lord sent it to me just as it is.' Then as much to the mother. Do you wonder I say better things than any body?"

But these brilliant scenes were soon mournfully ended. Lady Sophia, the haughty, the idolized, the Juno of that gay circle, was suddenly carried off by a fever. With real feeling Horace thus tells the tale:

"Before I talk of any public news, I must tell you what you will be very sorry for. Lady Granville (Lady Sophia Fermor) is dead. She had a fever for six weeks before her lying-in, and could never get it off. Last Saturday they called in another physician, Dr. Oliver. On Monday he pronounced her out of danger; about seven in the evening, as Lady Pomfret and Lady Charlotte (Fermor) were sitting by her, the first notice they had of her immediate danger was her sighing and saying, 'I feel death come very fast upon me!' She repeated the same words frequently, remained perfectly in her senses and calm, and died about eleven at night. It is very shocking for any body so young, so handsome, so arrived at the height of happiness, to be so quickly snatched away."

So vanished one of the brightest stars of the court. The same autumn (1745) was the epoch of a great event; the marching of Charles Edward into England. While the Duke of Cumberland was preparing to head the troops to oppose him, the Prince of Wales was inviting a party to supper, the main feature of which was the citadel of Carlisle in sugar, the company all besieging it with sugar-plums. It would, indeed, as Walpole declared, be impossible to relate all the *Caligulisms* of this effeminate, absurd prince. But buffoonery and eccentricity were the order of the day. "A ridiculous thing happened," Horace writes, "when the princess saw company after her confinement. The new-born babe was shown in a mighty pretty cradle, designed by Kent, under a canopy in the great drawing-room. Sir William Stanhope went to look at it. Mrs. Herbert, the governess, advanced to unmantle it. He said, 'In wax, I suppose?' 'Sir?' 'In wax, madam?' 'The young prince, sir?' 'Yes, in wax, I suppose?' This is his odd humor. When he went to see the duke at his birth, he said, 'Lord, it sees!'"

The recluse of Strawberry was soon consoled by hearing that the rebels were driven back from Derby, where they had penetrated, and where the remembrance of the then gay, sanguine, brave young Chevalier long lingered among the old inhabitants. One of the last traces of his short-lived possession of the town is gone: very recently, Exeter House, where he lodged and where he received his adherents, has been pulled down; the ground on which it stood, with its court and garden—somewhat in appearance like an old French hotel—being too valuable for the relic of by-gone times to be spared. The paneled chambers, the fine staircase, certain pictures—one by Wright of Derby, of him—one of Miss Walkinshaw—have all disappeared.

Of the capture, the trial, the death of his adherents, Horace Walpole has left the most graphic and therefore touching account that has been given; while he calls a "rebellion on the defensive" a "despicable affair." Humane, he reverted with horror to the atrocities of General Hawley, "the Chief Justice," as he was designated, who had a "passion for frequent and sudden executions." When this savage commander gained intelligence of a French spy coming over, he displayed him at once before the army on a gallows, dangling in his muff and boots. When one of the surgeons begged for the body of a deserter to dissect, "Well," said the wretch, "but you must let me have the skeleton to hang up in the guard-room." Such was the temper of the times; vice, childishness, levity at court, brutality in the camp, were the order of the day. Horace, even Horace, worldly in all, indifferent as to good and bad, seems to have been heart-sick. His brother's matrimonial infidelity vexed him also sorely. Lady Orford, "tired," as he expresses it, of "sublunary affairs," was trying to come to an arrangement with her husband, from whom she had been long separated; the price was to be, he fancied, £2000 a year. Meantime, during the convulsive state of political affairs, he interested himself continually in the improvement of Strawberry Hill. There was a rival building, Mr. Bateman's Monastery, at Old Windsor, which is said to have had more uniformity of design than Strawberry Hill. Horace used indeed to call the house of which he became so proud a paper house; the walls were at first so slight, and the roof so insecure in heavy rains. Nevertheless, his days were passed as peacefully there as the premature infirmities which came upon him would permit.

From the age of twenty-five his fingers were enlarged and deformed by chalk-stones, which were discharged twice a year. "I can chalk up a score with more rapidity than any man in England," was his melancholy jest. He had now adopted as a necessity a strict temperance: he sat up very late, either writing or conversing, yet always breakfasted at nine o'clock. After the death of Madame du Deffand, a little fat dog, scarcely able to move for age and size—her legacy—used to proclaim his approach by barking. The little favorite was placed beside him on a sofa; a tea-kettle, stand, and heater were brought in, and he drank two or three cups of tea out of the finest and most precious china of Japan—that of a pure white. He breakfasted with an appetite, feeding from his table the little dog and his pet squirrels.

Dinner at Strawberry Hill was usually served up in the small parlor in winter, the large dining-room being reserved for large parties. As age drew on, he was supported down stairs by his valet; and then, says the compiler of Walpoliana, "he ate most moderately of chicken, pheasant, or any light food. Pastry he disliked, as difficult of digestion, though he would taste a morsel of venison-pie. Never but once, that he drank two glasses of white wine, did the editor see him taste any liquor, except ice-water. A pail of ice was placed under the table, in which stood a decanter of water, from which he supplied himself with his favorite beverage."

No wine was drunk after dinner, when the host of Strawberry Hill called instantly to some one to ring the bell for coffee. It was served up stairs, and there, adds the same writer, "he would pass about five o'clock, and generally resuming his place on the sofa, would sit till two in the morning, in miscellaneous chit-chat, full of singular anecdotes, strokes of wit, and acute observations, occasionally sending for books, or curiosities, or passing to the library, as any reference happened to arise in conversation. After his coffee, he tasted nothing; but the snuff-box of *tabac d'etrennes*, from Fribourg's, was not forgotten, and was replenished from a canister lodged in an ancient marble urn of great thickness, which stood in the window seat, and served to secure its moisture and rich flavor."

In spite of all his infirmities, Horace Walpole took no care of his health, as far as out-door exercise was concerned. His friends beheld him with horror go out on a dewy day: he would even step out in his slippers. In his own grounds he never wore a hat: he used to say, that on his first visit to Paris he was ashamed of his effeminacy, when he saw every meagre little Frenchman whom he could have knocked down in a breath walking without a hat, which he could not do without a certainty of taking the disease which the Germans say is endemical in England, and which they call *to catch cold.* The first trial, he used to tell his friends, cost him a fever, but he got over it. Draughts of air, damp rooms, windows open at his back, became matters of indifference to him after once getting through the hardening process. He used even to be vexed at the officious solicitude of friends on this point, and with a half smile would say, "My back is the same as my face, and my neck is like my nose." He regarded his favorite iced-water as a preservative to his stomach, which, he said, would last longer than his bones. He did not take into account that the stomach is usually the seat of disease.

One naturally inquires why the amiable recluse never, in his best days, thought of marriage: it is in many instances a difficult question to be answered. In men of that period, a dissolute life, an unhappy connection, too frequently explained the problem. In the case before us, no such explanation can be offered. Horace Walpole had many votaries, many friends, several favorites, but no known mistress. The marks of the old bachelor fastened early on him, more especially after he began to be governed by his *valet de chambre.* The notable personage who ruled over the pliant Horace was a Swiss, named Colomb. This domestic tyrant was despotic; if Horace wanted a tree to be felled, Colomb opposed it, and the master yielded. Servants, in those days, were intrinsically the same as in ours, but they differed in manner. The old familiarity had not gone out, but existed as it still does among the French. Those who recollect Dr. Parr will remember how stern a rule his factotum Sam exercised over him. Sam put down what wine he chose, nay, almost invited the guests; at all events, he had his favorites among them. And in the same way as Sam ruled at Hatton, Colomb was, *de facto*, the master of Strawberry Hill.

With all its defects, the little "plaything house," as Horace Walpole called it, must have been a charming house to visit in. First, there was the host. "His engaging manners," writes the editor of Walpoliana, "and gentle, endearing affability to his friends, exceed all praise. Not the smallest hau-

N

teur, or consciousness of rank or talent, appeared in his familiar conferences; and he was ever eager to dissipate any constraint that might occur, as imposing a constraint upon himself, and knowing that any such chain enfeebles and almost annihilates the mental powers. Endued with exquisite sensibility, his wit never gave the smallest wound, even to the grossest ignorance of the world, or the most morbid hypochondriac bashfulness."

He had, in fact, no excuse for being doleful or morbid. How many recourses were his! what an even destiny! what prosperous fortunes! what learned luxury we revel in! he was enabled to "pick up all the roses of science, and to leave the thorns behind." To how few of the gifted have the means of gratification been permitted! to how many has hard work been allotted! Then, when genius has been endowed with rank, with wealth, how often it has been degraded by excess! Rochester's passions ran riot in one century; Beckford's gifts were polluted by his vices in another—signal landmarks of each age. But Horace Walpole was prudent, decorous, even respectable: no elevated aspirations, no benevolent views ennobled under the *petitesse* of his nature. He had neither genius nor romance: he was even devoid of sentiment; but he was social to all, neighborly to many, and attached to some of his fellow-creatures.

The "prettiest bawble" possible, as he called Strawberry Hill, "set in enameled meadows in filigree hedges," was surrounded by "dowagers as plenty as flounders;" such was Walpole's assertion. As he sat in his library, scented by caraway, heliotropes, or pots of tuberose, or orange-trees in flower; certain dames would look in upon him, sometimes *malgré lui;* sometimes to his bachelor heart's content.

"Thank God!" he wrote to his cousin Conway, "the Thames is between me and the Duchess of Queensberry!" Walpole's dislike to his fair neighbor may have originated in the circumstance of her birth, and her grace's presuming to plume herself on what he deemed an unimportant distinction. Catherine Hyde, Duchess of Queensberry, was the great-granddaughter of the famous Lord Clarendon, and the great-niece of Anne, Duchess of York. Prior had in her youth celebrated her in the "Female Phaëton," as "Kitty;" in his verse he begs Phaëton to give Kitty the chariot, if but for a day.

In reference to this, Horace Walpole, in the days of his admiration of her grace, had made the following impromptu:

"On seeing the Duchess of Queensberry walk at the funeral of the Princess Dowager of Wales—

"To many a Kitty, Love his car
Would for a day engage;
But Prior's Kitty, ever fair,
Obtained it for an age."

It was Kitty who took Gay under her patronage, who resented the prohibition of the "Beggar's Opera," remonstrated with the king and queen, and was thereupon forbidden the court. She took the poet to her house. She may have been ridiculous, but she had a warm, generous heart. "I am now," Gay wrote to Swift in 1729, "in the Duke of Queensberry's house, and have been so ever since I left Hampstead; where I was carried at a time that it was thought I could not live a day. I must acquaint you (because I know it will please you) that during my sickness I had many of the kindest proofs of friendship, particularly from the Duke and Duchess of Queensberry; who, if I had been their nearest relation and dearest friend, could not have treated me with more constant attendance then, and they continue the same to me now."

The duchess appears to have been one of those willful, eccentric, spoiled children, whom the world at once worships and ridicules: next to the Countess of Pomfret, she was Horace Walpole's pet-aversion. She was well described as being "very clever, very whimsical, and just not mad." Some of Walpoles touches are strongly confirmatory of this description. For instance, her grace gives a ball, orders every one to come at six, to sup at twelve, and go away directly after: opens the ball herself with a minuet. To this ball she sends strange invitations; "yet," says Horace, "except these flights, the only extraordinary thing the duchess did was to do nothing extraordinary, for I do not call it very mad that some pique happening between her and the Duchess of Bedford, the latter had this distich sent to her:

"'Come with a whistle—come with a call;
Come with good-will, or come not at all.'

I do not know whether what I am going to tell you did not border a little upon Moorfields. The gallery where they danced was very cold. Lord Lorn, George Selwyn, and I, retired into a little room, and sat comfortably by the fire. The duchess looked in, said nothing, and sent a smith to take the hinges of the door off. We understood the hint—left the room—and so did the smith the door."

"I must tell you," he adds in another letter, "of an admirable reply of your acquaintance, the Duchess of Queensberry: old Lady Granville, Lord Carteret's mother, whom they call *the queen-mother*, from taking upon her to do the honors of her son's power, was pressing the duchess to ask her for some place for herself or friends, and assured her that she would procure it, be it what it would. Could she have picked out a fitter person to be gracious to? The duchess made her a most grave courtesy, and said, 'Indeed, there was one thing she had set her heart on.' 'Dear child, how you oblige me by asking any thing! What is it? tell me.' 'Only that you would speak to my Lord Carteret to get me made lady of the bed-chamber to the Queen of Hungary.'"

The duchess was, therefore, one of the dowagers, "thick as flounders," whose proximity was irritating to the fastidious bachelor. There was, however, another Kitty between whom and Horace a tender friendship subsisted: this was Kitty Clive, the famous actress; formerly Kitty Ruftar. Horace had given her a house on his estate, which he called sometimes "Little Strawberry Hill," and sometimes "Cliveden;" and here Mrs. Clive lived with her brother, Mr. Ruftar, until 1785. She formed, for her friend, a sort of outer-home, in which he passed his evenings. Long had he admired her talents. Those were the days of the drama in all its glory; the opera was unfashionable. There were, Horace writes in 1742, on the 26th of May, only two-and-forty people in the Opera House, in the pit and boxes: people were running to see "Miss Lucy in Town," at Drury Lane, and to admire Mrs. Clive, in her imitation of the Muscovites; but the greatest crowds assembled to wonder at Garrick, in "Wine Merchant turned Player;" and great and small alike rushed to Goodman's Fields to see him act all parts, and to laugh at his admirable mimicry. It was, perhaps, somewhat in jealousy of the counter attractions, that Horace declared he saw nothing wonderful in the acting of Garrick, though it was then heresy to say so. "Now I talk of players," he adds in the same letter; "tell Mr. Chute that his friend Bracegirdle breakfasted with me this morning." Horace delighted in such intimacies, and in recalling old times.

Mrs. Abingdon, another charming and clever actress, was also a denizen of Twickenham, which became the most fashionable village near the metropolis. Mrs. Pritchard, likewise, was attracted there; but the proximity of the Countess of Suffolk, who lived at Marble Hill, was the delight of a great portion of Horace Walpole's life. Her reminiscences, her anecdotes, her experience, were valuable as well as entertaining to one who was forever gathering up materials for history, or for biography, or for letters to absent friends.

In his own family he found little to cheer him: but if he hated one or two more especially—and no one could hate more intensely than Horace Walpole—it was his uncle, Lord

Walpole, and his cousin, that nobleman's son, whom he christened Pigwiggin; "my monstrous uncle;" "that old buffoon, my uncle," are terms which occur in his letters, and he speaks of the bloody civil wars between "Horatio Walpole" and "Horace Walpole."

Horatio Walpole, the brother of Sir Robert, was created in June, 1756, Baron Walpole of Wolterton, as a recompense for fifty years passed in the public service—an honor which he only survived nine months. He expired in February, 1757. His death removed one subject of bitter dislike from the mind of Horace; but enough remained in the family to excite grief and resentment.

Toward his own two brothers, Robert, Earl of Orford, and Edward Walpole, Horace the younger, as he was styled in contradistinction to his uncle, bore very little affection. His feelings, however, for his nephew George, who succeeded his father as Earl of Orford in 1751, were more creditable to his heart; yet he gives a description of this ill-fated young man in his letters, which shows at once pride and disapprobation. One lingers with regret over the character and the destiny of this fine young nobleman, whose existence was rendered miserable by frequent attacks, at intervals, of insanity.

Never was there a handsomer, a more popular, a more engaging being than George, third Earl of Orford. When he appeared at the head of the Norfolk regiment of militia, of which he was colonel, even the great Lord Chatham broke out into enthusiasm: "Nothing," he wrote, "could make a better appearance than the two Norfolk battalions; Lord Orford, with the front of Mars himself, and really the greatest figure under arms I ever saw, was the theme of every tongue."

His person and air, Horace Walpole declared, had a noble wildness in them: crowds followed the battalions when the king reviewed them in Hyde Park; and among the gay young officers in their scarlet uniforms, faced with black, in their buff waistcoats and gold buttons, none was so conspicuous for martial bearing as Lord Orford, although classed by his uncle "among the knights of shires who had never in their lives shot any thing but woodcocks."

But there was a peculiarity of character in the young peer which shocked Horace. "No man," he says in one of his letters, "ever felt such a disposition to love another as I did to love him. I flattered myself that he would restore some lustre to our house—at least not let it totally sink; but I am forced to give him up, and all my Walpole views. . . . . He has a good breeding, and attention when he is with you that is even flattering. . . . . He promises, offers every thing one can wish; but this is all: the instant he leaves you, all the world are nothing to him; he would not give himself the least trouble in the world to give any one satisfaction; yet this is mere indolence of mind, not of body: his whole pleasure is outrageous exercise."

"He is," in another place Horace adds, "the most selfish man in the world: without being in the least interested, he loves nobody but himself, yet neglects every view of fortune and ambition. Yet," he concludes, "it is impossible not to love him when one sees him: impossible to esteem him when one thinks on him."

The young lord, succeeding to an estate deeply encumbered, both by his father and grandfather, rushed on the turf, and involved himself still more. In vain did Horace the younger endeavor to secure for him the hand of Miss Nicholls, an heiress with £50,000, and, to that end, placed the young lady with Horace the elder (Lord Walpole), at Wolterton. The scheme failed: the crafty old politician thought he might as well benefit his own sons as his nephew, for he had himself claims on the Houghton estate which he expected Miss Nicholls's fortune might help to liquidate.

At length the insanity and recklessness displayed by his nephew—the handsome, martial George—induced poor Horace to take affairs in his own hands. His reflections, on his paying a visit to Houghton, to look after the property there, are pathetically expressed:

"Here I am again at Houghton," he writes in March, 1761, "and alone; in this spot where (except two hours last month) I have not been in sixteen years. Think what a crowd of reflections! . . . Here I am probably for the last time of my life: every clock that strikes, tells me I am an hour nearer to yonder church—that church into which I have not yet had courage to enter; where lies that mother on whom I doted, and who doted on me! There are the two rival mistresses of Houghton, neither of whom ever wished to enjoy it. There, too, is he who founded its greatness—to contribute to whose fall Europe was embroiled; there he sleeps in quiet and dignity, while his friend and his foe—rather his false ally and real enemy—Newcastle and Bath, are exhausting the dregs of their pitiful lives in squabbles and pamphlets."

When he looked at the pictures—that famous Houghton collection—the surprise of Horace was excessive. Accustomed to see nothing elsewhere but daubs, he gazed with ecstasy on them. "The majesty of Italian ideas," he says, "almost sinks before the warm nature of Italian coloring! Alas! don't I grow old?"

As he lingered in the Gallery, with mingled pride and sadness, a party arrived to see the house—a man and three women, in riding-dresses—who "rode post" through the apartments. "I could not," he adds, "hurry before them fast enough; they were not so long in seeing the whole gallery as I could have been in one room, to examine what I knew by heart. I remember formerly being often diverted with this kind of *seers;* they come, ask what such a room is called in which Sir Robert lay, write it down, admire a lobster or a cabbage in a Market Piece, dispute whether the last room was green or purple, and then hurry to the inn, for fear the fish should be overdressed. How different my sensations! not a picture here but recalls a history; not one but I remember in Downing Street, or Chelsea, where queens and crowds admired them, though seeing them as little as these travelers!"*

After tea he strolled into the garden. They told him it was now called a *pleasure-ground.* To Horace it was a scene of desolation—a floral Nineveh. "What a dissonant idea of pleasure! those groves, those *allées*, where I have passed so many charming moments, were now stripped up or overgrown—many fond paths I could not unravel, though with an exact clew in my memory. I met two gamekeepers, and a thousand hares! In the days when all my soul was tuned to pleasure and vivacity (and you will think perhaps it is far from being out of tune yet), I hated Houghton and its solitude; yet I loved this garden, as now, with many regrets, I love Houghton—Houghton, I know not what to call it—a monument of grandeur or ruin!"

Although he did not go with the expectation of finding a land flowing with milk and honey, the sight of all this ruin long saddened his thoughts. All was confusion, disorder, debts, mortgages, sales, pillage, villainy, waste, folly, and madness. The nettles and brambles in the park were up to his shoulders; horses had been turned into the garden, and banditti lodged in every cottage.

The perpetuity of livings that came up to the very park palings had been sold, and the farms let at half their value. Certainly, if Houghton were bought by Sir Robert Walpole with public money, that public was now avenged.

The owner of this ruined property had just stemmed the torrent; but the worst was to come. The pictures were sold, and to Russia they went.

While thus harassed by family misfortunes, other annoy-

* Sir Robert Walpole purchased a house and garden at Chelsea in 1722, near the college adjoining Gough House.—Cunningham's "London."

ances came. The mournful story of Chatterton's fate was painfully mixed up with the tenor of Horace Walpole's life.

The gifted and unfortunate Thomas Chatterton was born at Bristol in 1752. Even from his birth fate seemed to pursue him, for he was a posthumous son: and if the loss of a father in the highest ranks of life be severely felt, how much more so is it to be deplored in those which are termed the working classes!

The friendless enthusiast was slow in learning to read; but when the illuminated capitals of an old book were presented to him, he quickly learned his letters. This fact, and his being taught to read out of a black-letter Bible, are said to have accounted for his facility in the imitation of antiquities.

Pensive and taciturn, he picked up education at a charity-school, until apprenticed to a scrivener, when he began that battle of life which ended to him so fatally.

Upon very slight accidents did his destiny hinge. In those days women worked with thread, and used thread-papers. Now paper was dear: dainty matrons liked tasty thread-papers. A pretty set of thread-papers, with birds or flowers painted on each, was no mean present for a friend. Chatterton, a quiet child, one day noticed that his mother's thread-papers were of no ordinary materials. They were made of parchment, and on this parchment were some of the black-letter characters by which his childish attention had been fixed to his book. The fact was, that his uncle was sexton to the ancient church of St. Mary Redcliffe, at Bristol; and the parchment was the fruit of theft. Chatterton's father had carried off, from a room in the church, certain ancient manuscripts, which had been left about; being originally extracted from what was called Mr. Canynge's coffin. Now, Mr. Canynge, an eminent merchant, had rebuilt St. Mary Redcliffe in the reign of Edward IV.: and the parchments, therefore, were of some antiquity. The antiquary groans over their loss in vain: Chatterton's father had covered his books with them; his mother had used up the strips for thread-papers; and Thomas Chatterton himself contrived to abstract a considerable portion also, for his own purposes.

He was ingenious, industrious, a poet by nature, and, wonderful to say, withal a herald by taste. Upon his nefarious possessions, he founded a scheme of literary forgeries; purporting to be ancient pieces of poetry found in Canynge's chest; and described as being the production of Thomas Canynge and of his friend, one Thomas Rowley, a priest. Money and books were sent to Chatterton in return for little strips of vellum, which he passed off as the original itself; and the successful forger might now be seen in deep thought, walking in the meadows near Redcliffe; a marked, admired poetic youth.

In 1769, Chatterton wrote to Horace Walpole, offering to send him some accounts of eminent painters who had flourished at Bristol, and at the same time mentioning the discovery of the poems, and inclosing some specimens. In a subsequent letter he begged Walpole to aid him in his wish to be freed from his then servile condition, and to be placed in one more congenial to his pursuits.

In his choice of a patron poor Chatterton made a fatal mistake. The benevolence of Horace was of a general kind, and never descended to any thing obscure or unappreciated. There was a certain hardness in that nature of his which had so pleasant an aspect. "An artist," he once said, "has his pencils—an author his pens—and the public must reward them as it pleases." Alas! he forgot how long it is before penury, even ennobled by genius, can make itself seen, heard, approved, repaid: how vast is the influence of *prestige!* how generous the hand which is extended to those in want, even if in error! All that Horace did, however, was strictly correct: he showed the poems to Gray and Mason, who pronounced them forgeries; and he wrote a cold and reproving letter to the starving author: and no one could blame him: Chatterton demanded back his poems; Walpole was going to Paris, and forgot to return them. Another letter came: the wounded poet again demanded them, adding, that Walpole would not have dared to use him so had he not been poor. The poems were returned in a blank cover: and here all Walpole's concern with Thomas Chatterton ends. All this happened in 1769. In August, 1770, the remains of the unhappy youth were carried to the burial-ground of Shoe Lane workhouse, near Holborn. He had swallowed arsenic; had lingered a day in agonies; and then, at the age of eighteen, expired. Starvation had prompted the act: yet on the day before he had committed it, he had refused a dinner, of which he was invited by his hostess to partake, assuring her that he was not hungry. Just or unjust, the world has never forgiven Horace Walpole for Chatterton's misery. His indifference has been contrasted with the generosity of Edmund Burke to Crabbe: a generosity to which we owe "The Village," "The Borough," and to which Crabbe owed his peaceful old age, and almost his existence. The cases were different; but Crabbe had his faults—and Chatterton was worth saving. It is well for genius that there are souls in the world more sympathizing, less worldly, and more indulgent, than those of such men as Horace Walpole. Even the editor of "Walpoliana" lets judgment go by default. "As to artists," he says, "he paid them what they earned, and he commonly employed mean ones, that the reward might be smaller."

Let us change the strain: stilled be the mournful note on which we have rested too long. What have wits and beaux and men of society to do with poets and beggars? Behold, Horace, when he has written his monitory letter, packs up for Paris. Let us follow him there, and see him in the very centre of his pleasures—in the *salon* of La Marquise du Deffand.

Horace Walpole had perfected his education, as a fine gentleman, by his intimacy with Madame Geoffrin, to whom Lady Hervey had introduced him. She called him *le nouveau Richelieu;* and Horace was sensible of so great a compliment from a woman at once "*spirituelle* and *pieuse*"—a combination rare in France. Nevertheless, she had the national views of matrimony. "What have you done, Madame," said a foreigner to her, "with the poor man I used to see here, who never spoke a word?"

"Ah, *mon Dieu!*" was the reply, "that was my husband: he is dead." She spoke in the same tone as if she had been specifying the last new opera, or referring to the latest work in vogue: things just passed away.

The *Marquise du Deffand* was a very different personage to Madame Geoffrin, whose great enemy she was. When Horace Walpole first entered into the society of the marquise, she was stone blind, and old; but retained not only her wit, and her memory, but her passions. Passions, like artificial flowers, are unbecoming to age; and those of the witty, atheistical marquise are almost revolting. Scandal still attached her name to that of Hénault, of whom Voltaire wrote the epitaph beginning

> "Hénault, fameux par vos soupers
> Et votre 'chronologie,'" etc.

Hénault was for many years deaf; and, during the whole of his life, disagreeable. There was something farcical in the old man's receptions on his death-bed; while, among the rest of the company, came Madame du Deffand, a blind old woman of seventy, who, bawling in his ear, aroused the lethargic man by inquiring after a former rival of hers, Madame de Castelmaron—about whom he went on babbling until death stopped his voice.

She was seventy years of age when Horace Walpole, at fifty, became her passion. She was poor and disreputable, and even the high position of having been mistress to the Regent could not save her from being decried by a large portion of that society which centred round the *bel esprit.* "She was," observes the biographer of Horace Walpole (the lamented author of the "Crescent and the Cross"), "always gay, always charming—every thing but a Christian." The loss of her eyesight did not impair the remains of her beauty: her replies, her compliments, were brilliant; even from one whose best organs of expression were mute.

A frequent guest at her suppers, Walpole's kindness, real or pretended, soon made inroads on a heart still susceptible. The ever-green passions of this venerable sinner threw out fresh shoots; and she became enamored of the attentive and admired Englishman. Horace was susceptible of ridicule: there his somewhat icy heart was easily touched. Partly in vanity, partly in playfulness, he encouraged the sentimental exaggeration of his correspondent; but, becoming afraid of the world's laughter, ended by reproving her warmth, and by chilling, under the refrigerating influence of his cautions, all the romance of the octogenarian.

In later days, however, after his solicitude—partly soothed by the return of his letters to Madame du Deffand, partly by her death—had completely subsided, a happier friendship was permitted to solace his now increasing infirmities, as well as to enhance his social pleasures.

It was during the year 1788, when he was living in retirement at Strawberry, that his auspicious friendship was formed. The only grain of ambition he had left, he declared, was to believe himself forgotten; that was "the thread that had run through his life;" "so true," he adds, "except the folly of being an author, has been what I said last year to the Prince" (afterward George IV.) "when he asked me 'if I was a Freemason,' I replied, 'No, sir; I never was any thing.'"

Lady Charleville told him that some of her friends had been to see Strawberry. "Lord!" cried one lady, "who is that Mr. Walpole?" "Lord!" cried a second; "don't you know the great epicure, Mr. Walpole?" "Who?" cried the first—"great epicure! you mean the antiquarian." "Surely," adds Horace, "this anecdote may take its place in the chapter of local fame."

But he reverts to his new acquisition—the acquaintance of the Miss Berrys, who had accidentally taken a house next to his at Strawberry Hill. Their story, he adds, was a curious one: their descent Scotch; their grandfather had an estate of £5000 a year, but disinherited his son on account of his marrying a woman with no fortune. She died, and the grandfather, wishing for an heir-male, pressed the widower to marry again: he refused; and said he would devote himself to the education of his two daughters. The second son generously gave up £800 a year to his brother, and the two motherless girls were taken to the Continent, whence they returned the "best-informed and most perfect creatures that Horace Walpole ever saw at their age."

Sensible, natural, frank, their conversation proved most agreeable to a man who was sated of grand society, and sick of vanity until he had indulged in vexation of spirit. He discovered by chance only—for there was no pedantry in these truly well-educated women—that the eldest understood Latin, and "was a perfect Frenchwoman in her language." Then the youngest drew well; and copied one of Lady Di Beauclerk's pictures, "The Gipsies," though she had never attempted colors before. Then, as to looks: Mary, the eldest, had a sweet face, the more interesting from being pale; with fine dark eyes that were lighted up when she spoke. Agnes, the younger, was "hardly to be called handsome, but almost;" with an agreeable, sensible countenance. It is remarkable that women thus delineated—not beauties, yet not plain—are always the most fascinating to men. The sisters doted on each other: Mary taking the lead in society. "I must even tell you," Horace wrote to the Countess of Ossory, "that they dress within the bounds of fashion, but without the excrescences and balconies with which modern hoydens overwhelm and barricade their persons." (One would almost have supposed that Horace had lived in the days of crinoline.)

The first night that Horace met the two sisters, he refused to be introduced to them: having heard so much of them that he concluded they would be "all pretension." The second night that he met them, he sat next Mary, and found her an "angel both inside and out." He did not know which he liked best; but Mary's face, which was formed for a sentimental novel, or still more, for genteel comedy, riveted him, he owned. Mr. Berry, the father, was a little "merry man with a round face," whom no one would have suspected of sacrificing "all for love, and the world well lost." This delightful family visited him every Sunday evening; the region of Twickenham being too "proclamatory" for cards to be introduced on the seventh day, conversation was tried instead; thankful, indeed, was Horace for the "pearls," as he styled them, thus thrown in his path. His two "Straw Berries," as he christened them, were henceforth the theme of every letter. He had set up a printing-press many years previously at Strawberry, and on taking the young ladies to see it, he remembered the gallantry of his former days, and they found these stanzas in type:

"To Mary's lips has ancient Rome
Her purest language taught;
And from the modern city home
Agnes its pencil brought.

"Rome's ancient Horace sweetly chants
Such maids with lyric fire;
Albion's old Horace sings nor paints,
He only can admire.

"Still would his press their fame record,
So amiable the pair is!
But, ah! how vain to think his word
Can add a Straw to Berry's."

On the following day, Mary, whom he terms the Latin Nymph, sent the following lines:

"Had Rome's famed Horace thus addrest
His Lydia or his Lyce,
He had ne'er so oft complained their breast
To him was cold and icy.

"But had they sought their joy to explain,
Or praise their generous bard,
Perhaps, like me, they had tried in vain,
And felt the task too hard."

The society of this family gave him the truest, and perhaps the only relish he ever had of domestic life. But his mind was harassed toward the close of the eighteenth century, by the insanity not only of his nephew, but by the great national calamity, that of the king. "Every *eighty-eight* seems," he remarks, "to be a favorite period with fate;" he was "too ancient," he said, "to tap what might almost be called a new reign;" of which he was not likely to see much. He never pretended to penetration, but his foresight, "if he gave it the rein," would not prognosticate much felicity to the country from the madness of his father, and the probable regency of the Prince of Wales. His happiest relations were now not with politics or literature, but with Mrs. Damer and the Miss Berrys, to whom he wrote: "I am afraid of protesting how much I delight in your society, lest I should seem to affect being gallant; but, if two negatives make an affirmative, why may not two ridicules compose one piece of sense? and, therefore, as I am in love with you both, I trust it is a proof of the good sense of your devoted—H. Walpole."

He was doomed, in the decline of life, to witness two great national convulsions: of the insurrection of 1745 he wrote feelingly—justly—almost pathetically: forty-five years later, he was tired, he said, of railing against French barbarity and folly. "Legislators! a Senate! to neglect laws, in order to annihilate coats-of-arms and liveries!" George Selwyn said, that Monsieur the king's brother was the only man of rank from whom they could not take a title. His alarm at the idea of his two young friends going to the Continent was excessive. The flame of revolution had burst forth at Florence: Flanders was not a safe road; dreadful horrors had been perpetrated at Avignon. Then he relates a characteristic anecdote of poor *Marie Antoinette.* She went with the king to see the manufacture of glass. As they passed the Halle, the *poissardes* hurraed them. "Upon my word," said the queen, "these folks are civiler when you visit them than when they visit you."

Walpole's affection for the Miss Berrys cast a glow of happiness over the fast-ebbing year of his life. "In happy days," he wrote to them when they were abroad, "I called you my dear wives; now I can only think of you as darling children, of whom I am bereaved." He was proud of their affection; proud of their spending many hours with "a very old man," while they were the objects of general admiration. These charming women survived until our own time: the centre of a circle of the leading characters in literature, politics, art, rank, and virtue. They are remembered with true regret. The fullness of their age perfected the promise of their youth. Samuel Rogers used to say that they had lived in the reign of Queen Anne, so far back seemed their memories which were so coupled to the past; but the youth of their minds, their feelings, their intelligence, remained almost to the last.

For many years Horace Walpole continued, in spite of incessant attacks of the gout, to keep almost open house at Strawberry; in short, he said, he kept an inn—the sign, the Gothic Castle: "Take my advice," he wrote to a friend, "never build a charming house for yourself between London and Hampton Court; every body will live in it but you."

The death of Lady Suffolk, in 1767, had been an essential loss to her partial, and not too rigid neighbors. Two days before the death of George II., she had gone to Kensington, not knowing that there was a review there. Hemmed in by coaches, she found herself close to George II. and to Lady Yarmouth. Neither of them knew her—a circumstance which greatly affected the countess.

Horace Walpole was now desirous of growing old with dignity. He had no wish "to dress up a withered person, nor to drag it about to public places;" but he was equally averse from "sitting at home, wrapped up in flannels," to receive condolences from people he did not care for—and attentions from relations who were impatient for his death. Well might a writer in the "Quarterly Review" remark, that our most useful lessons in reading Walpole's Letters are not only derived from his sound sense, but from "considering this man of the world, full of information and sparkling with vivacity, stretched on a sick-bed, and apprehending all the tedious languor of helpless decrepitude and deserted solitude." His later years had been diversified by correspondence with Hannah More, who sent him her poems of the *Bas Bleu*, into which she had introduced his name. In 1786 she visited him at Strawberry Hill. He was then a martyr to the gout, but with spirits gay as ever: "I never knew a man suffer pain with such entire patience," was Hannah More's remark. His correspondence with her continued regularly; but that with the charming sisters was delightfully interrupted by their residence at Little Strawberry Hill—*Cliveden*, as it was also called, where day after day, night after night, they gleaned stores from that rich fund of anecdote which went back to the days of George I., touched even on the anterior epoch of Anne, and came in volumes of amusement down to the very era when the old man was sitting by his parlor fire, happy with his *wives* near him, resigned and cheerful. For his young friends he composed his "Reminiscences of the Court of England."

He still wrote cheerfully of his physical state, in which eyesight was perfect; hearing little impaired; and though his hands and feet were crippled, he could use them; and since he neither "wished to box, to wrestle, nor to dance a hornpipe," he was contented.

His character became softer, his wit less caustic, his heart more tender, his talk more reverent, as he approached the term of a long, prosperous life—and knew, practically, the small value of all that he had once too fondly prized.

His later years were disturbed by the marriage of his niece Maria Waldegrave to the Duke of Gloucester; but the severest interruption to his peace was his own succession to an earldom.

In 1791, George, Earl of Orford, expired; leaving an estate encumbered with debt, and, added to the bequest, a series of lawsuits threatened to break down all remaining comfort in the mind of the uncle, who had already suffered so much on the young man's account.

He disdained the honors which brought him such solid trouble, with such empty titles, and for some time refused to sign himself otherwise, but "Uncle to the late Earl of Orford." He was certainly not likely to be able to walk in his robes to the House of Lords, or to grace a levee. However, he thanked God he was free from pain. "Since all my fingers are useless," he wrote to Hannah More, "and that I have only six hairs left, I am not very much grieved at not being able to comb my head!" To Hannah More he wrote, in all sincerity, referring to his elevation to the peerage: "For the other empty metamorphosis that has happened to the outward man, you do me justice in believing that it can do nothing but tease me; it is being called names in one's old age:" in fact, he reckoned on being styled "Lord Methusalem." He had lived to hear of the cruel deaths of the once gay and high-born friends whom he had known in Paris, by the guillotine: he had lived to execrate the monsters who drove the grandest heroine of modern times, Marie Antoinette, to madness; he lived to censure the infatuation of religious zeal in the Birmingham riots. "Are not the devils escaped out of the swine, and overrunning the earth headlong?" he asked in one of his letters.

He had offered his hand, and all the ambitious views which it opened, to each of the Miss Berrys successively, but they refused to bear his name, though they still cheered his solitude: and, strange to say, two of the most admired and beloved women of their time remained single.

In 1796, the sinking invalid was persuaded to remove to Berkeley Square, to be within reach of good and prompt advice. He consented unwillingly, for his "Gothic Castle" was his favorite abode. He left it with a presentiment that he should see it no more; but he followed the proffered advice, and in the spring of the year was established in Berkeley Square. His mind was still clear. He seems to have cherished to the last a concern for that literary fame which he affected to despise. "Literature has," he says, "many revolutions; if an author could rise from the dead, after a hundred years, what would be his surprise at the adventures of his works! I often say, perhaps my books may be published in Paternoster Row!" He would indeed have been astonished at the vast circulation of his Letters, and the popularity which has carried them into every aristocratic family in England. It is remarkable that among the middle and lower classes they are far less known. He was essentially the chronicler, as well as the wit and beau, of St. James's, of Windsor, and Richmond. At last he declared that he should "be content with a sprig of rosemary" thrown on him when the parson of the parish commits his "dust to dust." The end of his now suffering existence was near at hand. Irritability, one of the unpitied accompaniments of weakness, seemed to compete with the gathering clouds of mental darkness as the last hour drew on. At intervals there were flashes of a wit that appeared at that solemn moment hardly natural, and that must have startled, rather than pleased, the watchful friends around him. He became unjust in his fretfulness, and those who loved him most could not wish to see him survive the wreck of his intellect. Fever came on, and he died on the 2d of March, 1797.

He had collected his letters from his friends: these epistles were deposited in two boxes, one marked with an A., the other with a B. The chest A. was not to be opened until the eldest son of his grandniece, Lady Laura, should attain the age of twenty-five. The chest was found to contain memoirs, and bundles of letters ready for publication.

It was singular, at the sale of the effects at Strawberry Hill, to see this chest, with the MSS. in the clean *Horatian* hand, and to reflect how poignant would have been the anguish of the writer could he have seen his Gothic Castle given up for fourteen days, to all that could pain the living or degrade the dead.

Peace to his manes, prince of letter-writers; prince companion of beaux; wit of the highest order! Without thy pen, society in the eighteenth century would have been to us almost as dead as the *beau monde* of Pompeii, or the remains of Etruscan leaders of the ton. Let us not be ungrateful to our Horace: we owe him more than we could ever have calculated on before we knew him through his works: prejudiced, he was not false; cold, he was rarely cruel; egotistical, he was seldom vainglorious. Every age should have a Horace Walpole; every country possess a chronicler so sure, so keen to perceive, so exact to delineate peculiarities, manners, characters, and events.

GEORGE SELWYN.

I HAVE heard, at times, of maiden ladies of a certain age who found pleasure in the affection of "spotted snakes with double tongue, thorny hedge-hogs, newts, and in live worms." I know that Leonardo da Vinci was partial to all that is horrible in nature. I frequently meet ladies who think conversation lacks interest without the recital of "melancholy deaths," "fatal diseases," and "mournful cases;" *on ne dispute pas les goûts*, and certainly the taste for the night side of nature seems immensely prevalent among the lower orders—in whom, perhaps, the terrible only can rouse from a sullen insensibility. What happy people, I always think to myself, when I hear of the huge attendance on the last tragic performance at Newgate; how very little they can see of mournful and horrible in common life, if they seek it out so eagerly, and relish it so thoroughly, when they find it! I don't know; for my own part, *gaudeamus.* I have always thought that the text, "Blessed are they that mourn," referred to the inner private life, not to a perpetual display of sackcloth and ashes; but I know not. I can understand the weeping-willow taste among people, who have too little wit or too little Christianity to be cheerful, but it is a wonder to find the luxury of gloom united to the keenest perception of the laughable in such a man as George Selwyn.

If human beings could be made pets, like Miss Tabitha's snake or toad, Selwyn would have fondled a hangman. He loved the noble art of execution, and was a connoisseur of the execution of the art. In childhood he must have decapitated his rocking-horse, hanged his doll in a miniature gallows, and burnt his bawbles at mimic stakes. The man whose calm eye was watched for the quiet sparkle that announced—and only that ever did announce it—the flashing wit within the mind, by a gay crowd of loungers at Arthur's, might be found next day rummaging among coffins in a damp vault, glorying in a mummy, confessing and preparing a live criminal, paying any sum for a relic of a dead one, or pressing eagerly forward to witness the dying agonies of a condemned man.

Yet Walpole and Warner both bore the highest testimony to the goodness of his heart; and it is impossible to doubt that his nature was as gentle as a woman's. There have been other instances of even educated men delighting in scenes of suffering; but in general their characters have been more or less gross, their hearts more or less insensible. The husband of Madame Récamier went daily to see the guillotine do its vile work during the Reign of Terror; but then he was a man who never wept over the death of a friend. The man who was devoted to a little child, whom he adopted and treated with the tenderest care, was very different from M. Récamier —and that he *had* a heart there is no doubt. He was an anomaly, and famous for being so; though, perhaps, his well-known eccentricity was taken advantage of by his witty friends, and many a story fathered on Selwyn which has no origin but in the brain of its narrator.

George Augustus Selwyn, then, famous for his wit, and notorious for his love of horrors, was the second son of a country gentleman, of Matson, in Gloucestershire, Colonel John Selwyn, who had been an aid-de-camp of Marlborough's, and afterward a frequenter of the courts of the first two Georges. He inherited his wit chiefly from his mother, Mary, the daughter of General Farington or Farringdon, of the county of Kent. Walpole tells us that she figured among the beauties of the court of the Prince and Princess of Wales, and was bedchamber-woman to Queen Caroline. Her character was not spotless, for we hear of an intrigue, which her own mistress imparted in confidence to the Duchess of Orleans (the mother of the Regent: they wrote on her tomb *Cy gist l'oisiveté*, because idleness is the *mother* of all vice), and which eventually found its way into the "Utrecht Gazette." It was Mrs. Selwyn, too, who said to George II., that he was the last person she should ever have an intrigue with, because she was sure he would tell the queen of it: it was well known that that very virtuous sovereign made his wife the confidante of his amours, which was even more shameless than young De Sévigné's taking advice from his mother on his intrigue with Ninon de l'Enclos. She seems to have been reputed a wit, for Walpole retains her *mots* as if they were worth it, but they are not very remarkable: for instance, when Miss Pelham lost a pair of diamond earrings, which she had borrowed, and tried to faint when the loss was discovered, some one called for lavender-drops as a restorative. "Pooh!" cried Mrs. Selwyn, "give her diamond-drops."

George Augustus was born on the 11th of August, 1719. Walpole says that he knew him at eight years old, and as the two were at Eton about the same time, it is presumed that they were contemporaries there. In fact, a list of the boys there, in 1732, furnished to Eliot Warburton, contains the names of Walpole, Selwyn, Edgecombe, and Conway, all in after life intimate friends and correspondents. From Eton to Oxford was the natural course, and George was duly entered at Hertford College. He did not long grace Alma Mater, for the *grand tour* had to be made, and London life to be begun, but he was there long enough to contract the usual Oxford debts, which his father consented to pay more than once. It is amusing to find the son getting Dr. Newton to write him a contrite and respectful letter to the angry parent, to liquidate the "small accounts" accumulated in London and Oxford as early as 1740. Three years later we find him in Paris, leading a gay life, and writing respectful letters to England for more money. Previously to this, however, he had obtained, through his father, the sinecure of Clerk of the Irons and surveyor of the Meltings at the Mint, a comfortable little appointment, the duties of which were performed by deputy, while its holder contented himself with honestly acknowledging the salary, and dining once a week, when in town, with the officers of the Mint, and at the Government's expense.

So far the young gentleman went on well enough, but in 1744 he returned to England, and his rather rampant character showed itself in more than one disgraceful affair.

Among the London shows was Orator Henley, a clergyman and clergyman's son, and a member of St. John's, Cambridge. He had come to London about this time, and instituted a series of lectures on universal knowledge and primitive Christianity. He styled himself a Rationalist, a title then more honorable than it is now; and, in grandiloquent language, "spouted" on religious subjects to an audience admitted at a shilling a head. On one occasion he announced a disputation among any two of his hearers, offering to give an impartial hearing and judgment to both. Selwyn and the young Lord Carteret were prepared, and stood up, the one to defend the ignorance, the other the impudence, of Orator Henley himself; so, at least, it is inferred from a passage in D'Israeli the Elder. The uproar that ensued can well be imagined. Henley himself made his escape by a back door. His pulpit, all gilt, has been immortalized by Pope, as "Henley's gilt tub;" in which

"Imbrown'd with native bronze, lo! Henley stands,
Tuning his voice and balancing his hands."

The affair gave rise to a correspondence between the Orator and his young friends; who, doubtless, came off best in the matter.

This was harmless enough, but George's next freak was not so excusable. The circumstances of this affair are narrated in a letter from Captain Nicholson, his friend, to George Selwyn; and may, therefore, be relied on. It appears that being at a certain club in Oxford, at a wine-party with his friends, George sent to a certain silversmith's for a certain chalice, intrusted to the shopkeeper from a certain church to be repaired in a certain manner. This being brought, Master George—then, be it remembered, not at the delicate and frivolous age of most Oxford boys, but at the mature one of six-and-twenty—filled it with wine, and handing it round, used the sacred words, "Drink this in remembrance of me." This, if any thing can be so, was a blasphemous parody of the most sacred rite of the Church. Selwyn was not a man to inquire whether that rite, so practiced, was in effect the rite instituted by our Savior. Had there even been that doubt in his mind, which certainly there is in the minds of some, the manner of indicating it would have been unpardonable. All he could say for himself was, that he was drunk when he did it. The other plea, that he did it in ridicule of the transubstantiation of the Romish Church, will not hold water at all; and was most weakly put forward. Let Oxford Dons be what they will; let them put a stop to all religious inquiry, and nearly expel Adam Smith for reading Hume's "Essay on Human Nature;" let them be, as many allege, narrow-minded, hypocritical, and ignorant; we can not charge them with wrong-dealing in expelling the originator of such open blasphemy, which nothing can be found to palliate, and of which its perpetrator did not appear to repent, rather complaining that the treatment of the Dons was harsh. The act of expulsion was, of course, considered in the same light by his numerous acquaintance, many of whom condoled with him on the occasion. It is true, the Oxford Dons are often charged with injustice and partiality, and too often the evidence is not sufficiently strong to excuse their judgments; but in this the evidence was not denied; only a palliative was put in, which every one can see through. The only injustice we can discover in this case is, that the head of Hart Hall, as Hertford College was called, seems to have been influenced in pronouncing his sentence of expulsion by certain previous *suspicions*, having no bearing on the question before him, which had been entertained by another set of tutors—those of Christchurch—where Selwyn had many friends, and where, probably enough, he indulged in many collegian's freaks. This knack of bringing up a mere suspicion, is truly characteristic of the Oxford Don, and since the same Head of his House—Dr. Newton—acknowledged that Selwyn was, during his Oxford career, neither intemperate, dissolute, nor a gamester, it is fair to give him the advantage of the doubt, that the judgment on the evidence had been influenced by the consideration of "suspicions" of former misdeeds, which had not been proved, perhaps never committed. Knowing the after life of the man, we can scarcely doubt that George had led a fast life at the University, and given cause for mistrust. But one may ask whether Dons, whose love of drinking, and whose tendency to jest on the most solemn subjects, are well known even in the present day, might not have treated Selwyn less harshly for what was done under the influence of wine? To this we are inclined to reply, that no punishment is too severe for profanation; and that drunkenness is not an excuse, but an aggravation. Selwyn threatened to appeal, and took advice on the matter. This, as usual, was vain. Many an expelled man, more unjustly treated than Selwyn, has talked of appeal in vain. Appeal to whom? to what? Appeal against men who never acknowledge themselves wrong, and who, to maintain that they are right, will listen to evidence which they can see is contradictory, and which they know to be worthless! An appeal from an Oxford decision is as hopeless in the present day as it was in Selwyn's. He wisely left it alone, but less wisely insisted on reappearing in Oxford, against the advice of all his friends, whose characters were lost if the ostracized man were seen among them.

From this time he entered upon his "profession," that of a wit, gambler, club-lounger, and man about town; for these many characters are all mixed in the one which is generally called "a wit." Let us remember that he was good-hearted, and not ill-intentioned, though imbued with the false ideas of his day. He was not a great man, but a great wit.

The localities in which the trade of wit was plied were, then, the clubs, and the drawing-rooms of fashionable beauties. The former were in Selwyn's youth still limited in the number of their members, thirty constituting a large club; and as the subscribers were all known to one another, presented an admirable field for display of mental powers in conversation. In fact, the early clubs were nothing more than dining-societies, precisely the same in theory as our breakfasting arrangements at Oxford, which were every whit as exclusive, though not balloted for. The ballot, however, and the principle of a single black ball suffering to negative an election, were not only, under such circumstances, excusable, but even necessary for the actual preservation of peace. Of course, in a succession of dinner-parties, if any two members were at all opposed to one another, the awkwardness would be intolerable. In the present day, two men may belong to the same club and scarcely meet, even on the stairs, oftener than once or twice in a season.

Gradually, however, in the place of the "feast of reason and flow of soul" and wine, instead of the evenings spent in toasting, talking, emptying bottles and filling heads, as in the case of the old Kit-kat, men took to the monstrous amusement of examining fate, and on club-tables the dice rattled far more freely than the glasses, though these latter were not necessarily abandoned. Then came the thirst for hazard that brought men early in the day to try their fortune, and thus made the club-room a lounge. Selwyn was an habitual frequenter of Brookes's.

Brookes's was, perhaps, the principal club of the day, though "White's Chocolate House" was almost on a par with it. But Selwyn did not confine his attention solely to this club. It was the fashion to belong to as many of them as possible, and Wilberforce mentions no less than five to which he himself belonged: Brookes's, Boodle's, White's, Miles and Evans's in New Palace Yard, and Goosetree's. As their names imply, these were all, originally, mere coffee-houses, kept by men of the above names. One or two rooms then sufficed for the requirements of a small party, and it was not till the members were greatly increased that the coffee-house rose majestically to the dignity of a bow-window, and was entirely and exclusively appropriated to the requirements of the club.

This was especially the case with White's, of which so many of the wits and talkers of Selwyn's day were members. Who does not know that bow-window at the top of St. James's Street, where there are sure, about three or four in the afternoon, to be at least three gentlemen, two old and one young, standing, to the exclusion of light within, talking and contemplating the oft-repeated movement outside. White's was established as early as 1698, and was thus one of the original coffee-houses. It was then kept by a man named Arthur: here Chesterfield gamed and talked, to be succeeded by Gilly Williams, Charles Townshend, and George Selwyn. The old house was burnt down in 1733. It was at White's—or as Hogarth calls it in his pictorial squib, Black's—that, when a man fell dead at the door, he was lugged in and bets made as to whether he was dead or no. The surgeon's operations were opposed, for fear of disturbing the bets. Here, too, did George Selwyn and Charles Townshend pit their wit against wit; and here Pelham passed all the time he was not forced to devote to politics. In short it was, next to Brookes's, the club of the day, and perhaps in some respects had a greater renown than even that famous club, and its play was as high.

In Brookes's and White's Selwyn appeared with a twofold fame, that of a pronouncer of *bon-mots*, and that of a lover of horrors. His wit was of the quaintest order. He was no inveterate talker, like Sydney Smith; no clever dissimulator, like Mr. Hook. Calmly, almost sanctimoniously, he uttered those neat and telling sayings which the next day passed over England as "Selwyn's last." Walpole describes his manner admirably—his eyes turned up, his mouth set primly, a look almost of melancholy in his whole face. Reynolds, in his Conversation-piece, celebrated when in the Strawberry Collection, and representing Selwyn leaning on a chair, Gilly Williams, crayon in hand, and Dick Edgecombe by his side, has caught the pseudo-solemn expression of his face admirably. The ease of the figure, one hand *empochée*, the other holding a paper of epigrams, or what not, the huge waistcoat with a dozen buttons and huge flaps, the ruffled sleeve, the bob-wig, all belong to the outer man; but the calm, quiet, almost inquiring face, the look half of melancholy, half of reproach, and, as the Milesian would say, the other half of sleek wisdom; the long nose, the prim mouth and joined lips, the elevated brow, and beneath it the quiet contemplative eye, contemplative not of heaven or hell, but of this world as it had seen it, in its most worldly point of view, yet twinkling with a flashing thought of incongruity made congruous, are the indices of the inner man. Most of our wits, it must have been seen, have had some other interest and occupation in life than that of "making wit:" some have been authors, some statesmen, some soldiers, some wildrakes, and some players of tricks: Selwyn had no profession but that of *diseur de bons mots;* for, though he sat in the House, he took no prominent part in politics; though he gambled extensively, he did not game for the sake of money only. Thus his life was that merely of a London bachelor, with a few incidents to mark it, and therefore his memoir must resolve itself more or less into a series of anecdotes of his eccentricities and list of his witticisms.

His friend Walpole gives us an immense number of both, not all of a first-rate nature, nor many interesting in the present day. Selwyn, calm as he was, brought out his sayings on the spur of the moment, and their appropriateness to the occasion was one of their greatest recommendations. A good saying, like a good sermon, depends much on its delivery, and loses much in print. Nothing less immortal than wit! To take first, however, the eccentricities of his character, and especially his love of horrors, we find anecdotes by the dozen retailed of him. It was so well known, that Lord Holland, when dying, ordered his servant to be sure to admit Mr. Selwyn if he called to inquire after him, "for if I am alive," said he, "I shall be glad to see him, and if I am dead, he will be glad to see me." The name of Holland leads us to an anecdote told by Walpole. Selwyn was looking over Cornbury with Lord Abergavenny and Mrs. Frere, "who loved one another a little," and was disgusted with the frivolity of the woman who could take no interest in any thing worth seeing. "You don't know what you missed in the other room," he cried at last, peevishly. "Why, what?" "Why, my Lord Holland's picture." "Well, what is my Lord Holland to me?" "Don't you know?" whispered the wit mysteriously, "that Lord Holland's body lies in the same vault in Kensington Church with my Lord Abergavenny's mother?" "Lord! she was so obliged," says Walpole, "and thanked him a thousand times!"

Selwyn knew the vaults as thoroughly as old Anthony Wood knew the brasses. The elder Craggs had risen by the favor of Marlborough, whose footman he had been, and his son was eventually a Secretary of State. Arthur Moore, the father of James Moore Smyth, of whom Pope wrote—

"Arthur, whose giddy son neglects the laws,
Imputes to me and my damned works the cause,"

had worn a livery too. When Craggs got into a coach with him, he exclaimed, "Why, Arthur, I am always getting up behind, are not you?" Walpole having related this story to Selwyn, the latter told him, as a most important communication, that Arthur Moore had had his coffin chained to that of his mistress. "Lord! how do you know?" asked Horace. "Why, I saw them the other day in a vault at St. Giles's." "Oh, your servant, Mr. Selwyn," cried the man who showed the tombs at Westminster Abbey, "I expected to see *you* here the other day when the old Duke of Richmond's body was taken up."

Criminals were, of course, included in his passion. Walpole affirms that he had a great share in bringing Lord Dacre's footman, who had murdered the butler, to confess his crime. In writing the confession, the ingenious plush coolly stopped and asked how "murder" was spelt. But it mattered little to George whether the criminal were alive or dead, and he defended his eccentric taste with his usual wit; and when rallied by some women for going to see the Jacobite Lord Lovat's head cut off, he retorted sharply—"I made full amends, for I went to see it sewn on again." He had indeed done so, and given the company at the undertaker's a touch of his favorite blasphemy, for when the man of coffins had done his work, and laid the body in its box, Selwyn, imitating the voice of the Lord Chancellor at the trial, muttered, "My Lord Lovat, you may *rise*." He said a better thing on the trial of a confederate of Lovat's, that Lord Kilmarnock, with whom the ladies fell so desperately in love as he stood on his defense. Mrs.

Bethel, who was famous for a *hatchet-face*, was among the fair spectators: "What a shame it is," quoth the wit, "to turn her face to the prisoners before they are condemned!" Terrible, indeed, was that instrument to those men, who had in the heat of battle so gallantly met sword and blunderbuss. The slow, sure approach of the day of the scaffold was a thousand times worse than the roar of cannon. Lord Cromarty was pardoned, solely, it was said, from pity for his poor wife, who was at the time of the trial far advanced in pregnancy. It was affirmed that the child born had a distinct mark of an axe on his neck. *Credat Judæus!* Walpole used to say that Selwyn never thought but *à la tête tranchée*, and that when he went to have a tooth drawn, he told the dentist he would drop his handkerchief by way of signal. Certain it is that he did love an execution, whatever he or his friends may have done to remove the impression of this extraordinary taste. Some better men than Selwyn have had the same, and Macaulay accuses Penn of a similar affection. The best-known anecdote of Selwyn's peculiarity relates to the execution of Damiens, who was torn with red-hot pincers, and finally quartered by four horses, for the attempt to assassinate Louis XV. On the day fixed, George mingled with the crowd plainly dressed, and managed to press forward close to the place of torture. The executioner observing him, eagerly cried out, "*Faites place pour Monsieur; c'est un Anglais et un amateur;* or, as another version goes, he was asked if he was not himself a *bourreau*. "*Non, Monsieur*," he is said to have answered, "*je n'ai pas cet honneur; je ne suis qu'un amateur*." The story is more than apocryphal, for Selwyn is not the only person of whom it has been told; and he was even accused, according to Wraxall, of going to executions in female costume. George Selwyn must have passed as a "remarkably fine woman," in that case.

It is only justice to him to say that the many stories of his attending executions were supposed to be inventions of Sir Charles Hanbury Williams, another wit, and of Chesterfield, another, and a rival. In confirmation, it is adduced that when the former had been relating some new account, and an old friend of Selwyn's expressed his surprise that he had never heard the tale before, the hero of it replied quietly, "No wonder at all, for Sir Charles has just invented it, and knows that I will not by contradiction spoil the pleasure of the company he is so highly entertaining."

Wit has been called "the eloquence of indifference;" no one seems ever to have been so indifferent about every thing but his little daughter, as George Selwyn. He always, however, took up the joke, and when asked why he had not been to see one Charles Fox, a low criminal, hanged at Tyburn, answered, quietly, "I make a point of never going to *rehearsals*."

Selwyn's love for this kind of thing, to believe his most intimate friend, Horace Walpole, was quite a fact. His friend relates that he even bargained for the High Sheriff's wand, after it was broken, at the condemnation of the gallant Lords, but said, "that he behaved so like an attorney the first day, and so like a pettifogger the second, that he would not take it to light his fire with."

The State Trials, of course, interested George more than any other in his eventless life: he dined after the sentence with the celebrated Lady Townshend, who was so devoted to Lord Kilmarnock—

"Pitied by gentle minds, Kilmarnock died"—Johnson.

that she is said to have even staid under his windows, when he was in prison; but he treated her anxiety with such lightness that the lady burst into tears, and "flung up stairs." "George," writes Walpole to Montagu, "coolly took Mrs. Dorcas, her woman, and bade her sit down to finish the bottle. 'And pray,' said Dorcas, 'do you think my lady will be prevailed upon to let me go and see the execution? I have a friend that has promised to take care of me, and I can lie in the Tower the night before.' Could she have talked more pleasantly to Selwyn?"

His contemporaries certainly believed in his love of Newgatism; for when Walpole had caught a housebreaker in a neighbor's area, he immediately dispatched a messenger to White's for the philo-criminalist, who was sure to be playing at the Club any time before daylight. It happened that the drawer at the "Chocolate-house" had been himself lately robbed, and therefore stole to George with fear and trembling, and muttered mysteriously to him, "Mr. Walpole's compliments, and he has got a housebreaker for you." Of course, Selwyn obeyed the summons readily, and the event concluded, as such events do nine times out of ten, with a quiet capture, and much ado about nothing.

The Selwyns were a powerful family in Gloucestershire, owning a great deal of property in the neighborhood of Gloucester itself. The old colonel had represented that city in Parliament for many years. On the 5th of November, 1751, he died. His eldest son had gone a few months before him. This son had been also at Eton, and was an early friend of Horace Walpole and General Conway. His death left George sole heir to the property, and very much he seemed to have needed the heritage.

The property of the Selwyns lay in the picturesque district of the Northern Cotswolds. Any body who has passed a day in the dull city of Gloucester, which seems to break into any thing like life only at an election, lying dormant in the intervals, has been glad to rush out to enjoy air and a fine view on Robin Hood's Hill, a favorite walk with the worthy citizens, though what the jovial archer of merry Sherwood had to do with it, or whether he was ever in Gloucestershire at all, I profess I know not. Walpole describes the hill with humorous exaggeration. "It is lofty enough for an alp, yet is a mountain of turf to the very top, has wood scattered all over it, springs that long to be cascades in many places of it, and from the summit it beats even Sir George Littleton's views, by having the city of Gloucester at its foot, and the Severn widening to the horizon." On the very summit of the next hill, Chosen-down, is a solitary church, and the legend saith that the good people who built it did so originally at the foot of the steep mount, but that the Virgin Mary carried up the stones by night, till the builder, in despair, was compelled to erect it on the top. Others attribute the mysterious act to a very different personage, and with apparently more reason, for the position of the church must keep many an old sinner from hearing service.

At Matson, then, on Robin Hood's Hill, the Selwyns lived: Walpole says that the "house is small, but neat. King Charles lay here at the siege, and the Duke of York, with typical fury, hacked and hewed the window-shutters of his chamber as a memorandum of his being there. And here is the very flower-pot and counterfeit association for which Bishop Sprat was taken up, and the Duke of Marlborough sent to the Tower. The reservoirs on the hill supply the city. The late Mr. Selwyn governed the borough by them—and I believe by some wine too." Probably, or at least by some beer, if the modern electors be not much altered from their forefathers.

Besides this important estate, the Selwyns had another at Ludgershall, and their influence there was so complete, that they might fairly be said to *give* one seat to any one they chose. With such double barrels George Selwyn was, of course, a great gun in the House, but his interest lay far more in piquet and pleasantry than in politics and patriotism, and he was never fired off with any but the blank cartridges of his two votes. His parliamentary career, begun in 1747, lasted more than forty years, yet was entirely without distinction. He, however, amused both parties with his wit, and by *snoring in unison* with Lord North. This must have been trying to Mr. Speaker Cornwall, who was longing, no doubt, to snore also, and dared not. He was probably the only Speaker who presided over so august an assembly as our English Parliament with a pewter pot of porter at his elbow, sending for more and more to Bellamy's, till his heavy eyes closed of themselves. A modern M. P., carried back by some fancies to "the Senate" of those days, might reasonably doubt whether his guide had not taken him by mistake to some Coal-hole or Cider-cellar, presided over by some former Baron Nicholson, and whether the furious eloquence of Messrs. Fox, Pitt, and Burke were not got up for the amusement of an audience admitted at sixpence a head.

Selwyn's political jokes were the delight of Bellamy's. He said that Fox and Pitt reminded him of Hogarth's Idle and Industrious Apprentices. When asked by some one, as he sauntered out of the House—"Is the House up?" he replied, "No, but Burke is." The length of Burke's elaborate spoken essays was proverbial, and obtained for him the name of the "Dinner-bell." Fox was talking one day at Brookes's of the advantageous peace he had made with France, and that he had even induced that country to give up the *gum* trade to England. "That, Charles," quoth Selwyn, sharply, "I am not at all surprised at; for having drawn your *teeth*, they would be d—d fools to quarrel with you about gums." Fox was often the object of his good-natured satire. As every one knows, his boast was to be called "The Man of the People," though perhaps he cared as little for the great unwashed as for the wealth and happiness of the waiters at his clubs. Every one knows, too, what a dissolute life he led for many years. In 1782, we are told by Walpole, he was "languishing at the feet" of the notorious and abandoned Mrs. Robinson. "Well," says Selwyn, calmly, "whom should 'The Man of the People' live with, but the *woman of the people*." Selwyn's sleepiness was well known. He slept in the House; he slept, after losing £800, "and with as many more before him," upon the gaming-table, with the dice-box "stamped close to his ears;" he slept, or half slept, even in conversation, which he seems to have caught by fits and starts. Thus it was that words he heard suggested different senses, partly from being only dimly associated with the subject on the *tapis*. So, when they were talking around of the war, and whether it should be a sea-war or a Continental war, Selwyn woke up just enough to say, "I am for a sea-war and a *Continent* admiral."

When Fox had ruined himself, and a subscription for him was talked of, some one asked how they thought "he would take it." "Take it," cried Selwyn, suddenly lighting up, "why, *quarterly* to be sure."

His parliamentary career was then quite uneventful; but at the dissolution in 1780, he found that his security at Gloucester was threatened. He was not Whig enough for that constituency, and had throughout supported the war with America. He offered himself, of course, but was rejected with scorn, and forced to fly for a seat to Ludgershall. Walpole writes to Lady Ossory: "They" (the Gloucester people) "hanged him in effigy, and dressed up a figure of Mie-Mie" (his adopted daughter), "and pinned on its breast these words, alluding to the gallows: 'This is what I told you you would come to!'" From Gloucester he went to Ludgershall, where he was received by ringing of bells and bonfires. "Being driven out of my capital," said he, "and coming into that country of turnips, where I was adored, I seemed to be arrived in my Hanoverian dominions"—no bad hit at George II. For Ludgershall he sat for many years, with Sir Nathaniel Wraxall, whose "Memoirs" are better known than trusted, as colleague. That writer says of him, that he was "thoroughly well versed in our history, and master of many curious as well as secret anecdotes, relative to the houses of Stuart and Brunswick."

Another *bon-mot*, not in connection with politics, is reported by Walpole as "incomparable." Lord George Gordon asked him if the Ludgershall electors would take him (Lord George) for Ludgershall, adding, "if you would recommend me, they would choose me, if I came from the coast of Africa." "That is according to what part of the coast you came from; they would certainly, if you came from the Guinea coast." "Now, Madam," writes his friend, "is not this true inspiration as well as true wit? Had any one asked him in which of the four quarters of the world Guinea is situated, could he have told?" Walpole did not perhaps know Master George thoroughly—he was neither so ignorant nor so indifferent as he seemed. His manner got him the character of being both; but he was a still fool that ran deep.

Though Selwyn did little with his two votes, he made them pay; and in addition to the post in the Mint, got out of the party he supported those of Registrar to the Court of Chancery in the Island of Barbadoes, a sinecure done by deputy, Surveyor of the Crown Lands, and Paymaster to the Board of Works. The wits of White's added the title of "Receiver General of Waif and Stray Jokes." It is said that his hostility to Sheridan arose from the latter having lost him the office in the Works in 1782, when Burke's Bill for reducing the Civil List came into operation; but this is not at all probable, as his dislike was shown long before that period. Apropos of the Board of Works, Walpole gives another anecdote. On one occasion, in 1780, Lord George Gordon had been the only opponent on a division. Selwyn afterward took him in his carriage to White's. "I have brought," said he, "the whole Opposition in my coach, and I hope one coach will always hold them, if they mean to take away the Board of Works."

Undoubtedly, Selwyn's wit wanted the manner of the man to make it so popular, for, as we read it, it is often rather mild. To string a list of them together:

Lady Coventry showed him her new dress all covered with spangles as large as shillings. "Bless my soul," said he, "you'll be change for a guinea."

Fox, debtor and bankrupt as he was, had taken lodgings with Fitzpatrick at an oilman's, in Piccadilly. Every one pitied the landlord, who would certainly be ruined. "Not a bit of it," quoth George; "he'll have the credit of keeping at his house the finest pickles in London."

Sometimes there was a good touch of satire on his times. When "High Life Below Stairs" was first acted, Selwyn vowed he would go and see it, for he was sick of low life above stairs; and when a waiter at his Club had been convicted of felony, "What a horrid idea," said he, "the man will give of *us* in Newgate!"

Dining with Bruce, the Abyssinian traveler, he heard him say, in answer to a question about musical instruments in the East, "I believe I saw one *lyre* there." "Ay," whispered the wit to his neighbor, "and there's one less since he left the country." Bruce shared the travelers' reputation of drawing the long-bow to a very considerable extent.

Two of Selwyn's best *mots* were about one of the Foley family, who were so deeply in debt that they had "to go to Texas," or Boulogne, to escape the money-lenders. "That," quoth Selwyn, "is a *pass-over* which will not be much relished by the Jews." And again, when it was said that they would be able to cancel their father's old will by a new-found one, he profanely indulged in a pun far too impious to be repeated in our day, however it may have been relished in Selwyn's time.

A picture called "The Daughter of Pharaoh," in which the princess royal and her attendant ladies figured as the saver of Moses and her handmaids, was being exhibited in 1782, at a house opposite Brookes's, and was to be the companion-piece to Copley's "Death of Chatham." George said he could recommend a better companion, to wit—the "Sons of Pharaoh" at the opposite house. It is scarcely necessary to explain that pharaoh or faro, was the most popular game of hazard then played.

Walking one day with Lord Pembroke, and being besieged

SELWYN ACKNOWLEDGES "THE SOVEREIGNTY OF THE PEOPLE."

by a troop of small chimney-climbers, begging—Selwyn, after bearing their importunity very calmly for some time, suddenly turned round, and with the most serious face thus addressed them—"I have often heard of the sovereignty of the people; I suppose your highnesses are in Court mourning." We can well imagine the effect of this sedate speech on the astonished youngsters.

Pelham's truculency was well known. Walpole and his friend went to the sale of his plate in 1755. "Lord," said the wit, "how many toads have been eaten off these plates!"

The jokes were not always very delicate. When, in the middle of the summer of 1751, Lord North, who had been twice married before, espoused the widow of the Earl of Rockingham, who was fearfully stout, Selwyn suggested that she had been kept in ice for three days before the wedding. So, too, when there was talk of another *embonpoint* personage going to America during the war, he remarked that she would make a capital *breast*-work.

One of the few epigrams he ever wrote—if not the only one, of which there is some doubt—was in the same spirit. It is on the discovery of a pair of shoes in a certain lady's bed:

"Well may Suspicion shake its head—
Well may Clorinda's spouse be jealous,
When the dear wanton takes to bed
Her very shoes—because they're *fellows*."

Such are a few specimens of George Selwyn's wit; and dozens more are dispersed through Walpole's Letters. As Eliot Warburton remarks, they do not give us a very high idea of the humor of the period; but two things must be taken into consideration before we deprecate their author's title to the dignity and reputation he enjoyed so abundantly among his contemporaries: they are not necessarily the *best* specimens that might have been given, if more of his *mots* had been preserved; and their effect on his listeners depended more on the manner of delivery than on the matter. That they were improvised and unpremeditated is another important consideration. It is quite unfair to compare them, as Warburton does, with the hebdomadal trash of "Punch," though perhaps they would stand the comparison pretty well. It is one thing to force wit with plenty of time to invent and meditate it—another to have so much wit within you that you can bring it out on any occasion; one thing to compose a good fancy for *money*—another to utter it only when it flashes through the brain.

But it matters little what we in the present day may think of Selwyn's wit, for conversation is spoiled by bottling, and should be drawn fresh when wanted. Selwyn's companions —all men of wit, more or less, affirmed him to be the most amusing man of his day, and that was all the part he had to play. No real wit ever hopes to *talk* for posterity; and written wit is of a very different character to the more sparkling, if less solid, creations of a moment.

We have seen Selwyn in many points of view, not all very creditable to him: first, expelled from Oxford for blasphemy; next, a professed gambler and the associate of men who led fashion in those days, it is true, but then it was very bad fashion; then as a lover of hangmen, a wit, and a lounger. There is reason to believe that Selwyn, though less openly reprobate than many of his associates, was, in his quiet way, just as bad as any of them, if we except the Duke of Queensberry, his intimate friend, or the disgusting "Franciscans" of Medmenham Abbey, of whom, though not the founder, nor even a member, he was, in a manner, the suggester in his blasphemy.

But Selwyn's real character is only seen in profile in all these accounts. He had at the bottom of such vice, to which his position, and the fashion of the day introduced him, a far better heart than any of his contemporaries, and in some respects a kind of simplicity which was endearing. He was neither knave nor fool. He was not a voluptuary, like his friend the duke; nor a continued drunkard, like many other "fine gentlemen" with whom he mixed; nor a cheat, though a gambler; nor a skeptic, like his friend Walpole; nor a blasphemer, like the Medmenham set, though he had once parodied profanely a sacred rite; nor was he steeped in debt, as Fox was; nor does he appear to have been a practiced seducer, as too many of his acquaintance were. Not that these negative qualities are to his praise; but if we look at the age and the society around him, we must, at least, admit that Selwyn was not one of the worst of that wicked set.

But the most pleasing point in the character of the old bachelor—for he was *too much* of a wit ever to marry—is his affection for children—not his own. That is, not avowedly his own, for it was often suspected that the little ones he took up so fondly bore some relationship to him, and there can be little doubt that Selwyn, like every body else in that evil age, had his intrigues. He did not die in his sins, and that is almost all we can say for him. He gave up gaming in time, protesting that it was the bane of four much better things—health, money, time, and thinking. For the last two, perhaps, he cared little. Before his death he is said to have been a Christian, which was a decided rarity in the fashionable set of his day. Walpole answered, when asked if he was a Freemason, that he never had been *any thing*, and probably most of the men of the time would, if they had had the honesty, have said the same. They were not atheists professedly, but they neither believed in nor practiced Christianity.

His love for children has been called one of his eccentricities. It would be a hard name to give it if he had not been a club-lounger of his day. I have sufficient faith in human nature to trust that two thirds of the men of this country have that most amiable eccentricity. But in Selwyn it amounted to something more than in the ordinary pater-familias: it was almost a passion. He was almost motherly in his celibate tenderness to the little ones to whom he took a fancy. This affection he showed to several of the children, sons or daughters, of his friends; but to two especially, Anne Coventry and Maria Fagniani.

The former was the daughter of the beautiful Maria Gunning, who became Countess of Coventry. Nanny, as he called her, was four years old when her mother died, and from that time he treated her almost as his own child.

But Mie-Mie, as the little Italian was called, was far more favored. No picture can better display the vice of the age than that of two men of the highest fashion, one of them the Duke of Queensberry, the greatest libertine and most disgusting profligate that ever disgraced the British peerage (which is saying much), vying for the honor of being the father of this poor little girl, while a reverend doctor attempted to decide the question, and advised one of them actually to *marry* her; and her own shameless mother encouraged each in his fancy, and alternately assured the one or the other that he was really its progenitor. The doubt of the paternity may afford a pleasant subject of investigation to certain precisionists of our day, but we beg to decline entering on such an inquiry. Whoever may have been the child's father, her mother was a rather beautiful and very immoral woman, the wife of the Marchese Fagniani. She seems to have desired to make the most of her daughter out of the extraordinary rivalry of the two English "gentlemen," and they were admirably taken in by her. Whatever the truth may have been, Selwyn's love for children showed itself more strongly in this case than in any other; and, oddly enough, it seems to have begun when the little girl was at an age when children scarcely interest other men than their fathers—in short, in infancy. Her parents allowed him to have the sole charge of her at a very early age, when they returned to the Continent; but in 1777, the marchioness, being then in Brussels, claimed her daughter back again;

though less, it seems, from any great anxiety on the child's account, than because her husband's parents, in Milan, objected to their granddaughter being left in England; and also, not a little, from fear of the voice of Mrs. Grundy. Selwyn seems to have used all kinds of arguments to retain the child; and a long correspondence took place, which the marchesa begins with "My very dear friend," and many affectionate expressions, and concludes with a haughty "Sir," and her opinion that his conduct was "devilish." The affair was, therefore, clearly a violent quarrel, and Selwyn was obliged at last to give up the child. He had a carriage fitted up for her expressly for her journey; made out for her a list of the best hotels on her route; sent his own confidential man-servant with her, and treasured up among his "relics" the childish little notes, in a large scrawling hand, which Mie-Mie sent him. Still more curious was it to see this complete man of the world, this gambler for many years, this club-lounger, drinker, associate of well-dressed blasphemers, of Franciscans of Medmenham Abbey, of women of morals as loose as their petticoats, devoting, not his money only, but his very time to this mere child, leaving town in the height of the season for dull Matson, that she might have fresh air. Quitting his hot club-rooms, his nights spent at the piquet-table and the rattle of the dice, for the quiet, pleasant terraces of his country-house, where he would hold the little innocent Mie-Mie by her tiny hand, as she looked up into his shriveled dissipated face; quitting the interchange of wit, the society of the Townshends, the Walpoles, the Williamses, the Edgecumbes; all the jovial, keen wisdom of Gilly, and Dick, and Horace, and Charles, as they called one another, for the meaningless prattle, the merry laughter of this half-English, half-Italian child. It redeems Selwyn in our eyes, and it may have done him real good: nay, he must have felt a keen refreshment in this change from vice to innocence; and we understand the misery he expressed, when the old bachelor's one little companion and only pure friend was taken away from him. His love for the child was well known in London society; and of it did Sheridan's friends take advantage, when they wanted to get Selwyn out of Brookes's, to prevent his black-balling the dramatist. The anecdote is given in the next Memoir.

In his later days Selwyn still haunted the clubs, hanging about, sleepy, shriveled, dilapidated in face and figure, yet still respected and dreaded by the youngsters, as the "celebrated Mr. Selwyn." The wit's disease—gout—carried him off at last, in 1791, at the age of seventy-two.

He left a fortune which was not contemptible: £33,000 of

it were to go to Mie-Mie—by this time a young lady—and as her "other papa," at his death, left her no less than £150,000, Miss was by no means a bad match for Lord Yarmouth,* who was too little apprehensive on points of "legitimacy" to look closely into the doubt between Selwyn, Queensberry, and the marchese. See what a good thing it is to have three papas, when two of them are rich! The duke made Lord Yarmouth his residuary legatee, and between him and his wife divided nearly half a million.

People who pass by a certain house in Regent's Park have generally some scandalous tale to tell you of "the late marquis." The story of the marchioness's three papas is quite scandalous enough to make us think we have said enough, and had better close this sketch of George Selwyn—only remembering that, wit, gambler, drinker, profaner, club-lounger, gallows-lover, and worse, though he was, he had yet two points to redeem him from utter condemnation—a good heart and a fondness for children.

* Afterward the well-known and dissolute Marquis of Hertford.

RICHARD BRINSLEY SHERIDAN.

Poor Sherry! poor Sherry! drunkard, gambler, spendthrift, debtor, godless and worldly as thou wert, what is it that shakes from our hand the stone we would fling at thee? Almost, we must confess it, thy very faults; at least those qualities which seem to have been thy glory and thy ruin; which brought thee into temptation; to which, hadst thou been less brilliant, less bountiful, thou hadst never been drawn. What is it that disarms us when we review thy life, and wrings from us a tear when we should utter a reproach? Thy punishment; that bitter, miserable end; that long battling with poverty, debt, disease, all brought on by thyself; that abandonment in the hour of need, more bitter than them all; that awakening to the terrible truth of the hollowness of man and rottenness of the world! surely this is enough: surely we may hope that a pardon followed. But now let us view thee in thy upward flight—the genius, the wit, the monarch of mind.

This great man, this wonderful genius, this eloquent senator, this most applauded dramatist was—hear it, oh, ye boys! and fling it triumphantly in the faces of your pedagogues—Sheridan, at your age, was a dunce! This was the more extraordinary, inasmuch as his father, mother, and grandfather were all celebrated for their quick mental powers. The last, in fact, Dr. Sheridan, was a successful and eminent schoolmaster, the intimate friend of Dean Swift, and an author. He was an Irishman and a wit, and would seem to have been a Jacobite to boot, for he was deprived of a chaplaincy he held under Government, for preaching, on King George's birthday, a sermon having for its text "Sufficient for the day is the evil thereof."

Sheridan's mother, again—an eccentric, extraordinary woman—wrote novels and plays; among the latter "The Discovery," which Garrick said was "one of the best comedies he ever read;" and Sheridan's father, Tom Sheridan, was famous, in connection with the stage, where he was so long the rival of David Garrick.

Born of such parents, in September, 1751, Richard Brinsley Sheridan was sent in due course to Harrow, where that famous old pedant, Dr. Parr, was at that time one of the masters. The Doctor has himself described the lazy boy, in whose face he discovered the latent genius, and whom he attempted to inspire with a love of Greek verbs and Latin verses, by making him ashamed of his ignorance. But Richard preferred English verses and no verbs, and the Doctor failed. He did not, even at that period, cultivate elocution, of which his father was so good a master; though Dr. Parr remembered one of his sisters, on a visit to Harrow, reciting, in accordance with her father's teaching, the well-known lines:

"*None* but the brave,
None but the *brave*,
None *but* the brave deserve the fair."

But the real mind of the boy who wouldn't be a scholar showed itself early enough. He had only just left Harrow, when he began to display his literary abilities. He had formed at school the intimate acquaintance of Halhed, afterward a distinguished Indianist, a man of like tastes with himself; he had translated with him some of the poems of Theocritus. The two boys had reveled together in boyish dreams of literary fame—ah, those boyish dreams! so often our noblest—so seldom realized. So often, alas! the aspirations to which we can look back as our purest and best, and which make us bitterly regret that they were but dreams. And now, when young Halhed went to Oxford, and young Sheridan to join his family at Bath, they continued these ambitious projects for a time, and laid out their fancy at full usury over many a work destined never to see the fingers of the printer's devil. Among these was a farce, or rather burlesque, which shows immense promise, and which, oddly enough, resembles in its cast the famous "Critic," which followed it later. It was called "Jupiter," and turned chiefly on the story of Ixion—

"Embracing cloud, Ixion like,"

the lover of Juno, who caught a cold instead of the Queen of Heaven; and who, according to the classical legend, tortured forever on a wheel, was in this production to be condemned forever to trundle the machine of a "needy knife-grinder," amid a grand musical chorus of "razors, scissors, and penknives to grind!" This piece was amusing enough, and clever enough, though it betrayed repeatedly the youthfulness of its authors; but less so their next attempt, a weekly periodical, to be called "Hernan's Miscellany," of which Sheridan wrote, or was to write, pretty nearly the whole. None but the first number was ever completed, and perhaps we need not regret that no more followed it; but it is touching to see these two young men, both feeling their powers, confident in them, and sunning their halcyon's wings in the happy belief that they were those of the eagle, longing eagerly, earnestly, for the few poor guineas that they hoped from their work. Halhed, indeed, wrote diligently, but his colleague was not true to the contract, and though the hope of gold stimulated him—for he was poor enough—from time to time to a great effort, he was always "beginning," and never completing.

The only real product of these united labors was a volume of Epistles in verse from the Greek of a poor writer of late age, Aristænetus. This volume, which does little credit to either of its parents, was positively printed and published in 1770, but the rich harvest of fame and shillings which they expected from it was never gathered in. Yet the book excited some little notice. The incognito of its authors induced some critics to palm it even on such a man as Dr. Johnson: others praised; others sneered at it. In the young men it raised hopes, only to dash them; but its failure was not so utter as to put the idea of literary success entirely out of their heads, nor its success sufficient to induce them to rush recklessly into print, and thus strangle their fame in its cradle. Let it fail, was Richard Sheridan's thought; he had now a far more engrossing ambition. In a word, he was in love.

Nonsense! Sherry in love, the idea is preposterous. Sherry, the disreputable, the licentious, the "Bardolph," as he was afterward called, still more the *Genius*—was Genius ever in love? Yes, he was in love for a time—only for a time, and not truly. But, be it remembered, Sheridan's evil days had not commenced. He sowed his wild oats late in life—alack for him! and he never finished sowing them. His was not the viciousness of nature, but the corruption of success. "In all time of wealth, good Lord deliver us!" What prayer can wild, unrestrained, unheeding Genius utter with more fervency? I own Genius is rarely in love. There is an egotism, almost a selfishness, about it, that will not stoop to such common worship. Women know it, and often prefer the blunt, honest, commonplace soldier to the wild erratic poet. Genius, grand as it is, is unsympathetic. It demands higher—the highest joys. It will not smack its lips over a beefsteak. Its banquet may be the richest, just to be tasted; or the poorest, just to try hunger. Genius claims to be loved, but to love is too much to ask it. In very sooth, it is not more nor less than madness; and who ever saw a madman in love? Who ever knew a madman cherish even the commonest passion? No, Genius is a disease, the mind overpowering the body. It is incapable of the honesty, despises the honor, of a pure love affair. And yet at this time Sheridan was not a matured Genius. When his development came, he cast off this very love for which he had fought, manœuvred, and struggled, and was unfaithful to the very wife whom he had nearly died to obtain.

Miss Linley was one of a family who have been called "a nest of nightingales." Young ladies who practice elaborate pieces and sing simple ballads in the voice of a white mouse, know the name of Linley well. For ages the Linleys have been the bards of England—composers, musicians, singers, always popular, always English. Sheridan's love was one of the most renowned of the family, but the "Maid of Bath," as she was called, was as celebrated for her beauty as for the magnificence of her voice. When Sheridan first knew her, she was only sixteen years old—very beautiful, clever, and modest, and—a flirt of the first water. She was a singer by profession, living at Bath, as Sheridan, only three years older than herself, also was, but attending concerts, oratorios, and so forth, in other places, especially at Oxford. Her adorers were legion; and the Oxford boys especially—always in love as they are—were among them. Halhed was among these last, and in the innocence of his heart confided his passion to his friend Dick Sheridan. At sixteen the young beauty began her conquests. A rich old Wiltshire squire, with a fine heart, as golden as his guineas, offered to or for her, and was readily accepted. But "Cecilia," as she was always called, could not sacrifice herself on the altar of duty, and she privately told him, that though she honored and esteemed, she could never love him. The old gentleman proved his worth. Did he storm? did he hold her to her engagement? did he shackle himself with a young wife, who would only learn to hate him for his pertinacity? Not a bit of it. He acted with a generosity which should be held up as a model to all old gentlemen who are wild enough to fall in love with girls of sixteen. He knew Mr. Linley, who was delighted with the match, would be furious if it were broken off. He offered to take on himself all the blame of the breach, and, to satisfy the angry parent, settled £1000 on the daughter. The offer was accepted, and the trial for breach of promise with which the père Linley had threatened Mr. Long, was of course withheld. Mr. Long afterward presented Mrs. Sheridan with £3000.

The "Maid of Bath" was now an heiress as well as a fascinating beauty, but her face and her voice were the chief enchantments with her ardent and youthful adorers. The Sheridans had settled in Mead Street, in that town which is celebrated for its gambling, its scandal, and its unhealthy situation at the bottom of a natural basin. Well might the swine of the Celtic shepherd discover its mineral waters; it has been a veritable sty of vice and dirt since then. Well might the Romans build their baths there: it will take more water than even Bath supplies to wash out its follies and iniquities. It certainly is strange how washing and cards go together. One would fancy there were no baths in Eden, for wherever there are baths, there we find idleness and all its attendant vices.

The Linleys were soon intimate with the Sheridans, and the Maid of Bath added to her adorers both Richard and his elder brother Charles; only, just as at Harrow every one thought Richard a dunce, and he disappointed them; so at Bath no one thought Richard would fall in love, and he *did* disappoint them—none more so than Charles, his brother, and Halhed, his bosom friend. As for the latter, he was almost mad in his devotion, and certainly extravagant in his expressions. He described his passion by a clever, but rather disagreeable simile, which Sheridan, who was a most disgraceful plagiarist, though he had no need to be so, afterward adopted as his own. "Just as the Egyptian pharmacists," wrote Halhed, in a Latin letter, in which he described the power of Miss Linley's voice over his spirit, "were wont, in embalming a dead body, to draw the brain out through the ears with a crooked hook, this nightingale has drawn out through mine ears not my brain only, but my heart also."

Then among other of her devotees were Norris, the singer, and Mr. Watts, a rich gentleman-commoner, who had also met her at Oxford. Surely with such and other rivals, the chances of the quiet, unpretending, undemonstrative boy of nineteen were small. But no, Miss Linley was foolish enough to be captivated by genius, and charmed by such poems as the quiet boy wrote to her, of which this is, perhaps, one of the prettiest:

"Dry that tear, my gentlest love;
Be hush'd that struggling sigh,
Nor seasons, day, nor fate shall prove
More fix'd, more true than I.
Hush'd be that sigh, be dry that tear;
Cease boding doubt, cease anxious fear—
Dry be that tear.

"Ask'st thou how long my love will stay,
When all that's new is past?
How long, ah Delia, can I say
How long my life will last?
Dry be that tear, be hush'd that sigh,
At least I'll love thee till I die:
Hush'd be that sigh.

"And does that thought affect thee too,
The thought of Sylvio's death,
That he who only breath'd for you,
Must yield that faithful breath?
Hush'd be that sigh, be dry that tear,
Nor let us lose our heaven here:
Be dry that tear."

The many adorers had not the remotest suspicion of this devotion, and "gave her" to this, that, or the other eligible personage; but the villainous conduct of a scoundrel soon brought the matter to a crisis. The whole story was as romantic as it could be. In a three-volume novel, critics, always so just and acute in their judgment, would call it far-fetched, improbable, unnatural; in short, any thing but what should be the plot of the pure "domestic English story." Yet, here it is with almost dramatic effect, the simple tale of what really befell one of our most celebrated men.

Yes, to complete the fiction-like aspect of the affair, there was even a "captain" in the matter—as good a villain as ever shone in short hose and cut doublet at the "Strand" or "Victoria." Captain Matthews was a married man, and a very naughty one. He was an intimate friend of the Linleys, and wanted to push his intimacy too far. In short, "not to put too fine a point on it" (too fine a point is precisely what never *is* put), he attempted to seduce the pretty, innocent girl, and not dismayed at one failure, went on again and again. "Cecilia," knowing the temper of Linley père, was afraid to expose him to her father, and with a course, which we of the present day can not but think strange, if nothing more, disclosed the attempts of her persecutor to no other than her own lover, Richard Brinsley Sheridan.

Strange want of delicacy, undoubtedly, and yet we can excuse the poor songstress, with a father who sought only to make money out of her talents, and no other relations to confide in. But Richard Brinsley, long her lover, now resolved to be both her protector and her husband. He persuaded her to fly to France, under cover of entering a convent. He induced his sister to lend him money out of that provided for the housekeeping at home, hired a post-chaise, and sent a sedan-chair to her father's house in the Crescent to convey her to it, and wafted her off to town. Thence, after a few adroit lies on the part of Sheridan, they sailed to Dunkirk; and there he persuaded her to become his wife. She consented, and they were knotted together by an obliging priest accustomed to these runaway matches from *la perfide Albion.*

The irate parent, Linley, followed, recaptured his daughter, and brought her back to England. Meanwhile, the elopement excited great agitation in the good city of Bath, and among others, the villain of the story, the gallant Captain Matthews, posted Richard Brinsley as "a scoundrel and a liar," the then polite method of expressing disgust. Home came Richard in the wake of Miss Linley, who rejoiced in the unromantic prænomen of "Betsy," and her angry parent, and found matters had been running high in his short absence. A duel with Matthews seems to have been the natural consequence, and up Richard posted to London to fight it. Matthews played the craven—Sheridan the impetuous lover. They met, fought, seized one another's swords, wrestled, fell together, and wounded each other with the stumps of their rapiers in true Chevy-Chase fashion. Matthews, who had behaved in a cowardly manner in the first affair, sought to retrieve his honor by sending a second challenge. Again the rivals—well represented in "The Rivals" afterward produced—met at Kingsdown. Mr. Matthews drew; Mr. Sheridan advanced on him at first; Mr. Matthews in turn advanced fast on Mr. Sheridan; upon which he retreated, till he very suddenly ran in upon Mr. Matthews, laying himself exceedingly open, and endeavoring to get hold of Mr. Matthews' sword. Mr. Matthews received him at point, and, I believe, disengaged his sword from Mr. Sheridan's body, and gave him another wound. The same scene was now enacted, and a *combat à l'outrance* took place, ending in mutual wounds, and fortunately no one dead.

Poor little Betsy was at Oxford when all this took place. On her return to Bath she heard something of it, and unconsciously revealed the secret of her private marriage, claiming the right of a wife to watch over her wounded husband. Then came the *dénouement*. Old Tom Sheridan rejected his son. The angry Linley would have rejected his daughter, but for her honor. Richard was sent off into Essex, and in due time the couple were legally married in England. So ended a wild, romantic affair, in which Sheridan took a desperate, but not altogether honorable, part. But the dramatist got more out of it than a pretty wife. Like all true geniuses, he employed his own experience in the production of his works, and drew from the very event of his life some hints or touches to enliven the characters of his imagination. Surely the bravado and cowardice of Captain Matthews, who on the first meeting in the Park is described as finding all kinds of difficulties in the way of their fighting, objecting now to the ground as unlevel, now to the presence of a stranger, who turns out to be an officer, and very politely moves off when requested, who, in short, delays the event as long as possible, must have supplied the idea of Bob Acres; while the very conversations, of which we have no record, may have given him some of those hints of character which made "The Rivals" so successful. That play—his first—was written in 1774. It failed on its first appearance, owing to the bad acting of the part of Sir Lucius O'Trigger, by Mr. Lee; but when another actor was substituted, the piece was at once successful, and acted with overflowing houses all over the country. How could it be otherwise? It may have been exaggerated, far-fetched, unnatural, but such characters as Sir Anthony Absolute, Sir Lucius, Bob Acres, Lydia Languish, and most of all Mrs. Malaprop, so admirably conceived, and so carefully and ingeniously worked out, could not but be admired. They have become household words; they are even now our standards of ridicule, and be they natural or not, these last eighty years have changed the world so little that Malaprops and Acreses may be found in the range of almost any man's experience, and in every class of society.

Sheridan and his divine Betsy were now living in their own house, in that dull little place, Orchard Street, Portman Square, then an aristocratic neighborhood, and he was diligent in the production of essays, pamphlets, and farces, many of which never saw the light, while others fell flat, or were not calculated to bring him any fame. What great authors have not experienced the same disappointments? What men would ever be great if they allowed such checks to damp their energy, or were turned back by them from the course in which they feel that their power lies?

But his next work, the opera of "The Duenna," had a yet more signal success, and a run of no less than seventy-five nights at Covent Garden, which put Garrick at Drury Lane to his wit's end to know how to compete with it. Old Linley himself composed the music for it; and to show how thus a family could hold the stage, Garrick actually played off the mother against the son, and revived Mrs. Sheridan's comedy of "The Discovery," to compete with Richard Sheridan's "Duenna."

The first night "The Rivals" was brought out at Bath came Sheridan's father, who, as we have seen, had refused to have any thing to say to his son. It is related, as an instance of Richard's filial affection, that during the representation he placed himself behind a side scene opposite to the box in which his father and sisters sat, and gazed at them all the time. When he returned to his house and wife, he burst into tears, and declared that he felt it too bitter that he alone should have been forbidden to speak to those on whom he had been gazing all the night.

In the following year this man of straw, who married on nothing but his brain, and had no capital, no wealthy friends, in short nothing whatever, suddenly appears in the most mysterious manner as a capitalist, and lays down his £10,000 in the coolest and quietest manner. And for what? For a share in the purchase of Garrick's moiety of the patent of Drury Lane. The whole property was worth £70,000; Garrick sold his half for £35,000, of which old Mr. Linley contributed £10,000, Doctor Ford £15,000, and penniless Sheridan the balance. Where he got the money nobody knew, and apparently nobody asked. It was paid, and he entered at once on the business of proprietor of that old house, where so many a Roscius has strutted and declaimed with more or less fame; so many a walking gentleman done his five shillings' worth of polite comedy, so many a tinsel king degraded the "legitimate drama" in the most illegitimate manner, and whose glories were extinguished with the reign of Macready, when we were boys, *nous autres.*

The first piece he contributed to this stage was "A Trip to Scarborough," which was only a species of "family edition" of Vanbrugh's obscene play, "The Relapse;" but in 1777 he reached the acme of his fame, in "The School for Scandal."

But alack and alas for these sensual days, when it is too much trouble to think, and people go to the play, if they go at all, to feast their eyes and ears, not their minds, to gaze, like clods, on a tinsel pageant of Mr. Charles Kean's, or, like a dull eastern prince, on the meretricious attitudes of half-clothed ballet-girls; nay, worse, to listen to the noise and clatter of Verdi or Balfe, and impudently call it music; to songs in a language they can not understand; and ridiculous ranting, to which they are not ashamed to give the name of acting. Can any sensible person believe that if "The School for Scandal," teeming as it does with wit, satire, and character, finer and truer than in any play produced since the days of Ben Jonson, Massinger, and Marlowe, were set on the boards of the Haymarket at this day, as a new piece by an author of no very high celebrity, it would draw away a single admirer from the flummery in Oxford Street, the squeaking at Covent Garden, or the broad, exaggerated farce at the Adelphi or Olympic? No: it may still have its place on the London stage when well acted, but it owes that to its ancient celebrity, and it can never compete with the tinsel and tailoring which alone can make even Shakspeare go down with a modern audience.

In those days of Garrick, on the other hand, those glorious days of true histrionic art, high and low were not ashamed to throng Drury Lane and Covent Garden, and make the appearance of a new play the great event of the season. Hundreds were turned away from the doors, when the "School for Scandal" was acted, and those who were fortunate enough to get in made the piece the subject of conversation in society for many a night, passing keen comment on every scene, every line, every word almost, and using their minds as we now use our eyes.

This brilliant play, the earliest idea of which was derived from its author's experience of the gossip of that kettle of scandal and backbiting, Bath, where if no other commandment were ever broken, the constant breach of the ninth would suffice to put it on a level with certain condemned cities we have somewhere read of, won for Sheridan a reputation of which he at once felt the value, and made his purchase of a share in the property of Old Drury for the time being a successful speculation. It produced a result which his good heart perhaps valued even more than the guineas which now flowed in; it induced his father, who had long been at war with him, to seek a reconciliation, and the elder Sheridan actually became manager of the theatre of which his son was part proprietor.

Old Tom Sheridan had always been a proud man, and when once he was offended, was hard to bring round again. His quarrel with Johnson was an instance of this. In 1762 the Doctor hearing they had given Sheridan a pension of two hundred a year, exclaimed, "What, have they given *him* a pension? then it is time for me to give up mine." A "kind friend" took care to repeat the peevish exclamation, without adding what Johnson had said immediately afterward, "However, I am glad that they have given Mr. Sheridan a pension, for he is a very good man." The actor was disgusted; and though Boswell interfered, declined to be reconciled. On one occasion he even rushed from a house at which he was to dine, when he heard that the great Samuel had been invited. The Doctor had little opinion of Sheridan's declamation. "Besides, sir," said he, "what influence can Mr. Sheridan have upon the language of this great country by his narrow exertions? Sir, it is burning a farthing candle at Dover to show light at Calais." Still, when Garrick attacked his rival, Johnson nobly defended him. "No, sir," he said, "there is to be sure, in Sheridan, something to reprehend, and every thing to laugh at; but, sir, he is not a bad man. No, sir; were mankind to be divided into good and bad, he would stand considerably within the ranks of the good."

However, the greatest bully of his age (and the kindest-hearted man) thought very differently of the son. Richard Brinsley had written a prologue to Savage's play of "Sir Thomas Overbury"—

"Ill-fated Savage, at whose birth was giv'n
No parent but the muse, no friend but Heav'n;"

and in this had paid an elegant compliment to the great lexicographer, winding up with these lines:

"So pleads the tale that gives to future times
The son's misfortunes and the parent's crimes;

THE FAMOUS "LITERARY CLUB."

> There shall his fame, if own'd to-night, survive,
> Fix'd by *the hand that bids our language live*—"

referring at once to Johnson's life of his friend Savage and to his great Dictionary. It was Savage, you remember, with whom Johnson in his days of starvation was wont to walk the streets all night, neither of them being able to pay for a lodging, and with whom, walking one night round and round St. James's Square, he kept up his own and his companion's spirits by inveighing against the minister, and declaring that they would "stand by their country."

Doubtless the Doctor felt as much pleasure at the meed awarded to his old companion in misery as at the high compliment to himself. Anyhow he pronounced that Sheridan "had written the two best comedies of his age," and therefore proposed him as a member of the Literary Club.

This celebrated gathering of wit and whimsicality, founded by Johnson himself in conjunction with Sir J. Reynolds, was the Helicon of London Letters, and the temple which the greatest talker of his age had built for himself, and in which he took care to be duly worshiped. It met at the Turk's Head in Gerrald Street, Soho, every Friday; and from seven in the evening to almost any hour of night was the scene of such talk, mainly on literature and learning, as has never been heard since in this country. It consisted at this period of twenty-six members, and there is scarcely one among them whose name is not known to-day as well as any in the history of our literature. Besides the high-priests, Reynolds and Johnson, there came Edmund Burke, Fox, Sheridan, and many another of less note, to represent the senate: Goldsmith, Gibbon, Adam Smith, Malone, Dr. Burney, Percy, Nugent, Sir William Jones, three Irish bishops, and a host of others, crowded in from the ranks of learning and literature. Garrick and George Colman found here an indulgent audience; and the light portion of the company comprised such men as Topham Beauclerk, Bennet Langton, Vesey, and a dozen of lords and baronets. In short, they were picked men, and if their conversation was not always witty, it was because they had all wit, and frightened one another.

Among them the bullying Doctor rolled in majestic grumpiness; scolded, dogmatized, contradicted, pished and pshawed, and made himself generally disagreeable; yet, hail the omen, Intellect! such was the force, such the fame of his mind, that the more he snorted, the more they adored him—the more he bullied, the more humbly they knocked under. He was quite "His Majesty" at the Turk's Head, and the courtiers waited for his coming with anxiety, and talked of him till he came in the same manner as the lackeys in the anteroom of a crowded monarch. Boswell, who, by the way, was also a member—of course he was, or how should we have had the great man's conversations handed down to us?—was sure to keep them up to the proper mark of adulation if they ever flagged in it, and was as servile in his admiration in the Doctor's absence as when he was there to call him a fool for his pains.

Thus, on one occasion while "King Johnson" tarried, the courtiers were discussing his journey to the Hebrides and his coming away "willing to believe the second sight." Some of them smiled at this, but Bozzy was down on them with more than usual servility. "He is only *willing* to believe," he exclaimed. "*I do* believe. The evidence is enough for me, though not for his great mind. What will not fill a quart bottle will fill a pint bottle. I am filled with belief." "Are you?" said Colman, slyly; "then cork it up."

As a specimen of Johnson's pride in his own club, which always remained extremely exclusive, we have what he said of Garrick, who, before he was elected, carelessly told Reynolds he liked the club, and "thought he would be of them."

"*He'll be of us!*" roared the Doctor indignantly, on hearing of this. "How does he know we will *permit* him? The first duke in England has no right to hold such language!"

It can easily be imagined that when "His Majesty" expressed his approval of Richard Brinsley, then a young man of eight-and-twenty, there was no one who ventured to blackball him, and so Sheridan was duly elected.

The fame of "The School for Scandal" was a substantial one for Richard Brinsley, and in the following year he extended his speculation by buying the other moiety of Drury Lane. This theatre, which took its name from the old Cockpit Theatre in Drury Lane, where Killigrew acted in the days of Charles II., is famous for the number of times it has been rebuilt. The first house had been destroyed in 1674; and the one in which Garrick acted was built by Sir Christopher Wren, and opened with a prologue by Dryden. In 1793 this was rebuilt. In 1809 it was burnt to the ground; and on its reopening the Committee advertised a prize for a prologue, which was supposed to be tried for by all the poets and poetasters then in England.* Horace Smith and his brother seized the opportunity to parody the style of the most celebrated in their delightful "Rejected Addresses." Drury Lane has always been grand in its prologue, for besides Dryden and

* None of the addresses sent in having given satisfaction, Lord Byron was requested to write one, which he did.

Byron, it could boast of Sam. Johnson, who wrote the address when Garrick opened the theatre in 1747. No theatre ever had more great names connected with its history.

It was in 1778, after the purchase of the other moiety of this property, that Sheridan set on its boards "The Critic." Though this was denounced as itself as complete a plagiarism as any Sir Fretful Plagiary could make, and though undoubtedly the idea of it was borrowed, its wit, so truly Sheridanian, and its complete characters, enhanced its author's fame, in spite of the disappointment of those who expected higher things from the writer of "The School for Scandal." Whether Sheridan would have gone on improving, had he remained true to the drama, "The Critic" leaves us in doubt. But he was a man of higher ambition. Step by step, unexpectedly, and apparently unprepared, he had taken by storm the outworks of the citadel he was determined to capture, and he seems to have cared little to garrison these minor fortresses. He had carried off from among a dozen suitors a wife of such beauty that Walpole thus writes of her in 1773:

"I was at the ball last night, and have only been at the opera, where I was infinitely struck with the Carrara, who is the prettiest creature upon earth. Mrs. Hartly I find still handsomer, and Miss Linley is to be the superlative degree. The king admires the last, and ogles her as much as he dares in so holy a place as an oratorio, and at so devout a service as Alexander's Feast."

Yet Sheridan did not prize Betsy as he should have done, when he had once obtained her. Again he had struck boldly into the drama, and in four years had achieved that fame as a play-writer to which even Johnson could testify so handsomely. He now quitted this, and with the same innate power—the same consciousness of success—the same readiness of genius—took a higher, far more brilliant flight than ever. Yet had he garrisoned the forts he captured, he would have been a better, happier, and more prosperous man. Had he been true to the Maid of Bath, his character would not have degenerated as it did. Had he kept up his connection with the drama, he would not have lost so largely by his speculation in Drury Lane. His genius became his temptation, and he hurried on to triumph and to fall.

Public praise is a siren which the young sailor through life can not resist. Political life is a fine aim, even when its seeker starts without a shred of real patriotism to conceal his personal ambition. No young man of any character can think, without a thrill of rapture, on the glory of having *his* name—now obscure—written in capitals on the page of his country's history.

A true patriot cares nothing for fame; a really great man is content to die nameless, if his acts may but survive him. Sheridan was not really great, and it may be doubted if he had any sincerity in his political views. But the period favored the rise of young men of genius. In former reigns a man could have little hope of political influence without being first a courtier; but by this time liberalism had made giant strides. The leaven of revolutionary ideas, which had leavened the whole lump in France, was still working quietly and less passionately in this country, and being less repressed, displayed itself in the last quarter of the eighteenth century in the form of a strong and brilliant opposition. It was to this that the young men of ambition attached themselves, rallying under the standard of Charles James Fox, since it was there only that their talents were sufficient to recommend them.

To this party, Sheridan, laughing in his sleeve at the extravagance of their demands—so that when they clamored for a "parliament once a year, or oftener if need be," he pronounced himself an "Oftener-if-need-be" man—was introduced, when his fame as a literary man had brought him into contact with some of its hangers-on. Fox, after his first interview with him, affirmed that he had always thought Hare and Charles Townsend the wittiest men he had ever met, but that Sheridan surpassed them both; and Sheridan was equally pleased with "the Man of the People."

The first step to this political position was to become a member of a certain club, where its leaders gambled away their money, and drank away their minds—to wit, Brookes's. Pretty boys, indeed, were these great Whig patriots when turned loose in these precincts. The tables were for stakes of twenty or fifty guineas, but soon ran up to hundreds. What did it matter to Charles James Fox, to the Man of the People, whether he lost five, seven, or ten thousand of a night, when the one half came out of his father's, the other out of Hebrew, pockets—the sleek, thick-lipped owners of which thronged his Jerusalem chamber, as he called his back sitting-room, only too glad to "oblige" him to any amount? The rage for gaming at this pandemonium may be understood from a rule of the club, which it was found necessary to make to interdict it *in the eating-room*, but to which was added the truly British exception, which allowed two members of Parliament in those days, or two "gentlemen" of any kind, to *toss up* for what they had ordered.

This charming resort of the dissipated was originally established in Pall Mall in 1764, and the manager was that same Almack who afterward opened a lady's club in the rooms now called Willis's, in King Street, St. James's; who also owned the famous Thatched House, and whom Gilly Williams described as having a "Scotch face, in a bag-wig," waiting on the ladies at supper. In 1778 Brookes—a wine-merchant and money-lender, whom Tickell, in his famous "Epistle from the Hon. Charles Fox, partridge-shooting, to the Hon. John Townsend, cruising," describes in these lines:

> "And know I've bought the best champagne from Brookes,
> From liberal Brookes, whose speculative skill
> Is hasty credit, and a distant bill:
> Who, nurs'd in clubs, disdains a vulgar trade;
> Exults to trust, and blushes to be paid"—

built and opened the present club-house in St. James's Street, and thither the members of Almack's migrated. Brookes's speculative skill, however, did not make him a rich man, and the "gentlemen" he dealt with were perhaps too gentlemanly to pay him. He died poor in 1782. Almack's at first consisted of twenty-seven members, one of whom was C. J. Fox. Gibbon, the historian, was actually a member of it, and says that in spite of the rage for play, he found the society there rational and entertaining. Sir Joshua Reynolds wanted to be a member of it too. "You see," says Topham Beauclerk thereupon, "what noble ambition will make a man attempt. That den is not yet opened," etc.

Brookes's, however, was far more celebrated, and besides Fox, Reynolds, and Gibbon, there were here to be found Horace Walpole, David Hume, Burke, Selwyn, and Garrick. It would be curious to discover how much religion, how much morality, and how much vanity there were among the set. The first two would require a microscope to examine, the last an ocean to contain it. But let Tickell describe its inmates:

> "Soon as to Brookes's thence thy footsteps bend,
> What gratulations thy approach attend!
> See Gibbon rap his box—auspicious sign,
> That classic compliment and wit combine;
> See Beauclerk's cheek a tinge of red surprise,
> And friendship give what cruel health denies;
> * * * *
> Of wit, of taste, of fancy we'll debate,
> If Sheridan for once be not too late.
> But scarce a thought on politics we'll spare,
> Unless on Polish politics with Hare.
> Good-natured Devon! oft shall there appear
> The cool complacence of thy friendly sneer;
> Oft shall Fitzpatrick's wit, and Stanhope's ease,
> And Burgoyne's manly sense combine to please."

To show how high gaming ran in this assembly of wits, even so early as 1772, there is a memorandum in the books, stating

P 2

that Mr. Thynne retired from the club in disgust, because he had only won £12,000 in two months. The principal games at this period were quinze and faro.

Into this eligible club Richard Sheridan, who ten years before had been agreeing with Halhed on the bliss of making a couple of hundred pounds by their literary exertions, now essayed to enter as a member; but in vain. One black ball sufficed to nullify his election, and that one was dropped in by George Selwyn, who would not have the son of an actor among them. Again and again he made the attempt; again and again Selwyn foiled him; and it was not till 1780 that he succeeded. The Prince of Wales was then his devoted friend, and was determined he should be admitted into the club. The elections at that time took place between eleven at night and one o'clock in the morning, and the "greatest gentleman in Europe" took care to be in the hall when the ballot began. Selwyn came down as usual, bent on triumph. The prince called him to him. There was nothing for it; Selwyn was forced to obey. The prince walked him up and down the hall, engaging him in an apparently most important conversation. George Selwyn answered him question after question, and made desperate attempts to slip away. The other George had always something more to say to him. The long finger of the clock went round, and Selwyn's long white fingers were itching for the black ball. The prince was only more and more interested, the wit only more and more abstracted. Never was the one George more lively, or the other more silent. But it was all in vain. The finger of the clock went round and round, and at last the members came out noisily from the balloting-room, and the smiling faces of the prince's friends showed to the unhappy Selwyn that his enemy had been elected.

So, at least, runs one story. The other, told by Sir Nathaniel Wraxall, is perhaps more probable. It appears that the Earl of Besborough was no less opposed to his election than George Selwyn, and these two individuals agreed at any cost of comfort to be always at the club at the time of the ballot to throw in their black balls. On the night of his success, Lord Besborough was there as usual, and Selwyn was at his rooms in Cleveland Row, preparing to come to the club. Suddenly a chairman rushed into Brookes's with an important note for my lord, who, on tearing it open, found to his horror that it was from his daughter-in-law, Lady Duncannon, announcing that his house in Cavendish Square was on fire, and imploring him to come immediately. Feeling confident that his fellow-conspirator would be true to his post, the earl set off at once. But almost the same moment Selwyn received a message informing him that his adopted daughter, of whom he was very fond, was seized with an alarming illness. The ground was cleared; and by the time the earl returned, having, it is needless to say, found his house in a perfect state of security, and was joined by Selwyn, whose daughter had never been better in her life, the actor's son was elected, and the conspirators found they had been duped.

But it is far easier in this country to get into that House, where one has to represent the interests of thousands, and take a share in the government of a nation, than to be admitted to a club where one has but to lounge, to gamble, and to eat dinner; and Sheridan was elected for the town of Stafford with probably little more artifice than the old and stale one of putting five-pound notes under voters' glasses, or paying thirty pounds for a home-cured ham. Whether he bribed or not, a petition was presented against his election, almost as a matter of course in those days, and his maiden speech was made in defense of the good burgesses of that quiet little county-town. After making this speech, which was listened to in silence on account of his reputation as a dramatic author, but does not appear to have been very wonderful, he rushed up to the gallery, and eagerly asked his friend Woodfall what he thought of it. That candid man shook his head, and told him oratory was not his forte. Sheridan leaned his head on his hand a moment, and then exclaimed with vehement emphasis, "It is in me, however, and, by Heaven! it shall come out."

He spoke prophetically, yet not as the great man who determines to conquer difficulties, but rather as one who feels conscious of his own powers, and knows that they must show themselves sooner or later. Sheridan found himself laboring under the same natural obstacles as Demosthenes—though in a less degree—a thick and disagreeable tone of voice; but we do not find in the indolent but gifted Englishman that admirable perseverance, that conquering zeal, which enabled the Athenian to turn these very impediments to his own advantage. He did, indeed, prepare his speeches, and at times had fits of that same diligence which he had displayed in the preparation of "The School for Scandal;" but his indolent, self-indulgent mode of life left him no time for such steady devotion to oratory as might have made him the finest speaker of his age, for perhaps his natural abilities were greater than those of Pitt, Fox, or even Burke, though his education was inferior to that of those two statesmen.

From this time Sheridan's life had two phases—that of a politician, and that of a man of the world. With the former we have nothing to do in such a memoir as this, and indeed it is difficult to say whether it was in oratory, the drama, or wit that he gained the greatest celebrity. There is, however, some difference between the three capacities. On the mimic stage, and on the stage of the country, his fame rested on a very few grand outbursts—some matured, prepared, deliberated—others spontaneous. He left only three great comedies, and perhaps we may say only one really grand. In the same way he made only two great speeches, or perhaps we may say only one. His wit, on the other hand—though that too is said to have been studied—was the constant accompaniment of his daily life, and Sheridan has not left two or three celebrated bon-mots, but a hundred.

But even in his political career his wit, which must then have been spontaneous, won him almost as much fame as his eloquence, which he seems to have reserved for great occasions. He was the wit of the House. Wit, ridicule, satire, quiet, cool, and easy sneers, always made in good temper, and always therefore the more bitter, were his weapons, and they struck with unerring accuracy. At that time—nor at that time only—the "Den of Thieves," as Cobbett called our senate, was a cockpit as vulgar and personal as the present Congress of the United States. Party spirit meant more than it has ever done since, and scarcely less than it had meant when the throne itself was the stake for which parties played some forty years before. There was, in fact, a substantial personal centre for each side. The one party rallied round a respectable but maniac monarch, whose mental afflictions took the most distressing form, the other round his gay, handsome, dissolute—nay disgusting—son, at once his rival and his heir. The spirit of each party was therefore personal, and their attacks on one another were more personal than any thing we can imagine in the present day in so respectably ridiculous a conclave as the House of Commons. It was little for one honorable gentleman to give another honorable gentleman the lie direct before the eyes of the country. The honorable gentlemen descended—or, as they thought, ascended—to the most vehement invective, and such was at times the torrent of personal abuse which parties heaped on one another, while good-natured John Bull looked on and smiled at his rulers, that, as in the United States of to-day, a debate was often the prelude to a duel. Pitt and Fox, Tierney, Adam, Fullarton, Lord George Germain, Lord Shelburne, and Governor Johnstone, all "vindicated their honor," as the phrase went, by "coffee and pistols for four." If Sheridan had not to repeat the Bob Acres scene with Captain Matthews, it was only because his wonderful good-humor could put up with a great deal that others thought could only be expiated by a hole in the waistcoat.

In the administration of the Marquis of Rockingham the dramatist enjoyed the pleasures of office for less than a year as one of the Under Secretaries of State in 1782. In the next year we find him making a happy retort on Pitt, who had somewhat vulgarly alluded to his being a dramatic author. It was on the American question, perhaps the bitterest that ever called forth the acrimony of parties in the House. Sheridan, from boyhood, had been taunted with being the son of an actor. He had been called "the player-boy" at school, and his election at Brookes's had been opposed on the same grounds. It was evidently his bitterest point, and Pitt probably knew this when, in replying to a speech of the ex-dramatist's, he said that "no man admired more than he did the abilities of that right honorable gentleman, the elegant sallies of his thought, the gay effusions of his fancy, his *dramatic* turns, and his epigrammatic point; and if they were reserved for the *proper stage*, they would, no doubt, receive what the hon. gentleman's abilities always did receive, the plaudits of the audience; and it would be his fortune *sui plausu gaudere theatri*. But this was not the proper scene for the exhibition of those elegancies." This was vulgar in Pitt, and probably every one felt so. But Sheridan rose, cool and collected, and quietly replied:

"On the particular sort of personality which the right hon. gentleman has thought proper to make use of, I need not make any comment. The propriety, the taste, the gentlemanly point of it, must have been obvious to the House. But let me assure the right hon. gentleman that I do now, and will at any time he chooses to repeat this sort of allusion, meet it with the most sincere good-humor. Nay, I will say more: flattered and encouraged by the right hon. gentleman's panegyric on my talents, if ever I again engage in the compositions he alludes to, I may be tempted to an act of presumption—to attempt an improvement on one of Ben Jonson's best characters, the character of the *Angry Boy*, in the 'Alchemist.'"

The fury of Pitt, contrasted with the coolness of the man he had so shamefully attacked, made this sally irresistible, and from that time neither "the angry boy" himself, nor any of his colleagues, were anxious to twit Sheridan on his dramatic pursuits.

Pitt wanted to lay a tax on every horse that started in a race. Lord Surrey, a *turfish* individual of the day, proposed one of five pounds on the winner. Sheridan, rising, told his lordship that the next time he visited Newmarket he would probably be greeted with the line:

"Jockey of Norfolk, be not so bold."

Lord Rolle, the butt of the Opposition, who had attacked him in the famous satire "The Rolliad," so popular that it went through twenty-two editions in twenty-seven years, accused Sheridan of inflammatory speeches among the operatives of the northern counties on the cotton question. Sheridan retorted by saying that he believed Lord Rolle must refer to "Compositions less prosaic, but more popular" (meaning the "Rolliad"), and thus successfully turned the laugh against him.

It was Grattan, I think, who said, "When I can't talk sense, I talk metaphor." Sheridan often talked metaphor, though he sometimes mingled it with sense. His famous speech about the Begums of Oude is full of it, but we have one or two instances before that. Thus on the Duke of Richmond's report about fortifications, he said, turning to the duke, that "holding in his hand the report made by the Board of Officers, he complimented the noble president on his talents as an *engineer*, which were strongly evinced in planning and constructing that very paper. . . . . He has made it a contest of posts, and conducted his reasoning not less on principles of trigonometry than of logic. There are certain assumptions thrown up, like advanced works, to keep the enemy at a distance from the principal object of debate; strong provisos protect and cover the flanks of his assertions: his very queries are his casemates," and so on.

When Lord Mulgrave said, on another occasion, that any man using his influence to obtain a vote for the crown *ought* to lose his head, Sheridan quietly remarked, that he was glad his lordship had said "*ought* to lose his head," not *would* have lost it, for in that case the learned gentleman would not have had that evening "a *face* to have shown among us."

Such are a few of his well-remembered replies in the House; but his fame as an orator rested on the splendid speeches which he made at the impeachment of Warren Hastings. The first of these was made in the House on the 7th of February, 1787. The whole story of the corruption, extortions, and cruelty of the worst of many bad rulers who have been imposed upon that unhappy nation of Hindoostan, and who, ignorant of how to *parcere subjectis*, have gone on in their unjust oppression, only rendering it the more dangerous by weak concessions, is too well known to need a recapitulation here. The worst feature in the whole of Hastings's misconduct was, perhaps, his treatment of those unfortunate ladies whose money he coveted, the Begums of Oude. The Opposition was determined to make the governor general's conduct a state question, but their charges had been received with little attention, till on this day Sheridan rose to denounce the cruel extortioner. He spoke for five hours and a half, and surpassed all he had ever said in eloquence. The subject was one to find sympathy in the hearts of Englishmen, who, though they beat their own wives, are always indignant at a man who dares to lay a little finger on any body else's. Then, too, the subject was Oriental: it might even be invested with something of romance and poetry; the zenanah, sacred in the eyes of the oppressed natives, had been ruthlessly violated; under a glaring Indian sun, amid the luxuriance of Indian foliage, these acts had been committed, etc., etc. It was a fertile theme for a poet, and however little Sheridan cared for the Begums and their wrongs—and that he did care little appears from what he afterward said of Hastings himself—he could evidently make a telling speech out of the theme, and he did so. Walpole says that he turned every body's head. "One heard every body in the street raving on the wonders of that speech; for my part, I can not believe it was so supernatural as they say." He affirms that there must be a witchery in Mr. Sheridan, who had no diamonds—as Hastings had—to win favor with, and says that the Opposition may be fairly charged with sorcery. Burke declared the speech to be "the most astonishing effort of eloquence, argument, and wit united, of which there was any record or tradition." Fox affirmed that "all he had ever heard, all he had ever read, when compared with it, dwindled into nothing, and vanished like vapor before the sun." But these were partisans. Even Pitt acknowledged "that it surpassed all the eloquence of ancient and modern times, and possessed every thing that genius or art could furnish to agitate and control the human mind." One member confessed himself so unhinged by it, that he moved an adjournment, because he could not, in his then state of mind, give an unbiased vote. But the highest testimony was that of Logan, the defender of Hastings. At the end of the first hour of the speech, he said to a friend, "All this is declamatory assertion without proof." Another hour's speaking, and he muttered, "This is a most wonderful oration!" A third, and he confessed "Mr. Hastings has acted very unjustifiably." At the end of the fourth, he exclaimed, "Mr. Hastings is a most atrocious criminal." And before the speaker had sat down, he vehemently protested that "Of all monsters of iniquity, the most enormous is Warren Hastings."

Such in those days was the effect of eloquence; an art which has been eschewed in the present House of Commons, and which our newspapers affect to think is much out of place in an assembly met for calm deliberation. Perhaps they are right; but oh! for the golden words of a Sheridan, a Fox—even a Pitt and Burke.

It is said, though not proved, that on this same night of Sheridan's glory in the House of Commons, his "School for Scandal" was acted with "rapturous applause" at Covent Garden, and his "Duenna" no less successfully at Drury Lane. What a pitch of glory for the dunce who had been shamed into learning Greek verbs at Harrow! Surely Dr. Parr must then have confessed that a man can be great without the classics—nay, without even a decent English education, for Sheridan knew comparatively little of history and literature, certainly less than the men against whom he was pitted or whose powers he emulated. He has been known to say to his friends, when asked to take part with them on some important question, "You know I'm an ignoramus—instruct me and I'll do my best." He had even to rub up his arithmetic when he thought he had some chance of being made Chancellor of the Exchequer; but, perhaps, many a statesman before and after him has done as much as that.

No wonder that after such a speech in the House the celebrated trial which commenced in the beginning of the following year should have roused the attention of the whole nation. The proceedings opened in Westminster Hall, the noblest room in England, on the 13th of February, 1788. The Queen and four of her daughters were seated in the Duke of Newcastle's box; the Prince of Wales walked in at the head of a hundred and fifty peers of the realm. The spectacle was imposing enough. But the trial proceeded slowly for some months, and it was not till the 3d of June that Sheridan rose to make his second great speech on this subject.

The excitement was then at its highest. Two thirds of the peers with the peeresses and their daughters were present, and the whole of the vast hall was crowded to excess. The sun shone in brightly to light up the gloomy building, and the whole scene was splendid. Such was the enthusiasm that people paid *fifty guineas* for a ticket to hear the first orator of his day, for such he then was. The actor's son felt the enlivening influence of a full audience. He had been long preparing for this moment, and he threw into his speech all the theatrical effect of which he had studied much and inherited more. He spoke for many hours on the 3d, 5th, and 6th, and concluded with these words:

"They (the House of Commons) exhort you by every thing that calls sublimely upon the heart of man, by the majesty of that justice which this bold man has libeled, by the wide fame of your own tribunal, by the sacred pledges by which you swear in the solemn hour of decision, knowing that that decision will then bring you the highest reward that ever blessed the heart of man, the consciousness of having done the greatest act of mercy for the world that the earth has ever yet received from any hand but heaven! My Lords, I have done."

Sheridan's valet was very proud of his master's success, and as he had been to hear the speech, was asked what part he considered the finest. Plush replied by putting himself into Sherry's attitude, and imitating his voice admirably, solemnly uttering, "My Lords, I have done!" He should have added the word "nothing." Sheridan's eloquence had no more effect than the clear proofs of Hastings's guilt, and the impeachment, as usual, was but a troublesome sham, to satisfy the Opposition and dust the eyeballs of the country. Oh! Sham, Sham, Sham! if you are ever deposed and want a kingdom in a quiet corner of the globe, come to this island. We have long honored you here, and sacrifice to you at every general election and in every parliamentary Commission. Sham, you will be always welcome to the land of Johannes Bull!

Sheridan's great speech was made. The orator has concluded his oration; fame was complete, and no more was wanted. Adieu, then, blue-books and parties, and come on the last grand profession of this man of many talents—that of the wit. That it was a profession there can be no doubt, for he lived on it: it was all his capital. He paid his bills in that coin alone: he paid his workmen, his actors, carpenters, builders with no more sterling metal; with that ready tool he extracted loans from the very men who came to be paid; that brilliant ornament maintained his reputation in the senate, and his character in society. But wit without wisdom—the froth without the fluid—the capital without the pillar—is but a poor fortune, a wretched substitute for real worth and honest utility. For a time men forgave to Mr. Sheridan—extravagant swindler, drunkard, and debauchee—what would long before have brought an honester, better, but less amusing man to a debtor's prison and the contempt of society; but only for a time.

Sheridan has now reached the pinnacle of his fame, and from this point we have to trace that decline which ended so awfully.

When we call him a swindler, we must not be supposed to imply that he was so in heart. It is pleaded for him that he swindled "for the fun of the thing," like a modern Robin Hood, and like that forester bold, he was mightily generous with other men's money. But Sheridan had the advantage of being born in a respectable station. Had his father been a tinker or cobbler instead of a comedian, no doubt the son would have ended his days in some salubrious colony, chained some equally inglorious fellow-swindler, and no one would have written his Life, or taken a moment's pains to prove him any better than a jury had pronounced him. Thieving is thieving whether in sport or earnest, and Sheridan, no doubt, made it a very profitable employment. He had always a taste for the art of duping, and he had begun early in life—soon after leaving Harrow. He was spending a few days at Bristol, and wanted a pair of new boots, but could not afford to pay for them. Shortly before he left, he called on two bootmakers, and ordered of each a pair, promising payment on delivery. He fixed the morning of his departure for the tradesmen to send in their goods. When the first arrived he tried on the boots, complained that that for the *right* foot pinched a little, and ordered Crispin to take it back, stretch it, and bring it again at nine the next morning. The second arrived soon after, and this time it was the boot for the *left* foot which pinched. Same complaint; same order given; each had taken away only the pinching boot, and left the other behind. The same afternoon Sheridan left in his new boots for town, and when the two shoemakers called at nine the next day, each with a boot in his hand, we can imagine their disgust at finding how neatly they had been duped.

Anecdotes of this kind swarm in every account of Dick Sheridan—many of them, perhaps, quite apocryphal, others exaggerated or attributed to this noted trickster, but all tending to show how completely he was master of this high art. His ways of eluding creditors used to delight me, I remember, when an Oxford boy, often inclined to imitate the great comedian, and they are only paralleled by Oxford stories. One of these may not be generally known, and was worthy of Sherry. Every Oxonian knows Hall, the boat-builder at Folly Bridge. Mrs. Hall was, in my time, proprietress of those dangerous skiffs and nutshell canoes which we young harebrains delighted to launch on the Isis. Some youthful Sheridanian had a long account with this elderly and bashful personage, who had applied in vain for her money, till, coming one day to his rooms, she announced her intention not to leave till the money was paid. "Very well, Mrs. Hall, then you must sit down and make yourself comfortable while I dress, for I am going out directly." Mrs. H. sat down composedly, and with equal composure the youth took off his coat. Mrs. H. was not abashed, but in another moment the debtor removed his waistcoat also. Mrs. H. was still immovable. Sundry other articles of dress followed, and the good lady began to be nervous. "Now,

Mrs. Hall, you can stay if you like, but I assure you that I am going to change *all* my dress." Suiting the action to the word, he began to remove his lower garments, when Mrs. Hall, shocked and furious, rushed from the room.

This reminds us of Sheridan's treatment of a female creditor. He had for some years hired his carriage-horses from Edbrooke in Clarges Street, and his bill was a heavy one. Mrs. Edbrooke wanted a new bonnet, and blew up her mate for not insisting on payment. The curtain lecture was followed next day by a refusal to allow Mr. Sheridan to have the horses till the account was settled. Mr. Sheridan sent the politest possible message in reply, begging that Mrs. Edbrooke would allow his coachman to drive her in his own carriage to his door, and promising that the matter should be satisfactorily arranged. The good woman was delighted, dressed in her best, and bill in hand, entered the M. P.'s chariot. Sheridan meanwhile had given orders to his servants. Mrs. Edbrooke was shown up into the back drawing-room, where a slight luncheon, of which she was begged to partake, was laid out; and she was assured that her debtor would not keep her waiting long, though for the moment engaged. The horse-dealer's wife sat down and discussed a wing of chicken and glass of wine, and in the mean time her victimizer had been watching his opportunity, slipped down stairs, jumped into the vehicle, and drove off. Mrs. Edbrooke finished her lunch and waited in vain; ten minutes, twenty, thirty, passed, and then she rang the bell: "Very sorry, ma'am, but Mr. Sheridan went out on important business half an hour ago." "And the carriage?" "Oh, ma'am, Mr. Sheridan never walks."

He procured his wine in the same style. Chalier, the wine-merchant, was his creditor to a large amount, and had stopped supplies. Sheridan was to give a grand dinner to the leaders of the Opposition, and had no port or sherry to offer them. On the morning of the day fixed he sent for Chalier, and told him he wanted to settle his account. The importer, much pleased, said he would go home and bring it at once. "Stay," cried the debtor, "will you dine with me to-day? Lord ———, Sir ——— ———, and So-and-so are coming." Chalier was flattered and readily accepted. Returning to his office, he told his clerk that he should dine with Mr. Sheridan, and therefore leave early. At the proper hour he arrived in full dress, and was no sooner in the house than his host dispatched a message to the clerk at the office, saying that Mr. Chalier wished him to send up at once three dozen of Burgundy, two of claret, two of port, etc., etc. Nothing seemed more natural, and the wine was forwarded, just in time for the dinner. It was highly praised by the guests, who asked Sheridan who was his wine-merchant. The host bowed toward Chalier, gave him a high recommendation, and impressed him with the belief that he was telling a polite falsehood in order to secure him other customers. Little did he think that he was drinking his own wine, and that it was not, and probably never would be, paid for!

In like manner, when he wanted a particular Burgundy from an innkeeper at Richmond, who declined to supply it till his bill was paid, he sent for the man, and had no sooner seen him safe in the house than he drove off to Richmond, saw his wife, told her he had just had a conversation with mine host, settled every thing, and would, to save them trouble, take the wine with him in his carriage. The condescension overpowered the good woman, who ordered it at once to be produced, and Sheridan drove home about the time that her husband was returning to Richmond, weary of waiting for his absent debtor. But this kind of trickery could not always succeed without some knowledge of his creditor's character. In the case of Holloway, the lawyer, Sheridan took advantage of his well-known vanity of his judgment of horse-flesh. Kelly gives the anecdote as authentic. He was walking one day with Sheridan, close to the church-yard of St. Paul's, Covent Garden, when, as ill-luck would have it, up comes Holloway on horseback, and in a furious rage, complains that he has called on Mr. Sheridan time and again in Hertford Street, and can never gain admittance. He proceeds to violent threats, and slangs his debtor roundly. Sheridan, cool as a whole bed of cucumbers, takes no notice of these attacks, but quietly exclaims, "What a beautiful creature you're riding, Holloway!" The lawyer's weak point was touched.

"You were speaking to me the other day about a horse for Mrs. Sheridan; now this would be a treasure for a lady."

"Does he canter well?" asked Sheridan, with a look of business.

"Like Pegasus himself."

"If that's the case, I shouldn't mind, Holloway, stretching a point for him. Do you mind showing me his paces?"

"Not at all," replies the lawyer, only too happy to show off his own; and touching up the horse, put him to a quiet canter. The moment is not to be lost; the church-yard gate is at hand; Sheridan slips in, knowing that his mounted tormentor can not follow him, and there bursts into a roar of laughter, which is joined in by Kelly, but not by the returning Holloway.

But if he escaped an importunate lawyer once in a way like

"A TREASURE FOR A LADY"—SHERIDAN AND THE LAWYER.

this, he required more ingenuity to get rid of the limbs of the law, when they came, as they did frequently in his later years. It was the fashionable thing in by-gone novels of the "Pelham" school, and even in more recent comedies, to introduce a well-dressed sheriff's officer at a dinner-party or ball, and take him through a variety of predicaments, ending, at length, in the revelation of his real character; and probably some such scene is still enacted from time to time in the houses of the extravagant: but Sheridan's adventures with bailiffs seem to have excited more attention. In the midst of his difficulties he never ceased to entertain his friends, and "why should he not do so, since he had not to pay?" "Pay your bills, sir? what a shameful waste of money!" he once said. Thus, one day a young friend was met by him and taken back to dinner, "quite in a quiet way, just to meet a very old friend of mine, a man of great talent, and most charming companion." When they arrived they found "the old friend" already installed, and presenting a somewhat unpolished appearance, which the young man explained to himself by supposing him to be a genius of somewhat low extraction. His habits at dinner, the eager look, the free use of his knife, and so forth, were all accounted for in the same way, but that he was a genius of no slight distinction was clear from the deep respect and attention with which Sheridan listened to his slightest remarks, and asked his opinion on English poetry. Meanwhile Sheridan and the servant between them plied the genius very liberally with wine; and the former, rising, made him a complimentary speech on his critical powers, while the young guest, who had heard nothing from his lips but the commonest platitudes in very bad English, grew more and more amused. The wine told in time, the "genius" sang songs which were more Saxon than delicate, talked loud, clapped his host on the shoulder, and at last rolled fairly under the table. "Now," said Sheridan, quite calmly to his young friend, "we will go up stairs; and, Jack" (to his servant) "take that man's hat and give him to the watch." He then explained in the same calm tone, that this was a bailiff of whose company he was growing rather tired, and wanted to be rid.

But his finest tricks were undoubtedly those by which he turned, harlequin-like, a creditor into a lender. This was done by sheer force of persuasion, by assuming a lofty indignation, or by putting forth his claims to mercy with the most touching eloquence, over which he would laugh heartily when his point was gained. He was often compelled to do this during his theatrical management, when a troublesome creditor might have interfered with the success of the establishment.

He talked over an upholsterer who came with a writ for £350, till the latter handed him, instead, a check for £200. He once, when the actors struck for arrears of wages to the amount of £3000, and his bankers refused flatly to Kelly to advance another penny, screwed the whole sum out of them in less than a quarter of an hour by sheer talk. He got a gold watch from Harris, the manager, with whom he had broken several appointments, by complaining that as he had no watch he could never tell the time fixed for their meetings; and, as for putting off pressing creditors, and turning furious foes into affectionate friends, he was such an adept at it, that his reputation as a dun-destroyer is quite on a par with his fame as comedian and orator.

Hoaxing, a style of amusement fortunately out of fashion now, was almost a passion with him, and his practical jokes were as merciless as his satire. He and Tickell, who had married the sister of his wife, used to play them off on one another like a couple of schoolboys. One evening, for instance, Sheridan got together all the crockery in the house and arranged it in a dark passage, leaving a small channel for escape for himself, and then, having teased Tickell till he rushed after him, bounded out and picked his way gingerly along the passage. His friend followed him unwittingly, and at the first step stumbled over a washhand-basin, and fell forward with a crash on piles of plates and dishes, which cut his face and hands in a most cruel manner, Sheridan all the while laughing immoderately at the end of the passage, secure from vengeance.

But his most impudent hoax was that on the Honorable House of Commons itself. Lord Belgrave had made a very telling speech which he wound up with a Greek quotation, loudly applauded. Sheridan had no arguments to meet him with; so rising, he admitted the force of his lordship's quotation (of which he probably did not understand a word), but added that had he gone a little farther, and completed the passage, he would have seen that the context completely altered the sense. He would prove it to the House, he said, and forthwith rolled forth a grand string of majestic gibberish so well imitated that the whole assembly cried, "Hear, hear!" Lord Belgrave rose again, and frankly admitted that the passage had the meaning ascribed to it by the honorable gentleman, and that he had overlooked it at the moment. At the end of the evening, Fox, who prided himself on his classical lore, came up to and said to him, "Sheridan, how came you to be so ready with that passage? It is certainly as you say, but I was not aware of it before you quoted it." Sherry was wise enough to keep his own counsel for the time, but must have felt delightfully tickled at the ignorance of the would-be savants with whom he was politically associated. Probably Sheridan could not at any time have quoted a whole passage of Greek on the spur of the moment; but it is certain that he had not kept up his classics, and at the time in question must have forgotten the little he ever knew of them.

This facility of imitating exactly the sound of a language without introducing a single word of it is not so very rare, but is generally possessed in greater readiness by those who know no tongue but their own, and are therefore more struck by the strangeness of a foreign one, when hearing it. Many of us have heard Italian songs in which there was not a word of actual Italian sung in London burlesques, and some of us have laughed at Levassor's capital imitation of English; but perhaps the cleverest mimic of the kind I ever heard was M. Laffitte, brother of that famous banker who made his fortune by picking up a pin. This gentleman could speak nothing but French, but had been brought by his business into contact with foreigners of every race at Paris, and when he once began his little trick, it was impossible to believe that he was not possessed of a gift of tongues. His German and Italian were good enough, but his English was so splendidly counterfeited, that after listening to him for a short time, I suddenly heard a roar of laughter from all present, for I had actually unconsciously *answered him*, "Yes," "No," "Exactly so," and "I quite agree with you!"

Undoubtedly much of Sherry's depravity must be attributed to his intimacy with a man whom it was a great honor to a youngster then to know, but who would probably be scouted even from a London club in the present day—the Prince of Wales. The part of a courtier is always degrading enough to play; but to be courtier to a prince whose favor was to be won by proficiency in vice and audacity in follies, to truckle to his tastes, to pander to his voracious lusts, to win his smiles by the invention of a new pleasure, and his approbation by the plotting of a new villainy, what an office for the author of "The School for Scandal," and the orator renowned for denouncing the wickednesses of Warren Hastings! What a life for the young poet who had wooed and won the Maid of Bath —for the man of strong domestic affections, who wept over his father's sternness, and loved his son only too well! It was bad enough for such mere worldlings as Captain Hanger or Beau Brummell, but for a man of higher and purer feelings, like Dick Sheridan, who, with all his faults, had some poetry in his soul, such a career was doubly disgraceful.

It was at the house of the beautiful, lively, and adventurous

Duchess of Devonshire, the partisan of Charles James Fox, who loved him or his cause—for Fox and Liberalism were often one in ladies' eyes—so well, that she could give greasy Steele, the butcher, a kiss for his vote, that Sheridan first met the prince—then a boy in years, but already more than an adult in vice. No doubt the youth whom Fox, Brummell, Hanger, Lord Surrey, Sheridan, the tailors, and the women combined to turn at once into the finest gentleman and greatest blackguard in Europe, was at that time as fascinating in appearance and manner as any one, prince or not, could be. He was by far the handsomest of the Hanoverians, and had the least amount of their sheepish look. He possessed all their taste and capacity for gallantry, with none of the German coarseness, which certain other Princes of Wales exhibited in their amorous address. *His* coarseness was of a more sensual, but less imperious kind. He *had* his redeeming points, which few of his ancestors had, and his liberal hand and warm heart won him friends, where his conduct could win him little else than contempt. Sheridan was introduced to him by Fox, and Mrs. Sheridan by the Duchess of Devonshire. The prince had that which always takes with Englishmen—a readiness of conviviality, and a recklessness of character. He was ready to chat, drink, and bet with Sheridan, or any new-comer equally well recommended, and an introduction to young George was always followed by an easy recognition. With all this he managed to keep up a certain amount of royal dignity under the most trying circumstances, but he had none of that easy grace which made Charles II. beloved by his associates. When the George had gone too far, he had no resource but to cut the individual with whom he had hobbed and nobbed, and he was as ungrateful in his enmities as he was ready with his friendship. Brummell had taught him to dress, and Sheridan had given him wiser counsels: he quarreled with both for trifles, which, if he had had real dignity, would never have occurred, and if he had had real friendship, would easily have been overlooked.

Sheridan's breach with the prince was honorable to him. He could not wholly approve of the conduct of that personage and his ministers, and he told him openly that his life was at his service, but his character was the property of the country. The prince replied that Sheridan "might impeach his ministers on the morrow—that would not impair their friendship;" yet turned on his heel, and was never his friend again. When, again, the "delicate investigation" came off, he sent for Sheridan, and asked his aid. The latter replied, "Your royal highness honors me, but I will never take part against a woman, whether she be right or wrong." His political courage atones somewhat for the want of moral courage he displayed in pandering to the prince's vices.

Many an anecdote is told of Sheridan and "Wales"—many, indeed, that can not be repeated. Their bets were often of the coarsest nature, won by Sheridan in the coarsest manner. A great intimacy sprang up between the two reprobates, and Sherry became one of the satellites of that dissolute prince. There are few of the stories of their adventures which can be told in a work like this, but we may give one or two specimens of the less disgraceful character:

The Prince, Lord Surrey, and Sheridan were in the habit of seeking nightly adventures of any kind that suggested itself to their lively minds. A low tavern, still in existence, was the rendezvous of the heir to the crown and his noble and distinguished associates. This was the "Salutation," in Tavistock Court, Covent Garden, a night-house for gardeners and countrymen, and the sharpers who fleeced both, and was kept by a certain Mother Butler, who favored in every way the adventurous designs of her exalted guests. Here wigs, smock-frocks, and other disguises were in readiness; and here, at call, was to be found a ready-made magistrate, whose sole occupation was to deliver the young Haroun and his companions from the dilemmas which their adventures naturally brought them into, and which were generally more or less concerned with the watch. Poor old watch! what happy days, when members of parliament, noblemen, and sucking monarchs condescended to break thy bob-wigged head! and—blush, Z 350, immaculate constable—to toss thee a guinea to buy plaster with.

In addition to the other disguise, *aliases* were of course assumed. The prince went by the name of Blackstock, Graystock was my Lord Surrey, and Thinstock Richard Brinsley Sheridan. The treatment of women by the police is traditional. The "unfortunate"—unhappy creatures!—are their pet aversion; and once in their clutches, receive no mercy. The "Charley" of old was quite as brutal as the modern Hercules of the glazed hat, and the three adventurers showed an amount of zeal worthy of a nobler cause, in rescuing the drunken Laïs from his grasp. On one occasion they seem to have hit on a "deserving case;" a slight skirmish with the watch ended in a rescue, and the erring creature was taken off to a house of respectability sufficient to protect her. Here she told her tale, which, however improbable, turned out to be true. It was a very old, a very simple one—the common history of many a frail, foolish girl, cursed with beauty, and the prey of a practiced seducer. The main peculiarity lay in the fact of her respectable birth, and his position, she being the daughter of a solicitor, he the son of a nobleman. Marriage was promised, of course, as it has been promised a million times with the same intent, and for the millionth time was not performed. The seducer took her from her home, kept her quiet for a time, and when the novelty was gone, abandoned her. The old story went on; poverty—a child—a mother's love struggling with a sense of shame—a visit to her father's house at the last moment, as a forlorn hope. There she had crawled on her knees to one of those relentless parents on whose heads lies the utter loss of their children's souls. The false pride, that spoke of the blot on his name, the disgrace of his house—when a Savior's example should have bid him forgive and raise the penitent in her misery from the dust—whispered him to turn her from his door. He ordered the footman to put her out. The man, a nobleman in plush, moved by his young mistress's utter misery, would not obey though it cost him his place, and the harder-hearted father himself thrust his starving child into the cold street, into the drizzling rain, and slammed the door upon her cries of agony. The footman slipped out after her, and five shillings—a large sum for him—found its way from his kind hand to hers. Now the common ending might have come; now starvation, the slow, unwilling recourse to more shame and deeper vice; then the forced hilarity, the unreal smile, which in so many of these poor creatures hides a canker at the heart; the gradual degradation—lower still and lower—oblivion for a moment sought in the bottle—a life of sin and death ended in a hospital. The will of Providence turned the frolic of three voluptuaries to good account; the prince gave his purseful, Sheridan his one last guinea for her present needs; the name of the good-hearted Plush was discovered, and he was taken into Carlton House, where he soon became known as Roberts, the prince's confidential servant; and Sheridan bestirred himself to rescue forever the poor lady, whose beauty still remained as a temptation. He procured her a situation, where she studied for the stage, on which she eventually appeared. "All's well that ends well;" her secret was kept, till one admirer came honorably forward. To him it was confided, and he was noble enough to forgive the one false step of youth. She was well married, and the boy for whom she had suffered so much fell at Trafalgar, a lieutenant in the navy.

To better men such an adventure would have been a solemn warning; such a tale, told by the ruined one herself, a sermon, every word of which would have clung to their memories. What effect, if any, it may have had on Blackstock and his companions must have been very fleeting.

It is not so very long since the Seven Dials and St. Giles's were haunts of wickedness and dens of thieves, into which the police scarcely dared to penetrate. Probably their mysteries would have afforded more amusement to the artist and the student of character than to the mere seeker of adventure, but it was still, I remember, in my early days, a great feat to visit by night one of the noted "cribs" to which "the profession" which fills Newgate was wont to resort. The "Brown Bear," in Broad Street, St. Giles's, was one of these pleasant haunts, and thither the three adventurers determined to go. This style of adventure is out of date, and no longer amusing. Of course a fight ensued, in which the prince and his companions showed immense pluck against terrible odds, and in which, as one reads in the novels of the "London Journal" or "Family Herald," the natural superiority of the well-born of course displayed itself to great advantage. Surely Bulwer has described such scenes too graphically in some of his earlier novels to make a minute description here at all necessary; but the reader who is curious in the matter may be referred to a work which has recently appeared under the title of "Sheridan and his Times," professing to be written by an Octogenarian, intimate with the hero. The fray ended with the arrival of the watch, who rescued Blackstock, Graystock, and Thinstock, and with Dogberryan stupidity carried them off to a neighboring lock-up. The examination which took place was just the occasion for Sheridan's fun to display itself on, and pretending to turn informer, he succeeded in bewildering the unfortunate parochial constable, who conducted it, till the arrival of the magistrate, whose duty was to deliver his friends from durance vile. The whole scene is well described in the book just referred to, with, we presume, a certain amount of idealizing; but the "Octogenarian" had probably heard the story from Sheridan himself, and the main points must be accepted as correct. The affair ended, as usual, with a supper at the "Salutation."

We must now follow Sheridan in his gradual downfall.

One of the causes of this—as far as money was concerned—was his extreme indolence and utter negligence. He trusted far too much to his ready wit and rapid genius. Thus when "Pizarro" was to appear, day after day went by, and nothing was done. On the night of representation, only four acts out of five were written, and even these had not been rehearsed, the principal performers, Siddons, Charles Kemble, and Barrymore, having only just received their parts. Sheridan was up in the prompter's room, actually writing the fifth act while the first was being performed, and every now and then appeared in the green-room with a fresh relay of dialogue, and setting all in good-humor by his merry abuse of his own negligence. In spite of this "Pizarro" succeeded. He seldom wrote except at night, and surrounded by a profusion of lights. Wine was his great stimulant in composition, as it has been to better and worse authors. "If the thought is slow to come," he would say, "a glass of good wine encourages it; and when it does come, a glass of good wine rewards it." Those glasses of good wine were, unfortunately, even more frequent than the good thoughts, many and merry as they were.

His neglect of letters was a standing joke against him. He never took the trouble to open any that he did not expect, and often left sealed many that he was most anxious to read. He once appeared with his begging face at the bank, humbly asking an advance of twenty pounds. "Certainly, sir; would you like any more?—fifty or a hundred?" said the smiling clerk. Sherry was overpowered. He *would* like a hundred. "Two or three?" asked the scribe. Sherry thought he was joking, but was ready for two or even three—he was always ready for more. But he could not conceal his surprise. "Have you not received our letter?" the clerk asked, perceiving it. Certainly he had received the epistle, which informed him that his salary as Receiver General of Cornwall had been paid in, but he had never opened it.

This neglect of letters once brought him into a troublesome lawsuit about the theatre. It was necessary to pay certain demands, and he had applied to the Duke of Bedford to be his security. The duke had consented, and for a whole year his letter of consent remained unopened. In the mean time Sheridan had believed that the duke had neglected him, and allowed the demands to be brought into court.

In the same way he had long before committed himself in the affair with Captain Matthews. In order to give a public denial of certain reports circulated in Bath, he had called upon an editor, requesting him to insert the said reports in his paper, in order that he might write him a letter to refute them. The editor at once complied, the calumny was printed and published, but Sheridan forgot all about his own refutation, which was applied for in vain till too late.

Other causes were his extravagance and intemperance. There was an utter want of even common moderation in every thing he did. Whenever his boyish spirits suggested any freak, whenever a craving of any kind possessed him, no matter what the consequences here or hereafter, he rushed heedlessly into the indulgence of it. Perhaps the enemy had never an easier subject to deal with. Any sin in which there was a show of present mirth, or easy pleasure, was as easily taken up by

Sheridan as if he had not a single particle of conscience or religious feeling, and yet we are not at all prepared to say that he lacked either; he had only deadened both by excessive indulgence of his fancies. The temptation of wealth and fame had been too much for the poor and obscure young man who rose to them so suddenly, and, as so often happens, those very talents which should have been his glory, were, in fact, his ruin.

His extravagance was unbounded. At a time when misfortune lay thick upon him, and bailiffs were hourly expected, he would invite a large party to a dinner, which a prince might have given, and to which one prince sometimes sat down. On one occasion, having no plate left from the pawnbroker's, he had to prevail on "my uncle" to lend him some for a banquet he was to give. The spoons and forks were sent, and with them two of his men, who, dressed in livery, waited, no doubt with the most vigilant attention, on the party. Such at that period was the host's reputation, when he could not even be trusted not to pledge another man's property. At one time his income was reckoned at £15,000 a year, when the theatre was prosperous. Of this he is said to have spent not more than £5000 on his household, while the balance went to pay for his former follies, debts, and the interest, lawsuits often arising from mere carelessness and judgments against the theatre! Probably a great deal of it was betted away, drunk away, thrown away in one way or another. As for betting, he generally lost all the wagers he made: as he said himself—"I never made a bet upon my own judgment that I did not lose; and I never won but one, which I had made against my judgment." His bets were generally laid in hundreds; and though he did not gamble, he could of course run through a good deal of money in this way. He betted on every possible trifle, but chiefly, it would seem, on political possibilities; the state of the funds, the result of an election, or the downfall of a ministry. Horse-races do not seem to have possessed any interest for him, and, in fact, he scarcely knew one kind of horse from another. He was never an adept at field-sports, though very ambitious of being thought a sportsman. Once, when staying in the country, he went out with a friend's gamekeeper to shoot pheasants, and after wasting a vast amount of powder and shot upon the air, he was only rescued from ignominy by the sagacity of his companion, who, going a little behind him when a bird rose, brought it down so neatly that Sheridan, believing he had killed it himself, snatched it up, and rushed bellowing with glee back to the house to show that he *could* shoot. In the same way, he tried his hand at fishing in a wretched little stream behind the Deanery at Winchester, using, however, a net, as easier to handle than a rod. Some boys, who had watched his want of success a long time, at last bought a few pennyworth of pickled herrings, and throwing them on the stream, allowed them to float down toward the eager disciple of old Izaak. Sheridan saw them coming, rushed in regardless of his clothes, cast his net, and in great triumph secured them. When he had landed his prize, however, there were the boys bursting with laughter, and Piscator saw he was their dupe. "Ah!" cried he, laughing in concert, as he looked at his dripping clothes, "this is a pretty *pickle* indeed!"

His extravagance was well known to his friends, as well as to his creditors. Lord Guildford met him one day. "Well, Sherry, so you've taken a new house, I hear." "Yes, and you'll see now that every thing will go on like clock-work." "Ay," said my lord, with a knowing leer, "*tick, tick*." Even his son Tom used to laugh at him for it. "Tom, if you marry that girl, I'll cut you off with a shilling." "Then you must borrow it," replied the ingenious youth.* Tom sometimes disconcerted his father with his inherited wit—his only inheritance. He pressed urgently for money on one, as on many an occasion. "I have none," was the reply, as usual; "there is a pair of pistols up stairs, a horse in the stable, the night is dark, and Hounslow Heath at hand."

"I understand what you mean," replied young Tom; "but I tried that last night, and unluckily stopped your treasurer, Peake, who told me you had been beforehand with him, and robbed him of every sixpence he had in the world."

So much for the respect of son to father!

Papa had his revenge of the young wit he had begotten, when Tom, talking of Parliament, announced his intention of entering it on an independent basis, ready to be bought by the highest bidder. "I shall write on my forehead," said he, "'To let.'"

"And under that, Tom, 'Unfurnished,'" rejoined Sherry the elder. The joke is now stale enough.

But Sheridan was more truly witty in putting down a young braggart whom he met at dinner at a country house. There are still to be found, like the bones of dead asses in a field newly plowed, in some parts of the country, youths, who are so hopelessly behind their age, and indeed every age, as to look upon authorship as degrading, all knowledge, save Latin and Greek, as "a bore," and all entertainment but hunting, shooting, fishing, and badger-drawing, as unworthy of a man.

* Another version is that Tom replied—"You don't happen to have it about you, sir, do you?"

In the last century these young animals, who unite the modesty of the puppy with the clear-sightedness of the pig, not to mention the progressiveness of another quadruped, were more numerous than in the present day, and in consequence more forward in their remarks. It was one of these charming youths, who was staying in the same house as Sheridan, and who, quite unprovoked, began at dinner to talk of "actors and authors, and those low sort of people, you know." Sherry said naught, but patiently bided his time. The next day there was a large dinner-party, and Sheridan and the youth happened to sit opposite to one another in the most conspicuous part of the table. Young Nimrod was kindly obliging his side of the table with the extraordinary leaps of his hunter, the perfect working of his new double-barreled Manton, etc., bringing of course number one in as the hero in each case. In a moment of silence, Sheridan, with an air of great politeness, addressed his unhappy victim. "He had not," he said, "been able to catch the whole of the very interesting account he had heard Mr. ——— relating." All eyes were turned upon the two. "Would Mr. ——— permit him to ask who it was who made the extraordinary leap he had mentioned?" "I, sir," replied the youth, with some pride. "Then who was it killed the wild duck at that distance?" "I, sir." "Was it your setter who behaved so well?" "Yes, mine, sir," getting rather red over this examination. "And who caught the huge salmon so neatly?" "I, sir." And so the questioning went on through a dozen more items, till the young man, weary of answering "I, sir," and growing redder and redder every moment, would gladly have hid his head under the table-cloth, in spite of his sporting prowess. But Sheridan had to give him the *coup de grâce.*

"So, sir," said he, very politely, "you were the chief *actor* in every anecdote, and the *author* of them all; surely it is impolitic to despise your own professions."

Sheridan's intemperance was as great and as incurable as his extravagance, and we think his mind, if not his body, lived only on stimulants. He could neither write nor speak without them. One day, before one of his finest speeches in the House, he was seen to enter a coffee-house, call for a pint of brandy, and swallow it "neat," and almost at one gulp. His friends occasionally interfered. This drinking, they told him, would destroy the coat of his stomach. "Then my stomach must digest in its waistcoat," laughed Sherry.

Where are the topers of yore? Jovial I will not call them, for every one knows that

"Mirth and laughter,"

worked up with a cork-screw, are followed by

"Headaches and hot coppers the day after."

But where are those Anakim of the bottle, who *could* floor their two of port and one of Madeira, though the said two and one floored them in turn? The race, I believe, has died out. Our heads have got weaker, as our cellars grew emptier. The arrangement was convenient. The daughters of Eve have nobly undertaken to atone for the naughty conduct of their primeval mamma, by reclaiming men, and dragging them from the Hades of the mahogany to that seventh heaven of muffins and English ballads prepared for them in the drawing-room.

We are certainly astounded, even to incredulity, when we read of the deeds of a David or a Samson; but such wonderment can be nothing compared to that which a generation or two hence will feel, when sipping, as a great extravagance and unpardonable luxury, two thimblefuls of "African Sherry," the young demirep of the day reads that three English gentlemen, Sheridan, Richardson, and Ward, sat down one day to dinner, and before they rose again—if they ever rose, which seems doubtful—or, at least, were raised, had emptied five bottles of port, two of Madeira, and one of brandy! Yet this was but one instance in a thousand; there was nothing extraordinary in it, and it is only mentioned because the amount drunk is accurately given by the unhappy owner of the wine, Kelly, the composer, who unfortunately, or fortunately, was not present, and did not even imagine that the three honorable gentlemen were discussing his little store. Yet Sherry does not seem to have believed much in his friend's vintages, for he advised him to alter his brass plate to "Michael Kelly, Composer of Wine and Importer of Music." He made a better joke, when, dining with Lord Thurlow, he tried in vain to induce him to produce a second bottle of some extremely choice Constantia from the Cape of Good Hope. "Ah," he muttered to his neighbor, "pass me that decanter, if you please, for I must return to Madeira, as I see I can not *double the Cape*."

But as long as Richard Brinsley was a leader of political and fashionable circles, as long as he had a position to keep up, an ambition to satisfy, a labor to complete, his drinking was, if not moderate, not extraordinary for his time and his associates. But when a man's ambition is limited to mere success—when fame and a flash for himself are all he cares for, and there is no truer, grander motive for his sustaining the position he has climbed to—when, in short, it is his own glory, not mankind's good, he has ever striven for—woe, woe, woe when the hour of success is come! I can not stop to name and examine instances, but let me be allowed to refer to that bugbear who is called up whenever greatness of any kind has to be illustrated—Napoleon the Great; or let me take any of the lesser Napoleons in lesser grades in any nation, any age—the men who have had no star but self and self-glory before them—and let me ask if any one can be named who, if he has survived the attainment of his ambition, has not gone down the other side of the hill somewhat faster than he came up it? Then let me select men whose guiding-star has been the good of their fellow-creatures, or the glory of God, and watch their peaceful useful end on that calm summit that they toiled so honestly to reach. The difference comes home to us. The moral is read only at the end of the story. Remorse rings it forever in the ears of the dying—often too long a-dying—man who has labored for himself. Peace reads it smilingly to him whose generous toil for others has brought its own reward.

Sheridan had climbed with the stride of a giant, laughing at rocks, at precipices, at slippery water-courses. He had spread the wings of genius to poise himself withal, and gained one peak after another, while homelier worth was struggling mid-way, clutching the brambles and clinging to the ferns. He had, as Byron said in Sherry's days of decay, done the best in all he undertook, written the best comedy, best opera, best farce; spoken the best parody, and made the best speech. Sheridan, when those words of the young poet were told him, shed tears. Perhaps the bitter thought struck him, that he had *not* led the best, but the *worst* life; that comedy, farce, opera, monody, and oration were nothing, nothing to a pure conscience and a peaceful old age; that they could not save him from shame and poverty—from debt, disgrace, drunkenness—from grasping, but long-cheated creditors, who dragged his bed from under the feeble, nervous, ruined old man. Poor Sherry! his end was too bitter for us to cast one stone more upon him. Let it be noted that it was in the beginning of his decline, when, having reached the climax of all his ambition and completed his fame as a dramatist, orator, and wit, that the hand of Providence mercifully interposed to rescue this reckless man from his downfall. It smote him with that common but powerful weapon—death. Those he best loved were torn from him, one after another, rapidly, and with little warning. The Linleys, the "nest of nightingales," were all delicate as nightingales should be; and it seemed as if this very time was chosen for their deaths, that the one erring soul—more precious, remember, than many just lives—might be called back. Almost within one year he lost his dear sister-in-law, the wife of his most intimate friend Tickell; Maria Linley, the last of the family; his own wife, and his little daughter. One grief succeeded another so rapidly that Sheridan was utterly unnerved, utterly brought low by them; but it was his wife's death that told most upon him. With that wife he had always been the lover rather than the husband. She had married him in the days of his poverty, when her beauty was so celebrated that she might have wed whom she would. She had risen with him and shared his later anxieties. Yet she had seen him forget, neglect her, and seek other society. In spite of his tender affection for her and for his children, he had never made a *home* of their home. Vanity Fair had kept him ever flitting, and it is little to be wondered at that Mrs. Sheridan was sometimes tempted to fill up his place from among her many admirers.* Yet, in spite of calumny, she died with a fair fame. Decline had long pressed upon her, yet her last illness was too brief. In 1792 she was taken away, still in the summer of her days, and with her last breath uttering her love for the man who had deserted her. His grief was terrible; yet it passed, and wrought no change. He found solace in his beloved son, and yet more beloved daughter. A few months —and the little girl followed her mother. Again his grief was terrible: again passed and wrought no change. Yes, it did work some change, but not for the better: it drove him to the goblet; and from that time we may date the confirmation of his habit of drinking. The solemn warnings had been unheeded: they were to be repeated by a long-suffering God in a yet more solemn manner, which should touch him yet more nearly. His beautiful wife had been the one restraint upon his folly and his lavishness. Now she was gone, they burst out afresh, wilder than ever.

For a while after these afflictions, which were soon completed in the death of his most intimate friend and boyish companion, Tickell, Sheridan threw himself again into the commotion of the political world. But in this we shall not follow him. Three years after the death of his first wife he married again. He was again fortunate in his choice. Though now forty-four, he succeeded in winning the heart of a most estimable and charming young lady with a fortune of £5000. She must indeed have loved or admired the widower very much to consent to be the wife of a man so notoriously irregular, to use a mild term, in his life. But Sheridan fascinated wherever he went, and young ladies like "a little wildness." His heart was always good, and where he gave it he gave it warmly, richly, fully. His second wife was Miss Esther Jane

* Lord Edward Fitzgerald was one of the most devoted of these: he chose his wife, Pamela, because she resembled Mrs. Sheridan.

Ogle, daughter of the Dean of Winchester. She was given to him on condition of his settling in all £20,000 upon her—a wise proviso with such a spendthrift—and he had to raise the money, as usual.

His political career was sufficiently brilliant, though his real fame as a speaker rests on his great oration at Hastings's trial. In 1806 he satisfied another point of his ambition, long desired, and was elected for the city of Westminster, which he had ardently coveted when Fox represented it. But a dissolution threw him again on the mercy of the popular party; and again he offered himself for Westminster; but, in spite of all the efforts made for him, without success. He was returned, instead, for Ilchester.

Meanwhile his difficulties increased; extravagance, debt, want of energy to meet both, brought him speedily into that position when a man accepts without hesitation the slightest offer of aid. The man who had had an income of £15,000 a year, and settled £20,000 on his wife, allowed a poor friend to pay a bill for £5 for him, and clutched eagerly at a £50 note when displayed to him by another. Extravagance is the father of meanness, and Sheridan was often mean in the readiness with which he accepted offers, and the anxiety with which he implored assistance. It is amusing in the present day to hear a man talk of "a debt of honor," as if all debts did not demand honor to pay them—as if all debts incurred without hope of repayment were not dishonorable. A story is told relative to the old-fashioned idea of "a debt of honor." A tradesman, to whom he had given a bill for £200, called on him for the amount. A heap of gold was lying on the table. "Don't look that way," cried Sheridan, after protesting that he had not a penny in the world, "that is to pay a debt of honor." The applicant, with some wit, tore up the bill he held. "Now, Mr. Sheridan," quoth he, "mine is a debt of honor too." It is to be hoped that Sherry handed him the money.

The story of Gunter's bill is not so much to his credit. Hanson, an iron-monger, called upon him and pressed for payment. A bill sent in by the famous confectioner was lying on the table. A thought struck the debtor, who had no means of getting rid of his importunate applicant. "You know Gunter?" he asked. "One of the safest men in London," replied the iron-monger. "Then will you be satisfied if I give you his *bill* for the amount?" "Certainly." Thereupon Sherry handed him the neatly-folded account and rushed from the room, leaving the creditor to discover the point of Mr. Sheridan's little fun.

Still Sheridan might have weathered through the storm. Drury Lane was a mine of wealth to him, and with a little care might have been really profitable. The lawsuits, the debts, the engagements upon it, all rose from his negligence and extravagance. But Old Drury was doomed. On the 24th of February, 1809, soon after the conclusion of the performances, it was announced to be in flames. Rather it announced itself. In a few moments it was blazing—a royal bonfire. Sheridan was in the House of Commons at the time. The reddened clouds above London threw the glare back even to the windows of the House. The members rushed from their seats to see the unwonted light, and in consideration for Sheridan, an adjournment was moved. But he rose calmly, though sadly, and begged that no misfortune of his should interrupt the public business. His independence, he said—witty in the midst of his troubles—had often been questioned, but was now confirmed, for he had nothing more to depend upon. He then left the House, and repaired to the scene of conflagration.

Not long after, Kelly found him sitting quite composed in "The Bedford," sipping his wine, as if nothing had happened. The musician expressed his astonishment at Mr. Sheridan's *sang froid.* "Surely," replied the wit, "you'll admit that a man has a right to take his wine by his own fireside." But Sherry was only drowning care, not disregarding it. The event was really too much for him, though perhaps he did not realize the extent of its effect at the time. In a word, all he had in the world went with the theatre. Nothing was left either for him or the principal shareholders. Yet he bore it all with fortitude, till he heard that the harpsichord, on which his first wife was wont to play, was gone too. Then he burst into tears.

This fire was the opening of the shaft down which the great man sank rapidly. While his fortunes kept up, his spirits were not completely exhausted. He drank much, but as an indulgence rather than as a relief. Now it was by wine alone that he could even raise himself to the common requirements of conversation. He is described, *before* dinner, as depressed, nervous, and dull; *after* dinner only did the old fire break out, the old wit blaze up, and Dick Sheridan was Dick Sheridan once more. He was, in fact, fearfully oppressed by the long-accumulated and never-to-be-wiped-off debts, for which he was now daily pressed. In quitting Parliament he resigned his sanctuary, and left himself an easy prey to the Jews and Gentiles, whom he had so long dodged and deluded with his ready ingenuity. Drury Lane, as we all know, was rebuilt, and the birth of the new house heralded with a prologue by Byron, about as good as the one in "Rejected Addresses," the cleverest parodies ever written, and suggested by this very occasion. The building-committee having advertised for a prize prologue, Samuel Whitbread sent in his own attempt, in which, as probably in a hundred others, the new theatre was compared to a Phœnix rising out of the ashes of the old one. Sheridan said Whitbread's description of a Phœnix was excellent, for it was quite a *poulterer's description.*

This same Sam Whitbread was now to figure conspicuously in the life of Mr. Richard B. Sheridan. The ex-proprietor was found to have an interest in the theatre to the amount of £150,000—not a trifle to be sneezed at; but he was now past sixty, and it need excite no astonishment that, even with all his liabilities, he was unwilling to begin again the cares of management, or mismanagement, which he had endured so many years. He sold his interest, in which his son Tom was joined, for £60,000. This sum would have cleared off his debts and left him a balance sufficient to secure comfort for his old age. But it was out of the question that any money matters should go right with Dick Sheridan. Of the rights and wrongs of the quarrel between him and Whitbread, who was chairman of the committee for building the new theatre, I do not pretend to form an opinion. Sheridan was not naturally mean, though he descended to meanness when hard pressed—what man of his stamp does not? Whitbread was truly friendly to him for a time. Sherry was always complaining that he was sued for debts he did not owe, and kept out of many that were due to him. Whitbread knew his man well, and if he withheld what was owing to him, may be excused on the ground of real friendship. All I know is, that Sheridan and Whitbread quarreled; that the former did not, or affirmed that he did not, receive the full amount of his claim on the property, and that, when what he had received was paid over to his principal creditors, there was little or nothing left for my lord to spend in banquets to parliamentary friends and jorams of brandy in small coffee-houses.

Because a man is a genius, he is not of necessity an upright, honest, ill-used, oppressed, and cruelly-entreated man. Genius plays the fool wittingly, and often enough quite knowingly, with its own interests. It is its privilege to do so, and no one has a right to complain. But then Genius ought to hold its tongue, and not make itself out a martyr, when it has had the dubious glory of defying common sense. If Genius despises gold, well and good, but when he has spurned it, he should not whine out that he is wrongfully kept from it. Poor Sherry may or may not have been right in the Whitbread quarrel;

he has had his defenders, and I am not anxious of being numbered among them; but whatever were now his troubles were brought on by his own disregard of all that was right and beautiful in conduct. If he went down to the grave a pauper and a debtor, he had made his own bed, and in it he was to lie.

Lie he did, wretchedly, on the most unhappy bed that old age ever lay in. There is little more of importance to chronicle of his latter days. The retribution came on slowly but terribly. The career of a ruined man is not a pleasant topic to dwell upon, and I leave Sheridan's misery for Mr. J. B. Gough to whine and roar over when he wants a shocking example. Sherry might have earned many a crown in that capacity, if temperance oratory had been the passion of the day. Debt, disease, depravity—these words describe enough the downward career of his old age. To eat, still more to drink, was now the troublesome enigma of the quondam genius. I say quondam, for all the marks of that genius were now gone. One after another his choicest properties made their way to "my uncle's." The books went first, as if they could be most easily dispensed with; the remnants of his plate followed; then his pictures were sold; and at last even the portrait of his first wife, by Reynolds, was left in pledge for a "farther remittance."

The last humiliation arrived in time, and the associate of a prince, the eloquent organ of a party, the man who had enjoyed £15,000 a year, was carried off to a low sponging-house. His pride forsook him in that dismal and disgusting imprisonment, and he wrote to Whitbread a letter which his defenders ought not to have published. He had his friends—stanch ones too—and they aided him. Peter Moore, iron-monger, and even Canning, lent him money and released him from time to time. For six years after the burning of the old theatre he continued to go down and down. Disease now attacked him fiercely. In the spring of 1816 he was fast waning toward extinction. His day was past; he had outlived his fame as a wit and social light; he was forgotten by many, if not by most, of his old associates. He wrote to Rogers, "I am absolutely undone and broken-hearted." Poor Sherry! in spite of all thy faults, who is he whose morality is so stern that he can not shed one tear over thy latter days! God forgive us, we are all sinners; and if we weep not for this man's deficiency, how shall we ask tears when our day comes? Even as I write I feel my hand tremble and my eyes moisten over the sad end of one whom I love, though he died before I was born. "They are going to put the carpets out of window," he wrote to Rogers, "and break into Mrs. S.'s room and *take me*. For God's sake let me see you!" See him!—see one friend who could and would help him in his misery! Oh! happy may that man count himself who has never wanted that one friend, and felt the utter helplessness of that want! Poor Sherry! had he ever asked, or hoped, or looked for that Friend out of *this* world it had been better; for "the Lord thy God is a jealous God," and we go on seeking human friendship and neglecting the divine till it is too late. He found one hearty friend in his physician, Dr. Bain, when all others had forsaken him. The spirit of White's and Brookes's, the companion of a prince and a score of noblemen, the enlivener of every "fashionable" table, was forgotten by all but this one doctor. Let us read Moore's description: "A sheriff's officer at length arrested the dying man *in his bed*, and was about to carry him off, in his blankets, to a sponging-house, when Dr. Bain interfered." Who would live the life of revelry that Sheridan lived to have such an end? A few days after, on the 7th of July, 1816, in his sixty-fifth year, he died.

Peace! there was not peace even in death, and the creditor pursued him even into the "waste wide"—even to the coffin. He was lying in state, when a gentleman in the deepest mourning called, it is said, at the house, and introducing himself as an old and much attached friend of the deceased, begged to be allowed to look upon his face. The tears which rose in his eyes, the tremulousness of his quiet voice, the pallor of his mournful face, deceived the unsuspecting servant, who accompanied him to the chamber of death, removed the lid of the coffin, turned down the shroud, and revealed features which had once been handsome, but long since rendered almost hideous by drinking. The stranger gazed with profound emotion, while he quietly drew from his pocket a bailiff's wand, and touching the corpse's face with it, suddenly altered his manner to one of considerable glee, and informed the servant that he had arrested the corpse in the king's name for a debt of £500. It was the morning of the funeral, which was to be attended by half the grandees of England, and in a few minutes the mourners began to arrive. But the corpse was the bailiff's property till his claim was paid, and naught but the money would soften the iron capturer. Canning and Lord Sidmouth agreed to settle the matter, and over the coffin the debt was paid.

Poor corpse! was it worth £500—diseased, rotting as it was, and about to be given for nothing to mother earth? Was it worth the pomp of the splendid funeral and the grand hypocrisy of grief with which it was borne to Westminster Abbey?

Was not rather the wretched old man, while he yet struggled on in life, worth this outlay, worth this show of sympathy? Folly; not folly only—but a lie! What recked the dead of the four noble pall-bearers—the Duke of Bedford, the Earl of Lauderdale, Earl Mulgrave, and the Bishop of London? What good was it to him to be followed by two royal highnesses—the Dukes of York and Sussex—by two marquises, seven earls, three viscounts, five lords, a Canning, a lord mayor, and a whole regiment of honorables and right honorables, who now wore the livery of grief, when they had let him die in debt, in want, and in misery? Far more, if the dead could feel, must he have been grateful for the honester tears of those two untitled men who had really befriended him to the last hour, and never abandoned him, Mr. Rogers and Dr. Bain. But peace; let him pass with nodding plumes and well-dyed horses to the great Walhalla, and amid the dust of many a poet let the poet's dust find rest and honor, secure at last from the hand of the bailiff. There was but one nook unoccupied in Poets' Corner, and there they laid him. A simple marble was afforded by another friend without a title—Peter Moore.

To a life like Sheridan's it is almost impossible to do justice in so narrow a space as I have here. He is one of those men who, not to be made out a whit better or worse than they are, demand a careful investigation of all their actions, or reported actions—a careful sifting of all the evidence for or against them, and a careful weeding of all the anecdotes told of them. This requires a separate biography. To give a general idea of the man, we must be content to give that which he inspired in a general acquaintance. Many of his "mots," and more of the stories about him, may have been invented for him, but they would scarcely have been fixed on Sheridan if they had not fitted more or less his character: I have therefore given them without inquiry as to their veracity. I might have given a hundred more, but I have let alone those anecdotes which did not seem to illustrate the character of the man. Many another good story is told of him, and we must content ourselves with one or two. Take one that is characteristic of his love of fun.

Sheridan is accosted by an elderly gentleman, who has forgotten the name of a street to which he wants to go, and who informs him precisely that it is an out-of-the-way name.

"Perhaps, sir, you mean John Street?" says Sherry, all innocence.

"No, an unusual name."

"It can't be Charles Street?"

Impatience on the part of the old gentleman.

"King Street?" suggests the cruel wit.

"I tell you, sir, it is a street with a very odd name!"

"Bless me, is it Queen Street?"

Irritation on the part of the old gentleman.

"It must be Oxford Street," cries Sheridan, as if inspired.

"Sir, I repeat," very testily, "that it is a very odd name. Every one knows Oxford Street!"

Sheridan appears to be thinking.

"An odd name! Oh! ah! just so; Piccadilly, of course?"

Old gentleman bounces away in disgust.

"Well, sir," Sherry calls after him, "I envy you your admirable memory!"

His wit was said to have been prepared, like his speeches, and he is even reported to have carried his book of *mots* in his pocket, as a young lady of the middle class *might*, but seldom does, carry her book of etiquette into a party. But some of his wit was no doubt extempore.

When arrested for non-attendance to a call in the House, soon after the change of ministry, he exclaimed, "How hard to be no sooner out of office than into custody!"

He was not an inveterate talker, like Macaulay, Sydney Smith, or Jeffrey: he seems rather to have aimed at a striking effect in all that he said. When found tripping, he had a clever knack of getting out of the difficulty. In the Hastings speech he complimented Gibbon as a "luminous" writer; questioned on this, he replied archly, "I said *vo*luminous."

I can't afford to be voluminous on Sheridan, and so I quit him.

BEAU BRUMMELL.

It is astonishing to what a number of insignificant things high art has been applied, and with what success. It is the vice of high civilization to look for it and reverence it, where a ruder age would only laugh at its employment. Crime and cookery, especially, have been raised into sciences of late, and the professors of both received the amount of honor due to their acquirements. Who would be so naïve as to sneer at the author of "The Art of Dining?" or who so ungentlemanly as not to pity the sorrows of a pious baronet, whose devotion to the noble art of appropriation was shamefully rewarded with accommodation gratis on board one of Her Majesty's transport-ships? The disciples of Ude have left us the literary results of their studies, and one at least, the graceful Alexis Soyer, is numbered among our public benefactors. We have little doubt that as the art, vulgarly called "embezzlement," becomes more and more fashionable, as it does every day, we shall have a work on the "Art of Appropriation." It is a pity that Brummell looked down upon literature: poor literature! it had a hard struggle to recover the slight, for we are convinced there is not a work more wanted than the "Art of Dressing," and "George the Less" was almost the last professor of that elaborate science.

If the maxim, that "whatever is worth doing at all is worth doing well," hold good, Beau Brummell must be regarded in the light of a great man. That dressing is worth doing at all, every body but a Fiji Islander seems to admit, for every body does it. If, then, a man succeeds in dressing better than any body else, it follows that he is entitled to the most universal admiration.

But there was another object to which this great man condescended to apply the principles of high art—I mean affectation. How admirably he succeeded in this his life will show. But can we doubt that he is entitled to our greatest esteem and heartiest gratitude for the studies he pursued with unremitting patience in these two useful branches, when we find that a prince of the blood delighted to honor, and the richest, noblest, and most distinguished men of half a century ago were proud to know him? We are writing, then, of no common man, no mere beau, but of the greatest professor of two of the most popular sciences—Dress and Affectation. Let us speak with reverence of this wonderful genius.

George Brummell was a "self-made man." That is, all that nature, the tailors, stags, and padding had not made of him, he made for himself—his name, his fame, his fortune, and his friends—and all these were great. The author of "Self-help" has most unaccountably omitted all mention of him, and most erroneously, for if there ever was a man who helped himself, and no one else, it was "very sincerely yours, George Brummell."

The founder of the noble house of Brummell, the grandfather of our hero, was either a treasury porter, or a confectioner, or something else.* At any rate he let lodgings in Bury Street, and whether from the fact that his wife did not purloin her lodgers' tea and sugar, or from some other cause, he managed to ingratiate himself with one of them—who afterward became Lord Liverpool—so thoroughly, that through his influence he obtained for his son the post of Private Secretary to Lord North. Nothing could have been more fortunate, except, perhaps, the son's next move, which was to take in marriage the daughter of Richardson, the owner of a well-known lottery-office. Between the lottery of office and the lottery of love, Brummell *père* managed to make a very good fortune. At his death he left as much as £65,000 to be divided among his three children—Raikes says as much as £30,000 apiece—so that the Beau, if not a fool, ought never to have been a pauper.

George Bryan Brummell, the second son of this worthy, honored by his birth the 7th of June, 1778. No anecdotes of his childhood are preserved, except that he once cried because he could not eat any more damson tart. In later years he would probably have thought damson tart "very vulgar." He first turns up at Eton at the age of twelve, and even there commences his distinguished career, and is known as "Buck Brummell." The boy showed himself decidedly father to the man here. Master George was not vulgar enough, nor so imprudent, it may be added, as to fight, row, or play cricket, but he distinguished himself by the introduction of a gold buckle in the white stock, by never being flogged, and by his ability in toasting cheese. We do not hear much of his classical attainments.

The very gentlemanly youth was in due time passed on to Oriel College, Oxford. Here he distinguished himself by a

* Mr. Jesse says that the Beau's grandfather was a servant of Mr. Charles Monson, brother to the first Lord Monson.

studied indifference to college discipline and an equal dislike to studies. He condescended to try for the Newdigate Prize poem, but his genius leaned far more to the turn of a coat-collar than that of a verse, and, unhappily for the British poets, their ranks were not to be dignified by the addition of this illustrious man. The Newdigate was given to another; and so, to punish Oxford, the competitor left it and poetry together, after having adorned the old quadrangle of Oriel for less than a year.

He was now a boy of seventeen, and a very fine boy, too. To judge from a portrait taken in later life, he was not strictly handsome; but he is described as tall, well built, and of a slight and graceful figure. Added to this, he had got from Eton and Oxford, if not much learning, many a well-born friend, and he was toady enough to cultivate those of better and dismiss those of less distinction. He was through life a celebrated "cutter," and Brummell's cut was as much admired—by all but the *cuttee*—as Brummell's coat. Then he had some £25,000 as capital, and how could he best invest it? He consulted no stock-broker on this weighty point; he did not even buy a shilling book of advice that we have seen advertised for those who don't know what to do with their money. The question was answered in a moment by the young worldling of sixteen: he would enter a crack regiment and invest his guineas in the thousand per cents. of fashionable life.

His namesake, the Regent, was now thirty-two, and had spent those years of his life in acquiring the honorary title of the "first gentleman of Europe," by every act of folly, debauch, dissipation, and degradation which a prince can conveniently perpetrate. He was the hero of London society, which adored and backbit him alternately, and he was precisely the man whom the boy Brummell would worship. The Regent was colonel of a famous regiment of fops—the 10th Hussars. It was the most expensive, the most impertinent, the best-dressed, the worst-moraled regiment in the British army. Its officers, many of them titled, all more or less distinguished in the trying campaigns of London seasons, were the intimates of the Prince Colonel. Brummell aspired to a cornetcy in this brilliant regiment, and obtained it; nor that alone; he secured, by his manners, or his dress, or his impudence, the favor and companionship—friendship we can not say—of the prince who commanded it.

By this step his reputation was made, and it was only necessary to keep it up. He had an immense fund of good-nature, and, as long as his money lasted, of good spirits, too. Good sayings—that is, witty if not wise—are recorded of him, and his friends pronounce him a charming companion. Introduced, therefore, into the highest circles in England, he could scarcely fail to succeed. Young Cornet Brummell became a great favorite with the fair.

His rise in the regiment was of course rapid: in three years he was at the head of a troop. The onerous duties of a military life, which vacillated between Brighton and London, and consisted chiefly in making one's self agreeable in the mess-room, were too much for our hero. He neglected parade, or arrived too late: it was such a bore to have to dress in a hurry. It is said that he knew the troop he commanded only by the peculiar nose of one of the men, and that when a transfer of men had once been made, rode up to the wrong troop, and supported his mistake by pointing to the nose in question. No fault, however, was found with the Regent's favorite, and Brummell might have risen to any rank if he could have supported the terrific labor of dressing for parade. Then, too, there came wars and rumors of wars, and our gallant captain shuddered at the vulgarity of shedding blood: the supply of smelling-salts would never have been liberal enough to keep him from fainting on the battle-field. It is said, too, that the regiment was ordered to Manchester. Could any thing be more gross or more ill-bred? The idea of figuring before the wives and daughters of cotton-spinners was too fearful; and from one cause or another our brave young captain determined to retire, which he did in 1798.

It was now, therefore, that he commenced the profession of a beau, and as he is the Prince of Beaux, as his patron was the Beau of Princes, and as his fame has spread to France and Germany, if only as the inventor of the trowser; and as there is no man who on getting up in the morning does not put on his clothes with more or less reflection as to whether they are the right ones to put on, and as beaux have existed since the days of the emperor of beaux, Alexander the Macedonian, and will probably exist to all time, let us rejoice in the high honor of being permitted to describe how this illustrious genius clothed his poor flesh, and made the most of what God had given him—a body and legs.

The private life of Brummell would in itself serve as a book of manners and habits. The two were his profoundest study; but, alas! his impudence marred the former, and the latter can scarcely be imitated in the present day. Still as a great example he is yet invaluable, and must be described in all detail.

His morning toilet was a most elaborate affair. Never was Brummell guilty of *déshabille*. Like a true man of business, he devoted the best and earliest hours—and many of them too—to his profession, namely—dressing. His dressing-room was a studio, in which he daily compared that elaborate portrait of George Brummell which was to be exhibited for a few hours in the club-rooms and drawing-rooms of town, only to be taken to pieces again, and again made up for the evening. Charles I. delighted to resort of a morning to the studio of Vandyck, and watch his favorite artist's progress. The Regent George was no less devoted to art, for we are assured by Mr. Raikes that he often visited his favorite beau in the morning to watch his toilet, and would sometimes stay so late that he would send his horses away, insisting on Brummell giving him a quiet dinner, "which generally ended in a deep potation."

There are, no doubt, many fabulous myths floating about concerning this illustrious man; and his biographer, Captain Jesse, seems anxious to defend him from the absurd stories of French writers, who asserted that he employed two glovers to cover his hands, to one of whom were intrusted the thumbs, to the other the fingers and hand, and three barbers to dress his hair, while his boots were polished with champagne, his cravats designed by a celebrated portrait painter, and so forth. These may be pleasant inventions, but Captain Jesse's own account of his toilet, even when the Beau was broken, and living in elegant poverty abroad, is quite absurd enough to render excusable the ingenious exaggerations of the foreign writer.

The *batterié de toilette*, we are told, was of silver, and included a spitting-dish, for its owner said "he could not spit into clay." Napoleon shaved himself, but Brummell was not quite great enough to do that, just as my Lord So-and-So walks to church on Sunday, while his neighbor, the Manchester millionaire, can only arrive there in a chariot and pair.

His ablutions took no less than two whole hours! What knowledge might have been gained, what good done in the time he devoted to rubbing his lovely person with a hair glove! Cleanliness was, in fact, Brummell's religion; perhaps because it is generally set down as "next to godliness," a proximity with which the Beau was quite satisfied, for he never attempted to pass on to that next stage. Poor fool, he might rub every particle of moisture off the skin of his body—he might be clean as a kitten—but he could not and did not purify his mind with all this friction; and the man who would have fainted to see a black speck upon his shirt, was not at all shocked at the indecent conversation in which he and his companions occasionally indulged.

The body cleansed, the face had next to be brought up as near perfection as nature would allow. With a small looking-glass in one hand, and tweezers in the other, he carefully removed the tiniest hairs that he could discover on his cheeks or chin, enduring the pain like a martyr.

Then came the shirt, which was in his palmy days changed three times a day, and then in due course the great business of the cravat. Captain Jesse's minute account of the process of tying this can surely be relied on, and presents one of the most ludicrous pictures of folly and vanity that can be imagined. Had Brummell never lived, and a novelist or play-writer described the toilet which Captain Jesse affirms to have been his daily achievement, he would have had the critics about him with the now common phrase—"This book is a tissue, not only of improbabilities, but of actual impossibilities." The collar, then, was so large, that in its natural condition it rose high above the wearer's head, and some ingenuity was required to reduce it by delicate folds to exactly that height which the Beau judged to be correct. Then came the all-majestic white neck-tie, a foot in breadth. It is not to be supposed that Brummell had the neck of a swan or a camel—far from it. The worthy fool had now to undergo, with admirable patience, the mysterious process known to our papas as "creasing down." The head was thrown back, as if ready for a dentist; the stiff white tie applied to the throat, and gradually wrinkled into half its actual breath by the slow downward movement of the chin. When all was done, we can imagine that comfort was sacrificed to elegance, as it was then considered, and that the sudden appearance of Venus herself could not have induced the deluded individual to turn his head in a hurry.

It is scarcely profitable to follow this lesser deity into all the details of his self-adornment. It must suffice to say that he affected an extreme neatness and simplicity of dress, every item of which was studied and discussed for many an hour. In the mornings he was still guilty of hessians and pantaloons, or "tops" and buckskins, with a blue coat and buff waistcoat. The costume is not so ancient, but that one may tumble now and then on a country squire who glories in it and denounces us juveniles as "bears" for want of a similar precision. Poor Brummell, he cordially hated the country squires, and would have wanted rouge for a week if he could have dreamed that his pet attire would, some fifty years later, be represented only by one of that class which he was so anxious to exclude from Watier's.

But it was in the evening that he displayed his happy invention of the trowser, or rather its introduction from Germany.

This article he wore very tight to the leg, and buttoned over the ankle, exactly as we see it in old prints of "the fashion." Then came the wig, and on that the hat. It is a vain and thankless task to defend Brummell from the charge of being a dandy. If one proof of his devotion to dress were wanted, it would be the fact that this hat, once stuck jauntily on one side of the wig, was never removed in the street even to salute a lady—so that, inasmuch as he sacrificed his manners to his appearance, he may be fairly set down as a fop.

The perfect artist could not be expected to be charitable to the less successful. Dukes and princes consulted him on the make of their coats, and discussed tailors with him with as much solemnity as divines might dispute on a mystery of religion. Brummell did not spare them. "Bedford," said he, to the duke of that name, fingering a new garment which his grace had submitted to his inspection, "do you call this *thing* a coat?" Again, meeting a noble acquaintance who wore shoes in the morning, he stopped and asked him what he had got upon his feet. "Oh! shoes are they?" quoth he, with a well-bred sneer, "I thought they were slippers." He was even ashamed of his own brother, and when the latter came to town, begged him to keep to the back streets till his new clothes were sent home. Well might his friend the Regent say, that he was "a mere tailor's dummy to hang clothes upon."

But in reality Brummell was more. He had some sharpness and some taste. But the former was all brought out in sneers, and the latter in snuff-boxes. His whole mind could have been put into one of these. He had a splendid collection of them, and was famous for the grace with which he opened the lid of his box with the thumb of the hand that carried it, while he delicately took his pinch with two fingers of the other. This and his bow were his chief acquirements, and his reputation for manners was based on the distinction of his manner. He could not drive in a public conveyance, but he could be rude to a well-meaning lady; he never ate vegetables—*one* pea he confessed to—but he did not mind borrowing from his friends money which he knew he could never return. He was a great gentleman, a gentleman of his patron's school—in short, a well-dressed snob. But one thing is due to Brummell: he made the assumption of being "a gentleman" so thoroughly ridiculous that few men of keen sense care now for the title: at least, not as a class distinction. Nor is it to be wondered at; when your tailor's assistant is "a gentleman," and would be mightily disgusted at being called any thing else, you, with your indomitable pride of caste, can scarcely care for the patent.

Brummell's claim to the title was based on his walk, his coat, his cravat, and the grace with which he indulged, as Captain Jesse delightfully calls it, "the nasal pastime" of taking snuff. All the rest was impudence; and many are the anecdotes—most of them familiar as household words—which are told of his impertinence. The story of Mrs. Johnson-Thompson is one of those oft-told tales, which, from having become Joe Millers, have gradually passed out of date and been almost forgotten. Two rival party-givers rejoiced in the aristocratic names of Johnson and Thompson. The former lived near Finsbury, the latter near Grosvenor Square, and Mrs. Thompson was somehow sufficiently fashionable to expect the Regent himself at her assemblies. Brummell, among other impertinencies, was fond of going where he was not invited or wanted. The two rivals gave a ball on the same evening, and a card was sent to the Beau by her of Finsbury. He chose to go to the Grosvenor Square house, in hopes of meeting the Regent, then his foe. Mrs. Thompson was justly disgusted, and with a vulgarity quite deserved by the intruder, told him he was not invited. The Beau made a thousand apologies, hummed, hawed, and drew a card from his pocket. It was the rival's invitation, and was indignantly denounced. "Dear me, how very unfortunate," said the Beau, "but you know Johnson and Thompson—I mean Thompson and Johnson—are so very much alike. Mrs. Johnson-Thompson, I wish you a very good-evening."

Perhaps there is no vulgarity greater than that of rallying people on their surnames, but our exquisite gentleman had not wit enough to invent one superior to such a puerile amusement. Thus, on one occasion, he woke up at three in the morning a certain Mr. Snodgrass, and when the worthy put his head out of the window in alarm, said quietly, "Pray, sir, is your name Snodgrass?" "Yes, sir, it is Snodgrass." "Snodgrass—Snodgrass—it is a very singular name. Good-by, Mr. *Snodgrass.*" There was more wit in his remark to Poodle Byng, a well-known puppy, whom he met one day driving in the Park with a French dog in his curricle. "Ah!" cried the Beau, "how d'ye do, Byng? a family vehicle, I see."

It seems incredulous to modern gentlemen that such a man should have been tolerated even at a club. Take, for instance, his vulgar treatment of Lord Mayor Combe, whose name we still see with others over many a public-house in London, and who was then a most prosperous brewer and thriving gambler. At Brookes's one evening the Beau and the Brewer were playing at the same table: "Come, *Mash-tub*," cried the "gentleman," "what do you set?" Mash-tub unresentingly set a pony, and the Beau won twelve of him in succession. Pocketing his cash, he made him a bow, and exclaimed, "Thank you, Alderman, in future I shall drink no porter but yours." But Combe was worthy of his namesake, Shakspeare's friend, and answered very aptly, "I wish, sir, that every *other* blackguard in London would tell me the same."

Then again, after ruining a young fool of fortune at the tables, and being reproached by the youth's father for leading his son astray, he replied with charming affectation, "Why, sir, I did all I could for him. I once gave him my arm all the way from White's to Brookes's!"

When Brummell really wanted a dinner, while at Calais, he could not give up his impertinence for the sake of it. Lord Westmoreland called on him, and, perhaps, out of compassion, asked him to dine at *three o'clock* with him. "Your lordship is very kind," said the Beau, "but really I could not *feed* at such an hour." Sooner or later he was glad to *feed* with any one who was toady enough to ask him. He was once placed in a delightfully awkward position from having accepted the invitation of a charitable but vulgar-looking Britisher at Calais. He was walking with Lord Sefton, when the individual passed and nodded familiarly. "Who's your friend, Brummell?" "Not mine, he must be bowing to you." But presently the man passed again, and this time was cruel enough to exclaim, "Don't forget, Brum, don't forget—goose at four!" The poor Beau must have wished the earth to open under him. He was equally imprudent in the way in which he treated old acquaintance who arrived at the town to which he had retreated, and of whom he was fool enough to be ashamed. He generally took away their characters summarily, but on one occasion was frightened almost out of his wits by being called to account for this conduct. An officer who had lost his nose in an engagement in the Peninsula called on him, and in very strong terms requested to know why the Beau had reported that he was a retired hatter. His manner alarmed the rascal, who apologized, and protested that there must be a mistake; he had never said so. The officer retired, and as he was going, Brummell added, "Yes, it must be a mistake, for now I think of it, I never dealt with a hatter without a nose."

So much for the good-breeding of this friend of George IV. and the Duke of York.

His affectation was quite as great as his impudence; and he won the reputation of fastidiousness—nothing gives more prestige by dint of being openly rude. No hospitality or kindness melted him, when he thought he could gain a march. At one dinner, not liking the champagne, he called to the servant to give him "some more of that cider:" at another, to which he was invited in days when a dinner was a charity to him, after helping himself to a wing of capon, and trying a morsel of it, he took it up in his napkin, called to his dog—he was generally accompanied by a puppy, even to parties, as if one at a time were not enough—and presenting it to him, said aloud, "Here, *Atons*, try if you can get your teeth through that, for I'm d—d if I can!"

To the last he resented offers of intimacy from those whom he considered his inferiors, and as there are ladies enough every where, he had ample opportunity for administering rebuke to those who pressed into his society. On one occasion he was sauntering with a friend at Caen under the window of a lady who longed for nothing more than to have the great *arbiter elegantiarum* at her house. When seeing him beneath, she put her head out, and called out to him, "Good-evening, Mr. Brummell, won't you come up and take tea?" The Beau looked up with extreme severity expressed on his face, and replied, "Madam, you take medicine—you take a walk—you take a liberty—but you *drink* tea," and walked on, having, it may be hoped, cured the lady of her admiration.

In the life of such a man there could not of course be much striking incident. He lived for "society," and the whole of his story consists in his rise and fall in that narrow world. Though admired and sought after by the women—so much so that at his death his chief assets were locks of hair, the only things he could not have turned into money—he never married. Wedlock might have sobered him, and made him a more sensible, if not more respectable, member of society, but his advances toward matrimony never brought him to the crisis. He accounted for one rejection in his usual way, "What could I do, my dear *fellar*," he lisped, "when I actually saw Lady Mary eat cabbage?" At another time he is said to have induced some deluded young creature to elope with him from a ball-room, but managed the affair so ill, that the lovers (?) were caught in the next street, and the affair came to an end. He wrote rather ecstatic love-letters to Lady Marys and Miss ——s, gave married ladies advice on the treatment of their spouses, and was tender to various widows, but though he went on in this way through life, he was never, it would seem, in love, from the mere fact that he was incapable of passion.

Perhaps he was too much of a woman to care much for women. He was certainly egregiously effeminate. About the only creatures he could love were poodles. When one of his dogs, from overfeeding, was taken ill, he sent for two dog-doctors, and consulted very gravely with them on the remedies to be applied. The canine physicians came to the conclusion that she must be bled. "Bled!" said Brummell, in horror; "I shall leave the room: inform me when the operation is over." When the dog died, he shed tears—probably the only ones he had shed since childhood; and though at that time receiving money from many an old friend in England, complained, with touching melancholy, "that he had lost the only friend he had!" His grief lasted three whole days, during which he shut himself up, and would see no one; but we are not told that he ever thus mourned over any human being.

His effeminacy was also shown in his dislike to field-sports. His shooting exploits were confined to the murder of a pair of pet pigeons perched on a roof, while he confessed, as regards hunting, that it was a bore to get up so early in the morning only to have one's boots and leathers splashed by galloping farmers. However, hunting was a fashion, and Brummell must needs appear to hunt. He therefore kept a stud of hunters, in his better days, near Belvoir, the Duke of Rutland's, where he was a frequent visitor, and if there was a near meet, would ride out in pink and tops to see the hounds break cover, follow through a few gates, and return to the more congenial atmosphere of the drawing-room. He, however, condescended to bring his taste to bear on the hunting-dress; and, it is said, introduced white tops instead of the ancient mahoganies. That he *could* ride there seems reason to believe, but it is equally probable that he was afraid to do so. His valor was certainly composed almost entirely of its "better part," and indeed had so much prudence in it that it may be doubted if there was any of the original stock left. Once when he had been taking away somebody's character, the "friend" of the maligned gentleman entered his apartment, and very menacingly demanded satisfaction for his principal, unless an apology were tendered "in five minutes." "Five minutes!" answered the exquisite, as pale as death, "five seconds, or sooner if you like."

Brummell was no fool, in spite of his follies. He had talents of a mediocre kind, if he had chosen to make a better use of them. Yet the general opinion was not in favor of his wisdom. He quite deserved Sheridan's cool satire for his affectation, if not for his want of mind.

The Wit and the Beau met one day at Charing Cross, and it can well be imagined that the latter was rather disgusted at being seen so far east of St. James's Street, and drawled out to Sheridan, "Sherry, my dear boy, don't mention that you saw me in this filthy part of the town, though, perhaps, I am rather severe, for his Grace of Northumberland resides somewhere about this spot, if I don't mistake. The fact is, my dear boy, I have been in the d—d City, to the Bank; I wish they would remove it to the West End, for re-all-y it is quite a bore to go to such a place; more particularly as one can not be seen in one's own equipage beyond Somerset House," etc., etc., etc., in the Brummellian style.

"Nay, my good fellow," was the answer to this peroration, "traveling from the East? impossible!"

"Why, my dear boy, why?"

"Because the wise men came from the East."

"So then, sa-ar, you think me a fool?"

"By no means; I know you to be one," quoth Sherry, and turned away. It is due to both the parties to this anecdote to state that it is quite apocryphal, and rests on the slenderest authority. However, whether fool or not, Brummell has one certain, though small, claim upon certain small readers. Were you born in a modern generation, when scraps of poetry were forbidden in your nursery, and no other pabulum was offered to your infant stomach, but the rather dull biographies of rather dull, though very upright men?—if so, I pity you. Old airs of a jaunty jig-like kind are still haunting the echoes of my brain. Among them is—

"The butterfly was a gentleman,
Which nobody can refute:
He left his lady-love at home,
And roamed in a velvet suit."

I remember often to have ruminated over this character of an innocent, and, I believe, calumniated insect. He was a gentleman, and the consequences thereof were twofold: he abandoned the young woman who had trusted her affections to him, and attired his person in a complete costume of the best Lyons silk-velvet—*not* the proctor's velvet, which Theodore felt with thumb and finger, impudently asking, "how much a yard?" I secretly resolved to do the same as Mr. Butterfly when I came of age. But the said Mr. Butterfly had a varied and somewhat awful history, all of which was narrated in various ditties chanted by my nurse. I could not quite join in her vivid assertion that she *would*

"Be a butterfly,
Born in a bower,
Christened in a tea-pot,
And dead in an hour."

Ætat. four, life is dear, and the idea of that early demise was far from welcome to me. I privily agreed that I would *not* be a butterfly. But there was no end to the history of this very inconstant insect in our nursery lore. We didn't care a drop of honey for Dr. Watts's "Busy Bee;" we infinitely preferred the account—not in the "Morning Post"—of the "Butterfly's Ball" and the "Grasshopper's Feast;" and few, perhaps, have ever given children more pleasures of imagination than William Roscoe, its author. There were some among us, however, who were already being weaned to a knowledge of life's mysterious changes, and we sought the third volume of the romance of the flitting gaudy thing in a little poem called "The Butterfly's Funeral."

Little dreamed we, when in our pretty little song-books we saw the initial "B." at the bottom of these verses, that a real human butterfly had written them, and that they conveyed a solemn prognostication of a fate that was *not* his. Little we dreamed, as we lisped out the verses, that the "gentleman who roamed in a" not velvet but "plum-colored suit," according to Lady Hester Stanhope, was the illustrious George Brummell. The Beau wrote these trashy little rhymes—pretty in their way—and, since I was once a child, and learnt them off by heart, I will not cast a stone at them. Brummell indulged in such trifling poetizing, but never went farther. It is a pity he did not write his memoirs; they would have added a valuable page to the history of "Vanity Fair."

Brummell's London glory lasted from 1798 to 1816. His chief club was Watier's. It was a superb assemblage of gamesters and fops—knaves and fools; and it is difficult to say which element predominated. For a time Brummell was monarch there; but his day of reckoning came at last. Byron and Moore, Sir Henry Mildmay and Mr. Pierrepoint, were among the numbers. Play ran high there, and Brummell once won nearly as much as his squandered patrimony, £26,000. Of course he not only lost it again, but much more—indeed his whole capital. It was after some heavy loss that he was walking home through Berkeley Street with Mr. Raikes, when he saw something glittering in the gutter, picked it up, and found it to be a crooked sixpence. Like all small-minded men, he had a great fund of superstition, and he wore the talisman of good luck for some time. For two years, we are told, after this finding of treasure-trove, success attended him in play—macao, the very pith of hazard, was the chief game at Watier's—and he attributed it all to the sixpence. At last he lost it, and luck turned against him. So goes the story. It is probably much more easily accountable. Few men played honestly in those days without losing to the dishonest, and we have no reason to charge the Beau with malpractice. However this may be, his losses at play first brought about his ruin. The Jews were, of course, resorted to; and if Brummell did not, like Charles Fox, keep a Jerusalem Chamber, it was only be-

R 2

cause the sum total of his fortune was pretty well known to the money-lenders.

> "Then came the change—the check, the fall:
> Pain rises up—old pleasures pall.
> There is one remedy for all."

This remedy was the crossing of the Channel, a crossing swept by beggars, who levy a heavy toll on those who pass over it.

The decline of the Beau was rapid, but not without its *éclat.* A breach with his royal patron led the way. It is presumed that every reader of these volumes has heard the famous story of "Wales, ring the bell!" but not all may know its particulars.

A deep impenetrable mystery hangs over this story. Perhaps some German of the twenty-first century—some future Gifford, or who not—will put his wits to work to solve the riddle. In very sooth *il ne vaut pas la chandelle.* A quarrel did take place between George the Prince and George the Less, but of its causes no living mortal is cognizant: we can only give the received versions. It appears, then, that dining with H. R. H. the Prince of Wales, Master Brummell asked him to ring the bell. Considering the intimacy between them, and that the Regent often sacrificed his dignity to his amusement, there was nothing extraordinary in this. But it is added that the Prince did ring the bell in question—unhappy bell to jar so between two such illustrious friends!—and when the servant came, ordered "Mr. Brummell's carriage!" Another version palms off the impertinence on a drunken midshipman, who, being related to the Comptroller of the Household, had been invited to dinner by the Regent. Another yet states that Brummell, being asked to ring the said bell, replied, 'Your Royal Highness is close to it." No one knows the truth of the legend, any more than whether Homer was a man or a myth. It surely does not matter. The friends quarreled, and perhaps it was time they should do so, for they had never improved one another's morals; but it is only fair to the Beau to add that he always denied the whole affair, and that he himself gave as the cause of the quarrel his own sarcasms on the Prince's increasing corpulency, and his resemblance to Mrs. Fitzherbert's porter, "Big Ben." Certainly some praise is due to the Beau for the *sang froid* with which he appeared to treat the matter, though in reality dreadfully cut up about it. He lounged about, made amusing remarks on his late friend and patron, swore he would "cut" him, and, in short, behaved with his usual *aplomb.* The "Wales, ring the bell," was sufficient proof of his impudence, but "Who's your fat friend?" was really good.

THE BEST THING BEAU BRUMMELL EVER SAID.

It is well known, in all probability, that George IV. contemplated with as much disgust and horror the increasing rotundity of his "presence" as ever a maiden lady of a certain age did her first gray hair. Soon after the bell affair, the royal beau met his former friend in St. James's Street, and resolved to cut him. This was attacking Brummell with his own pet weapon, but not with success. Each antagonist was leaning on the arm of a friend. "Jack Lee," who was thus supporting the Beau, was intimate with the Prince, who, to make the cut the more marked, stopped and talked to him without taking the slightest notice of Brummell. After a time both parties moved on, and then came the moment of triumph and revenge. It was sublime! Turning round half way, so that his words could not fail to be heard by the retreating Regent, the Beau asked of his companion in his usual drawl, "Well, Jack, who's your fat friend?" The coolness, presumption, and impertinence of the question perhaps made it the best thing the Beau ever said, and from that time the Prince took care not to risk another encounter with him.*

Brummell was scotched rather than killed by the Prince's indifference. He at once resolved to patronize his brother, the Duke of York, and found in him a truer friend. The duchess, who had a particular fondness for dogs, of which she is said to have kept no fewer, at one time, than a hundred, added the puppy Brummell to the list, and treated him with a kindness in which little condescension was mixed. But neither impudence nor the blood-royal can keep a man out of debt, especially when he plays. The Beau got deeper and deeper into the difficulty, and at last some mysterious quarrel about money with a gentleman who thenceforward went by the name of Dick the Dandy-killer, obliged him to think of place and poverty in another land. He looked in vain for aid, and among others Scrope Davies was written to to lend him "two hundred," "because his money was all in the three per cents." Scrope replied laconically—

"MY DEAR GEORGE,

"It is very unfortunate, but *my* money is all in the three per cents. Yours, S. DAVIES."

It was the last attempt. The Beau went to the opera, as usual, and drove away from it clear off to Dover, whence the packet took him to safety and slovenliness in the ancient town

* Another version, given by Captain Jesse, represents this to have taken place at a ball given at the Argyle Rooms in July, 1813, by Lord Alvanley, Sir Henry Mildmay, Mr. Pierrepoint, and Mr. Brummell.

of Calais. His few effects were sold after his departure. Porcelain, buhl, a drawing or two, double-barreled Mantons (probably never used), plenty of old wine, linen, furniture, and a few well-bound books, were the Beau's assets. His debts were with half the chief tradesmen of the West End and a large number of his personal friends.

The climax is reached: henceforth Master George Bryan Brummell goes rapidly and gracefully down the hill of life.

The position of a Calais beggar was by no means a bad one, if the reduced individual had any claim whatever to distinction. A black-mail was sedulously levied by the outcasts and exiles of that town on every Englishman who passed through it; and in those days it was customary to pass some short time in this entrance of France. The English "residents" were always on the look-out, generally crowding round the packet-boat, and the new arrival was sure to be accosted by some old and attached friend, who had not seen him for years. Just as Buttons, who is always breaking the plates and tumblers, has the invariable mode of accounting for his carelessness, "they fell apart, sir, in my 'ands!" so these expatriated Britons had always a tale of confidence misplaced—security for a bond—bail for a delinquent, or in short any hard case, which compelled them, much against their wills, to remain "for a period" on the shores of France. To such men, whom you had known in seven-guinea waistcoats at White's and Watier's, and found in seven-shilling coats on the Calais pier, it was impossible to refuse your five-pound note, and in time the black-mail of Calais came to be reckoned among the established expenses of a Continental tour.

Brummell was a distinguished beggar of this description, and managed so adroitly that the new arrivals thought themselves obliged by Mr. Brummell's acceptance of their donations. The man who could not eat cabbages, drive in a hackney-coach, or wear less than three shirts a day, was now supported by voluntary contributions, and did not see any thing derogatory to a gentleman in their acceptance. If Brummell had now turned his talents to account; if he had practiced his painting, in which he was not altogether despicable; or his poetry, in which he had already had some trifling success: if he had even engaged himself as a waiter at Quillacq's, or given lessons in the art of deportment, his fine friends from town might have cut him, but posterity would have withheld its blame. He was a beggar of the merriest kind. While he wrote letters to friends in England, asking for remittances, and describing his wretched condition on a bed of straw and eating bran bread, he had a good barrel of Dorchester ale in his lodgings, his usual glass of maraschino, and his bottle of claret after dinner; and though living on charity, could order new snuff-boxes to add to his collection, and new knick-knacks to adorn his room. There can be no pity for such a man, and we have no pity for him, whatever the rest of the world may feel.

Nothing can be more contemptible than the gradual downfall of the broken Beau. Yet, if it were doubted that his soul ever rose above the collar of a coat or the brim of a hat, his letters to Mr. Raikes in the time of his poverty would settle the question. "I heard of you the other day in a waistcoat that does you considerable credit, spick-and-span from Paris, a broad stripe, salmon color, and *cramoisé*. Don't let them laugh you into a relapse—into the Gothic—as that of your former English simplicity." He speaks of the army of occupation as "rascals in red coats waiting for embarkation." "English education," he says in another letter, "may be all very well to instruct the hemming of handkerchiefs, and the ungainly romps of a country dance, but nothing else; and it would be a poor consolation to your declining years to see your daughters come into the room upon their elbows, and to find their accomplishments limited to broad native phraseology in conversation, or thumping the 'Woodpecker' upon a discordant spinet." And he proceeds to recommend "a good French formation of manners," and so forth.

Nor did he display any of that dignity and self-respect which are generally supposed to mark the "gentleman." When his late friend and foe, by this time a king, passed through Calais, the Beau, broken in every sense, had not pride enough to keep out of his way. Many stories are told of the manner in which he pressed himself into George IV.'s notice, but the various legends mostly turn upon a certain snuff-box. According to one quite as reliable as any other, the Prince and the Beau had in their days of amity intended to exchange snuff-boxes, and George the Greater had given George the Less an order on his jeweler for a *tabatière* with his portrait on the top. On their quarrel this order was, with very bad taste, rescinded, although Brummell's snuff-box had already passed into the Prince's hands and had not been returned. It is said that the Beau employed a friend to remind the king of this agreement, and ask for his box; to whom the latter said that the story was all nonsense, and that he supposed "the poor devil," meaning his late intimate friend, wanted £100 and should have it. However, it is doubtful if the money ever reached the "poor devil." The story does not tell over well, for whatever George IV.'s failings and faults, he seems to have had a certain amount of good-nature, if not absolutely of good heart, at least sufficient sense of what became a prince, to prevent his doing so shabby an act, though he may have defrauded a hundred tradesmen. In these days there *were* such things as "debts of honor," and they were punctiliously attended to. There are, as we have said, various versions of this story, but all tend to show that Brummell courted the notice of his late master and patron on his way through the place of his exile; and it is not remarkable in a man who borrowed so freely from all his acquaintances, and who was, in fact, in such a state of dependence on their liberality.

Brummell made one grand mistake in his career as a Beau: he outlived himself. For some twenty-four years he survived his flight from England, to which country he never returned. For a time he was an assiduous writer of begging-letters and the plague of his friends. At length he obtained the appointment of consul at the good old Norman town of Caen. This was almost a sinecure, and the Beau took care to keep it so. But no one can account for the extraordinary step he took soon after entering on his consular duties. He wrote to Lord Palmerston, stating that there were no duties attached to the post, and recommending its abolition. This act of suicide is partly explained by a supposed desire to be appointed to some more lively and more lucrative consulate; but in this the Beau was mistaken. The consulate at Caen was vacated in accordance with his suggestion, and Brummell was left penniless, in debt, and to shift for himself. With the aid of an English tradesman, half grocer, half banker, he managed to get through a period of his poverty, but could not long subsist in this way, and the punishment of his vanity and extravagance came at last in his old age. A term of existence in prison did not cure him, and when he was liberated he again resumed his primrose gloves, his Eau de Cologne, and his patent *vernis* for his boots, though at that time literally supported by his friends with an allowance of £120 per annum. In the old days of Caen life this would have been equal to £300 a year in England, and certainly quite enough for any bachelor; but the Beau was really a fool. For whom, for what should he dress and polish his boots at such a quiet place as Caen? Yet he continued to do so, and to run into debt for the polish. When he confessed to having, "so help him Heaven," not four francs in the world, he was ordering this *vernis de Guiton*, at five francs a bottle, from Paris, and calling the provider of it "a scoundrel," because he ventured to ask for his money. What foppery, what folly was all this! How truly worthy of the man who built his fame on the reputation of a coat! Terrible indeed was the hardship that followed his extravagance; he was actually compelled to exchange his white for a black cravat. Poor martyr! after such a trial it is impossible to be hard upon him. So, too, the man who sent repeated begging-letters to the English grocer, Armstrong, threw out of window a new dressing-gown because it was not of the pattern he wished to have.

Retribution for all this folly came in time. His mind went even before his health. Though only some sixty years of age, almost the bloom of some men's life, he lost his memory and his powers of attention. His old ill-manners became positively bad manners. When feasted and fêted, he could find nothing better to say than "What a half-starved turkey!" At last the Beau was reduced to the level of that slovenliness which he had considered as the next step to perdition. Reduced to one pair of trowsers, he had to remain in bed till they were mended. He grew indifferent to his personal appearance, the surest sign of decay. Driveling, wretched, in debt, an object of contempt to all honest men, he dragged on a miserable existence. Still with his boots in holes, and all the honor of beaudom gone forever, he clung to the last to his Eau de Cologne, and some few other luxuries, and went down, a fool and a fop, to the grave. To indulge his silly tastes he had to part with one piece of property after another; and at length he was left with little else than the locks of hair of which he had once boasted.

I remember a story of a laborer and his dying wife. The poor woman was breathing her last wishes. "And, I say, William, you'll see the ould sow don't kill her young uns?" "Ay, ay, wife, set thee good." "And, I say, William, you'll see Lizzy goes to schule reg'lar?" "Ay, ay, wife, set thee good." "And, I say, William, you'll see Tommy's breeches is mended against he goes to schule again?" "Ay, ay, wife, set thee good." "And, I say, William, you'll see I'm laid proper in the yard?" William grew impatient. "Now never thee mind them things, wife, I'll see to 'em all, you just go on with your dying." No doubt Brummell's friends heartily wished that he would go on with his dying, for he had already lived too long; but he would live on. He is described in his last days as a miserable, slovenly, half-witted old creature, creeping about to the houses of a few friends he retained or who were kind enough to notice him still, jeered at by the *gamins*, and remarkable now, not for the cleanliness, but the filthiness and raggedness of his attire.

Poor old fool! one can not but pity him, when wretched, friendless, and miserable as he was, we find him, still graceful, in a poor *café* near the Place Royale, taking his cup of coffee, and when asked for the amount of his bill, answering very vaguely, "Oui, Madame, à la pleine lune, à la pleine lune."

The drivelings of old age are no fit subject for ridicule, yet in the case of a man who had sneered so freely at his fellow-creatures, they may afford a useful lesson. One of his fancies was to give imaginary parties, when his tallow dips were all set alight and his servant announced with proper decorum, "The Duchess of Devonshire," "Lord Alvanley," "Mr. Sheridan," or whom not. The poor old idiot received the imaginary visitors with the old bow, and talked to them in the old strain, till his servant announced their imaginary carriages, and he was put driveling to bed. At last the idiocy became mania. He burnt his books, his relics, his tokens. He ate enormously, and the man who had looked upon beer as the *ne plus ultra* of vulgarity, was glad to imagine it champagne. Let us not follow the poor maniac through his wanderings. Rather let us throw a veil over all his driveling wretchedness, and find him at his last gasp, when coat and collar, hat and brim, were all forgotten, when the man who had worn three shirts a day was content to change his linen once a month. What a lesson, what a warning! If Brummell had come to this pass in England, it is hard to say how and where he would have died. He was now utterly penniless, and had no prospect of receiving any remittances. It was determined to remove him to the Hospice du Bon Sauveur, a *Maison de Charité*, where he would be well cared for at no expense. The mania of the poor creature took, as ever, the turn of external preparation. When the landlord of his inn entered to try and induce him to go, he found him with his wig on his knee, his shaving apparatus by his side, and the quondam beau deeply interested in lathering the peruke as a preliminary to shearing it. He resisted every proposal to move, and was carried down stairs kicking and shrieking. Once lodged in the Hospice, he was treated by the sœurs de charité with the greatest kindness and consideration. An attempt was made to recall him to a sense of his future peril, that he might at least die in a more religious mood than he had lived; but in vain. It is not for us, erring and sinful as we are, to judge any fellow-creature; but perhaps poor Brummell was the last man to whom religion had a meaning. His heart was good; his sins were more those of vanity than those of hate; it may be that they are regarded mercifully where the fund of mercy is unbounded. God grant that they may be so; or who of us would escape? None but devils will triumph over the death of any man in sin. Men are not devils; they must and will always feel for their fellow-men, let them die as they will. No doubt

Brummell was a fool—a fool of the first water—but that he was equally a knave is not so certain. Let it never be certain to blind man, who can not read the heart, that any man is a knave. He died on the 30th of March, 1840, only twenty years ago, and so the last of the Beaux passed away. People have claimed, indeed, for D'Orsay, the honor of Brummell's descending mantle, but D'Orsay was not strictly a beau, for he had other and higher tastes than mere dress. It has never been advanced that Brummell's heart was bad, in spite of his many faults. Vanity did all. Vanitas vanitatum. O young men of this age, be warned by a Beau, and flee his doubtful reputation! Peace then to the coat-thinker. Peace to all—to the worst. Let us look within and not judge. It is enough that we are not tried in the same balance.

THEODORE EDWARD HOOK.

If it be difficult to say what wit is, it is well-nigh as hard to pronounce what is not wit. In a sad world, mirth hath its full honor, let it come in rags or in purple raiment. The age that patronizes a "Punch" every Saturday, and a pantomime every Christmas, has no right to complain if it finds itself barren of wits, while a rival age has brought forth her dozens. Mirth is, no doubt, very good. We would see more, not less, of it in this unmirthful land. We would fain imagine the shrunken-cheeked factory-girl singing to herself a happy burden, as she shifts the loom—the burden of her life—and fain believe that the voice was innocent as the skylark's. But if it be not so—and we know it is not so—shall we quarrel with any one who tries to give the poor care-worn, money-singing public a little laughter for a few pence? No, truly; but it does not follow that a man who raises a titter is, of necessity, a wit. The next age, perchance, will write a book of "Wits and Beaux," in which Mr. Douglas Jerrold, Mr. Mark Lemon, and so on, will represent the *wit* of this passing day; and that future age will not ask so nicely what wit is, and not look for that last solved of riddles, its definition.

Hook has been, by common consent, placed at the head of modern wits. When kings were kings, they bullied, beat, and browbeat their jesters. Now and then they treated them to a few years in the Tower for a little extra impudence. Now that the people are sovereign, the jester fares better—nay, too well. His books or his bon-mots are read with zest and grins; he is invited to his Grace's and implored to my Lord's; he is waited for, watched, pampered like a small Grand Llama, and, in one sentence, the greater the fool, the more fools he makes.

If Theodore Hook had lived in the stirring days of King Henry VIII., of blessed (?) memory, he would have sent Messrs. Patch and Co. sharply to the right-about, and been presented with the caps and bells after his first comic song. No doubt he was a jester, a fool in many senses, though he did not, like Solomon's fool, "say in his *heart*" very much. He jested away even the practicals of life, jested himself into disgrace, into prison, into contempt, into the basest employment—that of a libeler tacked on to a party. He was a mimic, too, to whom none could send a challenge; an improvisatore, who beat Italians, Tyroleans, and Styrians hollow, sir, hollow. And lastly—oh! shame of the shuffle-tongued—he was, too, a punster. Yes, a glorier in puns, a maker of pun upon pun, a man whose whole wit ran into a pun as readily as water rushes into a hollow, who could not keep out of a pun, let him loathe it or not, and who made some of the best and some of the worst on record, but still puns.

If he was a wit withal, it was *malgré soi*, for fun, not wit, was his "aspiration." Yet the world calls him a wit, and he has a claim to his niche. There were, it is true, many a man in his own set who had more real wit. There were James Smith, Thomas Ingoldsby, Tom Hill, and others. Out of his set, but of his time, there was Sydney Smith, ten times more a wit; but Theodore could amuse, Theodore could astonish, Theodore could be at home any where; he had all the impudence, all the readiness, all the indifference of a jester, and a jester he was.

Let any one look at his portrait, and he will doubt if this be the king's jester, painted by Holbein, or Mr. Theodore Hook, painted by Eddis. The short, thick nose, the long upper lip, the sensual, whimsical mouth, the twinkling eyes, all belong to the regular maker of fun. Hook was a certificated jester, with a lenient society to hear and applaud him, instead of an irritable tyrant to keep him in order: and he filled his post well. Whether he was more than a jester may well be doubted; yet Coleridge, when he heard him, said, "I have before in my time met with men of admirable promptitude of intellectual power and play of wit, which, as Stillingfleet says,

" 'The rays of wit gild wheresoe'er they strike,'

but I never could have conceived such readiness of mind and resources of genius to be poured out on the mere subject and impulse of the moment." The poet was wrong in one respect. Genius can in no sense be applied to Hook, though readiness was his chief charm.

The famous Theodore was born in the same year as Byron, 1788, the one on the 22d of January, the other on the 22d of September; so the poet was only nine months his senior. Hook, like many other wits, was a second son. Ladies of sixty or seventy well remember the name of Hook as that which accompanied their earliest miseries. It was in learning Hook's exercises, or primers, or whatever they were called, that they first had their fingers slapped over the pianoforte. The father of Theodore, no doubt, was the unwitting cause of much unhappiness to many a young lady in her teens. Hook *père* was an organist at Norwich. He came up to town, and was engaged at Marylebone Gardens and at Vauxhall; so that Theodore had no excuse for being of decidedly plebeian origin, and, Tory as he was, he was not fool enough to aspire to patricianism.

Theodore's family was, in real fact, Theodore himself. He made the name what it is, and raised himself to the position he at one time held. Yet he had a brother whose claims to celebrity are not altogether ancillary. James Hook was fifteen years older than Theodore. After leaving Westminster School, he was sent to immortal Skimmery (St. Mary's Hall), Oxford, which has fostered so many great men—and spoiled them. He was advanced in the Church from one preferment to another, and ultimately became Dean of Worcester. The character of the reverend gentleman is pretty well known, but it is unnecessary here to go into it farther. He is only mentioned as Theodore's brother in this sketch.* He was a dabbler in literature, like his brother, but scarcely to the same extent a dabbler in wit.

The younger son of "Hook's Exercises" developed early enough a taste for ingenious lying—so much admired in his predecessor, Sheridan. He "fancied himself" a genius, and therefore, from school-age, not amenable to the common laws of ordinary men. Frequenters of the now fashionable prize-ring—thanks to two brutes who have brought that degraded pastime into prominent notice—will hear a great deal about a man "fancying himself." It is common slang, and needs little explanation. Hook "fancied himself" from an early period, and continued to "fancy himself," in spite of repeated disgraces, till a very mature age. At Harrow, he was the contemporary, but scarcely the friend, of Lord Byron. No two characters could have been more unlike. Every one knows, more or less, what Byron's was; it need only be said that Hook's was the reverse of it in every respect. Byron felt where Hook laughed. Byron was morbid where Hook was gay. Byron abjured with disgust the social vices to which he was introduced; Hook fell in with them. Byron indulged in vice in a romantic way; Hook in the coarsest. There is some excuse for Byron, much as he has been blamed. There is little or no excuse for Hook, much as his faults have been palliated. The fact is that goodness of heart will soften, in men's minds, any or all misdemeanors. Hook, in spite of many vulgar witticisms and cruel jokes, seems to have had a really good heart.

I have it on the authority of one of Hook's most intimate

* Dr. James Hook, Dean of Worcester, was father to Dr. Walter Farquhar Hook, now the excellent Dean of Chichester, late Vicar of Leeds.

friends, that he was capable of any act of kindness, and by way of instance of his goodness of heart, I am told by the same person that he on one occasion quitted all his town amusements to solace the spirit of a friend in the country who was in serious trouble. I, of course, refrain from giving names; but the same person informs me that much of his time was devoted, in a like manner, to relieving, as far as possible, the anxiety of his friends, often, indeed, arising from his own carelessness. It is due to Hook to make this impartial statement before entering on a sketch of his "Sayings and Doings," which must necessarily leave the impression that he was a heartless man.

Old Hook, the father, soon perceived the value of his son's talents; and, determined to turn them to account, encouraged his natural inclination to song-writing. At the age of sixteen Theodore wrote a kind of comic opera, to which his father supplied the music. This was called "The Soldier's Return." It was followed by others, and young Hook, not yet out of his teens, managed to keep a Drury Lane audience alive, as well as himself and family. It must be remembered, however, that Liston and Mathews could make almost any piece amusing. The young author was introduced behind the scenes through his father's connection with the theatre, and often played the fool under the stage while others were playing it for him above it, practical jokes being a passion with him which he developed thus early. These tricks were not always very good-natured, which may be said of many of his jokes out of the theatre.

He soon showed evidence of another talent, that of acting as well as writing pieces. Assurance was one of the main features of his character, and to it he owed his success in society; but it is a remarkable fact, that on his first appearance before an audience he entirely lost all his nerve, turned pale, and could scarcely utter a syllable. He rapidly recovered, however, and from this time became a favorite performer in private theatricals, in which he was supported by Mathews and Mrs. Mathews, and some amateurs who were almost equal to any professional actors. His attempts were, of course, chiefly in broad farce and roaring burlesque, in which his comic face, with its look of mock gravity, and the twinkle of the eyes, itself excited roars of laughter. Whether he would have succeeded as well in sober comedy or upon public boards may well be doubted. Probably he would not have given to the profession that careful attention and entire devotion which are necessary to bring forward properly the highest natural talents. It is said that for a long time he was anxious to take to the stage as a profession, but, perhaps—as the event seems to show—unfortunately for him, he was dissuaded from what his friends must have thought a very rash step, and in after years he took a violent dislike to the profession. Certainly the stage could not have offered more temptations than did the society in which he afterward mixed; and perhaps, under any circumstances, Hook, whose moral education had been neglected, and whose principles were never very good, would have lived a life more or less vicious, though he might not have died as he did.

Hook, however, was not long in coming very prominently before the public in another capacity. Of all stories told about him, none are more common or more popular than those which relate to his practical jokes and hoaxes. Thank Heaven, the world no longer sees amusement in the misery of others, and the fashion of such clever performance is gone out. It is fair, however, to premise, that while the cleverest of Hook's hoaxes were of a victimizing character, a large number were just the reverse, and his admirers affirm, not without some reason, that when he had got a dinner out of a person he did not know, by an ingenious lie, admirably supported, he fully paid for it in the amusement he afforded his host and the ringing metal of his wit. As we have all been boys—except those that were girls—and not all of us very good boys, we can appreciate that passion for robbery which began with orchards and passed on to knockers. It is difficult to sober middle-age to imagine what entertainment there can be in that breach of the eighth commandment, which is generally regarded as innocent. As Sheridan swindled in fun, so Hook, as a young man, robbed in fun, as hundreds of medical students and others have done before and since. Hook, however, was a proficient in the art, and would have made a successful "cracksman" had he been born in the Seven Dials. He collected a complete museum of knockers, bell-pulls, wooden Highlanders, barbers' poles, and shop signs of all sorts. On one occasion he devoted a whole fortnight to the abstraction of a golden eagle over a shop window, by means of a lasso. A fellow-dilettante in the art had confidentially informed him of its whereabouts, adding that he himself despaired of ever obtaining it. At length Hook invited his friend to dinner, and on the removal of the cover of what was supposed to be the joint, the work of art appeared served up and appropriately garnished. Theodore was radiant with triumph; but the friend, probably thinking that there ought to be honor among thieves, was highly indignant at being thus surpassed.

Another achievement of this kind was the robbery of a life-sized Highlander, who graced the door of some unsuspecting tobacconist. There was little difficulty in the mere displacement of the figure; the troublesome part of the business was to get the bare-legged Celt home to the museum, where probably many a Liliputian of his race was already awaiting him. A cloak, a hat, and Hook's ready wit effected the transfer. The first was thrown over him, the second set upon his bonneted head, and a passing hackney-coach hailed by his captor, who, before the unsuspecting driver could descend, had opened the door, pushed in the prize, and whispered to Jehu, "My friend —very respectable man—but rather tipsy." How he managed to get him out again at the end of the journey we are not told.

Hook was soon a successful and valuable writer of light pieces for the stage. But farces do not live, and few of Hook's are now favorites with a public which is always athirst for something new. The incidents of most of the pieces—many of them borrowed from the French—excited laughter by their very improbability; but the wit which enlivened them was not of a high order, and Hook, though so much more recent than Sheridan, has disappeared before him.

But his hoaxes were far more famous than his collection of curiosities, and quite as much to the purpose; and the impudence he displayed in them was only equaled by the quaintness of the humor which suggested them. Who else would have ever thought, for instance, of covering a white horse with black wafers, and driving it in a gig along a Welsh high-road, merely for the satisfaction of being stared at? It was almost worthy of Barnum. Or who, with less assurance, could have played so admirably on the credulity of a lady and daughters fresh from the country, as he did at the trial of Lord Melville? The lady, who stood next to him, was naturally anxious to understand the proceedings, and betrayed her ignorance at once by a remark which she made to her daughter about the procession of the Lords into the House. When the bishops entered in full episcopal costume, she applied to Hook to know who were "those gentlemen?" "Gentlemen," quoth Hook, with charming simplicity; "ladies, I think you mean; at any rate, those are the dowager peeresses in their own right." Question followed question as the procession came on, and Theodore indulged his fancy more and more. At length the Speaker, in full robes, became the subject of inquiry. "And pray, sir, who is that fine-looking person?" "That, ma'am, is Cardinal Wolsey," was the calm and audacious reply. This was too much even for Sussex; and the lady drew herself up in majestic indignation. "We know better than that, sir," she replied; "Cardinal Wolsey has been dead many a good year." Theodore was unmoved. "No such thing, my dear madam," he answered, without the slightest sign of perturbation: "I know it has been generally reported so in the country, but without the slightest foundation; the newspapers, you know, will say any thing."

But the hoax of hoaxes, the one which filled the papers of the time for several days, and which, eventually, made its author the very prince of hoaxsters, if such a term can be admitted, was that of Berners Street. Never, perhaps, was so much trouble expended, or so much attention devoted, to so frivolous an object. In Berners Street there lived an elderly lady, who, for no reason that can be ascertained, had excited the animosity of the young Theodore, who was then just of age. Six weeks were spent in preparation, and three persons were engaged in the affair. Letters were sent off in every direction, and Theodore Hook's autograph, if it could have any value, must have been somewhat low in the market at that period, from the number of applications which he wrote. On the day in question he and his accomplices seated themselves at a window in Berners Street, opposite to that of the unfortunate Mrs. Tottenham, of No. 54, and there enjoyed the fun. Advertisements, announcements, letters, circulars, and what not, had been most freely issued, and were as freely responded to. A score of sweeps, all "invited to attend professionally," opened the ball at a very early hour, and claimed admittance, in virtue of the notice they had received. The maid-servant had only just time to assure them that all the chimneys were clean, and their services were not required, when some dozen of coal-carts drew up as near as possible to the ill-fated house. New protestations, new indignation. The grimy and irate coal-heavers were still being discoursed with, when a bevy of neat and polite individuals arrived from different quarters, bearing each under his arm a splendid ten-guinea wedding-cake. The maid grew distracted; her mistress was single, and had no intention of doubling herself; there must be some mistake; the confectioners were dismissed, in a very different humor to that with which they had come. But they were scarcely gone when crowds began to storm the house, all "on business." Rival doctors met in astonishment and disgust, prepared for an *accouchement;* undertakers stared one another mutely in the face, as they deposited at the door coffins made to order—elm or oak—so many feet and so many inches; the clergymen of all the neighboring parishes, high church or low church, were ready to minister to the spiritual wants of the unfortunate moribund, but retired in disgust when they found that some forty fishmongers had been engaged to purvey "cod's head and lobsters" for a person professing to be on the brink of the grave.

The street now became the scene of fearful distraction. Furious tradesmen of every kind were ringing the house-bell, and rapping the knocker for admittance—such, at least, as could press through the crowd as far as the house. Bootmakers arrived with Hessians and Wellingtons—"as per order"—or the most delicate of dancing-shoes for the sober old lady; haberdashers had brought the last new thing in evening dress, "quite the fashion," and "very chaste;" hatmakers, from Lincoln and Bennett down to the Hebrew vendor in Marylebone Lane, arrived with their crown-pieces; butchers' boys, on stout little nags, could not get near enough to deliver the legs of mutton which had been ordered; the lumbering coal-carts still "stopped the way." A crowd—the easiest curiosity in the world to collect—soon gathered round the motley mob of butchers, bakers, candlestick-makers, and makers and sellers of every thing else that mortal can want; the mob thronged the pavement, the carts filled the road, and soon the carriages of the noble of the land dashed up in all the panoply of state, and a demand was made to clear the way for the Duke of Gloucester, for the Governor of the Bank, the Chairman of the East India Company, and last, but oh! not least, the grandee whose successor the originator of the plot afterward so admirably satirized—the great Lord Mayor himself. The consternation, disgust, and terror of the elderly female, the delight and chuckling of Theodore and his accomplices, seated at a window on the opposite side of the road, "can be more easily imagined than described;" but what were the feelings of tradesmen, professional men, gentlemen, noblemen, and grand officials, who had been summoned from distant spots by artful lures to No. 54, and there battled with a crowd in vain only to find that they were hoaxed, people who had thus lost both time and money, can be neither described nor imagined. It was not the idea of the hoax—simple enough in itself—which was entitled to the admiration accorded to ingenuity, but its extent and success, and the clever means taken by the conspirators to insure the attendance of every one who ought not to have been there. It was only late at night that the police succeeded in clearing the street, and the dupes retired, murmuring and vowing vengeance. Hook, however, gloried in the exploit, which he thought "perfect."

But the hoaxing dearest to Theodore—for there was something to be gained by it—was that by which he managed to obtain a dinner when either too hard up to pay for one, or in the humor for a little amusement. No one who has not lived as a bachelor in London and been reduced—in respect of coin—to the sum of twopence halfpenny, can tell how excellent a strop is hunger to sharpen wit upon. We all know that

"Mortals with stomachs can't live without dinner;"

and in Hook's day the substitute of "heavy teas" was not invented. Necessity is very soon brought to bed, when a man puts his fingers into his pockets, finds them untenanted, and remembers that the only friend who would consent to lend him five shillings is gone out of town; and the infant, Invention, presently smiles into the nurse's face. But it was no uncommon thing in those days for gentlemen to invite themselves where they listed, and stay as long as they liked. It was only necessary for them to make themselves really agreeable, and deceive their host in some way or other. Hook's friend, like little Tom Hill, of whom it was said that he knew every body's affairs far better than they did themselves, was famous for examining kitchens about the hour of dinner, and quietly selecting his host according to the odor of the viands. It is of him that the old "Joe Miller" is told of the "haunch of venison." Invited to dinner at one house, he *happens* to glance down into the kitchen of the next, and seeing a tempting haunch of venison on the spit, throws over the inviter, and ingratiates himself with his neighbor, who ends by asking him to stay to dinner. The fare, however, consisted of nothing more luxurious than an Irish stew, and the disappointed guest was informed that he had been "too cunning by half," inasmuch as the venison belonged to his original inviter, and had been cooked in the house he was in by kind permission, because the chimney of the owner's kitchen smoked.

The same principle often actuated Theodore; and, indeed, there are few stories which can be told of this characteristic of the great frolicker, which have not been told a century of times. For instance: two young men are strolling, toward 5 P. M., in the then fashionable neighborhood of Soho; the one is Terry, the actor—the other, Hook, the actor, for surely he deserves the title. They pass a house, and sniff the viands cooking underground. Hook quietly announces his intention of dining *there.* He enters, is admitted and announced by the servant, mingles with the company, and is quite at home before he is perceived by the host. At last the *dénouement* came; the dinner-giver approached the stranger, and with great politeness asked his name. "Smith" was, of course, the reply, and reverting to mistakes made by servants in announcing, etc., Smith hurried off into an amusing story, to put his host in good-humor. The conversation that followed is taken from "Ingoldsby:"

"But, really, my dear sir," the host put in, "I think the mistake on the present occasion does not originate in the source you allude to; I certainly did not anticipate the honor of Mr. Smith's company to-day."

"No, I dare say not. You said *four* in your note, I know, and it is now, I see, a quarter past five; but the fact is, I have been detained in the City, as I was going to explain—"

"Pray," said the host, "whom do you suppose you are addressing?"

"Whom? why Mr. Thompson, of course, old friend of my father. I have not the pleasure, indeed, of being personally known to you, but having received your kind invitation yesterday," etc., etc.

"No, sir, my name is not Thompson, but Jones," in highly indignant accents.

"Jones!" was the well-acted answer: "why, surely, I can not have—yes I must—good heaven! I see it all. My *dear* sir, what an unfortunate blunder; wrong house—what must you think of such an intrusion? I am really at a loss for words in which to apologize; you will permit me to retire at present, and to-morrow—"

"Pray, don't think of retiring," rejoined the host, taken with the appearance and manner of the young man. "Your friend's table must have been cleared long ago, if, as you say, four was the hour named, and I am too happy to be able to offer you a seat at mine."

It may be easily conceived that the invitation had not to be very often repeated, and Hook kept the risible muscles of the company upon the constant stretch, and paid for the entertainment in the only coin with which he was well supplied.

There was more wit, however, in his visit to a retired watchmaker, who had got from government a premium of £10,000 for the best chronometer. Hook was very partial to journeys in search of adventure; a gig, a lively companion, and sixpence for the first turnpike being generally all that was requisite; ingenuity supplied the rest. It was on one of these excursions that Hook and his friend found themselves in the neighborhood of Uxbridge, with a horse and a gig, and not a sixpence to be found in any pocket. Now a horse and gig are property, but of what use is a valuable of which you can not dispose or deposit at a pawnbroker's, while you are prevented proceeding on your way by that neat white gate with the neat white box of a house at its side? The only alternative left to the young men was to drive home again, dinnerless, a distance of twenty miles, with a jaded horse, or to find gratuitous accommodation for man and beast. In such a case Sheridan would simply have driven to the first inn, and by persuasion or stratagem contrived to elude payment, after having drunk the best wine and eaten the best dinner the house could afford. Hook was really more refined, as well as bolder in his pillaging.

The villa of the retired tradesman was perceived, and the gig soon drew up before the door. The strangers were ushered in to the watchmaker, and Hook, with great politeness and a serious respectful look, addressed him. He said that he felt he was taking a great liberty—so he was—but that he could not pass the door of a man who had done the country so much service by the invention of what must prove the most useful and valuable instrument, without expressing to him the gratitude which he, as a British subject devoted to his country's good, could not but feel toward the inventor, etc., etc. The flattery was so delicately and so seriously insinuated, that the worthy citizen could only receive it as an honest expression of sincere admiration. The Rubicon was passed; a little lively conversation, artfully made attractive by Hook, followed, and the watchmaker was more and more gratified. He felt, too, what an honor it would be to entertain two real gentlemen, and remarking that they were far from town, brought out at last the longed-for invitation, which was, of course, declined as out of the question. Thereupon the old gentleman became pressing: the young strangers were at last prevailed upon to accept it, and very full justice they did to the larder and cellar of the successful chronometer-maker.

There is nothing very original in the act of hoaxing, and Hook's way of getting a hackney-coach without paying for it was, perhaps, suggested by Sheridan's, but was more laughable. Finding himself in the vehicle, and knowing that there was nothing either in his purse or at home to pay the fare, he cast about for expedients, and at last remembered the address of an eminent surgeon in the neighborhood. He ordered the coachman to drive to his house and knock violently at the door, which was no sooner opened than Hook rushed in, terribly agitated, demanded to see the doctor, to whom, in a few incoherent and agitated sentences, he gave to understand that his wife needed his services immediately, being on the point of becoming a mother.

"I will start directly," replied the surgeon; "I will order my carriage at once."

"But, my dear sir, there is not a moment to spare. I have a coach at the door, jump into that."

The surgeon obeyed. The name and address given were those of a middle-aged spinster of the most rigid virtue. We can imagine her indignation, and how sharply she rung the bell, when the surgeon had delicately explained the object of his visit, and how eagerly he took refuge in the coach. Hook had, of course, walked quietly away in the mean time, and the Galenite had to pay the demand of Jehu.

The hoaxing stories of Theodore Hook are numberless. Hoaxing was the fashion of the day, and a childish fashion too. Charles Mathews, whose face possessed the flexibility of an acrobat's body, and who could assume any character or disguise on the shortest notice, was his great confederate in these plots. The banks of the Thames were their great resort. At one point there was Mathews talking gibberish in a disguise intended to represent the Spanish embassador, and actually deceiving the Woolwich authorities by his clever impersonation. At another, there was Hook landing uninvited with his friends upon the well-known, sleek-looking lawn of a testy little gentleman, drawing out a note-book and talking so authoritatively about the survey for a canal, to be undertaken by government, that the owner of the lawn becomes frightened, and in his anxiety attempts to conciliate the mighty self-made official by the offer of dinner—of course accepted.

Then the *Arcades ambo* show off their jesting tricks at Croydon fair, a most suitable place for them. On one occasion Hook personates a madman, accusing Mathews, "his brother," of keeping him out of his rights and in his custody. The whole fair collects around them, and begins to sympathize with Hook, who begs them to aid in his escape from his "brother." A sham escape and sham capture take place, and the party adjourn to the inn, where Mathews, who had been taken by surprise by the new part suddenly played by his confederate, seized upon a hearse, which drew up before the inn, on its return from a funeral, persuaded the company to bind the "madman," who was now becoming furious, and would have deposited him in the gloomy vehicle if he had not succeeded in snapping his fetters, and so escaped. In short, they were two boys, with the sole difference that they had sufficient talent and experience of the world to maintain admirably the parts they assumed.

But a far more famous and more admirable talent in Theodore than that of deception was that of improvising. The art of improvising belongs to Italy and the Tyrol. The wonderful gift of ready verse to express satire and ridicule, seems, as a rule, to be confined to the inhabitants of these two lands. Others are, indeed, scattered over the world, who possess this gift, but very sparsely. Theodore Hook stands almost alone in this country as an improviser. Yet, to judge of such of his verses as have been preserved, taken down from memory or what not, the grand effect of them—and no doubt it *was* grand—must have been owing more to his manner and his acting than to any intrinsic value in the verses themselves, which are, for the most part, slight, and devoid of actual wit, though

THEODORE HOOK'S ENGINEERING FROLIC.

abounding in puns. Sheridan's testimony to the wonderful powers of the man is, perhaps, more valuable than that of any one else, for Sherry was a good judge both of verse and of wit. One of Hook's earliest displays of his talent was at a dinner given by the Drury Lane actors to Sheridan at the Piazza Coffee House in 1808. Here, as usual, Hook sat down to the piano, and, touching off a few chords, gave verse after verse on all the events of the entertainment, on each person present, though he now saw many of them for the first time, and on any thing connected with the matters of interest before them. Sheridan was delighted, and declared that he could not have believed such a faculty possible if he had not witnessed its effects; that no description "could have convinced him of so peculiar an instance of genius," and so forth.

One of his most extraordinary efforts in this line is related by Mr. Jordan. A dinner was given by Mansell Reynolds to Lockhart, Luttrell, Coleridge, Hook, Tom Hill, and others. The grown-up schoolboys, pretty far gone in Falernian, of a home-made and very homely vintage, amused themselves by breaking the wine-glasses, till Coleridge was set to demolish the last of them with a fork thrown at it from the side of the table. Let it not be supposed that any teetotal spirit suggested this iconoclasm, far from it—the glasses were too small, and the poets, the wits, the punsters, the jesters, preferred to drink their port out of tumblers. After dinner Hook gave one of his songs, which satirized successively, and successfully, each person present. He was then challenged to improvise on any given subject, and by way of one as far distant from poetry as could be, *cocoanut oil* was fixed upon. Theodore accepted the challenge; and after a moment's consideration began his lay with a description of the Mauritius, which he knew so well, the negroes dancing round the cocoanut-tree, the process of extracting the oil, and so forth, all in excellent rhyme and rhythm, if not actual poetry. Then came the voyage to England, hits at the Italian warehousemen, and so on, till the oil is brought into the very lamp before them in that very room, to show them with the light it feeds, and make them able to break wine-glasses and get drunk from tumblers. This we may be sure Hook himself did, for one, and the rest were probably not much behind him.

In late life this gift of Hook's—improvising I mean, not getting intoxicated—was his highest recommendation in society, and at the same time his bane. Like Sheridan, he was ruined by his wonderful natural powers. It can well be imagined that to improvise in the manner in which Hook did it, and at a moment's notice, required some effort of the intellect. This effort became greater as circumstances depressed his spirits more and more, and yet, with every care upon his mind, he was expected, wherever he went, to amuse the guests with a display of his talent. He could not do so without stimulants, and, rather than give up society, fell into habits of drinking, which hastened his death.

We have thrown together the foregoing anecdotes of Hook, irrespective of time, in order to show what the man's gifts were, and what his title to be considered a wit. We must proceed more steadily to a review of his life. Successful as Hook had proved as a writer for the stage, he suddenly and without any sufficient cause rushed off into another branch of literature, that of novel-writing. His first attempt in this kind of fiction was "The Man of Sorrow," published under the *nom de plume* of *Alfred Allendale*. This was not, as its name would seem to imply, a novel of pathetic cast, but the history of a gentleman whose life from beginning to end is rendered wretched by a succession of mishaps of the most ludicrous but improbable kind. Indeed, Theodore's novels, like his stage-pieces, are gone out of date in an age so practical that even in romance it will not allow of the slightest departure from reality. Their very style was ephemeral, and their interest could not outlast the generation to amuse which they were penned. This first novel was written when Hook was one-and-twenty. Soon after he was sent to Oxford, where he had been entered at St. Mary's Hall, more affectionately known by the nickname of "Skimmery." No selection could have been worse. Skimmery was, at that day, and until quite recently, a den of thieves, where young men of fortune and folly submitted to be pillaged in return for being allowed perfect license, as much to eat as they could possibly swallow, and far more to drink than was at all good for them. It has required all the enterprise of the present excellent Principal to convert it into a place of sober study. It was then the most "gentlemanly" residence in Oxford; for a gentleman in those days meant a man who did nothing, spent his own or his father's guineas with a brilliant indifference to consequences, and who applied his mind solely to the art of frolic. It was the very place where Hook would be encouraged instead of restrained in his natural propensities, and had he remained there, he would probably have ruined himself and his father long before he had put on the sleeves.

At the matriculation itself he gave a specimen of his "fun." When asked, according to the usual form, "if he was willing to sign the Thirty-nine Articles," he replied, "Certainly, sir; *forty* if you please." The gravity of the stern Vice-Chancellor was upset, but as no Oxford Don can ever pardon a joke, however good, Master Theodore was very nearly being dismissed, had not his brother, by this time a Prebendary of Winchester, and "an honor to his college, sir," interceded in his favor.

The night before, he had given a still better specimen of his impudence. He had picked up a number of old Harrowvians, with whom he had repaired to a tavern for song, supper, and sociability, and as usual in such cases, in the lap of Alma Mater, the babes became sufficiently intoxicated, and not a little uproarious. Drinking in a tavern is forbidden by Oxonian statutes, and one of the proctors happening to pass in the street outside, was attracted into the house by the sound of somewhat unscholastic merriment. The effect can be imagined. All the youths were in absolute terror, except Theodore, and looked in vain for some way to escape. The wary and faithful "bull-dogs" guarded the doorway; the marshal, predecessor of the modern omniscient Brown, advanced respectfully behind the proctor into the room, and passing a penetrating glance from one youth to the other, all of whom —except Theodore again—he knew by sight—for that is the pride and pleasure of a marshal—mentally registered their names in secret hopes of getting half a crown apiece to forget them again.

No mortal is more respectful in his manner of accosting you than an Oxford proctor, for he may make a mistake, and a mistake may make him very miserable. When, for instance, a highly respectable lady was the other day lodged, in spite of protestations, in the "Procuratorial Rooms," and there locked up on suspicion of being somebody very different, the over-zealous proctor who had ordered her incarceration was sued for damages for £300, and had to pay them too! Therefore the gentleman in question most graciously and suavely inquired of Mr. Theodore Hook—

"I beg your pardon, sir, but are you a member of this university?"—the usual form.

"No, sir, I am not. Are you?"

The suavity at once changed to grave dignity. The proctor lifted up the hem of his garment, which being of broad velvet, with the selvage on it, was one of the insignia of his office, and sternly said, "You see this, sir."

"Ah!" said Hook, cool as ever, and quietly feeling the material, which he examined with apparent interest, "I see; Manchester velvet: and may I take the liberty, sir, of inquiring how much you have paid per yard for the article?"

A roar of laughter from all present burst out with such vehemence that it shot the poor official, red with suppressed anger, into the street again, and the merrymakers continued their bout till the approach of midnight, when they were obliged to return to their respective colleges.

Had Theodore proceeded in this way for several terms, no doubt the outraged authorities would have added his name to the list of the great men whom they have expelled from time to time most unprophetically. As it was, he soon left the groves of Academus, and sought those of Fashion in town. His matriculation into this new university was much more auspicious; he was hailed in society as already fit to take a degree of bachelor of his particular arts, and ere long his improvising, his fun, his mirth—as yet natural and overboiling—his wicked punning, and his tender wickedness, induced the same institution to offer him the grade of "Master" of those arts. In after years he rose to be even "Doctor," and many, perhaps, were the minds diseased to which his well-known mirth ministered.

It was during this period that some of his talents were displayed in the manner we have described, though his great fame as an improvisatore was established more completely in later days. Yet he had already made himself a name in that species of wit—not a very high one—which found favor with the society of that period. We allude to imitation, "taking off," and punning. The last contemptible branch of wit-making, now happily confined to "Punch," is as old as variety of language. It is not possible with simple vocabularies, and accordingly is seldom met with in purely-derived languages. Yet we have Roman and Greek puns; and English is peculiarly adapted to this childish exercise, because, being made up of several languages, it necessarily contains many words which are like in sound and unlike in meaning. Punning is, in fact, the vice of English wit, the temptation of English mirth-makers, and, at last, we trust, the scorn of English good sense. But in Theodore's day it held a high place, and men who had no real wit about them could twist and turn words and combinations of words with great ingenuity and much readiness, to the delight of their listeners. Pun-making was a fashion among the conversationists of that day, and took the place of better wit. Hook was a disgraceful punster, and a successful one. He strung puns together by the score—nothing more easy—in his improvised songs and conversation. Take an instance from his quiz on the march of intellect:

"Hackney-coachmen from *Swift* shall reply, if you feel
Annoyed at being needlessly shaken;
And butchers, of course, be flippant from *Steele*,
And pig-drivers well versed in *Bacon*.

> From *Locke*, shall the blacksmiths authority brave,
> And gas-men cite *Coke* at discretion;
> Undertakers talk *Gay* as they go to the *grave*,
> And watermen *Rowe* by profession."

I have known a party of naturally stupid people produce a whole century of puns one after another, on any subject that presented itself, and I am inclined to think that nothing can, at the same time, be more nauseous, or more destructive to real wit. Yet Theodore's strength lay in puns, and when shorn of them, the Philistines might well laugh at his want of strength. Surely his title to wit does not lie in that direction.

However, he amused, and that gratis; and an amusing man makes his way any where if he have only sufficient tact not to abuse his privileges. Hook grew great in London society for a time, and might have grown greater if a change had not come.

He had supported himself, up to 1812, almost entirely by his pen; and the goose-quill is rarely a staff, though it may sometimes be a walking-stick. It was clear that he needed—what so many of us need and can not get—a certainty. Happy fellow; he might have begged for an appointment for years in vain, as many another does, but it fell into his lap, no one knows how, and at four-and-twenty Mr. Theodore Edward Hook was made treasurer to the Island of Mauritius, with a salary of £2000 per annum. This was not to be, and was not, sneezed at. In spite of climate, musquitoes, and so forth, Hook took the money and sailed.

We have no intention of entering minutely upon his conduct in this office, which has nothing to do with his character as a wit. There are a thousand and one reasons for believing him guilty of the charges brought against him, and a thousand and one for supposing him guiltless. Here was a young man, gay, jovial, given to society entirely, and not at all to arithmetic, put into a very trying and awkward position—native clerks who would cheat if they could, English governors who would find fault if they could, a disturbed treasury, an awkward currency, liars for witnesses, and undeniable evidence of defalcation. In a word, an examination was made into the state of the treasury of the island, and a large deficit found. It remained to trace it home to its original author.

Hook had not acquired the best character in the island. Those who know the official dignity of a small British colony can well understand how his pleasantries must have shocked those worthy big-wigs who, exalted from Pump Court, Temple, or Paradise Row, Old Brompton, to places of honor and high salaries, rode their high horses with twice the exclusiveness of those "to the manor born." For instance, Hook was once, by a mere chance, obliged to take the chair at an official dinner, on which occasion the toasts proposed by the chairman were to be accompanied by a salute from guns without. Hook went through the list, and seemed to enjoy toast-drinking so much that he was quite sorry to have come to the end of it, and continued, as if still from the list, to propose successively the health of each officer present. The gunners were growing quite weary, but, having their orders, dared not complain. Hook was delighted, and went on to the amazement and amusement of all who were not tired of the noise, each youthful sub, taken by surprise, being quite gratified at the honor done him. At last there was no one left to toast; but the wine had taken effect, and Hook, amid roars of laughter inside, and roars of savage artillery without, proposed the health of the waiter who had so ably officiated. This done, he bethought him of the cook, who was sent for to return thanks; but the artillery officer had by this time got wind of the affair, and feeling that more than enough powder had been wasted on the health of gentlemen who were determined to destroy it by the number of their potations, took on himself the responsibility of ordering the gunners to stop.

On another occasion he incurred the displeasure of the governor, General Hall, by fighting a duel—fortunately as harmless as that of Moore and Jeffrey—

"When Little's leadless pistol met his eye,
And Bow-street myrmidons stood laughing by,"

as Byron says. The governor was sensible enough to wish to put down the "Gothic appeal to arms," and was therefore the more irate.

These circumstances must be taken into consideration in Hook's favor in examining the charge of embezzlement. It must also be stated that the information of the deficit was sent in a letter to the governor by a man named Allan, chief clerk in the Treasury, who had, for irregular conduct, been already threatened with dismissal. Allan had admitted that he had known of the deficit for fifteen months, and yet he had not, till he was himself in trouble, thought of making it known to the proper authorities. Before his examination, which of course followed, could be concluded, Allan committed suicide. Now, does it not, on the face of it, seem of the highest probability that this man was the real delinquent, and that, knowing that Hook had all the responsibility, and having taken fair precautions against his own detection, he had anticipated a discovery of the affair by a revelation, incriminating the treasurer? *Quien sabe;*—dead men tell no tales.

The chest, however, was examined, and the deficit found far greater yet than had been reported. Hook could not explain, could not understand it at all; but if not criminal, he had necessarily been careless. He was arrested, thrown into prison, and by the first vessel dispatched to England to take his trial, his property of every kind having been sold for the Government. Hook, in utter destitution, might be supposed to have lost his usual spirits, but he could not resist a joke. At St. Helena he met an old friend going out to the Cape, who, surprised at seeing him on his return voyage after a residence of only five years, said, "I hope you are not going home for your health." "Why," said Theodore, "I am sorry to say they think there is something wrong in the *chest*." "Something wrong in the chest" became henceforward the ordinary phrase in London society in referring to Hook's scrape.

Arrived in England, he was set free, the Government here having decided that he could not be criminally tried; and thus Hook, guilty or not, had been ruined and disgraced for life for simple carelessness. True, the custody of a nation's property makes negligence almost criminal; but that does not excuse the punishment of a man before he is tried.

He was summoned, however, to the Colonial Audit Board, where he underwent a trying examination; after which he was declared to be in the debt of Government: a writ of extent was issued against him; nine months were passed in that delightful place of residence—a sponging-house, which he then exchanged for the "Rules of the Bench"—the only rules which have no exception. From these he was at last liberated, in 1825, on the understanding that he was to repay the money to Government if at any time he should be in a position to do so.

His liberation was a tacit acknowledgment of his innocence of the charge of robbery; his encumberment with a debt caused by another's delinquencies was, we presume, a signification of his responsibility and some kind of punishment for his carelessness. Certainly it was hard upon Hook, that, if innocent, he should not have gone forth without a stain on his character for honesty; and it was unjust that, if guilty, he should not have been punished. The judgment was one of those compromises with stern justice which are seldom satisfactory to either party.

The fact was that, guilty or not guilty, Hook had been both incompetent and inconsiderate. Doubtless he congratulated himself highly on receiving, at the age of twenty-five, an appointment worth £2000 a year in the paradise of the world; but how short-sighted his satisfaction, since this very appointment left him some ten years later a pauper to begin life anew with an indelible stain on his character. It was absurd to give so young a man such a post; but it was absolutely wrong in Hook not to do his utmost to carry out his duties properly. Nay, he had trifled with the public money in the same liberal —perhaps a *more* liberal—spirit as if it had been his own—made advances and loans here and there injudiciously, and taken little heed of the consequences. Probably, at this day, the common opinion acquits Hook of a designed and complicated fraud; but common opinion never did acquit him of misconduct, and even by his friends this affair was looked upon with a suspicion that preferred silence to examination.

But why take such pains to exonerate Hook from a charge of robbery, when he was avowedly guilty of as bad a sin, of which the law took no cognizance, and which society forgave far more easily than it could have done for robbing the state? Soon after his return from the Mauritius, he took lodgings in the cheap but unfashionable neighborhood of Somers Town. Here, in the moment of his misfortune, when doubting whether disgrace, imprisonment, or what not awaited him, he sought solace in the affection of a young woman, of a class certainly much beneath his, and of a character unfit to make her a valuable companion to him. Hook had received little moral training, and had he done so, his impulses were sufficiently strong to overcome any amount of principle. With this person—to use the modern slang which seems to convert a glaring sin into a social misdemeanor—"he formed a connection." In other words, he destroyed her virtue. Hateful as such an act is, we must, before we can condemn a man for it without any recommendation to mercy, consider a score of circumstances which have rendered the temptation stronger and the result almost involuntary. Hook was not a man of high moral character—very far from it—but we need not therefore suppose that he sat down coolly and deliberately, like a villain in a novel, to effect the girl's ruin. But the Rubicon once passed, how difficult is the retreat! There are but two paths open to a man who would avoid living a life of sin: the one, to marry his victim; the other, to break off the connection before it is too late. The first is, of course, the more proper course; but there are cases where marriage is impossible. From the latter a man of any heart must shrink with horror. Yet there *are* cases, even, where the one sin will prove the least—where she who has loved too well may grieve bitterly at parting, yet will be no more open to temptation than if she had never fallen. Such cases are rare, and it is not probable that the young person with whom Hook had become connected would have retrieved the fatal error. She became a mother, and there was no retreat. It is clear that Hook ought to have married her. It is evident that he was selfish and wrong not to do so; yet he shrank from it weakly, wickedly, and he was punished for his shrinking. He had sufficient feeling not to throw his victim over, yet he was content to live a life of sin and to keep her in such a life. This is, perhaps, the blackest stain on Hook's character. When Fox married, in consequence of a similar connection, he "settled down," retrieved his early errors, and became a better man, morally, than he had ever been. Hook *ought* to have married. It was the cowardly dread of public opinion that deterred him from doing so, and, in consequence, he was never happy, and felt that this connection was a perpetual burden to him.

Wrecked and ruined, Hook had no resource but his literary talents, and it is to be deplored that he should have prostituted these to serve an ungentlemanly and dishonorable party in their onslaught upon an unfortunate woman. Whatever may be now thought of the queen of "the greatest gentleman"—or *roué*—of Europe, those who hunted her down will never be pardoned, and Hook was one of those. We have cried out against an Austrian general for condemning a Hungarian lady to the lash, and we have seen, with delight, a mob chase him through the streets of London and threaten his very life. But we have not only pardoned, but even praised, our favorite wit for far worse conduct than this. Even if we allow, which we do not, that the queen was one half as bad as her enemies, or rather her husband's toadies, would make her out, we can not forgive the men who, shielded by their incognito, and perfectly free from danger of any kind, set upon a woman with libels, invectives, ballads, epigrams, and lampoons, which a lady could scarcely read, and of which a royal lady, and many an English gentlewoman, too, were the butts.

The vilest of all the vile papers of that day was the "John Bull," now settled down to a quiet periodical. Perhaps the real John Bull, heavy, good-natured lumberer as he is, was never worse represented than in this journal which bore his name, but had little of his kindly spirit. Hook was its originator, and for a long time its main supporter. Scurrility, scandal, libel, baseness of all kinds formed the fuel with which it blazed, and the wit, bitter, unflinching, unsparing, which puffed the flame up, was its chief recommendation.

No more disgraceful climax was ever reached by a disgraceful dynasty of profligates than that which found a King of England—long, as Regent, the leader of the profligate and degraded—at war with his injured queen. None have deserved better the honest gratitude of their country than those who, like Henry Brougham, defended the oppressed woman in spite of opposition, obloquy, and ridicule.

But we need not go deeply into a history so fresh in the minds of all, as that blot which shows John Bull himself upholding a wretched dissipated monarch against a wife, who, whatever her faults, was still a woman, and whatever her spirit—for she had much of it, and showed it grandly at need—was still a lady. Suffice it to say that "John Bull" was the most violent of the periodicals that attacked her, and that Theodore Hook, no Puritan himself, was the principal writer in that paper.

If you can imagine "Punch" turned Conservative, incorporated in one paper with the "Morning Herald," so that a column of news was printed side by side with one of a jocular character, and these two together devoted without principle to the support of a party, the attack of Whiggism, and an unblushing detractation of the character of one of our princesses, you can form some idea of what "John Bull" was in those days. There is, however, a difference: "Punch" attacks public characters, and ridicules public events; "John Bull" dragged out the most retired from their privacy, and attacked them with calumnies, for which, often, there was no foundation. Then, again, "Punch" is not nearly so bitter as was "John Bull:" there is not in the "London Charivari" a determination to say every thing that spite can invent against any particular set or party; there is a good-nature, still, in Master "Punch." It was quite the reverse in "John Bull," established for one purpose, and devoted to that. Yet the wit in Theodore's paper does not rise much higher than that of our modern laughing philosopher.

Of Hook's contributions the most remarkable was the "Ramsbottom Letters," in which Mrs. Lavinia Dorothea Ramsbottom describes all the *memory billions* of her various tours at home and abroad, always, of course, with more or less allusion to political affairs. The "fun" of these letters is very inferior to that of "Jeames" or of the "Snob Papers," and consists more in Malaprop absurdities and a wide range of bad puns, than in any real wit displayed in them. Of the style of both, we take an extract any where:

"Oh! Mr. Bull, Room is raley a beautiful place. We entered it by the Point of Molly, which is just like the Point and Sally at Porchmouth, only they call Sally there Port, which is not known in Room. The Tiber is a nice river; it looks yellow, but it does the same there as the Tames does here. We hired a carry-lettz and a cocky-olly to take us to the Church of Salt Peter, which is prodigious big; in the centre of the pizarro there is a basilisk very high, on the right and left two handsome foundlings; and the farcy, as Mr. Fulmer called it, is ornamented with collateral statutes of some of the Apostates."

We can quite imagine that Hook wrote many of these letters in his cups. Some are laughable enough, but the majority are so deplorably stupid, reeking with puns and scurrility, that when the temporary interest was gone, there was nothing left to attract a reader. It is scarcely possible to laugh at the Joe-Millerish mistakes, the old-world puns, and the trite stories of Hook "remains." Remains! indeed; they had better have remained where they were.

Besides prose of this kind, Hook contributed various jingles—there is no other name for them—arranged to popular tunes, and intended to become favorites with the country people. These, like the prose effusions, served the purpose of an hour, and have no interest now. Whether they were ever really popular remains to be proved. Certes, they are forgotten now, and long since even in the most conservative corners of the country. Many of these have the appearance of having been originally *recitati*, and their amusement must have depended chiefly on the face and manner of the singer—Hook himself; but in some he displayed that vice of rhyming which has often made nonsense go down, and which is tolerable only when introduced in the satire of a "Don Juan" or the first-rate mimicry of "Rejected Addresses." Hook had a most wonderful facility in concocting out-of-the-way rhymes, and a few verses from his song on Clubs will suffice for a good specimen of his talent:

"If any man loves comfort, and has little cash to buy it, he
Should get into a crowded club—a most select society;
While solitude and mutton-cutlets serve *infelix uxor*, he
May have his club (like Hercules), and revel there in luxury.
Bow, wow, wow, etc.

"Yes, clubs knock houses on the head; e'en Hatchett's can't demolish them;
Joy grieves to see their magnitude, and Long longs to abolish them.
The inns are out; hotels for single men scarce keep alive on it;
While none but houses that are in the family way thrive on it.
Bow, wow, wow, etc.

"There's first the Athenæum Club, so wise, there's not a man of it
That has not sense enough for six (in fact, that is the plan of it);
The very waiters answer you with eloquence Socratical;
And always place the knives and forks in order mathematical.
Bow, wow, wow, etc.

* * * * *

"E'en Isis has a house in town, and Cam abandons her city.
The master now hangs out at the Trinity University.

* * * * *

"The Union Club is quite superb; its best apartment daily is
The lounge of lawyers, doctors, merchants, beaux, *cum multis aliis.*

* * * * *

"The Travelers are in Pall Mall, and smoke cigars so cosily,
And dream they climb the highest Alps, or rove the plains of Moselai.

* * * * *

"These are the stages which all men propose to play their parts upon,
For *clubs* are what the Londoners have clearly set their *hearts* upon.
Bow, wow, wow, tiddy-iddy-iddy-iddy, bow, wow, wow," etc.

This is one of the harmless ballads of "Bull." Some of the political ones are scarcely fit to print in the present day. We can not wonder that ladies of a certain position gave out that they would not receive any one who took in this paper. It was scurrilous to the last degree, and Theodore Hook was the soul of it. He preserved his incognito so well that, in spite of all attempts to unearth him, it was many years before he could be certainly fixed upon as a writer in its columns. He even went to the length of writing letters and articles against himself, in order to disarm suspicion.

Hook now lived and thrived purely on literature. He published many novels—gone where the bad novels go, and unread in the present day, unless in some remote country town, which boasts only a very meagre circulating library. Improbability took the place of natural painting in them; punning supplied that of better wit; and personal portraiture was so freely used, that his most intimate friends—old Mathews, for instance—did not escape.

Meanwhile Hook, now making a good fortune, returned to his convivial life, and the enjoyment—if enjoyment it be—of general society. He "threw out his bow-window" on the strength of his success with "John Bull," and spent much more than he had. He mingled freely in all the London circles of thirty years ago, whose glory is still fresh in the minds of most of us, and every where his talent as an improvisatore, and his conversational powers, made him a general favorite.

Unhappy popularity for Hook! He, who was yet deeply in debt to the nation—who had an illegitimate family to maintain, who owed in many quarters more than he could ever hope to pay—was still fool enough to entertain largely, and receive both nobles and wits in the handsomest manner. Why did he not live quietly? why not, like Fox, marry the unhappy woman whom he had made the mother of his children, and content himself with trimming vines and rearing tulips? Why, forsooth? because he was Theodore Hook, thoughtless and foolish to the last. The jester of the people must needs be a fool. Let him take it to his conscience that he was not as much a knave.

In his latter years Hook took to the two dissipations most likely to bring him into misery—play and drink. He was utterly unfitted for the former, being too gay a spirit to sit down and calculate chances. He lost considerably, and the more he lost the more he played. Drinking became almost a necessity with him. He had a reputation to keep up in society, and had not the moral courage to retire from it altogether. Writing, improvising, conviviality, play, demanded stimulants. His mind was overworked in every sense. He had recourse to the only remedy, and in drink he found a temporary relief from anxiety, and a short-lived sustenance. There is no doubt that this man, who had amused London circles for many years, hastened his end by drinking.

It is not yet twenty years since Theodore Hook died. He left the world on August the 24th, 1841, and by this time he remains in the memory of men only as a wit that was, a punster, a hoaxer, a story-jester, with an ample fund of fun, but not as a great man in any way. Allowing every thing for his education—the times he lived in, and the unhappy error of his early life—we may admit that Hook was not, in character, the worst of the wits. He died in no odor of sanctity, but he was not a blasphemer or reviler, like others of his class. He ignored the bond of matrimony, yet he remained faithful to the woman he had betrayed; he was undoubtedly careless in the one responsible office with which he was intrusted, yet he can not be taxed, taking all in all, with deliberate peculation. His drinking and playing were bad—very bad. His improper connection was bad—very bad; but perhaps the worst feature in his career was his connection with "John Bull," and his ready giving in to a system of low libel. There is no excuse for this but the necessity of living; but Hook, had he retained any principle, might have made enough to live upon in a more honest manner. His name does, certainly, not stand out well among the wits of this country, but, after all, since all were so bad, Hook may be excused as not being the worst of them. *Requiescat in pace.*

SYDNEY SMITH.

"SMITH'S reputation"—to quote from Lord Cockburn's "Memorials of Edinburgh"—"here, then, was the same as it has been throughout his life, that of a wise wit." A wit he was, but we must deny him the reputation of being a beau. For that, nature, no less than his holy office, had disqualified him. Who that ever beheld him in a London drawing-room, when he went to so many dinners that he used to say he was a walking patty—who could ever miscall him a beau? How few years have we numbered since one perceived the large bulky form in canonical attire—the plain, heavy, almost ugly face, large, long, unredeemed by any expression, except that of sound hard sense—and thought, "can this be the Wit?" How few years is it since Henry Cockburn, hating London, and coming but rarely to what he called the "devil's drawing-room," stood near him, yet apart, for he was the most diffident of men; his wonderful luminous eyes, his clear, almost youthful, vivid complexion, contrasting brightly with the gray, pallid, prebendal complexion of Sydney? how short a time since Francis Jeffrey, the smallest of great men, a beau in his old age, a wit to the last, stood hat in hand to bandy words with Sydney ere he rushed off to some still gayer scene, some more fashionable circle: yet they are all gone—gone from sight, living in memory alone.

Perhaps it was time: they might have lived, indeed, a few short years longer; we might have heard their names among us; listened to their voices; gazed upon the deep hazel, ever-sparkling eyes, that constituted the charm of Cockburn's handsome face, and made all other faces seem tame and dead: we might have marveled at the ingenuity, the happy turns of expression, the polite sarcasm of Jeffrey; we might have reveled in Sydney Smith's immense natural gift of fun, and listened to the "wise wit," regretting, with Lord Cockburn, that so much worldly wisdom seemed almost inappropriate in one who should have been in some freer sphere than within the pale of holy orders: we might have done this, but the picture might have been otherwise. Cockburn, whose intellect rose, and became almost sublime, as his spirit neared death, might have sunk into the depression of conscious weakness; Jeffrey might have repeated himself, or turned hypochondriacal; Sydney Smith have grown garrulous: let us not grieve; they went in their prime of intellect, before one quality of mind had been touched by the frost-bite of age.

Sydney Smith's life is a chronicle of literary society. He was born in 1771, and he died in 1845. What a succession of great men does that period comprise! Scott, Jeffrey, Mackintosh, Dugald Stewart, Horner, Brougham, and Cockburn were his familiars—a constellation which has set, we fear, forever. Our world presents nothing like it: we must look back, not around us, for strong minds, cultivated up to the nicest point. Our age is too diffused, too practical for us to hope to witness again so grand a spectacle.

From his progenitors Sydney Smith inherited one of his best gifts, great animal spirits—the only spirits one wants in this racking life of ours; and his were transmitted to him by his father. That father, Mr. Robert Smith, was odd as well as clever. His oddities seem to have been coupled with folly; but that of Sydney was soberized by thought, and swayed by intense common sense. The father had a mania for buying and altering places: one need hardly say that he spoiled them. Having done so, he generally sold them; and *nineteen* various places were thus the source of expense to him and of injury to the pecuniary interests of his family.

This strange spendthrift married a Miss Olier, the daughter of a French emigrant from Languedoc. Every one may remember the charming attributes given by Miss Kavanagh, in her delicious tale, "Nathalie," to the French women of the South. This Miss Olier seems to have realized all one's ideas of the handsome, sweet-tempered, high-minded Southrons of *la belle France.* To her Sydney Smith traced his native gayety; her beauty did not, certainly, pass to him as well as to some of her other descendants. When Talleyrand was living in England as an emigrant, on intimate terms with Robert Smith, Sydney's brother, or Bobus, as he was called by his intimates, the conversation turned one day on hereditary beauty. Bobus spoke of his mother's personal perfections: "*Ah! mon ami,*" cried Talleyrand, "*c'était apparemment, monsieur: votre père qui n'était pas bien.*"

This Bobus was the schoolfellow at Eaton of Canning and Frere; and, with John Smith and those two youths, wrote the "Microcosm." Sydney, on the other hand, was placed, on the Foundation, at Winchester, which was then a stern place of instruction for a gay, spirited, hungry boy. Courtenay, his younger brother, went with him, but ran away twice. To owe one's education to charity was, in those days, to be half starved. Never was there enough, even of the coarsest food, to satisfy the boys, and the urchins, fresh from home, were left to fare as they might. "Neglect, abuse, and vice were," Sydney used to say, "the pervading evils of Winchester; and the system of teaching, if one may so call it, savored of the old monastic narrowness. . . . I believe, when a boy at school, I made above ten thousand Latin verses, and no man in his senses would dream of ever making another in after-life. So much for life and time wasted." The verse-inciting process is, nevertheless, remorselessly carried on during three years more at Oxford, and is much oftener the test of patient stupidity than of aspiring talent. Yet of what stupendous importance it is in the attainment of scholarships and prizes; and how zealous, how tenacious are dons and "coaches" in holding to that which far higher classics, the Germans, regard with contempt!

Sydney's proficiency promoted him to be captain of the school, and he left Winchester for New College, Oxford—one of the noblest and most abused institutions then of that grand university. Having obtained a scholarship, as a matter of course, and afterward a fellowship, he remarked that the usual bumpers of port wine at college were as much the order of the day among the Fellows as Latin verses among the under-graduates. We may not, however, picture to ourselves Sydney as partaking in the festivities of the common room; with more probability let us imagine him wandering with steady gait, even *after* Hall—a thing not either then or now certain in colleges—in those evergreen, leafy, varied gardens, flanked by that old St. Peter's church on the one side, and guarded by the high wall, once a fortification, on the other. He was poor, and therefore safe, for poverty is a guardian angel to an undergraduate, and work may protect even the Fellow from utter deterioration.

He was turned out into the world by his father with his hundred a year from the Fellowship, and never had a farthing from the old destroyer of country-seats afterward. He never owed a sixpence; nay, he paid a debt of thirty pounds, which Courtenay, who had no *iron* in his character, had incurred at Winchester, and had not the courage to avow. The next step was to choose a profession. The bar would have been Sydney's choice; but the Church was the choice of his father. It is the cheapest channel by which a man may pass into genteel poverty; "wit and independence do not make bishops," as Lord Cockburn remarks. We do not, however, regard, as he does, Sydney Smith as "lost" by being a churchman. He was happy, and made others happy; he was good, and made others good. Who can say the same of a successful barrister, or of a popular orator? His first sphere was in a curacy on Salisbury Plain; one of his earliest clerical duties was to marry his brother Robert (a barrister) to Miss Vernon, aunt to Lord Lansdown. "All I can tell you of the marriage," Sydney wrote to his mother, "is that he cried, she cried, I cried." It was celebrated in the library at Bowood, where Sydney so often enchanted the captivating circle afterward by his wit.

Nothing could be more gloomy than the young pastor's life on Salisbury Plain: "the first and poorest pauper of the hamlet," as he calls a curate, he was seated down among a few scattered cottages on this vast flat; visited even by the butcher's cart only once a week from Salisbury; accosted by few human beings; shunned by all who loved social life. But the probation was not long; and after being nearly destroyed by a thunder-storm in one of his rambles, he quitted Salisbury Plain, after two years, for a more genial scene.

There was a hospitable squire, a Mr. Beach, living in Smith's parish; the village of Netherhaven, near Amesbury. Mr. Beach had a son; the quiet Sundays at the Hall were enlivened by the curate's company at dinner, and Mr. Beach found his guest both amusing and sensible, and begged him to become tutor to the young squire. Smith accepted; and went away with his pupil, intending to visit Germany. The French Revolution was, however, at its height. Germany was impracticable, and "we were driven," Sydney wrote to his mother, "by stress of politics, into Edinburgh."

This accident—this seeming accident—was the foundation of Sydney Smith's opportunities; not of his success, for that his own merits procured, but of the direction to which his efforts were applied. He would have been eminent wherever destiny had led him; but he was thus made to be useful in one especial manner: "his lines had, indeed, fallen in pleasant places."

Edinburgh, in 1797, was not, it is almost needless to say, the Edinburgh of 1860. An ancient, picturesque, high-built looking city, with its wynds and closes, it had far more the characteristics of an old French *ville de Province* than of a northern capital. The foundation-stone of the new College was laid in 1789, but the building was not finished until more than forty years afterward. The edifice then stood in the midst of fields and gardens. "Often," writes Lord Cockburn, "did we stand to admire the blue and yellow crocuses rising through the clean earth in the first days of spring, in the house of Doctor Monro (the second), whose house stood in a small field entering from Nicolson street, within less than a hundred yards from the college."

The New Town was in progress when Sydney Smith and

his pupil took refuge in "Auld Reekie." With the rise of every street some fresh innovation in manners seemed also to begin. Lord Cockburn, wedded as he was to his beloved Reekie, yet unprejudiced and candid in all points, ascribes the change in customs to the intercourse with the English, and seems to date it from the Union. Thus the overflowing of the old town into fresh spaces "implied," as he remarks, "a general alteration of our habits."

As the dwellers in the Faubourg St. Germain regard their neighbors across the Seine, in the Faubourg St. Honoré, with disapproving eyes, so the sojourners in the Canongate and the Cowgate considered that the inundation of modern population vulgarized their "prescriptive gentilities." Cockburn's description of a Scottish assembly in the olden time is most interesting.

"For example, Saint Cecilia's Hall was the only public resort of the musical; and, besides being our most selectly fashionable place of amusement, was the best and most beautiful concert-room I have ever seen. And there have I myself seen most of our literary and fashionable gentlemen, predominating with their side curls and frills, and ruffles, and silver buckles; and our stately matrons stiffened in hoops, and gorgeous satin; and our beauties with high-heeled shoes, powdered and pomatumed hair, and lofty and composite head-dresses. All this was in the Cowgate; the last retreat nowadays of destitution and disease. The building still stands, though raised and changed. When I last saw it, it seemed to be partly an old-clothesman's shop and partly a brazier's." Balls were held in the beautiful rooms of George Square, in spite of the "New Town piece of presumption," that is, an attempt to force the fashionable dancers of the reel into the George Street apartments.

"And here," writes Lord Cockburn, looking back to the days when he was that "ne'er-do-weel" Harry Cockburn, "were the last remains of the ball-room discipline of the preceding age. Martinet dowagers and venerable beaux acted as masters and mistresses of ceremonies, and made all the preliminary arrangements. No couple could dance unless each party was provided with a ticket prescribing the precise place, in the precise dance. If there was no ticket, the gentleman or the lady was dealt with as an intruder, and turned out of the dance. If the ticket had marked upon it—say for a country-dance, the figures 3, 5, this meant that the holder was to place himself in the 3d dance, and 5th from the top; and if he was any where else, he was set right or excluded. And the partner's ticket must correspond. Woe on the poor girl who, with ticket 2, 7, was found opposite a youth marked 5, 9! It was flirting without a license, and looked very ill, and would probably be reported by the ticket director of that dance to the mother."

All this had passed away; and thus the aristocracy of a few individuals was ended; and society, freed from some of its restraints, flourished in another and more enlightened way than formerly.

There were still a sufficient number of peculiarities to gratify one who had an eye to the ludicrous. Sydney Smith soon discovered that it is a work of time to impart a humorous idea to a true Scot. "It requires," he used to say, "a surgical operation to get a joke well into a Scotch understanding." "They are so imbued with metaphysics, that they even make love metaphysically. I overheard a young lady of my acquaintance, at a dance in Edinburgh, exclaim in a sudden pause of the music, 'What you say, my Lord, is very true of love in the *abstract*, but—' here the fiddlers began fiddling furiously, and the rest was lost." He was, however, most deeply touched by the noble attribute of that nation which retains what is so rare—the attribute of being true friends. He did ample justice to their kindliness of heart. "If you meet with an accident," he said, "half Edinburgh immediately flocks to your doors to inquire after your *pure* hand, or your *pure* foot." "Their temper," he observed, "stands any thing but an attack on their climate; even Jeffrey can not shake off the illusion that myrtles flourish at Craig Crook." The sharp reviewer stuck to his myrtle allusions, and treated Smith's attempts with as much contempt as if he had been a "wild visionary, who had never breathed his caller air," nor suffered under the rigors of his climate, nor spent five years in "discussing metaphysics and medicine in that garret end of the earth—that knuckle end of England—that land of Calvin, oat-cakes, and sulphur," as Smith termed Scotland.

During two years he braved the winters in which he declared hackney-coaches were drawn by four horses on account of the snow; where men were blown flat down on the face by the winds; and where even "experienced Scotch fowls did not dare to cross the streets, but sidled along, tails aloft, without venturing to encounter the gale." He luxuriated, nevertheless, in the true Scotch supper, than which nothing more pleasant and more unwholesome has ever been known in Christendom. Edinburgh is said to have been the only place where people dined twice a day. The writer of this memoir is old enough to remember the true Scottish *Attic* supper before its final "fading into wine and water," as Lord Cockburn describes its decline. "Suppers," Cockburn truly says, "are cheaper than dinners," and Edinburgh, at that time, was the cheapest place in Great Britain. Port and sherry were the staple wines; claret, duty free in Scotland until 1780, was indeed beginning to be a luxury; it was no longer the ordinary beverage, as it was when—as Mackenzie, the author of the "Man of Feeling," described—it used, upon the arrival of a cargo, to be sent through the town on a cart with a horse before it, so that every one might have a sample, by carrying a jug to be filled for sixpence: still even at the end of the eighteenth century it was in frequent use. Whisky toddy and plotty (red wine mulled with spices) came into the supper-room in ancient flagons or *stoups*, after a lengthy repast of broiled chickens, roasted moorfowl, pickled mussels, flummery, and numerous other good things had been discussed by a party who ate as if they had not dined that day. "We will eat," Lord Cockburn used to say after a long walk, "a profligate supper," a supper without regard to discretion or digestion; and he usually kept his word.

In Edinburgh, Sydney Smith formed the intimate acquaintance of Lord Jeffrey, and that acquaintance ripened into a friendship only closed by death. The friendship of worthy, sensible men he looked upon as one of the greatest pleasures in life.

The "old suns," Lord Cockburn tells us, "were setting when the band of great thinkers and great writers, who afterward concocted the 'Edinburgh Review,' were rising into celebrity." Principal Robertson, the historian, had departed this life in 1793, a kindly old man. With beaming eyes underneath his frizzed and curled wig, and a trumpet tied with a black ribbon to the button-hole of his coat, for he was deaf, this most excellent of writers showed how he could be also the most zealous of diners. Old Adam Ferguson, the historian of Rome, had "set" also: one of the finest specimens of humanity had gone from among his people in him. Old people, not thirty years ago, delighted to tell you how "Adam," when chaplain to the Black Watch, that glorious 42d, refused to retire to his proper place, the rear, during an action, but persisted in being engaged in front. He was also gone; and Dugald Stewart filled his vacant place in the professorship of moral philosophy. Dr. Henry, the historian, was also at rest: after a long, laborious life, and the compilation of a dull, though admirable History of England, the design of which, in making a chapter on arts, manners, and literature separate from the narrative, appears to have suggested to Macaulay his inimitable disquisition on the same topics. Dr. Henry showed to a friend a pile of books which he had gone through merely to satisfy himself and the world as to what description of trowsers was worn by the Saxons. His death was calm as his life. "Come out to me directly," he wrote to his friend, Sir Harry Moncrieff: "I have got something to do this week; I have got to die."

It was in 1801 that Dugald Stewart began his course of lectures on political economy. Hitherto all public favor had been on the side of the Tories, and independence of thought was a sure way to incur discouragement from the Bench, in the Church, and from every government functionary. Lectures on political economy were regarded as innovations; but they formed a forerunner of that event which had made several important changes in our literary and political hemisphere: the commencement of the "Edinburgh Review." This undertaking was the work of men who were separated from the mass of their brother-townsmen by their politics, their isolation as a class binding them the more closely together by links never broken, in a brotherhood of hope and ambition to which the natural spirits of Sydney Smith, of Cockburn, and of Jeffrey gave an irresistible charm.

Among those who the most early in life ended a career of promise was Francis Horner. He was the son of a linen-draper in Edinburgh; or, as the Scotch called it, following the French, a merchant. Horner's best linen for sheets, and tablecloths, and all the *under garments* of housekeeping, are still highly esteemed by the trade.

"My desire to know Horner," Sydney Smith states, "arose from my being cautioned against him by some excellent and feeble-minded people to whom I brought letters of introduction, and who represented him as a person of violent political opinions." Sydney Smith interpreted this to mean that Horner was a man who thought for himself; who loved truth better than he loved Dundas (Lord Melville), then the tyrant of Scotland. "It is very curious to consider," Sydney Smith wrote, in addressing Lady Holland, in 1817, "in what manner Horner gained, in so extraordinary a degree, the affections of such a number of persons of both sexes—all ages, parties, and ranks in society; for he was not remarkably good-tempered, nor particularly lively and agreeable; and an inflexible politician on the unpopular side. The causes are, his high character for probity, honor, and talents; his fine countenance; the benevolent interest he took in the concerns of all his friends; his simple and gentlemanlike manners; his untimely death." "Grave, studious, honorable, kind, every thing Horner did," says Lord Cockburn, "was marked by thoughtfulness and kindness;" a beautiful character, which was exhibited but briefly to his contemporaries, but long remembered after his death.

Henry Brougham was another of the Edinburgh band of young spirits. He was educated in the High School under Luke Fraser, the tutor who trained Walter Scott and Francis Jeffrey. Brougham used to be pointed out "as the fellow who had beat the master." He had dared to differ with Fraser, a hot pedant, on some piece of Latinity. Fraser, irritated, punished the rebel, and thought the matter ended. But the next day "Harry," as they called him, appeared, loaded with books, renewed the charge, and forced Luke to own that he was beaten. "It was then," says Lord Cockburn, "that I first saw him."

After remaining two years in Edinburgh, Sydney Smith went southward to marry a former schoolfellow of his sister Maria's—a Miss Pybus, to whom he had been attached and engaged at a very early period of his life. The young lady, who was of West Indian descent, had some fortune; but her husband's only stock, on which to begin housekeeping, consisted of six silver tea-spoons, worn away with use. One day he rushed into the room and threw these attenuated articles into her lap: "There, Kate, I give you all my fortune, you lucky girl!"

With the small *dôt*, and the thin silver spoons, the young couple set up housekeeping in the "garret end of the earth." Their first difficulty was to know how money could be obtained to begin with, for Mrs. Smith's small fortune was settled on herself by her husband's wish. Two rows of pearls had been given her by her thoughtful mother. These she converted into money, and obtained for them £500. Several years afterward, when visiting the shop at which she sold them, with Miss Vernon and Miss Fox, Mrs. Smith saw her pearls, every one of which she knew. She asked what was the price. "£1500" was the reply.

The sum, however, was all important to the thrifty couple. It distanced the nightmare of the poor and honest—debt. £750 was presented by Mr. Beach, in gratitude for the care of his son, to Smith. It was invested in the funds, and formed the nucleus of future savings—"*Ce n'est que le premier pas qui coûte*," is a trite saying. "*C'est le premier pas qui gagne*," might be applied to this and similar cases. A little daughter —Lady Holland, the wife of the celebrated physician, Sir Henry Holland—was sent to bless the sensible pair. Sydney had wished that she might be born with one eye, so that he might never lose her; nevertheless, though she happened to be born with two, he bore her secretly from the nursery, a few hours after her birth, to show her in triumph to the future Edinburgh Reviewers.

The birth of the "Edinburgh Review" quickly followed that of the young lady. Jeffrey—then an almost starving barrister, living in the eighth or ninth flat of a house in Buccleuch Place—Brougham, and Sydney Smith were the triumvirate who propounded the scheme, Smith being the first mover. He proposed a motto: "Tenui Musam meditamur avena:" We cultivate literature on a little oatmeal; but this being too near the truth, they took their motto from Publius Syrus; "of whom," said Smith, "none of us had, I am sure, read a single line." To this undertaking Sydney Smith devoted his talents for more than twenty-eight years.

Meantime, during the brief remainder of his stay in Edinburgh, his circumstances improved. He had done that which most of the clergy are obliged to do—taken a pupil. He had now another, the son of Mr. Gordon, of Ellon; for each of these young men he received £400 a year. He became to them a father and a friend; he entered into all their amusements. One of them saying that he could not find conversation at the balls for his partners; "Never mind," cried Sydney Smith, "I'll fit you up in five minutes." Accordingly, he wrote down conversations for them amid bursts of laughter.

Thus happily did years, which many persons would have termed a season of adversity, pass away. The chance which brought him to Edinburgh introduced him to a state of society never likely to be seen again in Scotland. Lord Cockburn's "Memorials" afford an insight into manners, not only as regarded suppers, but on the still momentous point, of dinners. Three o'clock was the fashionable hour so late as the commencement of the present century. That hour, "not without groans and predictions," became four—and four was long and conscientiously adhered to. "Inch by inch," people yielded, and five continued to be the standard polite hour from 1806 to 1820. "Six has at length prevailed."

The most punctilious ceremony existed. When dinner was announced, a file of ladies went first in strict order of precedence. "Mrs. Colonel Such a One;" "Mrs. Doctor Such a One," and so on. Toasts were *de rigueur:* no glass of wine was to be taken by a guest without comprehending a lady, or a covey of ladies. "I was present," says Lord Cockburn, "when the late Duke of Buccleuch took a glass of sherry by himself at the table of Charles Hope, then Lord Advocate, and this was noticed as a piece of ducal contempt." Toasts, and, when the ladies had retired, *rounds* of toasts, were drunk. "The prandial nuisance," Lord Cockburn wrote, "was horrible. But it was nothing to what followed."

At these repasts, though less at these than at boisterous suppers, a frequent visitor at the same table with Sydney Smith was the illustrious Sir James Mackintosh, a man to whose deep-thinking mind the world is every day rendering justice. The son of a brave officer, Mackintosh was born on the banks of Loch Ness: his mother, a Miss Fraser, was aunt to Mrs. Fraser Tytler, wife of Lord Woodhouselee, one of the judges of the Court of Session, and mother of the late historian of that honored name.

Mackintosh had been studying at Aberdeen, in the same classes with Robert Hall, whose conversation, he avowed, had a great influence over his mind. He arrived in Edinburgh about 1784, uncertain to what profession to belong, somewhat anxious to be a bookseller, in order to revel in "the paradise of books;" he turned his attention, however, to medicine, and became a Brunonian, that is, a disciple of John Brown, the founder of a theory which he followed out to the extent in practice. The main feature of the now defunct system, which set scientific Europe in a blaze, seems to have been a mad indulgence of the passions, and an unbridled use of intoxicating liquors. Brown fell a victim to his vices. Years after he had been laid in his grave, his daughter, Euphemia, being in great indigence, received real kindness from Sir James and Lady Mackintosh, the former of whom used to delight in telling a story of her father's saying to her, "Effy, bring me the mood-erate stimulus of a hoondred draps o' laudanum in a glass o' brandy."

Mackintosh had not quitted Edinburgh when Sydney Smith reached it. Smith became a member of the famous Speculative Society. Their acquaintance was renewed years afterward in London. Who can ever forget the small, quiet dinners given by Mackintosh when living out of Parliament, and out of office, in Cadogan Place? Simple but genial were those repasts, forming a strong contrast to the Edinburgh dinners of yore. He had then long given up both the theory and practice of the Brunonians, and took nothing but light French and German wines, and these in moderation. His tall, somewhat high-shouldered, massive form; his calm brow, mild, thoughtful; his dignity of manner, his gentleness to all; his vast knowledge; his wonderful appreciation of excellence; his discrimination of faults—all combined to form one of the finest specimens ever seen even in that illustrious period, of a philosopher and historian.

Jeffrey and Cockburn were contrasts to one whom they honored. Jeffrey, "the greatest of British critics," was eight years younger than Mackintosh, having been born in 1773.

He was the son of one of the deputy clerks to the Supreme Court, not an elevated position, though one of great respectability. When Mackintosh and Sydney Smith first knew him in Edinburgh, he was enduring, with all the impatience of his sensitive nature, what he called a "slow, obscure, philosophical starvation" at the Scotch bar.

"There are moments," he wrote, "when I think I could sell myself to the ministers or to the devil, in order to get above these necessities." Like all men so situated, his depression came in fits. Short, spare, with regular, yet *not* aristocratic features, speaking, brilliant, yet *not* pleasing eyes; a voice consistent with that *mignon* form; a somewhat precise and anxious manner, there was never in Jeffrey that charm, that *abandon*, which rendered his valued friend, Henry Cockburn, the most delightful, the most beloved of men, the very idol of his native city.

The noble head of Cockburn, bald, almost in youth, with its pliant, refined features, and its fresh tint upon a cheek always clear, generally high in color, was a strong contrast to the rigid *petitesse* of Jeffrey's physiognomy; much more so to the large proportions of Mackintosh; or to the ponderous, plain, and, later in life, swarthy countenance of Sydney Smith. Lord Webb Seymour, the brother of the late Duke of Somerset, gentle, modest, intelligent—Thomas Thomson, the antiquary—and Charles and George Bell, the surgeon and the advocate—Murray, afterward Lord Murray, the generous pleader, who gave up to its rightful heirs an estate left him by a client—and Brougham—formed the staple of that set now long since extinct.

It was partially broken up by Sydney Smith's coming, in 1803, to London. He there took a house in Doughty Street, being partial to legal society, which was chiefly to be found in that neighborhood.

Here Sir Samuel Romilly, Mackintosh, Scarlett (Lord Abinger), the eccentric unhappy Mr. Ward, afterward Lord Dudley, "Conversation" Sharp, Rogers, and Luttrell, formed the circle in which Sydney delighted. He was still very poor, and obliged to sell the rest of his wife's jewels; but his brother Robert allowed him £100 a year, and lent him, when he subsequently removed into Yorkshire, £500.

He had now a life of struggling, but those struggles were the lot of his early friends also; Mackintosh talked of going to India as a lecturer; Smith recommended Jeffrey to do the same. Happily, both had the courage and the sense to await for better times at home; yet Smith's opinion of Mackintosh was, that "he never saw so theoretical a head which contained so much practical understanding;" and to Jeffrey he wrote:

"You want nothing to be a great lawyer, and nothing to be a great speaker, but a deeper voice—slower and more simple utterance—more humility of face and neck—and a greater contempt for *esprit* than men *who have so much* in general attain to."

The great event of Sydney Smith's first residence in London was his introduction at Holland House; in that "gilded room which furnished," as he said, "the best and most agreeable society in the world," his happiest hours were passed. John Allen, whom Smith had introduced to Lord Holland, was the peer's librarian and friend. Mackintosh, who Sydney Smith thought only wanted a few bad qualities to get on in the world, Rogers, Luttrell, Sheridan, Byron, were among the "suns" that shone where Addison had suffered and studied.

Between Lord Holland and Sydney Smith the most cordial friendship existed; and the eccentric and fascinating Lady Holland was his constant correspondent. Of this able woman it was said by Talleyrand: "*Elle est toute assertion; mais quand on demande la preuve c'est là son sécret.*" Of Lord Holland, the keen diplomatist observed: "*C'est la bienveillance même, mais la bienveillance la plus perturbatrice, qu'on ait jamais vue.*"

Lord Holland did not commit the error ascribed by Rogers, in his Recollections, to Marlay, Bishop of Waterford, who, when poor, with an income of only £400 a year, used to give the best dinners possible; but, when made a bishop, enlarged his table, and lost his fame—had no more good company—there was an end of his enjoyment: he had lords and ladies to his table—foolish people—foolish men—and foolish women—and there was an end of him and us. "Lord Holland selected his lords and ladies, not for their rank, but for their peculiar merits or acquirements." Then even Lady Holland's oddities were amusing. When she wanted to get rid of a fop, she used to say, "I beg your pardon, but I wish you would sit a little farther off; there is something on your handkerchief which I don't quite like." Or when a poor man happened to stand, after the fashion of the lords of creation, with his back to the chimney-piece, she would cry out, "Have the goodness, sir, to stir the fire."

Lord Holland never asked any one to dinner ("not even *me*," says Rogers, "whom he had known so long") without asking Lady Holland. One day, shortly before his lordship's death, Rogers was coming out from Holland House when he met him. "'Well, do you return to dinner?' I answered, 'No, I have not been invited.'" The precaution, in fact, was necessary, for Lord Holland was so good-natured and hospitable that he would have had a crowd daily at his table had he been left to himself.

The death of Lord Holland completely broke up the unrivaled dinners, and the subsequent evenings in the "gilded chamber." Lady Holland, to whom Holland House was left for her lifetime, declined to live there. With Holland House, the mingling of aristocracy with talent; the blending ranks by force of intellect; the assembling, not only of all the celebrity that Europe could boast, but of all that could enhance private enjoyment, has ceased. London, the most intelligent of capitals, possesses not one single great house in which pomp and wealth are made subsidiary to the true luxury of intellectual conversation.

On the morning of the day when Lord Holland's last illness began, these lines were written by him, and found after his death on his dressing-table:

"Nephew of Fox, and friend of Grey,
Sufficient for my fame;
If those who know me best shall say
I tarnished neither name."

Of him his best friend, Sydney Smith, left a short but discriminative character. "There was never (among other things he says) a better heart, or one more purified from all the bad passions—more abounding in charity and compassion—or which seemed to be so created as a refuge to the helpless and oppressed."

Meantime Sydney Smith's circumstances were still limited; £50 a year as evening preacher to the Foundling Hospital was esteemed as a great help by him. The writer of this memoir remembers an amusing anecdote related of him at the table of an eminent literary character by a member of Lord Woodhouselee's family, who had been desirous to obtain for Sydney the patronage of the godly. To this end she persuaded Robert Grant and Charles Grant (afterward Lord Glenelg) to go to the Foundling to hear him, she hoped, to advantage; to her consternation he broke forth into so familiar a strain, couched in terms so bordering on the jocose—though no one had deeper religious convictions than he had—that the two saintly brothers listened in disgust. They forgot how South let loose the powers of his wit and sarcasm; and how the lofty-minded Jeremy Taylor applied the force of humor to lighten the prolixity of argument. Sydney Smith became, nevertheless, a most popular preacher; but the man who prevents people from sleeping once a week in their pews is sure to be criticised.

Let us turn to him, however, as a member of society. His

A DROLL SCENE AT SYDNEY SMITH'S.

circle of acquaintance was enlarged, not only by his visits to Holland House, but by his lectures on moral philosophy at the Royal Institution. Sir Robert Peel, not the most impressionable of men, but one whose cold shake of the hand is said—as Sydney Smith said of Sir James Mackintosh—"to have come under the genus *Mortmain*," was a very young man at the time when Albemarle Street was crowded with carriages from one end of the street to the other, in consequence of Sydney Smith's lectures; yet he declared that he had never forgotten the effect given to the speech of Logan, the Indian chief, by Sydney's voice and manner.

His lectures produced a sum sufficient for Sydney to furnish a house in Orchard Street. Doughty Street—raised to celebrity as having been the residence, not only of Sydney Smith, but of Charles Dickens—was too far for the *habitué* of Holland House and the orator of Albemarle Street long to sojourn there. In Orchard Street Sydney enjoyed that domestic comfort which he called the "grammar of life;" delightful suppers to about twenty or thirty persons, who came and went as they pleased. A great part of the same amusing and gifted set used to meet once a week also at Sir James Mackintosh's at a supper, which, though not exactly Cowper's "radish and an egg," was simple but plentiful—yet most eagerly sought after. "There are few living," writes Sydney Smith's daughter, "who can look back to them, and I have always found them do so with a sigh of regret."

One night, a country cousin of Sydney Smith's was present at a supper. "Now, Sydney," whispered the simple girl, "I know all these are very remarkable people; do tell me who they are." "Oh, yes; there's Hannibal," pointing to a grave, dry, stern man, Mr. Whishaw; "he lost his leg in the Carthaginian war: there's Socrates," pointing to Luttrell: "that," he added, turning to Horner, "is Solon."

Another evening, Mackintosh brought a raw Scotch cousin —an ensign in a Highland regiment—with him. The young man's head could carry no idea of glory except in regimentals. Suddenly, nudging Sir James, he whispered, "Is that the great Sir Sidney Smith?" "Yes, yes," answered Sir James; and instantly telling Sydney who he was supposed to be, the grave evening preacher at the Foundling immediately assumed the character ascribed to him, and acted the hero of Acre to perfection, fighting his battles over again—even charging the Turks—while the young Scot was so enchanted by the great Sir Sidney's condescension, that he wanted to fetch the pipers of his regiment, and pipe to the great Sir Sydney, who had never enjoyed the agonizing strains of the bagpipe. Upon this the party broke up, and Sir James carried the Highlander off, lest he should find out his mistake, and cut his throat from shame and vexation. One may readily conceive Sydney Smith's enjoying this joke, for his spirits were those of a boy: his gayety was irresistible; his ringing laugh, infectious; but it is difficult for those who knew Mackintosh in his later years—the quiet, almost pensive invalid—to realize in that remembrance any trace of the Mackintosh of Doughty Street and Orchard Street days.

One day Sydney Smith came home with two hackney-coaches full of pictures, which he had picked up at an auction. His daughter thus tells the story: "Another day he came home with two hackney-coach loads of pictures, which he had met with at an auction, having found it impossible to resist so many yards of brown-looking figures and faded landscapes going for 'absolutely nothing, unheard-of sacrifices.' 'Kate' hardly knew whether to laugh or cry when she saw these horribly dingy-looking objects enter her pretty little drawing-room, and looked at him as if she thought him half mad; and half mad he was, but with delight at his purchase. He kept walking up and down the room, waving his arms, putting them in fresh lights, declaring they were exquisite specimens of art, and if not by the very best masters, merited to be so. He invited his friends, and displayed his pictures; discovered fresh beauties for each new comer; and for three or four days, under the magic influence of his wit and imagination, these gloomy old pictures were a perpetual source of amusement and fun."

At last, finding that he was considered no authority for the fine arts, off went the pictures to another auction, but all rechristened by himself with unheard-of names. "One, I remember," says Lady Holland, "was a beautiful landscape, by Nicholas de Falda, a pupil of Valdezzio, the only painting by that eminent artist. The pictures sold, I believe, for rather less than he gave for them under their original names, which were probably as real as their assumed ones."

Sydney Smith had long been styled by his friends the "Bishop of Mickleham," in allusion to his visits to, and influence in, the house of his friend, Richard Sharp, who had a cottage at that place. A piece of real preferment was now his. This was the living of Foston le Clay, in Yorkshire, given him by Lord Erskine, then Chancellor. Lady Holland never rested till she had prevailed on Erskine to give Sydney Smith a living. Smith, as Rogers relates, went to thank his lordship. "Oh," said Erskine, "don't thank me, Mr. Smith; I gave you the living because Lady Holland insisted on my doing so; and if she had desired me to give it to the devil, *he* must have had it."

Notwithstanding the prediction of the saints, Sydney Smith

proved an excellent parish priest. Even his most admiring friends did not expect this result. The general impression was, that he was infinitely better fitted for the bar than for the Church. "Ah! Mr. Smith," Lord Stowell used to say to him, "you would be in a far better situation, and a far richer man, had you belonged to us."

One *jeu d'esprit* more, and Smith hastened to take possession of his living, and to enter upon duties of which no one better knew the mighty importance than he did.

Among the Mackintosh set was Richard Sharp, to whom we have already referred, termed, from his great knowledge and ready memory, "Conversation Sharp." Many people may think that this did not imply an agreeable man, and they were, perhaps, right. Sharp was a plain, ungainly man. One evening, a literary lady, now living, was at Sir James Mackintosh's, in company with Sharp, Sismondi, and the late Lord Denman, then a man of middle age. Sir James was not only particularly partial to Denman, but admired him personally. "Do you not think Denman handsome?" he inquired of the lady after the guests were gone. "No? Then you must think Mr. Sharp handsome," he rejoined; meaning that a taste so perverted as not to admire Denman must be smitten with Sharp. Sharp is said to have studied all the morning before he went out to dinner, to get up his wit and anecdote, as an actor does his part. Sydney Smith having one day received an invitation from him to dine at Fishmongers' Hall, sent the following reply:

"Much do I love
The monsters of the deep to eat;
To see the rosy salmon lying,
By smelts encircled, born for frying;
And from the china boat to pour
On flaky cod the flavored shower.
Thee above all I much regard,
Flatter than Longman's flattest bard,
Much honor'd turbot! sore I grieve
Thee and thy dainty friends to leave.
Far from ye all, in snuggest corner,
I go to dine with little Horner;
He who with philosophic eye
Sat brooding o'er his Christmas pie;
Then firm resolved, with either thumb,
Tore forth the crust-enveloped plum;
And mad with youthful dreams of deathless fame,
Proclaimed the deathless glories of his name."

One word before we enter on the subject of Sydney Smith's ministry. In this biography of a great Wit, we touch but lightly upon the graver features of his character, yet they can not wholly be passed over. Stanch in his devotion to the

Church of England, he was liberal to others. The world in the present day is afraid of liberality. Let it not be forgotten that it has been the fanatic and the intolerant, not the mild and practical among us who have gone from the Protestant to the Romish faith. Sydney Smith, in common with other great men, had no predilection for dealing damnation round the land. How noble, how true, are Mackintosh's reflections on religious sects! "It is impossible, I think, to look into the interior of any religious sect without thinking better of it. I ought, indeed, to confine myself to those of Christian Europe, but with that limitation it seems to me the remark is true, whether I look at the Jansenists of Port Royal, or the Quakers in Clarkson, or the Methodists in these journals. All these sects, which appear dangerous or ridiculous at a distance, assume a much more amicable character on nearer inspection. They all inculcate pure virtue, and practise mutual kindness; and they exert great force of reason in rescuing their doctrines from the absurd or pernicious consequences which naturally flow from them. Much of this arises from the general nature of religious principle—much also from the genius of the Gospel."

Nothing could present a greater contrast with the comforts of Orchard Street than the place on which Sydney Smith's "lines" had now "fallen." Owing to the non-residence of the clergy, one third of the parsonage-houses in England had fallen into decay, but that of Foston le Clay was pre-eminently wretched. A hovel represented what was still called the parsonage-house: it stood on a glebe of three hundred acres of the stiffest clay in Yorkshire: a brick-floored kitchen, with a room above it, both in a ruinous condition, was the residence which, for a hundred and fifty years, had never been inhabited by an incumbent. It will not be a matter of surprise that for some time, until 1808, Sydney Smith, with the permission of the Archbishop of York, continued to reside in London, after having appointed a curate at Foston le Clay.

The first visit to his living was by no means promising. Picture to yourself, my reader, Sydney Smith, in a carriage, in his superfine black coat, driving into the remote village, and parleying with the old parish clerk, who, after some conversation, observed, emphatically, striking his stick on the ground, "Master Smith, it stroikes me that people as comes froe London is such *fools*." "I see *you* are no fool," was the prompt answer; and the parson and the clerk parted mutually satisfied.

The profits arising from the sale of two volumes of sermons carried Sydney Smith, his family, and his furniture to Foston

SYDNEY SMITH'S WITTY ANSWER TO THE OLD PARISH CLERK.

le Clay in the summer of 1809, and he took up his abode in a pleasant house about two miles from York, at Heslington.

Let us now, for a time, forget the wit, the editor of the "Edinburgh Review," the diner out, the evening preacher at the Foundling, and glance at the peaceful and useful life of a country gentleman. His spirits, his wit, all his social qualities, never deserted Sydney Smith, even in the retreat to which he was destined. Let us see him driving in his second-hand carriage, his horse "Peter the Cruel," with Mrs. Smith by his side, summer and winter, from Heslington to Foston le Clay. Mrs. Smith at first trembled at the inexperience of her charioteer; but "she soon," said Sydney, "raised my wages, and considered me an excellent Jehu." "Mr. Brown," said Sydney to one of the tradesmen of York, through the streets of which he found it difficult to drive, "your streets are the narrowest in Europe." "Narrow, sir? there's plenty of room for two carriages to pass each other, and an inch and a half to spare!"

Let us see him in his busy, peaceful life, digging an hour or two every day in his garden to avoid sudden death by preventing corpulency; then galloping through a book, and when his family laughed at him for so soon dismissing a quarto, saying, "Cross-examine me, then," and going well through the ordeal. Hear him, after finishing his morning's writing, saying to his wife, "There, Kate, it's done; do look over it, put the dots to the i's, and cross the t's;" and off he went to his walk, surrounded by his children, who were his companions and confidants. See him in the lane, talking to an old woman whom he had taken into his gig as she was returning from market, and picking up all sorts of knowledge from her; or administering medicine to the poor, or to his horses and animals, sometimes committing mistakes next to fatal. One day he declared he found all his pigs intoxicated, grunting "God save the King" about the sty. He nearly poisoned his red cow by an over-dose of castor-oil; and Peter the Cruel, so called because the groom said he had a cruel face, took two boxes of opium pills (boxes and all) in his mash without ill consequences.

See him, too, rushing out after dinner—for he had a horror of long sittings after that meal—to look at his "scratcher." He used to say, Lady Holland (his daughter) relates, "I am all for cheap luxuries, even for animals; now all animals have a passion for scratching their back-bones; they break down your gates and palings to effect this. Look! there is my universal scratcher, a sharp-edged pole, resting on a high and a low post, adapted to every height, from a horse to a lamb.

Even the Edinburgh Reviewer can take his turn: you have no idea how popular it is; I have not had a gate broken since I put it up; I have it in all my fields."

Then his experiments were numerous. Mutton fat was to be burned instead of candles; and working people were brought in and fed with broth, or with rice, or with porridge, to see which was the most satisfying diet. Economy was made amusing, benevolence almost absurd, but the humorous man, the kind man, shone forth in all things. He was one of the first, if not the first, who introduced allotment-gardens for the poor: he was one who could truly say at the last, when he had lived sixty-six years, "I have done but very little harm in the world, and I have brought up my family."

We have taken a glimpse—and a glimpse merely—of the "wise wit" in London, among congenial society, where every intellectual power was daily called forth in combative force. See him now in the provincial circles of the remote county of York. "Did you ever," he once asked, "dine out in the country? What misery do human beings inflict on each other under the name of pleasure!" Then he describes driving in a broiling sun through a dusty road, to eat a haunch of venison at the house of a neighboring parson. Assembled in a small house, "redolent of frying," talked of roads, weather, and turnips: began, that done, to be hungry. A stripling, caught up for the occasion, calls the master of the house out of the room, and announces that the cook has mistaken the soup for dirty water, and thrown it away. No help for it—agreed: they must do without it; perhaps as well they should. Dinner announced; they enter the dining-room: heavens! what a gale! the venison is high!

Various other adverse incidents occur, and the party return home, grateful to the post-boys for not being drunk, and thankful to Providence for not being thrown into a wet ditch.

In addition to these troubles and risks, there was an enemy at hand to apprehend—prejudice. The Squire of Heslington —"the last of the Squires"—regarded Mr. Smith as a Jacobin; and his lady, "who looked as if she had walked straight out of the Ark, or had been the wife of Enoch," used to turn aside as he passed. When, however, the squire found "the peace of the village undisturbed, harvests as usual, his dogs uninjured, he first bowed, then called, and ended by a pitch of confidence;" actually discovered that Sydney Smith had made a joke; nearly went into convulsions of laughter, and finished by inviting the "dangerous fellow," as he had once thought him, to see his dogs.

In 1813 Sydney Smith removed, as he thought it his duty

to do, to Foston le Clay, and, "not knowing a turnip from a carrot," began to farm three hundred acres, and, not having any money, to build a parsonage-house.

It was a model parsonage, he thought, the plan being formed by himself and "Kate." Being advised by his neighbors to purchase oxen, he bought (and christened) four oxen, "Tug and Lug," "Crawl and Haul." But Tug and Lug took to fainting, Haul and Crawl to lie down in the mud, so he was compelled to sell them, and to purchase a team of horses.

The house plunged him into debt for twenty years; and a man-servant being too expensive, the "wise Wit" caught up a country girl, "made like a mile-stone," and christened her "Bunch," and Bunch became the best butler in the county.

He next set up a carriage, which he christened the "Immortal," for it grew, from being only an ancient green chariot, supposed to have been the earliest invention of the kind, to be known by all the neighbors; the village dogs barked at it, the village boys cheered it, and "we had no false shame."

One could linger over the annals of Sydney Smith's useful, happy life at Foston le Clay, visited there, indeed, by Mackintosh, and each day achieving a higher and higher reputation in literature. We see him as a magistrate, "no friend to game," as a country squire in Suffolk solemnly said of a neighbor, but a friend to man; with a pitying heart, that forbade him to commit young delinquents to jail, though he would lecture them severely, and call out, in bad cases, "John, bring me out my *private gallows*," which brought the poor boys on their knees. We see him making visits, and even tours, in the "Immortal," and receiving Lord and Lady Carlisle in their coach and four, which had stuck in the middle of a plowed field, there being scarcely any road, only a lane up to the house. Behold him receiving his poor friend, Francis Horner, who came to take his last leave of him, and died at Pisa in 1817, after earning honors paid, as Sir James Mackintosh remarked, to intrinsic claims alone—"a man of obscure birth, who never filled an office." See Sydney Smith, in 1816, from the failure of the harvest (he who was in London "a walking patty"), sitting down with his family to repasts without bread, thin, unleavened cakes being the substitute. See his cheerfulness, his submission to many privations: picture him to ourselves trying to ride, but falling off incessantly; but obliged to leave off riding "for the good of his family and the peace of his parish" (he had christened his horse Calamity). See him suddenly prostrate from that steed in the midst of the streets of York, "to the great joy of Dissenters," he declares: another time flung, as if he had been a shuttlecock, into a neighboring parish, very glad that it was not a neighboring planet, for somehow or other his horse and he had a "trick of parting company." "I used," he wrote, "to think a fall from a horse dangerous, but much experience has convinced me to the contrary. I have had six falls in two years, and just behaved like the Three per Cents., when they fell—I got up again, and am not a bit the worse for it, any more than the stock in question."

His country life was varied by many visits. In 1820 he went to visit Lord Grey, then to Edinburgh, to Jeffrey. Traveling by the coach, a gentleman, with whom he had been talking, said, "There is a very clever fellow lives near here, Sydney Smith, I believe—a devilish odd fellow." "He may be an odd fellow," cried Sydney, taking off his hat, "but here he is, odd as he is, at your service."

Sydney Smith found great changes in Edinburgh—changes, however, in many respects for the better. The society of Edinburgh was then in its greatest perfection. "Its brilliancy," Lord Cockburn remarks, "was owing to a variety of peculiar circumstances, which only operated during this period." The principal of these were "the survivance of several of the eminent men of the preceding age, and of curious old habits, which the modern flood had not yet obliterated; the rise of a powerful community of young men of ability; the exclusion of the British from the Continent, which made this place, both for education and for residence, a favorite resort of strangers; the war, which maintained a constant excitement of military preparation and of military idleness; the blaze of that popular literature which made this the second city in the empire for learning and science; and the extent and the ease with which literature and society embellished each other, without rivalry, and without pedantry."

Among the "best young," as his lordship styles them, were Lord Webb Seymour and Francis Horner; while those of the "interesting old" most noted were Elizabeth Hamilton and Mrs. Grant of Laggan, who had "unfolded herself," to borrow Lord Cockburn's words, in the "Letters from the Mountains," "an interesting treasury of good solitary thoughts." Of these two ladies, Lord Cockburn says, "They were excellent women, and not *too* blue. Their sense covered the color." It was to Mrs. Hamilton that Jeffrey said, "That there was no objection to the blue stocking, provided the petticoat came low enough to cover it." Neither of these ladies possessed personal attractions. Mrs. Hamilton had the plain face proper to literary women; Mrs. Grant was a tall, dark woman, with much dignity of manner: in spite of her life of misfortune, she had a great flow of spirits. Beautifully, indeed, does Lord Cockburn render justice to her character: "She was always under the influence of an affectionate and delightful enthusiasm, which, unquenched by time and sorrow, survived the wreck of many domestic attachments, and shed a glow over the close of a very protracted life."

Both she and Mrs. Hamilton succeeded in drawing to their *conversazioni*, in small rooms of unpretending style, men of the highest order, as well as attractive women of intelligence. Society in Edinburgh took the form of Parisian *soireés*, and, although much divided into parties, was sufficiently general to be varied. It is amusing to find that Mrs. Grant was at one time one of the supposed "Authors of 'Waverley,'" until the disclosure of the mystery silenced reports. It was the popularity of "Marmion" that made Scott, as he himself confesses, nearly lose his footing. Mrs. Grant's observation on him, after meeting the Great Unknown at some brilliant party, has been allowed, even by the sarcastic Lockhart, to be "witty enough." "Mr. Scott always seems to me to be like a glass, through which the rays of admiration pass without sensibly affecting it; but the bit of paper* that lies beside it will presently be in a blaze—and no wonder."

Scott endeavored to secure Mrs. Grant a pension; merited, as he observes, by her as an authoress, "but much more," in his opinion, "by the firmness and elasticity of mind with which she had borne a great succession of domestic calamities." "Unhappily," he adds, "there was only about £100 open on the Pension List, and this the minister assigned in equal portions to Mrs. G—— and a distressed lady, granddaughter of a forfeited Scottish nobleman. Mrs. G——, proud as a Highlandwoman, vain as a poetess, and absurd as a blue-stocking, has taken this partition in *malam partem*, and written to Lord Melville about her merits, and that her friends do not consider her claims as being fairly canvassed, with something like a demand that her petition be submitted to the king. This is not the way to make her *plack* a *bawbee*, and Lord M——, a little *miffed* in turn, sends the whole correspondence to me to know whether Mrs. G—— will accept the £50 or not. Now, hating to deal with ladies when they are in an unreasonable humor, I have got the good-humored Man of Feeling to find out the lady's mind, and I take on myself the task of making her peace with Lord M——. After all, the poor lady is greatly to be pitied; her sole remaining daughter deep and far gone in a decline."

The Man of Feeling proved successful, and reported soon

* Alluding to Lady Scott.

afterward that the "dirty pudding" was eaten by the almost destitute authoress. Scott's tone in the letters which refer to this subject does little credit to his good taste and delicacy of feeling, which were really attributable to his character.

Very few notices occur of any intercourse between Scott and Sydney Smith in Lockhart's "Life." It was not, indeed, until 1827 that Scott could be sufficiently cooled down from the ferment of politics which had been going on to meet Jeffrey and Cockburn. When he dined, however, with Murray, then Lord Advocate, and met Jeffrey, Cockburn, the late Lord Rutherford, then Mr. Rutherford, and others of "that file," he pronounced the party to be "very pleasant, capital good cheer, and excellent wine, much laugh and fun. I do not know," he writes, "how it is, but when I am out with a party of my Opposition friends, the day is often merrier than when with our own set. Is it because they are cleverer? Jeffrey and Harry Cockburn are, to be sure, very extraordinary men, yet it is not owing to that entirely. I believe both parties meet with the feeling of something like novelty. We have not worn out our jests in daily contact. There is also a disposition on such occasions to be courteous, and of course to be pleased."

On his side, Cockburn did ample justice to the "genius who," to use his own words, "has immortalized Edinburgh and delighted the world." Mrs. Scott could not, however, recover the smarting inflicted by the critiques of Jeffrey on her husband's works. Her "And I hope, Mr. Jeffrey, Mr. Constable paid you well for your article" (Jeffrey dining with her that day), had a depth of simple satire in it that even an Edinburgh reviewer could hardly exceed. It was, one must add, impertinent and in bad taste. "You are very good at cutting up."

Sydney Smith found Jeffrey and Cockburn rising barristers. Horner, on leaving Edinburgh, had left to Jeffrey his bar wig, and the bequest had been lucky. Jeffrey was settled at Craigcrook, a lovely English-looking spot, with wooded slopes and green glades, near Edinburgh; and Cockburn had, since 1811, set up his rural gods at Bonally, near Colinton, just under the Pentland Hills, and he wrote, "Unless some avenging angel shall expel me, I shall never leave that Paradise." And a paradise it was. Beneath those rough, bare hills, broken here and there by a trickling burn, like a silver thread on the brown sward, stands a Norman tower, the addition, by Playfair's skill, to what was once a scarcely-habitable farm-house. That tower contained Lord Cockburn's fine library, also his ordinary sitting-rooms. There he read, and wrote, and received such society as will never meet again, there or elsewhere—among them Sydney Smith. Beneath—around the tower—stretches a delicious garden, composed of terraces, and laurel-hedged walks, and beds of flowers, that blossomed freely in that sheltered spot. A bowling-green, shaded by one of the few trees near the house, a sycamore, was the care of many an hour; for, to make the turf velvety, the sods were fetched from the hills above—from "yon hills," as Lord Cockburn would have called them. And this was, for many years, one of the rallying-points of the best Scottish society, and, as each autumn came round, of what the host called his carnival. Friends were summoned from the north and the south—"death no apology." High jinks within doors, excursions without. Every Edinburgh man reveres the spot, hallowed by the remembrance of Lord Cockburn. "Every thing except the two burns," he wrote, "the few old trees, and the mountains, are my own work. Human nature is incapable of enjoying more happiness than has been my lot here. I have been too happy, and often tremble in the anticipation that the cloud must come at last." And come it did; but found him not unprepared, although the burden that he had to bear in after life was heavy. In their enlarged and philosophic minds, in their rapid transition from sense to nonsense, there was an affinity in the character of Sydney Smith and of Lord Cockburn which was not carried out in any other point. Smith's conversation was wit—Lord Cockburn's was eloquence.

From the festivities of Edinburgh Sydney Smith returned contentedly to Foston le Clay and to Bunch. Among other gifted visitors was Mrs. Marcet. "Come here, Bunch," cries Sydney Smith one day; "come and repeat your crimes to Mrs. Marcet." Then Bunch, grave as a judge, began to repeat: "Plate-snatching, gravy-spilling, door-slamming, blue-bottle-fly catching, and courtesy-bobbing." "Blue-bottle-fly catching" means standing with her mouth open, and not attending; and "courtesy-bobbing" was courtesying to the centre of the earth.

One night in the winter, during a tremendous snow-storm, Bunch rushed in, exclaiming, "Lord and Lady Mackincrush is com'd in a coach and four." The lord and lady proved to be Sir James and his daughter, who had arrived to stay with his friends in the remote parsonage of Foston le Clay a few days, and had sent a letter, which arrived the day afterward, to announce their visit. Their stay began with a blunder; and when Sir James departed, leaving kind feelings behind him, books, his hat, his gloves, his papers, and other articles of apparel, were found also. "What a man that would be," said Sydney Smith, "had he one particle of gall, or the least knowledge of the value of red tape!" It was true that the indolent, desultory character of Mackintosh interfered perpetually with his progress in the world. He loved far better to lie on the sofa reading a novel than to attend a Privy Council; the slightest indisposition was made on his part a plea for avoiding the most important business.

Sydney Smith had said that when "a clever man takes to cultivating turnips and retiring, it is generally an imposture;" but in him the retirement was no imposture. His wisdom shone forth daily in small and great matters. "Life," he justly thought, "was to be fortified by many friendships," and he acted up to his principles, and kept up friendships by letters. Cheerfulness he thought might be cultivated by making the rooms one lives in as comfortable as possible. His own drawing-room was papered, on this principle, with a yellow flowering pattern, and filled with "irregular regularities;" his fires were blown into brightness by *Shadrachs*, as he called them —tubes furnished with air opening in the centre of each fire. His library contained his rheumatic armor; for he tried heat and compression in rheumatism; put his leg into narrow buckets, which he called his jack-boots; wore round his throat a tin collar; over each shoulder he had a large tin thing like a shoulder of mutton; and on his head he displayed a hollow helmet filled with hot water. In the middle of a field into which his windows looked was a skeleton sort of a machine, his Universal Scratcher, with which every animal, from a lamb to a bullock, could scratch itself. Then on the Sunday the Immortal was called into use, to travel in state to a church like a barn; about fifty people in it; but the most original idea was farming through the medium of a tremendous speaking-trumpet from his own door, with its companion, a telescope, to see what his people are about! On the 24th of January, 1828, the first notable piece of preferment was conferred on him by Lord Lyndhurst, then Chancellor, and of widely differing political opinions to Sydney Smith. This was a vacant stall in the cathedral at Bristol, where, on the ensuing 5th of November, the new canon gave the Mayor and Corporation of that Protestant city such a dose of "toleration as should last them many a year." He went to court on his appointment, and appeared in shoestrings instead of buckles. "I found," he relates, "to my surprise, people looking down at my feet: I could not think what they were at. At first I thought they had discovered the beauty of my legs; but at last the truth burst on me, by some wag laughing and thinking I had done it as a good joke. I was, of course, exceedingly annoyed to have been supposed capable of such a vulgar, unmeaning piece of disrespect, and kept my feet as coyly under my petticoats as the veriest prude in the country, till I should make my escape." His circumstances were now improved, and though moralists, he said, thought property an evil, he declared himself happier every guinea he gained. He thanked God for his animal spirits, which received, unhappily, in 1829, a terrible shock from the death of his eldest son, Douglas, aged twenty-four. This was the great misfortune of his life; the young man was promising, talented, affectionate. He exchanged Foston le Clay at this time for a living in Somersetshire, of a beautiful and characteristic name—Combe Florey.

Combe Florey seems to have been an earthly paradise, seated in one of those delicious hollows, or combes, for which that part of the west of England is celebrated. His withdrawal from the Edinburgh Review, Mackintosh's death, the marriage of his eldest daughter, Saba, to Dr. Holland (now Sir Henry Holland), the termination of Lord Grey's Administration, which ended Sydney's hopes of being a bishop, were the leading events in his life for the next few years.

It appears that Sydney Smith felt to the hour of his death pained that those by whose side he had fought for fifty years, in their adversity, the Whig party, should never have offered what he declared he should have rejected, a bishopric, when they were constantly bestowing such promotions on persons of mediocre talent and claims. Waiving the point whether it is right or wrong to make men bishops because they have been political partisans, the cause of this alleged injustice may be found in the tone of the times, which was eminently tinctured with cant. The Clapham sect were in the ascendency; and Ministers scarcely dared to offend so influential a body. Even the gentle Sir James Mackintosh refers, in his Journal, with disgust to the phraseology of the day:

"They have introduced a new language, in which they never say that A. B. is good, or virtuous, or even religious; but that he is an 'advanced Christian.' Dear Mr. Wilberforce is an 'advanced Christian.' Mrs. C. has lost three children without a pang, and is so 'advanced a Christian' that she could see the remaining twenty, 'with poor dear Mr. C.,' removed with perfect tranquillity."

Such was the disgust expressed toward that school by Mackintosh, whose last days were described by his daughter as having been passed in silence and thought, with his Bible before him, breaking that silence—and portentous silence—to speak of God, and of his Maker's disposition toward man. His mind ceased to be occupied with speculations; politics interested him no more. His own "personal relationship to his Creator" was the subject of his thoughts. Yet Mackintosh was not by any means considered as an advanced Christian, or even as a Christian at all by the zealots of his time.

Sydney Smith's notions of a bishop were certainly by no means carried out in his own person and character. "I never remember in my time," he said, "a real bishop; a grave, elderly man, full of Greek, with sound views of the middle voice and preterpluperfect tense; gentle and kind to his poor clergy, of powerful and commanding eloquence in Parliament, never to be put down when the great interests of society were concerned, leaning to the Government when it was right, leaning to the people when they were right; feeling that if the Spirit of God had called him to that high office, he was called for no mean purpose, but rather that seeing clearly, acting boldly, and intending purely, he might confer lasting benefit upon mankind."

In 1831 Lord Grey appointed Sydney Smith a Canon Residentiary of St. Paul's; but still the mitre was withheld, although it has since appeared that Lord Grey had destined him for one of the first vacancies in England.

Henceforth his residence at St. Paul's brought him still more continually into the world, which he delighted by his "wise wit." Most London dinners, he declared, evaporated in whispers to one's next neighbors. He never, however, spoke to his neighbor, but "fired" across the table. One day, however, he broke this rule, on hearing a lady, who sat next him, say in a sweet, low voice, "No gravy, sir." "Madam," he cried, "I have all my life been looking for a person who disliked gravy; let us swear immortal friendship." She looked astonished, but took the oath, and kept it. "What better foundation for friendship," he asks, "than similarity of tastes?"

He gave an evening party once a week, when a profusion of wax-lights was his passion. He loved to see young people decked with natural flowers; he was, in fact, a blameless and benevolent Epicurean in every thing; great indeed was the change from his former residence at Foston, which he used to say was twelve miles from a lemon. Charming as his parties at home must have been, they wanted the *bonhommie* and simplicity of former days, and of the homely suppers in Orchard Street. Lord Dudley, Rogers, Moore, "Young Macaulay," as he was called for many years, formed now his society. Lord Dudley was then in the state which afterward became insanity, and darkened completely a mind sad and peculiar from childhood. Bankes, in his "Journal," relates an anecdote of him about this time, when, as he says, "Dudley's mind was on the wane; but still his caustic humor would find vent through the cloud that was gradually overshadowing his masterly intellect." He was one day sitting in his room soliloquizing aloud; his favorite Newfoundland dog was at his side, and seemed to engross all his attention. A gentleman was present who was good-looking and good-natured, but not overburdened with sense. Lord Dudley at last, patting his dog's head, said, "Fido mio, they say dogs have no souls. Humph, and still they say ——" (naming the gentleman present) "has a soul!" One day Lord Dudley met Mr. Allen, Lord Holland's librarian, and asked him to dine with him. Allen went. When asked to describe his dinner, he said, "There was no one there. Lord Dudley talked a little to his servant, and a great deal to his dog, but said not one word to me."

Innumerable are the witticisms related of Sydney Smith, when seated at a dinner-table, having swallowed in life what he called a "Caspian Sea" of soup. Talking one day of Sir Charles Lyell's book, the subject of which was the phenomena which the earth might, at some future period, present to the geologists—"Let us imagine," he said, "an excavation on the site of St. Paul's; fancy a lecture by the Owen of his future era on the thigh-bone of a minor canon, or the tooth of a dean: the form, qualities, and tastes he would discover from them." "It is a great proof of shyness," he said, "to crumble your bread at dinner. Ah! I see," he said, turning to a young lady, "you're afraid of me; you crumble your bread. I do it when I sit by the Bishop of London, and with both hands when I sit by the Archbishop."

He gave a capital reproof to a lively young M. P. who was accompanying him after dinner to one of the solemn evening receptions at Lambeth Palace during the life of the late Archbishop of Canterbury. The M. P. had been calling him "Smith," though they had never met before that day. As the carriage stopped at the Palace, Smith turned to him and said, "Now don't, my good fellow, don't call the Archbishop 'Howley.'"

Talking of fancy balls—"Of course," he said, "if I went to one, I should go as a Dissenter." Of Macaulay he said, "To take him out of literature and science, and to put him in the House of Commons, is like taking the chief physician out of London in a pestilence."

Nothing amused him so much as the want of perception of a joke. One hot day a Mrs. Jackson called on him, and spoke of the oppressive state of the weather. "Heat! it was dreadful," said Sydney; "I found I could do nothing for it but take off my flesh and sit in my bones." "Take off your flesh and sit in your bones! Oh, Mr. Smith, how could you do that?"

the lady cried. "Come and see next time, ma'am—nothing more easy." She went away, however, convinced that such a proceeding was very unorthodox. No wonder, with all his various acquirements, it should be said of him that no "dull dinners were ever remembered in his company."

A happy old age concluded his life, at once brilliant and useful. To the last he never considered his education as finished. His wit, a friend said, "was always fresh, always had the dew on it." He latterly got into what Lord Jeffrey called the vicious habit of water-drinking. Wine, he said, destroyed his understanding. He even "forgot the number of the Muses, and thought it was thirty-nine of course." He agreed with Sir James Mackintosh that he had found the world more good and more foolish than he had thought when young. He took a cheerful view of all things; he thanked God for small as well as great things, even for tea. "I am glad," he used to say, "I was not born before tea." His domestic affections were strong, and were heartily reciprocated.

General society he divided into classes: "The noodles—very numerous and well known. The affliction woman—a valuable member of society, generally an ancient spinster in small circumstances, who packs up her bag and sets off in cases of illness or death, 'to comfort, flatter, fetch, and carry.' The up-takers—people who see from their fingers' ends, and go through a room touching every thing. The clearers—who begin at a dish and go on tasting and eating till it is finished. The sheep-walkers—who go on forever on the beaten track. The lemon-squeezers of society—who act on you as a wet blanket; see a cloud in sunshine; the nails of the coffin in the ribbons of a bride; extinguish all hope; people whose very look sets your teeth on an edge. The let-well-aloners, cousin-german to the noodles—yet a variety, and who are afraid to act, and think it safer to stand still. Then the washerwomen—very numerous! who always say, "Well, if ever I put on my best bonnet, 'tis sure to rain,' etc.

"Besides this, there is a very large class of people always treading on your gouty foot, or talking in your deaf ear, or asking you to give them something with your lame hand," etc.

During the autumn of the year 1844, Sydney Smith felt the death-stroke approaching. "I am so weak, both in body and mind," he said, "that I believe, if the knife were put into my hand, I should not have strength enough to stick it into a Dissenter." In October he became seriously ill. "Ah! Charles," he said to General Fox (when he was being kept very low), "I wish they would allow me even the wing of a roasted butterfly." He dreaded sorrowful faces around him, but confided to his old servant, Annie Kay—and to her alone—his sense of his danger.

Almost the last person Sydney Smith saw was his beloved brother Bobus, who followed him to the grave a fortnight after he had been laid in the tomb.

He lingered till the 22d of February, 1845. His son closed his eyes. His last act was bestowing on a poverty-stricken clergyman a living.

He was buried at Kensal Green, where his eldest son, Douglas, had been interred.

It has been justly and beautifully said of Sydney Smith, that Christianity was not a dogma with him, but a practical and most beneficent rule of life.

As a clergyman, he was liberal, practical, stanch; free from the latitudinarian principles of Hoadley, as from the bigotry of Laud. His wit was the wit of a virtuous, a decorous man; it had pungency without venom; humor without indelicacy; and was copious without being tiresome.

GEORGE BUBB DODINGTON, LORD MELCOMBE.

"It would have been well for Lord Melcombe's memory," Horace Walpole remarks, "if his fame had been suffered to rest on the tradition of his wit and the evidence of his poetry." And, in the present day, that desirable result has come to pass. We remember Bubb Dodington chiefly as the courtier whose person, houses, and furniture were replete with costly ostentation, so as to provoke the satire of Foote, who brought him on the stage under the name of Sir Thomas Lofty in "The Patron."

We recall him most as "*l'Amphytrion chez qui on dine*:" "My Lord of Melcombe," as Mallett says,

> "Whose soups and sauces duly season'd,
> Whose wit well timed and sense well reason'd,
> Give Burgundy a brighter stain,
> And add new flavor to Champagne."

Who now cares much for the court intrigues which severed Sir Robert Walpole and Bubb Dodington? Who now reads without disgust the annals of that famous quarrel between George II. and his son, during which each party devoutly wished the other dead? Who minds whether the time-serving Bubb Dodington went over to Lord Bute or not? Who cares whether his hopes of political preferment were or were not gratified? Bubb Dodington was, in fact, the dinner-giving lordly poet, to whom even the saintly Young could write,

> "You give protection—I a worthless strain."

Born in 1691, the accomplished courtier answered, till he had attained the age of twenty-nine, to the not very euphonious name of Bubb. Then a benevolent uncle with a large estate died, and left him, with his lands, the more exalted surname of Dodington. He sprang, however, from an obscure family, who had settled in Dorchester; but that disadvantage, which, according to Lord Brougham's famous pamphlet, acts so fatally on a young man's advancement in English public life, was obviated, as most things are, by a great fortune.

Mr. Bubb had been educated at Oxford. At the age of twenty-four he was elected M. P. for Winchelsea; he was soon afterward named Envoy at the Court of Spain, but returned home after his accession of wealth to provincial honors, and became Lord-Lieutenant of Somerset. Nay, poets began to worship him, and even to pronounce him to be well born:

"Descended from old British sires;
Great Dodington to kings allied;
My patron then, my laurels' pride."

It would be consolatory to find that it is only Welsted who thus profaned the Muse by this abject flattery, were it not recorded that Thomson dedicated to him his "Summer." The dedication was prompted by Lord Binning; and "Summer" was published in 1727, when Dodington was one of the Lords of the Treasury, as well as Clerk of the Pells in Ireland. It seemed, therefore, worth while for Thomson to pen such a passage as this: "Your example, sir, has recommended poetry with the greatest grace to the example of those who are engaged in the most active scenes of life; and this, though confessedly the least considerable of those qualities that dignify your character, must be particularly pleasing to *one* whose only hope of being introduced to your regard is thro' the recommendation of an art in which you are a master." Warton adding this tribute:

"To praise a Dodington, rash bard, forbear!
What can thy weak and ill-tuned voice avail,
When on that theme both Young and Thomson fail?"

Yet even when midway in his career, Dodington, in the famous political caricature called the "Motion," is depicted as "the Spaniel," sitting between the Duke of Argyle's legs, while his grace is driving a coach at full speed to the Treasury, with a sword instead of a whip in his hand, with Lord Chesterfield as postillion, and Lord Cobham as a footman, holding on by the straps; even then the servile though pompous character of this true man of the world was comprehended completely; and Bubb Dodington's characteristics never changed.

In his political life, Dodington was so selfish, obsequious, and versatile as to incur universal opprobrium; he had also another misfortune for a man of society—he became fat and lethargic. "My brother Ned," Horace Walpole remarks, "says he is grown of less consequence, though more weight." And on another occasion, speaking of a majority in the House of Lords, he adds, "I do not count Dodington, who must now always be in the minority, for no majority will accept him."

While, however, during the factious reign of George II., the town was declared, even by Horace, to be "wondrous dull; operas unfrequented, plays not in fashion, and amours old as marriages," Bubb Dodington, with his wealth and profusion, contrived always to be in vogue as a host, while he was at a discount as a politician. Politics and literature are the high-roads in England to that much-craved-for distinction, an admittance into the great world; and Dodington united these passports in his own person: he was a poetaster, and wrote political pamphlets. The latter were published and admired; the poems were referred to as "very pretty love verses" by Lord Lyttelton, and were never published—and never ought to have been published, it is stated.

His *bon mots*, his sallies, his fortune and places, and continual dangling at court, procured Bubo, as Pope styled him, one pre-eminence. His dinners at Hammersmith were the most *recherché* in the metropolis. Every one remembers, or ought to remember, Brandenburgh House, when the hapless Caroline of Brunswick held her court there, and where her brave heart —burdened probably with many sins—broke at last. It had been the residence of the beautiful and famous Margravine of Anspach, whose loveliness in vain tempts us to believe her innocent, in despite of facts. Before those eras—the presence of the Margravine, whose infidelities were almost avowed, and the abiding of the queen, whose errors had, at all events, verged on the very confines of guilt—the house was owned by Dodington. There he gave dinners; there he gratified a passion for display which was puerile; there he indulged in eccentricities which almost implied insanity; there he concocted his schemes for court advancement; and there, later in life, he contributed some of the treasures of his wit to dramatic literature. "The Wishes," a comedy, by Bentley, was supposed to owe much of its point to the brilliant wit of Dodington.*

At Brandenburgh House, a nobler presence than that of Dodington still haunted the groves and alleys, for Prince Rupert had once owned it. When Dodington bought it, he gave it—in jest, we must presume—the name of La Trappe; and it was not called Brandenburgh House until the fair and frail Margravine came to live there.

Its gardens were long famous, and in the time of Dodington were the scene of revel. Thomas Bentley, the son of Richard Bentley, the celebrated critic, had written a play called "The Wishes," and during the summer of 1761 it was acted at Drury Lane, and met with the especial approbation of George III., who sent the author, through Lord Bute, a present of two hundred guineas as a tribute to the good sentiments of the production.

This piece, which, in spite of its moral tendency, has died out, while plays of less virtuous character have lived, was rehearsed in the gardens of Brandenburgh House. Bubb Dodington associated much with those who give fame; but he

* See Walpole's "Royal and Noble Authors."

courted among them also those who could revenge affronts by bitter ridicule. Among the actors and literati who were then sometimes at Brandenburgh House were Foote and Churchill; capital boon companions, but, as it proved, dangerous foes.

Endowed with imagination; with a mind enriched by classical and historical studies; possessed of a brilliant wit, Bubb Dodington was, nevertheless, in the sight of some men, ridiculous. While the rehearsals of "The Wishes" went on, Foote was noting down all the peculiarities of the Lord of Brandenburgh House, with a view to bring them to account in his play of "The Patron." Lord Melcombe was an aristocratic Dombey: stultified by his own self-complacency, he dared to exhibit his peculiarities before the English Aristophanes. It was an act of imprudence, for Foote had long before (in 1747) opened the little theatre of the Haymarket with a sort of monologue play, "The Diversions of the Morning," in which he convulsed his audience with the perfection of a mimicry never beheld before, and so wonderful, that even the persons of his models seemed to stand before the amazed spectators.

These entertainments, in which the contriver was at once the author and performer, have been admirably revived by Mathews and others, and in another line by the lamented Albert Smith. The Westminster justices, furious and alarmed, opposed the daring performance, on which Foote changed the name of his piece, and called it "Mr. Foote giving Tea to his Friends," himself still the sole actor, and changing with Proteus-like celerity from one to the other. Then came his "Auction of Pictures," and Sir Thomas de Veil, one of his enemies, the justices, was introduced. Orator Henley and Cock the auctioneer figured also; and year after year the town was enchanted by that which is most gratifying to a polite audience, the finished exhibition of faults and follies. One stern voice was raised in reprobation, that of Samuel Johnson; he, at all events, had a due horror of buffoons; but even he owned himself vanquished.

"The first time I was in Foote's company was at Fitzherbert's. Having no good opinion of the fellow, I was resolved not to be pleased; and it is very difficult to please a man against his will. I went on eating my dinner pretty sullenly, affecting not to mind him; but the dog was so very comical that I was obliged to lay down my knife and fork, throw myself back in my chair, and fairly laugh it out. Sir, he was irresistible." Consoled by Foote's misfortunes and ultimate complicated misery for his lessened importance, Bubb Dodington still reigned, however, in the hearts of some learned votaries. Richard Bentley, the critic, compared him to Lord Halifax—

"That Halifax, my lord, as you do yet,
Stood forth the friend of poetry and wit,
Sought silent merit in the secret cell,
And Heav'n, nay, even man, repaid him well."

A more remorseless foe, however, than Foote, appeared in the person of Charles Churchill, the wild and unclerical son of a poor curate of Westminster. Foote laughed Bubb Dodington down, but Churchill perpetuated the satire; for Churchill was wholly unscrupulous, and his faults had been reckless and desperate. Wholly unfit for a clergyman, he had taken orders, obtained a curacy in Wales at £30 a year; not being able to subsist, took to keeping a cider-cellar, became a sort of bankrupt, and, quitting Wales, succeeded to the curacy of his father, who had just died. Still, famine haunted his home; Churchill took, therefore, to teaching young ladies to read and write, and conducted himself in the boarding-school, where his duties lay, with wonderful propriety. He had married at seventeen; but even that step had not protected his morals: he fell into abject poverty. Lloyd, father of his friend Robert Lloyd, then second master at Westminster, made an arrangement with his creditors. Young Lloyd had published a poem called "The Actor;" Churchill, in imitation, now produced "The Rosciad," and Bubb Dodington was one whose ridiculous points were salient in those days of personality. "The Rosciad" had a signal success, which completed the ruin of its author: he became a man of the town, forsook the wife of his youth, and abandoned the clerical character. There are few sights more contemptible than that of a clergyman who has cast off his profession, or whose profession has cast him off. But Churchill's talents for a time kept him from utter destitution. Bubb Dodington may have been consoled by finding that he shared the fate of Dr. Johnson, who had spoken slightingly of Churchill's works, and who shone forth, therefore, in "The Ghost," a later poem, as Dr. Pomposo.

Richard Cumberland, the dramatist, drew a portrait of Lord Melcombe, which is said to have been taken from the life; but perhaps the most faithful delineation of Bubb Dodington's character was furnished by himself in his "Diary;" in which, as it has been well observed, he "unveiled the nakedness of his mind, and displayed himself as a courtly compound of mean compliance and political prostitution." It may, in passing, be remarked, that few men figure well in an autobiography; and that Cumberland himself, proclaimed by Dr. Johnson to be a "learned, ingenious, accomplished gentleman," adding, the "want of company is an inconvenience, but Mr. Cumberland is a million"—in spite of this eulogium, Cumberland has betrayed in his own autobiography unbounded vanity, worldliness, and an undue estimation of his own perishable fame. After all, amusing as personalities must always be, neither the humors of Foote, the vigorous satire of Churchill, nor the careful limning of Cumberland, while they can not be ranked among talents of the highest order, imply a sort of social treachery. The delicious little colloquy between Boswell and Johnson places low personal ridicule in its proper light.

Boswell.—"Foote has a great deal of humor." Johnson. —"Yes, sir." Boswell.—"He has a singular talent of exhibiting characters." Johnson.—"Sir, it is not a talent—it is a vice; it is what others abstain from. It is not comedy, which exhibits the character of a species—as that of a miser gathered from many misers—it is farce which exhibits individuals." Boswell.—"Did he not think of exhibiting you, sir?" Johnson.—"Sir, fear restrained him; he knew I would have broken his bones. I would have saved him the trouble of cutting off a leg; I would not have left him a leg to cut off."

Few annals exist of the private life of Bubb Dodington, but those few are discreditable.

Like most men of his time, and like many men of all times, Dodington was entangled by an unhappy and perplexing intrigue.

There was a certain "black woman," as Horace Walpole calls a Mrs. Strawbridge, whom Bubb Dodington admired. This handsome brunette lived in a corner house of Saville Row, in Piccadilly, where Dodington visited her. The result of their intimacy was his giving this lady a bond of ten thousand pounds to be paid if he married any one else. The real object of his affections was a Mrs. Behan, with whom he lived seventeen years, and whom, on the death of Mrs. Strawbridge, he eventually married.

Among Bubb Dodington's admirers and disciples was Paul Whitehead, a wild specimen of the poet, rake, satirist, dramatist, all in one; and, what was quite in character, a Templar to boot. Paul—so named from being born on that saint's day—wrote one or two pieces which brought him an ephemeral fame, such as the "State Dunces," and the "Epistle to Dr. Thompson," "Manners," a satire, and the "Gymnasiad," a mock heroic poem, intended to ridicule the passion for boxing then prevalent. Paul Whitehead, who died in 1774, was an infamous, but not, in the opinion of Walpole, a despicable poet, yet Churchill has consigned him to everlasting infamy as a reprobate in these lines:

"May I (can worse disgrace on manhood fall?)
Be born a Whitehead, and baptized a Paul."

Paul was not, however, worse than his satirist Churchill; and both of these wretched men were members of a society long the theme of horror and disgust, even after its existence had ceased to be remembered, except by a few old people. This was the "Hell-fire Club," held in appropriate orgies at Medmenham Abbey, Buckinghamshire. The profligate Sir Francis Dashwood, Wilkes, and Churchill were among its most prominent members.

With such associates, and living in a court where nothing but the basest passions reigned and the lowest arts prevailed, we are inclined to accord with the descendant of Bubb Dodington, the editor of his "Diary," Henry Penruddocke Wyndham, who declares that all Lord Melcombe's political conduct was "wholly directed by the base motives of vanity, selfishness, and avarice." Lord Melcombe seems to have been a man of the world of the very worst *calibre;* sensual, servile, and treacherous; ready, during the lifetime of his patron, Frederick, Prince of Wales, to go any lengths against the adverse party of the Pelhams, that prince's political foes—eager, after the death of Frederick, to court those powerful men with fawning servility.

The famous "Diary" of Bubb Dodington supplies the information from which these conclusions have been drawn. Horace Walpole, who knew Dodington well, describes how he read with avidity the "Diary" which was published in 1784.

"A nephew of Lord Melcombe's heirs has published that lord's 'Diary.' Indeed, it commences in 1749, and I grieve it was not dated twenty years later. However, it deals in topics that are twenty times more familiar and fresh to my memory than any passage that has happened within these six months. I wish I could convey it to you. Though drawn by his own hand, and certainly meant to flatter himself, it is a truer portrait than any of his hirelings would have given. Never was such a composition of vanity, versatility, and servility. In short, there is but one feature wanting in it, his wit, of which in the whole book there are not three sallies."

The editor of this "Diary" remarks "that he will no doubt be considered a very extraordinary editor, the practice of whom has generally been to prefer flattery to truth, and partiality to justice." To understand, not the flattery which his contemporaries heaped upon Bubb Dodington, but the opprobrium with which they loaded his memory—to comprehend, not his merits, but his demerits—it is necessary to take a brief survey of his political life from the commencement. He began life, as we have seen, as a servile adherent of Sir Robert Walpole. A political epistle to the minister was the prelude to a temporary alliance only, for in 1737 Bubb went over to the adverse party of Leicester House, and espoused the cause of Frederick, Prince of Wales, against his royal father. He was therefore dismissed from the Treasury. When Sir Robert fell, Bubb expected to rise, but his expectations of preferment were not realized. He attacked the new administration forthwith, and succeeded so far in becoming important that he was made Treasurer of the Navy, a post which he resigned in 1749, and which he held again in 1755, but which he lost the next year. On the accession of George III., he was not ashamed to appear altogether in a new character, as the friend of Lord Bute: he was, therefore, advanced to the peerage by the title of Baron of Melcombe Regis, in 1761. The honor was enjoyed for one short year only, and on the 28th of July, 1762, Bubb Dodington expired. Horace Walpole, in his Royal and Noble Authors, complains that "Dodington's 'Diary' was mangled, in compliment, before it was imparted to the public." We can not, therefore, judge of what the "Diary" was before, as the editor avows every anecdote was cut out, and all the little gossip so illustrative of character and manners which would have brightened its dull pages, fell beneath the power of a merciless pair of scissors. Mr. Penruddocke Wyndham conceives, however, that he was only doing justice to society in these suppressions. "It would," he says, "be *no* entertainment to the reader to be informed who daily dined with his lordship, or whom he daily met at the table of other people."

Posterity thinks differently: a knowledge of a man's associates forms the best commentary on his life; and there is much reason to rejoice that all biographers are not like Mr. Penruddocke Wyndham. Bubb Dodington, more especially, was a man of society: inferior as a literary man, contemptible as a politician, it was only at the head of his table that he was agreeable and brilliant. He was, in fact, a man who had no domestic life: a courtier, like Lord Hervey, but without Lord Hervey's consistency. He was, in truth, a type of that era in England: vulgar in aims; dissolute in conduct; ostentatious, vain-glorious—of a low, ephemeral ambition, but, at the same time, talented, acute, and lavish to the lettered. The public is now the patron of the gifted. What writer cares for individual opinion, except as it tends to sweep up the gross amount of public blame or censure? What publisher will consent to undertake a work because some lord or lady recommended it to his notice? The reviewer is greater in the commonwealth of letters than the man of rank.

But in these days it was otherwise; and they who, in the necessities of the times, did what they could to advance the interests of the *belles lettres*, deserve not to be forgotten.

It is with a feeling of sickness that we open the pages of this great wit's "Diary," and attempt to peruse the sentences in which the most grasping selfishness is displayed. We follow him to Leicester House, that ancient tenement—(wherefore pulled down, except to erect on its former site the narrowest of streets, does not appear): that former home of the Sydneys had not always been polluted by the dissolute, heartless *clique* who composed the court of Frederick, Prince of Wales. Its chambers had once been traversed by Henry Sydney, by Algernon, his brother. It was their *home*—their father, Robert Sydney, Earl of Leicester, having lived there. The lovely Dorothy Sydney, Waller's Saccharissa, once, in all purity and grace, had danced in that gallery where the vulgar, brazen Lady Middlesex and her compliant lord afterward flattered the weakest of princes, Frederick. In old times, Leicester House had stood on Lammas land—land, in the spirit of the old charities, open to the poor at Lammas-tide; and even "the Right Hon. the Earl of Leicester"—as an old document hath it—was obliged, if *he* chose to turn out his cows or horses on that appropriated land, to pay a rent for it to the overseers of St. Martin's parish, then really "in the fields." And here this nobleman not only dwelt in all state himself, but let or lent his house to persons whose memory seems to hallow even Leicester Fields. Elizabeth of Bohemia, after what was to her indeed "life's fitful fever," died at Leicester House. It became then, temporarily, the abode of embassadors. Colbert, in the time of Charles II., occupied the place; Prince Eugène, in 1712, held his residence here; and the rough soldier, famous for all absence of tact—brave, loyal-hearted, and coarse—lingered at Leicester House in hopes of obstructing the peace between England and France.

All that was good and great fled forever from Leicester House at the instant that George II., when Prince of Wales, was driven by his royal father from St. James's, and took up his abode in it until the death of George I. The once honored home of the Sydneys henceforth becomes loathsome in a moral sense. Here William, Duke of Cumberland—the hero, as court flatterers called him; the butcher, as the poor Jacobites designated him of Culloden—first saw the light. Peace and respectability then departed the old house forever. Prince Frederick was its next inmate: here the Princess of Wales, the mother of George III., had her lyings-in, and her royal husband held his public tables; and at these and in every assembly, as well as in private, one figure is conspicuous.

Grace Boyle—for she unworthily bore that great name—was the daughter and heiress of Richard, Viscount Shannon.

She married Lord Middlesex, bringing him a fortune of thirty thousand pounds. Short, plain, "very yellow," as her contemporaries affirm, with a head full of Greek and Latin, and devoted to music and painting; it seems strange that Frederick should have been attracted to one far inferior to his own princess both in mind and person. But so it was, for in those days every man liked his neighbor's wife better than his own. Imitating the forbearance of her royal mother-in-law, the princess tolerated such of her husband's mistresses as did not interfere in politics: Lady Middlesex was the "my good Mrs. Howard" of Leicester House. She was made Mistress of the Robes: her favor soon "grew," as the shrewd Horace remarks, "to be rather more than Platonic." She lived with the royal pair constantly, and sat up till five o'clock in the morning at their suppers; and Lord Middlesex saw and submitted to all that was going on with the loyalty and patience of a *Georgian* courtier. Lady Middlesex was a docile politician, and, on that account, retained her position probably long after she had lost her influence.

Her name appears constantly in the "Diary," out of which every thing amusing has been carefully expunged.

"Lady Middlesex, Lord Bathurst, Mr. Breton, and I, waited on their Royal Highnesses to Spitalfields, to see the manufacture of silk." In the afternoon off went the same party to Norwood Forest, in private coaches, to see a "settlement of gipsies." Then returning, went to find out Bettesworth, the conjuror, but, not discovering him, went in search of the "little Dutchman." Were disappointed in that, but "concluded," relates Bubb Dodington, "the particularities of this day by supping with Mrs. Cannon, the princess's *midwife*."

All these elegant modes of passing the time were not only for the sake of Lady Middlesex, but, it was said, of her friend, Miss Granville, one of the maids of honor, daughter of the first Lord Lansdown, the poet. This young lady, Eliza Granville, was scarcely pretty: a fair, red-haired girl.

All this thoughtless, if not culpable gallantry, was abruptly checked by the rude hand of death. During the month of March, Frederick was attacked with illness, having caught cold. Very little apprehension was expressed at first, but, about eleven days after his first attack, he expired. Half an hour before his death he had asked to see some friends, and had called for coffee and bread and butter: a fit of coughing came on, and he died instantly from suffocation. An abscess, which had been forming in his side, had burst; nevertheless, his two physicians, Wilmot and Lee, "knew nothing of his distemper." According to Lord Melcombe, who thus refers to their blunders, "They declared, half an hour before his death, that his pulse was like a man's in perfect health. They either would not see or did not know the consequences of the black thrush, which appeared in his mouth, and quite down into his throat. Their ignorance, or their knowledge of his disorder, renders them equally inexcusable for not calling in other assistance."

The consternation in the prince's household was great, not for his life, but for the confusion into which politics were thrown by his death. After his relapse, and until just before his death, the princess never suffered any English man or woman above the degree of valet-de-chambre to see him; nor did she herself see any one of her household until absolutely necessary. After the death of his eldest born, George II. vented his diabolical jealousy upon the cold remains of one thus cut off in the prime of life. The funeral was ordered to be on the model of that of Charles II., but private counter-orders were issued to reduce the ceremonial to the smallest degree of respect that could be paid.

On the 13th of April, 1751, the body of the prince was entombed in Henry VII.'s chapel. Except the lords appointed to hold the pall and attend the chief mourner, when the attendants were called over in their ranks, there was not a *single* English lord, not *one* bishop, and only one Irish lord (Lord Limerick), and three sons of peers. Sir John Rushout and Dodington were the only privy councilors who followed. It rained heavily, but no covering was provided for the procession. The service was performed without organ or anthem. "Thus," observes Bubb Dodington, "ended this sad day."

Although the prince left a brother and sisters, the Duke of Somerset acted as chief mourner. The king hailed the event of the prince's death as a relief, which was to render happy his remaining days; and Bubb Dodington hastened, in a few months, to offer to the Pelhams "his friendship and attachment." His attendance at court was resumed, although George II. could not endure him; and the old Walpolians, nicknamed the Black-tan, were also averse to him.

Such were Bubb Dodington's *actions*. His expressions, on occasion of the prince's death, were in a very different tone.

"We have lost," he wrote to Sir Horace Mann, "the delight and ornament of the age he lived in—the expectations of the public: in this light I have lost more than any subject in England; but this is light; public advantages confined to myself do not, ought not, to weigh with me. But we have lost the refuge of private distress—the balm of the afflicted heart—the shelter of the miserable against the fury of private adversity;

the arts, the graces, the anguish, the misfortunes of society, have lost their patron and their remedy.

"I have lost my companion—my protector—the friend that loved me, that condescended to hear, to communicate, to share in all the pleasures and pains of the human heart: where the social affections and emotions of the mind only presided, without regard to the infinite disproportion of my rank and condition. This is a wound that can not, ought not to heal. If I pretended to fortitude here, I should be infamous—a monster of ingratitude—and unworthy of all consolation, if I was not inconsolable."

"Thank you," writes the shrewd Horace Walpole, addressing Sir Horace Mann, "for the transcript from *Bubb de Tristibus*. I will keep your secret, though I am persuaded that a man who has composed such a funeral oration on his master had himself fully intended that its flowers should not bloom and wither in obscurity."

Well might George II., seeing him go to court, say: "I see Dodington here sometimes; what does he come for?"

It was, however, clearly seen what he went for, when, in 1753, two years after the death of his "benefactor," Dodington humbly offered His Majesty his services in the house, and "five members," for the rest of his life, if His Majesty would give Mr. Pelham leave to employ him for His Majesty's service. Nevertheless, he continued to advise with the Princess of Wales, and to drop into her house as if it had been a sister's house—sitting on a stool near the fireside, and listening to her accounts of her children.

In the midst of these intrigues for favor on the part of Dodington, Mr. Pelham died, and was succeeded by his brother, the Duke of Newcastle, the issue of whose administration is well known.

In 1760 death again befriended the now veteran wit, beau, and politician. George II. died; and the intimacy which Dodington had always taken care to preserve between himself and the Princess of Wales ended advantageously for him; and he instantly, in spite of all his former professions to Pelham, joined hand and heart with that minister, from whom he obtained a peerage. This, as we have seen, was not long enjoyed. Lord Melcombe, as this able, intriguing man was now styled, died on the 28th of July, 1762, and with him terminated the short-lived distinction for which he had sacrificed even a decent pretext of principle and consistency.

So general has been the contempt felt for his character, that it seems almost needless to assert that Bubb Dodington was eminently to be despised. Nothing much more severe can be said of him than the remarks of Horace Walpole upon his "Diary," in which he observes that Dodington records little but what is to his own disgrace; as if he thought that the world would forgive his inconsistencies as readily as he forgave himself. "Had he adopted," Horace well observes, "the French title '*Confessions*,' it would have seemed to imply some kind of penitence."

But vain-glory engrossed him: "he was determined to raise an altar to himself, and, for want of burnt-offerings, lighted the pyre, like a great author (Rousseau), with his own character."

It was said by the same acute observer, both of Lord Hervey and of Bubb Dodington, that "they were the only two persons he ever knew that were always aiming at wit and never finding it." And here, it seems, most that can be testified in praise of a heartless, clever man, must be summed up.

Lord Melcombe's property, with the exception of a few legacies, devolved upon his cousin, Thomas Wyndham, of Hammersmith, by whom his lordship's papers, letters, and poems were bequeathed to Henry Penruddocke Wyndham, with an injunction that only such as "might do honor to his memory should be made public."

After this, in addition to the true saying, defend us from our friends, one may exclaim, "defend us from our executors and editors."

X

THE END.

It is a work of real historical value, the result of accurate criticism, written in a liberal spirit, and from first to last deeply interesting.—*Athenæum.*

The style is excellent, clear, vivid, eloquent; and the industry with which original sources have been investigated, and through which new light has been shed over perplexed incidents and characters, entitles Mr. Motley to a high rank in the literature of an age peculiarly rich in history.—*North British Review.*

It abounds in new information, and, as a first work, commands a very cordial recognition, not merely of the promise it gives, but of the extent and importance of the labor actually performed on it.—*London Examiner.*

Mr. Motley's "History" is a work of which any country might be proud.—*Press* (London).

Mr. Motley's History will be a standard book of reference in historical literature.—*London Literary Gazette.*

Mr. Motley has searched the whole range of historical documents necessary to the composition of his work.—*London Leader.*

This is really a great work. It belongs to the class of books in which we range our Grotes, Milmans, Merivales, and Macaulays, as the glories of English literature in the department of history. * * * Mr. Motley's gifts as a historical writer are among the highest and rarest.—*Nonconformist* (London).

Mr. Motley's volumes will well repay perusal. * * * For his learning, his liberal tone, and his generous enthusiasm, we heartily commend him, and bid him good speed for the remainer of his interesting and heroic narrative.—*Saturday Review.*

The story is a noble one, and is worthily treated. * * * Mr. Motley has had the patience to unravel, with unfailing perseverance, the thousand intricate plots of the adversaries of the Prince of Orange; but the details and the literal extracts which he has derived from original documents, and transferred to his pages, give a truthful color and a picturesque effect, which are especially charming.—*London Daily News.*

M. Lothrop Motley dans son magnifique tableau de la formation de notre République.—G. GROEN VAN PRINSTERER.

Our accomplished countryman, Mr. J. Lothrop Motley, who, during the last five years, for the better prosecution of his labors, has established his residence in the neighborhood of the scenes of his narrative. No one acquainted with the fine powers of mind possessed by this scholar, and the earnestness with which he has devoted himself to the task, can doubt that he will do full justice to his important but difficult subject.—W. H. PRESCOTT.

The production of such a work as this astonishes, while it gratifies the pride of the American reader.—*N. Y. Observer.*

The "Rise of the Dutch Republic" at once, and by acclamation, takes its place by the "Decline and Fall of the Roman Empire," as a work which, whether for research, substance, or style, will never be superseded.—*N. Y. Albion.*

A work upon which all who read the English language may congratulate themselves.—*New Yorker Handels Zeitung.*

Mr. Motley's place is now (alluding to this book) with Hallam and Lord Mahon, Alison and Macaulay in the Old Country, and with Washington Irving, Prescott, and Bancroft in this.—*N. Y. Times.*

THE authority, in the English tongue, for the history of the period and people to which it refers.—*N. Y. Courier and Enquirer.*

This work at once places the author on the list of American historians which has been so signally illustrated by the names of Irving, Prescott, Bancroft, and Hildreth.—*Boston Times.*

The work is a noble one, and a most desirable acquisition to our historical literature.—*Mobile Advertiser.*

Such a work is an honor to its author, to his country, and to the age in which it was written.—*Ohio Farmer.*

By William C. Prime.

Boat Life in Egypt & Nubia.

Boat Life in Egypt and Nubia. By WILLIAM C. PRIME, Author of "The Old House by the River," "Later Years," &c. Illustrations. 12mo, Muslin, $1 25.

Tent Life in the Holy Land.

By WILLIAM C. PRIME, Author of "The Old House by the River," "Later Years," &c. Illustrations. 12mo, Muslin, $1 25.

The Old House by the River.

By WILLIAM C. PRIME, Author of the "Owl Creek Letters." 12mo, Muslin, 75 cents.

Later Years.

By WILLIAM C. PRIME, Author of "The Old House by the River." 12mo, Muslin, $1 00.

Harper's Catalogue.

A NEW DESCRIPTIVE CATALOGUE OF HARPER & BROTHERS' PUBLICATIONS is now ready for distribution, and may be obtained gratuitously on application to the Publishers personally, or by letter inclosing SIX CENTS in postage stamps. The attention of gentlemen, in town or country, designing to form Libraries or enrich their literary collections, is respectfully invited to this Catalogue, which will be found to comprise a large proportion of the standard and most esteemed works in English Literature—COMPREHENDING MORE THAN TWO THOUSAND VOLUMES—which are offered, in most instances, at less than one half the cost of similar productions in England. To Librarians and others connected with Colleges, Schools, &c., who may not have access to a reliable guide in forming the true estimate of literary productions, it is believed this Catalogue will prove especially valuable as a manual of reference. To prevent disappointment, it is suggested that, whenever books can not be obtained through any bookseller or local agent, applications with remittance should be addressed direct to the Publishers, which will meet with prompt attention.

www.ingramcontent.com/pod-product-compliance
Lightning Source LLC
LaVergne TN
LVHW020917110826
845150LV00004B/697

* 9 7 8 1 4 2 5 5 5 6 2 4 2 *